I0819976

New Directions in Medieval Manuscript Studies and Reading Practices

Derek Pearsall

NEW DIRECTIONS *in* MEDIEVAL MANUSCRIPT STUDIES *and* READING PRACTICES

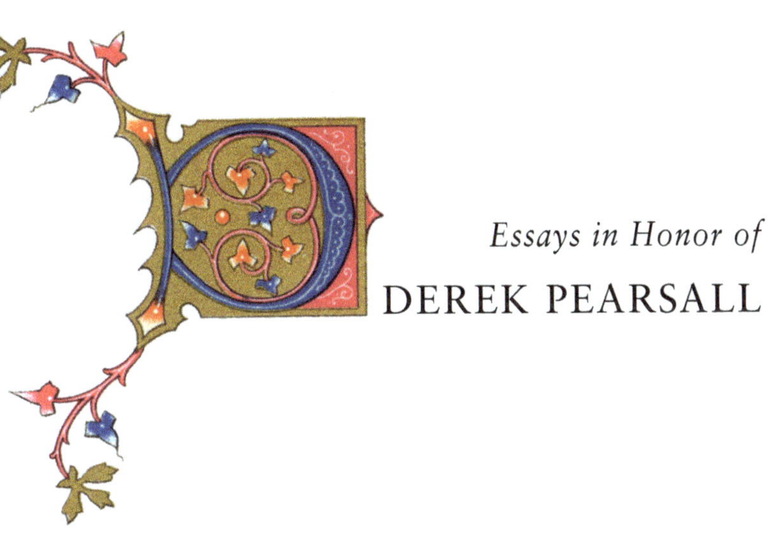

Essays in Honor of

DEREK PEARSALL

Edited by

Kathryn Kerby-Fulton, John J. Thompson,

and

Sarah Baechle

UNIVERSITY OF NOTRE DAME PRESS · NOTRE DAME, INDIANA

Notre Dame, Indiana 46556
www.undpress.nd.edu

Published in the United States of America

The Press gratefully acknowledges the support of the Institute for Scholarship in the Liberal Arts, University of Notre Dame, in the publication of this book.

Library of Congress Cataloging-in-Publication Data

New directions in medieval manuscript studies and reading practices : essays in honor of Derek Pearsall / edited by Kathryn Kerby-Fulton, John J. Thompson and Sarah Baechle.
pages cm
Includes index.
ISBN 978-0-268-03327-9 (hardback) — ISBN 0-268-03327-7 (hardcover)
1. Manuscripts, Medieval—England. 2. English literature—Middle English, 1100–1500—Manuscripts. 3. Books and reading—England—History—To 1500. I. Kerby-Fulton, Kathryn, editor. II. Thompson, John J., 1955– editor. III. Baechle, Sarah, editor. IV. Pearsall, Derek, honouree.
Z106.5.G7N49 2014
091'.0942—dc23

2014022368

∞ *The paper in this book meets the guidelines for permanence and durability of the Committee on Production Guidelinesfor Book Longevity of the Council on Library Resources.*

New Directions in Medieval Manuscript Studies and Reading Practices

Proceedings of the Robert M. Conway Notre Dame London Center Conferences, I

About the Conway Conferences

As a University of Notre Dame alumnus and trustee, Robert M. Conway has long been a generous supporter of the Medieval Institute, not only endowing the prestigious Conway lecture series and the director's position but also providing funds for programming. He recently also gave a special gift to fund conferences to be held in the Notre Dame Center in London. Since he lives in London, Bob Conway's idea was to bring together academics from Notre Dame and from British universities to talk about medieval topics. After this gift was announced, two Notre Dame faculty members, Kathryn Kerby-Fulton (English) and Margot Fassler (Theology), proposed the topics for these Conway London Conferences, one on medieval manuscript culture (Conference I) and the other on the musicology of historian-cantors in monastic houses (Conference II). These proposals not only fulfill the spirit of the gift, as proposed by Bob Conway, but they are interdisciplinary, which is in keeping with the mission of the Medieval Institute. The more recent conference, the Cantor-Historian Symposium, was held at the Notre Dame London Center on October 20–23, 2013. The first of these conferences, New Directions in Medieval Manuscript Studies and Reading Practices in Honour of the 80th Birthday of Derek Pearsall, was held on October 20–22, 2011, and selections from its proceedings are gathered here.

Remie Constable
Director, Medieval Institute
University of Notre Dame

Contents

Part II. England and International: Studies in Courtly Verse and Affectivity Inspired by the Work of Elizabeth Salter and Derek Pearsall at York

Part III. The Making of a Field: York's 1981 *Manuscripts and Readers* Thirty Years Later

Part IV. Newer Directions in Manuscript Studies I: Regional and Scribal Identities

Part V. Newer Directions in Manuscript Studies II: Women, Children, and Literacy at Work in Late Medieval and Early Tudor England

Part VI. Chaucerian and Post-Chaucerian Reading Practices

Part VII. What a Poet Is "Entitled to Be Remembered By": Editorial Philosophies and the Langlandian Legacy of Derek Pearsall

Illustrations

Preface

Like the conference in honor of Derek Pearsall it commemorates, this volume focuses on new research prompted by his rich and ongoing legacy as a literary critic and founding father of Middle English manuscript studies. Essays here are explicitly framed to indicate that relationship, and to indicate the many ways in which the latest research grows out of but now goes well beyond that legacy. The conference New Directions in Medieval Manuscript Studies and Reading Practices in Honour of the 80th Birthday of Derek Pearsall was held on October 20–22, 2011. The event was three years in the making, beginning as a plan to celebrate Derek's eightieth birthday by gathering his students together somehow. At the time we had not imagined that we would be able to afford a large, spectacular, international event, but the University of Notre Dame's loyal donor, Robert M. Conway, gave a generous amount of money to the Medieval Institute for conferences at the Notre Dame London Center. Bob's simple stipulation was that we "do something really good." Honoring Derek seemed to be the quintessential "something really good" that we could do for the field of Middle English literary studies as a whole.

This book, like the conference, covers a range of issues from the study of medieval literary manuscripts to the history of medieval books, libraries, literacy, censorship, and the social classes who used books: nobility, laymen, women, children, schoolmasters, monks, priests, merchants, and more. The reading practices dimension covers marginal commentaries, images and interpretive methods, international transmission, and early print and editorial methods. The conference was greeted with great excitement and was colloquially called the "party of the decade" in the Middle English literary field. Its participants included many of the major figures in North America and the United Kingdom in late medieval English studies, whether students of Derek's or close colleagues. The publication of the selected proceedings, now revamped as a coherent volume in honor of Derek Pearsall's legacy, and indicating new directions well beyond that legacy, captures the state of the field for the twenty-first century.

I called the conference New Directions in Manuscript Studies and Reading Practices for many reasons: as a way of revisiting the marvelous 1998 conference Derek hosted at Harvard on the same subject and as a way of revisiting the even earlier 1981 York conference on manuscript studies that in effect christened the field. Sections of the present volume offer retrospectives on both these benchmark events. In naming the conference I also wanted to draw attention to the fact that manuscript studies is seeping beyond the purview of paleographers and codicologists, even beyond its splendid home in the Early Book Society, to take on the larger world of literary criticism—that is, via "reading practices." In this event, then, we also honored an idea whose time has come, an idea that Derek more than anyone has fostered, as only a brilliant codicologist, editor, and literary critic could do. Since 1998 interest in this area of study has grown exponentially, and this volume contributes to the urgent need for groundbreaking scholarship in the field.

The conference was enhanced by a supplementary grant from the British Academy (for which John Thompson applied on our behalf and for which he expresses his great gratitude) and by the generosity of King's College London, Derek's first employer as a young academic. It ended with Derek's onetime King's colleague, Ron Waldron, offering a retrospective called "The Same Young Derek: Reminiscences of Those Early Years at King's College in the Strand," beginning with tales of the days when Derek's office was a broom closet in the college library and ending with a meditation on the secret of his eternal youthfulness. We wish to thank Clare Lees of King's College London, the British Academy, the University of Notre Dame London Center's director, Greg Kucich, and his assistant, Charlotte Parkyn, as well as the Notre Dame Conference Services staff. For assistance with both the conference and the volume, Sarah Baechle and I would especially like to thank Katie Bugyis, Amanda Bohne, and the many Notre Dame PhD students who worked tirelessly as organizers. More recently we owe an enormous debt to

Amanda Bohne, especially for her dedicated work as a research assistant, copy editor, and indexer. Through the special kindness of Robert M. Conway and of the Graduate Office, University of Notre Dame graduate students, many of whom are trained in manuscript studies, were able to attend and perform at this conference. This was a once-in-a-lifetime experience for our graduate students, and six of their essays are included in the volume. One of the anonymous reader's reports made this assessment of the contribution of the Notre Dame graduate students (most of them now already employed at other universities and scholars in their own right):

> The collection . . . has a possibly-unanticipated fringe benefit that might turn out to be its greatest strength in the long run. It introduces the reader to stimulating work by an upcoming generation of more recent practitioners . . . all of whom open dazzling perspectives on exactly what this collection should care most about: the particulars of individual manuscripts, including scribal practice, marginal commentary and other evidence of external circumstance and audience reception. I suspect that, in its longer history, this collection will be most esteemed as the place where a whole new generation of manuscript scholars, pursuing original and distinctive methodologies, got their start. As a result, this collection is at once canonical in some respects and innovative in others. To borrow a term from manuscript studies, it points toward certain forms of "mouvance" in manuscript study itself, suggesting at every point that manuscript study has not been standing still but remains a young and dynamic and developing field.

The present volume contains an enticing sampling of some of the best of the forty-three papers offered at the conference, now in revised form. Senior scholars who acted as respondents to most of the original conference sessions have here provided short forewords to discrete sections of the volume, situating the essays or guiding readers new to the field. This book blends the study of medieval manuscripts with literary criticism and direct evidence of how medieval people read. It aims not only to address manuscript specialists but also to introduce the complexities of interdisciplinary manuscript studies to students and instructors already familiar with medieval literature.

Kathryn Kerby-Fulton

A Brief Biographical Sketch of Derek Pearsall

Born and educated in Birmingham, Derek Pearsall was a lecturer at King's College London from 1959 to 1965 before being hired by the Department of English at York in the early years of the university. He rose from lecturer to professor in the Department of English and Related Literature, where he taught for twenty years. In 1985 he was hired by Harvard University to take up its prestigious Gurney Professorship of English Literature. He remained there until his retirement in 2000, when he returned to his home in York. He has remained active in the Department of English and Related Literature and the Centre for Medieval Studies at York as an honorary professor (since 1989).

Derek is known worldwide in the field of medieval English literature. His fifteen books on Chaucer and his contemporaries are landmark studies read and cited so frequently that it would be difficult to tally them. His books include biographies of Geoffrey Chaucer and his disciple John Lydgate, editions of texts ranging from William Langland's *Piers Plowman* to the anonymous *Floure and the Leaf* and *Assembly of Ladies*, an acclaimed critical book on Chaucer's *Canterbury Tales*, wide-ranging studies introducing medieval literature to readers of all backgrounds, and anthologies of medieval English writings used in undergraduate and postgraduate teaching. In the 1970s and 1980s, he was a leader in rejuvenating the study of medieval English texts from their original manuscript sources and initiated the York Manuscripts Conferences (still ongoing) in which distinguished scholars and postgraduates alike could come together to share their discoveries from original source materials. He has served in prestigious positions in scholarly organizations, including president of the New Chaucer Society, member of the Editorial Board of the Early English Text Society, president of the International Association of University Professors of English, fellow of the American Academy of Arts and Sciences, and fellow of the Medieval Academy of America. In addition to the fifteen books he has written or edited, Derek has edited nine volumes of essays by other scholars and written over seventy essays in scholarly journals or essay collections. A complete list of his publications, which will continue to be updated, is available online, at http://www3.nd.edu/~pearsall/. Derek has been invited to visiting professorships at numerous universities in the United Kingdom and the United States and is a frequent plenary speaker at conferences and invited speaker at universities in the United Kingdom, the United States, Canada, Australia, Denmark, the Netherlands, Italy, Germany, Switzerland, Sweden, Finland, Taiwan, and Japan.

Linne Mooney

PART I

Celebrating Pearsallian Reading Practices

FOREWORD TO PART I

In recent years Derek Pearsall has written a series of essays and given a number of talks that recommend the practice of "close reading."[1] At a moment when many in literary studies are rushing back to what has now been called the "surface" of the text, the recommendation hardly needs justification, and yet the occasion of Derek's eightieth birthday prompts nothing so strongly as the recognition that this insistence has a deep and important history.[2] To read through the canon of his criticism, in other words, is to note that this interest represents a return to the mode Derek adopted in one of his earliest articles, "Gower's Narrative Art" (1966).[3] The focus there was on the structure of the narrative frame of the *Confessio Amantis* rather than its style,[4] but, by Derek's own account, this article was a response to Charles Muscatine's *Chaucer and the French Tradition* (1957), which, to many, was itself an attempt to bring the techniques of the New Criticism to bear on medieval works.[5] Although he spent a great deal of his career editing both major and minor Middle English texts, as well as promoting the study of manuscripts, this early essay makes clear that Derek's first love was the description of what meanings are "released" (as he often puts it) by sufficiently careful description of "poetic expression."[6] Aspects of the essays in Part I, by A. C. Spearing, Oliver Pickering, and Martha Driver, document the influence of this mode, and this too makes it the right moment not only to celebrate "Pearsallian" close reading, but to define it with some care.

To anyone who has read through Derek's criticism with anything like his characteristic attention it will be clear that his more recent readings display a marked decrease in what he himself once described as "caustic criticisms."[7] In his earlier work, Derek's object of analysis was often "literary value," and his larger purpose was a kind of ranking (as he put it, "sneering and laughing . . . disguised . . . as judgment . . . comparing all literary works against a few accepted classics, and assigning them to classes and leagues").[8] As a collection of the most pointed barbs in an essay characterizing Middle English romances clearly demonstrates, the method of this earlier work was "scathing dismissal":

> "grotesquely inept" (*Arthur*); "hack-work" (*Guy*); "every possible concession to popular taste[;] . . . vivid, gross and ridiculous by turns, though never dull" (*Beves*); "a not at all contemptible example of what the professional romancer could knock together when pressed" (*Degarre*); "third-rate fumbling in an enfeebled tradition[,] . . . a wretched piece of work" (*Roland and Vernagu*); "a mechanical shuffling-together of stock incidents" (*Eglamour*); and finally "There may not be much interest in what is going on, but at least there is always something going on" (*Tryamour*).[9]

Derek himself now understands this mode as historically determined (a "fashion" that "died out in the 1970s"), and more recent writers on romance have judged it a failure of understanding that "obscured" a particular, and particularly medieval, "cultural-literary aesthetic."[10] It is, in that sense, ripe for "recantation," and Derek, with characteristic generosity, has obliged his detractors, not only by foregoing the "diatribe of abuse" as a rule in his recent readings, but by focusing instead on the carefully historicized "pleasure" medieval texts might have given their readers.[11]

And yet a broader history of reading than Derek allows himself finds a place for such diatribes in the "inflexible honesty" that Matthew Arnold for one insisted was necessary to criticism.[12] As Eliot had it a few generations later, the "testing" and "discrimination" that constitute "critical labor" are most properly allied to the "heat of creation," a process and skill so far from abusive that, in its purest form, is that which brings "art" into being.[13] Such a mode of apprehension is "critical" because it insists upon measuring every work against its own ambitions and presumes that it is now only possible to see works written long in the past—to see "the object as in itself it really is," in Arnold's other ringing phrase—by allowing for the tastes and predilections by which the modern reader inevitably sees.[14] Although, as I have suggested, this mode determined almost all of Derek's writing until the recent relaxation, it virtually constituted the purpose of *Old English and Middle English Poetry*, where the object at issue was how the whole of the medieval poetic tradition might still matter.[15] The volume is itself a chrestomathy of caustic criticism. "Layamon," it teaches us, "is a massive erratic in the history of English poetry" and "proves nothing about the continuity of the alliterative tradition but his own obstinacy" (112). The "over 10,000 septenary lines of inexorable 15-syllable regularity" of *The Ormulum* have "no appeal of any kind," and therefore "the first line will speak for all" (102). "Accumulation" is "the whole principle" of the *South English Legendary*, where "if one saint's life is good, three score are better . . . and the same with tortures and miracles" (104). *Piers Plowman* is "by any standards but its own . . . near to artistic breakdown" (178). "Lydgate can seldom be confidently quoted at length, even where there are legitimate grounds for admiration" (228). In the alliterative *Morte Arthure*, metrical requirements so often determine meaning that it is "unfortunate for the giant that he shares a palatal initial with so few portions of the anatomy" (164). And "John Metham is [a] writer whose admiration for Lydgate, if it persuaded him to try his hand at poetry, proved his undoing" (239). In such cases judgment *is* the method of careful historical account, because it is not simply an opinion about form or poetic purpose or aesthetic tendency, but the placing of that form and purpose in the history of all literary valuations. The precision of the abuse is also profoundly pedagogical, humorous in its concision, and memorable because of its pith.

Criticism so worthy of its name requires what Martha Driver calls (quoting Derek in a characteristic phrase) the "power of imaginative penetration," but it also often recruits the very resources of language it describes, judging by means of the apposite image or metaphor. Thus Chaucer is said to have left the Cook's Tale unfinished because he "saw the tunnel that realism might go into," and the Nun's Priest's Tale "recoils" like a snake "upon all systematic attempts at interpretation."[16]

These formulations often draw, too, on less ostentatious forms of styling, such as euphony and balance ("Chaucer's eminence obscures Gower's excellence" [208]). Most characteristically, however, is the Pearsallian period, an imitative form, in which the complex but controlled and gradually cumulative syntax follows the contours of the object as if in intricate outline, arcing neatly toward its own precise conclusion:

> Henryson absorbs into his poetry a good deal of learning, in law, medicine, music and allegorised classical mythology as well as in other fields; he is scrupulously attentive to detail; and he is an artist of great technical expertness and resource, admirable not so much in *tours de force* like the majestic *Prayer for the Pest*, with its stanzas of triple internal rhyme, as in the systematic conciseness of his style, in which every word is weighed. (276)

Derek himself might have observed (borrowing an image from Keats he is particularly fond of), every rift here is loaded with ore, and so the simultaneous collection and ordering of disparate parts in the observation is almost as rich as the object itself.[17]

Because it has its roots in a common mode and because the technique virtually requires Derek's native wit, there is no straightforward lineage to trace from Derek's example (at least so far). And yet the practice is distinctive enough for it to be right to say that Tony Spearing is "Pearsallian" in his metaphors when he says here that the "impersonal . . . [and] . . . first-personal . . . melt into one another and merge" in *Troilus and Criseyde*'s narration, and, again, when he observes that so many subjectivities are drawn into the "orbit of Criseyde's own consciousness" that she is "surrounded by a luminous halo of feeling." Oliver Pickering can also be said to be "Pearsallian" in this way when he describes how the "long, complex verse sentences" of the *South English Legendary* "overflow the couplet boundaries" or how distinctive styles of this poet "seem to emerge naturally (as if representing peaks of inspiration) from the lower level." No moment in these essays is more densely Pearsallian, however, as when Spearing's description of a passage in *Troilus and Criseyde* approximates its complexity by entwining critical description with the poem's own language in order to describe a similar sort of entwining in the poem's form: "a kind of *dit* twined round the heterodiegesis 'as aboute a tree, with many a twiste, / Bytrent and writh the swote wodebynde' (III.1230–31)."

What makes any reading Pearsallian, however, is the conviction that, no matter how nuanced and well informed our historical understanding of the aesthetic criterion by which poetry was produced, the very ambitions that make language poetic require us to say whether it continues to measure up. Such reading is not peppered with but consists of what Driver characterizes as, in a slightly different connection (but in a wholly Pearsallian manner), "skewering." Derek's powers have therefore tended to come most fully into their own where poetry has the least to commend it. This is already clear in the quotations above on *The Ormulum*, Metham, and Lydgate—and accounts in itself for the fact that Derek was able to write such a gripping book on the last of these figures—but it reaches its zero degree when Derek dares to describe solely by identifying flaws:

> Of the mystery cycles it must be said that, though they contain some of what is good in the religious verse of the century, they contain more of what is bad, and that whatever interest these plays have from the point of view of theatre, social history or theology, little of that interest derives from any use of language that might be called effectively "poetic." (252)

Or:

> Of [the poets of the N-town plays] it is possible to say that at least they know what poetry should do, even if they cannot do it. (256)

Equally important to such reading is the courage to be as "outspoken" as the *Legendary* poet Pickering so fittingly describes in his essay. And it is in this sense equally fitting that Driver begins her essay by describing Derek as a "great *critic*," for he is one of a select few readers of medieval literature to have dared to criticize it. Such criticism is not informed by the belief that this literature falls short, however, but rather by an inspiring faith in its capacities and durability: Derek could never have found such fault did he not simply expect Old English and Middle English poetry to stand its ground against the literature produced in any period and for all time.

Christopher Cannon

NOTES

1. For the phrase, in an essay insisting that this mode of analysis "should not be ignored," see Derek Pearsall, "Towards a Poetics of Chaucerian Narrative," in *Drama, Narrative and Poetry in the "Canterbury Tales,"* ed. Wendy Harding (Toulouse: Presses Universitaires du Mirail, 2003), 112 (99–112).

2. See Stephen Best and Sharon Marcus, "Surface Reading: An Introduction," *Representations* 108 (2009): 1–21.

3. Derek Pearsall, "Gower's Narrative Art," *PMLA* 81 (1966): 475–84.

4. See Pearsall, "Gower's Narrative Art," 475, 478, 483.

5. See Lee Patterson, *Negotiating the Past: The Historical Understanding of Medieval Literature* (Madison: University of Wisconsin Press, 1987), 22–26; Charles Muscatine, *Chaucer and the French Tradition: A Study in Style and Meaning* (Berkeley: University of California Press, 1957).

6. Pearsall, "Gower's Narrative Art," 477 ("released") and 484 ("poetic").

7. The characterization is Derek's own. See his "The Pleasure of Popular Romance: A Prefatory Essay," in *Medieval Romance, Medieval Contexts*, ed. Rhiannon Purdie and Michael Cichon (Cambridge: D. S. Brewer, 2011), 9 (9–18).

8. Pearsall, "Pleasure of Popular Romance," 10.

9. Ibid.

10. Ibid. ("died out"); Julie Nelson Couch, "The Vulnerable Hero: *Havelok* and the Revision of Romance," *Chaucer Review* 42 (2008): 330, and see also 347 n. 3.

11. Pearsall, "Pleasure of Popular Romance," 11.

12. Matthew Arnold, "The Function of Criticism at the Present Time," in his *Essays in Criticism* (London: Macmillan, 1865), 19; reprinted in *Literary Theory Full-Text Database* (Cambridge: Chadwyck-Healey, 1999), online at http://gateway.proquest.com/openurl?ctx_ver=Z39.88-2003&xri:pqil:res_0.2&res_id=xri:lion-us&rft_id=xri:lion:ft:pr:Z100738761:1.

13. T. S. Eliot, "The Function of Criticism," in his *Selected Essays* (New York: Harcourt, Brace & World, 1950), 13–14 ("art") and 19 ("heat" and "critical") (12–22).

14. Arnold, "Function of Criticism," 1.

15. Derek Pearsall, *Old English and Middle English Poetry* (London: Routledge & Kegan Paul, 1977). Hereafter this volume is cited by page number in the text.

16. Derek Pearsall, *The Canterbury Tales* (Boston: George Allen & Unwin, 1985), 193 ("saw") and 238 ("recoils").

17. See, e.g., Derek Pearsall, *Arthurian Romance: A Short Introduction* (Oxford: Blackwell, 2003), 72.

CHAPTER 1

Narrative and Freedom in *Troilus and Criseyde*

A. C. Spearing

Derek Pearsall and I have never been colleagues, and Derek is much too young to have been my teacher; but I have known him, admired his work, and enjoyed his company for many years. (I believe we first met in Cambridge, as examiners of Jill Mann's PhD dissertation—the one that soon became her influential book *Chaucer and Medieval Estates Satire*.) So I felt my accidental place as first speaker in the conference to celebrate his eightieth birthday to be a great honor. Yet it made me very nervous, because it seemed so unlikely that I would be able to say anything worth saying that Derek had not already said, with deep learning, penetrating insight, luminous clarity, unimpugnable good sense, and engaging wit—"And if he have noght seyd it, leve brother, / In o book, he hath seyd it in another." But it also struck me that it would have been worse to be speaking last, when so many brilliant scholars would have said more brilliant things than I could possibly compete with, and it was even conceivable that Derek, for all his robustness and vigor, might be feeling a little tired. So I ceased to procrastinate, and began.

Narrative and Freedom is the title of a book by the Slavic scholar and literary theorist Gary Saul Morson. Morson begins from the constraints imposed by narrative itself as a "form of thought" and a means by which "we understand our lives," and he points out how "narratives, insofar as they rely on structure, are predisposed to convey a sense of fatalism, determinism, or otherwise closed time." "Life as it is experienced," Morson writes, "does not have closure or an Aristotelian ending, a point at which continuation is unthinkable and at which all loose ends are tied up."[1] His main concern is with the ways in which great Russian writers of the nineteenth and twentieth centuries, such as Dostoevsky and Tolstoy, escaped from the determinism imposed by the very form of narrative into something more like the freedom of "life as it is experienced." One way in which they did that, he explains, was by taking the risk of incorporating into their narratives real-life events which had not reached their conclusion at the time when they were writing. Scholars of medieval literature are no longer resistant to theory in general, but they have shown little interest in narrative theory, and Morson's work does not seem to have had much impact on medieval studies; yet it has illuminating implications for medieval narrative, and that is why I take it as the starting point for an essay on *Troilus and Criseyde.*

If narrative itself imposes structure and thus a certain determinism, in the Middle Ages that effect was greatly reinforced by the expectation that third-person narratives would be retellings of stories that already existed. We all know that medieval storytellers—and this applies especially to the more serious kinds of narrative—generally claim to be giving versions of stories already established by the authority of tradition: Malory's "Frensshe book," or "the authentic version as told by Thomas of Britain" invoked by Gottfried von Strassburg, or Chaucer's "olde stories" or his "auctour called Lollius."[2] We all know too that these authoritative sources were often invented or deceptively invoked, yet it really is the case that serious medieval third-person narrative—what Gérard Genette calls heterodiegesis, narrative "with the narrator absent from the story he tells"—almost always consists of the renarration of tales already told in the past.[3] As Derek has noted, "The story of Troilus and Criseyde was well known in fourteenth-century England," both in French from Benoît de Sainte-Maure's widely read twelfth-century *Roman de Troie* and in Latin from Guido delle Colonne's thirteenth-century *Historia destructionis Troiae*, a work still more widely read by those who knew Latin.[4] Chaucer made use of both of these, though his *Troilus* has as its chief source Giovanni Boccaccio's fourteenth-century *Filostrato*, an authority apparently known only to himself (presumably as a result of his visits to Italy) and carefully concealed from his readers.[5] In that sense *Troilus and Criseyde* was a renarration and would surely have been received as such; but retelling is still more in the foreground when a story is based in what is taken to be history. Lollius may be a fiction, but Chaucer, finding in Boccaccio a huge elaboration of a love story that already existed as part of the accepted history of Troy, must have seen himself as retelling a story that derived not just from earlier writings but from events that had actually occurred and been completed in the distant past. This is shaky ground, because medieval conceptions of "history" are hard to grasp. It was possible, certainly, for the truth of what was presented as history to be questioned, as when William of Newburgh denounced Geoffrey of Monmouth's *Historia regum Britanniae*, writing that "none except those ignorant of ancient histories can possibly doubt the extent of his wanton and shameless lying virtually throughout his book, which he calls *A History of the Britons*, when they come across it. He has not learnt the truth about events, and so without discrimination he gives space to fables without substance."[6] In general, though, what was narrated in old books, especially if they were in Latin, does not seem to have been distinguished from what had really happened. I find it hard to believe that Chaucer regarded his book of Troilus as fable. A great many personal details could only be speculation, as he repeatedly indicates, but the main outline of the story and its conclusion were predetermined and could not be changed.[7] And of course the "sense of fatalism, determinism, or otherwise closed time" that Morson refers to is evoked in *Troilus and Criseyde* in the characters' frequent glances back and forward, and is made perfectly explicit in Chaucer's addition of the soliloquy in Book IV, in which Troilus repeats Boethius's discussion of predestination and free will but omits the concluding stage of Lady Philosophy's argument, so as to leave fatalism as the only possibility. It was not until a century later that Henryson felt free to change the story's existing ending, so as to leave Criseyde dead of leprosy and Troilus alive, a situation incompatible with the outline followed by Chaucer.

At this point I want to bring to bear on Chaucer's poem a concept put forward in a book completed but not yet published at the time of the New Directions conference; it has now appeared as *Medieval Autographies: The "I" of the Text*.[8] By "autographies" I mean extended nonlyrical writings in the first person, texts of a kind that began to be prevalent in French in the thirteenth century, with dream poems from the *Roman de la Rose* onward and with *dits* such as those of Rutebeuf, but that did not emerge in English until the second half of the fourteenth century. In the anonymous dream poem *Winner and Waster*, probably from the early 1350s, the textual "I" is little more than an observer and reporter, but by the next decade, with the earliest version of *Piers Plowman* and Chaucer's *Book of the Duchess*, we encounter English dream poems that are genuinely homodiegetic, to use another term of Genette's, that is, examples of narrative "with the narrator present as a character in the story he tells."[9] But it may be that "narrative," as generally understood, is a misleading description of those and similar poems, which can incorporate within themselves more or less autonomous sections of lyric, letter, catalogue, doctrine, and other kinds of non-narrative material. In identifying this category of writing, I have been influenced by the attempts of French scholars to define an elusive genre known as the *dit*.[10] The *dit*'s elusiveness is indicated by their descriptions of it as "a genre formless in itself," one which "does not appear *a priori* to be very clearly defined by any particular formal or thematic characteristic" and one whose "specificity would lie precisely in not having any."[11] But though the *dit* is unbounded by existing generic limits, it has been pinned down more exactly in a seminal article by Jacqueline Cerquiglini.[12] To summarize her findings, the *dit* is a montage of discontinuous elements, a textual performance that stages an "I," that uses writing to create the illusion of speech, and that is often *about* writing, a form of *méta-écriture*. This is roughly what I mean by autography, which, however, I see as also appearing in dependent forms such as long prologues to heterodiegetic narratives and in first-person interventions in and commentaries on such narratives. It is distinct from auto*bio*graphy in that it exists as an autonomous mode of first-person writing not committed to any consistent relation to a real person seen as the origin of the text; nor is it a kind of dramatic monologue, presented as the utterance of a fictional person inside the text, an individual "narrator" or "speaker." Autography is autobiography with the *bio* left out; or, to put it differently, in autography "I" functions less as a pronoun, standing in place of a real or fictional person, than as an unanchored proximal deictic, serving to evoke proximality itself and thus experientiality—the effect of experience, as created, for example, in most cinematic narratives by the presence of the camera detached from any specific experiencing subject within the cinematic fiction.[13]

Autography can be seen as a reaction against the earlier predominance in medieval culture of the retelling of existing stories. While it was still felt, as it evidently was when Chaucer wrote *Troilus and Criseyde*, that the shape and outcome of serious heterodiegesis were predetermined not only by the requirements of narrative itself but also by what had already been written and perhaps had already occurred in reality, it seems likely that there was a growing wish, one felt by Chaucer himself, to find some way of escaping from that predetermination into a freer and less predictable kind of discourse. Morson contrasts the closure imposed by narrative form with the freedom or open-endedness of "life as it is experienced." It might be added that in writing, unlike film, "life as it is experienced" will usually be conveyed in the first person (regardless of the relation of that grammatical person to any specific human person), because that is what experience primarily means: *my* experience. In a book first published half a century ago, one that in the English-speaking world has proved to be the most influential study of narrative ever since, *The Rhetoric of Fiction*, Wayne Booth wrote that the most overworked distinction in narrative analysis was that of person. "To say that a story is told in the first or the third person," he declared, "will tell us nothing of importance." Twenty-two years later, in a second edition, he admitted that he was wrong; and he surely *was* wrong, because homodiegesis is potentially the language of life as it is experienced, indeterminate and open-ended (in the sense that we never get to the end of our experience until we cease to experience anything), while heterodiegesis, at least in the Middle Ages, implied fixedness and closure.[14]

Chaucer, learning from the French poets of the fourteenth century who were probably his favorite leisure reading, had written three dream poems before *Troilus and Criseyde*, all liberated in structure from the requirements of the retold story, all genuinely unpredictable in their forward movement. *Troilus and Criseyde* differs from the dream poems in that its fundamental narrative substance, its *matere*, is predetermined. In *The Book of the Duchess* the narrative is free to follow a path that is "litel used"—in fact entirely new, though put together from a miscellany of French sources.[15] In *Troilus and Criseyde* that is not so, yet it is generally agreed that its narratorial element owes much to those earlier experiments of Chaucer's in first-person writing. What critics have usually said is that the "narrator" of *Troilus and Criseyde* develops out of the "narrators" of *The Book of the Duchess*, *The House of Fame*, and *The Parliament of Fowls*. I once put it that way myself, writing that in all his major poems after *The Book of the Duchess*, "Chaucer conceals himself behind a similarly naïve narrator. The idiot-dreamer of *The Book of the Duchess* develops into the idiot-historian of *Troilus and Criseyde*."[16]

I have come to realize that this is misleading, first, because the narratorial elements in medieval narratives do not necessarily cohere as the utterances of an individual person, and second, because, in practice, use of the term *narrator* almost invariably involves a confusion of the poet as creator of the poetic text with a fictional storyteller who supposedly has internal responsibility for the entire contents of the poem. The historical development that led to this situation is summarized as follows by Ann Banfield:

> The term *narrator* entered the critical vocabulary as a legacy of the New Criticism and of Russian Formalism as the first person who recounts a story, a persona quite distinct from the author. The distinction was once necessary because Romantically inspired literary criticism often assumed that any first person in the text represented the author. Today, much criticism still recognizes only one notion, but, by a curious reversal of literary history, the term *narrator* replaces the now taboo *author* for both concepts.[17]

In some versions of the "narrator" approach, the responsibility of this internal storyteller is imagined to include even the text's formatting or *dispositio*; in others he is held to be responsible only for some parts of the text, those parts being arbitrarily selected by the critic.[18]

I heartily agree with Derek Pearsall that the conventional assumption that "first-person narrative is fallible and the voice of the narrator, when heard, is false" is mistaken.[19] If I had to choose between, on the one hand, referring to the textual "I" of *Troilus and Criseyde* as "the narrator" (adding a sprinkle of the usual disparaging epithets such as "unreliable," "foolish," "naive," "confused," or "obtuse") and, on the other, describing that "I," as Derek did in 1992, as "in the most literal sense, . . . Chaucer"—if I had to make that choice, I'd unhesitatingly follow Derek.[20] Certainly, the textual "I" is often a means of expressing the attitudes, views, and discoveries of the Chaucer who wrote the poem, and this is especially the case in first-person passages discussing the poem's narrative and poetic art. There indeed the "I" is closest to being a textual representation of the Chaucer who wrote the poem, though that Chaucer adopts a variety of roles. (And for this reason, in what follows, I often refer to the narratorial "I" as "Chaucer" rather than use some clumsy circumlocution to avoid calling him "the narrator.") But fictional narrator and literal poet are not the only possible options, and that is why I put forward the concept of autography, to refer to first-person writing in which the "I," rather than being an indicator of a distinct human person, whether fictional or real, is a means of introducing proximality, experientiality, and a liberating openness.

In Book I of *Troilus and Criseyde* the autographic "I" is relatively rare, but it emerges much more noticeably in Book II.[21] One reason for this, I believe, is that it was in writing Book II that Chaucer began to realize that the task he had undertaken in composing the poem could not be fulfilled on the terms he had originally intended. In the first line of Book I he announced his plan as being to tell of "the double sorwe of Troilus," but, as he translated and adapted the *Filostrato*, he gradually came to see that for him the interest of the story lay as much in its flawed heroine as in its doomed hero. What he referred to in the *Retractions* as "the book of Troilus" (X 1085) would have to become what he called it in *The Legend of Good Women*, "the bok / How that Crisseyde Troylus forsok" (G 264–65)—a narrative of the complicated process by which a woman worthy of Troilus's idealizing love could have become the deceptive female required by the existing history. Criseyde's infidelity to Troilus, he saw, was not simply something laid down in historical sources as the inevitable consequence of female fickleness, but was contingent on a whole variety of circumstances, the most fundamental of which was that of the vulnerability of a young widow, her need to rely on the protection of others and on what others think and say of her.[22] A woman whose husband is dead and father an absent traitor is the guardian of her own reputation and must always be concerned with it, something that Chaucer brings out (to give a single illustration) when he represents her as thinking:

> What men wolde of hit deme I kan nat seye;
> It nedeth me ful sleighly for to pleie. (II.461–62)

Chaucer understood better than Boccaccio the kinds of pressure a young woman could be under in such a situation: what she takes to be her autonomy (her ability to "play slyly" and even to understand her own motives) is really nothing of the kind, and in certain ways Criseyde's very claim to independent judgment, action, and choice makes her more of a victim—a somewhat Jamesian insight, if we think of *Troilus and*

Criseyde as *The Portrait of a Lady*. As in Boccaccio, she has a just sense of her own value as an attractive woman, and Chaucer reveals her awareness of this but also her wish to keep the awareness secret from others:

> For wel woot I myself, so God me spede—
> Al wolde I that noon wiste of this thought—
> I am oon the faireste . . . (744–46)

In Boccaccio she possesses this awareness but not the desire to conceal it. Boccaccio's Criseida, delightful though she is, is essentially an elaborated compound of the male stereotypes that were transmitted by the earlier histories known to Chaucer's audience.

Criseyde correctly foresees how those histories will define her—

> Allas, of me, unto the worldes ende,
> Shal neyther ben ywriten nor ysonge
> No good word, for thise bokes wol me shende (V.1058–60)

—but what came to interest Chaucer, and what he wanted his audience to imagine and judge for themselves, was the working of the internal and external factors, the intricate interaction of personal psychology and politics (including sexual and cultural politics), that led to this closure. The closure could not be changed, but we can recognize in the poem signs of change in Chaucer's understanding of the story he had to tell.[23] Morson observes:

> The creative process typically traces not a straight line to a goal but a series of false leads, missed opportunities, new possibilities, improvisations, visions, and revisions. It is constituted by an intention that evolves over time. To be sure, authors typically remove the traces of this process and present their work as if it were the product of a clear plan, known from the outset.[24]

In *Troilus and Criseyde* many such traces are not removed, a particularly striking instance being the retention in the proem to Book IV of the "false lead" according to which the fourth book was to have been the last.[25] What Chaucer did was to combine the predetermined narrative, enacted entirely by third persons, with a flexible autographic commentary, and in that way he was able to sustain the possibility of experiential openness up to the very moment that the story reached its unavoidable end.

Of course Chaucer was by no means the first medieval narrative poet to incorporate first-person commentary into heterodiegesis: in the romances of Chrétien de Troyes, to take a single example, we already find a largely narratorless narrative interspersed with patches of narratorial commentary. But once autography had developed as an independent kind of writing, autographic commentary on retold third-person narratives also began to flourish more vigorously. A major topic of the homodiegesis in *Troilus and Criseyde* is the task of telling the story: it evokes what Bakhtin, quoted by Morson, calls "the real present of the creative process," through a textual performance in which the "I" is a storyteller of no fixed address or identity responding freely, in a flexible variety of ways, to a fixed story.[26] The storytelling "I" is sometimes that of a humanistic poet, sometimes that of a bard appealing for inspiration, sometimes that of a humble entertainer, sometimes that of a historian baffled by his sources as he investigates and reassembles them. Sometimes too it is that of a writer as reteller increasingly aware of the necessary gap between language and historical reality—for his audience might expect him to convey "every word, or soonde, or look, or cheere" (III.492) of the lovers, but

> For sothe, I have naught herd it don er this
> In story non, ne no man here, I wene. (III.498–99)

This is indeed *méta-écriture*, a kind of *dit* twined round the heterodiegesis "as aboute a tree, with many a twiste, / Bytrent and writh the swote wodebynde" (III.1230–31). The two elements, romance and *dit*, heterodiegesis and autography, are almost inextricably bound together, and the combination is crucial to the poem's effect. Moreover, explicit commentary merges into modes of subjectless subjectivization—subjectivizing effects encoded in the narrative itself and not associated with any one definable human consciousness. The overall effect is to immerse the story told in feelings that do not have to be attributed either to the author or to a fictional narrator, and to evoke feelings in its audience that will differ for different readers and may indeed differ for a single reader on different readings of the poem. In what follows I attempt to illustrate this, in a way that was not possible in a brief conference paper.

It is in Book II above all that Chaucer adds passages of subjectivization and *méta-écriture* to the existing narrative. The chief effect of the additions is to enable us to enter into Criseyde's experience with greater empathy and to convey the problems for the poet that arise from this opening up of the story. Many of the additions directly report what Criseyde says or thinks and feels, or, like the narratorial intervention beginning at line 666 ("Now myghte som envious jangle thus . . ."), defend her against possible criticism of her behavior. My main focus here is not on these explicit redressings of the balance against the antifeminist bias of the story as previously told but on passages about the writing of the poem and on the subtler modes of subjectivization that loosen the narrative's fixity by bringing it closer to the experiential; and I consider only passages that have no equivalent in Boccaccio's *Filostrato*. My account cannot hope to be complete because the modes of subjectivization, ranging from the entirely impersonal to the explicitly first-personal, melt into one another and merge, at one extreme, into "pure narrative" that appears not to be subjectivized at all, and, at the other, into what appears as direct address by Chaucer to his readers or listeners.

The "I" that functions as a commentator on the heterodiegetic narrative of the lovers merges into the homodiegetic "I" concerned with the problems of telling their story. Book II begins with an extended homodiegetic passage of *méta-écriture* in which a composing "I" addresses "you." This is the seven-stanza proem, sharply focused on the problems of composition—Chaucer's need for assistance from Clio, the muse of history, his reliance on his Latin *auctour* (18, 49), and the strangeness caused by historical and cultural difference. The first-personalization is exceptionally strong. The proem's forty-nine lines include 23 first-person pronouns, 22 of them singular ("I," "me," "my") and one plural (24–25: "now wonder nyce and straunge / *Us* thinketh hem"). The first person implies the second: in an imagined scene of oral delivery, an "I" is addressing a plural "you" made up of many singular individuals whose possible responses are uncontrollably varied—"For to *thi* purpos this may liken *the*, / And *the* right nought" (45–46)—and the address occurs "now" (7, 24, 26) and "here" (11, 39) in "this place" (30, 43). There are many proximal deictics beyond the fundamental "I-now-here" cluster, in particular nine occurrences of "this" or "these"—two in the instances of "this place" just mentioned, the others probably all examples of textual deixis, pointing to what we are or have been reading: "thise blake wawes" (1) and "this see" (3, 5), referring to the "tempestous matere" (5) of Book I; "this book" (10), "this werk" (16), and simply "this" in "I this endite" (13); and "fro this forth" (9), meaning from this moment onward, a moment both in the story and in its telling. Textual and nontextual deixis mingle so closely together that they can hardly be distinguished: "here" in "Me nedeth here noon other art to use" (11) probably means "in this poem," while "here" in "If that they ferde in love as men don here" (39) blends the imagined place of recitation with a larger sense of this land, England, as opposed to the other lands where lovers may behave differently. (Similarly the plural first-person pronoun in "Us thinketh hem" [25] means us people in the place of recitation but also us living now as opposed to those who lived in the distant past of the story.) The overall effect is complex, but what predominates is the evocation of an overwhelmingly subjectivized and proximal present which is at once that of the *énonciation* and of the *énoncé*, the narration and the narrated—a present free from any determined future.

An autographic passage also concludes Book II; like the proem, it textualizes an imagined scene of oral delivery but is far shorter, only a single stanza. Within the diegesis, Pandarus has set up a complicated arrangement by which Criseyde will be alone with Troilus for the first time (alone except of course for Pandarus himself) but in a way that will not seem to be a romantic rendezvous that would compromise her reputation. Troilus, supposedly overcome by sickness when visiting Deiphebus's house—and, as he says, truly suffering from lovesickness—is lying in bed there in a small room separate from "the grete chaumbre" (1712), waiting with extreme nervousness for Pandarus to bring Criseyde to visit him. He can hear or half-hear Pandarus outside the room, urging his niece sotto voce not to waste time in hesitation but to make best use of this opportunity to embark upon a relationship while "folk is blent" (1743) and "ther yet devyneth noon / Upon yow two" (1741–42). (Yet Pandarus's words, as so often, are studiously vague as to what exactly he is urging Criseyde to do: she is as much the victim of her uncle's duplicity, of the deep-rooted ambiguity of courtly language, and of the imbalance of power served by that ambiguity as of her own conflicted longings.) At this moment of acute suspense comes an intervention from the storytelling "I":

> But now to yow, ye loveres that ben here,
> Was Troilus nought in a kankedort,

That lay, and myghte whisprynge of hem here,
And thoughte, "O Lord, right now renneth my sort
Fully to deye, or han anon comfort!"
And was the firste tyme he shulde hire preye
Of love; O myghty God, what shal he seye? (1751–57)

Unlike the proem, this cannot be described as *méta-écriture*: it is concerned not with the problems of the poet but with those of the lover, a character within the story; but as in the proem the imagined audience is plural, and its options are not fixed. The predetermined nature of the story dissolves into the freedom of a creative process in which the reader is invited to participate, and a space for that participation is provided by the gap between Books II and III.

In Book II, and especially in its second half, there are several passages in which a Chaucerian "I" comments reflexively on questions of poetry and narrative. In the extended scene that culminates in Criseyde's dream, the fall of night is described:

The dayes honour, and the hevenes yë,
The nyghtes foo—al this clepe I the sonne—
Gan westren faste, and downward for to wrye,
As he that hadde his dayes cours yronne. (904–7)

In this *chronographia*, the series of circumlocutory expressions, three metaphors and a simile, that contribute to saying but not saying that the sun was setting, are markers of stylistic elevation. The statement explaining the kennings for "the sun" reminds us of the poem's textuality; it may imply some self-mockery, but probably we should assume that some at least of Chaucer's public would need the explanation but might also be willing to smile at themselves for needing it. A few lines later, when Criseyde's women have put her to bed, Chaucer writes:

Whan al was hust, than lay she stille and thoughte
Of al this thing; the manere and the wise
Reherce it nedeth nought, for ye ben wise. (915–17)

Here the address to a plural "you" explicitly invites readers to complete the scene out of their own individual imaginations, sharing in the "creative process" in a freedom beyond Chaucer's control.

From this point on, there is an increasing number of instances of *méta-écriture*. The most important, and the one that helps to explain the others, occurs shortly before Book II's open conclusion. The morning after Troilus has gone to visit Deiphebus and taken to his bed there, other guests arrive for dinner, all this being in accordance with Pandarus's scheme. Eleyne arrives, and so do Criseyde and Antigone and Antigone's sister Tharbe; and at this point the composing "I" intervenes, subsumed in a "we," to request the audience's or reader's assistance in hastening things along:

But fle we now prolixitee best is,
For love of God, and lat us faste go
Right to th'effect, withouten tales mo,
Whi al this folk assembled in this place;
And lat us of hire saluynges pace. (1564–68)

"Prolixitee" is a somewhat technical term, and we listeners or readers are invited to share in responsibility for the craft of storytelling. In the absence of any rule of courtly romance requiring an account to be given of the "saluynges" whenever a social group convenes, we shall probably not object. The motive for this desire to flee prolixity must surely be Chaucer's awareness that in adding so much detail to his sources he may really seem unacceptably prolix to his readers, because, as he wrote in the passage from Book III quoted above:

For sothe, I have naught herd it don er this
In story non, ne no man here, I wene. (III.498–99)

Textual symptoms of that underlying anxiety appear in other references in the latter part of Book II to the need to abbreviate the narrative. In answer to Troilus's letter to Criseyde, she, at Pandarus's bidding, writes one to Troilus,

Of which to telle in short is myn entente
Th'effect, as fer as I kan understonde. (1219–20)

Pandarus reluctantly accepts for the moment his niece's hesitance to meet Troilus in person, and Chaucer asks, "What sholde I make of this a long sermoun?" (1299)—perhaps also a gesture toward the complexity of a situation that defies brief and explicit narration, leaving us to work it out for ourselves if we choose. Pandarus approaches Deiphebus to collaborate in his scheme to bring about the meeting, and an explanation of his established friendship with Deiphebus is cut short with "To telle in short, withouten wordes mo . . ." (1405). "To telle in short" is repeated in the account of Pandarus's visit to Troilus to explain the scheme to him (1492). A more elaborate *occupatio* fits into the same pattern:

What nedeth yow to tellen al the cheere
That Deiphebus unto his brother made,
Or his accesse, or his sikliche manere,
How men gan hym with clothes for to lade
Whan he was leyd, and how men wolde hym glade? (1541–45)

The anxiety about excessive detail emerges again more explicitly when a justification of Criseyde's secret pleasure in her power over a man so much admired as Troilus is cut short:

For who is that ne wolde hire glorifie,
To mowen swich a knyght don lyve or dye?
But al passe I, lest ye to longe dwelle;
For for o fyn is al that evere I telle. (1593–96)

And there is yet another rhetorical question about delay in getting to that "fyn" when Chaucer cuts short an account of the company's denunciations of Poliphete, Criseyde's supposed enemy, with "What shold I lenger in this tale tarien?" (1622).[27]

This rhetorical question is a repetition of one asked by Pandarus a few lines earlier in abbreviating his account of Poliphete's alleged malicious actions: "'What sholde I lenger,' quod he, 'do yow dwelle?'" (1614). It is striking that the many indications of the need for haste in the later stages of Book II come not only from the narrating "I" but from the characters themselves, and especially from Pandarus. In an important sense, Pandarus is the poet's surrogate within the poem, devising the schemes that drive the action; and near the end of Book I it was Pandarus who was responsible for a notable yet half-concealed instance of *méta-écriture*, when a passage from Geoffrey of Vinsauf's *Poetria nova* that likens the advance planning of a poem to the designing of a house was adapted to refer to the planning of a love affair:

For everi wight that hath an hous to founde
Ne renneth naught the werk for to bygynne
With rakel hond, but he wol bide a stounde,
And sende his hertes line out fro withinne
Aldirfirst his purpos for to wynne.
Al this Pandare in his herte thoughte,
And caste his werk ful wisely or he wroughte. (I.1065–71)[28]

Only after the house-building analogy is complete do we learn that it represents Pandarus's thought; in its immediate context, line 1065 seems to introduce one of the many purported explanations beginning with "For" that form part of the poem's general narratorial discourse. The accepted teaching of the medieval *ars poetica* that a poem must be, to borrow Morson's words quoted above, "the product of a clear plan, known from the outset," or in Geoffrey of Vinsauf's words, *prius archetypus quam sensilis* (an idea before becoming a sensible reality), is just what autography undermines, allowing evidence of changes of plan arrived at in the process of composition itself to remain in the text.[29] We cannot know at exactly what stage in composing *Troilus and Criseyde* Chaucer came to recognize that he must diverge from his original "double sorwe of Troilus" plan, but, since Pandarus's careful planning eventually comes to nothing, it seems likely enough that by the end of Book I Chaucer already had in mind that the poem too would in part have to be about a poet's struggles to reshape his material, to open up the closed narrative that was his source, and then eventually to submit to closing it down again with Criseyde's infidelity and Troilus's death.

Pandarus is also the source of a section of *méta-écriture*, not found in Boccaccio, early in Book II. Preparing to heighten Criseyde's interest in the "thyng to doon yow pleye" (121) that he has temptingly mentioned but not specified (it is the news that Troilus loves her), he remarks:

How so it be that som men hem delite
With subtyl art hire tales for to endite,
Yet for al that, in hire entencioun
Hire tale is al for som conclusioun. (256–59)

Here there are many terms alluding to the storyteller's art: "art" itself and "tale(s)," the concepts of *intentio* and *conclusio*, and "endite," referring specifically to composition in writing. (Cerquiglini notes the association of *dit* and *ditié* with "the Latin *dictare*, meaning in Old French: *to write, to draw up, to teach*.")[30] Deceptively abjuring the very subtlety he is using, Pandarus goes on:

> And sithe th'ende is every tales strengthe,
> And this matere is so bihovely,
> What sholde I peynte or drawen it on lengthe . . . ? (260–62)

"Matere" (Latin *materia*) is a fundamental term in the *ars poetica*, and "peynte" has a general reference to the idea of *ut pictura poesis* and to the use of terms such as "colours" to refer to rhetorical elaboration. Finally we are told what Pandarus is thinking:

> If I my tale endite
> Aught harde, or make a proces any whyle,
> She shal no savour have therin but lite . . . (267–69)

Once again "endite" is used, and perhaps the underlying idea is what the *artes poeticae* call *ornatus difficilis*. Pandarus's words and thoughts correspond to the themes of autography as found in the French *dit*.

To return now to the final stages of Book II, we can see that the increasingly frequent references to the need to avoid delay, coming equally from Chaucer and from Pandarus, pervade the whole narrative discourse. Chaucer's interventions to stress the need to avoid delay in telling the story merge into the need Pandarus feels to avoid delay if his scheme to bring Criseyde and Troilus together is not to fall apart. Words such as "tarry," "anon," "com of" (italicized in the following quotations), along with others relating to shortness of time and the necessity for speed, occur again and again:

"and that *anon*, iwys" (1635: Pandarus)
"So ther be no *taryinge*" (1642: Pandarus)
"in short" (1658: Pandarus)
"Withouten more" (1666: Chaucer)[31]
"As sone as I may gon" (1684: Troilus)
"Now lat hem rede, and torne we *anon* / To Pandarus" (1709–10: Chaucer)
"and that in hye" (1712: Chaucer)

"*com of anon!* / Thynk al swich *taried* tyde, but lost it nys" (1738–39: Pandarus)
"*come of* now, if ye konne!" (1742: Pandarus)
"titeryng, and pursuyte, and delayes" (1744: Pandarus)
"Las, tyme ilost!" (1749: Pandarus)
"*Com of*, therfore" (1750: Pandarus)

The main effect is to bring about a convergence of the world of the story with that of the telling in an overwhelming sense of urgency. The many references to abbreviation do not come from any single source: the effect is not to point to a clumsy "narrator" but to convey the breathless haste of what is being narrated.

As I noted above, a whole range of modes of subjectivization are employed in Book II to loosen the fixed narrative and move it toward a more fluid experientiality. In an earlier study of *Troilus and Criseyde*, I observed, "When we look closely at almost any narrative passage in Chaucer, we find not a single shaping subjectivity but the traces of many different centres of consciousness."[32] To give a comprehensive account of such traces in Book II would be intolerably tedious, for they are an intrinsic element in the fabric of Chaucerian narrative, but I give here a few random illustrations, focusing especially on ways they invite readers to be more than consumers of a retelling and to bring their own feelings and imaginations to take part in the creative process.[33] The least noticeable subjectivizing effect, one not peculiar to Chaucer, is encoded in the narrative text itself, with deixis as the predominant means. Examples include unobtrusive linking phrases such as "So after this" in

> So after this, with many wordes glade,
> And frendly tales, and with merie chiere,
> Of this and that they pleide . . . (148–50)

or "With that" in lines such as "With that thei gonnen laughe" (99), "With that she gan hire eighen down to caste" (253), "With that the teris breste out of his yën" (326), or "Wyth that she gan ful sorwfully to syke" (428). There the distal deictic "that" places what has preceded in the past of both narrative time and the reader's experience while establishing continuity with what follows. "With that word" (250) works similarly, as does "With this" in "With this he stynte, and caste adown the heed" (407) or "With this he took his leve, and hom he wente" (596). Here the deictics are proximal, but more important, probably, than the difference between proximal "this" and distal "that" is the general effect of deixis in rendering the diegetic sequence experiential. An interesting example of how proximal deictics can imply the experiential copresence of poet and audience, even though neither is explicitly present as "I" and "you," is this account of Criseyde's curiosity to read the letter from Troilus that Pandarus has thrust "in hire bosom" (1155) but to do so without attracting attention:

> But of hire besynesses this was on—
> Amonges othere thynges, out of drede—
> Ful pryvely this lettre for to rede. (1174–76)
>
> ———
>
> [But *this* was one of her concerns—
> among other things, no doubt—
> to read *this* letter in great secrecy.]

The first "this" is cataphoric, pointing forward over the parenthesis of line 1175 to what is going to be mentioned next, while the second is anaphoric, indicating that the letter has been mentioned in the preceding text; but both have an effect of proximal demonstrativity that goes beyond their textual functions, so that, taken together, they imply a subjective relation of proximality in which both poet and reader or listener participate. And "out of drede" also subjectivizes the narration in a more explicit way, offering assurance that reading the letter must have been only one of the things she was anxious to do. The source of the assurance is undefined: it could be interpreted ironically, but if so the irony would surely not be directed (as the "narrator" way of reading would suggest) toward a fictional storyteller anxious to downplay Criseyde's curiosity but toward Criseyde herself, pretending to have other concerns when what she really wants is to read the letter.

Of the many other implicit means of subjectivization, I want to mention just one that is common in *Troilus and Criseyde*: the insertion of statements purporting to explain what happens in the story in terms of generalizations about human behavior which, it is assumed, will be shared by the reader or listener. (Such generalizations, "made in a collective and anonymous voice originating in traditional human experience," were identified by Roland Barthes in his famous analysis of Balzac's *Sarrasine* as "cultural codes.")[34] A simple example in Book II occurs immediately after lines 148–50 quoted above, when Pandarus comes to visit Criseyde in her palace and it is stated that they exchange "wordes glade" and "frendly tales" (148–49) "As frendes doon whan thei ben mette yfere" (152). We all know (it's implied) how friends behave when they meet; but in *Troilus and Criseyde* such generalizations have a purpose beyond what they serve for less historically minded medieval storytellers: they are part of a larger attempt by Chaucer to help us think of the pagan past as, in most ways, simply human, and thus familiar rather than alien. A cluster of generalizations of this kind occurs later when Troilus reads Criseyde's letter. His careful reading gives him hope, "But as we may alday oureselven see" (1331), hope increases his desire; "Wherefore I seye alwey" (1338) that he persevered under Pandarus's guidance

> And dide also his other observaunces
> That til a lovere longeth in this cas. (1345–46)

Chaucer enters sympathetically into Troilus's feelings but at the same time shares with his audience the understanding that they are not unique to him but follow a recognizable pattern for young lovers—a pattern that belongs to the medieval present as much as to the Trojan past.

Near the end of Book II, a similar generalization is inserted when Troilus is lying sick in Deiphebus's house. Those present lament his sickness, and then,

> After compleynte, hym gonnen they to preyse,
> As folk don yet whan som wight hath bygonne
> To preise a man, and up with pris hym reise
> A thousand fold yet heigher than the sonne. (1583–86)

Here the appeal to an accepted and transhistorical truth is more explicit: the unconscious lack of historical sense found in earlier medieval romances (and many later ones) gives way to a conscious emphasis on the shared human experience of past and present times. A more complex use of this kind of cultural generalization occurs before this, when Criseyde has seen Troilus riding past her window and Pandarus first urges her to "spek with hym in esyng of his herte" (1287) and then hurries to visit Troilus. He finds him "allone abedde," lying, "as do thise lovers, in a traunce" (1305–6). We medieval readers all know how lovers behave (or at least how they behave in courtly romances), but this is just one element in a more fundamental insight, that what for Troilus is a unique experience—here one of tension between hope and despair—is actually the common experience of all lovers. A "narrator" reading would perhaps see line 1306 as coming from a naive fictional storyteller who can only report on love from the outside, but a richer reading will recognize a humane amusement at adolescent extremes of emotion—and perhaps, beyond that, a more general perception of the paradox that for all lovers the experience of love is unique, yet it always leads them to behave in the same way.

Sometimes such generalizations about human behavior, instead of floating in total anonymity, seem to be pulled magnetically toward the consciousness of one of the characters, to produce something like free indirect discourse. A large part of what Chaucer added in Book II to his hidden Italian source was devoted to filling in Criseyde's thoughts and feelings, especially when she is left alone. Once Pandarus has departed, after his first revelation that Troilus loves her, she retires to "hire closet" (599), a small private room, the objective setting for the expression of private subjectivity, and ponders on what he has said:

> And wex somdel astoned in hire thought
> Right for the newe cas; but whan that she
> Was ful avysed, tho fond she right nought
> Of peril why she ought afered be,
> For man may love, of possibilite,
> A womman so, his herte may tobreste,
> And she naught love ayein, but if hire leste. (603–9)

The last three lines present a generalization about what is possible in human relations—what can sometimes happen but also what is socially acceptable or ethically permissible. The two "may"s in lines 607 and 608 are delightfully ambiguous, and a third is to be understood in line 609: a man *may* so love a woman that his heart *may* break, yet she *may* not return his love unless she wishes. The context strongly implies that this train of thought is Criseyde's; yet the explanatory "For" (found as the first word in so many of the poem's lines) seems to place it in the realm of commentary coming from elsewhere, a realm of "traditional human experience" outside the fiction. To interpret it as coming from a simple-minded narrator who truly accepts it as an adequate justification for Criseyde to be convinced that she is in no danger is to weaken it by resolving its many uncertainties.

A somewhat similar effect is found in a later passage, when Pandarus is urging his niece to show greater "routhe" (1280) toward Troilus and "Lat nycete nat do yow bothe smerte" (1288). These lines follow:

> But theron was to heven and to doone.
> Considered al thing it may nat be;
> And whi? For speche; and it were ek to soone
> To graunten hym so gret a libertee. (1289–92)

The absence of attribution is striking, and leaves us free to imagine for ourselves whose thought is being represented. Given that Pandarus has just been speaking, line 1289 seems most likely to represent his recognition that still further exertion on his part will be needed to achieve his goal. But then whose consideration is implied by the absolute construction "Considered al thing," and what are all those things, and what is the "it" that may not be? Line 1291 begins with a question whose source is again not specified, and which is answered by the equally unattributed statement that also ("ek") it would be ("were") too soon to grant Troilus so great a liberty. Whose sense of propriety is determining that it would be too soon? And if it *would* be too soon, that implies possible circumstances in which it *would not* be too soon—but what are they? We have surely moved from Pandarus's thoughts to Criseyde's, by way of an apparently anonymous but perhaps authorial question and answer. Cultural codes are in play but with a vagueness that begs for our participation; and the consciousnesses evoked cannot be clearly distinguished one from another. This is very free, very indirect discourse.

To return to the scene in Criseyde's "closet" previously discussed: at this point Troilus comes riding slowly past,

> Right as his happy day was, sooth to seyne,
> For which, men seyn, may nought destourbed be
> That shal bityden of necessitee. (621–23)

Here the uncertainty about where the commentary is coming from is very explicit, in the gap between the full endorsement of "sooth to seyne" and the more doubtful "men seyn." This section of Book II includes much description, for example, in the *effictio* of Troilus returning from battle in lines 624–48—armed but with his head bare, his horse wounded and bleeding, his helmet and shield battered by the enemy. He is described largely in terms of sight, and after the description (not before) we are told that "Criseÿda gan al his chere aspien" (649), so that retrospectively we can feel that he has been seen through her admiring eyes. But others are also looking: her household has cried out, "A, go we se!" (615), and there are also "the peple" (643), common onlookers whose shouts of praise make Troilus blush. No specific *origo* can be identified, either within the text or without, for what is seen and what is asserted, especially since so many of the constructions concerning sight are impersonal, with verbs in the infinitive. As the italicized words in the following quotations indicate, a lot of seeing is going on, but it is not specified who is doing it:

"swich a knyghtly *sighte* . . . / As was on hym, was nought . . . / To *loke* on Mars" (628–30)
"So lik a man of armes and a knyght / He was to *seen*" (631–32)
"to *seen* hym . . . so weldy *semed* he . . . / It was an heven upon hym for to *see*" (635–37)
"His sheeld . . . / In which men myghte many an arwe *fynde* [discern]" (640–41)
"to *byholde* [his blushes] it was a noble game" (647)

In this passage, with no narratorial "I," the underlying formal *effictio* is almost dissolved into a widely diffused experientiality; yet the subjectivity is not entirely subjectless, because it is drawn into the orbit of Criseyde's own consciousness and self-consciousness, as Troilus's blushes give way to Criseyde's:

Criseÿda gan al his chere aspien,
And leet it so softe in hire herte synke,
That to hireself she seyde, "Who yaf me drynke?"

For of hire owen thought she wex al reed . . . (649–52)

The recollection of the Tristan legend in "Who yaf me drynke?" may ultimately be seen as part of what Barry Windeatt has called the "disenchantment of romance" in *Troilus and Criseyde*, yet at this moment

Criseyde's experience of love remains enchanted, and perhaps all the more so because, in an almost Virginia Woolf way, it is surrounded by a luminous halo of feeling not hers.[35]

In the brief but penetrating and still enormously stimulating account of Chaucer that Derek Pearsall gave thirty-five years ago in his *Old English and Middle English Poetry*, the word *freedom* occurs many times. Derek puts special emphasis on the freedom that Chaucer enjoyed and achieved from the merely doctrinal purposes of writing: the freedom from censorship and self-censorship available in the years before the campaign against Lollardy, the freedom from "the potential embarrassments of authorial narrative" that he achieved in the *Canterbury Tales* and retained by not "committing himself to a consistent dramatic ethic," and "the freedom to explore the world" that he sought throughout his career as a poet. In *Troilus and Criseyde* Derek finds "an unprecedented quality of dramatic life, freedom and actuality," and he sees that freedom as secured "by subtle manipulative shifts of emphasis and angle which keep alive the audience's sense of continuous living process" and "by techniques of layered and multi-levelled narration."[36] What I have tried to investigate in this essay is some other aspects of the narrative freedom that Derek recognized in Chaucer's greatest poem. Though Christopher Cannon finds traces of Pearsallian style in this essay, I am afraid that my employment of jargon such as "homodiegetic," "heterodiegetic," "proximal," and "cataphoric" may not be very appealing to a scholar as skilled as Derek in using the common language to express subtle meanings. But I hope he will believe in the sincerity of my tribute to his work, from which I have learned so much.

Notes

1. Gary Saul Morson, *Narrative and Freedom: The Shadows of Time* (New Haven: Yale University Press, 1994), 5, 8, 38.

2. Sir Thomas Malory, *Le Morte Darthur*, ed. Stephen H. A. Shepherd (New York: Norton, 2004), 8 ("whether it were Powlis or not, the Frensshe book maketh no mencyon") and many other places; Gottfried von Strassburg, *Tristan*, trans. A. T. Hatto (Harmondsworth: Penguin, 1967), 43; *Knight's Tale* A 859 and *Troilus* I 394, both ed. Larry D. Benson, *The Riverside Chaucer*, 3rd ed. (Boston: Houghton Mifflin, 1987). All subsequent Chaucer quotations are taken from this edition, with book or fragment and line numbers given in the text.

3. Gérard Genette, *Narrative Discourse: An Essay in Method*, trans. Jane E. Lewin (Ithaca: Cornell University Press, 1980), 244.

4. Derek Pearsall, *The Life of Geoffrey Chaucer: A Critical Biography* (Oxford: Blackwell, 1992), 169.

5. Conceivably a few of Chaucer's intimates might have known of his debt to Boccaccio, but it seems clear that he wished to give the impression of relying on Latin sources such as those indicated in the (possibly authorial) marginal glosses in the best *Troilus* manuscripts.

6. Preface to William of Newburgh, *A History of English Affairs, Book I*, ed. and trans. P. G. Walsh and M. J. Kennedy (Warminster: Aris & Phillips, 1988), 31.

7. E.g., *Troilus* I 132–33: "But wheither that she children hadde or noon, / I rede it naught."

8. A. C. Spearing, *Medieval Autographies: The "I" of the Text* (Notre Dame: University of Notre Dame Press, 2012). The book originated as the Robert M. Conway Lectures, given at Notre Dame in 2007, and I was glad to be able to draw on it at the "New Directions" conference, sponsored by the Notre Dame Medieval Institute through Mr. Conway's generosity.

9. Genette, *Narrative Discourse*, 245.

10. The connection was first noted by John Burrow, "Hoccleve and the Middle French Poets," in *The Long Fifteenth Century: Essays for Douglas Gray*, ed. Helen Cooper and Sally Mapstone (Oxford: Clarendon Press, 1997), 35–49. See also Burrow's earlier comment on the neglect of "Gower's debt to the fourteenth-century French *dits amoreux*," in J. A. Burrow, "The Portrayal of Amans in *Confessio Amantis*," in *Gower's Confessio Amantis: Responses and Reassessments*, ed. A. J. Minnis (Cambridge: D. S. Brewer, 1983), 5–24, at 6.

11. Michel Zink, *The Invention of Literary Subjectivity*, trans. David Sices (Baltimore: Johns Hopkins University Press, 1999), 50; Michel Zink, "Dit," in *Dictionnaire des lettres françaises*, ed. Robert Bossuat et al., rev. ed. (Paris: Fayard, 1992), 38 (my translation); Anthime Fourrier, ed., *Dits et Debats, Jean Froissart* (Geneva: Droz, 1979), 13 (my translation).

12. Jacqueline Cerquiglini, "Le clerc et l'écriture: Le *Voir Dit* de Guillaume de Machaut et la définition du *dit*," in *Literatur in der Gesellschaft des Spätmittelalters*, ed. Hans Ulrich Gumbrecht (Heidelberg: C. Winter, 1980), 151–68.

13. Cf. Ann Banfield, "Describing the Unobserved: Events Grouped around an Empty Centre," in *The Linguistics of Writing: Arguments between Language and Literature*, ed. Nigel Fabb et al. (Manchester: Manchester University Press, 1987), 265–85.

14. Wayne Booth, *The Rhetoric of Fiction* (Chicago: University of Chicago Press, 1961), 150; 2nd ed. (Chicago: University of Chicago Press, 1983), 412.

15. *Book of the Duchess*, 400.

16. A. C. Spearing, "Chaucer the Writer," in *An Introduction to Chaucer*, by Maurice Hussey, A. C. Spearing, and James Winny (Cambridge: Cambridge University Press, 1965), 121.

17. Ann Banfield, "The Formal Coherence of Represented Speech and Thought," *PTL: A Journal for Descriptive Poetics and Theory of Literature* 3 (1978): 289–314, at 296.

18. I gave a detailed account of these developments in *Troilus* criticism in A. C. Spearing, *Textual Subjectivity: The Encoding of Subjectivity in Medieval Narratives and Lyrics* (Oxford: Oxford University Press, 2005), chap. 3. For one illustration of the confusion, see Donald W. Rowe, *O Love O Charite! Contraries Harmonized in Chaucer's Troilus* (Carbondale: Southern Illinois University Press, 1976): "The *narrator*'s efforts to deal with the poem he has created continue in the epilogue and remain inadequate, ambiguous, and often comic" (164; my emphasis).

19. Pearsall, *Life of Geoffrey Chaucer*, 174.

20. Ibid., 173. This is something about which Derek's opinion, like mine, has shifted. In his *Old English and Middle English Poetry* (London: Routledge & Kegan Paul, 1977), 204, he referred, by contrast, to Chaucer's "consistent use . . . of a fictionalised narrative *persona*."

21. It may not be by chance that this book includes a scene, that of Antigone's song, in which the instability of a textual "I" is conspicuously underlined. In the seven stanzas of the "Troian song" (825) sung by Antigone in praise of love and in vehement defense of it against its detractors, first-person-singular pronouns occur no fewer than 28 times; and as we read these stanzas we are surely lulled into assuming that the "I" of the song is Antigone herself. But then in the next stanza Criseyde asks her, "Who made this song?" (878), and Antigone explains that the composer was "the goodlieste mayde / Of gret estat in al the town of Troye" (880–81), though without revealing who that might be. In this episode entirely of his own invention, Chaucer seems to go out of his way to remind us that the grammatical first person is a shifter, though human persons are not. As I was writing this essay I came upon a reference, in a review of a recent novel, to "the fraudulence of the first-person narrator, who is pretending to be speaking to the reader off the cuff even as the novel has been rewritten a thousand times by the laboring author" (James Wood, "Broken Record," *New Yorker*, May 21, 2012, 74–76, at 75). No doubt there is some such "fraudulence" in the narratorial discourse of *Troilus and Criseyde*, but I think it likely that Chaucer really was shaping his story as he was telling it, was sometimes responding to discoveries made in the course of telling it, and chose not to cover up all such discoveries by revision.

22. Gretchen Mieszkowski, "The Reputation of Criseyde, 1155–1500," *Transactions of the Connecticut Academy of Arts and Sciences* 43 (1971): 71–153, notes that "for at least three centuries, Criseyde was a type figure, a standard example of a fickle woman," and that this stereotyping "derives from the earliest version of her story, Benoît de Sainte-Maure's Old French poem, *Le Roman de Troie*" (79). Mieszkowski assumes that Chaucer reproduces the

stereotype, while his "narrator" foolishly rejects it. Before the "narrator" interpretation was imposed on *Troilus and Criseyde*, J. S. P. Tatlock had been able to see that "knowing his readers to be aware of what Criseyde will finally do, Chaucer feels no responsibility for making it seem inevitable, and devotes himself to making her *simpatica*" (Tatlock, "The Epilog of Chaucer's *Troilus*," *Modern Philology* 18 [1920–21]: 625–59, at 636 n. 1).

23. This case was persuasively argued by Derek Pearsall's colleague and collaborator, Elizabeth Salter, in "*Troilus and Criseyde*: A Reconsideration" (1966) and "*Troilus and Criseyde*: Poet and Narrator" (1982), both reprinted in Salter, *English and International: Studies in the Literature, Art and Patronage of Medieval England*, ed. Derek Pearsall and Nicolette Zeeman (Cambridge: Cambridge University Press, 1988), 215–38. See also Barry Windeatt, "*Troilus and Criseyde*: Love in a Manner of Speaking," in *Writings on Love in the English Middle Ages*, ed. Helen Cooney (New York: Palgrave, 2006), 81–97.

24. Morson, *Narrative and Freedom*, 24.

25. See Spearing, *Medieval Autographies*, 110–11, elaborated in A. C. Spearing, "Time in *Troilus and Criseyde*," in *Traditions and Innovations in the Study of Medieval English Literature: The Influence of Derek Brewer*, ed. Charlotte Brewer and Barry Windeatt (Cambridge: D. S. Brewer, 2013), 60–72.

26. M. M. Bakhtin, *Problems of Dostoevsky's Poetics*, ed. and trans. Caryl Emerson (Minneapolis: University of Minnesota Press, 1984), 63. We need to remember, though, that in a retold story "creation" is not out of nothing.

27. There is another kind of *méta-écriture* in Book II in the form of Pandarus's advice to Troilus on the *ars dictandi* (1023–43), followed by a first-person summary of the letter that Troilus actually writes (1065–85) and of Criseyde's reply (1221–25). The summaries obliquely indicate the conventionality, wearying length, and excessively convoluted syntax of the lovers' letters, and (for modern readers who can consult the 88-line and 56-line Boccaccian originals) become an amusingly pointed Chaucerian critique of his Italian source. The statement, in the passage quoted above about Criseyde's letter, that Chaucer intends to give a brief account of the gist of it "as fer as I kan understonde" (1220), thus serves two purposes: not only to emphasize the need for haste, but to point to the unnecessary length and difficulty of the letter as an obstacle to haste. I discuss the way the letters are summarized in Spearing, *Medieval Autographies*, 261–62.

28. As has often been pointed out, lines 1065–69 are based on *Poetria nova* 43–48, in *Les arts poétiques du XIIe et du XIIIe siècle*, ed. Edmond Faral (Paris: Honoré Champion, 1926), 198.

29. *Poetria nova*, ed. Faral, line 48.

30. Cerquiglini, "Le clerc et l'écriture," 159–60.

31. Though the most obvious sense of this phrase is "without anything further," it might also mean "without delay," recalling the use of Latin *mora* (delay) in treatises on rhetoric or poetics to refer to the means of amplification.

32. Spearing, *Textual Subjectivity*, 95.

33. The element of readerly participation in Book II was brilliantly explored by Donald Howard, "Experience, Language and Consciousness: *Troilus and Criseyde*, II, 596–931," in *Medieval Literature and Folklore Studies*, ed. Jerome Mandel and B. A. Rosenberg (New Brunswick, NJ: Rutgers University Press, 1970), 173–92.

34. Roland Barthes, *S/Z*, trans. Richard Miller (New York: Hill and Wang, 1974), 18. The example Barthes discusses—"I was deep in one of those daydreams which overtake even the shallowest of men, in the midst of the most tumultuous parties"—is more oblique in that it implies rather than states the generalization that even shallow men can have daydreams in noisy surroundings.

35. Barry Windeatt, "*Troilus* and the Disenchantment of Romance," in *Studies in Medieval English Romances: Some New Approaches*, ed. Derek Brewer (Cambridge: D. S. Brewer, 1988), 129–47.

36. Pearsall, *Old English and Middle English Poetry*, 195, 207, 204, 206.

CHAPTER 2

How Good Is the Outspoken *South English Legendary* Poet?

A New Edition of the Prologue to the *Conception of Mary*

Oliver Pickering

I first introduced the so-called Outspoken *South English Legendary* Poet at the 1991 York Manuscripts Conference, and I was particularly encouraged by the generous support I received from Derek Pearsall at the time. He bolstered my belief that Middle English literary study can include identifying, describing, and illustrating the individual poetic voice, even if that voice has to remain anonymous. And Derek's own way of writing about Middle English poetry, succinctly characterizing virtues and failings, seems to me to have liveliness and individuality similar to those of the author under discussion here.

Questions surround the Outspoken Poet, principally relating to the distinguishing features of his writing and the certainty with which his verse can be identified. Speaking generally, he was a major contributor to the late-thirteenth-century *South English Legendary* collection (*SEL*), being the principal reviser and expander of an earlier form of the legendary. Using Manfred Görlach's terms, he represents work done in Gloucestershire as part of the "A" version of the *SEL*, as opposed to the original "Z" version that Görlach located in Worcestershire.[1] His hand can also be seen, at length, in some of the *temporale* narratives—mainly poems on the life of Christ and Mary—which sit alongside the saints' lives; and it seems clear that he also made a significant contribution to the chronicle that goes under the name of Robert of Gloucester.[2]

Again speaking generally, his writing is distinguished first by his "outspoken" characteristics, namely, decidedly personal comments praising or blaming the behavior of the good or bad characters with whom he is dealing, or scorning those who are defeated,[3] expressed in a lively, colloquial, conversational style with often striking vocabulary and phrasing. This extends also to the way he tells illustrative stories (which are often anecdotes of contemporary medieval life) and to the way in which he engages with his imaginary audience, haranguing or otherwise appealing to them. The second distinguishing feature of his writing is his ability to construct long, complex verse sentences that overflow the couplet boundaries, which differs from the style of writing elsewhere in the *SEL*, where each couplet normally forms a separate grammatical unit. Quite often the poet expresses a sense of wonderment, as in the following extract from the *temporale* narrative now known (because of his filling out of an existing poem) as the *Expanded Nativity*.[4] The subject matter is the behavior of the ox and ass said to have been present at Christ's birth:

Now was þis a wonder dede and aȝe kunde inow,
Vor wel ichot þat oxen kunne bet now drawe ate plow
And asses bere sackes and corn aboute to bringe
Þan to make meri gleo and knele bi fore a kinge . . .
. . . How couþen heo here legges bowen & here knen so to
wende
To knele bifore a king? Who made hem so hende?
(331–34, 337–38)

——

[Now this was a wonderful thing to do, and against their nature, for I know well that oxen are more fitted to pulling ploughs, and asses to carrying sacks and bringing corn, than to rejoicing and kneeling before a king. How were they able to bend their legs and move their knees so as to kneel before a king? Who made them so skillful?]

A little earlier, lines about the circumstances of Christ's birth evince touching personal concern about the Virgin Mary:[5]

Whar was as al þe nobleye þat fel to a quene,
At a kinges burþtime, whar was hit isene?
Ledies and chamberleins, scarlet to drawe and grene,
To winden ynne þe ȝonge king? Al was lute, ich wene. (315–18)

[Where was all the magnificence that should attend a queen when a king is born, where was it to be seen? (Where were) ladies and chamberlains bringing scarlet and green (cloth) in which to wrap the young king? It seems to me there was very little.]

in contrast to which a harshly written passage scorns those who claim that Saint Anastasia was present at the birth of Christ:[6]

Þe lesinge of mani foles telleþ of seint anastase
Þat heo scholde wiþ oure ledi beo: hit nis bote þe mase,
Vor heo ne seiȝ neuer oure ledi her, vor to hundred ȝer bifore
And more ar heo come an erþe oure lord was ibore.
Som wrecche bifond þis lesinge wiþ onriȝte,
Vor as muche as me makeþ of hire munde a midewinter niȝte.
(355–60)

[The lies of many fools relate of Saint Anastasia that she attended Our Lady, but that is nothing but fantasy, because she never saw Our Lady, for the reason that Our Lord was born more than two hundred years before she lived on earth. Some wretch made up this lie without any basis of truth, on the grounds that she is commemorated on Christmas night.]

The above characteristics, however, are not sufficient to identify all of the Outspoken Poet's contributions to the legendary and its associated poems: in practice it is difficult to say that this or that line or passage of *SEL* verse was written by him, because it appears that he was also capable of writing in a more ordinary style, using less special vocabulary and largely closed couplets. Manuscript evidence of revision shows that there are undoubtedly occasions where he has inserted anecdotes or comments into preexisting narrative in order to liven it up (or correct it), but there are many places where lines in one or other of his distinctive styles seem to emerge naturally (as if representing peaks of inspiration) from the lower level of their surrounding narrative; and in these cases it may make sense to regard him as the author of both the ordinary and the heightened verse. There is further complication in that textual evidence demonstrates that subsequent scribes or editors sometimes removed lines that were apparently regarded as too outspoken, most obviously the extended passage on the defense of women from scandalous attack that the Outspoken Poet included in the *temporale* narrative known as the *Southern Passion*.[7] One consequence of the uncertainty about his contribution is that there can be no such thing as an edition of "The Works of the Outspoken *South English Legendary* Poet," because it is hard to bring forward examples of poems of which it can be said he is the sole author:[8] he is essentially a reviser, as can most easily be demonstrated by his major achievements among the *temporale* narratives, namely, the *Expanded Nativity* and the *Southern Passion*.[9] When it comes to assessing the overall merits of the *SEL*, the difficulty of isolating his work is, of course, not such a serious matter. It is more important that passages such as those quoted above (and many comparable) are recognized as examples of successful writing—lively, imaginative, skillful—even if they are not sustained and remain relatively isolated.

One instance of the Outspoken Poet's work that has been printed but never studied is the Prologue to the *temporale* narrative known as the *Conception of Mary*, a composition of some eighty-two lines. The *Conception of Mary* itself is a slight but distinct revision of the first part of another narrative, the *South English Nativity of Mary and Christ*, which tells the story from the marriage of Joachim and Anne, the Virgin Mary's parents, up to Joseph's betrothal to Mary. The revision consists of half a dozen textual changes, in ordinary *SEL* style, apparently made because the reviser was unhappy with points of detail in the narrative before him.[10] In one of the three manuscripts in which it is found complete (British Library, MS Egerton 1993), it is immediately followed by the *Expanded Nativity*. This is a revision of the remainder of the *South English Nativity of Mary and Christ*, far more obvious because in this case the narrative has been filled out with translations of those liturgical gospels that tell the Christmas story (though often at the expense of repetition that the more or less skillful dovetailing of parallel passages does not disguise). But despite the slightness of the changes in the *Conception of Mary*, the three-part sequence Prologue / *Conception* / *Expanded Nativity* can with confidence be wholly attributed to the Outspoken Poet.[11] The case for the Prologue occupies the remainder of this essay.

The Prologue to the *Conception of Mary* survives in four manuscripts: Bodleian Library, Ashmole 61, fols. 208v–209r (A); British Library, Egerton 1993, fol. 27r–v (E); Bodleian Library, Laud Misc. 622, fol. 71r–v (L); and Magdalene College, Cambridge, Pepys 2344, pp. 353–54 (P). A and E were printed in parallel by Carl Horstmann in 1875, and L—where the Prologue occurs independently of the *Conception of Mary*—by Furnivall in 1878.[12] The poem is written in the *SEL*'s familiar septenary couplets, but most unusually it also uses internal rhyme, which distinguishes it not only from most other *SEL* verse, but from other of the Outspoken Poet's compositions. This and the generally celebratory nature of the subject matter (mankind's good fortune in Christ's incarnation) give the verse a lyrical feel, very noticeable at the poem's opening, quoted here from the new edition of the text that I provide below:

Of joye and blisse is my song, kare to byleve,
And to herye him among that al oure sorwe schal reve.
Ycome is the swete thing, the swete hony drope,
Jesus kyng of alle kynges to whan is al oure hope. (1–4)

These lines could, indeed, be set out as quatrains, in lyric fashion:

Of joye and blisse is my song,
  Kare to byleve,
And to herye him among
  That al oure sorwe schal reve.
Ycome is the swete thing,
  The swete hony drope,
Jesus kyng of alle kynges
  To whan is al oure hope.

The essential character of the Prologue is, however, discursive, and the poet makes no attempt to avoid repetition as he puts across his main points. As elsewhere in his writing, his involvement in his subject matter leads to prolixity and duplication, and it is not suggested that the present text is among the very best examples of his work. (One difficulty results from the poet's having adapted a couplet from the *South English Nativity of Mary and Christ*, as I demonstrate.) Nevertheless there is both subtlety in the way he deploys his arguments—causing some problems for the scribes of the extant manuscripts—and a noticeably outspoken passage about the possibility of Christ descending to hell that could not easily be defended against a charge of irreverence.

The content of the Prologue's eighty-two lines can be summarized as follows. The divisions correspond to the paragraphs in the edited text below (detailed glosses follow this text).

1–4 Exclamation of happiness because of the Incarnation of Christ.

5–16 As a result of this, and of Christ's redemption of mankind, we are now his brothers, unlike those who lived on earth earlier. Mankind now has the highest status in heaven, closest to God's throne.

17–32 In particular, we have a higher status in heaven than angels, whom Christ did not redeem in the same way and who are only his messengers—and who indeed will act as our servants once we are in heaven.

33–42 In contrast, those who lived on earth before Christ all went to hell when they died, without exception. The prophets yearned for him, knowing he would come eventually, and wrote about it in their books, but they did not know when.

43–52 They hoped that heaven might split open so that Christ would come down and save them; or even fall down and save them, in which case they would have kept him there if they could.

53–55 King David made a particular appeal for Christ to come down and save them.

56–64 There was also an appeal by Simeon, who had made an earlier request when alive to know when he would see Christ, but he did not complain in vain, for he did not die until he saw the infant Christ in the temple on Candlemas Day.

65–72 Again, our good fortune in being able to go to heaven contrasts with that of those who came before us, as Christ himself pointed out. Because of his redemption of mankind we can now get to heaven without difficulty.

73–82 But those who had to go to hell called on Christ without success, and seeing no change in their condition they eventually gave up their appeals, bowed to God's will, and "spoke of it no more."

Essentially the poem has two main themes, which alternate and which occupy almost exactly equal space: our joy in being able to go to heaven (1–32, 65–72) contrasted with the suffering of those who had to go to hell (33–64, 73–82). Lines 5–32, following the lyrical opening, provide a good example of the strengths and weaknesses of the poet's discursive style as he works through the question of mankind's status in heaven particularly in relation to angels. Lines 5–16 are transitional in that they continue to be mainly exclamatory, anticipating the more carefully argued subject matter to come. The rhetorical question in line 5 ("whar was he so longe?") foreshadows the cries of those in hell, who are introduced briefly in line 8. Mankind's brotherhood with Christ—and consequent place in heaven—is declared to be the result of both the incarnation and the redemption,[13] and man's now being reconciled with angels ("ysome," heightened by an effective anadiplosis across ll. 10–11) is also confidently attributed to both events.[14]

Already, however, we begin to see the poet's enthusiasm (and facility) leading him into repetition of both phrases and ideas, a seemingly inherent trait of his writing that becomes more apparent in 17–32 when he argues the case that angels are inferior to mankind and (21–27) no more than our servants.[15] But along with repetition, lines 21–32 illustrate his engaged, questioning manner of writing and the ease with which he avoids couplet boundaries when his rhetoric demands a longer sentence, as in lines 28–32:

Ne aungel nys nevere-the-mo bote as his messager
—How mighte hit thanne go to beo his brother her?
And in hevene hi scholleth also, whanne we beoth there,
Oure hestes and oure wille do as hi oure hynen were,
And to oure heste servy us to fot and to honde;
Oure owene we mowe hem holde thus, as ich understonde.
Ne mowe we thanne glade beo to habbe such an hyne?
The sothe ye mowe her yseo, as we seoth atte fine,
That we beoth alre kunde hext withoute God alone
And in hevene also him next among his aungeles echone,
And alle that now late come suthe oure lord alighte
And oure flesch hath her ynome—yhered beo his mighte!

When the poet turns to those consigned to hell—their yearning for Christ, their knowledge that he would come to them at some point—the livelier scenes ahead are anticipated by the colloquial "ech ynche ham thoughte a spanne" (40), a foretaste of the marked informality with which the "prophetes" are about to be treated. The *Middle English Dictionary* quotes the line (from MS A) as an example of the proverbial use of the word *span* (meaning a hand's breadth),[16] but "figurative" might be a better term as spatial measurements are here applied to time, making the phrase even more striking. It is then in lines 43–52, where those in hell hope that heaven will split open, that the author's individual voice becomes most noticeable. The idea of heaven opening to allow the Lord to come down derives from Psalm 144:5 ("Domine inclina celos tuos et descende"), and its application here is reasonable enough in itself.[17] But the poet, using strong vocabulary, describes those in hell as becoming increasingly impatient. They do not simply want heaven to divide (except, it seems, at the edges); they want it to burst open so that Christ falls down:

Somdel ham longede tho, whanne hi nolde abyde,
That hevene clove evene a-two, to savy eyther syde,
Ak scholde al to-rive and oure lord falle adoun.

However, the following line ("Ak he ne hyyede nought so blive ak com softe al ysoun") asserts, in contrast, that Christ did not in the end come down in a rush (i.e., when he descended to hell after the Crucifixion) but came down softly and unharmed ("al ysoun"), which—one is asked to imagine—might not have been the case if he had actually fallen.

But the most outspoken couplet is the next wholly gratuitous comment,

Myghte hi him habbe yhent faste by the croune,
Hi wolde narwe him habbe ywent, ak he held ham ther doune,

which appears to say that if those in hell had been able to grasp Christ by his head ("faste by the croune") they would have bound him tightly ("narwe him habbe ywent"), presumably to prevent his escape. But he held them down there. With an exclamatory "Parde" (By God!) the following two lines then emphasize the point that Christ would come in his own good time.[18]

Lines 43–52 constitute a remarkable passage, which is typical of the Outspoken Poet's work in identifying with the all too human frustrations of the people in question—never mind that they are souls in hell—and attributing extravagant reactions to them. There is an element of fantasy, but it could be said to have an understandable psychological cause. At the end of the Prologue, returning to the subject, the poet sympathetically describes how those in hell become tired of appealing to God, realize there is no point in continuing, and decide to drop the subject because, like ordinary human beings, they need a rest.

Before then, in lines 53–64, the poet turns in more sober fashion to the appeals made first by King David and more particularly by Simeon. In contrast to the Prologue's earlier fluency, the passage on Simeon (56–64) is distinctly awkward, because of the clumsiness of the author's apparent attempt to reference the two separate contexts, from different time periods, in which Simeon traditionally features: his encounter with the infant Christ in the temple, from Luke 2, and his presence in hell before the Harrowing of Hell, as in the apocryphal *Gospel of Nicodemus*. In summary, the former event occupies 57b–59 and 62–64, the latter (more by implication) 56–57a and 60. Simeon, on his initial appearance, is clearly suffering in hell alongside David, and at first sight his anxious questioning about the time of Christ's coming and his own ability to hold out is akin to David's appeal:

> Him longede after his face also the holy Symeon,
> For alle blisse him was bynome and ofte gradde byfore:
> "Lord, whanne woltou come and whanne woltou beo ybore?
> Wene ye ich mowe dure? Wene ye ich mowe yseo?" (56–59)

But the time is not that of the Harrowing, which is not the poet's concern,[19] and the word *byfore* at the end of line 57 (repeated at the end of 61 with explicit reference to the episode in the temple in 62–64) reveals that the poet is imagining that Simeon made such heartfelt appeals to Christ while waiting for him to be born, contrary to the quiet and dignified foreknowledge described by Luke. In contrast, Simeon's supposed cries from hell, not narrated, are said to be "ayen" (61), that is, on a subsequent occasion. In between there is the anomalous "Hare mone was deol to hure, ne gamede ham no gleo" (60), which must refer to the souls in hell—who might seem also to be anticipated by Simeon's switch to plural address in 59—and we can only conclude that at this point the author is conflating the two episodes.

One explanation for the awkwardness of this passage is that lines 58–59 are not original to the Outspoken Poet but derive from lines relating to Simeon in the *South English Nativity of Mary and Christ*.[20] The story as related there is that Simeon had prayed to God throughout his life to be allowed to see Christ before he died, and was so desperate to do so that he questioned any wise man who came his way, subsequently receiving reassurance from the Holy Ghost:[21]

> So grete wil he hadde him to abyde þat whanne any wis man com,
> For he hopede here of him tidinge esche he wolde ylome:
> "Wenestou out þat he wole be ybore, and þat ich mowe him yse?
> Wenestou out þat Y dure mowe fort he ybore be?" (585–88)

The second couplet, further evidence of the Outspoken Poet's knowledge of the *Nativity* poem, provides him, after small adaptation, with a ready-made appeal to Christ to be put into Simeon's mouth. But its unavoidable reference to Christ's nativity, though relevant to the opening theme of the Incarnation, brings with it problems that he does not satisfactorily resolve.

In its inconsistent level of achievement—at times freely moving and strikingly individual, at others repetitious and clumsy, especially when reusing existing material—the Prologue to the *Conception of Mary* is a typical example of the Outspoken Poet's work. Given that his motivation was essentially didactic, we would not necessarily expect him to display authorial self-consciousness, and (as has been indicated) his most rewarding passages occur as if the result of natural inspiration rather than anything contrived. He is good at deploying arguments and very good at lively and imaginative narration and comment. The literary value of his work derives from such successes and from his creative use of words, and his particular qualities deserve to be much better known. He could not be said to display an overarching poetic intelligence, but he is a distinctive voice among English-language writers of the time.[22]

The base text for the following edition of the Prologue is that of P, which has not previously been printed. P has been dated to the second half of the fourteenth century, possibly after 1378,[23] and is thus significantly later than A and E, which have been dated to the first and second quarters of the century, respectively.[24] Like them, however, P has been localized linguistically in Gloucestershire, the probable area in which the Outspoken Poet was working.[25] The fourth manuscript, L, which is datable to the middle of the second half of the fourteenth century, has been localized linguistically in Essex and is very likely a London production, as demonstrated recently by Ralph Hanna.[26] Analysis of the readings of the four manuscripts shows that P, on balance, appears to preserve as good a text of the Prologue as A (its only real competitor as base manuscript) and a better one than the more divergent E (for which see below and the Textual Notes). Its text is also complete, unlike A's, which omits lines 79b–81a, and E's, which omits lines 47–50. L's text often agrees with P and like it is complete (but it reverses ll. 48–49). However, L is not a *South English Legendary* manuscript, and its divergent linguistic forms make it unrepresentative.[27]

Following Derek Pearsall's editorial aim, in his *Chaucer to Spenser*, of accessibility without loss of authenticity,[28] I have introduced modern letter forms in place of thorn and yogh (changing the latter to *gh* or *y* as appropriate) and normalized *u/v* and *i/j* according to modern usage. I have also reduced the scribe's habitual double *ff* to single *f*. The spelling of the manuscript is otherwise unaltered. Abbreviations and contractions have been silently expanded, including the single occurrence of an ampersand in line 58, and capitalization, punctuation, word division, and paragraphing are all editorial.

I have emended the text of P on some twenty-eight occasions for reasons of sense, internal rhyme, or (rarely) meter. In cases of minor lexical difference P's reading has been allowed to stand irrespective of the readings of the other manuscripts. To increase readability, the emendations are not signaled in the edited text but are recorded in the textual apparatus, where readings from other manuscripts are supplied as necessary.[29] Emendations taken from other manuscripts are made to conform to P's usual spelling system. All readings in the textual apparatus, other than the quoted edited text, are given in manuscript spelling, the first manuscript in a list of manuscript sigla supplying that spelling. Variant readings are not otherwise recorded, partly for reasons of space, partly because the other three manuscript texts are already available in print.

In taking decisions about emendation it has been assumed that the author of the poem generally expressed himself in a compact rather than an awkwardly explicit way, and that every couplet originally contained an internal rhyme or near equivalent. These assumptions may not always be correct, but there is no possibility of recovering the author's own form of words, and it has seemed best to give him the benefit of the doubt, again partly for reasons of readability. Thus in lines 2 and 6 "that al oure sorwe schal reve" and "that boughte us so stronge," supported by the other manuscripts, have been preferred to P's clumsier "þat schal al oure sorwe vs byreue" and "þat vs bouȝte ffram deþ stronge." The decision to restore internal rhymes apparently lost from MS P (taken on eight occasions) is complicated by the fact that the chief witness to "correct" rhymes is MS E, whose scribe elsewhere transmits what are quite clearly rewritings of more original phrasing (though at other times it is the sole witness to crucial readings, such as the pronoun *hare* in l. 17). There is therefore the possibility that MS E's text contains nonoriginal internal rhymes. Nevertheless the principle that the author would have endeavored to keep his rhyme scheme going seems reasonable, and so MS E's guidance has quite frequently been accepted. Discussion of individual emendations can be found in the textual notes.

The Prologue to the *Conception of Mary*

Of joye and blisse is my song, kare to byleve,
And to herye evere among that al oure sorwe schal reve.
Ycome is the swete thing, the swete hony drope,
Jesus kyng of alle kynges to whan is al oure hope.
Bycome he is oure brother—whar was he so longe?
He hit is and non other that boughte us so stronge.
Oure brother we mowe him clupye, and so seith himsulf ylome;
So ne mighte hi nevere a del that byfore us come.
He nas oure brother nought ar he oure flesch nome;
Ther-myd he hath us deore abought to make us ysome.
Ysome nere we nought byfore, aungeles and oure kunde,
Ar swete Jesus were ybore that to selde is in munde.
Ak now he hath oure flesch ynome and oure brother is,
Oure kunde is wel heye ycome among alle othere ywis,
For he is with oure kunde hext, save his godhede,
And aboute his throne is next, so noble is manhede.
Aungel ne worth him nought so ney for he nys hare brother nought,
Ak oure kunde is so hey for he hath us deore abought.
Ne aungeles he boughte nought—we beoth him therfore the ner;
Whanne he hath us so deore abought wel aughte we him lovye her.
Ne aungel nys nevere-the-mo bote as his messager
—How mighte hit thanne go to beo his brother her?
And in hevene hi scholleth also, whanne we beoth there,
Oure hestes and oure wille do as hi oure hynen were,
And to oure heste servy us to fot and to honde;
Oure owene we mowe hem holde thus, as ich understonde.
Ne mowe we thanne glade beo to habbe such an hyne?

The sothe ye mowe her yseo, as we seoth atte fine,
That we beoth alre kunde hext withoute God alone
And in hevene also him next among his aungeles echone,
And alle that now late come suthe oure lord alighte
And oure flesch hath her ynome—yhered beo his mighte!
  Thulke that byfore us come whanne hi than deth founde,
Thanne were hi ycast adoun into helle grounde.
Were hi nevere so holy ne so goed, ther nas tho forbore non;
Therfore ham longede in hare mode after oure lord echon.
The prophetes that were so goede and so holy alle,
That of oure lord understode and what scholde byfalle,
Hi wuste that he wolde come ak hi nuste whanne;
The tyme ham thoughte swithe longe, ech ynche ham thoughte a spanne.
Hi gradde after him wel ofte in hare prophecye
And on the bokes that hi wroughte that he scholde hye.
  "God yeve," quath on of ham, "that hevene to-borste a-two
That he mighte alighte adoun and savy us fram wo."
Somdel ham longede tho, whanne hi nolde abyde,
That hevene clove evene a-two, to savy eyther syde,
Ak scholde al to-rive and oure lord falle adoun
—Ak he ne hyyede nought so blive ak com softe al ysoun.
Myghte hi him habbe yhent faste by the croune,
Hi wolde narwe him habbe ywent, ak he held ham ther doune.
Parde, yut ne com he nought, nere ham nevere so wo;
Hi hadde the grounde of helle ysought ar he com ham to.
  Seint David after his anuy after him gradde thus:
"Lord thin hevene to us abowe and alight doun to us.
Schewe us thin holy face and we worth hole anon."
  Him longede after his face also the holy Symeon,
For alle blisse him was bynome and ofte gradde byfore:
"Lord, whanne woltou come and whanne woltou beo ybore?
Wene ye ich mowe dure? Wene ye ich mowe yseo?"
Hare mone was deol to hure, ne gamede ham no gleo.
Ak he ne menede him for nought, ayen othere byfore,
For he nas nought to deth ybrought ar God were ybore,
Ak lyvede forto he him ysey and on his armes nom
Tho he a Candelmasse day to the temple com.
  Lord, wel may us beo bet than ham mighte tho,
That ne mighte nowher fleo ak to helle hi moste go.

Therfore oure lord sede, tho he was ybore,
That we mighte beo wel glad over othere that were byfore:
The prophetes wilnede for to seo and monye kynges also
That we yseoth yif hit mighte beo, ak hi ne mighte hit nought do.
We mowe as hit were for nought to hevene come
Suthe oure lord us hath ybought and the develes power bynome.
   Ak hi that such grace nadde, that tofore us come,
After oure lord hi gradde in hare prophecyes ylome.
After him hi gradde so heye with gret wil and longe,
Ak non amendement hi ne seye bote the pyne stronge
—So longe that hi wery were and lete al beo stille,
And har gredynge forbere and turnde to Godes wille,
For hi ne seye non other won, they ham thoughte longe;
Oure lord let hare wille agon ar he wolde flesch afonge.
And tho hi were wery ynow, as whoso seith for sore,
Eche of ham to reste drow and speke of him namore.

Glosses

1 kare to byleve] *in order to set unhappiness aside.* 2 herye evere among] *praise repeatedly*; that] *him who*; reve] *take away.* 4 to whan] *in whom.* 5 whar was he so longe] *where was he for such a long time?* 6 boughte us so stronge] *redeemed us so bravely.* 7 mowe him clupye] *may call him*; ylome] *often.* 8 *Those who lived before us (on earth) could never do that at all.* 9 ar . . . nome] *before he became incarnate.* 10 deore abought] *redeemed us for a high price*; ysome] *reconciled (to God).* 11 kunde] *kind (species).* 12 to . . . munde] *too seldom is in mind.* 13 Ak] *but.* 14 is . . . othere] *has become highly placed compared to all other species (of beings).* 15 *For our kind is highest alongside Christ, leaving aside his divinity.* 16 is next] *(our kind) is nearest*; manhede] *mankind.* 17 Aungel ne worth] *angels are not*; nys . . . nought] *is not their brother.* 19 beoth] *are*; ner] *nearer.* 20 Whanne] *seeing that.* 21 Ne . . . as] *angels are no more than.* 22 hit . . . beo] *they then be.* 23 scholleth] *shall*; beoth] *(shall) be.* 24 hestes] *commands*; do] *carry out*; hynen] *servants.* 25 servy . . . honde] *wait upon us hand and foot.* 26 Oure . . . thus] *in this way we may consider them ours (i.e. our servants).* 27 Ne . . . beo] *shouldn't we then be glad.* 28 sothe] *truth*; seoth . . . fine] *shall see at the end (of life).* 29 *That we are highest of all species only excepting God.* 31 And . . . suthe] *and (that this includes) all who lived (on earth) since.*

32 yhered] *praised.* 33 Thulke] *those*; come] *lived (on earth before Christ's incarnation)*; deth founde] *died.* 35 goed] *good*; ther . . . non] *none were exempted.* 36 *Therefore each of them yearned in their mind for our lord.* 39 wuste] *knew.* 40 spanne] *hand's breadth.* 41 gradde] *implored.* 42 hye] *hasten.* 43 yeve] *grant.* 45 Somdel] *greatly*; nolde abyde] *could not remain patient.* 46 clove . . . syde] *should split completely in two, except for either side.* 47 Ak] [in this case] *and*; to-rive] *break open.* 48 blive] *quickly*; ysoun] *uninjured.* 49 yhent] *seized hold of*; croune] *(top of the) head.* 50 narwe] *tightly*; ywent] *bound* (?). 51 Parde] *by God*; yut] *at that time*; nere . . . wo] *never mind how sorrowful they were.* 52 grounde] *depths*; ysought] *visited* (*i.e. got to know*). 53 after his anuy] *in his affliction.* 55 worth] *will become.* 57 bynome] *taken away*; byfore] *earlier.* 58 woltou] *will you.* 59 Wene] *think*; dure] *stay alive.* 60 ne . . . gleo] *nothing gave them pleasure.* 61 *But he did not cry out in vain this second time or earlier.* 63 forto] *until.* 65 wel . . . tho] *i.e. we have a much better chance (of going to heaven) than they did.* 68 over] *more than.* 71 for nought] *easily.* 75 heye] *loudly.* 76 pyne] *torment (of hell).* 77 lete . . . stille] *i.e. let the matter rest.* 78 har gredynge forbere] *ceased their outcry.* 79 won] *alternative*; they] *although.* 80 wille agon] *desire disappear*; flesch afonge] *receive flesh (i.e. become incarnate).* 81 as . . . sore] *that is to say, as a result of their misery.* 82 to reste drow] *settled down to rest.*

Textual Apparatus

2 that . . . reve] reue AEL, þat schal al oure sorwe vs byreue P. 3 thing] þeng E, diew PAL. 4 kynges] AL, þing PE. 6 boughte us so] boȝte ous so AL, bouȝte vs vrom pine E, vs bouȝte ffram deþ P. 16 is] AEL, is his P. 17 hare] heore E, oure PAL. 18 for] vor E, wher wiþ P, *omitted* AL. 19 him therfore the] þerfore him þe E, him wel PAL. 25 servy us] seruy ous AEL, hi scholleþ seruy vs P. 26 hem holde thus] hem holden þus E, holden ous A, holden hem L, þus holde P. 28 The sothe] þe soþe E, þat soþe A, And suþþe PL. 34 ycast adoun] anon ycast adoun P, anon icast AL, forþ inome E. 35 hi] A, he PL, *omitted* E. 36 in hare mode] in here mod E, sore PL, more A. 40 swithe longe] swiþe long E, longe ynow PAL. 42 wroughte] wrouȝhten E, writen PAL. 43 yeve] ȝeue AEL, wolde P. 46 That] þat AEL, and P. 47 to-rive] *conjectural*, to berste PAL. 48 blive] bliue A, swiþe PL; softe al ysoun] softe al isoun A, soft adoun L, wiþ a softe soun P. 50 ywent] iwent A, yhent L, yholde P. 54

þin] E, in PAL. 57 For] vor E, and PAL. 61 ne menede him for] menede him for E, ne mened hem A, ne meuede him P, hym ne greued L; othere] oþer AEL, þe oþere P. 62 to deth ybrought] to deþe ibroȝt AEL, ded P. 75 so heye] so heiȝe E, *omitted* PAL.

Textual Notes

1 Unusually, given the extent of its later efforts to maintain internal rhyme, E reads *þouȝt* (apparently a scribal or editorial choice rather than a corruption) in place of PAL's *song*.
3 Conversely, E's *þeng*, i.e., "thing," is necessary for the internal rhyme in this next couplet, despite PAL's alternative reading, *dew*, which is much more akin to *hony drope* in the second half of the line. But "dew" may be a later improvement of the line by someone who found "thing" too prosaic, a theory possibly supported by the apparent displacement of "thing" to the first half of 4 (in place of *kynges*) in PE—although the result in E is the occurrence of the same internal rhyme word (*þeng, þing*) in two successive lines. The matter is complicated further by A's reversal of the half-lines 3b and 4b.
7 *and so seith himsulf ylome*. For Christ's referring to men as his brothers, see, e.g., Matthew 12:49–50, Mark 4:34–35.
16 The first half-line appears to be elliptical, with the subject of *is next* being mankind. E has *men worþ* in place of *is*, but the resulting repetition of *men* / *man-* suggests that it is a later elucidation.
22 E has *þat angel were* in place of *to beo*, another apparent clarification of an elliptical construction.
25 P's unemended line alone places the midline mark before *servy* (*And to oure heste hi schólleþ . seruy vs to ffot and to honde*), adding to the clumsiness of the repetitive and seemingly unoriginal *hi scholleþ*.
26 The second line of P's couplet then lacks an internal rhyme, but so does L's, and only E has the adopted solution. Its *holden þus* is however supported by P's *þus holde*.
34 P alone has *adoun*, which it places after the midline mark, but it is to be preferred as a (near) internal rhyme to E's *inome*, which appears to be a weak substitution for PAL's *ycast* (at some stage of the textual transmission) in an attempt to provide a purer rhyme with 33's *come* (though replaced in E itself by *were*). The rhyme *come* / *adoun* is supported by *ham* / *adoun* in 43–44, attested in all manuscripts except E, which reads *adoun anon*, very likely another attempt to create a closer rhyme.

36 *ham longede*, impersonal construction for "they yearned" (cf. 45 and 56, and also 40 and 79, *ham thoughte*, "it seemed to them"). There then appears to be no alternative to adopting E's *in here mod* for the purposes of internal rhyme. PAL's *sore / more* seem weak in respect of both sense and meter.

40 E's *swiþe long* has been adopted, as providing a closer internal rhyme for 39's *come* than PAL's *longe ynow*, despite the latter's possibly deliberate understatement.

42 Similarly E's *wrouȝten* furnishes a closer rhyme for 41's *ofte* than PAL's *writen*. The adopted preterite form *wroughte* could derive from either *writen* "write" or *werken* "create."

43–44 See note to 34 above.

47–50 E omits these lines.

47 All four manuscripts read *to berste* in 47, but internal rhyme with 48 is quite lacking. I conjecture that the original rhyme was between *to riue* (47)—a verb of very similar meaning—and A's *bliue* (48).

48–49 L reverses these two lines.

48 A's *softe al isoun* ("softly and wholly uninjured") has been adopted as the harder reading. See *MED* s.v. *isound*, where the line from A is quoted.

50 P's *yholde* loses the internal rhyme with *yhent* in 49. A's *iwent* (speculatively "bound," "restrained") has been adopted as the harder reading. See *MED* s.v. *winden*, v. (1), 5(e), not recording past participle forms in *-e-* but noting some overlap of forms with *wenden*.

54 E's *þin* reflects the biblical source, "Domine inclina celos tuos" (Psalm 144:5), which underlies the idea of the "bowing down" of heaven in ll. 43–48 above. E alone has a marginal note at this point, written against ll. 54–57 and combining phrases from Psalms 144:5 and 80:4: "Domine inclina celos tuos et ostende faciem tuam et salui erimus."

56 Here, however, it would seem that E's reading *grace*, instead of *face* as in the other manuscripts, is a substitution to avoid the self-rhyme of *face* across the two lines of the couplet. In Luke 2:26, the source, Simeon has been promised that he will see Christ in person.

61 *ayen othere byfore* would seem to mean "this second time or earlier," *byfore* referring to Simeon's wait, while still alive, for Christ to be born, and *ayen* to his appeal from hell after death (see the discussion above). E's *for nouȝt* "in vain," necessary in the light of 62–64, applies more directly to the first occasion but is not inapplicable to the second

because Christ's eventual Harrowing of Hell took place relatively soon after Simeon's death.
68–70 The source is Luke 10:23–24, "Beati oculi, qui vident quae vos videtis. Dico enim vobis, quod multi prophetae, et reges voluerunt videre quae vos videtis, et non viderunt" (Blessed are the eyes which see the things that ye see: for I tell you, that many prophets and kings have desired to see those things which ye see, and have not seen them).
68 In place of *glad* E reads *glade & lute dede* in another apparent attempt to create a purer internal rhyme.
75 E alone preserves an internal rhyme. PAL's first half-line appears distinctly short.
79–81 A omits 79b–81a, presumably as a result of eye skipping.

Notes

1. Manfred Görlach, *The Textual Tradition of the South English Legendary*, Leeds Texts and Monographs, 6 (Leeds: School of English, University of Leeds, 1974).

2. See O. S. Pickering, "The Outspoken *South English Legendary* Poet," in *Late-Medieval Religious Texts and Their Transmission: Essays in Honour of A.I. Doyle*, ed. A. J. Minnis (Cambridge: D. S. Brewer, 1994), 21–37; and "*South English Legendary* Style in Robert of Gloucester's *Chronicle*," *Medium Aevum* 70 (2001): 1–18, recently combined and abridged as Oliver Pickering, "Outspoken Style in the *South English Legendary* and Robert of Gloucester," in *Rethinking the South English Legendaries*, ed. Heather Blurton and Jocelyn Wogan-Browne (Manchester: Manchester University Press, 2011), 106–45.

3. See Oliver Pickering, "Black Humour in the *South English Legendary*," in Blurton and Wogan-Browne, *Rethinking the South English Legendaries*, 427–42.

4. Quoted, with revised punctuation, from the poem printed as "Geburt Jesu" in *Altenglische Legenden*, ed. Carl Horstmann (Paderborn: Schöningh, 1875), 64–109 (92). "Geburt Jesu" comprises poems I have distinguished as the *Conception of Mary* (64–81) and the *Expanded Nativity* (81–109): see O. S. Pickering, "The *Temporale* Narratives of the *South English Legendary*," *Anglia* 91 (1973): 425–55 (438–40). Horstmann's text is from British Library, MS Egerton 1993, with variant readings (for this part of the poem) from Bodleian Library, MS Bodley 779, which I have drawn on in emending line 335.

5. Horstmann, *Altenglische Legenden*, 91.

6. Ibid., 93.

7. See O. S. Pickering, "The 'Defence of Women' from the *Southern Passion*: A New Edition," in *The South English Legendary: A Critical Assessment*, ed. Klaus P. Jankofsky (Tübingen: Francke, 1992), 154–76; and, more generally, Pickering, "The Outspoken *South English Legendary* Poet," 33–35.

8. For the case for "All Souls' Day," see Oliver Pickering, "Preaching in the *South English Legendary*: A Study and Edition of the Text for All Souls' Day," in *Preaching the Word in Manuscript and Print in Late Medieval England: Essays in Honour of Susan Powell*, ed. Martha W. Driver and Veronica O'Mara, Sermo, 11 (Turnhout: Brepols, 2013), 277–316, but it is shown that the text we have apparently incorporates lines from earlier compositions.

9. See O. S. Pickering, "Three *South English Legendary* Nativity Poems," *Leeds Studies in English*, n.s., 8 (1975): 105–19; and "The *Southern Passion* and the *Ministry and Passion*: The Work of a Middle English Reviser," *Leeds Studies in English*, n.s., 15 (1984): 33–56.

10. The changes are analyzed in Pickering, "Three *South English Legendary* Nativity Poems," 106–10. For his source poem, see *The South English Nativity of Mary and Christ*, ed. O. S. Pickering, Middle English Texts, 1 (Heidelberg: Winter, 1975).

11. In "Three *South English Legendary* Nativity Poems," 110, I argued, to the contrary, that the *Conception* and the *Expanded Nativity* were the work of different writers, partly because I believed that the former was devised to fill a gap in the calendrical sequence of saints' legends. My view now is that a later scribe or editor detached the *Conception* for this purpose. In MS Egerton 1993 the *temporale* material is gathered together at the beginning of the manuscript, before the calendrical sequence.

12. Horstmann, *Altenglische Legenden*, 64–69 (A on even-numbered and E on odd-numbered pages); and *Adam Davy's Five Dreams about Edward II, etc.*, ed. F. J. Furnivall, EETS, o.s., 69 (London: Trübner, 1878), 93–96. The Prologue is *NIMEV* 2632.

13. Cf. William Langland, *Piers Plowman: An Edition of the C-text*, ed. Derek Pearsall, York Medieval Texts, 2nd ser. (London: Edward Arnold, 1978), 338: "Ac alle þat beth myn hole brethrene, in bloed and in baptisme, / Shal neuere in helle eft come, be he ones oute" (XX, 419–20).

14. For mankind and angels being reconciled in Christ (deriving ultimately from Colossians 1:20), and also for the point that Christ did not die for angels (ll. 17–19), see Augustine, *Enchiridion*, chap. 61, in Saint Augustine, *On the Holy Trinity, Doctrinal Treatises, Moral Treatises*, ed. Philip Schaff, Select Library of the Nicene and Post-Nicene Fathers of the Christian Church, 1st ser., 3 (New York: Christian Literature Company, 1887), 257: "Now it was not for the angels that Christ died. Yet what was done for the redemption of man

through his death was in a sense done for the angels, because the enmity which sin had put between men and the holy angels is removed, and friendship is restored between them."

15. Cf. Hebrews 1.14, "Are they not all ministering spirits, sent forth to minister for them who shall be heirs of salvation?"

16. The *MED*'s only other example of so-called proverbial use (*spanne* n., 1d), from Gower's *Confessio Amantis*, is not comparable.

17. The words of the psalm are put into David's mouth in l. 54, and see further the textual note on this line following the edited text.

18. This reading of the passage naturally depends on my analysis of the different manuscript readings (more numerous than at some points, suggesting that the scribes had difficulty with the unconventional vocabulary and subject matter) and my editorial interpretation of the meaning of the lines. See the textual notes and glosses provided. We may note in particular that MS E omits ll. 47–50, the most controversial section, apparently an example of the censoring of the Outspoken Poet's work referred to above.

19. Simeon, in the *Gospel of Nicodemus*, does not appeal to Christ, and David's appeal for heaven to open is also not found there.

20. As pointed out in passing in Pickering, "Three *South English Legendary* Nativity Poems," 110.

21. I quote from Pickering, *The South English Nativity of Mary and Christ*, 90.

22. For assessments of the literary achievements of certain other poets not part of the central canon of Middle English literature, see, e.g., *Individuality and Achievement in Middle English Poetry*, ed. O. S. Pickering (Cambridge: D. S. Brewer, 1997).

23. See Rosamond McKitterick and Richard Beadle, comps., *Catalogue of the Pepys Library at Magdalene College Cambridge*, vol. 5, *Manuscripts*, pt. 1, *Medieval* (Cambridge: D. S. Brewer, 1992), 66–74, referring to Görlach, *Textual Tradition*, 94 and 182, who suggests that the positioning of the Prologue / *Conception of Mary* for the feast of Saint Anne in MS P may reflect the establishment of this feast in England in 1378.

24. Cf. Görlach, *Textual Tradition*, 74 and 81.

25. See Angus McIntosh, M. L. Samuels, and Michael Benskin, *A Linguistic Atlas of Late Mediaeval English*, 4 vols. (Aberdeen: Aberdeen University Press, 1986), LP (i.e., linguistic profile) 6990 (P), 7130 (E), and 7170 (A).

26. *Linguistic Atlas*, LP 6260. See Ralph Hanna, *London Literature, 1300–1380* (Cambridge: Cambridge University Press, 2005), 6–7 (and also 105–6). L was written by the same scribe as Magdalene College, Cambridge, MS Pepys 2498, and British Library, MS Harley 874; Hanna dates this writing activity to 1365–75.

27. After the Prologue itself PAE have two lines introducing the *Conception of Mary* that then follows, quoted here from E because PA are defective: "Þat swete bern oure kuinde nam . in vlesch & in velle. / Of þe kunde of wham he com . somwat imot telle." But L, where the Prologue is self-contained, expands this couplet to four lines and looks ahead instead to Christ's redemption of man on the cross. See Furnivall, *Adam Davy's Five Dreams about Edward II, etc.*, 96.

28. Derek Pearsall, ed., *Chaucer to Spenser: An Anthology of Writings in English, 1375–1575* (Oxford: Blackwell, 1999), xviii.

29. The readings of the manuscripts printed by Horstmann and Furnivall have been checked against the originals.

CHAPTER 3

Derek Pearsall, Secret Shakespearean

Martha W. Driver

What makes a great critic? Derek Pearsall is famously noted for his sensitive interpretation of the works of Geoffrey Chaucer, John Lydgate, and William Langland, but unlike many academics who are specialists in one or two areas, he is remarkable for the breadth of his reading. This essay examines his references to Shakespeare as his way of clarifying or explaining a medieval text to a literate audience. References to Shakespeare occur in his critical analysis of *The Canterbury Tales*, in his volume *Old English and Middle English Poetry* for the Routledge History of English Poetry, in his anthology of works from Chaucer to Spenser, in his Chaucer biography, and even in *The Medieval Python*, a festschrift for Terry Jones.[1]

Allusions to Shakespeare appear as well in *English and International* by Elizabeth Salter, which was edited by Pearsall and Nicolette Zeeman after Salter's untimely death. Shakespeare is used illustratively and is sometimes connected more directly with earlier writers, as Salter explains in her introduction to that book: "We are bound, therefore, to anticipate with pleasure the decades in which *Troilus and Criseyde*, the *Pearl*, and the *Cloud of Unknowing* were written, and to feel, however imprecisely, that here, once more, we are in touch with an 'English tradition' which will lead us naturally to Shakespeare."[2] This delight in the observation of a developing English literary tradition is also expressed in Pearsall's readings of earlier works against Shakespeare's plays.

Among the many plays cited in Pearsall's own criticism are histories (*Richard II*; *Richard III*; *Henry IV*, *Parts 1 and 2*), comedies (*Love's Labor's Lost*, *As You Like It*, *Midsummer Night's Dream*, *Measure for Measure*, *Merchant of Venice*, *Troilus and Cressida*), tragedies (*King Lear*, *Othello*, *Hamlet*), and romances (*Cymbeline*, *Winter's Tale*, *Tempest*), representing all four of Shakespeare's genres. These references are always temperate, used to elucidate or clarify the motives of medieval authors. Pearsall compares Chaucer to Shakespeare in terms of his genius, his "power of imaginative penetration" that can reshape even "traditional material from the dreariest sources . . . and by a shift of perspective, a new context, . . . detach it from its antique moorings and push it out into the full stream of his drama."[3] Chaucer and other medieval writers, like Shakespeare later, not only draw upon older texts, as is well known, but compose in a common cultural setting, with Shakespeare seeming to emerge fully formed out of the rich English literary tradition that precedes him. In addition to looking at a range of references to Shakespeare culled from Pearsall's criticism and the ways in which Shakespeare is interpolated into his discussion of medieval texts, I examine the ways in which Shakespeare himself employs medieval reference in order to show how a shared literary tradition can illuminate the work of authors, both major and minor, and how the critic may productively employ the works of one writer to elucidate or develop his observations on those of another.

Talking to Derek in 2012, I learned that his two favorite Shakespeare plays are *Henry IV, Part 1*, with its "three plots cunningly intertwined with a succession of great moments," and *Troilus and Cressida*, with its "almost mock elaboration of the speeches, especially [those of] Agamemnon." The latter play's "erotic language is very heated" and includes "intense, low sex." It is, in fact, "very unusual for Shakespeare to write a play in which not one character is likeable, and no other play is like it." When I asked what he thought makes a great critic, Derek replied, "Careful attention to what you are reading, reading everything with a critical eye but with no prejudgments."[4] In other words, great criticism is without pretense: the prose is lucid, witty, and engaging; and it opens the eyes of a reader to new possibilities, new readings of old texts. Other qualities include "the belief that [one] is in the presence of a masterpiece and with the recognition that [one's] own role is that of acolyte," along with open-mindedness and respect for the author and the work.[5] In Pearsall's writing, there is an assumption that the culturally literate reader will know and remember various allusions to Shakespeare (though not all Shakespeareans are perhaps as adept with medieval references). Before examining how Shakespeare's texts can inform a reading of medieval poetry, it is helpful to trace, however briefly, the influence of medieval literature on Shakespeare.

Source Hunting

In *The Swan at the Well: Shakespeare Reading Chaucer*, published in 1985, E. Talbot Donaldson pointed out that "Shakespeareans are naturally interested in showing how the Chaucerian background can illuminate the plays, but this perfectly proper interest often has the effect of assuming that, although the play is a puzzle requiring answers, the Chaucerian works that may help provide answers have settled—one might almost say static—meanings that are available to any reader."[6] In other words, Shakespeare scholars tend to view Chaucer as a static and readily understandable resource without considering Chaucer's own complexities. Ann Thompson, in *Shakespeare's Chaucer: A Study in Literary Origins*, a comprehensive and detailed survey of secondary materials on this subject, also tends to assume that Chaucer's text is fixed.[7] Even Harold Bloom, who puts forward a convincing case for Shakespeare's use of the Wife of Bath and the Pardoner as models for several flamboyant or corrupt characters in his plays, among them Falstaff and Iago, relies more directly on the criticism of G. K. Chesterton and the Chaucer biography by Donald Howard than on any readings of sixteenth-century editions of Chaucer's *Works* or the book or books that Shakespeare himself might have read.[8]

Thompson has, however, quite rightly pointed to several of the pitfalls of close textual analysis of editions of Chaucer alongside those of Shakespeare. Both use stories commonly known and in general circulation concerning tamed shrews, for example, or best friends vying for a woman's love, or the death of noble Lucrece. More detailed examinations become difficult because "there is very little hope of finding close verbal similarity, perhaps the most convincing kind of evidence in a source-study, and when one does find a phrase or sentence which seems almost a quotation from Chaucer it invariably turns out to have been proverbial in the sixteenth century, as it probably was in the fourteenth."[9]

There are some exceptions. For example, several critics have pointed to verbal parallels between Chaucer's description of Tarquin as a stalking thief in the *Legend of Good Women* ("And in the night thefely gan he stalke"; 1781) and Shakespeare's in *The Rape of Lucrece* ("creeping thief"; 305) and later descriptively ("Into the chamber wickedly he stalks"; 365), and to certain of the narrative details in this poem that could only have come from Chaucer.[10] Faint but unmistakable allusions to Chaucer occur in *A Midsummer Night's Dream*, with Shakespeare echoing three times the phrase "to doon his observaunce to May" from the Knight's Tale and with the apostrophe to the "wikked wal" in the play of Pyramus and Thisbe, derived from *Legend of Good Women*, for example.[11] There are, of course, other kinds of influences from Chaucer and medieval literature more generally that I subsequently explore, though these may be indirect.

But most text references are more general in Shakespeare plays, as when Petruchio says of Kate in *Taming of the Shrew*, "For patience she will prove a second Grissel" (II.i.287) and names his dog Troilus ("Where's my spaniel Troilus?"; IV.i.134).[12] In *Much Ado about Nothing*, Benedick refers to Troilus as "the first employer of pandars" (V.ii.30), and in *The Merry Wives of Windsor*, Pistol asks, "Shall I Sir Pandarus of Troy become, / And by my side wear steel?" (I.iii.80–81). There are also references to the Nun's Priest's Tale in *Henry IV, Part 1* ("How now, Dame Partlet the hen!"; III.iii.57), and in *The Winter's Tale*, when Leontes exclaims, "Thou art woman-tired, unroosted / By thy dame Partlett here" (II.iii.74–75), noted in the Arden edition as traditional names of the cock and hen.[13] While simple source hunting yields a degree of pleasure (and a fair amount of debate), Shakespeare can also be read productively through the lens of medieval literature, as R. W. Chambers, in a memorandum dictated to R. Kapp on March 13, 1942, pointed out: "I am convinced that Shakespeare can be best understood in his great tragedies if we read him in connection with the literature of Christian England which preceded him."[14] This is not only true of the tragedies; Shakespeare can also be employed to elucidate aspects of medieval poetry, as found often in Pearsall's commentary on the writings he knows so well, both the primary sources—the manuscripts and the printed editions—and the secondary sources.

Comparisons

In his criticism, Pearsall invokes Shakespeare as a touchstone of excellence that is also achieved in medieval literature. In addition to a wealth of sources and highly charged verse, medieval poets share with Shakespeare a richness of language. Commenting on the verse of the alliterative *Morte Arthure*, Pearsall notes, "Only again in Shakespeare's time, one would think, was the language so hospitable. Even with less exotic words there is a spirit of adventure abroad in the new extensions of meaning and new juxtapositions which is often marvelously effective."[15] Chaucer, like Shakespeare, "has a power of imaginative penetration through which he can make anything he borrows inviolably his own."[16] Shakespeare's plays share a freshness and originality with works like the *Canterbury Tales*, each giving new life to older sources, in some cases the same sources.

Characters from the *Canterbury Tales* can also sometimes be more directly understood by reading them against Shakespearean ones. While the Pardoner's persona is drawn partially from the Vice character in morality plays, his monologue may be compared with the soliloquies of Richard III and Iago, for both of whom the Vice figure may also serve as an antecedent: "for just as the Pardoner is derived from an allegorical personification in a moral poem, so the Shakespeare villains take much of their dramatic character and role-playing from the 'Vice' of the morality plays."[17] In the Summoner's Tale, the friar is described as "Falstaff-like" in turning the death of the couple's child "into another triumph for himself and his order."[18] Like the Pardoner, Iago, and Richard III, Shakespeare's Sir John Falstaff, the fat knight, is also partly drawn from the Vice, the antagonist in early morality plays. Appearing as comic relief in *Henry IV, Parts 1 and 2*, and in *The Merry Wives of Windsor*, which is set chronologically between the two, Falstaff is best known for his self-serving remark after he plays dead to escape confrontation in battle: "The better part of valor is / discretion, in the which better part I have sav'd my life" (*Hen. IV, pt. 1*, V.iv.119–20). In Pearsall's reference to the Summoner's Tale, then, knowledge of Falstaff's general tendency to turn every misadventure to his own advantage helps to clarify the characterization of Chaucer's friar. Pearsall notes further, this time in his discussion of William Dunbar's satire "The Two Married Women and the Widow," that the Scottish flyting form is "an exchange of bravura invective . . . as between Falstaff and Prince Hal in *Henry IV, Part I*," the famous scene in which Falstaff escapes responsibility for his rude remarks to the disguised Prince Hal by quickly qualifying his insults and then by flatly denying them ("No abuse, Hal"; II.iv.343).[19] In each case, Falstaff is invoked as a figure readers will readily recognize and is used to explain an older character, Chaucer's friar, or poetic form, the flyting, which might not be quite so accessible.

Despite their skewering in the poetry of William Langland and Chaucer and in Wycliffite poetry and prose, medieval friars, Pearsall points out, do appear as more benign and genial figures later: "when it has all ceased to matter, William Shakespeare uses friars as well-intentioned and obliging agents for sorting out marital and related problems, like their medieval forebears: so with the unlucky Friar Lawrence in *Romeo and Juliet*, the deus ex machina friar in *All's Well*, and the Duke-cum-friar of *Measure for Measure*," though in these cases there is also a certain irony, for example, in the activities of Friar Lawrence, which seem ill-timed at the very least.[20] On the other hand, Chaucer's Reeve is described as "an early Malvolio ('a kind of Puritan')," the comparison between the humorless steward of *Twelfth Night* and Chaucer's judgmental, hateful, ascetic Reeve serving as a vivid and effective anachronism.[21] The magician of Chaucer's Franklin's Tale is further seen as perhaps one progenitor of Prospero in *The Tempest*. In the case of the Franklin's Tale, the magician creates illusions to impress Aurelius and his brother, and then "clapte his handes two, And farwel! Al oure revel was ago" (1204). In a footnote, Pearsall speculates whether Shakespeare remembered these Chaucerian lines when he wrote Prospero's speech following the masque Prospero conjures for Miranda and Ferdinand: "Our revels now are ended. These our actors, / were all spirits, and / Are melted into air" (IV.i.148–50).[22]

Further resonance in Pearsall's literary criticism is created by comparing a medieval character to several in Shakespeare. Chaucer's Griselda is described, for example, as an anticipation of *Lear*'s Cordelia, the one faithful child who remains constant to Lear through all adversity, "especially in the emphasis on her depth and resilience of character, her 'rype and sad corage.' "[23] Griselda's poignant prayer before her baby daughter is taken, " 'For this nyght shaltow dyen for my sake' (560), with its enigmatic echo of the concluding formula of Christian prayer, asserts her recognition that the child dies, as she thinks, to preserve the integrity of her will in its submission to the higher will." This scene is explained as analogous "with a difference" to Isabella's farewell to Claudio in *Measure for Measure*, when she tells her beloved brother, "O, were it but for my life, / I'd throw it down for your deliverance / As frankly as a pin" (III.i.104–6). Pearsall's phrase "with a difference" is barbed here, as the reader recalls that Isabella's remark to her brother is quickly retracted when she learns she might rescue him if she gives up her virginity, and she refuses to do so. Summoning Isabella, the nun-heroine of one of the most uncomfortable of Shakespeare's comedies, to explain the actions of patient Griselda in Chaucer's challenging tale opens a panoply of perspectives on each character, both of whom remain obdurate, though in different ways, and are somewhat opaque. Griselda's monstrous husband, Walter, is described "as a mysterious and inscrutable figure, a kind of 'Duke of dark corners,' manipulating Griselda's suffering as a means of offering her the opportunity to demonstrate the temper of her will," though Chaucer's Walter is given more dimension than Shakespeare's Vincentio (*Measure for Measure*, IV.v.164–65) through the sustained narrative commentary on Walter's cruelty.[24] Images of Griselda and Shakespeare's heroines appear elsewhere, too. Writing of "The Nut Brown Maid" in Balliol MS 354, Pearsall points to the title character's unswerving fidelity to her lover, "which echoes the Clerk's Tale as it anticipates Child Waters and *As You Like It*," the latter with analogues as well to the Robin Hood stories and *The Tale of Gamelyn*.[25]

Numerous Shakespearean plays are sometimes invoked in Pearsall's discussion of Chaucer to provide a sense of critical dimension, almost as though comparison to one play is not quite enough. The Franklin's Tale, for example, is explained as a mixed genre, a romance that is so realistically dramatized that the reader is momentarily moved into the world of "domestic tragedy—rather as *Cymbeline* and *The Winter's Tale* inhabit for a time the world of *Othello*."[26] And when the rocks seem magically removed in the Franklin's Tale, the action of the story returns to "the optimistic harmonies of romance," a resolution also embraced by Shakespeare in *The Merchant of Venice* and *The Winter's Tale*.[27]

The satire of the Merchant's Tale, in which January's inherent misogyny and self-delusion provide subjects for ridicule along with the tale's cynical view of sexuality, is seen again in Shakespeare: the same "voice can be heard in Shakespeare, sometimes strident, as in the venomous outbursts of Timon or of Thersites in *Troilus and Cressida*, sometimes contained within higher art, as with many passages in *Hamlet*,

Othello and *The Winter's Tale*." "The great imaginative writers," Pearsall continues, "seem to be able to go beyond the tempting rhetoric of male cynicism, to recognize the cause of disorder in a disordered consciousness, and to isolate this consciousness through the power of their art."[28] The deus ex machina ending of the Merchant's Tale provided by the intervention of Pluto and Proserpina and the witty rejoinder quickly supplied by May when January sees her and Damian in the pear tree help to create a happy ending to the tale, though "the darkness is not entirely dissipated . . . any more than it is at the end of *Merchant of Venice* or *Cymbeline*."[29]

Shakespeare's *Lear* is cited often, as when Pearsall is speculating about whether Thomas of Erceldoune's Prophecy in Harley 2253 is a forerunner of the Fool's prophecy (III.ii.80–95),[30] and in his analysis of Chaucer's Knight's Tale, in which Pearsall remarks that Chaucer, like Shakespeare later, understands "the poignancy and power . . . [of] the affairs of men who live without God" when a character is "placed naked before the realities of his existence and the forces that seem to control it, and without the consolation of the faith that answers all such questions."[31] In this case, Pearsall is no doubt thinking of the play's turning point during the storm scene when Lear meets "Poor Tom" and suddenly, after a lifetime of selfishness, becomes compassionate ("Is man no more than this?"; III.iv.107), as analogous to the speeches of Egeus ("This world nys but a thurghfare ful of wo"; 2842–49) and Theseus's consolatory answer to the larger question of mortality ("Thanne is it wisdom, as it thynketh me, / To maken vertu of necessitee"; 3041–42) after the untimely death of Arcita in the Knight's Tale.

References to *A Midsummer Night's Dream* are frequent, too, whether Pearsall is noting Shakespeare's burlesque bashing ("medieval alliterative poetry . . . by Shakespeare's day was a source of ridicule ['Whereat, with blade, with bloody blameful blade'"; V.i.147])[32] or wittily comparing Chaucer's satiric Sir Thopas with the play-within-a-play thought up by the rude mechanicals. Sir Thopas "almost seems to have been made up by a latter-day Peter Quince from some list of instructions on 'How to write a romance.' Yet everything is wrong—not always or absolutely wrong, for a judicious admixture of sense is necessary to give the nonsense its full relish, but subtly, knowingly and hilariously wrong."[33] In addition to his propensity for alliteration and his comical attempts to compose a compelling romance, Peter Quince is credited with incorporating the figure of the man in the moon into his Pyramus and Thisbe play. Commenting on Robert Henryson's *The Testament of Cresseid*, Pearsall notes that the man in the moon painted on the breast of Lady Cynthia, the moon goddess ("on hir breast ane churle paintit full evin / Beirand ane bunche of thornis on his bak, / Quhilk for his thift micht clim na nar the hevin"; 261–63), in Henryson's poem alludes to "the old story of the 'man in the moon' as a thief banished there because he stole a bundle of thorns (Peter Quince puts him in his play of Pyramus and Thisbe in *A Midsummer Night's Dream*)."[34] In this example, the critic imaginatively inhabits the Shakespearean text, giving Peter Quince full rights of authorship of the play-within-a-play while simultaneously clarifying the image in Henryson's poetry.

Another stylistic similarity is found in the repetitive and silly verses of Sir Thopas and in the Pyramus and Thisbe play. In both, the couplet, the "basic unit" of Middle English romance (including the stanzaic romances), is exploited to comic effect.[35] Not only alliteration but also the jangling internal rhymes of Thopas as he wonders at his newfound love for the fairy queen ("O Seinte Marie, benedicite! / What eyleth this love at me / To bynde me so soore? / Me dremed al this nyght, pardee, / An elf-queene shal my lemman be / And slept under my gore"; 784–89) appear in the Pyramus play, for example, when Pyramus finds the bloodied mantle ("But stay! O spite! / But mark, poor knight? / What dreadful dole is here? / Eyes, do you see? / How can it be? / O dainty duck! O dear!"; V.i.265–70).

Hamlet is another play to which Pearsall frequently alludes. In the anonymous Middle English poem "Farewell, this World," for example, the speaker says he is "arrested to appere afore Goddes face," and the image of death as a form of arrest is linked by Pearsall to a line in Hamlet's dying speech, "this fell sergeant, Death, Is strict in his arrest" (V.ii.288–89).[36] In the Knight's Tale, Palamon is seen as the likelier lover of Emily because he shows "a consciousness, albeit only fitful, of a 'divinity that shapes our ends', where Arcite thinks he alone may 'roughhew' them"; to explicate Chaucer's characters, Pearsall quotes two lines of the speech by Hamlet telling Horatio about escaping the pirates and sending Rosencrantz and Guildenstern to their deaths (V.ii.10–11).[37] In this case, Pearsall seems to point to Palamon's ultimate faith in his love and his prayer to Venus, the goddess of love, "That if yow list, I shal wel have my love" (3.2250), that triumphs over Arcite's confidence in his ability to win the lady through his own prowess, as shown in his prayer to Mars: "do that I tomorowe have victorie. Myn be the travaille, and thyn be the glorie!" (3.2405). Pearsall also cites Hamlet's famous gravedigger scene when glossing Lydgate's lines in *The Dance Macabree* that describe John Rickhill, Henry V's juggler as well as the organizer of his court spectacles and entertainments:

> *Deeth to the Tregetour*
> Maistir John Rikele, some-tyme tregetour
> Of noble Harry, kyng of Engelond
> And of Fraunce the mighty conqueror,
> For alle the sleightes and turning of thin hond
> Thou must come ner, this daunce to undirstond:
> Nought may availe al thi conclusiouns,
> For deeth, shortly, nouther on see ne lond
> Is nought deceived by none illusions. (512–20)

Pearsall here remarks that the lines spoken by Death to the juggler sound "a little like Hamlet on 'poor Yorick,'" although in Lydgate's poem Rickhill replies, unlike Hamlet's jawless jester ("Quite chop-fallen?"; V.i.186).[38] Certainly the sentiments are similar, however, and there is shared irony, too, in the deaths of Yorick and Rickhill: both were formerly known for their court entertainments. As Hamlet inquires of Yorick's skull, "Where be your gibes now, your gambols, your songs, your flashes of merriment, that were wont to set the table on a roar?" (V.i.183–85). In this verse, Lydgate captures the inescapability of death and the related loss of earthly power also seen in *Hamlet*: "Imperious Caesar, dead and turn'd to clay, / Might stop a hole to keep the wind away" (V.i.206–7).

Writing about early Tudor poetry, Pearsall addresses the repetitions employed by Thomas Wyatt in Poem 15 of British Library MS Egerton 2711, Wyatt's manuscript with notes in his own hand. In this poem, which opens "Hevyn and erth and all that here me plain," each end line of nine stanzas includes a verbal repetition, for example, "Mercy, madame, alas, I dy, I dy!" (4), and "Why do I dy? Alas, for shame, for shame!" (28). Pearsall points out that the echoing final line of each stanza "creates emphasis but also an effect of a mind distracted ('. . . except my life, my life, my life')."[39] Pearsall's parenthetical line alludes, of course, to Hamlet's madness, specifically in his teasing (and manipulative) replies to Polonius, the "tedious old fool." When Polonius asks to take his leave of Hamlet, he replies, "You cannot, sir, take from me anything that I will not more willingly part withal—except my life, except my life, except my life" (II.ii.215–17); the statement is both literal and figurative.

Pearsall again invokes *Hamlet* in a discussion of Wyatt's verse paraphrase of the *Seven Penitential Psalms*, composed after the execution of Wyatt's patron, Thomas Cromwell:

> For, Lord, if thou do observe what men offend
> And putt thy natyf mercy in restraint,
> If just exaction demaund recompense,
> Who may endure, O Lord? Who shall not faynt
> At such acompt? (12–15)

Here comparison is made to Hamlet's reply, again to Polonius, in their discussion of where the players are to be housed in Elsinore. When Polonius says he will "use them according to their desert" (II.ii.523), or rank, Hamlet replies, "Use every man after his desert, and who shall scape whipping?" (II.ii.525), again reading Polonius's lines more broadly and philosophically.[40] While Wyatt's poem seems to echo the words of the Psalmist, "If you, Lord, were to note what is done amiss, / O Lord, who could stand?" (Psalm 130), thinking about *Hamlet* in this different context not only enriches the experience of reading Wyatt but also enlarges our thinking about Shakespeare.

While Derek Pearsall is not the only critic of medieval literature to allude to Shakespeare, his helpful Shakespearean references elucidate otherwise obscure passages as well as more familiar ones and shed light on medieval characters and narratives while providing both new perspectives and contexts for reading.[41] His many methods of employing Shakespeare in the cause of closely reading medieval poetry and prose, whether to clarify various aspects of the texts, to contextualize characters, or even to speculate further on which medieval stories Shakespeare might have known, are but briefly detailed here. As these several examples (I hope) have shown, Pearsall's analogies create striking parallels which readers might not have thought of previously, lending fuller dimension to considerations of character and narrative. His approach to the text, whether medieval or Shakespearean, is humble and open-minded, feeling and imaginative, sure signs of a great critic at work.

Notes

All Shakespeare quotes in this chapter are from Arden editions.

1. Elizabeth Salter, *English and International: Studies in the Literature, Art and Patronage of Medieval England*, ed. Derek Pearsall and Nicolette Zeeman (Cambridge: Cambridge University Press, 1988); Derek Pearsall, *The Canterbury Tales* (London: Unwin Hyman, 1985); Derek Pearsall, *Old English and Middle English Poetry*, Routledge History of English Poetry, 1 (London: Routledge & Kegan Paul, 1977); Derek Pearsall, ed., *Chaucer to Spenser: An Anthology of Writings in English, 1375–1575* (Oxford: Blackwell, 1999); Derek Pearsall, *The Life of Geoffrey Chaucer: A Critical Biography* (Oxford: Blackwell, 1992); and Derek Pearsall, "Medieval Monks and Friars: Differing Literary Perceptions," in *The Medieval Python: The Purposive and Provocative Work of Terry Jones*, ed. R. F. Yeager and Toshiyuki Takamiya (New York: Palgrave Macmillan, 2012), 59–73. Quotations from Chaucer are taken from *The Riverside Chaucer*, ed. Larry D. Benson, 3rd ed. (Oxford: Oxford University Press, 1988).

2. Salter, *English and International*, 2. See also Derek Pearsall, "Chaucer and Englishness," in *Chaucer's Cultural Geography*, ed. Kathryn L. Lynch (New York: Routledge, 2002), 281–301, cautioning that the "idealization of Chaucer as the poet of Englishness has little or no basis in his poetry" (288) but that Chaucer is certainly seen as early as the fifteenth century to be the first poet "to give high status to English as a literary language" (292), the sense that Salter is presenting here. For more on Chaucer and Englishness, see also Derek Pearsall, "The Idea of Englishness in the Fifteenth Century," in *Nation, Court and Culture: New Essays on Fifteenth-Century English Poetry*, ed. Helen Cooney (Dublin: Four Courts Press, 2001), 15–27.

3. Pearsall, *Old English and Middle English Poetry*, 203–4. For further elaboration on Chaucer as a dramatist, as an actor, and as a responder in the narration of his stories, see A. C. Spearing, "Narrative and Freedom in *Troilus and Criseyde*," chap. 1 this volume.

4. Derek Pearsall, interview by author, Kalamazoo, 2012. It may seem obvious that to be a good writer, one must be a good reader, but there is more. From childhood, Derek has been a keeper of commonplace books, jotting notes and anecdotes into little diaries, along with phrases that are "sonorous and memorable, written down as a substitute for memory." It has also been his practice when reading a lengthy classic to write summaries of plots or character and to include favorite quotations. As a pleasurable exercise, for example, Derek summarized each volume of Moncrieff's Proust translation and jotted down many striking quotations, as an aid to memory but also just because he liked the way they sounded. As a child, he wrote down passages, any aphoristic turn of phrase, from a range of writers, including Shakespeare, Dryden, and Pope.

5. Derek Pearsall, "Reviewing Literary History (Medieval)," in *Literary Reviewing*, ed. James O. Hoge (Charlottesville: University Press of Virginia, 1987), 19–28, 22, 23. In his foreword to Part I of this volume, Christopher Cannon notes that this respectfulness toward texts is a comparatively recent trend in the Pearsallian discourse, and Cannon provides several choice examples of Pearsall's critical comments; I would observe, however, that Derek can rarely resist making a joke, and his comic remarks about medieval texts (perhaps perversely) inspire me to want to read or reread the works he so deftly lampoons.

6. E. Talbot Donaldson, *The Swan at the Well: Shakespeare Reading Chaucer* (New Haven: Yale University Press, 1985), 2. It is interesting to note that Donaldson, the great medievalist, uses as his exemplar for commentary Stow's 1561 printing, with modernized punctuation and line numbers from "standard modern texts" (141 n. 1), though he never explains precisely why he has chosen this particular text.

7. Ann Thompson, *Shakespeare's Chaucer: A Study in Literary Origins* (Liverpool: Liverpool University Press, 1978), draws all of her Chaucer quotations from the 1957 Robinson edition (F. N. Robinson, ed., *The Poetical Works of Chaucer* [Cambridge, MA: Houghton Mifflin, 1933; 2nd rev. ed., 1957]), though she qualifies this approach in her bibliography by saying that she has consulted the editions of Thynne (1532), Stow (1561), and Speght (1598 and 1602) and that "quotations are always taken from the most recent [edition] at the time of the work on which I am claiming an influence" (222). There are, however, very few direct references in her text to the early editions of *Chaucer's Works* published by Speght and none at all to those of Thynne or Stow.

8. Harold Bloom, "Chaucer: The Wife of Bath, the Pardoner, and Shakespearean Character," in *The Western Canon: The Books and School of the Ages* (New York: Harcourt Brace, 1994; rev. ed. Papermac, 1995), 105–25.

9. Thompson, *Shakespeare's Chaucer*, 10.

10. Ibid., 87. David Bevington, ed., *William Shakespeare: The Poems* (New York: Bantam, 1988), 88, 90.

11. Harold F. Brooks, ed., *A Midsummer Night's Dream: The Arden Shakespeare* (New York: Methuen, 1983), lix and notes. Dramatic versions of the Knight's Tale seem to have circulated simultaneously with early printed editions of Chaucer's *Works*. Elizabeth I was familiar with the story from the 1560s, when the play by Richard Edwardes, now lost, titled *Palamon and Arcite* was performed before the queen at Oxford in two parts on September 2 and 4, 1566; Thompson, *Shakespeare's Chaucer*, 29. The "sounding dogs" featured in Edwardes's play are later alluded to by Hippolyta and Theseus in *Midsummer Night's Dream* (IV.i.105–17). See also notes on these passages in Arden. Donaldson includes a convincing argument that Shakespeare is rewriting Chaucer's "Tale of Sir Thopas"; see Donaldson, *Swan at the Well*, 9–18.

12. Brian Morris, ed., *The Taming of the Shrew: The Arden Edition of the Works of William Shakespeare* (New York: Routledge, 1989), 247. Petruchio's reference to his dog as "Troilus" must surely be a comic reference, though the Arden edition comments, "possibly so named as a type of faithfulness."

13. J. H. P. Pafford, ed., *The Winter's Tale* (New York: Methuen, 1984), 47 n. 75. See also allusions to Gower and Chaucer in Derek Pearsall, "The Gower Tradition," in Gower's *Confessio Amantis: Responses and Reassessments*, ed. A. J. Minnis (Cambridge: D. S. Brewer, 1983), 179–97, 192–93; R. F. Yeager, "Shakespeare as Medievalist: What It Means for Performing *Pericles*," in *Shakespeare and the Middle Ages: Essays on the Performance and Adaptation of the Plays with Medieval Sources or Settings*, ed. Martha W. Driver and Sid Ray (Jefferson, NC: McFarland, 2009), 215–31; Kelly Jones, "'The Quick and the Dead': Performing the Poet Gower in *Pericles*," in Driver and Ray, *Shakespeare and the Middle Ages*, 201–14; and Martha Driver, "Conjuring Gower in *Pericles*," in *John Gower, Trilingual Poet: Language, Translation, and Tradition*, ed. Elisabeth Dutton with John Hines and R. F. Yeager (Cambridge: Boydell and Brewer, 2010), 315–25.

14. EETS Archive, Box 2/1, folder 2, cited by H. L. Spencer, "The Early English Text Society 1930–1950: Wartime and Reconstruction," in *Probable Truth: Editing Medieval Texts from Britain in the Twenty-First Century*, ed. Vincent Gillespie and Anne Hudson (Turnhout: Brepols, 2013), 21.

15. Pearsall, *Old English and Middle English Poetry*, 163. Salter, *English and International*, 42, comments on the thirteenth-century debate poem "The Owl and the Nightingale," in which the lonely Owl inhabits a winter world of "bright evergreens, the night-frosts, the indoor warmth, and conviviality—there is just a hint of that sharply etched pastoral of *Love's Labour's Lost*—'When icicles hang by the wall . . . ,'" a reference to the ending poem of the comedy (V.ii.921–39), spoken by an allegorical Winter describing the paradoxical pleasures of the colder months; the owl also appears in the song of Winter that concludes the play.

16. Pearsall, *Old English and Middle English Poetry*, 203–4.

17. Pearsall, *Canterbury Tales*, 96.

18. Ibid., 225.

19. Giorgio Melchiori, ed., *The Merry Wives of Windsor: The Arden Shakespeare* (London: Methuen, 2000), 21, 27; Pearsall, *Chaucer to Spenser*, 511 n. 89–92. The figure of Falstaff is said to be loosely based on the martyr Sir John Oldcastle, who was executed for Lollardy in 1417. The name "Falstaff" is taken from that of another fifteenth-century knight, Sir John Fastolf. Due to his tactical retreat from the battle of Patay, Fastolf later entered into protracted litigation when Sir John Talbot contested Fastolf's right to membership in the Order of the Garter on grounds of cowardice. Talbot's lawsuit is also described in the first part of *Henry VI*, which was written before 1592 and is the only

Shakespeare play other than *Merry Wives* to include substantial mention of the Order of the Garter. The historical Fastolf was finally vindicated in the 1440s, after rebutting Talbot's charge before the king and his peers, although the stigma of his trial for "conduct unbecoming" remained. John A. F. Thomson, "Oldcastle, John, Baron Cobham (*d.* 1417)," in *Oxford Dictionary of National Biography* (Oxford: Oxford University Press, 2004), online ed, January 2008, www.oxforddnb.com/view/article/20674; G. L. Harriss, "Fastolf, Sir John (1380–1459)," *ODNB*, www.oxforddnb.com/view/article/9199. Unlike Falstaff in *Merry Wives*, neither Oldcastle nor Fastolf seems to have wooed married women for their money, nor did they find themselves stowed in laundry baskets and flung into the Thames or cross-dress to escape jealous husbands.

20. Pearsall, "Medieval Monks and Friars," 59–71, 71; see also Carl F. Grindley, " 'We're Everyone You Depend On': Filming Shakespeare's Peasants," in Driver and Ray, *Shakespeare and the Middle Ages*, 89–104, describing *Romeo and Juliet*'s Friar Lawrence as an "alchemical hobbyist," 94.

21. Pearsall, *Canterbury Tales*, 186. In *Twelfth Night, or What You Will*, a line spoken by Maria about Olivia's humorless servant, "sometimes, he is a kind of Puritan" (II.iii.150), has been read variously to allude to the devil taking the shape of a Puritan or to describe Malvolio as "the character of a pompous egotist, finally constant to no religion but his own self-advancement" (Maurice Hunt, "Malvolio, Viola, and the Question of Instrumentality: Defining Providence in *Twelfth Night*," *Studies in Philology* 90, no. 3 [Summer 1993]: 277–97 [279]), characteristics shared by Chaucer's Reeve. Keir Elam, ed., *Twelfth Night, or What You Will, The Arden Shakespeare* (London: Methuen, 2008).

22. Pearsall, *Canterbury Tales*, 154; Pearsall, *Chaucer to Spenser*, 155.

23. Pearsall, *Canterbury Tales*, 268.

24. Ibid., 270, 273–74. Oliver Pickering identifies in the Outspoken *South English Legendary* Poet a writer who, like Chaucer, uses "a lively, colloquial, conversational style" (chap. 2 this volume).

25. Pearsall, *Old English and Middle English Poetry*, 266, 144.

26. Pearsall, *Canterbury Tales*, 152.

27. Ibid., 154–55.

28. Ibid., 194–95.

29. Ibid., 206, 207.

30. Pearsall, *Old English and Middle English Poetry*, 125. While this is a helpful gloss on Thomas of Erceldoune, the Fool's prophecy in *Lear* more likely comes from apocrypha that first find their way into Caxton's edition of Chaucer, which is then repeated in sixteenth-century editions through Speght. The Arden edition of *Lear* says, rather unhelpfully, that "Shakespeare probably derived his knowledge of Merlin's prophecies from Holinshed," when clearly Shakespeare is drawing his text directly from one or more of the early

printed Chaucer editions. This, in fact, is one of the closest sustained references by Shakespeare to late medieval material, elegantly expanding the sense of the original satiric commentary on priests, law, crime, and lechery, and a comparison is worth further analysis. The Arden *Lear* notes say:

> The verses that follow are a parody of some pseudo-Chaucerian verses to be found in Puttenham, *Arte of English Poesie* (ed. Arber, p. 232). Thynne's edition of Chaucer prints them as follows: "When faith fayleth in preestes saws / And lordes hestes are holden for lawes / And robbery is holden purchase / And lechery is holden solace / Than shal the londe of albyon / Be brought to great confusyon." Warburton pointed out that ll. 81–84 refer to the actual state of affairs, while 85–90 are Utopian. He suggested, perhaps rightly, that 91–92 be inserted after 84.

A later note refers to Samuel L. Bethell, *Shakespeare and the Popular Dramatic Tradition* (Durham, NC: Duke University Press, 1944, 86), which "points out that the Fool's concluding remark makes him step out of the remote period as a contemporary," which seems a misreading of the passage. The Fool's lines here actually provide a setting in prehistory for the play, describing it as earlier than the Arthurian period. See *King Lear: The Arden Edition of the Works of William Shakespeare*, ed. Kenneth Muir (New York: Methuen, 1982), 104–5, n. 80, n. 95.

31. Pearsall, *Canterbury Tales*, 120; see further Pearsall, *Life of Chaucer*, 154, which again refers to a world without "the faith that answers all such questions as 'What is this world? What asketh men to have?' (I.2777) with the assertion of a mystery in which they are transcended."

32. Pearsall, *Old English and Middle English Poetry*, 188.

33. Pearsall, *Canterbury Tales*, 162. See also Martha Driver, "Reading *A Midsummer Night's Dream* through Middle English Romance," in Driver and Ray, *Shakespeare and the Middle Ages*, 140–60, esp. 140–45, tracing various medieval sources for Shakespeare's play.

34. Pearsall, *Chaucer to Spenser*, 476 n. 261. The man in the moon is also mentioned in *The Tempest.* See further Kim Zarins, "Caliban's God: The Medieval and Renaissance Man in the Moon," in Driver and Ray, *Shakespeare and the Middle Ages*, 245–62, 245–52.

35. A. C. Baugh, "Improvisation in the Middle English Romance," *Proceedings of the American Philosophical Society* 103 (1959): 418–54, 428, observes that romances typically use a "predictable complement": "Certain statements seem to call up in the mind of a poet or recite a conventional way of completing the thought. It was as though he were subject to a kind of conditioned reflex. Generally the statement and its predictable complement form a couplet and this feature of composition is the result of the fact that the couplet is the basic unit of most Middle English romances, even the stanzaic romances."

36. Pearsall, *Chaucer to Spenser*, 394 n. 2. References to *Hamlet* also occur frequently in the writings of P. G. Wodehouse, the comic writer who is a favorite of Pearsall's (and mine). One example from Wodehouse's classic *Joy in the Morning* (London: Arrow Books, 2008) will suffice. Bertie is speaking to Jeeves about insulting the ferocious Uncle Percy in order to bring two lovebirds together: "I shall shortly be telling Uncle Percy things about himself which will do something to his knotted and combined locks which at the moment has slipped my memory." Jeeves gently corrects, " 'Make his knotted and combined locks to part and each particular hair to stand on end like quills upon the fretful porpentine,' sir." "Porpentine?" "Yes, sir." "That can't be right. There isn't such a thing" (185), and later, "You're sure it's porpentine?" "Yes, sir." "Very odd. But I suppose half the time Shakespeare just shoved down anything that came into his head" (188).

37. Pearsall, *Life of Chaucer*, 155–56.

38. Pearsall, *Chaucer to Spenser*, 359 n. 516–18.

39. Ibid., 616 n.

40. Ibid., 629 n. 12–15.

41. See, e.g., Helen Cooper, *Oxford Guides to Chaucer: The Canterbury Tales* (Oxford: Oxford University Press, 1996); Helen Cooper, *The English Romance in Time: Transforming Motifs from Geoffrey of Monmouth to the Death of Shakespeare* (Oxford: Oxford University Press, 2004); Curtis Perry and John Watkins, *Shakespeare and the Middle Ages* (Oxford: Oxford University Press, 2009); and passing references in John Scattergood, "*The Libelle of Englysche Polycye*: The Nation and Its Place," in Cooney, *Nation, Court and Culture*, 28–49, 47; Toril Moi, "Desire in Language: Andreas Capellanus and the Controversy of Courtly Love," in *Medieval Literature: Criticism, Ideology and History*, ed. David Aers (New York: St. Martin's Press, 1986), 11–57, 26–27, and passim.

Part II

England and International

Studies in Courtly Verse and Affectivity Inspired by the Work of Elizabeth Salter and Derek Pearsall at York

Foreword to Part II

The work of Elizabeth Salter and Derek Pearsall at the Centre for Medieval Studies, University of York, spanned the period from the late 1960s until Elizabeth's death in May 1980. Their influence on research and teaching—particularly the supervision of research students—has been extensive. In that period the idea that research students should be guided by a supervisory team had not yet become a feature of British universities, but Elizabeth and Derek provided for their students joint supervision that drew the best out of research topics and the students themselves. To be supervised by Derek and Elizabeth was a unique privilege. In addition to supporting research students, Elizabeth and Derek along with other medievalists at York created a scholarly environment that was indeed international, with visitors from North America, Europe, and Japan making their way to York and the King's Manor to give seminar papers and lectures and to discuss their research.

Interdisciplinary approaches to teaching and research foster the exchange of ideas and methodologies across the boundaries of scholarly disciplines. It was this kind of approach to research that Elizabeth and Derek encouraged among postgraduate students and developed in their own work. It is therefore fitting that for her contribution to this part of the collection Susan Powell should revisit Elizabeth's essay "The

Timeliness of *Wynnere and Wastoure*," which first appeared in 1978 in *Medium Aevum*. The essay is a classic as much for the way it demonstrates the value of the interdisciplinary investigation of literature as for its critical acumen and its challenges to long-established assumptions that were central to writing about the "alliterative revival." Indeed, this was not Elizabeth's first venture into this question and its historical implications. Her two essays—in fact one essay in two parts—published in 1966 in *Modern Philology* questioned a number of entrenched ideas about the origin and provenance of this phenomenon in fourteenth-century English literature. In later years Elizabeth returned again and again to questions of the function and aesthetics of alliterative poetry in Middle English. This was an interest she shared with Derek, who addressed the question a number of times and published his own classic essay "The Alliterative Revival: Origins and Social Backgrounds" in the collection edited by David Lawton, *Middle English Alliterative Poetry and Its Background* (1982).

Like Elizabeth's essay, Susan Powell's begins with a review of the reading of *Wynnere and Wastoure* that Israel Gollancz set out in the introduction to his edition of 1920 and that came to define much about the poem and the alliterative revival itself. One of the striking arguments of Elizabeth's essay was that the arms worn by the Second Knight in *Wynnere and Wastoure* were not, as was commonly assumed, those of the Black Prince but of the Wingfields. In many ways this was a plausible alternative to Gollancz's interpretation but not, at the time, conclusive, and I recall Elizabeth saying that she would not mind if she were proved wrong; her principal concern had been to engage in a critical reading of the evidence for Gollancz's conclusions about the text. For Elizabeth, a rigorous assessment of evidence was the foremost task of a scholar. Powell uses her essay to pick up where Elizabeth's left off. Where there was uncertainty over Elizabeth's conclusions about the identity of the Second Knight, Powell has brought together evidence about the career of John Wingfield and another historical individual who figures in the text, William Shareshull, Chief Justice of the King's Bench, that has emerged in different contexts since Elizabeth published her article. Powell demonstrates tenacity in pursuing the implications of this new evidence, and the effect is to support and make convincing much of Elizabeth's original argument about *Wynnere and Wastoure* and its implications for the literary history of fourteenth-century England.

A significant aspect of the work of Elizabeth and Derek—and in the light of subsequent history possibly the most significant aspect—was the way in which they developed manuscript studies. During the period in which they worked together at York, Elizabeth's and Derek's interests were steadily moving toward the investigation of the medieval manuscript as the basis of research that went beyond its function as the source for critical editions. Derek's brief but trenchant introduction to the collection of essays that emerged from the first York medieval manuscripts conference (1981), *Manuscripts and Readers in Fifteenth-Century England: The Literary Implications of Manuscript Study* (1983), summarizes the discussions and debates that were taking place throughout the 1970s at the King's Manor and, read today, can be seen to have served as a prologue to one of the important directions that research in medieval studies took in the years that followed and which show no sign of abating. The essays in *Manuscripts and Readers* give indications of new directions in research while they reinforce and indeed refresh traditional objectives such as textual editing, and it is notable that in one way or another all of the contributors were students and, in the broadest sense, colleagues of Elizabeth and Derek.

Among the papers in *Manuscripts and Readers* was Kate Harris's essay on some of the witnesses to Gower's *Confessio Amantis*. This is subtitled "The Virtues of Bad Texts" and is an investigation of variant readings in manuscripts of Gower that might routinely be dismissed as errors and of no importance. Harris shows how these are not misunderstandings so much as the work of scribes or medieval editors intended to improve or make aspects of Gower's text acceptable to contemporary taste. Derek says of the essay that it demonstrates "how in the work of interfering and meddling scribes . . . can be seen the activities of our first literary critics." Although the subject matter is much different, the essay here by Katie Ann-Marie Bugyis follows in the tradition of investigating what could be seen as marginal but which has value as evidence of the reception of and response to a text. This is a subtle investigation of scribal intervention in the sole surviving manuscript of the *Book of Margery Kempe* by what has come to be known as the Red Ink Annotator. In an essay that thoroughly convinces, Bugyis gives coherence to the work of this annotator by showing how the interventions—far from being mere meddling—are driven by an understanding of contemplative theology and designed to make Margery Kempe's spiritual autobiography an exemplary Carthusian text.

One of Elizabeth's enduring interests—and one that she sought to promote among her students—was the international character of the literature of medieval Britain. Her work in this area is most fully realized in her later publications but has its roots in the subject of her earliest research project, Nicholas Love's Middle English translation of one of the classic European medieval Latin devotional texts, the *Meditationes Vitae Christi*. Sarah McNamer has introduced into scholarship on the Latin text an argument that would have intrigued Elizabeth, that the *MVC* had its origins as a vernacular text, in Italian, and that this version, more tightly focused on affectivity, was compiled by a woman. However, it was the Latin version (translation or otherwise) that ultimately had the most influence on medieval vernacular literatures in medieval England through the translation by Nicholas Love and a host of anonymous translations of parts of the text that were concerned principally with the passion. The essay by Sarah McNamer, which focuses on what she argues is the original Italian text, echoes the kind of work that Elizabeth was best at, a reading that is alert to nuances and shows a willingness to pursue their implications.

Jocelyn Wogan-Browne's essay, which begins Part II, also uses the literature on the passion of Christ to explore internationalism in the culture of medieval England. She turns first to the thirteenth century and the court of Henry III and Eleanor of Provence and recovers something of the cultural and spiritual aesthetics of John of Howden's *Rossignos*, a poem written in the French of England. However, whereas the *MVC* reveals an imagination that celebrates the humanity of Christ, John of Howden's *Rossignos*, a nightingale poem, is a tour de force of high style, remarkable and at the same time challenging to the reader, the work of a poet whom one might describe as clever and possibly a bit of a show-off but with a profound spiritual understanding and purpose. Wogan-Browne makes a compelling case for *Rossignos* and demonstrates how it reflects the cosmopolitan courtly and spiritual aesthetic cultivated by Henry III and Eleanor of Provence. The latter part of her essay turns to a much later poem, the Middle English pseudo-Lydgate *Nightingale* of the mid-fifteenth century that was written for Anne Neville, duchess of Buckingham. This too has as its subject the redemptive work of Christ but reflects a pragmatic spirituality that is more widely accessible. Both poems are evidence of the multilingualism of medieval English culture and through this its internationalism.

These four essays stand as a tribute to the work of Elizabeth and Derek and the enduring value of their joint contributions to the development of the study of the Middle Ages.

William Marx

CHAPTER 4

The Tongues of the Nightingale

"hertely redyng" at English Courts

Jocelyn Wogan-Browne

"Laüstic ad nun . . . russignol en franceis / E nihtegale en dreit engleis": the nightingale, "this bridde so small" that "syngeth as that she wold hirself dismember," sang in many tongues in medieval England, voicing and symbolizing sacred and secular passions.[1] This essay is concerned with two meditations on Christ's passion, John of Howden's late-thirteenth-century *Rossignos*, a remarkable poem rarely discussed but included in the cosmopolitan vision of literary culture in England taken by Elizabeth Salter and Derek Pearsall, and the pseudo-Lydgate *Nightingale* of [? late in] 1446 for Anne, duchess of Buckingham (d. 1480).[2]

Rossignos in particular exemplifies some of the rewarding complexities of meditation on Christ's passion. Recent work on models of emotion and cognition provides fuller understanding of the theological underpinning of meditative reading and complicates the "affective" categorization through which such texts have often been read. Michelle Karnes has emphasized the cognitive work in gospel meditations as practiced by lettered and unlettered; Lydia Schumacher has argued for a new theologically based account of the varieties of late-thirteenth-century Franciscan philosophical thought on divine illumination, in which Bonaventura reformulates it on a new Averroist basis and Aquinas on a neo-Augustinian one.[3] Alongside debates, medieval and modern, over the status of meditative knowledge, the cultural politics of affectivity—of "hertely redyng"—have also attracted renewed interest. Alexandra Barratt showed in a 1998 essay that Middle English meditation could be written as well as consumed by women.[4] More recently Sarah McNamer has argued that medieval European passion meditation is not simply an expression of the personal devotional fervor of Christian churchmen: a large percentage of such texts were composed at the request or command of women known to their writers, who saw pastoral and spiritual work for women as part of their professional responsibilities.[5] While this is no license for gendering passion meditation and affectivity as in some way essentially feminine, McNamer's argument fits well with what is known of women's patronage in medieval England.[6] Neither this, nor what McNamer calls the "invention of compassion" as feminine in the thirteenth century, precludes male writers, readers, and texts from passion meditation, which they undoubtedly continued to write and to practice. Nor does it preclude women patrons and readers from a compassion that involves more than intense private feeling within the heart.

Eleanor of Provence (d. 1291), queen of Henry III of England, is the dedicatee of *Rossignos*, composed by John of Howden, *clerc la roine d'Engleterre* (Prol., 1–2) between 1273 and 1282 (so after Henry III's death in 1272 but before Eleanor retired to the nunnery of Amesbury in 1286).[7] Howden's own *Philomena* (itself drawing on Anselm of Lucca's *Desere iam, anima, lectulo saporis*) was used by him as a starting point for the 5,272 lines of his Anglo-Norman poem.[8] Howden was highly regarded in the late Middle Ages and beyond.[9] Charles d'Orléans, for instance, borrowed a copy of Howden's *Philomena* from the Franciscans' London library during his English imprisonment, had it copied, and in 1440 took it back to France, where he composed an imitation of the poem.[10]

A major difference between *Rossignos* and *Philomena* is the tailoring of the vernacular work to its inscribed female patron ("la roïne . . . Mere au roi Edward," 5269–70). Although love of Christ is presented as a deeply emotional and refined courtly love ("*fin' amour*"), the poem does not urge a purely affective spirituality or one constitutive of a private self: the poem is also directed toward Eleanor's various public identities—her queenship, active queen motherhood, crusading Christianity, the aesthetics of her court, and her own high level of cultivation.

Rossignos, says its manuscript's anonymous prose prologue, "was made so that the heart of its reader will be kindled with love of our Lord" (Et pur ce fu il faiz que li quor celi qui le lira soit esprys en l'amour nostre Seignour), but the poem engenders sensuous and affective response while following an athletic metaphoric logic, and one that frequently incorporates broad cultural reference (as in the poem's many rhetorical lists—of saints, rivers, flowers, sounds, etc). Christ is a bush blooming with roses, the cross the cage of the nightingale (2711); Christ's side, cut by love's blade, is the fenestrated Ark (2529–36); devotees of the name of Jesus deploy a royal banner when they pleat his name between their lips (3463–64), a name lavishly imagined as the armament of heavenly chivalry (3517–612), and so on.

Rossignos moves in sections of different lengths, irregularly marked off by changing apostrophes (*Amor*, *Mort*, *Quors*, *Jhesu*, *Lance*, *Tu moers*, *Cest nom Jesu*, etc.), but it uses monorhymed quatrains of an unusually regular syllable count, so that the poem proceeds with a strong forward pulse and, like the Nightingale, draws "diverse matters into a single harmony" (Prol., 4–5). The poem enacts self-conscious literariness and belief in the Word by finding connections and echoes in the very texture and sound of human language: puns abound in its rhymes. In verbal play on quotidian and legal meanings, for example, Christ is addressed as a lord whom love of us controls (*nostre amor te justise*), and whose *franchise* of his flesh has given humanity a *jointure* in his *manoir* for all who rightly (*a droiture*) take this flesh and fully join him (*sanz desjointure*) (271–88).[11] Especially striking in a Latin poet of Howden's accomplishment is the fact that *Rossignos*, as its editor points out, borrows almost no vocabulary from Latin: the poem's lexis is repeatedly created for the occasion, but by adapting, suffixing, prefixing, and more rarely by semantic neologism in Anglo-Norman (many words of course ultimately derived from Latin, but, even at their most Latinate, fully established in French).[12] From the moment of its opening incitement to feeling ("*Alme, lesse lit de peresse* . . . ," 1), the poem creates a heightened register whose business is less to evoke Latin than to elevate literary French in illustrious vernacular courtliness.[13]

The aesthetic of *Rossignos* is continuous with the many lavish and exquisite things—stained glass, sculptures, statues, wall paintings—which (along with beautiful gardens) filled Henry and Eleanor's palaces.[14] Henry III has often been perceived as a weak king, and was of course eventually challenged for his throne by his sister's husband, Simon de Montfort, the most successful leader of the baronial rebellions of the reign. Henry nevertheless stayed on the throne for fifty-six years, from 1216 to 1272. During this time, his heavy taxation of his subjects frequently served his tastes as a royal patron of the arts: arts of and for pleasure, for spiritual and political purposes, and often for all three together. In rebuilding Westminster Abbey, for instance, Henry imitated the saint he most fervently honored, Edward the Confessor (r. 1041–66), who had himself rebuilt the abbey.[15] Henry, characteristically, did not just commission the building, but took a keen interest in its decoration, every aspect of which expresses an intricate mixture of aspiration, policy, and the sacred nature of regal power. The glorious Cosmati marble and glass work installed for the king as Westminster Abbey's sanctuary pavement by Italian craftsmen in 1268–72, for example, is not simply decorative, but constitutes a cosmology, depicting the universe; and functioning too, some have thought, as a practical liturgical map.[16]

Like all queens Eleanor had to take on the dynastic responsibilities and cultural preferences of her husband, but this was if anything congenial to her and conducive to the development and exercise of her own tastes. She became a formidable consort, strategist, troop gatherer, and ally for Henry, as well as a queen well aware of her own prerogatives and influence (which she used to the limit). She was elegant, cosmopolitan, and well informed, and she and Henry lived among visual and material renderings of subjects from the Old and New Testaments, images of their heavenly patron Edward the Confessor and other saints, and of Alexander the Great, the Siege of Antioch, Richard Coeur de Lion's duel with Saladin, *mappae mundi*, allegorical vices and virtues, and much else.[17] But, as the Westminster sanctuary pavement suggests, this is not just luxury for luxury's sake: there is gravity and a political charge here. Henry and Eleanor's model of courtliness proclaimed the sacredness of royalty in the most exalted aesthetic registers available. In their long and frequently vulnerable reign, it was important to demonstrate transcendent and charismatic royal (rather than baronial) courtliness. So, too, the highly wrought words and images of *Rossignos* can be seen as an equivalent to the Cosmati pavement's intensely polished marble and glass tesserae, designed to express a cosmological seriousness and making up an overall pattern of meaning from a variety of intensely crafted individual surface elements. Such a poem might be used in private meditation but is not fully accounted for by that function.

Intensified attention to the somatics of medieval reading is one result among many of Derek Pearsall's hugely influential practice of manuscript studies. Models of both the book and the reading body play a role here. In the case of *Rossignos*, one factor that complicates any assumption that the poem produces a straightforward internalized affectivity is the question of the reading heart and how it is imagined. Often the poem's model of the heart is the more familiar one of an enclosed inscriptional site of feeling, as in the medieval iconography studied by Eric Jager.[18] Love is a pen to write in the book of the heart, a divine charter in holy parchment (*la sainte pel agneline*, 1815–28), for example, and this heart is often resistant and unloving and needs to be pierced by a thorn of remembrance (773–75), or to become wax, with love of Christ its stylus (2579–80).

But another model is also in play, as in this extended passage from the center of the poem:

Par ceste mort bien remembree
Et einz eu quor encimentee
Est alme a Dieu droit marïee;
Il est l'espous, ele esposee.
Li queors ou cist penser repose
Pur la vertu qu'i est enclose
Devient com une fresche rose
Devant Dieu overte e declose.
Cist pensers est droit *alöé*
Que, quant eu coer est *aloué*,
Dieu meismes i est lors vowé
Com a l'offrende de Nöé:
Escrit est que Deus *odora*
Le don dont Nöé l'onora:
Mes cist penser tant de *odor a*
Que les sainz d'amor estora.
Cist pensiers est *une chaëne*
Que Dieu au quor droit *enchaëne*:
Il est respons, il est antenne
Qui gloire por löer desrenne.
Quoers, a touz les jours de ta vie
Cist pensiers soit ta melodie,
Tes matines e ta complie
Et tes heures, quoi que nul die.
Je di ke c'est chose provee
Que cist pensers est une espee

Dont la teste est adés trenchee
3924 De la beste deffiguree . . .

La memoire est abalsamee
Quant entient a ceste pensee;
Lors est li quors chambre acemee
3936 Du Rei de Gloire enhabitee.
Cist pensers a la voiz si saine
Que, quant il chante a gorge plaine,
Li rossignos pur nient se paine
3940 Chaunter a li, ne la siraine.
Si seint Pere ou seint Jake estoie,
De cest penser messal ferroie,
Mon coer auter, e chaunteroie,
3944 Lors jesqu'eu ciel oï seroie.
Qui en cest penser se delite
En son coer [a] la Bible escrite:
Li reguarders est grant merite
3948 Et la leson est joie eslite.
[fol. 83v] Qui a cest livre se prendra
Devinité si aprendra.

(Emphasis mine.)

[By recollecting this death properly and setting it firmly in the heart, the soul is well and truly married to God: he is the spouse and she is the bride. The heart where this meditation reposes becomes, through the power enclosed in it, a fresh rose, open and revealed before God. This meditation is the true incense which, once placed in the heart, invokes God himself there: just as it is written of Noah's offering that God smelt the gift with which Noah honoured him. But this meditation has so intense a fragrance that it provisions all the saints with love: this meditation is a chain that tightly binds God within the heart. It is both response and antiphon, winning heaven's *gloria* for its praise. Heart, for all the days of your life let this meditation be your melody, your matins, your compline and your hours, whatever may be said to you. I say that it is a proven thing that this meditation is a sword with which the ugly beast's head can instantly be cut off (3897–3924) . . . /

> Truly, the heart where this meditation is harboured ought to experience great joy, for then it can terrify the wicked more than the stooping goshawk does his prey. Memory itself is made fragrant when it sets itself to this meditation: then the heart is a chamber bedecked, inhabited by the King of Glory. This meditation has a voice so wholesome that, when it sings with full sound, the nightingale by comparison strives in vain to sing, as does the siren. If I were St. Peter or St. James, I would make a missal of this thought, an altar of my heart, and I would sing until I could be heard in heaven. Whoever delights in this meditation has the Bible written in their heart: contemplation of it is great merit, and the reading of it a rare joy. Whoever gives themselves over to this book learns divine knowledge thereby. (3933–50)]

In this passage, each metaphor grows out of its predecessor: the scent that is the memory of the passion in the opened rose of the heart becomes in line 3904 the "true incense" (*alöé* in 3905 is the aromatic wood burned in sacrifice), a bitter smoke wreathing at line 3909 into God's nostrils like the incense offered by Noah, but more powerfully feeding all the saints (3912). Then the incense spirals into a chain binding God into the heart (3914), while the heart's rising and flowering odor is transformed into the melody of the liturgical office (3915–20). Here the heart in relation with God provides at once its own versicle and response, together making up the antiphon of the liturgy.[19] So the relation between the believer and God is inhaled and exhaled from the heart to heaven and back again, transforming into a melodious circuit between the two. In the second part of the passage, the heart, in the fragrance of its recollection of God, is an adorned nuptial chamber for God, and capable of outsinging both the nightingale and the siren song of secular love (3940). Now sacralized, the heart is also an altar for the missal, a service book for its own devotions: it is a heart inscribed with the Bible and one that has learned the divinity of scripture (3946–50).

This passage thus enacts and indeed produces the sensation of opening up to the divine and being transformed by it in a transfusion of feeling across the distance between heaven and earth. The model for somatic response here involves reading with a different kind of heart from ours. In this passage, the heart inflates and exhales. The medieval heart was not a simple muscle pumping and circulating blood, with its psychological and spiritual dimensions confined to the metaphorical.

As Heather Webb has recently shown, one important model of the medieval heart is as a respiratory organ.[20] The heart concocted blood from air and vital spirit and sent a flow of blood out from itself to the other members of the body. But the only circulations *through* the heart were not of blood but of air, breath, spirit. Thus, the medieval heart is a breathing heart, by definition open to the sensations produced by the flow of airborne spirits through it. This, as Webb argues, has profound implications: instead of assuming the body as a self-sustaining source (powered by blood pumped round in a closed circuit and ceasing when the pump wears out), we could think of individual corporeality as sustained by a "radical state of relatedness to the external world."[21] Devotional vision and feeling *can* be modeled as the inscription of images on the heart in an interiorized subjectivity but can also be seen as a reciprocal and potentially generative mixing of external and innate spirits within the heart of the viewer. In *Rossignos*, the reading heart interacts with the divine along airborne pathways, in a psycho-physiology where human beings are innately designed in connection to an outer, divinely created world.

Like the heart with which it might be read and which it desires to inflame, the poem is porously connected with the world around it. Just after the passage quoted above, the poem follows its own metaphors to see Christ's pale face, drained of color by suffering, as an appropriate ensign on the heart's banner, and one that evokes the white lamb of God. In its longest *occupatio*, the poem now goes on to declare that when the blood of that lamb is poured out to paint the heart's armorial bearings no hero can equal the battle prowess of "*l'Agneau sanz maille*" (the spotless lamb, and perhaps the lamb without armor, 3971). Not (among many others) Judas Maccabeus, Hector of Troy, not Caesar, Charlemagne, Roland, Godfrey of Boulogne, not Tancred, Lancelot, Richard the Lionheart, Eleanor's husband, King Henry, not the Chatelain de Coucy, not Alexander the Great, King Arthur, or Eleanor's son Edward I on crusade, not Eleanor's brother-in-law Charles of Anjou, King of Sicily—not one of these, the poem sings triumphantly, can overcome an army as readily as someone who wills to read in their heart the blood and torment of Christ (3971–4048).

For Eleanor, the lamb of God must have been closely identified both with the soul's bridegroom and with battle through apocalypse books.[22] *Rossignos*'s biblical, classical, romance, and contemporary crusading heroes must also have evoked the paintings on Eleanor of Provence's palace walls, the images in her books, and the armorial bearings and faces known to her from both books and life.[23] As she heard or read this passage's resonant names from scripture, legend, history, romance, and contemporary politics, a most vivid succession of images must have passed before her, a pantheon immediately pertinent in her world.

So, too, the cultural and political freight of blood and blood shedding. Eleanor herself had active experience of war in the baronial rebellions of England, and she and Henry were aware for many reasons of the crusades. Successive thirteenth-century crusades failed to recover Jerusalem other than temporarily, and Henry and Eleanor vowed themselves to crusade in 1250 (just after the failure of the seventh crusade, led by Eleanor's sister's husband, Louis IX of France), though they were in the event unable to fulfill their vow. Henry III and Louis IX also responded by relic campaigns at home. Louis built the Sainte Chapelle, designing it as a grand reliquary for his recently acquired crown of thorns and true cross relics, which he displayed there in 1241. He thus resignified Paris as an alternative Holy Land in which contact with the passion could be treasured. Henry, in 1247, procured a relic of the Holy Blood of Christ and tried to promote a cult of it. In the associated ceremonies, the court heard a disquisition on blood and the heart by Eleanor's friend, Bishop Grosseteste, who was brought in to explain the different kinds of blood shed by Christ, and how Christ could be resurrected in perfection and yet leave bodily fluids on earth.[24]

Henry and Louis IX's mobilization of Christianity's most sacred relics from the Holy Land into northwestern Europe is paralleled in the development of medieval Grail Quest narratives and their attachment to Arthurian legend in the thirteenth century. With the Grail as a mobile chivalric-Eucharistic relic, contact with Christ's presence on earth and his passion becomes independent of physical access to Jerusalem. Copies of the developing French prose Lancelot-Grail cycle were owned and sometimes made in England from the second half of the thirteenth century on.[25] In narrating how Joseph of Arimathea's son Joseph brought blood from Christ to Britain in the Paschal platter,[26] this cycle's *Estoire del Saint Grail* makes Britain the first territory of the Holy Blood (in a matter where Glastonbury and Saint Denis competed for primacy).[27]

Dynastic, spiritual, theological, and political questions thus mass around questions of heart's blood and blood shedding at Henry and Eleanor's court. This was a society that believed in bloodlines as a vital element in the right to power. And it was a society that focused much of its foreign policy through the sacrifice of Christ's blood and the rationale that outpouring provided for extensive expenditure of blood and treasure in the lands where Christ had lived on earth. In her passion meditation poem, Christ's blood circulates through the whole of Eleanor's sacred, royal, dynastic, warring world and the earthly and heavenly chivalry serving that world in the heart's devotions. Moreover, reverence for Christ's blood enables Eleanor's courtly world to be seen as the very expression of high purpose and *fin' amour* (as the poem repeatedly calls Christ's sacrifice and appropriate response to it). As M. A. Michael has observed of the Wilton Diptych, this kind of art is transnational: metaphysical as well as geographical boundaries are crossed; the audience is removed from their ordinary reality, and no distinction operates between spiritual and political power.[28] *Rossignos* is a thirteenth-century equivalent of, say, Lydgate's fifteenth-century high linguistic aesthetic of aureation, deployed to protect "the space of the transcendent represented by the saints and the monasteries which house their relics."[29] *Rossignos*'s fine art, *fin' amour*, and transregional language reinforces the refinement and sacredness of Eleanor's court to contemporaries at home and abroad.

Rossignos connects God, the heart, and the world and also validates laypeople's devotions: the church's offices are sung within the believer's heart, and the heart's knowledge gives knowledge of divine scripture (ll. 3945–50, above). As earlier noted, the question of whether and how human beings could receive divine illumination engaged Bonaventura and other thirteenth-century thinkers: how ineffable such knowledge was and how far it required a human partner with agency was a key question. *Rossignos* does not explicitly address such issues, but its model of divine knowledge suggests something of the theological and epistemological concerns informing contemporary devotional meditation. So, too, without directly inhabiting academic registers of discussion, Eleanor may well have been aware of them. Like many elite brides, she was well educated in preparation for marriage, and at Henry's court she is revealed (in a letter by Adam Marsh) as planning to discuss the salvation of souls with the Countess of Leicester.[30] As Margaret Howell has shown, she repeatedly stretched out "for guidance and friendship towards men who combined their spirituality with a high degree of learning": most prominently among them Grosseteste and Adam Marsh himself, reader to the Oxford Franciscans, but also Thomas of Hales, William Batale,

Richard of Chichester, and probably Edmund of Canterbury.[31] Eleanor maintained various kinds of contact with the Benedictines and Cistercians, but the Franciscans were her spiritual directors and the particular object of her patronage.

A feminized model of divine illumination is offered in *Rossignos*: Christ's passion and response to it is at the poem's center, but the poem begins and ends with the Virgin. An opening meditation on the *virgo lactans* (53–100) celebrates the Virgin's milk as the bread of eternal life, fountain of sweetness, fine nurture and medicine for humanity, a remedy (*trïacle*, 80) against the poison of the apple. The Virgin is God's butler (*botellere*, 95): her chest is a wine cellar from which, in one of the poem's characteristic paradoxes, the divine vine drinks (97–98). Suckling the Christ child offers no simple representation of maternal affectivity: the Virgin is a mother to power, and a queen.[32] In Eleanor's world, exquisite thirteenth-century ivories and other images and statues of the Virgin and Child represented her both as *virgo lactans* and as Mother of God whose lap becomes *sedum sapientiae* "a throne for the incarnation of Divine Wisdom."[33] Lactation had a complex discursive career in the spirituality of men (Aelred of Rievaulx images wisdom as sucked from Christ's breast, for example, and Henry of Lancaster asks for the Virgin's milk to cleanse his wounds of sin).[34] In the Virgin's suckling, *Rossignos* sees "sapience pardurable" feeding on the Virgin's "amor fine," a wonder, the poem claims, equally incomprehensible to Plato and the Seraphim (145–88).

The poem ends with the Virgin's assumption, but not before she has given a speech of 389 lines (4199–588). She reflects on the passion, her motherhood, lactation, and nurturing (4205–88), and so unites the poem's opening *virgo lactans* with the Virgin as empress of heaven. She links knowledge and illumination to feeling, recalling her joy in learning "the profound subtleties of scripture and its meaning[,] . . . the unity of the three persons and the Trinity in one God" (4289–340). This is "kynde knowledge" imbibed as she breast-feeds God's Word but also knowledge expounded to her by her child, the *logos* incarnate.[35] God himself serves as her book (4477–84) so that she has knowledge beyond that of the angels (4489–508). Her grief, as well as her joy, is informed by her consequent understanding of creation and of Christ's two natures:[36] "Because of your divine nature, all creation bows to you: / Because of your human nature, the hard thorn / Lords it over your head" (*prent de ta teste la seisine*, 4521–24), she says, among many other such lamentations (4521–68). Her paradoxes are expressive of feeling rather than opposed to it: her speech comes to a moving conclusion, in which, resisting the temptation to "efface this sweet history" (4577) from her memory, the Virgin submits her desires to her son, and gives him back to God:

> . . . te command, ou qe je soie,
> A li de qui don je t'avoie;
> Qui te me dona te repreinge
> De moun don, e a li remaigne
> Ta vie adés, e soit ensaigne
> De sa peis . . . (4584–88)
>
> ———
>
> [wherever I may be, I commend you to him from whose gift I had you: may he who gave you to me take you back as a gift from me, and may your life remain his from now on and be a sign of his peace]

Howden thus presents the Virgin to Eleanor as a royal mother and cosmic player, supported by heavenly chivalry and by her knowledge of divine wisdom.[37] His passion meditation for the queen-mother offers a sacralized model for Eleanor's own royal power. But it also shows how the registers of that sacredness mattered: the refined love claimed here is not just any kind of courtliness or maternal intensity, but a form of transcendent, chaste, culturally literate power of (in all senses) the blood.

In the fifteenth-century nightingale passion meditation composed for Anne, duchess of Buckingham, there are continuities with Eleanor's poem but also a different timbre of courtly politics and devotion. The later poem is based on another notable Latin nightingale poem of Eleanor and Henry III's reign, the *Philomena praevia* of John Pecham, Franciscan archbishop of Canterbury (d. 1292) and translator, for Eleanor of Provence's daughter-in-law, of the Pseudo-Dionysian *Hierarchies*.[38] The English *Nightingale* was composed late in or soon after 1446 (shortly after Howden's *Philomena* went to France with Charles d'Orléans). Anne Neville (d. 1480) spent her life in circles close to the king's court. She was the third daughter of Ralph Neville, first earl of Westmoreland (d. 1425), a supporter of Bolingbroke, who continued to serve under his son, Henry V, and she married Humphrey Stafford, duke of Buckingham (killed at Northampton, 1460).[39] In her nightingale poem, Anne's own interests are represented as courtly and spiritual, and the well-documented literary and spiritual interests of her mother, Joan Beaufort (a legitimated daughter of John of Gaunt, duke of Lancaster, married to Ralph Neville as his second wife in 1396), suggest a highly and multilingually literate family.[40] The prologue to Anne's *Nightingale* requests a place "amonge hyre bokys" for the poem,[41] and it is possible that she is the "Anne Neville" whose signature appears in the famous Corpus manuscript of *Troilus and Criseyde*.[42] But if Anne, duchess of Buckingham, enjoyed pagan love stories, her *Nightingale* offered her reorientation toward another literary garden that was "nothyng towardes the gardyn of the Rose."[43]

As with Eleanor of Provence's poem, politics and devotion are not separate spheres. Anne's *Nightingale* follows Pecham's *Philomena* in using the last day of a dying nightingale to tell the story of salvation from the creation to the passion, and in structuring the narrative as a series of parallels between the hours of the cross and the ages of man, but it exemplifies from contemporary history. From among all the fifteenth century's sudden deaths in high places, that of Henry, duke of Warwick (d. 1446), godson to Anne's mother, Joan, is cited as a monitory example to "myghty princes and lordes of astate" (323).

The poem is no stranger to self-conscious aesthetic effects,[44] but it is composed in a plainer style than *Rossignos*, and, indeed, purports to be "right bare of eloquence" (18). Knowledge, order, instruction, and authority are key: the nightingale has been found not in a garden but

> In latyn . . . in a boke well versed,
> Ande what in morall sense it signifiede,
> The whech in englysh y wold were notified
> To all that lusty are it for to here . . . (108–12)

Anne herself is put in charge of the poem's mission and imagined as converting her household to a bracing spirituality. The poem's prologue envisages "hyr ladyly goodnesse" summoning "such of hyre peple . . . [as are] desyrous for to here the amerouse sentensce / Of the nyghtyngale" and "commanding theym to here with tendernesse / Of this your nightingale the gostly sense" (8–16). Whether Anne is to be seen as reading the poem or having it read and perhaps expounded by her clerics, this corrective reordering of feeling under the authority of a large household's mistress seems as Lancastrian as *Rossignos*'s high courtliness seems Plantagenet.

With English having become a high literary language as well as entering some documentary registers, the multilingualism of the culture which produced the fifteenth-century nightingale poem is if anything more polyglot than that of Eleanor of Provence's court. The extensive echoes and parallels in English, French, and Latin noted by the editor of Anne's *Nightingale* themselves eloquently show the trilingual discourse inhabited by passion meditations in the fifteenth century, even after what subsequent tradition has often taken as Henry V's successful association of English and nation.[45] As Derek Pearsall has pointed out, although Henry V encouraged poems such as Lydgate's *Lyf of oure Ladye* (1421–22) as "quasi-liturgical composition in the high style" that could "strike at the claims of the Lollards to own the religious vernacular," Henry himself had a French translation of Bonaventura's *Meditationes vitae Christi*, presented to him by its author, Jean Galopes, in 1420. It was subsequently used (perhaps at Henry's instigation) in Lydgate's *Lyf*.[46]

Rossignos is a poem in a specially crafted register of passion meditation, and it may be more useful to think in terms of register here than languages.[47] The history of nightingale passion meditation—in and out of Latin, insular and continental Frenches and Englishes—makes it useful to see each work as participating in a common polyglot "nightingale" discourse in a culture where not only the multiplicity of languages, but the diversity created within them in their varying linguistic and cultural contacts is important. Eleanor of Provence herself knew Frenches rather than French. Daughter of the count of Toulouse, she must have arrived at the English court speaking Provençal and some northern French, and probably reading these and some liturgical Latin. She will have had little trouble adapting to the French spoken by English royalty as their first language from the late eleventh to the end of the fourteenth century and will have moved among the Frenches of England, of Henry's Lusignan kin, and of her own Savoyard and Poitevin relatives. And in her England, English, Latin, and French all cross-fertilized each other. Around the same date as Eleanor's *Rossignos*, for instance, a poem in English from the South West Midlands (with the incipit "Ci commence le cunt[ek] parentre le Mauvis e la russinole" in one of its manuscripts) has its Nightingale argue for the Virgin as a validation of all women, using English's ability to call upon its own ingested

Frenchness. The Thrush doubts women's virtue, but the Nightingale repeatedly defends them as full of "hendiness" (the "English" English word, not yet downgraded by association with Chaucer's "hende Nicholas") *and* "curteysi" (the "French" English word), with the Virgin as supreme example.[48]

The linguistic system of English, like England's other languages, is shot through with opportunities for different registers and resonances across the genres. And though English was never more than a regional language in the Middle Ages, this makes it extremely rich. But a still richer medieval culture emerges when we follow manuscripts and their multilingualism to include England's participation in the transregional languages of Latin and French, and attempt to go further down the paths where Derek Pearsall and Elizabeth Salter have long shown us the way.

NOTES

I thank Carolyn Collette, Thelma Fenster, and Christopher Baswell for generously helpful readings of this essay, my colleague Nicholas Paul for helpful discussion, and Kathryn Kerby-Fulton for her invitation to participate in honoring Derek Pearsall. As is so often the case, I have been unable to take this essay to any place where Derek had not been before, a fact that increases one's respectful admiration and affection for him.

1. Quotations from Marie de France, *Lais*, ed. A. Ewert, introd. G. S. Burgess (London: Bristol Classical Press, 1995), 97 (3–6); Otto Glauning, ed., *Lydgate's Minor Poems: The Two Nightingale Poems*, EETS, e.s., 80 (London: Kegan Paul, Trench, Trübner & Co., 1900), poem I, 70–71.

2. On the ps.-Lydgate poem, see Derek Pearsall, *John Lydgate* (Charlottesville: University Press of Virginia, 1970), 267–68. On *Rossignos*, see Elizabeth Salter, *English and International: Studies in the Literature, Art and Patronage of Medieval England*, ed. Derek Pearsall and Nicolette Zeeman (Cambridge: Cambridge University Press, 1988), 90–91; Louise W. Stone, "Jean de Howden, poète anglo-normand du xiii siècle," *Romania* 69 (1946–47): 496–519. Denis Renevey, "1215–1349: The Texts," in *Medieval English Mysticism*, ed. Samuel Fanous and Vincent Gillespie (Cambridge: Cambridge University Press, 2011), 103–5. The recent edition by Glynn Hesketh, *Rossignos*, ANTS 63 (London: ANTS, 2006), and the digitization of the manuscript (Corpus Christi College, Cambridge MS 471) transform access to the poem.

3. Michelle Karnes, *Imagination, Meditation, and Cognition in the Middle Ages* (Chicago: University of Chicago Press, 2011); Lydia Schumacher,

Divine Illumination: The History and Future of Augustine's Theory of Knowledge (Oxford: Wiley-Blackwell, 2011). I thank Professor Nigel Palmer of Oxford for stimulating discussion and a prepublication copy of his *Medium Aevum* review of these books.

4. Alexandra Barratt, "*Stabant matres dolorosae*: Women as Readers and Writers of Passion Prayers, Meditations and Visions," in *The Broken Body: Passion Devotion in Late Medieval Culture*, ed. A. A. MacDonald, H. N. B. Ridderbos, and R. M. Schlusemann (Groningen: Forsten, 1998), 55–70.

5. Sarah McNamer, *Affective Meditation and the Invention of Medieval Compassion* (Philadelphia: University of Pennsylvania Press, 2010).

6. See Salter, *English and International*; Loveday L. Gee, *Women, Art, and Patronage from Henry III to Edward III: 1216–1377* (New York: Boydell Press, 2002); J. Wogan-Browne, "'Cest livre liseez . . . chescun jour': Women and Reading *c.* 1230–*c.* 1430," in *Language and Culture in Medieval Britain: The French of England c. 1100–c. 1500*, ed. J. Wogan-Browne, with Carolyn Collette, Maryanne Kowaleski, Linne Mooney, Ad Putter, and David Trotter (York: York Medieval Press, 2009), 239–53.

7. Hesketh, *Rossignos*, 10, 33. Citations of the poem henceforth by line number in the text. The *Rossignos* author is now accepted as the John of Howden recorded as Queen Eleanor's clerk between 1268 and 1275 (Hesketh, *Rossignos*, 3–6): he was formerly confused with the astrologer, John of London (A. G. Rigg, *ODNB*, s.v. "John of Howden").

8. For the identification of Pseudo-Anselm as a source for Howden, see Nigel Wilkins, *Catalogue des manuscrits français de la bibliothèque Parker (Parker Library) Corpus Christi College, Cambridge* (Cambridge: Corpus Christi College, 1993), 148; for the text, "Meditationes de gestis Jhesu Christi," in Anselm of Lucca's *opuscula spuria* (PL 149.591–602).

9. For Howden's known Latin poems (except *Philomena*), see F. J. E. Raby, ed., *The Poems of John of Howden* (Durham: Andrews and Co., 1939); for *Philomena*, Clemens Blume, ed., *John Hovedens Nachtigallenlied* (Leipzig: O. R. Reisland, 1930). On Howden's influence, see A. G. Rigg, *A History of Anglo-Latin Literature* (Cambridge: Cambridge University Press, 1992), 208–11; on the manuscript circulation of Howden's poems, his influence on Rolle and importance as a link between the twelfth and fifteenth centuries, see M. R. Moyes, *Richard Rolle's Expositio super Novem Lectiones Mortuorum* (Salzburg: Institut für Anglistik und Amerikanistik Universität Salzburg, 1988), vol. 1, 50–53. See also F. J. E. Raby, "A Middle English Paraphrase of John of Hoveden's 'Philomena' and the Text of His 'Viola,'" *Modern Language Review* 30 (1935): 339–43 (340–41); and for the Middle English text, Charlotte D'Evelyn, ed., *Meditations on the Life and Passion of Christ*, EETS, o.s., 158 (Oxford: Oxford University Press, 1921), and her "Meditations on the Life and Passion of Christ: A Note on Its Literary Relationships," in *Essays*

and Studies in Honor of Carleton Brown (New York: New York University Press, 1940), 79–90. *Rossignos*'s (professional but plain and occasionally corrected and commented) extant manuscript is late fourteenth century, suggesting diffusion beyond Eleanor's late-thirteenth-century court. For prints and early modern admiration of *Philomena*, see Blume, *Nachtigallenlied*, xiv–xv; Moyes, *Richard Rolle's Expositio*, 50 n. 133.

10. Gilbert Ouy, "Un poème mystique de Charles d'Orléans: Le 'Canticum Amoris,'" *Studi Francesi* 20 (1959): 415–56; and "Charles d'Orléans and His Brother Jean d'Angoulême in England: What Their Manuscripts Have to Tell," in *Charles d'Orléans in England (1415–1440)*, ed. Mary-Jo Arn (Cambridge: D. S. Brewer, 2000), 47–60 (52–53).

11. See also 505–8, 549–56, 1229–32, 4408–16, etc., and the extended quotation below. On puns, see Catherine Batt, "'De celle mordure vient la mort dure': Perspectives on Puns and Their Translation in Henry, duke of Lancaster's *Le Livre de Seyntz Medicines*," in *The Medieval Translator 10*, ed. Jacqueline Jenkins and Olivier Bertrand (Turnhout: Brepols, 2007), 405–17.

12. Hesketh, *Rossignos*, 24–25.

13. ["Soul, leave the bed of laziness . . ."] Howden's metrical regularity and lexical sonority is not, I would argue, an effort to escape the irregularities, or better, flexibility of Anglo-Norman prosody. Rather, like Gower's deliberately *un*-"anglo-normanisant" French (see Brian Merrilees and Heather Pagan, "John Barton, John Gower and Others: Variation in Late Anglo-French," in Wogan-Browne et al., *Language and Culture*, 118–34), and, as Derek Pearsall long ago showed, like Chaucer's development of English (see his "Chaucer and Englishness," *Proceedings of the British Academy* 101 [1998]: 77–99), *Rossignos* reaches for a transregional high *koinē*.

14. Howell, *Eleanor of Provence*, 71–92. Pearsall and Salter note a direction from Henry III for the queen's garden at Woodstock which, as they say, "could have served lyric or romance." *Landscapes and Seasons of the Medieval World* (London: Elek, 1973), 77.

15. Paul Binski, *Westminster Abbey and the Plantagenets: Kingship and the Representation of Power, 1200–1400* (New Haven: Yale University Press, 1995), and *Becket's Crown: Art and Imagination in Gothic England, 1170–1300* (New Haven: Yale University Press, 2004).

16. Lindy Grant and Richard Mortimer, eds., *Westminster Abbey: The Cosmati Pavements* (Aldershot: Ashgate, 2002): see the essays by Paul Binski, "The Cosmati and *Romanitas* in England: An Overview"; and David Carpenter, "Westminster Abbey and the Cosmati Pavements in Politics, 1258–1269."

17. Tancred Borenius, "The Cycle of Images in the Palaces and Castles of Henry III," *Journal of the Warburg and Courtauld Institutes* 6 (1943): 40–50.

18. Eric Jager, *The Book of the Heart* (Chicago: University of Chicago Press, 2000).

19. Hesketh points out that vv. 3915–16 play on glory as heavenly glory and the Gloria of the mass, and play, too, on the double meaning of "desrenne" (*desrainier*) as "to win by combat" and "to recite" (*Rossignos*, 217, n. to 3916).

20. Heather Webb, *The Medieval Heart* (New Haven: Yale University Press, 2010), esp. chap. 2, "The Porous Heart." For the changing model of the heart in the late thirteenth century, see Paul Zarowny, "The Heart of Christ at Helfta: The Influence of Aristotelian Cardiology on the Vitae of St Gertrude the Great and St Mechtild of Hackeborn" (PhD diss., Fordham University, 1999 [UMI 9955977]).

21. Webb, *Medieval Heart*, 4.

22. The Trinity Apocalypse from the inner court circle ca. 1255–57 and with text and commentary both in French shows a *female* saint battling the Beast (fol. 14v), and heraldry of Henry's rebellious brother-in-law Simon de Montfort appears in the Beast's army (fol. 23r): David McKitterick, ed., *The Trinity Apocalypse: Cambridge, Trinity College MS R. 16.2* (London: British Library, 2005); Adrian Ailes, "Heraldry in Medieval England: Symbols of Politics and Propaganda," in *Heraldry, Pageantry, and Social Display in Medieval England*, ed. Peter D. Coss and Maurice Keen (Woodbridge: Boydell Press, 2002), 84–85. In the Douce Apocalypse made for Edward I and his bride, the Lamb proffers a ring to his soul-bride at Rev. 19:6–7: Bodleian Library Luna website, MS Douce 180, p. 079 (http://bodley30.bodley.ox.ac.uk).

23. Eleanor herself bought manuscript romances (titles unknown) and owned other genres of books and texts (Howell, *Eleanor of Provence*, 82–83, 87–92).

24. Nicholas Vincent, *The Holy Blood: King Henry III and the Westminster Blood Relic* (Cambridge: Cambridge University Press, 2001), 87–100. Grosseteste argued that the inmost blood of the heart is consubstantial with God: not only does it not circulate, but it is not available on earth. Of the outer, more superfluous kinds of blood produced in the heart and sent round the body, by far the most valuable is that shed from Christ's heart and right side, the kind of blood, said Grosseteste, in Henry's relic: see *Matthei Parisiensis Chronica majora*, ed. H. R. Luard, 7 vols., RS 57 (London: Longman and Co., 1872–91), vol. 4: 641–45.

25. Roger Middleton, "Manuscripts of the Lancelot-Grail Cycle in England and Wales: Some Books and Their Owners," in *A Companion to the Lancelot-Grail Cycle*, ed. Carol Dover, Arthurian Studies 4 (Cambridge: D. S. Brewer, 2003), 218–35.

26. See Jean-Paul Ponceau, ed., *L'Estoire del Saint Graal*, Classiques français du Moyen Age (Paris: Champion, 1997–), vol. 1, xix–xxii, for a summary.

27. Grosseteste may have known the Grail stories: on this and the St. Denis and Glastonbury rivalry, see Vincent, *Holy Blood*, 90–91 and nn. 24–28. Interrelations between Grail and crucifixion iconography appear in the Amesbury

Psalter (Oxford, All Souls MS 6, ca. 1250–55) from Eleanor's retirement nunnery. On fol. 3/5 of the psalter (reproduced in Nigel J. Morgan, *Early Gothic Manuscripts II (1250–1285)* [London: Harvey Miller, 1988, vol. 2, pl. 29), Christ's blood trickles down to Adam, in resurrection posture at the foot of the cross, his hands clasped in prayer. In the Grail manuscript subsequently owned by Elizabeth Woodville, Edward IV's queen, Joseph of Arimathea, in similar but reversed resurrection posture, holds up a dish to receive Christ's blood (London, British Library, Royal 14 E III, fol. 7r), www.bl.uk/catalogues/illuminated manuscripts/ILLUMIN. ASP?Size=mid&IllID=43455.

28. M. A. Michael, "Transnationality in the Wilton Diptych as Text," in *Tributes to Nigel Morgan: Contexts of Medieval Art: Images, Objects and Ideas*, ed. Julian Luxford and M. A. Michael (Turnhout: Brepols [Harvey Miller], 2010), 365–74.

29. See Catherine Sanok, "Saints' Lives and the Literary after Arundel," in *After Arundel*, ed. Kantik Ghosh and Vincent Gillespie (Turnhout: Brepols, 2011), 469–86, as summarized by Nicholas Watson in the same volume, " 'A Clerke schulde have it of kinde for to kepe conseil,' " 563–89 (575). Far from emerging through the loss or rejection of an earlier religious sensibility, Sanok argues, the literary becomes, for fifteenth-century hagiographers, a means of differentiating literature from the *secular* order (485–86).

30. Howell, *Eleanor of Provence*, 94–95: letter (in Latin and French) available in *Epistolae*: Medieval Women's Latin Letters, http://epistolae.ccnmtl .columbia.edu/letter/688.html.

31. Howell, *Eleanor of Provence*, 95. On Franciscan influence in a book from Eleanor's circle, see Pamela Tudor-Craig, "Patronage, Iconography, and Franciscan Thought in the Alphonso Psalter, BL Additional MS 24686," in Luxford and Michael, *Tributes to Nigel Morgan*, 77–92.

32. The display of female breasts contravened class sanctions requiring wet nurses for elite mothers: but *ostentatio* was part of the iconography of humble intercession by the most powerful (as in the Virgin's pleading atop the Hereford *mappa mundi* ca. 1290): see Beth Williamson, "The Virgin *lactans* as Second Eve: Image of the Salvatrix," *Studies in Iconography* 19 (1998):105–38; and her *The Madonna of Humility: Development, Dissemination and Reception, c. 1340–1400* (Cambridge: Boydell and Brewer, 2009).

33. Ilene H. Forsyth, *The Throne of Wisdom: Wood Sculptures of the Madonna in Romanesque France* (Princeton: Princeton University Press, 1972), 2.

34. On Aelred, see Caroline Walker Bynum, *Jesus as Mother: Studies in the Spirituality of the High Middle Ages* (Berkeley: University of California Press, 1982), 123. For Henry of Lancaster, see Catherine Batt, *The Book of Holy Medicines*, French of England Translation Series 8 (Tempe, AZ: MRTS, forthcoming); and Naoë Kukita Yoshikawa, "Holy Medicine and Diseases of

the Soul: Henry of Lancaster and *Le Livre de Seyntz Medicines*," *Medical History* 53, no. 3 (2009): 397–414.

35. The Virgin is represented as asking detailed questions of the Christ child about his incarnation and the Trinity in the apocryphal gospels and their devotional derivatives: see Hilda Graef, *Mary: A History of Doctrine and Devotion*, rev. ed., with T. A. Thompson (Notre Dame: Christian Classics, 2009), 204; and the dialogue in the *Vita beate virginis Marie et salvatoris*, ed. A. Vögtlin (Tübingen: Bibliothek des litterarischen Vereins, 1888), 119–24. *Rossignos* explicitly follows [Luke's] Gospel in moving directly from Christ's infancy to his baptism (see ll. 225–28): though the poem shares some themes with apocryphal infancy and Marian gospels, its account of the Virgin's knowledge is differently toned.

36. Schumacher argues that for Bonaventura, Christ acts as the metaphysical center uniting the Creator and the created: through him the fullness of the Father's love overflows into countless instances of his divine ideas (Schumacher, *Divine Illumination*, 122–24); and see further, *De scientia Christi*, ed. and trans. Zachary Hayes, in *Works of St. Bonaventure*, vol. 4 (New York: Franciscan Institute Publications, 2005). Consonant with this is the fact that with Christ in her embrace the Virgin has knowledge of all created things (*Rossignos*, 4389–444).

37. On the importance of performed and visible piety in Eleanor and her daughter-in-law's queenship and support of their husbands' rule, see John Carmi Parsons, "Piety, Power and the Reputations of Two Thirteenth-Century English Queens," in *Queens, Regents and Potentates*, ed. Theresa M. Vann (Cambridge: Academia Press, 1993), 107–23.

38. See Benjamin Thompson, *Oxford Dictionary of National Biography* (Oxford: Oxford University Press, 2004), s.v. "John Pecham." Pecham's *Philomena praevia*, sometimes wrongly attributed to Bonaventura, was translated into (continental) French as well as English (ed., with parallel Latin and French texts, by Claudia Napoli, *Le Livre du rossignolet: Traduction médiévale de la* Philomena praevia [Palermo: I. L. A. Palma, 1979]).

39. *ODNB* has no entry for Anne, but see *ODNB*, s.v. "Ralph Neville, ca. 1364–1425"; "Humphrey Stafford, 1402–60"; and "Walter Blount, Lord Mountjoy (*d.* 1474)."

40. See Anthony Tuck, *ODNB*, s.v. "Joan Beaufort." Joan was the dedicatee of a manuscript collection of Hoccleve's poems and owned French crusade histories (one of which she lent to Henry V, whose father, Henry IV, was Joan's half brother), a Gower "in English," and a *Tristram* (in English?). She was visited by Margery Kempe, ca. 1413, and is associated with a manuscript of prayers, devotions, and Rolle's *Meditations on the Passion*, and perhaps also with a text of Love's *Myrrour of the Blessed Lyf of Jesu Christ.*

41. Glauning, ed., *Lydgate's . . . Nightingale poems*, poem I, 7: henceforth quoted by line number in the text.

42. If this is not Anne Neville, wife of Warwick the Kingmaker, Joan Beaufort's grandson (see *ODNB*, s.v. "Joan Beaufort").

43. The line is Lydgate's: see Glauning, ed. *Lydgate's . . . Nightingale Poems*, poem II, 53. On Anne and her poem, see further the valuable discussion in Rebecca Krug, *Reading Families: Women's Literate Practice in late Medieval England* (Ithaca: Cornell University Press, 2002), 77–82, esp. 81.

44. See, e.g., the homology between the poet's longing and the piercing rays of dawn (53–54) and the account of Christ hanging on the cross from sext to none until Longinus has "thirled and persed thorgh" his heart and side—across a stanza break (386–87). So, too, *Rossignos* speaks of the Virgin capturing "him whom the heavens cannot comprehend, . . . so powerfully could her song sway him" (*tant le pout sa chanzon sospendre*, 136) in one of the poem's rare hypermetric lines (9 syllables instead of 8, with a pun on *suspendre*: the Virgin suspends Christ's normal course by bringing him down from heaven); or again, *tresgrant amor* bows the unicorn down to the young woman across a line ending ("*. . . ki encline / Jus le unicorne a la meschine*," 1397–98).

45. For valuable complications to the "triumph of English" narrative, see W. M. Ormrod, "The Use of English: Language, Law and Political Culture in Fourteenth-Century England," *Speculum* 78 (2003): 750–87; Richard Ingham, "The Persistence of Anglo-Norman, 1230–1362: A Linguistic Perspective"; and T. W. Machan, "French, English and the Late Medieval Linguistic Repertoire," in Wogan-Browne et al., *Language and Culture*, 44–54 and 363–72 respectively; Ardis Butterfield, *The Familiar Enemy: Chaucer, Language and Nation in the Hundred Years War* (Oxford: Oxford University Press, 2010), 317–28.

46. Derek Pearsall, *John Lydgate (1371–1449): A Bio-Bibliography* (Victoria, BC: University of Victoria Press, 1997), 19–20. For the dating, see Joseph A. Lauritis, *A Critical Edition of Lydgate's "Lyf of our Lady"* (Pittsburgh: Duquesne University Press, 1961), 4–10 (7–8, 10). On the Lollard creation of vernacular theology as exclusively English, see Nicholas Watson, "Lollardry: The Anglo-Norman Heresy?," in Wogan-Browne et al., *Literature and Culture*, 334–36. Derek Pearsall observes that the patron of Lydgate's *Life of St Margaret* commands him to search out French and Latin sources and "thereof make a compilacyoun [in English]" (*Lydgate: A Bio-Bibliography*, 31).

47. This argument is developed in J. Wogan-Browne, "What Voice Is That Language? / What Language Is That Voice? Multilingualism in a Tri-lingual Medieval Letter-Treatise," in *Medieval Multilingualism in Later Medieval Britain: Sources and Analysis*, ed. Judith Jefferson and Ad. Putter (Turnhout: Brepols, 2013), 126–41.

48. Carleton Brown, ed., *English Lyrics of the XIIIth Century* (Oxford: Oxford University Press, 1932), 101–7.

CHAPTER 5

Wings, Wingfields, and *Wynnere and Wastoure*

Susan Powell

It may seem presumptuous of me, as a scholar of religious and devotional prose, to venture into the area of alliterative poetry, and indeed I do so with trepidation. My original paper at Derek Pearsall's eightieth birthday conference related to Syon Abbey and one of its abbesses in particular. I admitted then that Derek was not, I thought, very interested in abbesses, and, traveling with him in Suffolk on a visit to former colleagues, I asked him what he had thought of my paper. When he said he had no memory of it, I knew I was in trouble, since his memory is formidable. On the same journey I mentioned a conference at Wingfield College in Suffolk, which I was due to attend.[1] This led into a discussion of Alice de la Pole, Chaucer's granddaughter, whose husband descended from the Wingfields, and praise for Elizabeth Salter's work on the Wingfields, which I was urged to read. Thus it was that I changed my title and essay in this volume in praise of Derek to one which, I hope, despite its deficiencies, will interest him more.

Elizabeth Salter's essay, "The Timeliness of *Wynnere and Wastoure*," is, as Derek had told me, a meticulous close reading of the statements of earlier critics of the poem, particularly Sir Israel Gollancz.[2] Without being cruel or gratuitous, it lays bare Gollancz's predisposition to read the text to suit his own theories, a predisposition which is hardly unique to Gollancz. In particular, Salter reviewed the evidence for dating the poem to 1352 and for taking the First Knight to be the Garter Herald and the Second Knight to be the Black Prince. As a much more convincing alternative to the Black Prince, Salter argued that the "thre wynges inwith wroghte in the kynde / Vmbygon with a gold wyre" (ll. 117–18),[3] worn by the Second Knight on the front and back of his jupon, were the arms of the Wingfields, not the ostrich feathers of the Prince of Wales.

The most recent editor of the poem, Stephanie Trigg, is doubtful of this, and I will quote her comments in full, since they are all relevant to this part of my essay.

> Gollancz contends that the herald's *thre wynges . . . wroghte in the kynde* are not wings, rather the ostrich feathers of the Black Prince's 'badge for peace'. Citing OE *feþera* pl. 'wings' he suggests that the terms 'wings' and 'feathers' may have coalesced in Middle English, and argues that the Prince's feather badge would be especially appropriate on this mission of peace. Salter comments firstly that there is no record of the Prince wearing this device on a jupon, and secondly, that the Prince's badge is always blazoned in English as bearing the 'plume' or 'feather', a literal translation of Latin *penna* or French *plume*. Furthermore, the phrase *in the kynde* makes poor sense in reference to feathers, whereas heraldic wings may be borne in a variety of ways, some highly stylized, but some more natural (cf. MED *kinde* n., 4(c) and Salter, pp. 50–1, 53–4).
>
> Salter none the less maintains that the herald's jupon is a 'distinguishing feature of some precision' and proposes that a member of the Wingfield family served as a model for the herald. Yet the poet's heraldic references remain suggestive rather than literal: we are not told the tincture of the field of the knight's jupon, nor is mention made of any ordinaries on the field. A reference to the *bend gules* on the Wingfield coat of arms would give greater support to Salter's theory. As it is, wings are a common heraldic charge, like the boars' heads on the banner of the Carmelites and cannot in themselves direct us to any individual.[4]

Salter had effectively demolished Gollancz's special pleading for the Black Prince (which extended to an indefensible emendation of l. 108 to suit his purpose).[5] Trigg does not seek to reinstate him, and her criticisms of the lack of precision in the arms (no mention of tinctures or ordinaries) are not of great value without an alternative proposal.[6] On the one hand, she urges a relaxed reading of the text ("suggestive rather than literal"); on the other, she criticizes Salter's interpretation as too relaxed and wants greater preciseness of detail. One might instead suggest that the poet was being both suggestive and literal, providing enough information to distinguish the Second Knight without giving a full heraldic description. As for Trigg's statement that "wings are a common heraldic charge," Salter had perhaps yielded too much ground in saying this herself, since the source she uses for her examples of different types of wings seems only to feature wings attached to birds.[7] The wings in the Wingfield "canting arms" (punning on the name) are all disembodied. Disembodied wings do exist, as in the Seymour shield ("Gules a pair of gold wings"), but that is a single set of wings.[8]

The Wingfield shield is blazoned (described), "Argent [silver, which was always painted white], on a bend [diagonal band] gules [red] cotised [with a narrow band on each side of, and parallel with, the bend] sable [black], three sets of wings conjoined in lure [with tips downward] argent [white]";[9] that is, the shield is white, with a red bend banded in black carrying three sets of white wings joined together with their tips downward. Salter herself had a little difficulty with the description of this in *Wynnere and Wastoure*: "thre wynges inwith wroghte in the kynde / Vmbygon with a gold wyre" (ll. 117–18). She argued that the phrase "wroghte in the kynde" was hard to explain in relation to the ostrich feathers of the Black Prince but "makes better sense in the context of the Wingfield arms."[10] As she explained, ostrich plumes are only shown in one form, whereas wings occur in various, sometimes elaborate and unnatural forms, and so she interpreted "in the kynde" as meaning "according to their nature, in natural form." Trigg appears to follow Salter in this interpretation (quoted above).

It is odd, however, that Trigg is not more specific here, given her interest in tinctures, ordinaries, fields, and bends gules, since the *MED* definition (4(c)) which she cites (from Salter) actually reads: "*her.* ?natural colors or form." Salter herself had realized that the phrase might be "a translation of a technical French or Anglo-French heraldic term," had cited the *MED* definition ("in natural colors or form"), and had quoted one of the two *MED* citations: "[Sable two spotted] lebardys of sylwyr yn her kynde" (ca. 1460).[11] This citation was the less useful of the two (as I shall explain), and I here quote the earlier one: "Siluer, a cheueron of Gowles, sitte betwene three Gaddes of Stele of Asure, on the cheueron three swevells of golde; with two lizardes of theire owne kynde" (1456).[12] This is a white shield with a red chevron (two slanting lines meeting in a point, infilled with color) set between three steel spikes in blue, with three gold swivels on the chevron, and two lizards *in their natural color*.

The italics above indicate my own interpretation of "of theire owne kynde," not, I admit, entirely my own, since Sir W. H. St John Hope had commented, slightly obliquely but authoritatively, in his *Grammar of English Heraldry*, revised by the then Richmond Herald: "There is no need for retaining the word 'proper' for a charge 'in his proper colour', as the late Tudor heralds liked it, or 'of theire owne kynde' as an earlier grant has it, when there is no doubt about the natural colour of a popinjay, a peacock, or a chough, or of an Australian piping shrike, a kangaroo, or an emu."[13] St John Hope is referring, a little disparagingly, to contemporary coats of arms: in a previous chapter he had dealt with "the final degradation of heraldry" and cited descriptions of arms from those of Horatio Nelson (1801) to the Commonwealth of Australia (1912), the last of which has as supporters (figures holding the shield on either side) "Dexter a kangaroo, sinister an emu, both proper."[14]

However, while it seems to me clear that "of his/their own kind" refers to color and obviates the need to cite one of the seven heraldic colors (azure, gules, sable, vert, purpure, tenné, murrey/sanguine) or two metals (or, argent), or numerous furs, none of which may be relevant (as St John Hope slyly suggests), the proposed definition "in his/their natural color" is not entirely unchallengeable. First, the phrase is clearly rare; and, second, Salter's quoted example refers to "[Sable two spotted] lebardys of sylwyr yn her kynde," that is, a black shield with two spotted silver (white) lions in their natural color.[15] Is white (or even silver) the natural color of lions, and why follow the phrase "of sylwyr" with the phrase "yn her kynde" if the latter means "in their natural color"? Certainly, "yn her kynde" does not here mean "according to their nature, in natural form," since it is hardly natural that lions should swivel their heads to look at one full-faced, while walking, three paws on the ground, the right forepaw raised, and the tail curved over the back.[16] However, although the inclusion of a color in addition to the phrase "yn her kynde" is annoying in the context of my argument, it seems clear that the phrase is a heraldic one meaning "in his/their natural color." Since the poem has been subjected to much emendation, I would make a simple one here, not essential but definitely an improvement: "Thre wynges inwith wroghte in the[r] kynde."

The Second Knight in *Wynnere and Wastoure* is described in armor, "With a jupown full juste joynede by the sydes, / A brod chechun at the backke, þe breste had anoþer, / Thre wynges inwith wroghte in the kynde" (ll. 115–18). This would therefore appear to mean that he wore a fine jupon (a short-sleeved, close-fitting tunic, with a scalloped or fringed lower edge) sewn at the sides, with a broad escutcheon (heraldic shield) on its front and back, with three wings embroidered on it in their natural color (which we must assume, from the blazon given above, was white).[17] There are two issues here. First, I believe that Salter was misled in taking the line to consist of two phrases, "thre wynges inwith" and "wroghte in the kynde"; even though it broaches the half-line, I assume the syntax to be "thre wynges inwith wroghte" and "in the[r] kynde": "three wings embroidered on it, in the[ir] natural color." Second, I take *wroghte* to mean "embroidered" (*MED werken* (v.(1)) 11(e) ?to do fancywork with (silk thread, gold, etc.) [1st 2 quots.]; *ppl. wrought*, decorated, adorned; also, embroidered). The question mark seems to me unnecessary: as the definition indicates, the first two citations amply demonstrate the use of *werken* to mean "embroider" (and we still talk of "needlework" today): "He loked in bitwix þe trese, And many maidens þare he sese Wirkand silk and gold-wire" and "We wirk here silver, silk, and golde" (both from *Ywain*). So, too, do most of the other citations (with the past participle), which refer to work on a garment, cushions, a crimson cloth ("wroght with ye nylde," i.e., worked with the needle), and a coverlet to a bed.[18]

Salter did not comment on "wroghte," probably assuming it to be self-evident, but my interpretation of "inwith wroghte" as "embroidered on it" links with Salter's convincing explanation that the next half-line of the description of the Second Knight's escutcheon ("Vmbygon with a gold wyre") refers to the charge of three wings having been "embroidered and then appliquéd upon the knight's jupon."[19] She dismissed Gollancz's translation, "bound together with a gold wire or band," as both unduly influenced by his desire to read the charge as the Black Prince's feathers and an improbable description of the scroll encircling the feathers (not used anyway until the sixteenth century).[20] She pointed out that "golde wyre" was "an accepted ME alternative to 'fildore' as a translation of the Latin 'filum aureum', the gold thread used so lavishly in medieval embroidery," and tentatively suggested what is clearly an excellent emendation (semantically and metrically), the removal of the indefinite article *a*.[21] *MED* oddly does not specifically list "gold ~" in its entry for *wir:* (n.(1)(b) "fine wire used for filigree or other delicate work; also, metallic thread; a piece of such thread" [etc.]). However, the meaning is well attested, and four of the eight citations in *MED* refer to gold wire, a fifth to yellow being the color of wire, and a sixth to silver wire.

As for *vmbygon*, Salter cites the *OED* in her preference for "ornamenting or decorative" to the usual sense of "vmbygon," which she defines as "encircling or surrounding."[22] However, *MED* provides sufficient evidence for the verb *umbegon* to mean "to trim or decorate (sth.) all around or all over, [etc.]." As Salter says, this refers to "the decorative outlining of the charge of three wings by 'a golde wyre' or 'a gold thread.'"[23] As an alternative (perhaps influenced by *MED* "or all over") she offers "the overall 'tinselling' of the embroidered devices upon the jupon," but this seems to me unnecessary and too remote from the first meaning of the verb.[24] It is clear that the poet is describing the three wings being stitched all around their edges with gold thread (it is past, rather than present, participle, as Salter's definitions might suggest).

Salter's identification of the Wingfield arms is unassailable. One can, however, explain Trigg's skepticism, quoted above. Salter was unable to proffer much evidence for Sir John Wingfield's connections with the West Midlands, the provenance of not just most alliterative poetry but also, it seems, the poet of *Wynnere and Wastoure* who appears to claim kinship with a "westren wy" (l. 7). Sir John was the likely candidate for the Second Knight, and Salter noted that he was granted lands in Cheshire in 1352 (when in the service of the earl of Salisbury) and that several branches of the family were later settled in Derbyshire and Shropshire. She established his career at Crécy and Poitiers, particularly in the service of the Black Prince; she designated him governor or lieutenant of the Black Prince's household; she noted his death, perhaps of plague, in 1361 and his postmortem foundation of Wingfield College. However, she concentrated on Sir John's London connections as providing a home for a western poet: "There is good historical evidence for the employ of clerks from western families in royal and aristocratic families during these years; such service would of necessity involve them in travel between the west-country and the capital, and substantial residence in both areas."[25] Moreover, she arguably weakened her case by saying, "We have, of course, no means of telling which fourteenth-century member of [the Wingfield family] may have been the object of the *Wynnere and Wastoure* poet's complimentary attention."[26] Thereafter she offered, as alternatives to Sir John, Michael de la Pole (husband of Sir John's daughter), Sir Thomas Wingfield (Sir John's younger brother), his son, another Sir John (d. 1389), or Sir William Wingfield (cousin to the older Sir John and his brother).

By the time Elizabeth Salter's *Medium Aevum* article was reprinted in *English and International*, in 1988, Thorlac Turville-Petre's anthology of alliterative poetry was well under way (published 1989).[27] The intention of the series in which *Alliterative Poetry of the Later Middle Ages: An Anthology* was published was to offer "sound, attractive editions of major works which are at present inaccessible." Texts were to be unmodernized apart from punctuation, annotated textually, and provided with "full but concise" explanatory notes and a full glossary. Introductions to each text were to be "succinct and incisive," offering "essential information" and a "carefully selected bibliography."[28] In this context it is unsurprising that, although Turville-Petre provided very useful information on Sir John Wingfield to support Salter's ascription, this was done in brief sentences and bibliographical references. The introduction to his edition of *Wynnere and Wastoure* notes, "Contacts between the north-west midlands and London were strong, since the Black Prince was Earl of Chester and he employed many Cheshire men in administration and the army. . . . Perhaps the writer was part of the administration at Chester Castle dealing with the affairs of the Black Prince"; and he referred students to Michael Bennett's then recent book on Cheshire and Lancashire society in the age of *Sir Gawain and the Green Knight*.[29] His note to lines 117–18 endorsed Salter's identification of the Second Knight's arms[30] and provided further information on Sir John Wingfield—that he was the Black Prince's chief administrator in the period 1351–61 and so "responsible for all aspects of his winning and wasting," that he visited Cheshire (in 1351 and 1353, for example), and that he "dealt constantly with Chester business." He noted that the Black Prince was earl of Chester and employed Cheshire men in both administration and the army. Turville-Petre's sources were *The Financial Administration of the Lordship and County of Chester, 1272–1377*, and *Community, Class and Careerism*, both published after Salter's article.[31] Given Turville-Petre's admirably "succinct and incisive" introduction and the fact that his annotations could offer only "essential information," it would seem useful to explore at greater length the career of Sir John Wingfield, his association with Cheshire, and his role in the poem *Wynnere and Wastoure*.[32]

John Wingfield was born around 1307, presumably at Wingfield in Suffolk.[33] In 1325 and 1327 he was in France, on at least the first occasion involved in the buying of bulk supplies for Edward II. In 1331 he married the Wingfield heiress Eleanor Glanville, thereby becoming lord of altogether ten Wingfield manors. Their only child, Katherine, was not born until nineteen years later, and indeed Sir John appears to have been rarely at Wingfield during the whole of his life. He fought at the siege of Berwick in 1333 and was rewarded for his service there. In 1335 he was granted two more Suffolk manors (many others, not only in Suffolk, accrued to him later) and placed his coat of arms in Brockdish church, near Wingfield but over the border in Norfolk. By this time he is referred to as "Sir John." In 1345 he embarked for France, in the Gascony campaign, in the retinue of Sir Bartholomew Burghersh, where he was responsible for the young earl of Salisbury, William Montacute.[34] In 1346 he was appointed to the Black Prince's Council of War, and he fought at Crécy on August 26 in the retinue of the king, which then moved to the siege of Calais.[35] By September of the following year Calais was won and Sir John returned to England.

From 1348 until the battle of Poitiers (September 19, 1356) Sir John appears to have been consolidating his role as administrator in the service of the Black Prince. In 1350 he became steward of the Black Prince's vast estates and his daughter, Katherine, was born. The following year he is recorded as visiting the Prince's Cornish and Cheshire estates, and from this time until his death he was receiver for the Cheshire estates.[36] In 1352–54 he spent time in Devon, Cornwall, and Cheshire, sometimes with the Black Prince,[37] and he sailed in his retinue from Plymouth for Aquitaine on September 8, 1354, recorded as a Knight Banneret, second only to the Knights of the Garter. He was with the Prince at the razing of the old city of Carcassone on November 6, 1355, and wrote home from Carcassone and then Libourne in 1355 and 1356, distinguishing himself at Poitiers in September. He returned to England soon after, and from this date he is recorded as the Prince's principal administrator ("Gouvernour de noz Busoignes").[38] In 1359 he was in Cheshire (where he now held manors at Holdershaw, Mardsley, Merton, and Wareham) and was raising 20,000 marks for the Prince's war debts, some of which he supplied himself (and part of which may have been repaid in the £400 given him by the Prince that year).[39] He seems to have been in London frequently in the period 1359–61, in particular in January, February, May, and June 1361 (in March he was in Chester with the Prince). His death in the second half of 1361 must be attributed to the plague. The Prince contributed to his funeral at Wingfield, where his tomb is now outside what was once the Wingfield chantry chapel.[40] His will left provision to rebuild the church and establish a college of secular canons alongside.[41]

This is an astonishing career. Sir John Wingfield was clearly both an outstanding soldier and a very able administrator, "the principal maker of policy for the prince's estate administration . . . until his death in 1361."[42] He is a fitting man to be ordered into the dispute between Winner and Waster by the king, who sits outside his garter-strewn tent, dressed in robes embroidered with birds holding garters in their beaks.[43] "One of the ferlyest frekes þat faylede hym neuer" (l. 102), dubbed knight by the king "with dynttis to dele" (l. 103), he puts on his armor, his jupon with the Wingfield coat of arms displayed on front and back, breaks off a branch to carry as a sign of parley, and trots off, as herald ("Sir sandisman," l. 204), toward the assembled hosts below.

Wingfield's close involvement with the earldom of Chester amply explains the seeming anomaly of a Suffolk man's appearance in the intensely regional medium of alliterative poetry.[44] The Black Prince, as earl of Chester, owned a huge area, larger than the county and including the Welsh county of Flintshire, and the palatinate was important beyond its local significance. Indeed, it had no resident noble family and was effectively managed by London.[45] (During the prominent last ten years of Wingfield's life, he is recorded from time to time at his London house, Wingfield's Inn, from where a letter was sent on December 12, 1351, by the Black Prince.) Chester was an important recruiting ground for soldiers, archers in particular.[46] When Wingfield sailed for Crécy, it was in an army of 9,000 to 12,000 men, half of them archers, many Welsh archers, and the skill of the English army's longbowmen became legendary. In October 1351 Wingfield is recorded in Chester arranging the recruitment or, more probably, repatriation of local archers. He was therefore a suitable man to parley with Waster's army, "sadde men of armes, / Bolde sqwyeres of blode, bowmen many" (ll. 193–94). After the lengthy description of the banners of the church, lawyers, and four orders of friars in Winner's army, these knights, squires, and archers are certainly described "very cursorily."[47] However, it is plain that they were intended as ample opponents, having acquired a formidable reputation.[48]

Richard II recruited the men of Cheshire as his private army, and by the end of the century, when they were fighting for their survival in the struggle between Richard II and Henry Bolingbroke/Henry IV, there are records of Richard's admitting into his livery Cheshire knights and gentlemen, using 2,000 Cheshire archers to subdue opponents in his last London parliament of 1397, and taking 2,000 Cheshire men to Ireland with him for his 1399 campaign.[49] It is this period which is dealt with in *Richard the Redeless*, where the Cheshire men are described as "chyders of Chester" (III.317), who subdued opponents by force: "constrewed quarellis to quenche the peple, / And pletid with pollaxis and poyntis of swerdis" (III.327–28).[50] After Richard lost the throne (Bolingbroke had reached Chester before him), true to their fierce reputation, Cheshire men supported the rising of the earls of Kent and Huntingdon by launching an attack on Chester castle, and in 1403 they joined the Percys in rebellion.[51]

During the period of Wingfield's involvement with Chester, the major problems seem to have related to the Black Prince's need for money to finance his French wars.[52] It is here that William Shareshull becomes pertinent to the story. The title of Elizabeth Salter's article alludes to a major source of dissension among scholars: the date of *Wynnere and Wastoure*. From the time of Gollancz's dogmatic statement that the poem had been composed for the events of 1352, critics had vigorously disputed it. The dispute centered on Gollancz's insistence that the Statute of Treason (1352) provided the occasion for a poem in which armies with banners confronted one another and that the poet's reference to Sir William Shareshull (l. 317), with his complaint that the military "prikkede with powere his pese to distourbe" (l. 318), confirmed the fact, since it echoed Shareshull's own words to Parliament in January 1352.[53] Salter's article began with a consideration of the Statute of Treason and moved on to a demolition of Gollancz's use of Shareshull as evidence for 1352. She pointed out that Shareshull had been unpopular throughout his legal career,[54] which extended from his appointment as King's Serjeant in 1330 through to Justice of the Common Bench and Knight Banneret (1333), Chief Baron of the Exchequer (1344), and then Chief Justice of the King's Bench (1350–61). As such, it was impossible to assign a specific date to the poet's excoriation of him: "Now wolde God that it were . . . / That alle schent were those schalkes and Scharshull itwiste" (l. 317). Salter quoted Bertha Putnam: "it was inevitable that in his life-long fight against humble and powerful law-breakers alike he should have become an object of hatred to the turbulent elements in all classes of society."[55] In isolation, this seems rather a benign view of Shareshull. As well as "the architect of the 1349/51 labour legislation," Shareshull has been seen as responsible for allying the Crown and the Commons against the people.[56] He resurrected the "eyre," a criminal justice court but one where local maladministration could also be dealt with.[57] He was therefore unpopular with lords and peasants alike. In 1347 an eyre of the earl's hunting forests had been much resented, and another was planned for 1357, postponed from 1353. It was often considered best to buy off an eyre rather than submit to it, and this is what happened with the general eyre proposed for Chester from August 19, 1353. In return for a huge fine of 5,000 marks over four years, Cheshire was granted certain rights (including no general eyre for at least thirty years), but the Black Prince instead put Shareshull and Roger Hillary in charge of sessions of "trailbaston" (a peripatetic judicial commission first created in Edward I's reign), during which criminal fines were collected amounting to well over £1,000: "The sums of revenue produced in 1353 have no parallel in Cheshire's medieval history."[58] When the 1357 forest eyre took place, it is recorded that Wingfield feared a local insurrection by the concerted forest communities. In fact, two, Wirral and Mara-Mondrem, accepted communal fines, while the stronger Macclesfield forest community refused, and very little was collected from them in individual fines.

There is, therefore, strong reason for criticism of Sir William Shareshull in *Wynnere and Wastoure*. Inevitably, Wingfield had much to do with Shareshull, who retired from the King's Bench in the year of Wingfield's death, 1361. Wingfield was certainly in Chester with the Black Prince at the time of the 1353 eyre, and he must have been involved in all Shareshull's judicial dealings in Cheshire. Six thousand letters for 1351–65 survive from the Black Prince's privy seal letter books, over two thousand of which have warrants,[59] and Wingfield was the man whose name is attached to "the largest number of letters in the prince's name, either on his own authority or in conjunction with other officials."[60] One of these other officials was William Shareshull.[61] In the context of the poem, Shareshull is presented as "bad cop" and Wingfield as "good cop." The king chooses "one of the ferlyest frekes þat faylede hym neuer" (l. 102) as herald of peace between the two armies, and it is the army of Waster, the "sadde men of armes, / Bolde sqwyeres of blode, bowmen many" (ll. 193–94) that excoriates all the forces of Lent against their Carnival:

> Now wolde God that it were als I wisse couthe
> That thou Wynnere, thou wriche and Wanhope thi brothir
> And eke ymbryne dayes and euenes of sayntes,
> The Frydaye and his fere one the ferrere syde
> Were drownede in the depe see . . .
> And thies beryns one the bynches with [bonets] one lofte . . .
> That alle schent were those schalkes and Scharshull itwiste . . .
> (ll. 308–17)[62]

Elizabeth Salter's masterly article on *Wynnere and Wastoure* addressed the "timeliness" of the poem, countering Gollancz's narrow dating by submitting his evidence to scrutiny and, in a groundbreaking argument, replacing the Black Prince by the unknown Sir John Wingfield. I hope in this essay to have made Wingfield less unknown, if largely by marshaling the research of others. It is not my intention to discuss matters which were not pertinent to Salter's article, interesting though I find the descriptions of the pavilion, the First Knight ("ane hathell . . . / Wroghte als a wodwyse," ll. 70–71), the king, and the six banners of Winner's army.[63] It seems to me that the date 1352 is a convenient *terminus post quem* for the writing of the poem, even though none of Gollancz's eleven points in favor of that precise date stands up to careful scrutiny.[64] He was clearly too dogmatic to insist on a single year, but he has amply paid for it in the criticism heaped on him in the past (almost) century. What he said made sense of the poem, demonstrated scholarship, and stimulated argument, and he was the first explicator, and indeed translator, of the poem at a time when his readership was as likely to be the educated man in the street as the undergraduate English student.[65] Inevitably he has been subjected to the revulsion of later generations to history-based literary criticism,[66] of which I am, perhaps less unfashionably than earlier in my career, an advocate. To me the basic argument of *Wynnere and Wastoure* would appear to be an economic issue, saving versus spending, a subject that is debated today by European governments torn between increasing public expenditure and imposing austerity measures. One finds in the poem (and in most medieval poetry) what one wants to find, and what the spirit of the age inclines toward.

As one biased toward history and place, I myself might choose to see in Waster's sheer bloody-mindedness something of the Cheshire forest dwellers of the 1350s, and in Winner's criticism of Waster's "sturte and thy stryffe" (l. 265) something of the Cheshire archers of the 1390s.[67] Quite what Shareshull, or indeed Richard II, made of these men is hard to imagine. They were certainly Other, and, as Derek Pearsall himself pointed out, thirty years ago, speaking of the alliterative corpus, "It is difficult . . . to abandon completely the sense of 'differentness' that clings to these poets."[68] He cited the alliteration, the serious approach to historical writing, the interest in British history, the "total absence of the theme of love," which he attributed to "a provincial household culture, inheriting the conservative and old-fashioned tastes of provincial Anglo-Norman society." He looked too at the northwesterners who composed, copied, and kept alliterative verse as late as the sixteenth century.[69] He cited the Baguley author of *Scottish Field*, which celebrates the Stanleys at Flodden Field, the ownership of *St Erkenwald* by a chantry priest of the Booth family in Eccles, the copying of *The Destruction of Troy* by Thomas Chetham of Nuthurst, and the composition of two *Gawain*-inspired poems by Humphrey Newton of Pownall. Of these, all but the Booth family were Cheshire men. They did not forget, and it has been good to remember them, and Elizabeth Salter, and to offer a tribute to Derek Pearsall in this volume of essays in his honor.

Notes

1. The Wingfield 650th Anniversary History Symposium, Wingfield College, Wingfield, Suffolk, June 9–10, 2012.

2. Elizabeth Salter, "The Timeliness of *Wynnere and Wastoure*," *Medium Aevum* 47 (1978): 40–65; reprinted as "The timeliness of *Wynnere and Wastoure*," in Elizabeth Salter, *English and International: Studies in the Literature, Art and Patronage of Medieval England*, ed. Derek Pearsall and Nicolette Zeeman (Cambridge: Cambridge University Press, 1988), 180–98, which is the source for all references here. Israel Gollancz, *A Good Short Debate between Winner and Waster: An Alliterative Poem on Social and Economic Problems in England in the Year 1352 with Modern English Rendering* (London: Humphrey Milford/Oxford University Press, 1920).

3. All quotations from the poem are based on *Wynnere and Wastoure*, ed. Stephanie Trigg, EETS, o.s., 297 (Oxford: Oxford University Press, 1990).

4. Trigg, *Wynnere and Wastoure*, 24 (note to l. 117).

5. For details, see Trigg, *Wynnere and Wastoure*, 23 (note to l. 108). Extant in only one manuscript (London, British Library, Additional MS 31042, the Thornton Manuscript), the poem has inevitably laid itself open to emendation, although Gollancz exaggerated its degree of corruption (see the comments of Thorlac Turville-Petre, "The Prologue of Wynnere and Wastoure," *Leeds Studies in English*, n.s., 18 (1987): 19–29 (19–20)).

6. Tinctures consist of two metals, seven colors, and various furs; the field is the face of the shield itself; ordinaries are the simplest forms in which bands of color are painted on the shield (such as the bend, which is two diagonal lines infilled with a color). For heraldic information, I am most indebted (as was Salter) to *Boutell's Heraldry*, rev. C. W. Scott-Giles (London, 1950). Other works consulted include W. H. St John Hope, *A Grammar of English Heraldry*, rev. Anthony R. Wagner (Cambridge: Cambridge University Press, 1953); and Thomas Woodcock and John Martin Robinson, *The Oxford Guide to Heraldry* (Oxford: Oxford University Press, 1990).

7. Salter, "The timeliness of *Wynnere and Wastoure*," 192, citing (n. 80) Boutell (see his 74–78). She needed to find examples of wings which were unnatural in order to defend the meaning of "in the kynde" as "according to nature." Trigg appears merely to have followed her statement.

8. St John Hope, *Grammar of English Heraldry*, 18 (fig. 60). For a variety of wings, see Gerard J. Brault, *Early Blazon: Heraldic Terminology in the Twelfth and Thirteenth Centuries with Special Reference to Arthurian Literature* (Oxford: Clarendon Press, 1972), 90–93 (figs. 176–207). Only fig. 176 features wings (a single pair) unattached to birds.

9. *Boutell's Heraldry*, 27. Salter, "The timeliness of *Wynnere and Wastoure*," quotes (192) from Bernard Burke, *The General Armory of England, Scotland, Ireland, and Wales: comprising a registry of armorial bearings from the earliest to the present time* (London: Harrison, 1884), 1123: "argent on a bend gules cotised sable three pairs of wings conjoined in lure of the field." John Fearne, *The blazon of gentrie deuided into two parts, the first named The glorie of generositie, the second, Lacyes nobilitie: comprehending discourses of armes and of gentry, wherein is treated of the beginning, parts and degrees of gentlenesse, vvith her lawes of the bearing and blazon of cote-armors, of the lawes of armes and of combats* (London: John Windet, 1586), 233: "Argent, on a bend G, three paire of wings as the first." In Burke "of the field" refers to the tincture being the same as the field, or background color, of the shield (i.e., argent); in Fearne, "as the first" means the same, that the first tincture, argent, is repeated on the wings.

10. Salter, "The timeliness of *Wynnere and Wastoure*," 192.

11. Ibid., 190 and n. 58.

12. Also quoted in St John Hope, *Grammar of English Heraldry*, 82, with a bracketed note: ". . . of thiere [*sic*] own [*sic*] kynde (i.e. *proper*)."

13. St John Hope, *Grammar of English Heraldry*, 85. See n. 12 above.

14. St John Hope, *Grammar of English Heraldry*, 75–77. (South Australia has the piping shrike.)

15. *Boutell's Heraldry*, 65: "The early heralds considered a lion walking and looking about him to be behaving like a leopard, and they consequently blazoned him as a *lion-leopardé*, or merely as a leopard, though they always drew him as a stylized lion without spots or other leopard-like characteristics. So it is that the lions of England were anciently blazoned as leopards. They are now termed lions passant guardant"; St John Hope, *Grammar of English Heraldry*, 86: "When a lion, instead of being side-faced, looks out of the shield full-faced, he becomes heraldically 'a leopard'; not the spotted beast of that name, but merely a lion who looks at you."

16. Description from *Boutell's Heraldry*, 65.

17. An unpaginated desk publication of the Wingfield family (available from Wingfield College) shows the Wingfield escutcheon on the cover and a photograph and sketch of Sir John Wingfield, mounted, in armor as plate 1 (Jocelyn Wingfield, *Sir John de Wingfield III (ca. 1307–1361): How a local Anglo-Saxton rose in Norman-run England to become Executive Officer for the Black Prince*, no place or publisher, no date, unpaginated). For several articles pertinent to the Wingfield family, see *Proceedings of the Suffolk Institute of Archaeology and Natural History* VII, Part 1 (1889).

18. Only two entries would perhaps better be translated as "decorated." One is the hobby-harness (a harness for a hawk, or a small horse) "enbrowdered and wroght with ageletts of silver and gilt" (*MED aglet* (n.) a metal point at the end of a cord or ribbon; *OED aglet/aiglet* (n.) 2(a) a gold or silver tag or pendent attched to a fringe). The second refers to glass windows "wrought with jmagerye." In these two cases, *wroght* is more likely to take its first meaning, "worked," or "decorated."

19. Salter, "The timeliness of *Wynnere and Wastoure*," 193. For appliqué work, see the entry Appliqué in *Encyclopedia of Medieval Dress and Textiles of the British Isles c. 450–1450*, ed. Gale Owen-Crocker, Elizabeth Coatsworth, Maria Hayward, and Karen Watts (Leiden: Brill, 2012). I am grateful to Professor Owen-Crocker for access to her database.

20. Salter, "The timeliness of *Wynnere and Wastoure*," 190.

21. Ibid., 193.

22. Ibid. This may be the meaning at l. 62, although, again, "embroidered all round" is likely, if the "caban" is assumed to be of fine material.

23. Ibid.

24. Admittedly, some of the citations attached to *MED umbegon* (v.) (b) ("To trim or decorate (sth.) all round or all over") suggest "decorate . . . all over," although the neutral "decorate" might be sufficient.

25. Salter, "The timeliness of *Wynnere and Wastoure*," 195.

26. Ibid., 195–96.

27. Thorlac Turville-Petre, *Alliterative Poetry of the Later Middle Ages: An Anthology* (London: Routledge, 1989). Trigg's edition will have been complete or at press (published 1990) when *Alliterative Poetry* appeared. I have not consulted the three postgraduate editions cited in Trigg's Select Bibliography: her own (PhD, Melbourne, 1984) and those of Karen Stern (MPhil, London, 1973) and Lon Mark Rosenfield (PhD, Columbia, 1975).

28. Routledge Medieval English Texts, General Editor Malcolm Andrew (*Alliterative Poetry*, [p. ii]).

29. The subtitle of M. J. Bennett, *Community, Class and Careerism* (Cambridge: Cambridge University Press, 1983).

30. He translated the lines: "Three wings inside, done in their natural form, encircled with a gold wire."

31. P. H. W. Booth, *The Financial Administration of the Lordship and County of Chester, 1272–1377*, Chetham Society, 3rd ser., 28 (Manchester: Manchester University Press, 1981). Bennett, *Community, Class and Careerism.*

32. When I had submitted this essay, it struck me that Turville-Petre might not have gone to so much trouble to elucidate these references without exploiting the material himself. This indeed turned out to be the case, and the reader is recommended to read Thorlac Turville-Petre, "*Wynnere and Wastoure:* When and Where?," in *Loyal Letters: Studies on Mediaeval Alliterative Poetry and Prose*, ed. L. A. J. R. Houwen and A. A. MacDonald (Groningen: Egbert Forsten, 1994), 155–66. I am gratified that Professor Turville-Petre has said, "I agree with all you say" (pers. comm.). I return the compliment to his own article.

33. I have selected material from Jocelyn Wingfield's desk publication (see n. 17 above) and from a lecture given by Professor Mark Bailey at the Wingfield 650th Anniversary History Symposium (see n. 1 above). Wingfield lists his manuscript and printed sources, of which the most cited are the *Register of Edward the Black Prince . . . [1346–1348, 1351–1367]*, 4 vols. (London, 1930–33) in the National Archives Kew (E36/144, 278–280); and T. F. Tout, *Chapters in the Administrative History of Medieval England* (Manchester: Manchester University Press, 1920), 6 vols., esp. vols. 3–6. Where no source is cited, statements are taken from the desk publication, where references may (or may not) be found. However, the Wingfield symposium proceedings are to be published as *Wingfield College and the Dukes of Suffolk: Proceedings of the Wingfield 650th Anniversary Symposium*, ed. Peter Bloore and Edward Martin (Woodbridge: Boydell, forthcoming). Statements made here must therefore be

subject to confirmation in this publication, details of which may be found at www.wingfieldcollege.com/The%20Book.htm.

34. Both were Founder Knights of the Order of the Garter, as, of course, was the Prince of Wales himself. Wingfield himself never attained Garter status, although his great-grandson, William, 1st duke of Suffolk, was a Garter knight, as was his son, John, 2nd duke of Suffolk. William's wife, Alice Chaucer, was a Lady of the Garter (see n. 40 below).

35. His brother, Thomas, mentioned by Salter, fought in the retinue of Richard Fitzalan, earl of Arundel and Surrey, which also moved on to Calais.

36. In Cheshire in February 1351 he was involved in the audit of the accounts for 1349–50 (Booth, *Financial Administration*, 74).

37. Booth, *Financial Administration*, 74.

38. In 1358 he became the Prince's attorney and auditor (perhaps temporarily).

39. Booth, *Financial Administration*, 136.

40. No Wingfield arms survive, although Sally Badham, in her lecture on the monuments at the Wingfield symposium, provided evidence for their having been visible on the *cote-armour* in the late eighteenth century. Sir John's daughter, Katherine, married Michael de la Pole, 1st earl of Suffolk; they were both buried in the charterhouse at Hull. Michael's son, Michael, 2nd earl of Suffolk, married Katherine Stafford. The southeastern area of the church was rebuilt ca. 1430 by their son, William de la Pole, 1st duke of Suffolk (but see n. 41 below); his parents' tomb on the north side of the Lady Chapel carries de la Pole leopard heads and Stafford knots, and the arch above it alternates these with single pairs of wings. William himself was buried at Hull, and his wife, Alice Chaucer, at her college foundation in Ewelme, Oxfordshire. Their son, John, 2nd duke of Suffolk, married Elizabeth Plantagenet; their tomb is north of the sanctuary, east of Sir John's tomb. The font carries the Wingfield arms quartered with the de la Pole arms on two sides (wings and leopards), the Wingfield arms alone (bend and three pairs of wings) on one side, and the Stafford arms (a chevron) on the other side.

41. At the Wingfield symposium (see nn. 1 and 33 above) papers were given on the Wingfield church, college, and castle by Sally Badham and John A. A. Goodall; both papers will appear in the final publication. In the meantime, for valuable material on Wingfield College and its collegiate church, see Goodall's publication on Ewelme, the Oxfordshire foundation of Alice Chaucer (see n. 40 above): John A. A. Goodall, *God's House at Ewelme: Life, Devotion and Architecture in a Fifteenth-Century Almshouse* (Aldershot: Ashgate, 2001), esp. 51–65. For the statement that William de la Pole rebuilt the southeastern area of the church ca. 1430, see D. P. Mortlock, *The Guide to Suffolk Churches* (Cambridge: Lutterworth Press, 2009), 514–16; Goodall (57) says it was rebuilt by Michael de la Pole before his death in 1415 and extended further by

Alice Chaucer de la Pole in the 1460s. For the Ewelme tomb effigy of Alice (with the Garter wound round her left arm, as worn by Ladies of the Garter), see Goodall, pl. VII; for photographs of Wingfield church and tombs, see Goodall, figs. 21–28.

42. Booth, *Financial Administration*, 74.

43. Although it is not uncommon to dismiss the attempts of Gollancz and others to find resemblance in the records of the king's wardrobe, these records are in fact a remarkable survival and bear fascinating information on the extensive use of the Garter device (and other images) by Edward III at the time of his founding of the Order of the Garter (spring 1348). The robe of cloth of gold "poudr*e* cu*m* volucribus *et* losenges textis de auro" (powdered, i.e., scattered, with birds and lozenges covered in gold), or the velvet harnesses embroidered with blue garters and wodewoses, certainly bear close comparison with the description at ll. 91–94. (Sir Nicholas Harris Nicolas, "Observations on the Institution of the Most Noble Order of the Garter . . . illustrated by the Accounts of the Great Wardrobe of King Edward the Third, from the 29th of September 1344 to the 1st of August 1345, and again from the 21st of December 1345 to the 31st of January 1349," *Archaeologia* 31 (1846): 1–163 (25/117, 122)).

44. *St. Erkenwald* is the exception, London-focused but in a Cheshire dialect.

45. Bennett, *Community, Class and Careerism*, 74.

46. Ibid., 164, 204.

47. Turville-Petre, *Alliterative Poetry*, 39. In the course of the bad-tempered exchange of communications in the pages of the *Athenaeum* between Sir Israel Gollancz and the "lawyer-antiquary," as "G. N." (George Neilson) termed himself, Neilson too observed that "it makes a very lopsided narrative if no detail whatever is found for one of the contending armies" (*Athenaeum* 118 [1901]: nos. 3849, 3852, 3854, 3855 [no. 3854, p. 319]).

48. Bennett, *Community, Class and Careerism*, 204.

49. Ibid., 168, 169, 209. The palatinate of Chester did not survive: it was dismantled by Henry IV (Bennett, 211), who made Cheshire men serve him at their own costs (170, 211). Thereafter it was Henry's adjoining palatinate of Lancaster which held royal favor.

50. *The Piers Plowman Tradition: A Critical Edition of Pierce the Ploughman's Crede, Richard the Redeless, Mum and the Sothsegger, and The Crowned King*, ed. Helen Barr (London: J. M. Dent, 1993).

51. Bennett, *Community, Class and Careerism*, 169–70, 211. There had been a notorious Cheshire rising earlier, in 1393, brokered for the king by Sir John Stanley of Lathom in Lancashire, a family that was to rise to prominence under Tudor, and Lancastrian, government (Booth, *Financial Administration*, 218).

52. As noted above, Wingfield raised, and contributed to, the Prince's debts in 1359.

53. *A Good Short Debate*, Preface (unpaginated). Gollancz cited eleven points (i–xi) in support of the dating, of which Shareshull was the eleventh. It was this point which occasioned the correspondence with Neilson in the *Athenaeum*.

54. Salter, "The timeliness of *Wynnere and Wastoure*," 184. For the full extent of his unpopularity, demonstrated in acts of violence against him and his property from 1329 to 1358, see Richard W. Kaeuper, "Shareshull, Sir William (1289/90–1370)," *ODNB online*, www.oxforddnb.com/view/article/25204, accessed September 11, 2012.

55. Bertha Putnam, *The Place in Legal History of Sir William Shareshull* (Cambridge: Cambridge University Press, 1950), 156. Quoted in Salter, "The timeliness of *Wynnere and Wastoure*," 185.

56. Booth, *Financial Administration*, 120 (the latter G. L. Harriss's opinion).

57. For what follows, see Booth, *Financial Administration*, 120–26.

58. Booth, *Financial Administration*, 122.

59. Ibid., 71.

60. Ibid., 73. Jocelyn Wingfield adds that Sir John's personal seal ("sigillum Johannis Wingefelt") was attached to all the documents signed "by (the assent of and) command of," "on the instructions of," "by order of," or actually by Sir John. (The seal is reproduced as plate 6 and on the cover of *Sir John de Wingfield III*.)

61. See, e.g., the warrant quoted by Booth, *Financial Administration*, 73: "par avis monsire William de Shareshull . . . monsire Johan de Wengfeld. . . ." Jocelyn Wingfield says that Wingfield sat with Shareshull and Sir Richard de Stafford as King's Justices at Lostwithiel, Cornwall, in September 1354.

62. Turville-Petre, *Alliterative Poetry*, does not emend "howes" to "bonets."

63. I might just point out that a John Wodehouse had been chamberlain of Chester from July 17, 1374, to June 3, 1394 (Booth, *Financial Administration*, 151, 173). Gollancz, in a note to ll. 70–71, had indicated an earlier Robert de Wodehouse, treasurer of the Exchequer (d. ca. 1345).

64. The date 1352 is to me convenient because it is at the start of Wingfield's career as the Black Prince's chief administrative officer.

65. His edition consisted of Preface, Text, Modernized Version, Explanatory and Illustrative Notes, and Glossary.

66. See, e.g., David Lawton: "I question Gollancz's dating of 1352–3 . . . and I certainly do not accept his judgement that this poem is 'a topical pamphlet . . . on the social and economic problems of the hour.'" Lawton, "Middle

English Alliterative Poetry: An Introduction," in *Middle English Alliterative Poetry*, 1–19 (3). Lawton, however, dedicates the volume, "In honour of Madden, Morris, Skeat, Gollancz and all editors without whom we would have had no alliterative revival."

67. Presumably, despite limited evidence, similar behavior was the norm even between the 1350s and the 1390s.

68. Derek Pearsall, "The Alliterative Revival: Origins and Social Backgrounds," in *Middle English Alliterative Poetry and Its Background*, ed. David A. Lawton (Cambridge: D. S. Brewer, 1982), 34–53 (47 ff.).

69. For earlier readers and owners, see Turville-Petre, *The Alliterative Revival*, 40–47; and Bennett, *Community, Class and Careerism*, 231–35. Much more research has been carried out in this area since Derek wrote, e.g., Deborah Youngs, *Humphrey Newton (1466–1536): An Early Tudor Gentleman* (Woodbridge: Boydell and Brewer, 2008).

CHAPTER 6

The Author of the Italian *Meditations on the Life of Christ*

Sarah McNamer

I had the rare good fortune to meet Derek Pearsall the month he arrived at Harvard. I was seeking a mentor to direct the undergraduate thesis I had begun on Julian of Norwich's *Book of Showings*, and Derek—not yet surrounded by swarms of avid students, as he had been at York and soon became at Harvard—gamely agreed. As we met to talk about Julian under the rickety eaves of Warren House, in an office he shared then with Larry Benson, Derek steered me toward three principles that have had an enduring influence on my work, including the present piece and the larger project it represents. First, manuscripts matter; our literary texts simply cannot be understood without attention to manuscript matrix and textual history. Second, multilingual and European contexts matter: "It is much more important to understand the international affiliations of English poetry during this period than to invoke native traditions. The intellectual environment is a European one and English poetry is unintelligible except in relation to Latin and French poetic tradition."[1] And third, the best critical work combines sensitive readings and exploratory modes of thought with what is sensible and rigorous—a scholarly style so fully exemplified in the work of Elizabeth Salter, including her earliest study, *Nicholas Love's "Myrrour of the Blessed Lyf of Jesu Christ."*[2] Little did I know, that September afternoon, where Derek's teaching and encouragement would lead; but it has led, among other things, to Italy, and to efforts to enrich our knowledge of Love's *Mirror* and related English affective writing with attention to the Italian tradition.

In this essay, I present some fruits of my continuing work on the Italian *Meditazioni della vita di Cristo* (*MVC*). As I have articulated most fully in "The Origins of the *Meditationes vitae Christi*," an examination of the Italian and Latin manuscripts and their textual affiliations, as well as close stylistic analysis, strongly suggests that the original version of the popular and influential pseudo-Bonaventuran *MVC* was a short Italian version consisting of a prologue and thirty chapters, treating only the infancy and passion and replete with the affective and dramatic characteristics for which the *MVC* came to be so widely admired; that this original version, witnessed uniquely by Oxford, Bodleian Library MS Canonici Italian 174 (and thus designated, in what follows, as the Canonici version or text), was composed by a nun; that this version was subsequently taken up, "corrected," and expanded into successively longer versions—first, the Italian *testo minore*, then the Italian *testo maggiore*, and finally the long Latin text—by a redactor who can confidently be identified as a Franciscan friar; and that it was under this redactor's hand that the text became amplified to include the public ministry and many didactic and theological passages, as well as passages that identify the work explicitly as a Franciscan text composed for a Poor Clare.[3] I have designated the first author as Author A and the redactor as Author B.

Setting aside the question of who Author B may have been, a question I gladly leave to other scholars, I offer in this essay further thoughts on the identity of Author A.[4] My aim here is not to repeat evidence that I have already advanced (although some repetition is unavoidable) or to offer final conclusions—however inconclusive—of the kind that will appear in the critical edition and translation of the Canonici version that I am completing. Rather, I present some of my ongoing research, which appears to confirm the priority of Canonici among the extant versions and to support the claim that the text was composed by a nun. In short, my current hypothesis is this: the original version of the *MVC*, the Canonici text, was composed by a Poor Clare in Pisa sometime during the first two decades of the fourteenth century, probably between about 1305 and 1315. Because the convent of Ognissanti was the only convent of Poor Clares in Pisa at this time, I would place our author there.[5]

In what follows, I take up the matters of date and Pisan provenance first; move on to the evidence for Franciscan affiliation, which is simultaneously, I argue, indirect evidence for female authorship; and then turn to other forms of evidence that suggest that the Canonici text is likely to have been composed by a woman. Hypotheses concerning women's authorship of anonymous medieval texts often meet with skepticism, of course, and the nature of the evidence in this case is such that it does not admit of certainty. There is no single, incontrovertible piece of evidence that "proves" that the original version of the *MVC* was composed by a woman, nor are ideal forms of proof likely to be discovered. Rather, it is the accumulation and interpretation of disparate kinds of evidence that gestures strongly, as I see it, toward this conclusion.

Date and Place: Pisa, 1300–1320

The question of the date of the various versions of the *MVC* remains a compelling subject for research, in part because of its implications for understanding the relationship between this text and the innovations in the visual arts of the early Trecento. This is not the place to offer full evidence for revised dates for the various versions. But to put it simply, none of the versions can have been written prior to 1298 or 1299, since all, including the Canonici text, include a brief allusion to what appears to be Mechthild of Hackeborn's *Liber specialis gratiae*.[6] Given that it may have taken a few years for Mechthild's text to begin circulating in Tuscany, I suggest here a likely date of after 1305 for the Canonici text.

As for a date *ante quem*, my earlier suggestion that the Canonici text may have been composed in the early decades of the fourteenth century now appears more likely.[7] Recent paleographic work on the substantial corpus of *testo minore* manuscripts held at the Biblioteca Riccardiana indicates, on the basis of script, that at least one of them, MS 1269, dates to the second decade of the Trecento.[8] If the Canonici text was, as I have argued, composed prior to the *testo minore*, then it would have had to have been composed no later than 1320, and more probably by about 1315.

Moreover, in an important recent article that deserves to be widely known, Dávid Falvay has argued that it is no longer necessary to posit a date *post quem* of ca. 1336 for the *MVC* in *any* of its first redactions,

Italian or Latin. That date, ca. 1336, was one I had advanced, in my earliest research on the *MVC*'s textual tradition, for all versions of the *MVC* except the Canonici text on the basis of the inclusion in those versions of material from the *Revelations of St. Elizabeth of Hungary*.[9] Falvay's examination of the relationships among cults of Hungarian saints and Italian hagiographic texts suggests that the identification of the "Elizabeth of Hungary" in the *Revelations* as Elizabeth of Töss, who died ca. 1336, is likely to be mistaken: the depiction of the saintly Elizabeth in that text is far more likely to be a conflation of *topoi* of royal saints circulating in Italy by the early fourteenth century.[10] It is a compelling and well-documented argument, and one that I find persuasive, especially in conjunction with other recent textual and art historical scholarship; I would now consider my earlier dating of the post-Canonici versions of the *MVC* to post-1336 obsolete.[11] To summarize, then: it now seems highly likely that the Canonici text was composed between about 1305 and 1315, that the redactor completed the *testo minore* by 1320, and that the *testo maggiore* and the long Latin text may have been composed soon after this.

The basis for deducing that Author A was Pisan can be summarized more briefly: this rests on linguistic evidence. According to Pär Larson of the Opera del Vocabolario Italiano, the language of the Canonici copy is overwhelmingly Venetian (from the Veneto region, not necessarily Venice), and my independent work on the watermarks and history of the manuscript confirms its Venetian provenance. However, the very frequent appearance of certain verb endings and lexemes—*pippione*, for example, used as a synonym of *tortora*, "turtledove"—reveals that the base text is Tuscan. Larson has traced the text more specifically to Pisa on the basis of a coincidence of forms of the *passato remoto* found only in Pisan texts and amply represented in the Canonici MS.[12]

Franciscan Affiliation

Author A does not openly advertise any connection to the Franciscan order. It is not impossible that the author was a Cistercian, given the prominence of Saint Bernard as spiritual authority; more will be said about this below. But on balance, the evidence strongly suggests Franciscan affiliation. First, the author has communicated with a friar ("frate") who has been to the Holy Land. This friar has told the author that there is a stone placed in a wall at one of the holy sites, a stone that is believed to have been used in place of a pillow for the infant Jesus, as his mother was so poor that she had no pillow for him. It is not impossible that the term *frate* refers to a Dominican, and there was indeed a strong Dominican presence in Pisa, and a thriving culture of spiritual direction, as the writings of Cavalca attest. But Pisa was home to the robust friary of San Francesco as well; and given the strong Franciscan presence in the Holy Land and tradition of pilgrimage there, this phrase is highly likely to refer to news from a Franciscan friar—and therefore to imply that the author was also affiliated with the Franciscan order. Further, this news about the stone was not gathered from a sermon or another form of public discourse but through what sounds like an intimate, one-on-one conversation about holy things: "according to what I have heard from a friar who told me . . . " (et secundo che io havi da uno frate che mi disse . . .") (fol. 19v). Such a conversation is most likely to have taken place within the same order, whether in the context of friars speaking to each other or a friar speaking to a Poor Clare in the context of spiritual direction. In addition, there is a passing reference to Bonaventure's *Legenda maior* concerning Saint Francis; a reference to the shame Christ endured when being stripped naked, which was a favored theme among the Franciscans; and perhaps most telling, an exhortation to the reader, "O soul who desires to glory in the passion of your Lord, pay attention here . . ." (O anima la qualle desideri de gloriarti nella passione del tuo Signore, stà qui attento . . .) (fol. 89v), which is almost certainly an allusion to the Franciscan order's motto, *Mihi absit gloriari nisi in cruce Domini*, rather than a more generally applicable citation from Galatians 6:14.

The frequent references to poverty support the hypothesis of Franciscan authorship. Poverty was by no means an ideal exclusive to those affiliated with the Franciscan order; one need only recall the fervent devotion to poverty depicted in late medieval vitae of holy women belonging to the whole range of orders, or to none; and poverty was of course a fundamental vow of all monastics. But the way poverty is depicted in this text gestures toward the conclusion that both reader and writer were Franciscan. The author passionately encourages the reader's devotion to poverty: "O mirror of poverty, have compassion and strive to love poverty!" (O spechio di povertade, hàbili compassione et attendi di amare povertade!) (fol. 11r). The reader is encouraged to imitate Mary, who has no possessions or money and makes a living by the work of her hands, and who, "like one zealous for poverty" (sì come çelatrice de povertade) (fol. 22r), accepts the treasure the kings offer to her son but then distributes most of it to the poor. That Christ is depicted not only as "maestro de la povertade" (fol. 33r) but also as a mendicant, begging for alms, sleeping in a hostel, and walking barefoot from Nazareth to the Jordan River, would seem to offer conclusive evidence of the author's devotion to Franciscan ideals.[13]

If we can deduce, then, that the author was a Franciscan, the question can be narrowed to this: to which order of the Franciscans did the author belong, First, Second, or Third? The possibility that the author was a Third Order Franciscan is unlikely: among other things, the author emphasizes the need not to contradict or oppose "our superiors," especially when they issue reprimands (fols. 30v, 46v). This implies that both reader and author are situated within an institutional hierarchy in which castigation by superiors is to be welcomed as part of regular spiritual training in humility.

Was the author, then, a First Order Franciscan—a Franciscan friar? Or a Second Order Franciscan, a Poor Clare? To frame this as a question about distinctions in institutional history—setting aside, for now, other ways of asking whether the text was composed by a woman—is useful, I believe, in that it can enable us to evaluate internal textual evidence in relation to what is known about the First and Second Orders in the first decade or so of the Trecento and to ask, on that basis, which is the likeliest conclusion.

Let us return to institutional affiliation itself as authorial preoccupation, for instance. It is a striking feature of the Canonici text that the author's Franciscan affiliation is something that needs to be *deduced* from clues embedded in the text; it is never—not once in the entire text—openly announced or asserted. In other words, this appears to be an author who espouses Franciscan ideals but for whom the overt claiming of allegiance and promotion of institutional identity per se is unimportant. This feature of the text, and of the author's mind-set, is especially noticeable when the Canonici version is situated next to the subsequent versions of the *MVC*, in which Author B is so plainly intent on asserting the Franciscan identity of his reader and himself and thus of defining the text as a *Franciscan* text. In the version of the *MVC* most familiar to scholars, the long Latin text, Author B writes in the prologue: "If you were to read about blessed Francis and about your sweetest mother, blessed Clare the virgin, you would discover that they emerged from their many tribulations, wants and infirmities not only long-suffering but even cheerful."[14] This practice of adding explicit references to Francis and Clare is evident even in the first of Author B's revisions, the *testo minore*.[15] Indeed, Author B can be seen as a typical Franciscan of the First Order in this regard. For the Order of Friars Minor, defining the order within and against other forms of religious life, bolstering a strong sense of institutional identity and allegiance, and assertively claiming various texts, practices, and saints as "Franciscan" were central preoccupations for the first century of the order's history and beyond. Particularly in the context of the fierce debates about poverty taking place at the beginning of the Trecento—at the time when I have proposed the Canonici text was composed—it would be very difficult to find a member of the O. F. M. who could be as unconcerned about asserting Franciscan identity as our author manifestly is. I know of no comparable male Franciscan writer from this period: a member of the First Order, that is, who is not also an apologist promoting the order and championing its founder, one way or another. The most obvious writer to take as a basis for comparison, in fact, would be Ubertino da Casale, whose *Arbor vitae crucifixae Jesu*, composed in 1305, so manifestly conflates affective meditation on the passion with Franciscan polemic.[16]

For the Poor Clares, however, institutional circumstances were different. From the very beginning, women who belonged to what would become the Second Order had a far more ambiguous and flexible relationship to institutional affiliation itself. This is not the place to rehearse the complex early history of the Poor Clares in relation to the Order of Friars Minor, or to trace the shifting institutional affiliations of particular women of the thirteenth and early fourteenth centuries.[17] But it can be confidently stated that there was far greater fluidity in institutional circumstances, identity, and allegiance among women religious at this time, including those we can identify as Poor Clares for at least part of their lives.

And so, to return to the Canonici text, and to its internal clues of institutional affiliation: we are now in a position to recognize these clues as, simultaneously, clues indicating that the author was probably a woman. In short, this author appears to be a Franciscan but to feel no pressure to promote the order—an attitude which is compatible with the hypothesis that a woman wrote the text, and more difficult to reconcile with a theory of male authorship.

Moreover, to take up the matter of Cistercian influence in the Canonici text: this, too, seems to suggest that the author was a Poor Clare rather than a Franciscan friar. During the first century of the Second Order's history, especially, there appears to have been an easy compatibility—forged in part of necessity—between the ideals, practices, and institutional structures of the Poor Clares and Cistercian nuns.[18] Indeed, there are manifest signs which suggest that Saint Bernard influenced this writer as much or even more than Saint Francis. The rendering of the nativity provides an especially revealing instance of this. Famously, of course, Francis worshipped the infant Christ at the crèche at Greccio, a gesture which made him an exemplary figure of affective devotion to the poor and humble child in the manger; yet our author makes no mention of Francis, preferring to offer Bernard's insights and words in the chapter on the nativity:

> Saint Bernard says that he wants that you know for certain that the infancy of Christ Jesus, and the tears and the manger and the stall, do not give consolation to angry people and deceivers and silly people and to those who delight in the pomp and honors of this world. But they give consolation to the afflicted and the poor of spirit; and the Virgin Mary had these qualities, for she was not put off by the stall or the animals nor the hay nor the other base things. And Saint Bernard also says, "O Jesus Christ, how poor and needy you are from first to last! A stranger in the shelter from the rain, a poor child in the manger, he flees into Egypt sitting on a donkey, and is presented in the temple with the poor, and placed naked on the cross." And here you can see the great blessing you have received from the Lord God.
>
> ——
>
> [Dice sancto Bernardo ch'el vole che tu sapi per lo fermo che la infantia de Cristo Iesù et le lacrime et la mang[i]adora et la stalla non dano consolatione a quelli che sono furiosi et inganatori et riditori et a quelli che si dilectano delle pompe et honori di questo mondo, ma dàno consolatione alli afflicti et poveri de spirito, et questo have in sì la vergene Maria madre del Figliolo de Dio, che lei non have in horore la stalla né le bestie né 'l feno, né tute le altre cose vile. Et ancho dice sancto Bernardo: "O Iesù Cristo, che sei povero et bisognoso, primo et ultimo! Forestiero nel casamento della pioba, povero nella mançatora, fug[e] in Egypto sede sopra l'asenelo, et

> cum gli poveri è presentato nel tempio, et nudo posto in su la croce." Et qui tu pòi vedere el grande beneficio che tu hai riceputo dal signore Dio.] (fols. 16v–17r)

Perhaps especially significant here, as an indicator of the author's openness to multiple institutional influences of the kind often found among female religious at this time, is the wording of the phrase, "Saint Bernard says that he wants you to know for certain." There is a suggestion here of a filial relationship between Bernard and the reader; the relationship is presented as a personal bond, in which Bernard cares for the reader's spiritual well-being and offers his written words as spiritual direction for her; and the writer is serving as go-between at this moment, one who has an intimate understanding of Bernard and has the authority to convey Bernard's special concern to the reader. It is a subtle moment. It does not necessarily imply that the reader, or author, belonged to the Cistercian order. But what it does indicate is an open, flexible attitude toward affiliation and spiritual influence—an attitude that appears to have been more common among female than among male Franciscans in the late thirteenth and early fourteenth centuries.

Sources and Citation Practices

The Canonici author drew on sources of the kind that might well have been available to a nun capable of reading Latin in the early decades of the fourteenth century. The limited range of frequently cited texts can be identified as the Gospels, especially those of Matthew and Luke; the *Glossa ordinaria*; the Psalms; Peter Comestor's *Historia scholastica*; the *Legenda aurea*; Bernard of Clairvaux's *Sermons on the Song of Songs* (22, 43, 61); and the *Gospel of Nicodemus*. The ease and confidence with which these sources are woven into the narrative suggests that the author was quite familiar with them and drew upon them directly. It is worth noting that no great library was required; indeed, we need only posit that the author had ready access to four or five volumes, including the Gospels and a psalter. The liturgy is another important source drawn upon with ease. Other sources, referred to briefly or in passing, can be identified as Bernard of Clairvaux's *In die natali Domini*, *In die sancto Paschae*, and *De psalmo Qui habitat*; John Chrysostom, *Homilies on the Gospel of Matthew*; Bonaventure, *Legenda maior*; Augustine, *Tractates on the Gospel of John*; Saint Ambrose, *In Lucam*; and pseudo-Origen's *Homily on Mary Magdalene*. It is less clear, given the brevity of the citations in this second category, that these latter sources were drawn upon directly from texts readily available to the author; some, like the Ambrose passage, may have been absorbed from the liturgy, or through hearing sermons or through spiritual conversation of the kind the author obviously enjoyed with the *frate* who had been to the Holy Land. Although there is still too little known about the contents of nuns' libraries in Tuscany in the decades around 1300, the sources used here appear to be compatible with the hypothesis that the work was composed by a nun.[19]

Equally telling, I would suggest, is the way that these sources are cited. Throughout, the citation practice is loose and informal. For example, when describing Magdalene's encounter with the risen Christ, the author writes, "according to what a commentator says about this, her soul was not within her, but was where the body of Lord Jesus Christ had been placed" (dice qui uno expositore che lei non havea l'anima sua cum lei, ma l'havea nel luocho dove fu posto el corpo de miser Iesù Cristo) (fol. 114r). The title and author of the source text are mentioned only on very rare occasions, and even then, in very vague terms. The particular conjunction of impulses here is distinctive: on the one hand, the author is intent on emphasizing that material comes from good sources; on the other hand, there is a lack of concern with providing clear citations to specific texts. Indeed, the author seems to conceive of written texts, including the scriptures, primarily as traces of oral communication. "St. Mark says . . ." (Dice miser san Marco . . .) (fol. 47v); "Here the commentator says" (Dice qui lo exponitore) (fol. 48v); "And the apostle revealed this plainly, where he says" (Et questo ne monstra manifestamente lo apostolo là dove el dice) (fol. 41r); "And Saint Bernard says that Joseph often took Lord Jesus in his arms and played with him" (Et sancto Bernardo dice che Ioseph spesse volte tegniva in braçio miser Iesu & solaçava cum lui) (fol. 24v); and so on. Yet the author's manifest ease with oral style, broadly considered, is not easy to align with techniques used in the dominant oral genre among Franciscan friars, that of preaching. There is no sign in the Canonici text of the author's knowledge of preaching manuals, and the general stance of the speaker is not didactic. The "orality" that marks this text is colloquial; it is not "oratory."[20]

This raises a further question, of course: could the simplicity of the Canonici text—simple in its sources, simple in its adducing of them—have been a deliberate choice by a Franciscan friar, one who perhaps chose to suppress his knowledge of a wider array of sources and his knowledge of the scholastic mode of citing sources, perhaps because he was writing for a nun and believed she would not wish to be troubled with the specifics? Or could we attribute the text to a Franciscan friar who had simply not read very widely and who had not been exposed to scholastic citation practices?

Such possibilities are unlikely. Widespread impressions of the Franciscans as men who, like Francis, conceived of themselves as *ignorans et idiota* are simply not accurate for the early fourteenth century. The battle over education and the value of theological training had been waged well before 1300—and won, by those who saw numerous advantages to the order of having its members embrace scholastic education and having prestige accrue to the order as a result. As Neslihan Şenocak observes, by 1244, "the backbone of an educational framework and the formation of an administrative culture that favored the pursuit of learning as a good and useful activity was complete."[21] After this date, the order actively recruited men from university circles; by 1310, the order required that all postulants have a knowledge of grammar and logic and undergo at least a year of theological education, with the option of advancing to *studia* established in every province. Even the Spiritual Franciscans, in theory devoted to radical simplicity and to a return to the ideals of Francis, did not hesitate to deploy in their writings the skills in exegesis and disputation that they acquired through the standard trajectory of Franciscan education. Here again, the example of Ubertino da Casale, who spent nine years studying in Paris, is useful: one of the foremost proponents of the Spiritual ideal and a critic of the educational system, he nonetheless displays the fruits of his own education very openly in the *Arbor vitae crucifixae Jesu*. The versions of the *MVC* composed by Author B provide further examples of the tendency among members of the Order of Friars Minor at this time to display their learning: Author B does not hesitate to cite sources with specificity, to draw on a wider range of sources, and to adopt the authoritative voice of the preacher, even though he, like Author A, addresses his versions of the text to a nun.

The simplest explanation for the limited range of sources and the "nonprofessional" mode of introducing them, then, would seem to be that the author never received the kind of education typical of Franciscan friars of this period. What kind of Franciscan does not receive such an education, in the early Trecento, yet reads Latin and exhibits a high degree of intellectual curiosity and literary skill? The likeliest answer would seem to be a Poor Clare.

Familiarity with Women's Social Practices

The *MVC* in its many versions and translations, of course, is recognized for the extraordinary attention it gives to female characters, to a woman's point of view, to domestic realism, and to *imitatio Mariae*. I have pointed out elsewhere that these elements are even more strongly present in the Canonici version than in the subsequent versions; while Author B preserved most of these woman-centered passages, he excised some, including the long lament of the Virgin in the Canonici text, and altered others. Significantly, too, Author B betrays a far more limited ability or desire to write from a woman's point of view.[22]

What can we make of this? Could Author A have been a male author who was particularly attentive to and knowledgeable about women's practices? Certainly, this is possible; gifted writers of any place and time can be credited with expansive imaginative capacities and a heightened degree of attunement to the lives of others. Yet just as specific knowledge of certain practices has been taken as a valid clue to the identity of a broad array of anonymous authors in the medieval period (knowledge of legal procedures suggesting lawyers, of priestly rituals suggesting priests, etc.), I would suggest that we cannot dismiss knowledge of women's practices as a potentially valuable clue to the identity of Author A.

Let me give just one example in this regard, an example that I believe is especially valuable because it does not call attention to itself. It occurs in the chapter depicting the return from Egypt to Nazareth. Jesus is now a small child, one who plays in the road and can speak full sentences; he is capable of walking but cannot walk very far; we also gather that he is still small enough to be carried. Together, these features imply that he is a toddler of about two or perhaps three years old. The meditator is asked to enter this scene as the one who leads the donkey by the halter, while Jesus rides with his mother and Joseph follows behind. As this procession ambles along, an ordinary moment, but one rich in affective potential, is introduced: "Now, if Our Lady wants to dismount sometimes to go a little on foot, be sure to hold the child Jesus so he doesn't fall. And if the child Jesus wants to dismount, take him in your arms and hold him until his mother comes, and then reverently give him to his mother, because it is a great comfort to her when she receives her son in her arms" (Or se alcuna volta la dona nostra volesse desmontare per andare uno puocho a piedi, fa che tu tegni il fançullo Iesu açio chel non cadesse. Et s'el fançullo Iesu volesse desmontare, fa che tu el pigli in braço & tienlo fin che la madre vegna, & poi reverentementa il da alla madre, impero che gran riposo era a lei quando la ricevea il figliolo in braço) (fol. 34r). Worth pointing out here are the author's awareness of a very young child's vulnerabilities, the pragmatic provision that his mother should ride with him, and the need to "hold the child Jesus so he doesn't fall," should his mother want a break, as she would. It is a small set of details, easily escaping notice—until it is compared to the revised versions of the text. In successive redactions, Author B first removes the child's mother from the donkey altogether, so that in the *testo minore* he rides alone, with his mother walking behind; in the long Latin text, the meditator's protective hand, holding the child on the donkey, has also been removed.[23] These changes may well have been motivated by a desire to present an image of "Jesus riding alone on a donkey" that could function as a prefiguration of the mature Christ's entry into Jerusalem prior to the passion. Whatever the motive, the scene as imagined by Author B illuminates, through contrast, the Canonici author's superior degree of attunement to a very young child's limited capacities and the specific practices that women typically caring for a child of this age would need to engage in, in order to keep such a child safe.

In itself, this scene does not by any means stand as evidence that the Canonici text was composed by a woman. But there are so many scenes like this. Moreover, the cumulative effect of this kind of evidence of a woman's point of view—the ease and confidence with which women's spaces and domestic rituals are depicted, the lively attention given to how women socialize and share beds and engage in intimate talk, the lack of hesitation in describing aspects of pregnancy and the care of a newborn, and so on—invites attention to more assertive moments in the Canonici text in which women's status or authority is heightened. Here, I will simply point out the way Magdalene is referred to near the end of the work. The Canonici author, summarizing the various appearances Jesus made after the Resurrection, defines Magdalene quite pointedly as "his beloved disciple": "But in a spirit of devotion, we may imagine that he, being benevolent, appeared more times to his mother, and also to her, his beloved disciple, that is, Magdalene" (Ma noi podemo piatosamente pensare che lui come benigno più volte apparse alla madre sua & anche a quella sua dillecta discipula, çioe Magdalena) (fol. 121v). While this appellation is certainly not unprecedented, it is particularly striking here, in part because Christ's band of male disciples, including "John, the beloved disciple," is not mentioned in this passage. The Canonici author has placed women at the center here in a striking way, one that challenges scriptural authority in its implicit substitution of Magdalene for John as "his beloved disciple."

Could a male author have composed such a thoroughly woman-centered text? Yes; such a hypothesis is not impossible. But that possibility should not prevent us from proposing the alternative—that the author's heightened awareness of women's domestic practices, spaces, and social relationships, combined with a manifest tendency to assert the authority and importance of women, deserves consideration as a possible indication of female authorship. It may not be naive, in other words, to deduce from this evidence the simplest explanation, that the author was a woman.

Cecilia as Author Portrait?

The implicit objection to all the above—that we cannot credit a woman with the capacity to write a text such as this—makes little sense. Literacy levels among women in Tuscany were especially high in the early fourteenth century; indeed, they may have been the highest in all Europe at this time.[24] My concern in this context is not to adduce further documentation of this general phenomenon but simply to point out that the burden of proof need not rest so heavily on those who would propose female authorship for a vernacular devotional text at this time and place.

By way of concluding this essay, then, I wish to focus on a key textual site: the work's opening invocation of Saint Cecilia as exemplary figure. Canonici's unique depiction of Cecilia deserves close attention not only for what it appears to assume about women's literacy at this time, but, more specifically, for what it might imply about the identity of Author A. In short, I suggest that it functions as a kind of author portrait; and further, that its potential significance as author portrait was suppressed by Author B.

Like the many versions and translations of the *MVC* that enjoyed wide circulation, the Canonici text presents Cecilia as exemplar of affective meditation: "she carried always the gospel of Jesus Christ hidden in her breast" (ela portava sempre lo evangelio de Cristo Iesù ascoxo nel suo pecto) (fol. 1r). Strikingly, however, the Canonici text—alone of all the extant Italian or Latin versions—goes on to describe Cecilia as a writer. She has not only selected, but *written out* passages from the Gospels for her use in meditation. Expanding on the *Legenda aurea*'s image of Cecilia carrying the gospel hidden in her breast, the Canonici author gives this gloss: "And you should consider this to mean that she had written for herself some selections from the more devotional aspects of the life of Lord Jesus Christ" (E questo dè' tu intender cusì, che ella se havea scrito algune electe cose più devote de la vita de miser Iesù Cristo) (fol. 1r). Cecilia is thus manifestly presented as woman-capable-of-authorship in the Canonici version. This intriguing image is related to other iconographic developments at this time: the renowned Altarpiece of Saint Cecilia now held at the Uffizi, for instance, which was made for the convent of Saint Cecilia in Florence in 1305, depicts Cecilia holding a pen as well as a book, suggesting that she herself has written the book she holds. At the very least, the image of Cecilia as writer suggests that a capacity for composition would not have been a foreign idea to religious women at this time: it suggests a horizon of expectations which credits Cecilia, whom the reader is asked to imitate, with both reading and writing meditations.

Would it be too far-fetched, then, to suggest that this depiction of Cecilia as writer may have functioned as an image of the author? Clearly it is an author portrait in an indirect and generic sense: Cecilia is advanced as a maker of meditations, as one who deliberately selects and composes a meditative text from those passages from the Gospels that have the greatest affective potential; indeed, it could be said that she is presented as author of the genre of affective meditation. Could this opening image of Cecilia be a kind of author portrait, an indirect and perhaps deliberately coded nod to the author of the text it prefaces? The question is inevitably speculative, and further research on the varieties of late medieval author portraits—including, especially, those of the more indirect, coded kind—is necessary. But to at least clarify the nature of the speculation, it could be pointed out that the function of the image in relation to the *reader* is taken for granted. Cecilia is an exemplary image for the reader; the reader is explicitly invited to model herself on Cecilia. Given this, isn't it plausible to posit that Cecilia may be a self-referential image for the author, that she functions as a saintly model who licenses and endorses the composition of a meditation on the life of Christ by a woman?

Here again, a comparison with the redactor's work can, if not answer the question, at least provide further intrigue. For it is a remarkable fact that the reference to Cecilia as writer is not present in the *testo minore* and subsequent versions of the *MVC*. The *testo minore* credits Cecilia with "choosing" but not "writing" gospel passages: "she had chosen some selections from the more devotional aspects of the life of Lord Jesus Christ" (ella s'avea iscelte alquante cose più divote della vita di Jesù Cristo).[25] As is the case with other alterations made by Author B, we have two choices: either the change was accidental or it was deliberate. It seems to me implausible that the omission of such a significant detail as Cecilia's authorship of her gospel florilegium could be accidental. For one thing, this is a significant site: these are the opening words of the text, the tone-setting, disposition-setting mise-en-scène, and opening words are highly likely to receive an author's most careful attention. Beyond this, there is the fact that the image of Cecilia as writer is indeed an image: it is not simply a passing phrase that is omitted, but a visual image of a memorable sort, an image crystallizing an activity and an identity.

Is there, then, a reasonable explanation for the deliberate omission of the image of Cecilia as writer? I would suggest that there is. To grant women within the Franciscan fold spiritual authority, even symbolically through the propagation of images of women as writers or preachers, is something that the friars were occasionally drawn to (as in the case of Angela of Foligno) but far more often found problematic and sought to limit or suppress.[26] The relation between Author A and Author B would seem to fit in this historical context of suppression.[27]

In the end, I would emphasize once again that the evidence is cumulative, and I certainly welcome any new evidence or reasoning that might alter this picture.[28] But as I see it, a Poor Clare was the original literary artist behind the *MVC*, and a Franciscan friar—while clearly valuing much of what she produced—actively censored her authorial role and altered her text. But whatever Author B's motives may have been, this was nonetheless a *felix culpa*; for even as he sought to "improve" the work through numerous excisions and expansions, he absorbed most of the lively, dramatic, and moving scenes of the Canonici text into the revised versions that made their way into what would have seemed, to many Italians, strange hinterlands, including Nicholas Love's Yorkshire, and from thence into the hands of Elizabeth Salter and Derek Pearsall and their many fortunate students.

Notes

1. Derek Pearsall, *Old English and Middle English Poetry*, Routledge History of English Poetry, 1 (Boston: Routledge & Kegan Paul, 1977), xii.

2. Elizabeth Salter, *Nicholas Love's "Myrrour of the Blessed Lyf of Jesu Christ"* (Salzburg: Institut für Englische Sprache und Literatur, Universität Salzburg, 1974).

3. Sarah McNamer, "The Origins of the *Meditationes vitae Christi*," *Speculum* 84 (2009): 905–55. This argument is put forward in more compact form in Sarah McNamer, *Affective Meditation and the Invention of Medieval Compassion* (Philadelphia: University of Pennsylvania Press, 2010). Salter was one of the first to comment on the stylistic discrepancies within the long Latin text, noting that the infancy and passion sections have an "impressive dramatic and descriptive quality" which the chapters on the public ministry lack; Salter, *Nicholas Love's "Myrrour,"* 43.

4. The ongoing work of Péter Tóth and Dávid Falvay appears to be very promising where the identity of the author I have designated as Author B is concerned. See Péter Tóth, "Pseudo-Apocryphal Dialogue as a Tool for the Memorization of Scholastic Wisdom: The Farewell of Christ to Mary and the *Liber de Vita Christi* by Jacobus," in *The Making of Memories in the Middle Ages*, ed. L. Dolezalova (Leiden: Brill, 2010), 161–98; and a forthcoming essay by Tóth and Falvay (not available to me at the time of writing), "From the Apostle James to Bonaventure the Cardinal: New Light on the Date and Authorship of the *Meditationes Vitae Christi*," in *"Diuerse Imaginaciouns of Cristes Life": Devotional Culture in England and Beyond, 1300–1560*, ed. Stephen Kelly and Ryan Perry (Turnhout: Brepols, forthcoming).

5. Arianna Pecorini Cignoni, "Gregorio IX e il francescanesimo femminile: Il Monastero di Ognissanti in Pisa," *Studi Francescani* 95 (1998): 383–406; Mauro Ronzani, "Il francescanesimo a Pisa fina alla metà del Trecento," *Bollettino storico pisano* 54 (1985): 1–57. Ognissanti no longer exists; in 1331, the Poor Clares were transferred from Ognissanti to the Pisan convent of Santa Chiara Novella at San Martino in Kinseca. Holly Flora has traced the provenance of the well-known illuminated manuscript, Paris, Bibliothèque national

MS Ital. 115, to Santa Chiara Novella; see *The Devout Belief of the Imagination: The Paris "Meditationes vitae Christi" and Female Franciscan Spirituality in Trecento Italy* (Turnhout: Brepols, 2009).

6. For references, see McNamer, "Origins," 946.

7. Ibid.

8. Tommaso Gramigni, "I manoscritti della lettaratura italiana delle origini conservati nella Biblioteca Riccardiana di Firenze: Analisi paleografica e codicologica" (MA thesis, Università degli Studi di Firenze, 2003–4). For my use of the term *testo minore* to categorize this group of Italian manuscripts, which treat the infancy and passion but not the public ministry, see McNamer, "Origins," 910.

9. Sarah McNamer, "Further Evidence for the Date of the Pseudo-Bonaventuran *Meditationes vitae Christi*," *Franciscan Studies* 50 (1990): 235–36.

10. Dávid Falvay, "St. Elizabeth of Hungary in Italian Vernacular Literature: *Vitae*, Miracles, Revelations, and the *Meditations on the Life of Christ*," in *Promoting the Saints: Cults and Their Contexts from Late Antiquity until the Early Modern Period: Essays in Honor of Gábor Klaniczay for His 60th Birthday*, ed. Ótto Gescer (Budapest: Central European University Press, 2011), 137–50.

11. In addition to the art historical scholarship of Dianne Phillips and Holly Flora (cited in McNamer, "Origins," 905), see the textual studies by Péter Tóth and Tobias Kemper analyzing the relationship between the *MVC* and the sermons of Michael of Massa (d. 1337): Tóth, "Pseudo-Apocryphal Dialogue"; Tobias A. Kemper, *Die Kreuzigung Christi* (Tübingen: Max Niemeyer, 2006).

12. Larson's full philological analysis will appear in the introduction to my edition. Larson has been very generous in sharing his expertise, and I wish to thank him for his kind collaboration.

13. For the relevant passages from MS Canon. Ital. 174, see McNamer, "Origins," 947–48.

14. Francis X. Taney, Anne Miller, and C. Mary Stallings-Taney, trans. and eds., *John of Caulibus: Meditations on the Life of Christ* (Asheville, NC: Pegasus Press, 2000), 2.

15. For example, Author B explicitly advances Francis and Clare as models for meditative practice and the spiritual life in the prologue: "E onde credi che santo Francesco pervenisse a tanta abundanzia di virtude e a così sottile intendimento della Scrittura divina, e ancora a così esperto conoscimento de l'inganni del nemico e de' vizi, se non per la famigliare usanza e meditazione della vita di Jesu Cristo?" (Francesco Sarri, ed., *"Le meditazioni della vita di Cristo" di un frate minore del secolo XIV* [Milan: Vita y pensiero, 1933], 4).

16. Ubertino da Casale, *Arbor vitae crucifixae Jesu*, ed. Charles T. Davis (Turin: Bottega d'Erasmo, 1961).

17. Lezlie Knox, *Creating Clare of Assisi: Female Franciscan Identities in Later Medieval Italy* (Leiden: Brill, 2008); and Maria Pia Alberzoni, *Clare of Assisi and the Poor Sisters in the Thirteenth Century*, ed. Jean-François Godet-Calogeras (St. Bonaventure: Franciscan Institute Publications, 2004).

18. Knox, *Creating Clare*. In this respect, potential connections between the Poor Clares of Ognissanti and the Cistercian convent of San Mateo in Pisa are worth investigating.

19. One wishes for a resource for Tuscany akin to what David N. Bell has provided for medieval England in *What Nuns Read: Books and Libraries in Medieval English Nunneries* (Kalamazoo, MI: Cistercian Publications, 1995).

20. This feature of the Canonici author's style is also more visible when compared to the work of Author B; for comments on the preaching style of the latter, see McNamer, "Origins," passim.

21. Neslihan Şenocak, *The Poor and the Perfect: The Rise of Learning in the Franciscan Order, 1209–1310* (Ithaca: Cornell University Press, 2012), 76.

22. Author B's limitations in this regard are especially noticeable in the chapters on the public ministry; see McNamer, "Origins," 918–21.

23. Sarri, *Le meditazioni*, 61; Taney, Miller, and Stallings-Taney, *Meditations*, 51.

24. McNamer, "Origins," 951.

25. Sarri, *Le meditazioni*, 1. My examination of manuscripts of the *testo minore* has revealed no instances in which Cecilia is depicted as writer.

26. Bert Roest, "*Ignorantia est mater omnium malorum*: The Validation of Knowledge and the Office of Preaching in Late Medieval Female Franciscan Communities," in *Saints, Scholars, and Politicians: Gender as a Tool in Medieval Studies*, ed. Mathilde van Dijk and Renée Nip (Turnhout: Brepols, 2005), 65–83.

27. See my "Origins" for further evidence of the redactor's censorship of the Canonici text, including the suppression of the phrase "nostro dolce spoxo" (fol. 53r), which I read as an indication that Author A was a nun. I am grateful to Richard Kieckhefer for calling my attention to the masculine ending of the adjective *solliciti* in the context of the "dolce spoxo" phrase; reasons why this is not dispositive evidence are forthcoming in my critical edition.

28. I look forward, in particular, to the results of the research currently under way among PhD students in Italian at Eötvös Loránd Tudományegyetem in Budapest. Under the direction of Dávid Falvay, this group is investigating the Italian manuscripts of the *MVC* in an effort to provide philological analysis that can lead to a more detailed picture of the relationships among the Italian and Latin witnesses. My hope is that this work will provide the basis for a much-needed critical edition of the *testo minore*.

CHAPTER 7

Handling *The Book of Margery Kempe*

The Corrective Touches of the Red Ink Annotator

Katie Ann-Marie Bugyis

By the second quarter of the sixteenth century, the sole surviving manuscript copy of *The Book of Margery Kempe*, London, British Library, Additional MS 61823, found itself in a different and rather unexpected textual location, with respect to both *where* and *how* the manuscript was read, from its original site of production. Before the dissolution of Mount Grace Priory in 1539, Kempe's *Book* made it into this Carthusian charterhouse's library and was annotated, corrected, and rubricated by at least one of its monks, whose name was undisclosed by his own hand but who has been dubbed by scholars the Red Ink Annotator.[1] This scribe was the last of as many as six and as few as four readers to interact marginally and interlinearly with the manuscript.[2] The striking appearance, the abundance, and the numerous interactions of his textual additions with those of the other readers all suggest that the Red Ink Annotator intended for his handling of the text to supersede or, at the very least, to build upon and organize earlier contributions to the manuscript page. So obtrusive are some of his additions that Kempe's *Book*, as it appears in the manuscript, could never be read in the same way that the manuscript's original scribe had copied it or the *Book*'s second writer had written it. Indeed, in order to read the manuscript differently than he did, one at times has to literally read underneath his red ink.

Scholars interested in the Red Ink Annotator's handiwork have attempted to reconstruct his operative hermeneutic by drawing our attention to his interest in *discretio spirituum*, to how he customizes the manuscript for future laywomen readers, and to the instances where he parallels Kempe's affective mystical experiences with those of Richard Rolle (1290–1349), John Norton (d. 1522), and Richard Methley (ca. 1451–1528), the last two of whom were the former prior and vicar of Mount Grace, respectively.[3] These accounts have persuasively identified the source texts for his frequently affirmative and often affectively engaged annotations to Kempe's text, particularly when they echo the autobiographical contemplative works of Norton and Methley. Yet to be fully explained, however, are the Red Ink Annotator's numerous corrections, the places where he alters the reading of the text, and how his annotations and corrections often work together to promote a sophisticated reading praxis, especially for passages where Kempe's experiences defy readerly expectations of spiritual vision and mystical union.

I contend that the Red Ink Annotator's annotations and corrections evidence a theological hermeneutic that was informed not only by his reading of Richard Methley's more devotional works—the *Scola amoris languidi*, the *Dormitorium dilecti dilecti*, and the *Refectorium salutis*[4]—but also, and more significantly, by his Latin translations of and glosses on *The Cloud of Unknowing* (*Diuina caligo ignorancie*) and Marguerite Porete's *Mirror of Simple Souls* (*Speculum animarum simplicium*).[5] Read through these two works, the moments in Kempe's text that concern the correcting hand of the Red Ink Annotator become intelligible. He carefully redefines the bounds of Kempe's mystical experiences, so that they are neither too bodily nor too super-substantial. He determinedly situates her visions within the Augustinian definition of "*visio spiritualis*,"[6] forestalling misinterpretations of her visions as being transgressively corporeal or as flirting with Free Spiritism.[7] So corrected, Kempe becomes a model not only of affective devotion for laywomen readers but also of perfect contemplation for Carthusians.

Richard Methley's name makes four appearances in the Red Ink Annotator's hand in the margins of Additional MS 61823, three times on its own and once with John Norton's. First, in the inner margin of fol. 14v, the annotator supplied "R Medlay. v. was wo*n*t so to say" next to the following passage found in chapter 13 of Kempe's *Book*: "Tha*n* aft*yr* þis sche was in gret rest of sowle a gret whyle & had hy co*n*templacyon day be day & many holy spech & dalyaw*n*s of owyr Lord Ih*es*u

Cryst boþe a-for-noon & aft*yr*-noon, wyth many swet terys of hy deuocyon so plentyvowsly & *con*tynualy þ*a*t it was m*er*uayle þ*a*t hir eyne enduryd er how hir hert mygth lestyn þ*a*t it was not co*n*sumyd wyt*h* ardowr of loue."[8] This annotation affirms Kempe's "ardowr of loue" and compassionate tears by revealing that Methley frequently experienced them too. Far from being the hysterical outpourings of a madwoman, as some of Kempe's contemporaries (and later scholarly observers) judged, they were the sweet profusions of Christ's most devout. Kempe's episodes of spiritual weeping were similarly endorsed by the next two marginal annotations in which Methley's name is explicitly mentioned; they appear in the outer margins of fol. 33v ("so fa RM | & f Norto*n* | of Wakenes & | of þe passion") and fol. 85r ("father M. | was wont | so to doo").[9] Finally, and even more surprisingly, the Red Ink Annotator likens Methley to a woman, "owt [of] hir mende," seemingly as a result of having recently delivered a child, whom Kempe comforted and prayed for in chapter 75 of her *Book*. In the outer margin of fol. 86v, next to the passage which describes Kempe's first visit to the new mother's home, the annotator added "d. R. fow | dyd so" to the mention made of "þe seke woman þ*a*t was alienyd of hir witte."[10] The alienation of mind that this woman experienced was seen to be akin to Methley's. So recharacterized, her apparent illness takes on a new, spiritual cast; indeed, her professed ability to see "many fayr awngelys a-bowte [Kempe]" suggests that her visionary sight may indeed bear a rightful similitude to Methley's.[11] The annotator's use of the past tense in all four annotations indicates that they were written after Methley's death in 1528, but the citations of his name in the margins of Kempe's *Book* seek to rekindle the memory of his exemplary devotion in the minds of later readers, especially Methley's brothers at Mount Grace, through the spiritual kinship that he shares with Kempe.

Far more numerous than the direct references to Methley, however, are the verbal and symbolic annotations that are suggestive of his devotional practices and contemplative theology. The Red Ink Annotator draws the reader's attention to episodes of Kempe's crying with verbal cues to her "ter*es*"[12] and, more enigmatically, with line drawings of a "3-pronged foliate image" that Kelly Parsons has termed a "weeping or tears symbol" (fig. 7.1).[13] Likely not coincidentally, a similar symbol also appears in the sole surviving manuscript copy containing Methley's *Scola*, *Dormitorium*, and *Refectorium*, Cambridge, Trinity College MS O.2.56. On fol. 18r of the *Scola*, in the upper margin, to the right of the word "lachrimis," a cloverleaf-like image appears (fig. 7.2). At the bottom of the page, a different hand inserted a related sign with the following note: "Velle quod dilectus vult scilicet morari [*sic*] in carne, et tamen affectuose et cum lachrimis" (To will what the Beloved wills namely to die to the flesh, and yet affectionately and with tears).[14] In the passage to which this note was supplied, Methley explains why uniting one's will to Christ's is inherently a contradictory act. It requires the martyrdom of one's desire, and yet one must desire this martyrdom; one comes to will as Christ but still wills with one's own will;[15] and, as the note recapitulates, one's very flesh must be both put to death and embraced as the fitting medium through which one's tearful languor for Christ is expressed. Only one who has undergone such an experience understands how willing and unwilling can harmoniously coincide in Christ's will, and Methley holds himself up as such an expert, not to set himself over his fellow monks, but to provide an imitable model of a (transitorily) perfected will. And, as we will see, Kempe's experiences of union with Christ are similarly highlighted as exemplary to the Carthusians of Mount Grace, though with a bit more editorial assistance from her Red Ink Annotator.

The coincidence of the cloverleaf-like symbols in Additional MS 61823 and Trinity College MS O.2.56 may additionally reveal a common symbolic annotation for tears among Carthusian reading circles or a specific symbol used by and/or for Methley, who, as he writes in the *Scola*, was once so "perfusus eram lacrimis, et quodammodo rebaptizatus" (soaked with tears, he was in a certain way rebaptized).[16] More significantly, both manuscripts share other verbal and symbolic annotations—from line drawings of human faces and hearts to the marginal annotation "oracio," marking out passages for prayer—which suggest that Methley's contemplative treatises and Kempe's *Book* were not handled all that differently by their later scribal readers.[17] With the right hermeneutical apparatus, both could be profitably read for their insights into the contemplative life.

Not surprisingly given the titles of his autobiographical contemplative treatises, Methley was interested in giving expression to the soul's cultivation and manifestation of love for God, particularly "sensible divine love," for as he writes in his *Experimentum veritatis*, "si sensibilem diuinu*m* amore*m* h*ab*uit . . . ei credendu*m* est, quia nullo modo in eius amore, s*cilicet* diuino, errare potest" (if one has sensible divine love . . . he is to be believed, since in no way is he able to err in

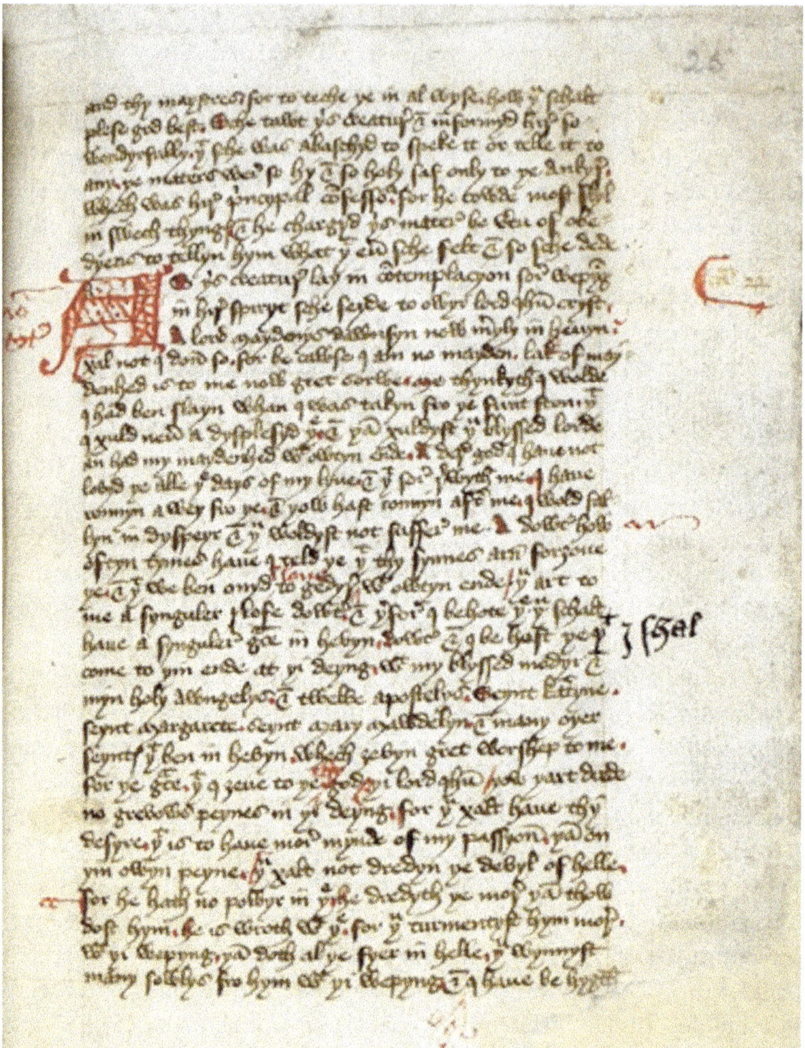

Fig. 7.1. London, British Library, MS Additional 61823 (*The Book of Margery Kempe*), fol. 25r. © British Library Board.

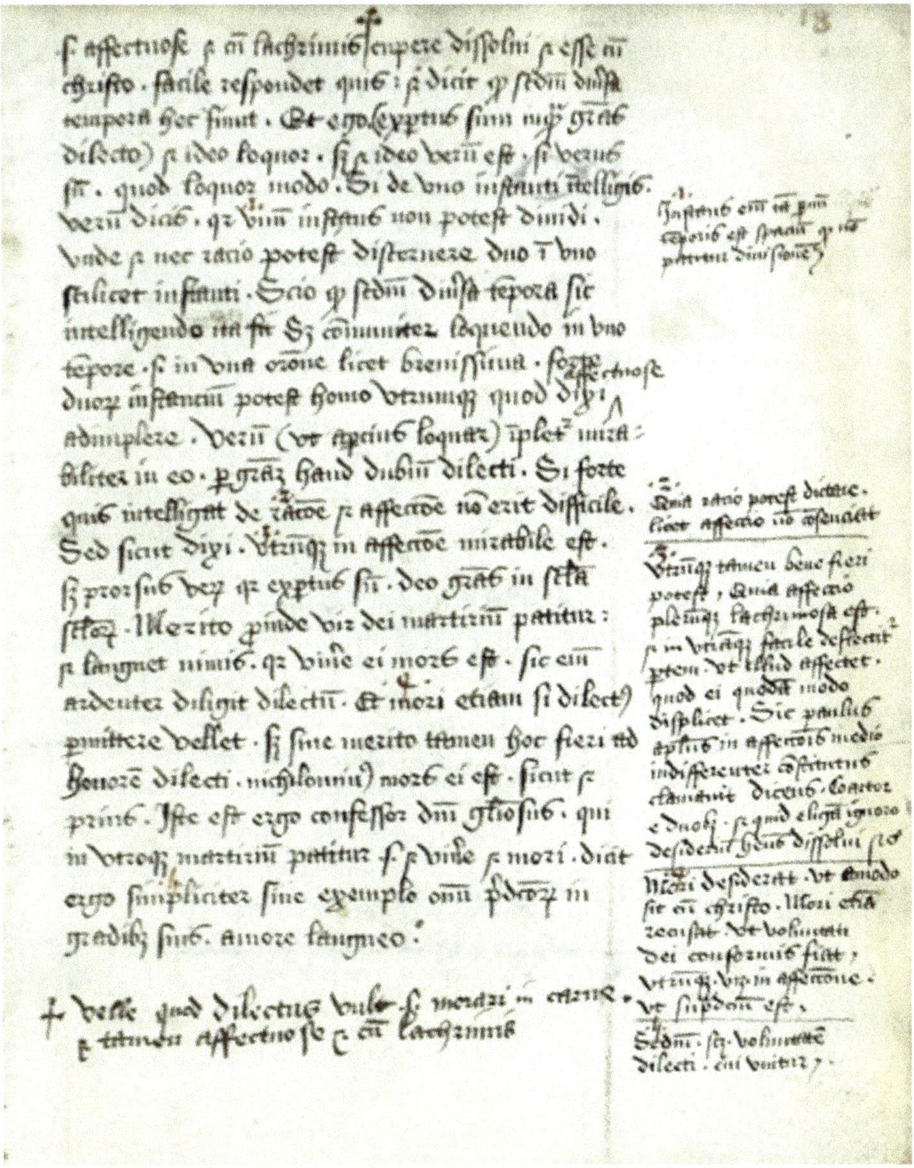

Fig. 7.2. Cambridge, Trinity College, MS O.2.56 (Methley's *Scola*), fol. 18r. By permission of the Master and Fellows of Trinity College Cambridge.

his love, namely divine love).[18] The Red Ink Annotator similarly makes love abound, both verbally and symbolically, on the pages of Additional MS 61823. Flames, hearts, and approving declarations of Kempe's "feruent loue" and "langor amoris" recall, among many other passages, the opening chapter of Methley's *Scola* in which he explains how "amor iste est status animi delectatione sensibili vulnerans et sanans, sanans et vulnerans, ita vt languor sit semper comes amoris ac amor languoris" (love is the state of the soul wounding and healing, healing and wounding, with sensible delight, such that languor is always the companion of love, and love of languor).[19] And the marginal gloss "ebrietatis sancta" found on fol. 48r of the Additional manuscript recalls not only Methley's own experience of "holy drunkenness" in contemplation that he details in his *Refectorium*[20] but also his fifth gloss on the third chapter of *Diuina caligo ignorancie*, in which he asserts:

> cum ad spiritualem mentis quietem perueneris in quadem ebrietate, tam sopiuntur sensus corporis et anime, quod homo quodammodo quiescit in caligne ignorancie, sicut ebrius vel sompnolentus non multum attendit quid agitur circa se ab alijs, vel quid ipse dixerit, fecerit, locutus fuerit de se.[21]
>
> ———
>
> [when you achieve a spiritual quiet of the mind in a kind of drunkenness, the senses of the body and soul are so asleep, in such a way that the person rests in the darkness of ignorance, as if drunk or drowsy, he does not attend very much to what is done around him by others, or to what he himself says, does, or speaks about himself.]

As the Red Ink Annotator's gloss highlights for Kempe's readers, she once was "so delectabely fed wyt*h* þe swet dalyawns of owr Lorde & so fulfilled of hys lofe" that she wept and stumbled "as a drunkyn man."[22] Instructed by Methley's writings, the Red Ink Annotator could see Kempe's seemingly besotted behavior for what it truly was: the outward manifestations of a holy woman whose soul delighted in the spiritual quiet of Christ's love.

The symbol for the Divine Name, "ihc," also frequently appears in the margins and rubricated capitals of the Additional manuscript, usually to draw the reader's attention to mentions of Christ in the text.[23] Although devotion to the Divine Name was not unique to Methley during this period,[24] his numerous accounts of his repeated invocations of the name "Iesu" in prayer in his *Dormitorium* and *Refectorium* are striking, especially when read on the manuscript page; frequently Jesus's name was written over and over, often for lines at a time.[25] Methley explains the importance of calling out Jesus's name in his *Scola*:

> Remedium vnum habeo, contra omnes temptaciones: Turris fortissima nomen domini, ad ipsam curret iustus et exaltabitur. In nomine Iesu, demonia eicio, linguis loquor nouis, serpentes tollo, et si mortiferum quid bibero, michi / non nocet; super egros manus impono et bene habent. Hec omnia spiritualiter impleo.[26]
>
> ———
>
> [I have one remedy against all temptations. The name of Jesus is the strongest tower; the just will run to it and be exalted. In the name of Jesus, I cast out demons; I speak in new tongues; I take up serpents; and if what I drink is deadly, it does not harm me; I lay my hands on the sick, and they are restored to health. I fulfill all these things spiritually.]

So too for the Red Ink Annotator. He inserted "ihc" in the outer margin beside the passage in Kempe's *Book* describing her first, salvific encounter with Christ: "þan on a tym, as sche lay a-loone and hir kepars wer fro hir, owyr merciful Lord Crist Ih*esu*, eu*yr* to be trostyd, worshypd be hys name, neu*yr* forsakyng hys s*er*uawnt in tyme of need, aperyd to hys creatur."[27] For the miraculous healing that Christ wrought in the ailing Kempe, his name indeed deserved to be "worshypd," and the Red Ink Annotator's annotation does just that.

More transgressively, at least to some scholarly readings of medieval orthodoxy, the Red Ink Annotator draws a wavy line down the outer margin of the vision in which Christ seems to promise Kempe that those whose thoughts are rightly occupied in contemplation may not sin for a time: "Lo, dowt*yr*, I haue ȝoue þe swech a lofe þ*a*t þu xalt non ypoc*ri*te be þ*er*in. And, dowt*yr*, þu xalt neu*yr* lesyn tyme whil þu art ocupijd þ*er*in, for ho-so thynkyth wel he may not synnyn for þe tyme. & þe Deuyl knowy*th* not þe holy thowt*ys* þ*a*t I ȝeue þe ne no man in erde knowy*th* how | wel & holily þu art ocupijd wy*th* me."[28] Such a passage resonates with the theology of Marguerite Porete's *Mirror of Simple Souls*. But, contrary to what we might expect given the wide circulation in standard canon law collections of the Council of Vienne's disposition, *Ad nostrum*, with its condemnation of the Beghard teaching that truly free souls are in no danger of sinning, this passage did not worry the correcting hand of the Red Ink Annotator.[29] Far from it. He draws attention to it, noting its significance. The approbative nature of this annotation is not surprising when viewed alongside Methley's glosses on similarly challenging passages in the *Speculum*. To cite one example, in his first gloss to chapter 126, he writes, "Peccatum est in nobis quamdiu viuimus, vel peccati pena, nisi pro tanto pro quanto quis vnitur Deo voluntate et raptu" (Sin, or the penalty of sin, remains in us for as long as we live, unless for as much or for as great as someone is united to God by will and rapture).[30] Indeed, Methley was taught this very lesson by God in a vision that he records in his *Dormitorium*: "nichil iniquitatum in illam scilicet contemplacionem intrat. Ergo peccatum non impediet te" (no iniquity enters into contemplation; therefore, sin will not impede you).[31]

The close of Methley's prologue to his translation of *The Cloud of Unknowing* reveals that he was not unfamiliar with the condemned errors of Free Spiritism. With respect to the degree of union that the soul is able to achieve with the Godhead *in via*, he maintains, "Vnio autem est illorum duorum copulacio, quorum vtrumque manet in sua substancia. Et hoc contra heresim Begardorum" (Union is the joining of God and the soul, both of whom remain in their own substance. And this is against the heresy of the Beghards).[32] Not unexpected, then, are Methley's glosses to the *Speculum* in which he warns the readers against certain misreadings of the radical oneing to the Divine that the text describes. In such a union, the essence of the soul does not change into God such that it ceases to be; rather, "Et ideo dicitur extra suum statum, quia tensione dileccionis tendit in infinitum, quod Deus ipse est" (It is said to be outside of its state, since by the tension of love it stretches into infinity, which is God himself).[33] The Red Ink Annotator similarly forestalls any misreading of the union that Kempe experienced with the Godhead. In chapter 22 of Kempe's *Book*, he intervened in the scene in which Kempe, while in contemplation, expressed to Christ her concern over the state of her salvation. She feared that because she was not a virgin, she would not be allowed to join the "maydenys [who] dawnsyn now m*er*yly in Heuyn."[34] To Kempe's desperate plea for mercy, Christ responded with the following question: "A, dowt*yr* how oftyn-tymes haue I teld þe þ*a*t thy synnes arn forȝoue þe & þ*a*t we ben onyd wyt*h*-owtyn ende?"[35] The Red Ink Annotator, however, did not allow the question to stand as it was originally copied in the manuscript. He inserted the prepositional phrase "in loue" interlinearly after the past participle "onyd." So corrected, there could be no danger of reading Christ's words as declaring that Kempe's soul had been substantially united to the Godhead. They united in love, not substance, just as Methley asserted was proper: "tam bene creauit, tam bene vnit sibi per dileccionem" (as God created well, so too he unites to himself through love well).[36] God always stands in relation to the soul as Creator to created, and, thus, his being always remains radically other than the soul's, uncontainable, ever exceeding human cognition.

The Red Ink Annotator reminds readers of this foundational theological distinction in his correction to chapter 85 of Kempe's *Book*, which describes the prayer of thanksgiving that she offered after an experience of deep contemplation of the Godhead: "& þa*n* sche thankyd God of al, for thorw þes gostly syt*ys* hir affeccyon was al drawyn in-to þe manhod of *Cri*st & in-to þe mynde of hys Passyon vn-to þ*at* tyme þ*at* it plesyd owr Lord to ȝeuyn hir vndirstondyng of hys *vndirstondabyl* Godhed."[37] With the interlinear insertion of the prefix *in-* before "vndirstondabyl," he makes clear that God always remains "<in>vndirstondabyl" to human understanding, even of those most illumined by the Spirit. Methley affirms this very point in his first gloss to chapter 34 of the *Diuina caligo ignorancie*:

> Nullus sanctus, nullus angelus in celo, contemplatur per speculum in enigmate, sed clare, nude, et aperte, facie ad faciem, quamuis Deum videant in creaturis; sed intencio autoris videtur insinuare quod cum Deus sit incomprehensibilis, nunquam posset in incomprehensibilem Deum ferri, nisi manu Dei supra nostram cognicionem.[38]
>
> ——
>
> [No saint or angel in heaven gazes through a mirror darkly, but clearly, nakedly, and openly, face-to-face, although they see God in creatures; but the intention of the author seems to suggest that since God is incomprehensible, one could never be carried into the incomprehensible God, except by the hand of God above our cognition.]

This side of death, contemplation of the Godhead never attains perfect, total comprehension; the Beatific Vision is only enjoyed by the perfected in heaven. Thus, the Red Ink Annotator had to clarify that heaven still awaited Kempe, for now she was more akin to her readers than they might suspect: she was another *viator*.

On the other end of the spectrum of the Red Ink Annotator's corrections are his interventions into Kempe's visionary experiences, where he makes clear that she did not see what she saw corporeally but spiritually. On three different occasions, he insists on the "gostly" nature of her visions. Again, in chapter 22, he departs from the manuscript's original record of Christ's exchange with the anxious matron Kempe. Christ once declared, "for-as-mech as þu art a mayden in þi sowle, I xal take þe be þe on hand in Hevyn & my Modyr be þe oþ*er* hand, & so xalt þu dawnsyn in Hevyn wy*th* oþ*er* holy maydens & v*ir*gynes, for I may clepyn þe dere a-bowte & myn owyn derworthy derlyng," but now, with an interlinear correction, declared that she shall "dawnsyn <gostly> in Hevyn," lest there be any confusion about where Kempe's body actually was in such a vision.[39] Similarly, in chapter 35, when Kempe's writer claimed that she once took hold of God the Father's hand in a vision, the Red Ink Annotator set her account straight with a "gostle" interlinear insertion: "And þan | þe Fadyr toke hir be þe hand <gostle> in hir sowle be-for þe Sone & þe Holy Gost & þe Modyr of Ih*es*u and alle þe xij apostelys & Seynt Kateryn & Seynt Margarete & many oþ*er* seynt*ys* & holy v*ir*gynes wy*th* gret multitude of awngelys."[40] Finally, in chapter 86, he intervened in Christ's expression of gratitude for the unfailing hospitality that Kempe extended to him and his mother, for surely not bodily did Kempe share her bed with Christ and Mary: "And also, dowt*yr*, I thank þe for alle þe tymys þ*at* þu hast herberwyd me & my blissyd Modyr in þi bed <gostly>."[41] Always "gostly" did Kempe populate her visions, neatly bound within the Augustinian definition of "spiritual vision," according to the Red Ink Annotator's reading. For, as Methley attests in the first gloss to chapter 57 of the *Speculum*, "Oculo corporali nec visa fuit nec vnquam videbitur Trinitas Sancta, sed spirituali, et hoc pro modulo vie, nam purius erit in peruencione" (The Holy Trinity has not nor will it ever be seen by the bodily eye, but by the spiritual eye, and this according to the manner of being *in via*, for in the yet-to-come it will be more pure).[42] Indeed, nearly *verbum pro verbo* with the *Cloud* author, Methley's translation chastises those who seek God with inappropriate curiosity in contemplative prayer:

> quia peruertunt sensus suos corporales in seipsos in corpora sua contra naturam, et seipsos constringunt, quasi vellent intus videre

> per oculos suos corporales, et intus audire auribus suis, et sic de similibus sensibus, odoratu, gustu, tactu introrsus. Et sic se peruertunt contra cursum nature, et hac curiositate labo/rant ymaginacione sua tam indiscrete, quod tandem vertunt cerebrum in capitibus suis.[43]
>
> [they turn their corporeal senses into themselves in their bodies against nature, and they strain themselves, as if they wish to see inwardly through their corporeal eyes, and to hear inwardly with their ears, and so forth concerning all similar senses, smelling, tasting, touching inwardly. And thus they turn themselves against the course of nature, and with this curiosity of their imagination they labor so indiscreetly that finally they turn their brain around in their heads.]

Concern over the curiosity of Kempe's imagination seems to have prompted the Red Ink Annotator to strike through the most dramatic moment of the vision detailed in chapter 85 in which she saw Christ cut down the middle of his chest with a dagger:

> Than, as sche lay stille in þe qwer, wepyng & mornyng for hir synnys, sodeynly sche was in a man*er* of slep. & a-non sche saw wyt*h* hir gostly eye owr Lordys body lying be-forn hir, & hys heuyd, as hir thowt, fast be hir wyt*h* hys blissyd face vpward, þe semeliest man þ*at* eu*yr* myth be seen er thowt. ~~And þa*n* cam on wyt*h* a baselard-knyfe to hir syght & kytt þ*at* p*re*cyows body al on long in þe brest~~.[44]

Likely troubled, as both the *Cloud* author and Methley would have been, that in this vision Kempe too nearly "make[s] such a God as it pleases [her] to make [and] invents much more curiously than Christ was ever depicted on earth," he decided to remove this passage from the text.[45] Or, at least, he nearly does. Readers can still read the passage under his red ink, because he did not commit as bold an act of correction as he could have. He did not scrape off or completely efface her words. Why did he stay his hand? Out of respect for the seer? I think so.

Read through both the Red Ink Annotator's annotations and corrections, Margery Kempe is transformed; she becomes, some might think, the unlikeliest of characters: a perfect model of the *vita contemplatiua* for a Carthusian monk. For, as he marginally remarks, we should indeed "no*ta* bene. | ei*us* p*er*fecc*ionem*" (note well her perfection).[46] With his guiding hand, she shares more than her tearful experiences with Richard Methley. She insists just as vehemently on the spiritual nature of her visions as Methley does: always "mentaliter" or "spiritualiter," never "corporaliter." Even more surprisingly, as I have argued, the Red Ink Annotator effects Kempe's transformation by reading her through a theological hermeneutic shaped by Methley's translations of and glosses on *The Cloud of Unknowing* and *The Mirror of Simple Souls*. Even though the Red Ink Annotator did not know that he was reading a woman-authored text through another woman-authored text, especially one that was burned at the stake with its author for heresy,[47] we need to be more sensitive to how Carthusian reading practices were informed by women's theologies and visionary experiences. For Carthusian libraries were not only populated with the works of Augustine, the Pseudo-Dionysius, Richard Rolle, and Walter Hilton, but also with those of Mechthild of Hackeborn, Catherine of Siena, Bridget of Sweden, and maybe even Margery Kempe's onetime spiritual director, Julian of Norwich,[48] and the words of these women were handled with just as much care and devotion by their Carthusian readers and copyists as those of their male shelf-mates, if not more.

Notes

1. For an overview of the spiritual and scribal activities of the Carthusians at Mount Grace, see James Hogg, "Mount Grace Charterhouse and Late Medieval English Spirituality," Analecta Cartusiana 82:3 (Salzburg: Institut für Anglistik und Amerikanistik, Universität Salzburg, 1980), 1–43. For the classic study of the history of the Carthusian order in England, see E. Margaret Thompson, *The Carthusian Order in England* (London: Society for Promoting Christian Knowledge, 1930).

2. Scholars, beginning with the first editors of the manuscript, Sanford Brown Meech and Hope Emily Allen, have noted that there are several scribal hands operating as annotators, correctors, and rubricators to Additional MS 61823, the earliest of which may have been the hand of the main scribe of the text, according to Joel Fredell. The question of the exact number of hands that appear in the manuscript has sparked no small debate among Kempe scholars. Recently, Fredell has argued that there are six different sets of annotations in the manuscript, involving as many as six different hands, which he identifies on

the basis of the color of ink and appearance of the script: Little Brown, Big Brown, Big Black, Ruby Paraph, Big Red N, and Red Ink Annotator. See Joel Fredell, "Design and Authorship in the *Book of Margery Kempe*," *Journal of the Early Book Society* 12 (2009): 1–28 (3). Most recently, however, Kathryn Kerby-Fulton has countered Fredell's thesis that there were at least two but likely three different scribes annotating in red ink; she has judged the red ink annotations, corrections, and rubrications to be the work of one scribe who returned to the manuscript repeatedly and sporadically over many years, not always employing exactly the same script or using the same batch of red ink. See Kathryn Kerby-Fulton, Maidie Hilmo, and Linda Olson, *Opening Up Middle English Manuscripts: Literary and Visual Approaches* (Ithaca: Cornell University Press, 2012), 238–39. With respect to the disagreements between Fredell and Kerby-Fulton, I agree with Kerby-Fulton's assessment.

3. For discussions of the Red Ink Annotator's interest in *discretio spirituum*, see both Rosalynn Voaden, *God's Words, Women's Voices: The Discernment of Spirits in the Writing of Late-Medieval Women Visionaries* (York: York Medieval Press, 1999), 153; and Kerby-Fulton, Hilmo, and Olson, *Opening Up Middle English Manuscripts*, 236–38. For his interest in adapting the manuscript for lay female use and for an accessible, comprehensive account of his annotations, corrections, and rubrications, see Kelly Parsons, "The Red Ink Annotator of *The Book of Margery Kempe* and His Lay Audience," in *The Medieval Professional Reader at Work: Evidence from Chaucer, Langland, Kempe, and Gower*, ed. Kathryn Kerby-Fulton and Maidie Hilmo (Victoria: English Literary Studies, 2001), 143–216; see also Johanne Paquette, "Male Approbation in the Extant Glosses to the *Book of Margery Kempe*," in *Women and the Divine in Literature before 1700: Essays in Memory of Margot Louis*, ed. Kathryn Kerby-Fulton (Victoria, BC: English Literary Series, 2009), 153–69. For his interest in comparing Kempe's affective mysticism with that of Richard Methley, see Karma Lochrie, *Margery Kempe and Translations of the Flesh* (Philadelphia: University of Pennsylvania Press, 1991), 209–20.

4. Methley's three autobiographical contemplative treatises survive in one manuscript, Cambridge, Trinity College MS O.2.56 (1160), which N. R. Ker tentatively dates to the end of the fifteenth century and places at Mount Grace Priory. See N. R. Ker, *Medieval Libraries of Great Britain: A List of Surviving Books*, 2nd ed. (London: Offices of the Royal Historical Society, 1964), 132. Methley's *Scola amoris languidi* (fols. 1r–24v) was written in 1484; *Dormitorium dilecti dilecti* (fols. 25r–48r) in 1485; and *Refectorium salutis* (fols. 49r–70v) in 1487. Two other works by Methley survive in London, Public Record Office Collection SP I/239: *Experimentum veritatis* (fols. 262r–265v, which begin at chapter 14) and *to hew heremyte—a pystyl of solitary lyfe nowadays* (fols. 266r–267v). In these works, Methley references other works that he had written but that do not survive: *Defensio solitarie siue contemplatiue*

vite (cited in *Experimentum veritatis*, fol. 264v), *Cellarium* (cited in *Dormitorium dilecti dilecti*, fol. 42r), *De maria nomine et sacramento altaris* (cited in *Refectorium salutis*, fol. 65v), and *Triuium excellencie* (cited in *Refectorium salutis*, fols. 66v–67r). For an insightful account of the unique conjunction of the autobiographical and mystical in the authorial persona that Methley constructs in these texts, especially as this persona compares with that constructed by Richard Rolle, see Katherine Zieman, "Monasticism and the Public Contemplative in Late Medieval England: Richard Methley and His Spiritual Formation," *Journal of Medieval and Early Modern Studies* 42 (2012): 699–724.

5. Methley's translations of the *Cloud* and the *Mirror* survive in one manuscript, Cambridge, Pembroke College MS 221, which was copied by William Darker (d. 1513), a monk of Sheen charterhouse, and annotated and corrected in part by James Grenehalgh (d. 1530), who originally professed at Sheen and then was a hospes at Coventry and finally at Hull. Methley wrote both translations in 1491 for his confrère Thurstan Watson. *Diuina caligo ignorancie* is found on fols. 1v–39v and *Speculum animarum simplicium* on fols. 41r–102r.

6. Augustine defines three forms of vision in his *De Genesi ad litteram*: "Hence let us call the first kind of vision corporeal, because it is perceived through the body and presented to the senses of the body. The second will be called spiritual, for whatever is not a body, and yet is something, is rightly called spirit: and certainly the image of an absent body, though it resembles a body, is not itself a body any more than is the act of vision by which it is perceived. The third kind will be intellectual from the word intellect. . . . [S]piritual vision is more excellent than corporeal, and intellectual is more excellent than spiritual"; *The Literal Meaning of Genesis: Books 7–12*, trans. J. H. Taylor, Ancient Christian Writers: The Works of the Fathers in Translation XLII (Mahwah, NJ: Paulist Press, 1982), 186, 213. The Augustinian position on the three forms of vision was profoundly influential on later theological and contemplative treatises. In chapter 17 of his *Experimentum veritatis*, Richard Methley rearticulates the Augustinian position in his discussion of the five-step discernment process of visions or auditions: "Quarto modus disc*er*ni debet vtrum s*cilicet* in extasi an in raptu in sp*irit*uali an in intellectuali aut in corporali visione fuerit. Estimo si p*r*oprie accipiant*ur* in suo saltem loco semp*er* in libris contemplatiuoru*m* inueneri q*uod* extasis & sp*irit*ualis visio q*ue* formas rer*um* accipiunt in sp*irit*u. Raptus si purus est & intellectualis visio sine formis visibiliu*m* corporalis vero, quod patet ocula" (fol. 263r) (In the fourth step it ought to be discerned namely whether it happened in ecstasy or in rapture, and whether in spiritual, intellectual, or corporeal vision. I think that in the books of contemplatives, it is always found that ecstasy and spiritual vision receive the forms of things in the spirit, if properly received in their own place at least. Rapture, if pure, and intellectual vision are without corporeal forms of visible things, but are apparent to the eyes). See "Self-Verification of Visionary

Phenomena: Richard Methley's *Experimentum veritatis*," in *Kartäusermystik und -Mystiker: Dritter Internationaler Kongress über die Kartäusergeschichte und -Spiritualität*, ed. Michael Sargent, Analecta Cartusiana 55:2 (Salzburg: Institut für Anglistik und Amerikanistik Universität Salzburg, 1981), 121–37 (128). All translations are my own unless specified otherwise.

7. The heresy of the Free Spirit, condemned at the Council of Vienne (1311–12), purportedly attempted, among other things, to overcome the body altogether this side of death through contemplative self-abnegation. The condemnation of this heresy and its relation to the Red Ink Annotator's theological hermeneutic is discussed at greater length later in the essay.

8. *The Book of Margery Kempe*, ed. Sanford Brown Meech and Hope Emily Allen, EETS, o.s., 212 (London: Oxford University Press, 1961), 29/9–17.

9. This first annotation was added to the following passage from chapter 28 of the *Book*: "& sche had hem [episodes of crying] so oftyn-tymes þ*a*t þei maydn hir ryth weyke in hir bodyly myghtys, & namely yf sche herd of owyr Lord*ys* Passyon" (68/30–69/1); and the second to the following passage from chapter 73: "Wha*n* sche beheld þis sygth in hir sowle, sche fel down in þe feld a-mong þe pepil. Sche cryid, sche roryd, sche wept as þow sche xulde a brostyn þ*er*-with" (174/19–22).

10. Ibid., 178/8. Though this annotation could have referred to someone else with the initials "d. R.," I list it as a reference to Methley given how his name appears in the *carta* of the Carthusian General Chapter, which records his death in 1528: "Domnus Richardus Methlei, monachus professus et vicarius domus Montisgracie" (Lord Richard Methley, professed monk and vicar of the house of Mount Grace). See Hogg's introduction to his edition of Methley's letter to Hugh the hermit: "Richard Methley: *to hew heremyte—a pystyl of solitary lyfe nowadays*," in *Boniface of Savoy; Carthusian and Archbishop of Canterbury, 1207–1270*, ed. James Hogg, Analecta Cartusiana 31 (Salzburg: Institut für Anglistik und Amerikanistik Universität Salzburg, 1977), 91–119 (100).

11. *The Book of Margery Kempe*, 178/12–13.

12. For Parsons's detailed tables of all of the red ink annotations, corrections, and rubrications found in Additional MS 61823, see her article, "The Red Ink Annotator of *The Book of Margery Kempe* and His Lay Audience," 164–216. The four verbal annotations that highlight episodes of Kempe's crying appear on the following folios: 23r/26–27 ("ters w^t | loue."), 68v/20–21 ("wel of ters."), 89r/12 ("ter*es*"), and 92v/24–26 (".racio hic | ponit*ur* q*ua*re | sic plor*ans* clama*ui*t").

13. The tears symbol appears on the following folios: 19r/8, 21v/6, 24r/18–19, 24r/34, 25r/34, 29v/19–21, 47v/1, 51v/21–28, 58r/1, 65r/1, 66r/1, 74v/1, 77r/33, 78v/1, 89r/12, 104v/34. For more images of such marks, see Paquette, "Male Approbation in the Extant Glosses to the *Book of Margery Kempe*," 165–69.

14. This leaf is not an insertion mark; for the facsimile of this manuscript, see James Hogg, ed., *Mount Grace Charterhouse and Late Medieval Spirituality*, vol. 2, *Trinity College Cambridge MS O.2.56*, Analecta Cartusiana 64 (Salzburg: Institut für Anglistik und Amerikanistik Universität Salzburg, 1978), 35. For a transcription of this manuscript, see "The *Scola amoris languidi* of Richard Methley of Mount Grace Charterhouse Transcribed from Trinity College Cambridge MS. O.2.56," in *Kartäusermystik und -Mystiker: Dritter Internationaler Kongress über die Kartäusergeschichte und -Spiritualität*, ed. James Hogg, Analecta Cartusiana 55:2 (Salzburg: Institut für Anglistik und Amerikanistik Universität Salzburg, 1981), 138–65 (159). I have emended "morari" to "mori" in my translation because "to die," rather than "to delay," fits better with Methley's description of the abnegation of one's will to Christ's as a kind of martyrdom.

15. "Loco nono ponitur principaliter, quod languet homo amore, quia voluntati dilecti suam (vt dignum est) voluntatem vnit voluntarie, et ideo ei martirium est pre nimio languore; puto quod nullus mortalis potest intelligere nisi expertus, quomodo in vno homine hec duo sensibiliter vel actualiter conueniant, / scilicet affectuose et cum lachrimis cupere dissolui et esse cum christo" ("The *Scola amoris languidi* of Richard Methley," fol. 17v–18r, p. 159) (In the ninth place it principally happens that man languishes with love, since he unites his will, when it is appropriate, to the will of the Beloved, and thus it is a martyrdom for him because of his great languor; I think that no mortal, except one who has experienced this, is able to understand, how in one man these two things should sensibly or actively come together, namely with feeling and with tears desire to be dissolved and to be with Christ).

16. Ibid., fol. 11r, p. 151.

17. A human face is found in the rubricated capital "I" on fol. 62v, which opens chapter 26 of Methley's *Refectorium*; in the Additional MS, similar drawings of human faces appear on fols. 19r/9–11, 49v/29–31, 79r/19–21, 82v/20–22, 96r/19–21, 100r/19–21, 100v/19–21, 101v/12–14, 105r/1. Two interlocking hearts were placed over the "est amor" of the line "Iesus est amor meus," which is found near the end of the closing prayer to Methley's *Scola* on fol. 22r; in the Additional MS, heart symbols appear on fols. 2r/2, 44v/8–9, 78v/9–10, 102r/9, 106r/3–4. And twice on fol. 15v, in the second half of chapter 16 of Methley's *Scola*, the word "oracio" appears to mark passages of exclamatory prayer that begin with the vocative "O"; in the Additional MS, the marginal annotation "oracio" appears on fol. 121v/1.

18. *Experimentum veritatis*, chap. 17, fol. 263r, p. 127.

19. *Scola amoris languidi*, chap. 1, fol. 2v, pp. 139, 140. The variations on "love" annotations that appear in the Additional MS are as follows: "loue" (fols. 14v/32, 15r/27, 40r/29), "no*ta* | feruent loue" (fol. 20r/7), "ters w^t | loue" (fol. 23r/26–27), a red box around an earlier brown ink annotation of

"loue" (fol. 24v/3–5), "singularis. C*risti*. | amatrix" (fol. 26r/5–6), "Ihc e*st* amor. t[u]*us*" (fol. 38v/7), "ig*n*is di*uin*i | amor*is*" enclosed in a line drawing of flames (fol. 43v/10–16), "amor | i*m*pacie*n*s" (fol. 52v/10–11), "fire of | loue" (fol. 54r/9–10), "Abu*n*dance | of loue" (fol. 67r/27–28), "langor amor*is*" (fol. 68r/19), "no*ta* | charit*atem* ei*us*" (fol. 68v/12–13), "fyre of loue" (fol. 71v/17–18), "Amor i*m*pacie*n*s" (fol. 72v/30), "pryk of loue" (fol. 75r/6), "no*ta* | loue" (fol. 76v/26–27), "no*ta* | la*n*gyng loue," (fol. 85v/29–30), "caritas di*uin*a" (f. 88r/5), "p*er*fect*a* caritas | foras mittit ti[morem]" (fol. 89r/4–5), "la*n*gyng loue" (fol. 96r/18), "no*ta* | feruor of loue" (fol. 96v/1–2).

20. See *Refectorium salutis*, chap. 29, fols. 64r–v; see "A Mystical Diary: The *Refectorium salutis* of Richard Methley of Mount Grace Charterhouse," in *Kartäusermystik und -Mystiker: Dritter Internationaler Kongress über die Kartäusergeschichte und -Spiritualität*, ed. James Hogg, Analecta Cartusiana 55:1 (Salzburg: Institut für Anglistik und Amerikanistik Universität Salzburg, 1981), 208–38 (230–31).

21. *Diuina caligo ignorancie*, chap. 3, gloss E, fol. 5va; see *Diuina caligo ignorancie: A Latin Glossed Version of "The Cloud of Unknowing,"* ed. John Clark, Analecta Cartusiana 119:3 (Salzburg: Institut für Anglistik und Amerikanistik Universität Salzburg, 2009), 12.

22. *The Book of Margery Kempe*, 98/28–29.

23. The marginal appearances of the symbol for the Divine Name occur on the following folios: 1r/1, 2r/2 (in a red heart), 2v/1, 4v/13, 26v/12, 51v/1, 87v/1, 106v/1, 110r/4; and the appearances of the symbol in rubricated capitals occur on the following folios: 6r/20–22, 14r/1–3, 23v/13–15, 44v/25–27, 52v/1–3, 55v/16–18, 69r/12–14, 77v/20–22, 83r/26–28, 85r/7–9.

24. Though devotion to the Divine Name was revitalized in the late thirteenth century in part through the establishment of the feast of Corpus Christi, it did not receive liturgical observance in England until the middle of the fourteenth century when votive masses of the Divine Name appeared in liturgical books. Subsequently, likely in the early fifteenth century, the votive mass of the Divine Name transitioned to a feast day mass, as Richard W. Pfaff has demonstrated. Francis Wormald's study of surviving English Benedictine liturgical calendars produced after about 1100 provides further evidence for Pfaff's claim; the feast day of the Divine Name, which was celebrated on August 7, is found in many fifteenth-century calendars and liturgical books. Devotion to the Divine Name infused the fourteenth-century writings of both Richard Rolle and Walter Hilton, as Denis Renevey has noted, but the cult did not receive widespread observance in England until the feast day mass was indulgenced by Robert Hallam, bishop of Salisbury, in 1411. See R.W. Pfaff, *New Liturgical Feasts in Later Medieval England* (Oxford: Clarendon Press, 1970), 62–83; Francis Wormald, *English Benedictine Kalendars after* A.D. *1100*, vol. 1, Henry Bradshaw Society 77 (London, 1939), 165; and Denis Renevey, "Name above

Names: The Devotion to the Name of Jesus from Richard Rolle to Walter Hilton's *Scale of Perfection I*," in *The Medieval Mystical Tradition, England, Ireland and Wales: Exeter Symposium VI*, ed. Marion Glasscoe (Cambridge: D. S. Brewer, 1999), 103–21. See also H. E. Allen, *Writings Ascribed to Richard Rolle*, Modern Language Association of America, Monograph Series 3 (London: Oxford University Press, 1927), 350–51.

25. See *Dormitorium dilecti dilecti*, chap. 21, fols. 36r–v; chap. 22, fol. 37r, in *Kartäusermystik und -Mystiker: Dritter Internationaler Kongress über die Kartäusergeschichte und -Spiritualität*, ed. James Hogg, Analecta Cartusiana 55:5 (Salzburg: Institut für Anglistik und Amerikanistik Universität Salzburg, 1982), 79–103; and *Refectorium salutis*, chap. 11, fol. 54v; chap. 25, fol. 62r.

26. *Scola amoris languidi*, chap. 14, fols. 13r–v, p. 153.

27. *The Book of Margery Kempe*, 8/10–14.

28. Ibid., 205/36–206/5.

29. See Kathryn Kerby-Fulton, *Books under Suspicion: Censorship and Tolerance of Revelatory Writing in Late Medieval England* (Notre Dame: University of Notre Dame Press, 2006), 260–71; and Sara Harris, "'In cordis tui scrinio conserva': Richard Methley, *The Cloud of Unknowing* and Reading for Affectivity," *Marginalia* 12 (2011): 14–26 (24).

30. *Speculum animarum simplicium*, chap. 126, Gloss A, fol. 79va; see *Speculum Animarum Simplicium: A Glossed Latin Version of "The Mirror of Simple Souls,"* vols. 1–2, ed. John Clark, Analecta Cartusiana 266 (Salzburg: Institut für Anglistik und Amerikanistik Universität Salzburg, 2010), 96. Similarly, in Gloss A to chap. 129, fol. 80rb, Methley asserts again that the soul through whom the Holy Spirit acts is not able to sin for a time: "Quicunque Spiritu Dei aguntur, hij filij sunt Dei; et cor regis in manu Domini, ad quodcunque voluerit vertet illud, et tunc homo non potest pro tanto peccare" (97) (Whosoever are led by the Holy Spirit are sons of God, and the heart of the king is in the hand of the Lord; he turns that one to whatever he wishes, and then the man is not able to sin for so much time).

31. *Dormitorium dilecti dilecti*, chap. 30, fol. 42v, p. 97.

32. *Diuina caligo ignorancie*, *Prologus*, fol. 1vb, p. 2.

33. *Speculum animarum simplicium*, chap. 156, Gloss B, fol. 88rb, p. 116.

34. *The Book of Margery Kempe*, 50/20.

35. Ibid., 50/31.

36. *Speculum animarum simplicium*, chap. 189, Gloss A, fol. 98rb, p. 139.

37. *The Book of Margery Kempe*, 208/24–28; emphasis mine.

38. *Diuina caligo ignorancie*, chap. 34, Gloss A, fol. 21rb, p. 51.

39. *The Book of Margery Kempe*, 52/26–31.

40. Ibid., 87/13–17.

41. Ibid., 214/5–7.

42. *Speculum animarum simplicium*, chap. 57, Gloss A, fol. 58vb, p. 45.

43. *Diuina caligo ignorancie*, chap. 52, fols. 28vb–29ra, p. 69. In the original Middle English version of the *Cloud*, this passage reads: "þei t*ur*ne þeire bodily wittes inwards to þeire body aȝens þe cou*r*s of kynde; & streynyn hem, as þei wolde see inwards wiþ þeire bodily iȝen, & heren inwards wiþ þeire eren, & so forþe of alle þeire wittes, smellen, taasten, & felyn inwards. & þus þei reuerse hem aȝens þe cou*r*s of ky*n*de, & wiþ þis coriouste þei t*r*auayle þeire ymaginac*io*n so vndiscreetly, þat at þe laste þei t*ur*ne here brayne i*n* here hedes"; see *The Cloud of Unknowing and the Book of Privy Counselling*, ed. Phyllis Hodgson, EETS, o.s., 218 (London: Oxford University Press, 1944), 96/17–24.

44. *The Book of Margery Kempe*, 208/3–10.

45. *Diuina caligo ignorancie*, chap. 57, fol. 31va, p. 75; the full passage reads: "Homines isti aliquando curiositate sue ymaginacionis penetrant planetas, et foramen faciunt in firmamento, vt inde in celum aspiciant. Homines isti talem Deum facere volunt, qualem sibi facere delectant, et vestire ditissime vestibus, et in throno eum sedere fingere multo curiosius quam vnquam pictus fuit in terris" (These men will sometimes with the curiosity of their imagination penetrate the planets and make a hole in the firmament to then gaze upon heaven. These men wish to make such a God as it pleases them to make, and to clothe him richly in clothes, and to sit him upon a throne, to invent much more curiously than he was ever depicted on earth). In the original, Middle English version of the *Cloud*, this passage reads: "Þees me*n* willen su*m*tyme wiþ þe coriouste of here ymaginac*io*n peerce þe planets, & make an hole in þe firmame*n*t to loke in þ*er*ate. Þees men wil make a God as hem lyst, & cloþe*n* hym ful richely in cloþes, & set hy*m* in a trone, fer more curiously þan eu*er* was he depynted in þis erþe" (105/9–14).

46. This annotation appears on the outer margin of fol. 84r/12–13, beside the following passage in chapter 72: "So be p*r*ocesse of tyme hir mende & hir thowt was so ioynyd to God þ*a*t sche neu*yr* forȝate hym but co*n*tynualy had mende of hym & behelde hym in alle creaturys" (*The Book of Margery Kempe*, 172/11–14). My translation of "perfeccionem" as "perfection" should be read according to its strong teleological meaning, which was operative in the Middle Ages. Thus in noting her "perfeccionem," the annotator sought to draw attention to the fact that here Kempe attained the ultimate completion or end of her divinely created human nature.

47. Neither Methley nor the earlier Middle English translator of the *Mirror*, who is only known to scholars by his initials "M. N.," seems to have known the identity of the work's original author, Marguerite Porete, who was ultimately condemned as a heretic and burned at the stake for her work on June 1, 1310, in Paris, though they would have likely thought that the text was written *for* women, given its "decidedly feminine approach." On this point, see Kerby-Fulton, Hilmo, and Olson, *Opening Up Middle English Manuscripts*, 322. For

further information about the Middle English translation of the *Mirror*, see Marilyn Doiron, "'The Mirror of Simple Souls': A Middle English Translation," *Archivio italiano per la storia della pietà* 5 (1968): 241–355; Edmund College and Romana Guarnieri, "The Glosses by M. N. and Richard Methley to the *Mirror of Simple Souls*," *Archivio italiano per la storia della pietà* 5 (1968): 357–82; Michael G. Sargent, "'Le Mirouer des simples ames' and the English Mystical Tradition," *Abendländische Mystik im Mittelalter: Symposion Kloster Engelberg 1984*, ed. Kurt Ruh (Stuttgart: Metzler, 1986), 443–65; Sargent, "Marguerite Porete," in *Medieval Holy Women in the Christian Tradition, c. 1100–1500*, ed. Alastair Minnis and Rosalynn Voaden (Turnhout: Brepols, 2010), 291–309; and Nicholas Watson, "Melting into God the English Way: Deification in the Middle English Version of Marguerite Porete's *Mirouer des simples âmes anienties*," in *Prophets Abroad: The Reception of Continental Holy Women in Late-Medieval England*, ed. Rosalynn Voaden (Cambridge: D. S. Brewer, 1996), 19–49.

48. Marleen Cré offers compelling arguments in favor of assigning a Carthusian provenance to London, British Library, Additional MS 37790, the mid-fifteenth-century English manuscript that contains the sole surviving copy of the Short Text of Julian's *Revelation of Love*, in her *Vernacular Mysticism in the Charterhouse: A Study of London, British Library, MS Additional 37790* (Turnhout: Brepols, 2006).

Part III

The Making of a Field

York's 1981 *Manuscripts and Readers* Thirty Years Later

Foreword to Part III

The 1981 York conference organized by Derek Pearsall, and the subsequent publication of its proceedings as *Manuscripts and Readers in Fifteenth-Century England*, represents an important milestone in the field of late medieval English manuscript study.[1] It was a time of significant retrenchment in the U.K. academic sphere and a period of recent sad change in York, so the conference itself can also be said to have celebrated a significant coming-of-age for the Centre for Medieval Studies based in the King's Manor. Derek marked this liminal event in characteristic style by bringing together a number of established scholars to discuss the literary implications of manuscript study with some of his graduate students and others of their peer group. These younger scholars were obviously still relative beginners in the English fair field that he and Elizabeth Salter had carefully nourished as part of the exciting interdisciplinary adventure in higher education in the United Kingdom that York represented. It was a simple idea and designed as a small-scale event on the Heslington campus—hardly a rival to Kalamazoo, or later to Leeds—but the success of that first conference evolved naturally into a series of other small biennial meetings at York on a similar model, the proceedings of which were also published by D. S. Brewer.

Although none of us present probably realized its full significance at the time, the 1981 conference was the first of its kind to foster the kinds of networking and collaboration for postgraduates and early career academics that have proved so important for establishing new interdisciplinary and cross-disciplinary opportunities in our field and that now regularly attract levels of financial support that were simply unavailable and unimaginable thirty years ago. The initial York manuscripts conference was important in the development of such future projects since it confirmed that literary scholars were beginning to take stock of how the codicological landscape of English manuscript study and book history in the preprinting era was already being shaped by the ready availability of major bibliographical reference works and modern facsimile editions of important English literary manuscripts. It established clearly the need for future laborers in a predominantly literary-critical field to advance our understanding of the place of highly technical analytical and descriptive work in paleography, linguistic analysis, and textual study as distinctive features of a much broader and more varied research landscape. The topography and boundaries of that landscape continue to be explored as part of the research agenda so clearly set out by that 1981 conference: put simply, the 1981 conference demonstrated the need for literary scholars in the burgeoning field of English medieval studies to develop a properly nuanced understanding of the socioliterary milieus in which the books and texts which interest them were written, produced, disseminated, collected, and read in the English Middle Ages and beyond.

The essays in this part are written by scholars who were present at the 1981 York conference and whose work continues to explore core aspects of that agenda. For her contribution to the 1981 conference, Julia Boffey took as the theme the manuscript context of fifteenth-century courtly love lyrics. Thirty years on, for this volume of essays, she reflects upon her enhanced conceptual understanding of ideas of intentionality and context in a characteristically insightful exploration of the collocation of items now found in San Marino, Henry E. Huntington Library, MS HM 136, a single manuscript that has at its core a mid-fifteenth-century copy of the much-copied Middle English prose *Brut*. If the *Brut* represents an anchor text in this manuscript, Boffey argues, then the assortment of items added later and surrounding it represent an archival remnant of other now imperfectly understood literary discourses and intertextual conversations, some of which speak to the Galfridian and Latinate interests in epigraphic and inscriptional verse by later readers of MS HM 136. The evidence for the existence of broadly similar such reading interests elsewhere can be gleaned from codicological analysis of other surviving *Brut* manuscripts and printed texts. Boffey here takes discussion of this kind of evidence to a new level. She can make a direct association between a short cluster of Latin flyleaf snippets copied by later historically inclined readers of this manuscript and similar Latin epigraphs copied and translated in the same order for "Fabyan's Chronicle," completed in 1504 and printed by Richard Pynson in 1516 as the *New Chronicles of England and of France*. Her example takes a closer look at the literary implications of what might at first appear to be a set of random snippets added casually by later hands but which turns out to offer much more useful insights than at first imagined between associated writing and copying activities in manuscripts, prints, and inscribed texts on other objects, all of which carry the weight of recording English history as part of their making and meaning.

Perhaps one of the most significant developments since the 1981 York conference is the exponential growth in our understanding of aspects of the metropolitan book trade in the period before, during, and after the arrival of Caxton and the printing press in England. In 1981 Carol M. Meale took as her theme the idea of a metropolitan compiler at work through a study of a single manuscript collection, London, British Library, MS Harley 2252, and what was then known about the early-sixteenth-century socioliterary milieu in which it was compiled by the London mercer and bookseller, John Colyns. In this pioneering work she outlined the importance of embedding Colyns in a matrix of professional and personal metropolitan contacts and activities that may help explain his activities as a compiler. She continues that process in her contribution to this volume where she moves beyond detailed codicological study of Colyns's manuscript collection to consider instead an event in 1526, recorded in the London Metropolitan Archives, at which Colyns is named as being present along with thirty other members of the London book trade. This assembly was called in order to hear Cuthbert Tunstall, bishop of London, warn those present (some perhaps for the second time) not to play any part in the spread of Lutheran and other heretical ideas through the printing and distribution of unapproved books and texts. Meale is not interested in whether Tunstall's Second Monition had any greater impact as an act of attempted censorship than his first but instead meticulously reconstructs biographical details for some of those present, particularly regarding their age, wealth, and place of residence and the likely nature of their engagement in the book trade. Using a steady and experienced eye to mine the available London archives for these names, she is able to establish in far greater detail than was possible thirty years ago how Colyns might now fit into this intriguing and partly unfamiliar picture of the metropolitan book trade that she has thus retrieved.

In the 1981 conference A. S. G. Edwards set out some directions for future research on Lydgate manuscripts and argued (from a position of bibliographical expertise about his topic that remains unrivaled) that a more systematic study of the relevant but geographically and socially widely scattered surviving Lydgate texts might well offer important literary-critical insights. Thirty years on and irrespective of his poetic merits or otherwise, Lydgate is now much more clearly seen as an important figure in the study of English literary history. Edwards's continuing work on the impact of Lydgate manuscripts—who copied them and why, who read them, their early provenance, and the company his short texts keep in larger and often more miscellaneous manuscripts and other collections—has led the way for others to follow. His long-standing commitment to understanding the ebb and flow of interest in Lydgate's poetical reputation among early English readers has greatly enhanced our understanding of the important place afforded to Lydgate's texts and literary reputation among key figures in the early English book trade. For his contribution to this volume, Edwards turns to an almost completely neglected aspect of the afterlife of Lydgate manuscripts but one in which he is probably uniquely knowledgeable, examining in impressive detail the prices paid for Lydgate manuscripts that have come up at auction over the past century. If Lydgate's poetical reputation in the first half of the twentieth century is to be judged by the prices buyers were prepared to pay for fifteenth-century manuscripts of his works, compared to the sale price reached at auction by other early printed texts that have also come up for sale, then one would be tempted to paint a sorry picture of Lydgate's achievement. Edwards alerts us to the need to consider other factors affecting the commercial sale of English manuscripts during the period and sensibly makes the point that it is impossible to make a judgment on how Lydgate's burgeoning reputation among modern literary critics over the past fifty years may well have driven prices skyward for the second half of his chosen period when so few Lydgate manuscripts have recently come up for sale.

In *Manuscripts and Readers in Fifteenth-Century England* A. I. Doyle contributed "Retrospect and Prospect" as the final essay in the volume. He used the opportunity to reflect on what the 1981 York conference represented both as a marker for his own research experience over thirty years and as a signpost for the future of Middle English manuscript research. It was clear to him then that the focus at the York conference was on the books themselves rather than on authors, texts, or language. Thirty years on and still in sparkling form, Doyle here contributes a manuscript-focused chapter in which he points to the value of studying marginalia as a means of asking questions about how manuscripts and printed books were read, used, and collected from their earliest times. His subject of inquiry is a small cluster of manuscripts associated with St. Mark's Hospital, Bristol, particularly those that can be associated through Doyle's extensive detective work with the name John Colman, a brother and last Master of St. Mark's before its dissolution in 1539. The books in question represent materials drawn together and copied down from a wide range of patristic and medieval Latin authors following a period of extensive and intensive reading and utilizing enviable library resources most likely to have been found in a university setting. Meanwhile, the marginalia points to an intended readership for Colman's books that is likely to have found bookish solace in difficult times from local libraries and collections held in the vicinity of St. Mark's.

Taken as a whole, therefore, the four essays in Part III pay tribute to the continuing value of interdisciplinary themes and motifs in English medieval studies and book history that were to some extent institutionalized at York by the establishment of the Centre for Medieval Studies and the appointment first of Elizabeth Salter and then of Derek Pearsall as the overseers of its rapid development as an internationally renowned research training ground for young scholars. The 1981 conference offered an opportunity for participants at the event to consider in "retrospect and prospect" how those values York exemplified had come of age. It is clear that all those who attended (regardless of their career stage) left the York conference with a determination to carry forward ideas about research interdisciplinarity, collaboration, and network building. It was thanks to Derek Pearsall's organizational genius and sense of timing that these values were clearly articulated at the conference. Thirty years later, as the event celebrated by the publication of this volume indicates, these same rigorous ideas and principles remain vital and indispensable components for next-generation research in our chosen field of study.

John J. Thompson

NOTE

1. Derek Pearsall, ed., *Manuscripts and Readers in Fifteenth-Century England: The Literary Implications of Manuscript Study. Essays from the 1981 Conference at the University of York* (Cambridge: D. S. Brewer, 1983).

CHAPTER 8

Assessing Manuscript Context

Visible and Invisible Evidence in a Copy of the Middle English *Brut*

Julia Boffey

In his introduction to the collection of essays *Manuscripts and Readers in Fifteenth-Century England*, the product of the 1981 York conference, Derek Pearsall reminded literary scholars that they should "learn the importance of close attention to the primary materials of their study." Signaling the important information to be gleaned from such things as "the methods of compilers and manuscript editors," "matters of layout and format," "excerpting, abridging and paraphrasing," and "the pictures provided by early illustrators," he also drew attention to the value of scrutinizing "the manuscript context of particular works."[1] In 1981 I was in the process of completing a DPhil thesis, begun under the supervision of Derek Pearsall and Elizabeth Salter and finished under Derek's guidance. It included the term *manuscript context* in its title, and at that point I was not only in complete agreement with my supervisor that it was something worth studying, but I also thought I knew what the phrase meant. What I did not fully appreciate then was the variety of meanings that *manuscript context* would come to encompass and the variety of ways in which following Derek's recommendation to investigate it both might and might not bear fruit.

"Contexts" of different kinds preoccupied a number of the contributors to the 1981 conference and the resulting volume. These included the local sociogeographic contexts in which manuscripts circulated and were read (Thorlac Turville-Petre discussed the characteristics of a number of fifteenth-century manuscripts of Middle English works copied in the North-East Midlands) and the immediate context of a manuscript's production (Carol Meale and John Thompson talked about the activities of individual manuscript compilers and of some of the factors determining their choice of texts to copy or of forms in which to copy them). Others of us outlined some specific manuscript contexts in which certain works circulated, in other words the company that these works kept (William Marx discussed this in relation to a Middle English prose translation of the *Gospel of Nicodemus*, and I did so in relation to some love lyrics that happen to survive in two different manuscripts alongside strikingly different bodies of material).[2] Identifying the companion pieces with which a work has survived in a manuscript copy seemed to me at that point central to any discussion of its manuscript context. The information gleaned from such identification appeared likely to be informative in a number of ways, not least because particular collocations of material might hold clues about the tastes of scribes and readers, or about medieval perceptions of the functions of particular genres.

Analysis of this sort can undoubtedly be meaningful, and some of what has been written about the selection and collocation of Middle English works in manuscript copies has opened the way to illuminating critical readings of those works. The not infrequent collocation of saints' lives with romances in fifteenth-century manuscript anthologies, for example, has prompted revealing commentary on features of both genres.[3] But to study assortments of textual material as if their collocation must always represent reasoned scribal or readerly decisions about the kinds of works that sit most effectively together is all too often to ignore pressures of much less predictable kinds which must have determined scribal choices. Derek Pearsall has highlighted some of these pressures in an article about fifteenth-century poetic miscellanies:

> What the compilers of these manuscripts did in bringing together poetic texts in their collections is often revealing of the assumptions about poetry that they consciously or unconsciously made. But it is sometimes revealing of no more than their ignorance or stupidity or confusion of mind, or, above all, of the practical limitations placed upon them by the availability or nonavailability of exemplars.[4]

In other words, the rationale in a particular sequence of works may reflect any number of things—and hardly ever a series of reasoned decisions about how one work can reinforce or, conversely, offer an ironic commentary on another. Sometimes it may simply reflect what the scribe had to hand, unreflectively transcribed from another copy: the fact that material for scribes to copy was in relatively short supply (the "exemplar poverty" to which Ralph Hanna has pointed) is all too easy to overlook.[5] The collocation of items in a compilation which has grown over time, with additions from different contributors made at different points in the compilation's history, offers still further challenges to those seeking to understand or justify the assortment of contents in a medieval manuscript book.

While Derek was suggesting what might be unknowable about the assortment of contents in any one manuscript, the term *manuscript context* was appearing with steadily greater frequency in the titles of books and articles on Old and Middle English topics. As used in the title of a collection of essays generated by a conference held at the Parker Library of Corpus Christi College, Cambridge, *Old English Literature in Its Manuscript Context*, it stretched to comprehend "ideas of textual identity, authorship and translation, and editorial standards and obligations."[6] In an article by Sylvia Huot titled "The Manuscript Context of Medieval Romance," it signified (quite usefully) something along the lines of "what medieval romances are like in the forms of their earliest survival rather than in modern editions."[7] And in applications where the phrase's already enlarged connotations were apparently felt to be too limiting, it was adapted and elaborated: recent studies have redefined the set of features comprehended in Huot's *manuscript context* in the new coinage *manuscript matrix*, described in one account as "an imagined, virtual dimension in which physical form and linguistic content function in dialectical reciprocity[,] . . . one overarching, category-crossing metasystem of systems of signs."[8]

In what ways might any of these conceptualizations of manuscript context be revealing in relation to a real book? This essay outlines a small exploration of the assortment of items in one volume, looking at what can plausibly be said about their collocation and at the same time signaling the challenges to definitions of *manuscript context* which are presented by a compilation which has grown over time. The volume at issue is a modest parchment manuscript mostly taken up with a copy of the Middle English prose *Brut*, the version of this rebarbative text classified by the late Lister Matheson as "the common version, sub-group c, to 1419"; copied by a single scribe writing a mid-fifteenth-century secretary hand, it now occupies the major part of San Marino, Henry E. Huntington Library, MS HM 136.[9] Other texts copied in the manuscript are additions apparently made by later readers or owners, mostly in the late fifteenth and/or the early sixteenth century. They include an extension to the prose *Brut*, in a later hand than that of the main copy; a short Latin verse epitome of English history, from William the Conqueror to Henry VI (front flyleaf ii^{v});[10] a copy of the Latin version of John of Bridlington's prophecy, added in space remaining in the lower margins of fols. 83v–86 and 102v–130;[11] some other Latin verses (front flyleaf iv); a group of English medical receipts (end flyleaf ix); and a whole series of notes along the top margins of the *Brut*, effectively a written conversation among a group of readers whose tastes have been discussed by Josephine Koster Tarvers.[12]

This is clearly an accretive compilation, one that took shape over a number of years as different readers or owners of the manuscript inserted material of their choice into available empty spaces in it. The collocation of items in the volume as it now exists came into being over many decades and reflects decisions made by a number of people who consulted it and made their own additions to it. To consider the rationale behind the assortment of items here is to confront a number of mostly irrecoverable circumstances in the manuscript's history and must seem to some extent a fool's errand. But a little drilling into the individual histories of the added items, investigating associations accumulated before the moment of their inscription in Huntington MS HM 136, may be a more worthwhile experiment. The additions that especially interest me are the Latin verses on front flyleaf iv, about which published descriptions of the manuscript have had notably little to say. They are in a hand which appears nowhere else in the compilation but looks on paleographic grounds to date either from the very late fifteenth or (probably more likely) the early sixteenth century (the *Guide to Medieval and Renaissance Manuscripts in the Huntington Library* suggests "s. XVIin.").[13] They are most clearly summarized as a list:

(i) "Oratio bruti ad dianam," beginning "Diva potens nemorum terror silvestribus apris . . ."; 6 lines. As the Huntington Catalogue description notes, number 4598 in Hans Walther's first-line index of Latin verse.

(ii) "Responsio diane ad brutum," beginning "Brute sub occasum solis trans gallica regna . . ."; 8 lines. Not separately identified in Walther, although presumably comprehended as part of the previous item.[14]

(iii) "Sede sedens ista iudex inflexibilis sta . . ."; 4 lines. Walther no. 17466.

(iv) "Epitaphium henrici secundi regis Anglie," beginning "Sufficit hic tumulus cui non suffecerat orbis . . ."; 10 lines. Walther no. 18695.

(v) "Epitaphium frederici imperatoris," beginning "Si probitas sensus virtutis gratia census . . ."; 3 lines. Walther no. 17866.

(vi) "Nullus in orbe fuit homo vivens nec vallet esse . . ."; 4 lines. Not in Walther.

(vii) "Funis cum lignis te miser ensis et ignis . . ."; 2 lines. Not in Walther.

The headings supplied to the fourth and fifth items indicate that these pieces constituted, or are extracts from, epitaphs, respectively for Henry II of England and for Emperor Frederick (information that is confirmed in Walther's index, which lists the verse used of Henry II as an epitaph for Alexander the Great). Some further burrowing reveals that the sixth item comes from a longer Latin verse epitaph, beginning "Mors est mesta nimis . . . ," accompanied in at least one surviving witness with the information "Isti versus sunt de Edwardo Rege nuper defuncto,"[15] and that the seventh item occurs in Thomas Walsingham's account of the execution of Hugh Despenser the younger in 1326.[16]

Discovering that at least some of these items survive in sources relating to early British history hints at a common thread which might explain their collocation, and suggests further places, beyond the witnesses listed by Walther, to search for copies. As it turns out, the first two items are to be found in one of the most widely circulating medieval sources of British history: Geoffrey of Monmouth's *Historia Regum Britannie*.[17] The third and the fifth appear in Ranulph Higden's *Polychronicon*, another Latin work with an extended English circulation.[18] The fourth item is included in the *Ymagines historiorum* of Ralph of Diceto, dean of St. Paul's Cathedral in London in the late twelfth century, recorded there as part of the funerary verses hung at the tomb of Henry II at Fontevraud, although evidently deriving from an epitaph on Alexander the Great incorporated in the *Alexandreis* of Gautier de Châtillon.[19]

Uncovering the range of sources in which these verse snippets appear makes it possible to discern a relatively straightforward connection to the original contents of Huntington MS HM 136, an extended version of the Middle English prose *Brut*. It is not hard to imagine why a reader might have wanted to insert them in some empty space on the flyleaves at the start of the volume to complement the *Brut*'s narration of British history. The fact that the added verses are in Latin also gives them a relationship to the historically oriented additions made to the manuscript at other, different points in its early existence: the verse epitome of English history added on the first flyleaf and the prophecy of John of Bridlington inserted in empty spaces later in the body of the volume. Even though it may not be possible to determine a precise chronology for these additions, the facts of their subject matter and their Latinness hold them together in some kind of grouping in what we might think of as the broad, flat context of the manuscript's contents.

Further penetration into the affiliations of the Latin verses on front flyleaf iv uncovers rather more precise reasons for their collocation here, however, and even some intimation of the form in which they might have been available to whoever copied them. Among the various things not previously noted about this group of additions to the manuscript is that all the short verse items appear in the work now generally known as "Fabyan's Chronicle": the *New Chronicles of England and of France,* as it is titled in Pynson's 1516 printed edition (STC 10659); or the *Concordance of Stories*, as Robert Fabyan refers to it in his two-volume autograph manuscript (now split between two libraries as Holkham Hall MS 671 and London, British Library, MS Cotton Nero C xi).[20] The *New Chronicles of England and of France* is, as the title suggests, an account of the histories of these two nations from the time of Brutus's journey from Troy until the late fifteenth century. It is peppered with Latin verses, in a variety of different forms and lengths, almost all of which are accompanied by English translations (also in verse) evidently made by Fabyan himself.[21] The order of the Latin verses on front flyleaf iv in Huntington MS HM 136 replicates the order in which these items appear in the *New Chronicles*, suggesting either that they were selected for transcription, in sequence, by someone with a copy of the *New Chronicles* to hand or that they constituted a source for Fabyan, whether directly or at some remove.

Could Fabyan have had access to Huntington MS HM 136? This cannot be ruled out, since he clearly knew the *Brut* chronicle, along with many other sources of English history, and he may well have owned a manuscript copy as well as had access to one or other of the editions printed in and after 1480 (STC 9991, etc.). The hand of the scribe who copied the Latin verses onto fol. iv of Huntington MS HM 136 cannot be dated with any precision, and its features do not altogether preclude the possibility that this scribe copied the Latin verses before or during the years when Fabyan was occupied with the compilation of his long work (completed in 1504) and that Fabyan somehow saw the verses and adapted them to his own uses. On balance, though, it seems more likely that the Latin verses were transcribed from the *New Chronicles*—either after 1516, when the first edition was printed, or if before that date, then from a manuscript copy which could have been Fabyan's autograph, or another version, or (just conceivably) his working notes.[22] The probability that the relationship took this shape is strengthened by the fact that the version of the sixth verse item (four lines from an epitaph of Edward I) in the *New Chronicles* is longer than the version copied into Huntington MS HM 136. That a reader of the manuscript should have imported into it elements garnered from another book, possibly a printed one, is not at all unlikely. There may indeed be precedent for such activity in other parts of the manuscript if, as Matheson has suggested, the scribe who added the continuation of the *Brut* used as his copy material from Caxton's 1480 printed edition, *The Chronicle of England* (STC 9991).[23] If the scribe of the Latin verses was working with a printed edition of Fabyan's *New Chronicles* to hand, he (or conceivably she) joins the large company of late medieval and early modern readers and compilers who engaged in what may seem to modern scholars the rather counterintuitive process of replicating printed text by hand.

Another feature not hitherto noted about these Latin snippets is their shared status as inscriptional verse. This is clear enough in the titles given to the third and fourth items, both headed "Epitaphium," and apparently deriving from funerary verses hung on tablets at tombs. The inscriptional status of the sixth item is not announced in a heading, but these lines are found elsewhere in a longer piece also apparently hung at a tomb, that of Edward I in Westminster Abbey. The seventh item, on the death of Hugh Despenser, was connected by Walsingham with the display of Despenser's severed head on London Bridge; and the third item was, according to Higden's *Polychronicon*, inscribed on a judge's chair.[24] Even the first and second items, with a wide manuscript circulation in Geoffrey of Monmouth's *Historia*, existed in tablet form: they were recorded in St. Paul's Cathedral, on a "great tablet" hanging near the tomb of Bishop Roger Walden.[25] Whoever selected and copied this little collection seems to have had a serious interest in commemorative and inscriptional verse—as did Fabyan himself, who included many examples of such writing among the Latin verse he incorporated in his *New Chronicles of England and of France*. Drilling into the associations of this small series of additions to Huntington MS HM 136 thus uncovers possible links to a printed exemplar, and (whether or not via that exemplar) to a range of inscriptional verse. Such associations invite us to imagine a reader-turned-scribe who was interested in written texts as things that might be found on chairs and tablets and tombs as well as on the parchment or paper leaves of a manuscript or printed book or pamphlet.

This small excavation of the associations of just a few of the contents of Huntington MS HM 136 stands as a representative demonstration of the often complex relationships between the items copied together in one volume. To survey the contents of this manuscript with manuscript context in mind (here perhaps especially the context in which the *Brut* now finds itself) is in the end to confront multiple contexts, whether the large and complicated one of the *Brut* or the smaller contexts of these tiny Latin items. Each item copied into the manuscript has its own affiliations and history, its own very particular assortment of reasons for being there, and very many aspects of these micro-histories are likely to remain hidden from us. Returning to my theme of manuscript context more generally, Huntington MS HM 136 instances further challenges. More strikingly than is the case with many manuscripts, its different layers of additions remind us that manuscript context is a fluid thing that changes over time. This volume seems to have begun life as a copy of the prose *Brut*, rather a distinctively well copied one. Only gradually over time did it turn into a "repository for historiographical texts," as it is now described on the *Imagining History* website: the kind of discursive environment in which texts spark off meanings against each other.[26] During at least the first century of its existence it must have changed significantly several times, and the difficulty of dating any of the additional hands means that the order of these changes is virtually impossible to track with any precision.

Detailed study of material aspects of the manuscript, and of the language of its contents, may refine our understanding of contexts of a different kind, in terms of the place and time of its original production. It is possible to construct the outline of later contexts of ownership and circulation from some of the details that have been inscribed in it (it belonged to a sixteenth-century John Leche, probably from Nantwich in Cheshire; and, rather gratifyingly for present purposes, to a "Will. Persall" at one point).[27] But trying to reconstruct the contexts of its use—exactly who read the manuscript; where, and how, and what they did with it—leaves us confronting a number of imponderables. Readers of Huntington MS HM 136 have left many traces behind them but of rather confusing kinds. On the evidence of tiny marginal marks, it has recently been argued that this copy of the *Brut* served as the exemplar for the major part of Caxton's 1480 printed edition of the *Chronicles of England*; thus the manuscript might have served time in Caxton's shop being effectively turned into print.[28] We know also that one and possibly two later readers copied into it material that they found in printed books: first the scribe of the *Brut* continuation, who used a printed copy of Caxton's same *Chronicles of England*; and then perhaps the copyist of the Latin verses on front flyleaf iv, who may have consulted a printed edition of Fabyan's *New Chronicles of England and of France*. While these activities are at least related by similar interests in British history, it is by contrast impossible to plumb the motives of whoever added the medical receipts and the notes about Dorothy Helbartun's ownership of the volume: these additions lead us to a realm in which the fact of the book's material existence was probably more significant than its contents and in which its available unused parchment, or its relationship to one specific owner and her associates, were what attracted attention.

So: how has my understanding of manuscript context changed since 1981? First, in relation to contents, manuscript context seems to me now something with depths to be plumbed as well as horizontal surfaces to be surveyed. Penetrating into the affiliations and wider circulation of all the contents of a manuscript can sometimes help us to understand why and how its contents have been brought together. In the instance explored here, the relationships that emerge have turned out very probably to include texts in printed form as well as in manuscript copies, and they are an important reminder of the need to remain aware of nonscribal forms of circulation (inscriptional and oral, as well as printed). Second, in relation to the contents and shape of a scribally produced book, manuscript context is unfixed and indeed protean: individual manuscripts can change over time, and their discursive environments just as much as their appearance can be endlessly re-formed or reconfigured. Third and last, among the numerous things about old manuscripts that we simply cannot know, very many relate to readers (and thus more broadly to "audience") and to circumstances of use. These aspects manage to hold endless allure while remaining mostly, and rather agreeably, resistant to recovery.

Notes

1. Derek Pearsall, ed., *Manuscripts and Readers in Fifteenth-Century England: The Literary Implications of Manuscript Study. Essays from the 1981 Conference at the University of York* (Cambridge: D. S. Brewer, 1983), 1.

2. Versions of all of these talks appear in Pearsall, *Manuscripts and Readers.*

3. George Shuffelton, ed., *Codex Ashmole 61: A Compilation of Popular Middle English Verse*, TEAMS: Middle English Texts Series (Kalamazoo: Western Michigan University, Medieval Institute Publications, 2008); Phillipa Hardman, ed., *The Heege Manuscript: A Facsimile of National Library of Scotland MS Advocates 19.3.1*, Leeds Texts and Monographs, n.s., 16 (Leeds: Leeds Studies in English, University of Leeds, 2000).

4. Derek Pearsall, "The Uses of Manuscripts: Late Medieval English," *Harvard Library Bulletin*, n.s., 4 (Winter 1993–94): 30–36.

5. On exemplar poverty, see Ralph Hanna III, "Booklets in Medieval Manuscripts: Further Considerations," reprinted in *Pursuing History: Middle English Manuscripts and Their Texts* (Stanford, CA: Stanford University Press, 1996), 21–34 (esp. 31); and Ralph Hanna III, "Miscellaneity and Vernacularity: Conditions of Literary Production in Late Medieval England," in *The Whole Book: Cultural Perspectives on the Medieval Miscellany*, ed. Stephen G. Nichols and Siegfried Wenzel (Ann Arbor: University of Michigan Press, 1996), 37–51 (esp. 47); Margaret Connolly, "Compiling the Book," in *The Production of Books in England, 1350–1500*, ed. Alexandra Gillespie and Daniel Wakelin (Cambridge: Cambridge University Press, 2011), 129–49 (esp. 129).

6. Joyce Tally Lionarons, ed., *Old English Literature in Its Manuscript Context* (Morgantown: West Virginia University Press, 2004); the quotation is taken from publicity on the publishers' website at http://wvupressonline.com.

7. Sylvia Huot, "The Manuscript Context of Medieval Romance," in *The Cambridge Companion to Medieval Romance*, ed. Roberta L. Krueger (Cambridge: Cambridge University Press, 2000), 60–77: "Anyone who has studied romances in their original manuscripts knows that the experience is markedly different from that of reading them in modern printed editions" (60).

8. Martha Dana Rust, *Imaginary Worlds in Medieval Books: Exploring the Manuscript Matrix* (New York: Palgrave Macmillan, 2007), 9. The phrase derives from Stephen G. Nichols's introduction to a special issue of *Speculum* devoted to the New Philology: see *Speculum* 65 (1990): 1–10 (7).

9. Lister Matheson, *The Prose "Brut": The Development of a Middle English Chronicle* (Tempe, AZ: Medieval & Renaissance Texts & Studies, 1998), 123–24, 163–64. For a full description of the manuscript, see Consuela Dutschke et al., *Guide to Medieval and Renaissance Manuscripts in the Huntington Library*, 2 vols. (San Marino, CA: Huntington Library, 1989), 1:181–83.

10. Beginning "Viribus armorum bastardus Willelmus agebat. . . ."

11. In T. Wright, ed., *Political Poems and Songs Relating to English History*, 2 vols., Rolls Series, 14 (London: Longman, Green, Longman and Roberts, 1859–61), 1:123–201; for further discussion of this work, see A. G. Rigg, "John of Bridlington's *Prophecy*: A New Look," *Speculum* 63 (1988): 596–613.

12. Josephine Koster Tarvers, "'Thys ys mystrys boke': English Women as Readers and Writers in Late Medieval England," in *The Uses of Manuscripts in Literary Studies: Essays in Memory of Judson Boyce Allen*, ed. Charlotte Morse, Penelope Reed Doob, and Marjorie Curry Woods (Kalamazoo: Western Michigan University, Medieval Institute Publications, 1992), 305–27; Anthony Bale, "Late Medieval Book-Owners Named John Leche," *Bodleian Library Record* 25 (2012): 105–12.

13. Dutschke et al., *Guide to Medieval and Renaissance Manuscripts in the Huntington Library*, vol. 1, 181.

14. Hans Walther, *Initia carminum ac versuum medii aevi posterioris latinorum*, Carmina medii aevi posterioris latina, 1 (Göttingen: Vandenhoeck & Ruprecht, 1959), no. 4598.

15. Walther, *Initia* 11241, Cambridge, Peterhouse MS 94, fol. iii^{v}; see M. R. James, *A Descriptive Catalogue of the Manuscripts in the Library of Peterhouse* (Cambridge: Cambridge University Press, 1899), 111 (a much longer version of the epitaph).

16. *Thomae Walsingham: Quondam monachi S. Albani, Historia Anglicana*, ed. Henry T. Riley, 2 vols, Rolls Series, 28 (London: Longman, Roberts and Green, 1863–64), vol. 1, 185.

17. *The Historia Regum Britannie of Geoffrey of Monmouth, I*, ed. Neil Wright (Cambridge: Cambridge University Press, 1984), 9.

18. Joseph Rawson Lumby, ed., *Polychronicon Ranulphi Higden Monachi Cestrensis, together with the English Translations of John Trevisa and of an Unknown Writer of the Fifteenth Century*, 9 vols., Rolls Series, 41 (London: Longman & Co., 1865–86), vol. 3, 174; vol. 7, 23.

19. W. Stubbs, ed., *Radulfi de Diceto decani Lundoniensis opera historica*, 2 vols., Rolls Series, 68 (London: Longman & Co., 1876), vol. 2, 65; Maura

Keyne Lafferty, “Mapping Human Limitations: The Tomb Ecphrases in Walter of Châtillon’s *Alexandreis*,” *Journal of Medieval Latin* 4 (1994): 64–81; and Maura Lafferty, “Walter of Châtillon’s *Alexandreis*,” in *A Companion to Alexander Literature in the Middle Ages*, ed. Z. David Zuwiyya (Leiden: Brill, 2011), 177–200; A. G. Rigg, *A History of Anglo-Latin Literature, 1066–1422* (Cambridge: Cambridge University Press, 1992), 156.

20. Henry Ellis, ed., *The New Chronicles of England and of France, in Two Parts; by Robert Fabyan* (London: F. C. and J. Rivington, 1811).

21. Julia Boffey, “The English Verse of Robert Fabyan,” in *In the Prayse of Writing: Early Modern Manuscript Studies. Essays in Honour of Peter Beal*, ed. S. P. Cerasano and Steven W. May (London: British Library, 2012), 1–24.

22. A second manuscript copy exists: now York Minster Library MS XVI. Q. 9 and Harvard University, Houghton Library MS Eng 766.

23. See above, n. 8.

24. See above, nn. 15 and 17; the judge’s chair was apparently covered in the flayed skin of his unjust father.

25. [N. H. Nicolas], *A Chronicle of London from 1089 to 1483* (London: Richard Taylor, 1827), 174–87 (177).

26. Description by Ryan Perry and Jason O’Rourke on the *Imagining History* website: www.qub.ac.uk/imagining-history/wordpress/index.php.

27. John Leche’s name appears on front flyleaf iii and back flyleaf i; see further Bale, “Late Medieval Book-Owners Named John Leche.” The name “Will. Persall” is on front flyleaf vi.

28. Daniel Wakelin, “Caxton’s Exemplar for *The Chronicle of England*?,” *Journal of the Early Book Society* 14 (2011): 75–113.

CHAPTER 9

Books with Marginalia from St. Mark's Hospital, Bristol

A. I. Doyle

When Derek Pearsall held the conference New Directions in the Study of Medieval Manuscripts at Harvard in 1998 it may have seemed perverse of me to open it rather on *recent* directions, but that was intended to introduce the questions of where we had already got to and how far we had not.[1] One focus of fresh attention has been the evidence for actual use of manuscript and printed books in the Middle Ages and later, as indicated by marginal annotations. I may be thought cynical to say that we have been driven to these edges by the exhaustion of other modes of study, such as the editing of new or old texts or exploration of their authors, illustrators, copyists, or owners. It is examples of the last two topics I am discussing, at the very end of the Middle Ages in England. I am concerned with a small group of manuscripts expertly produced and annotated by one man or his collaborators in a community, employing equally printed books as sources, and not only for internal benefit, and undeservedly truncated.

In 1967, before I got to know Derek Pearsall, I believe, which was after my friend of Cambridge postgraduate days, Elizabeth Salter, had become professor of English at the then-new University of York (U.K.), I gave the Lyell Lectures in Bibliography in the University of Oxford on the topic "Some English Scribes and Scriptoria of the Later Middle Ages." They have never been published as a whole, but I have used parts of them, with improvements, for other lectures, like the one delivered at the "New Directions" conference, and subsequent publications.[2] One of them was on the books which can be connected with John Colman, a brother and the last Master of the hospital of St. Mark, Billeswick, on what is now College Green, opposite St. Augustine's Abbey (now the cathedral), outside the walls of medieval Bristol. Commonly called "the Gaunts" after its founders in the early thirteenth century, it grew from dependence on the abbey to be a minor religious house, following the same Augustinian rule, with particular obligations of feeding the poor and the education of boys. Bristol was the third largest city in England after London and York, with comparable civic life and regional importance.[3] By the end of the fifteenth century St. Mark's had become a place for patronage and resort by both citizens and wealthy gentry, its tower added in 1483–87, the chancel of the church rebuilt after 1500, a south aisle chapel added in about 1510 and another in 1520–23, with armorial stained glass and burials of benefactors, not merely local, but also with metropolitan links.[4] Mary Erler has given a richly researched and perceptive account of three wealthy widows: one from the West Midlands, who in 1489 made generous bequests to the fabric and community and asked to be buried there in the chapel of St. Nicholas; the second, whose husband had been a leading Bristol citizen in the 1480s and 1490s, in her will of 1509/10 asked for burial in the midst of the choir, where she could have watched services from a chamber decorated with devotional paintings of her time; the third, who had long attended ladies of the Lancastrian and Tudor royal families, after the death of her second husband in 1532/33 and his burial in the new chantry chapel built by his father, appears to have resided in the precincts off and on until 1538, when the dissolution was imminent. The first two of these widows mention in their wills particular brothers of the convent in terms which suggest they were their spiritual guides, while the third wrote to Thomas Cromwell, the king's vice-regent, on behalf of John Colman as Master in performance of his duties outside. She had been living there "to serve God now in my old days" and accustomed to go to her chapel through the cloister instead of "the common way through the church." But she finally died and was buried in London.[5]

At its surrender in December 1539, the hospital's personnel consisted of the Master, three other priest brethren, sixteen men and children, servants, and choristers, quite a sizable establishment.[6] It seems that it had held more than a song school, for Thomas Tyler, Master in the period 1486–1516, said in 1496 that he had been "brought furth in the said place of Gauntes from youth."[7]

When the Bodleian Library in Oxford received the bequests of James Lyell in the early 1960s, Richard Hunt, then Keeper of Western Manuscripts, showed me, as was his wont, some of the manuscripts before they were cataloged, in the hope of information, and I quickly recognized the elegant monogram **IC**, of white capitals on a rectangular black background, on folio 34 of what would be Lyell MS 38, as identical to those in two other Oxford manuscripts, Bodley 618 and St. John's College 173, the latter specifying the scribe as John Colman and with an ownership inscription of St. Mark's hospital, Bristol (fig. 9.1).[8] During my Lyell lectures these three books (and others) were shown in a temporary Bodleian exhibition.

I had already published a note on the St. John's manuscript, where I observed that almost all its contents in English matched those of *A Ryght Profytable Treatyse* by Thomas Betson, brother of Syon Abbey (Middlesex), printed at Westminster by Wynkyn de Worde in about 1500 (fig. 9.2). I observed also that the manuscript had an added note, erased but recoverable under ultraviolet light, of having been sent to Richard Pynson at Fleet Street in London (where he was printing from 1500 to 1530).[9]

John Colman was a brother and a priest by 1508 and became Master possibly from 1517 until the suppression in 1539.[10] His monogram, on an upright rectangle placed centrally on one page of each of the three manuscripts, is humanist in style, obviously imitated from a printer's device like those of a number of French presses in the 1470s and 1480s, and particularly the first of Pynson's (a Norman) in London.[11] The writing of the main and subsidiary contents of the three books is not, however, at all humanist in character. In St. John's 173 the motto "Delectare in domino" is in expert Textura alongside the **IC** monogram, below four lines in the set Secretary of most of the contents, while the two lines of Colman's scribal claim are in a small, more formalized Secretary. The first item of Lyell 38 up to the page with the monogram is in expert Littera Textualis (Textura), and so are quotations within the next item, which is otherwise in what may be called upright Bastard Secretary or Semi-Hybrida (fig. 9.3).[12] In Bodley 618 the monogram follows a contents list of the first item in Textura like St. John's 173 and the following item of a smaller module compatible in detail. It has a later inscription asking prayers for Colman as once Master of the Gaunts, having given it

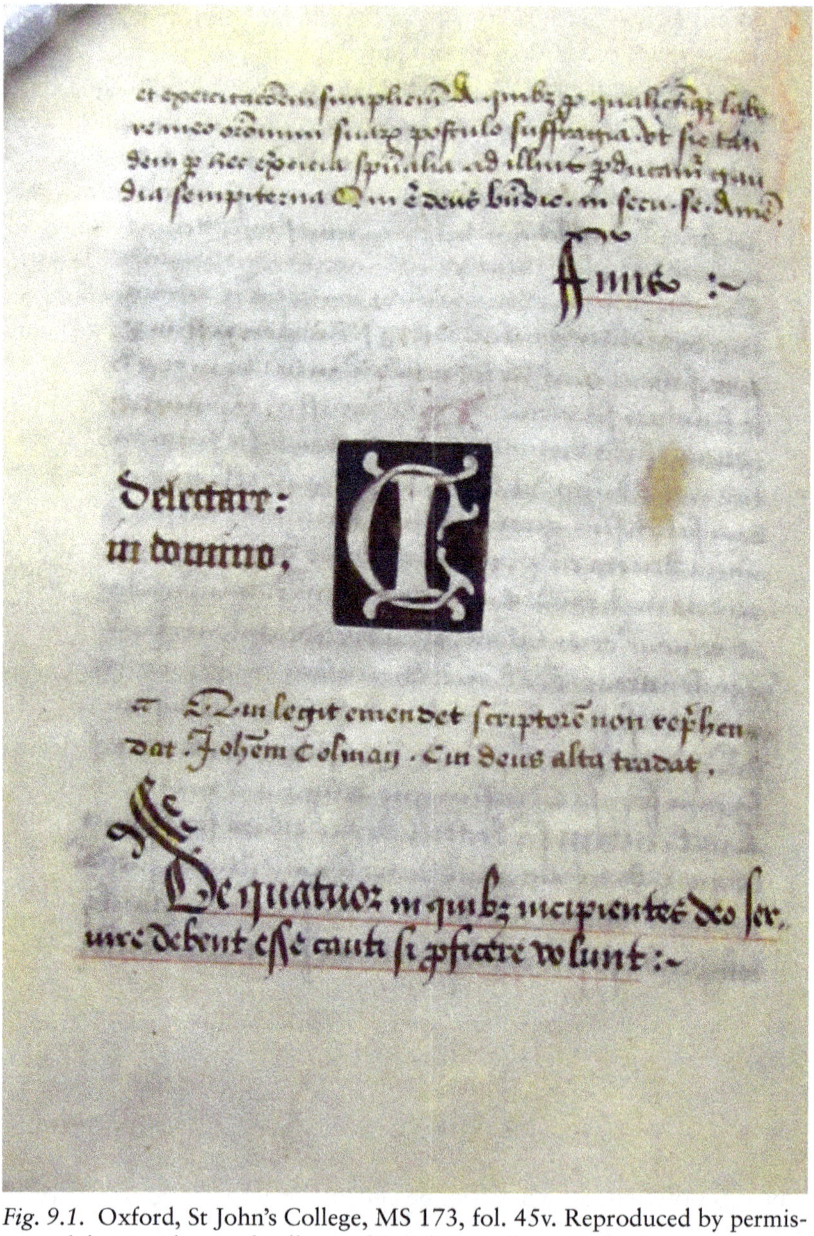

Fig. 9.1. Oxford, St John's College, MS 173, fol. 45v. Reproduced by permission of the President and Fellows of St John's College, Oxford.

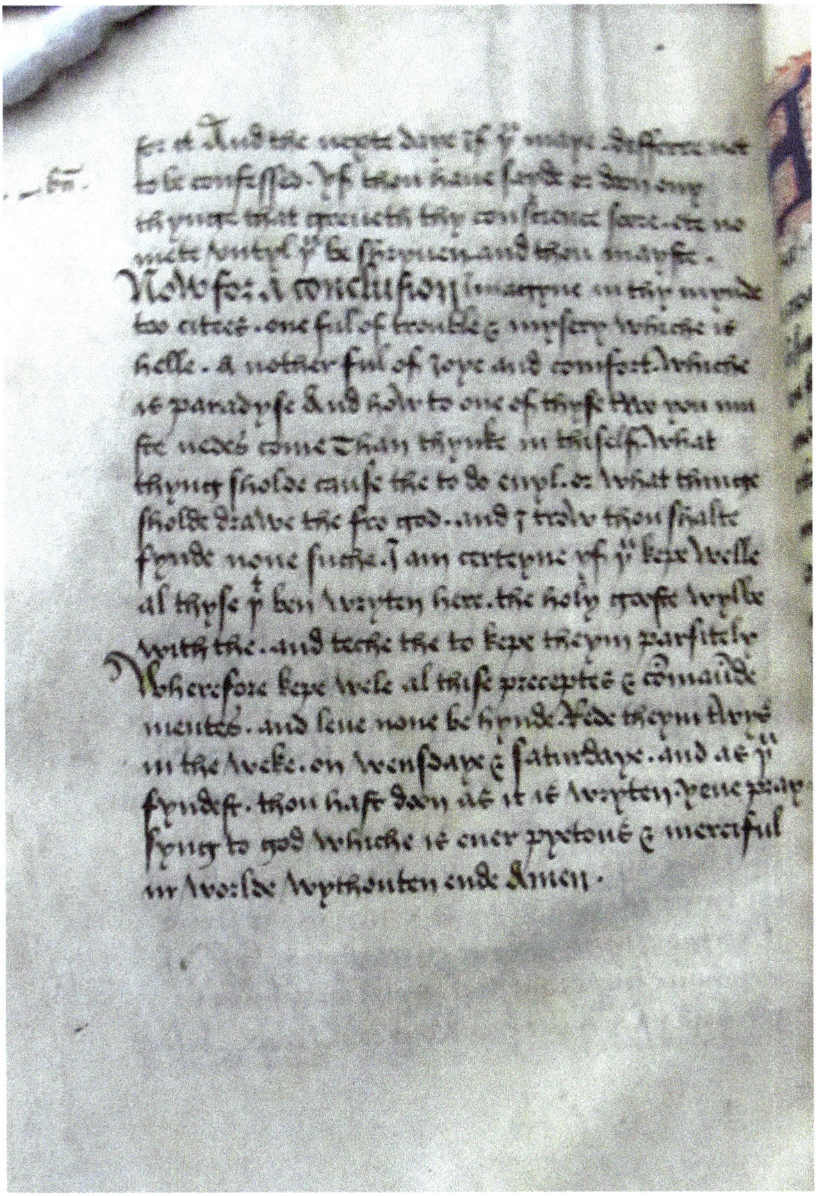

Fig. 9.2. Oxford, St John's College, MS 173, fol. 143v. Reproduced by permission of the President and Fellows of St John's College, Oxford.

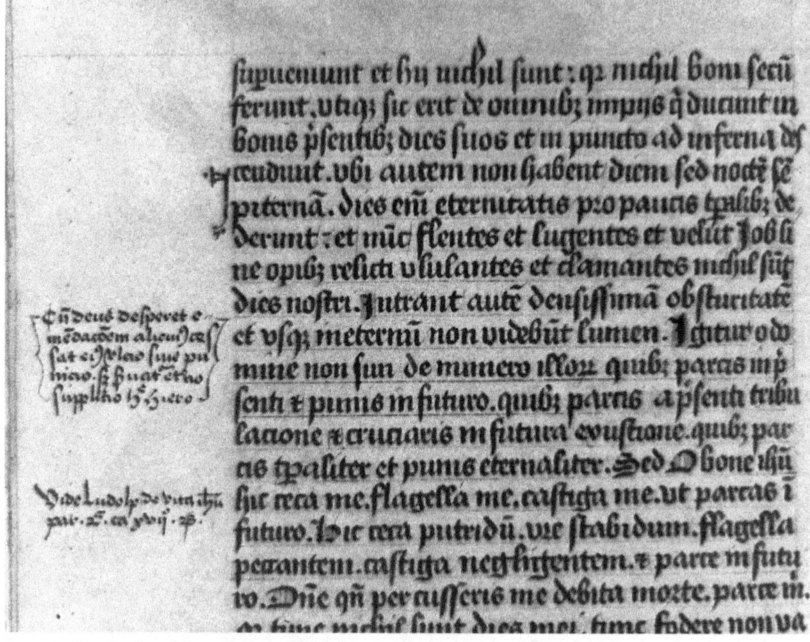

Fig. 9.3. Oxford, Bodleian Library, MS Lyell 38, fol. 36v. By permission of the Bodleian Libraries, University of Oxford.

to John Bradley, clerk, who is elsewhere recorded as being a chantry priest in the parish church of St. Mary Redcliffe, pensioned off in 1548, when Colman was still living on his generous pension of £40 a year in a rented home in the precincts of the Gaunts.[13]

Those are not the only books which may have been written by Colman. Bristol Central Reference Library MS 6, a collection of Latin liturgical and English spiritual treatises, of which the first part is dated at St. Mark's September 13 (fol. 47) and October 31, 1502 (fol. 119), that is, 72 leaves or 144 pages, amounts to two or three pages a day if written regularly (fig. 9.4). It is in a set Secretary of two sizes, very like the English in St. John's 173, with strapwork top-line ascenders larger than those there. Erler has shown that some of its English items are adapted to be read by or to devout women such as the widows she describes.[14] And in a cartulary of St. Mark's properties in the Bristol Record Office, 31101/1, a similar small Secretary writes two lines (perhaps on an erasure) on fol. 100 in a document of 1505, the last in date of the Bristol

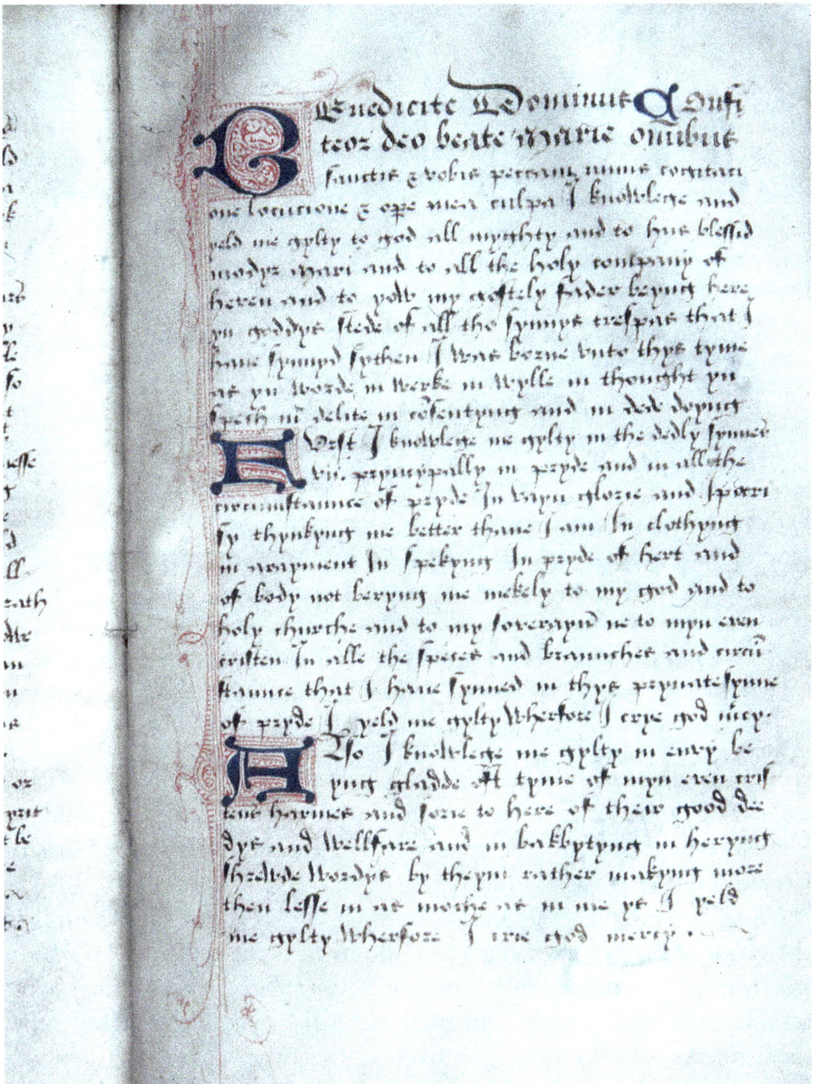

Fig. 9.4. Bristol, Bristol City Central Library, MS 6. By permission of the Bristol Reference Library.

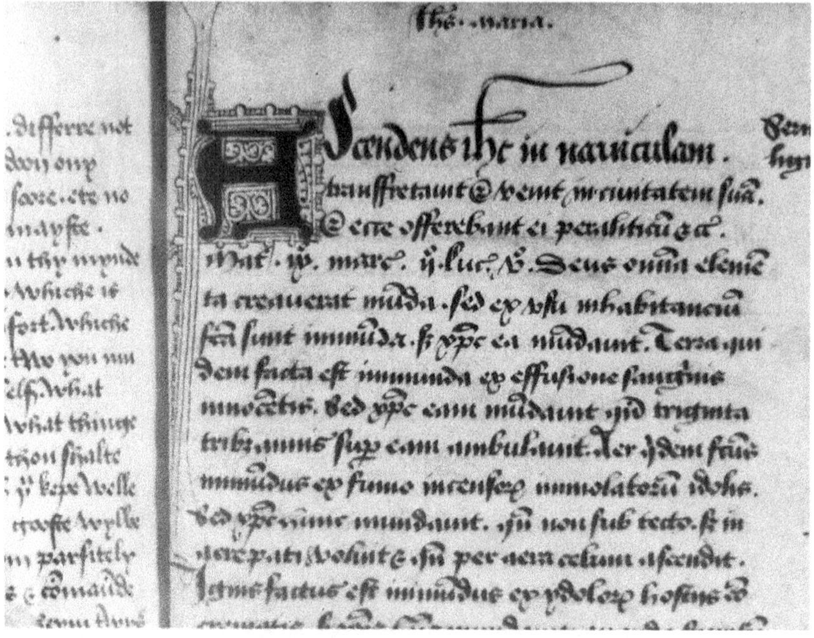

Fig. 9.5. Oxford, St John's College, MS 173, fol. 144r. Reproduced by permission of the President and Fellows of St John's College, Oxford.

section, whereas the rest of the contents are in a "common-law" Anglicana. The flourishing of the colored initials, although of the standard English type, has penwork details closely resembling those of Bristol Central Library 6 and St. John's 173.[15]

Since it was probably taught in the house, it is not surprising that the script of the first two signatures, John Colman and John Helys, on the original acknowledgment of royal supremacy in 1534 closely resemble each other and the informal Secretary style of the manuscripts mentioned, whereas the signatures of the other three brethren are larger and untidier, and a letter from Colman to Cromwell in 1538 could have been written by one of them on his behalf.[16] But we must allow for more than one hand contributing to the books, especially the final portion of St. John's 173, fols. 144–71v, in a more elaborate Bastard Secretary (fig. 9.5).

The marginalia in the manuscripts are not only brief notes by the same pen and ink as the adjacent texts, possibly copied from the exemplars or supplied at once by the scribe, some with distinctive features like an elongated **N**[ota] with **bene**, and well-drawn pointing hands, and also in the three Oxford manuscripts there are longer ones, mostly in Latin, some evidently added later, though apparently by the same hand, and even lengthier passages of Latin prose on endleaves by an expert Secretary or Hybrida like some of the additional notes, sometimes showing difficulty in fitting the space. These longer pieces, including some in margins, commonly have specific citations of their literary sources.

They embrace a wide range of authors and works, mostly patristic or medieval: Anselm, Augustine, Bernard, Boethius, Bonaventure, Birgitta, Cassiodorus, Chrysostom, Dionysius, Fulgencius, Gennadius, Gratian, Gregory, Holkot, Hugh of St. Victor, Hugo of Vienna, Humbert of Rome, Jerome, Ludolphus, Lathbury, Nicholas of Lyra, Peter Lombard, Peter of Blois, Thomas Aquinas, the *Rosarium*, *Speculum Spiritualium*, *Vitas Patrum*, and Philosophus (presumably Aristotle). Most of them are not just short "sententiae" which might have been taken from a florilegium, but longer quotations demanding thought of their relevance to the subjects of the volume or independently. What were these pieces transcribed from, and for whose benefit? The same questions may be asked about some of the main contents of the three or four manuscripts. They must have been drawn from an unusually extensive and intensive reading. Where were the books they all came from? Only one other manuscript book is known with an inscription from St. Mark's, St. John's College, Oxford, MS 165, of the late twelfth century, with fifteenth-century marginalia more cursive than those already discussed. Colman may have been a graduate of Oxford and brought books with him, yet hardly so many.[17]

He or the hospital did have the use of at least one printed book, a copy of the first edition of Walter Hylton's *Scale of Perfection*, printed at Westminster by Wynkyn de Worde in 1494 with the patronage of Lady Margaret Beaufort, King Henry VII's mother. A now defective copy in the British Library, IB 55165, was made up in the nineteenth century with leaves at the beginning and end from another copy.[18] The major middle portion (sig. b1–r6) is annotated by more than one hand, one recognizable as the same as in the three Oxford manuscripts, with the same elongated **N** in "Nota bene," "Nota optime," and "Exemplum"; "Nota adhuc," "fac hoc et vives," "Cape tecum" are new ones, with advisory ones such as "Notabilia religiosis," "Attende religiose," "The ground where uppon thou shal set alle thy good dedys," and "Discrecyon in redyng." And there are lengthy Latin passages from named authors: Augustine, Bonaventure (in fact David of Augsburg), Chrysostom, Lyra with book and chapter references, neatly written in upper and lower margins (fig. 9.6). Who were these for? Like many marginalia of all periods they reflect the copyists' own interests but equally encourage others, especially in a religious community, and here also the English notes for lay readers or hearers, such as the widows described by Erler.

There were three proximate outside sources for the quotations from Latin authors and texts: St. Augustine's Abbey, just across College Green, whose library no doubt contained many of the works of Saint Augustine or attributed to him;[19] the library of the Bristol Guild of Kalendars at All Saints Church, founded by Bishop Carpenter in 1442, of which we know disappointingly little;[20] and more immediately the personal collection of Miles Salley, bishop of Llandaff (South Wales) from 1500, who in that year is said to have paid for the rebuilding of the chancel of St. Mark's.[21] In his will of 1516 he asked to be buried there, where his effigy survives, leaving it vestments, a chalice, and a missal, with bequests to the brethren including John Colman, who was a witness. It said further that "my writen bokis in parchment here and my prent bokis of hugo de vienna be delivered to Ensham," the Benedictine monastery near Oxford, where he had been a monk, almoner, and abbot.[22] It appears he had habitually stayed at St. Mark's on the way to Llandaff and had kept his books in the house. While he left his manuscripts to Eynsham and specifies the set of Hugo de Vienna on the Bible (which is quoted on fol. 5 of St. John's 173, so probably before 1516/17), there is no mention of his other printed books, which possibly remained at St. Mark's. It is hardly a coincidence that among the books still belonging to All Saints Church, sometimes supposed to have been part of the library of the Guild of Kalendars, is an edition of Saint Thomas Aquinas on the Epistles printed at Bologna in 1481, in a contemporary English binding, with an inscription, "Liber milonis abbatis egoynshamie & landavensis episcopi," the last three words added—surely a stray from St. Mark's.[23] By 1516/17 almost all the sources quoted in marginalia and endleaves of the St. Mark's books were available in print, and that may also be true of some of the less common main contents of the manuscripts, though others probably had manuscript exemplars.[24]

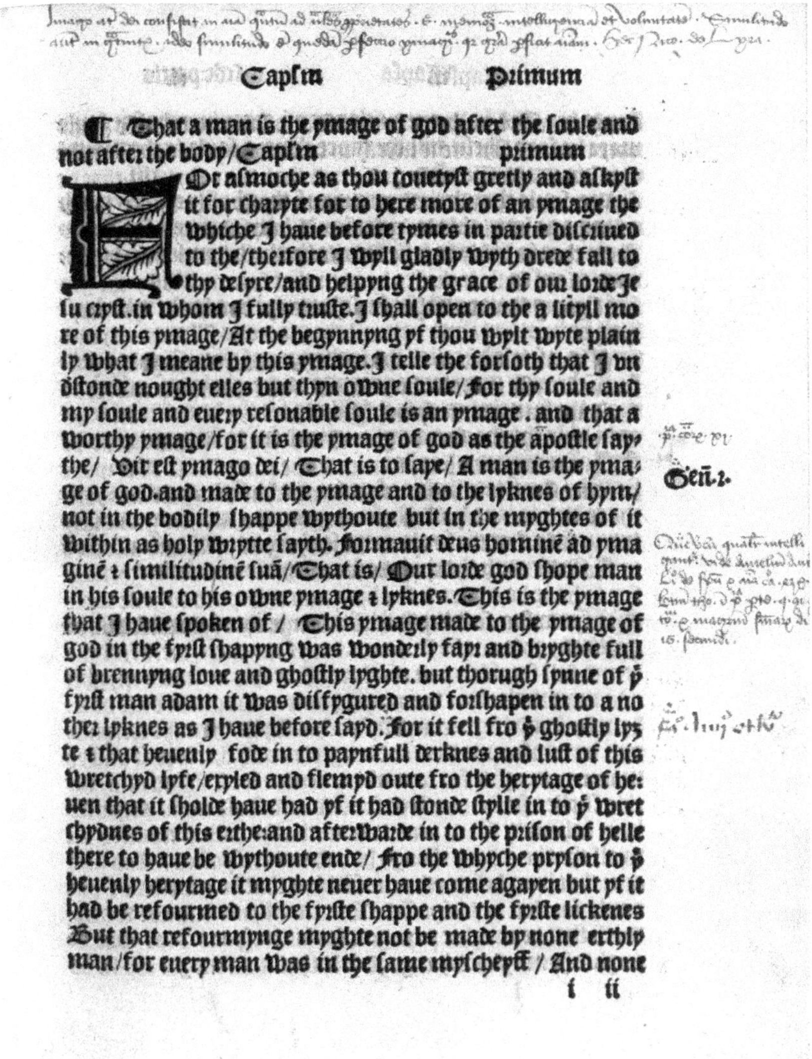

Capl'm Primum

¶ That a man is the ymage of god after the soule and
not after the body/Capl'm primum

For asmoche as thou coueytyst gretly and askyst
it for charyte for to here more of an ymage the
whiche I haue before tymes in partie discriued
to the/therfore I wyll gladly wyth drede fall to
thy desyre/and helpyng the grace of our lorde Je
su cryst.in whom I fully truste.I shall open to the a lityll mo
re of this ymage/At the begynnyng yf thou wylt wyte plain
ly what I meane by this ymage.I telle the forsoth that I vn
derstonde nought elles but thyn owne soule/For thy soule and
my soule and euery resonable soule is an ymage . and that a
worthy ymage/for it is the ymage of god as the apostle say
the/ Vir est ymago dei/ That is to saye/ A man is the yma Gen. 1.
ge of god.and made to the ymage and to the lyknes of hym/
not in the bodily shappe wythoute but in the myghtes of it
within as holy wrytte sayth. Formauit deus hominē ad yma
ginē & similitudinē suā/That is/ Our lorde god shope man
in his soule to his owne ymage & lyknes.This is the ymage
that I haue spoken of / This ymage made to the ymage of
god in the fyrst shappyng was wonderly fayr and bryghte full
of brennyng loue and ghostly lyghte. but thorugh synne of þe
fyrst man adam it was disfygured and forshapen in to a no
ther lyknes as I haue before sayd.For it fell fro þe ghostly lyg
te & that heuenly fode in to paynfull derknes and lust of this
wretchyd lyfe/exyled and flemyd oute fro the herytage of he:
uen that it sholde haue had yf it had stonde stylle in to þe wret
chydnes of this erthe:and afterwarde in to the prison of helle
there to haue be wythoute ende/ Fro the whyche pryson to þe
heuenly herytage it myghte neuer haue come agayen but yf it
had be refourmed to the fyrste shappe and the fyrste lickenes
But that refourmynge myghte not be made by none erthly
man/for euery man was in the same myschepff / And none

I ii

Fig. 9.6. London, British Library, IB 55165, sig. I2, upper half. © British Library Board.

Notes

1. A.I. Doyle, "Recent Directions in Medieval Manuscript Study," in *New Directions in Later Medieval Manuscript Studies: Essays from the 1998 Harvard Conference*, ed. Derek Pearsall (Woodbridge: Boydell and Brewer, 2000), 1–14.

2. E.g., A.I. Doyle, "Stephen Dodesham of Witham and Sheen," in *Of the Making of Books: Medieval Manuscripts, Their Scribes and Readers: Essays Presented to M.B. Parkes*, ed. Pamela Robinson and Rivkah Zim (Aldershot: Ashgate, 1997), 94–117; "William Darker: The Work of an English Carthusian Scribe," in *Medieval Manuscripts, Their Makers and Users: A Special Issue of VIATOR in Honor of Richard and Mary Rouse* (Turnhout: Brepols, 2011), 199–211.

3. Nicholas Orme and Margaret Webster, *The English Hospital, 1070–1570* (New Haven: Yale University Press, 1995), 51 (map of Bristol), 64–65; David Knowles and R.N. Hadcock, *Medieval Religious Houses, England and Wales,* 1st ed. (Cambridge: Cambridge University Press, 1953), wrongly as Benedictine, followed by Rose Graham in *Victoria County History: Gloucestershire*, ed. W. Page (London, 1907?), vol. 2, 115–17. That it followed the Augustinian rule is consistently clear from the Worcester episcopal registers.

4. William Robert Barker, *St. Mark's; or, The Mayor's Chapel, Bristol (formerly called the Church of the Gaunts)* (Bristol: W.C. Hemmons, 1892).

5. Mary Erler, "Widows in Retirement: Region, Patronage, Spirituality, Reading at the Gaunts, Bristol," *Religion and Literature* 37, no. 2 (2005): 51–75, where she gives more references. There are further instances of lay, particularly male, bequests to it and with brethren: e.g., Walter Wrattisley, gentleman, to be buried in the chancel like his wife, leaving the house revenues in Bristol, Somerset, and Wiltshire, 1502 (Public Record Office [now the National Archives]: Prerogative Court of Canterbury [PCC], register Blamyr 18); John Seyntabyne, "squyer," to be buried there and a chantry priest for a year, 1508, Thomas Tyler, Master, an executor, and John Colman, a witness (PCC Bennett 6).

6. Barker, *St. Mark's; or, The Mayor's Chapel, Bristol*, 47–56.

7. Bristol Record Office, *Great White Book*, ed. Elizabeth Ralph (Bristol Record Soc. 32, 1979), fol. 31v–32, evidence by Tyler, June 28, 11 *Hen.VII*; Orme and Webster, *The English Hospital, 1070–1570*, 65–66, for poor scholars to be housed and educated, twelve at St. Mark's.

8. Albinia C. de la Mare, *Catalogue of the Collection of Medieval Manuscripts Bequeathed to the Bodleian Library by James P.R. Lyell* (Oxford: Clarendon Press, 1971), 105–7 and pl. VII, showing monogram and different scripts from fols. 34, 35, and 188. For Bodley 618, see *Summary Catalogue of Western Manuscripts* (*SC*), 2149, vol. 2, 241–42, dating it earlier fifteenth century and from the Netherlands (?), without identifying the first item, an *Ammonicio*

addressed to a woman, lacking its prologue; but see Morton W. Bloomfield, *Incipits of Latin Works on the Virtues and Vices* (Cambridge, MA: Medieval Academy of America, 1979), no. 0722, also with prologue and 29 chapters in Bodley 797, an English volume (*SC* 2649, II, 469–70), and Clermont-Ferrand 155. The two following treatises attributed to Albertus Magnus occur with the same beginnings and endings in a quarto edition printed by G. Leeu, Antwerp, 1489.

9. A. I. Doyle, "Thomas Betson of Syon Abbey," *The Library*, 5th ser., 11 (1956): 115–18; R. Hanna, *Descriptive Catalogue of the Western Medieval Manuscripts in St. John's College, Oxford* (Oxford: Clarendon Press, 2002), 240–43, could not read or recognize "Gaunts" in the note about Pynson. The binding is now modern, but when I first saw the book in the 1950s it was still medieval, with staggered fore-edge tags for content divisions. The foliation has also been changed in part.

10. Barker, *St. Mark's; or, The Mayor's Chapel, Bristol*, 45, has Tyler until his death as 1515 and Richard Bromfield occurring in 1527, but the latter was Master of the hospital of St. John the Baptist from 1513 to at least 1537. Tyler was still alive and in office at the time of Miles Salley's will in November 1516. The bishop's license for an election after his death is undated but follows one for Bromfield's resignation of the vicarage of All Saints on May 8, 1517 (Worcester \Episcopal register \Silvester de Giglis, II, fol. 124v). Colman was Master by the acknowledgment of royal supremacy, September 12, 1534: PRO E25/18; Deputy Keeper's Report 7, app. 2, 281.

11. Ronald B. McKerrow, *Printers' and Publishers' Devices in England and Scotland, 1485–1640* (London: Bibliographical Society, 1913), no. 48, earliest state ca. 1491–92; cf. L. C. Silvestre, *Marques Typographiques* (Paris, 1867), nos. 73, 93, 133, and notably 86, Le Talleur (Rouen, 1487–93), who printed for Pynson in 1490; Lotte Hellinga, *William Caxton and Early Printing in England* (London: British Library, 2010), 115. The "reserved" white line just inside the black rectangle occurs in both Bodley 618 and Lyell 38 but not in St. John's 173, where the interlaced I and C also lack the decorative cusps and recesses found on the other instances.

12. For nomenclature of scripts, see Albert Derolez, *The Palaeography of Gothic Manuscript Books from the Twelfth to the Early Sixteenth Century* (Cambridge: Cambridge University Press, 2003), 160–74; M. B. Parkes, *English Cursive Book Hands, 1250–1500* (Oxford: Clarendon Press, 1969), xix–xxii, pls. 11–15.

13. Barker, *St. Mark's; or, The Mayor's Chapel, Bristol*, 64; Edith E. Williams, *The Chantries of William Canynges in St Mary Redcliffe Bristol* (Bristol: W. George, 1950), 37.

14. Norris Mathews, *Early Printed Books and Manuscripts in the City Reference Library Bristol* (Bristol: Hemmons, 1899), 66–67. Erler does not

emphasize the interest of the *Epistle of Discerning of Spirits*, associated elsewhere with the *Cloud of Unknowing* and often attributed to its author.

15. Bristol Record Office, St. Mark's Cartulary, ref. 31101/1, ed. Charles D. Ross (Bristol Record Society, 1959), fol. 100. Quire signatures and marginalia on fols. 54v, 55, 59, 73v, 77, 83v, 98v, 99, 142v, 153, 215, in set Secretary or Hybrida, like those of notes in other books described from St. Mark's. For flourishing in the Cartulary, compare St. John's 173, fol. 134v, but not fol. 144 with a different hand.

16. PRO/TNA, S.P.1/96, fol. 97.

17. A.B. Emden, *Biographical Register of the University of Oxford, 1501–1540* (Oxford: Clarendon Press, 1974), 131, has a John Colman as B.A. by 1515. Another person of that name had been vicar of St. Ewen's, Bristol, in 1501–2 (Worcester episcopal register S. de Giglis II, fol. 20) and left books to his church, one printed (*Transactions of the Bristol and Gloucestershire Archaeological Society*, 15, 155).

18. L. Hellinga, *Catalogue of Books Printed in the XVth Century Now in the British Library*, XI (2007), 190–1, without part 3 ("Mixed Life"), made up probably (from collation and dimensions) the Spencer copy, now Manchester University John Rylands Library 15046; see Henry Guppy, ed., *English Incunabula in the John Rylands Library* (Manchester: Manchester University Press 1930), 47.

19. Neil R. Ker, *Medieval Libraries of Great Britain*, 2nd ed., Guides and Handbooks 3 (London: Royal Historical Society, 1964), 13; T. Webber and A.G. Watson, eds., *Libraries of the Austin Canons*, Corpus of British Medieval Library Catalogues (CBMLC) 6 (London: British Library, 1998), 19–25.

20. N. Ramsay and J. Willoughby, eds., *Hospitals, Towns, and the Professions*, CBMLC 14 (London: British Library, 2009), 23; see N. Orme, "A Bristol Library for the Clergy," in *Education and Society in Medieval and Renaissance England* (London: Hambledon, 1988), 209–19. Ker, *Medieval Libraries of Great Britain*, 13, rejects books now at All Saints as from the Kalendars.

21. Barker, *St. Mark's; or, The Mayor's Chapel, Bristol*, 163–65.

22. PRO/TNA, PCC register Holder, made November 29, 1516, proved January 22, 1517: incomplete abridgment in *Testamenta Vetusta*, ed. N.H. Nicolas (London: Nichols, 1826), vol. 2, 538.

23. Bristol, All Saints Church 5, now Bristol Record Office P. AS/B/13, in a contemporary blind-stamped binding with two elementary small round tools not recognizably from a known binder, so perhaps by a monastic workshop.

24. Of works cited by name, the *Rosarium* is possibly the *Rosarium Sermonum* of Bernardus de Bustis (Lyon, 1513): it is probably not the Wycliffite alphabetical dictionary of theological quotations, for which see Christina Van Nolcken, ed., *The Middle English Translation of the Rosarium Theologie; a Selection . . .*, Middle English Texts 10 (Heidelberg: C. Winter, 1979), for the

citation is from chapter 12 into which it is not divided in the fairly numerous manuscripts. The only other printed book with that title is a very small devotional manual. The *Speculum Spiritualium* was printed in Paris for an English publisher in London, 1510, so in time to be cited in additions on the preliminary pages (fols. 2v–3r) of St. John's 173, and it was used for corrections to the text of Rolle's *Emendatio Vite* in Lyell 38. In addition to many surviving copies of the two issues of the printed edition on both sides of the Channel, there are 17 manuscripts of all or parts, without the *Emendatio*: A. I. Doyle, "The *Speculum Spiritualium* from Manuscript to Print," *Journal of the Early Book Society* 11 (2008): 145–53.

CHAPTER 10

John Colyns, Mercer and Bookseller of London, and Cuthbert Tunstall's Second Monition of 1526

Carol M. Meale

On October 25, 1526, an assortment of individuals associated with the book trade in London were summoned to appear before Cuthbert Tunstall, bishop of that city, in the "capella" of the London dwelling of the bishop of Norwich, known as Norwich Place, near "þe Charyng Crosse." These individuals, termed "bibliopolae," or booksellers, were subjected to what has become known as the Second Monition of Tunstall, in which they were told, in the translation by F. S. Siebert, not to "sell, hold, give or in any way part with any books containing Lutheran heresies or any other books conceived either in Latin or English, and that they neither print nor cause to be printed any other works whatsoever (except only works approved by the Church) unless first they exhibit the same to the Lord Legate [Thomas Wolsey], the Archbishop of Canterbury [William Warham], or the Bishop of London."[1] This document still survives, as City of London, London Metropolitan Archives DL/C/330, fol. 123r,[2] with its list of the thirty-one assembled booksellers attached, in which latter respect it differs from the monition issued two years previously, which has no such appendage.

The Second Monition is therefore of importance in several ways. Not only does it signify the increasing worries on the part of the authorities as to the possible spread of heretical, that is, Protestant, and perhaps especially Lutheran, ideas at a particular time, it also takes its place in the history of book censorship.[3] On another level it gives glimpses into the world of the book trade in London which are not otherwise possible, by naming individuals whom it is then possible to research further, looking at relative ages, wealth (where this can be established by, e.g., lay subsidy rolls, used for assessing taxes),[4] and the particular aspects of the book business in which they were involved. In relation to this latter point, while all those named were clearly booksellers, some were printers, some publishers, some retailers, and some importers, with a few combining some or all of these roles. In terms of nationality, some were natives, some denizens, and some aliens.[5] Not only this: the document also offers early evidence for the activities of some of those named, evidence for whose involvement with books is otherwise found later. My own curiosity was piqued not just because of the document's intrinsic interest for the history of the book trade, but principally because of the occurrence toward the end of the list of the name "Joh*an*nes Collyns," the London mercer the compilation of whose commonplace book, London, British Library, MS Harley 2252, was the subject of my 1981 paper.

At this time all I knew about Colyns was his place of residence in 1517, "in the p*ar*ysshe of *our* lady / of wolchyrche hawe anexid the Stock*ys* in þe /pultre" (London, British Library, MS Harley 2252, fol. 133v), the same parish in which he died some twenty-three or twenty-four years later;[6] that he was married to Alice Bohun;[7] his main area of trade, according to the Mercers' Company, the "Selling of Prynted bokes and other small tryfylles";[8] and the fact that he had provided Wynkyn de Worde with the setting copy for his edition of the romance of *Ipomydon*, ca. 1522, perhaps through the agency of Robert Copland, since the fullest of the two remaining copies contains an epilogue by him.[9] That Colyns's connection with de Worde lay through Copland is, possibly, rendered more likely by the fact that the name "Robert*us* copland" follows that of Colyns in the 1526 list, which appears to be organized in a completely arbitrary way—perhaps simply that of physical proximity in the "capella."

If that were the case, then it is worth remarking that the man whose name precedes that of Colyns, "ric*ard*us bank*es*," was a near neighbor of his. Listed as "Bokebynder" in the lay subsidy rolls of 1523, he operated from the "long shop," no. 24 on the north side of Poultry, next to St. Mildred's church and six doors from the Stocks Market.[10] In addition to bookbinding, he is known to have been active in printing in the mid-1520s. The following ten years are a blank, until he began to print again in 1539/40, by which time he had moved, "dwellynge in gracious street, beside the cundyte"; some of his later editions are stated to have been printed next to the White Hart in Fleet Street, or to have been sold there by one Anthony Clerke.[11] While he was a neighbor of Colyns, however, he was assessed at 100s, £5 being the lowest valuation recorded by the assessors.[12]

Another neighbor in Colyns's Walbrook Ward was John Richardson, who, although he does not appear in the monition list, was a "Stacyoner" and "doche" householder perhaps living, again, near the Stocks Market;[13] and yet another neighbor in the parish of St. Mary Woolchurch, one Richard Baas, scrivener, held no. 24b north of the Stocks between 1523 and 1527, and we know that the two men knew each other since at a parish meeting held on April 9, 1526, they appear as two of the ten "awdytors" appointed to settle fees for the clerk and any of his chosen helpers who aided in the celebration of the feast of St. Anne in the church, where there was a fraternity (to which Colyns belonged, as his will makes clear) dedicated to the saint.[14] "Johannes Gowghe," meanwhile, who does appear on the list, moved at one point in his religiously controversial, not to say tumultuous, career, in 1538/39, to the sign of the Mermaid in Lombard Street, "against the stockes market."[15]

Colyns's status as a mercer in the monition document is not as unusual as might at first appear. Other of the booksellers were members of mercantile companies: "Joh*an*nes Heron" was a haberdasher and stationer,[16] Robert Wyer was a salter,[17] and "Thomas petyt" was made free of the Drapers' Company in 1519,[18] although his master, John Hutton, may have taken up bookselling prior to Petyt's apprenticeship.[19] However, there are no sponsors or commercial backers of the stature of Caxton's patrons, or others such as the draper William Wilcock, who backed John Lettou in 1480; the haberdasher and sheriff of London, Henry Somer; or William Bretton, grocer and merchant of the staple, who was a major book importer in the early 1500s.[20]

Anne Sutton has called Colyns "a very unsuccessful businessman."[21] Yet he took an active role in his company from his early years. Made free in 1492, in 1494 "John Collyns Junior" appears as one of four men "extra liueratura" (i.e., Bachelors of the Company, who did not hold the status or seniority of men of the Livery) who participated in the election of the "weyer of silk" at the General Court held on February 20 (what may be of significance is that one of his companions was Roger Thorney, patron of Wynkyn de Worde);[22] he was present at the Quarterday Court in March 1510 at which the decision was made for negotiations to be begun with the "Maister" of Saint Thomas of Acres "for the Purchase of suche houses of his whiche be necessary to the Enlargyng of oure Chapell, Hall and other necessary Roumes adionyng to the same";[23] and he even, albeit without success, stood for the position of clerk of the company in 1516.[24] In his private, as opposed to public, life he was elected to two parish committees of auditors.[25] And then professionally, once more, his probable trade as a distributor and not simply a retailer of books was sufficient for him to be summoned to Bishop Tunstall's meeting in 1526, in the company of all but one of the London printers of the time and in that of a majority of stationers.[26]

The reason for Colyns's specialization in the selling of books can, in all probability, be traced back to his apprenticeship. As noted, he was made free of the company in 1492, being described as late apprentice to "William Tenaker."[27] Tenaker, or Tenacre, had himself been apprenticed to William Pratte (he was made free in 1473). Pratte is a name well known to historians of the book, for he was the "special frende" and "synguler frende and of olde knowledge" of Caxton, who provided the printer with the French morality and scriptural work known as *The Book of Good Manners*, translated by Caxton and published after Pratte's death, in May 1487.[28] Tenacre was one of Pratte's executors and also one of Pratte's wife's executors.[29] As Sutton has pointed out, it may have been possible for Tenacre to have met Caxton at his onetime master's house after Caxton's return from abroad,[30] and it may equally well be that the two men shared an interest in books, which Tenacre passed on to his apprentice. Be that as it may, although Colyns was astute enough to realize that the romance of *Ipomydon* would be a best-seller (it ran to two editions, in around 1522 and 1530/31, and he presumably sold at least some of the copies as part of his stock), he clearly lacked the capital to invest in larger, or potentially more profitable, projects. There is no lay subsidy return for him in the 1520s, for example, which was probably a sign that his goods amounted to less than the lowest valuation of £5; and in 1540, in the area of St. Mary Woolchurch in which it is thought he lived, four houses were let for the yearly rent of £5 6s 8d.

They were 12 feet 6 inches square, and each comprised a cellar with three floors above. None of the residents who lived there were taxed.[31] It is perhaps not surprising, taking this information into account, that Colyns's wife, Alice, died a "paup*er*" in 1542: her executor, one Browne (presumably the man to whom administration of Colyns's goods had been granted), swore that no goods remained to her on her death.[32]

This turn of events for Colyns and his wife is all the more puzzling since her father, Edmund Bohun, a clerk of the King's Exchequer from 1471 and an auditor there by 1490,[33] a man who has been described as having "every appearance of being one of those indispensable officials whom everyone discovers he cannot do without,"[34] was armigerous (his coat of arms, gules, between an orle of martlets golde, a crescent ermine, was granted by Clarenceux king at arms in 1486),[35] and from relatively humble beginnings, acquired plentiful lands mostly in Suffolk but also in Essex and London. He had compiled for him a cartulary of his lands in his home village of Fressingfield in the Waveney valley, Suffolk,[36] which bears testimony to his acquisitions. He was known and respected among a wide circle of the East Anglian gentry. He was one of the executors of the will of Thomasin Hopton, book owner and third wife of the eponymous subject of Colin Richmond's 1981 study,[37] and was retained as a councillor by her stepson, Sir William Hopton, and his son, Sir George Hopton, from 1480/81.[38] He was also known to the Paston family. While awaiting payment of his and his retinue's first quarter wages in 1475, for attendance at Calais, John Paston III wrote to his mother, Margaret, from Norwich, saying that he had been recommended to wait in that city until he had been paid by "oon Edmund Bowen of the Cheker, a specyall frend of myn."[39]

It is clear from the Paston documents that Bohun was close to Edward Hastings, Edward IV's Lord Chamberlain, and this has led Richmond to suggest that the latter man was Bohun's patron.[40] But this theory would not account for Bohun's rapid rise in the king's service from a remote village in Suffolk, and it seems more likely that he early caught the eye of the de la Pole family, dukes of Suffolk, whose principal East Anglian seat of Wingfield was two miles away, in the parish adjacent to that of Fressingfield.[41] By 1480 Bohun was described as gentleman of London, and it was presumably in that city that his daughter Alice met Colyns.[42] She and her two sisters, Agnes and Margaret, however, did not profit as much as they might have done from their father's achievements. In his will, dated May 14, 1499, and proved January 31, 1501, in the absence of a male heir, Edmund left the majority of his lands to his two nephews ("nepotes"), Nicholas and John, who were also executors.[43] Alice, as we shall see, was left some land, but she and her sisters, plus their husbands (Margaret, who was unmarried at the date of Edmund's death, had by this time married one William Thomas), took court action to challenge the will. The two cousins then took counteraction against Agnes's husband, John Cooke, but after Nicholas's death in 1505 matters were resolved in favor of John.[44] That there was no bad feeling on John Bohun's part, at least, is indicated by the fact that in his will, proved in Norwich on August 9, 1511, John left his godson, Edmund Colyns, 6s 8d. This Edmund is the only one of John and Alice's children whose name is known, all his other (unnumbered) offspring having predeceased him, as Colyns states in his own will.

It may be that Alice was, in comparison to her sisters, particularly favored by her father, for she was left property in Wood Street, London (a part of which was left to John for his life, with reversion to Alice upon his death), and lands in Essex. It is possible, though, that John and Alice were under some financial pressure as early as 1506, for in this year they jointly conveyed parcels of her inherited lands in Mount Bures, Wakes Colne, and Great Tey, all in Essex, to a London citizen and mercer, Robert Wentworth, and Richard Kemp, for a consideration of 40 marks.[45] Twelve years later, on July 8, 1518, they conveyed the bakehouse in Wood Street, in the parish of St. Alban, to four goldsmiths of the City.[46] The assumption is, though it cannot be a certainty, that they were in need of money to invest in Colyns's business venture. Whatever the truth of the matter, the life journey of Alice Bohun, from a secure, even quite elevated, beginning, to her death as a widow and pauper, was a sad one.[47]

In 1526, however, her husband was clearly still regarded as a man of some importance as a retailer and distributor of books when he was summoned to the chapel of the bishop of Norwich to meet Cuthbert Tunstall. The generally well-known nature of the rest of the company assembled is demonstrated by the names of the individuals who attended the meeting, all of whom except three are familiar to literary historians working on the early years of the sixteenth century. The first printer, and bookseller, to be mentioned is "wynkyn de word," and he is followed by "mestres andrewe," probably the wife of the printer Laurence Andrewe, a significant presence because it marks the potential power of women within the book trade;[48] among the stationers, "Thomas kellyt" (Kele) is the first to be mentioned. Later in the column appears the Norman John Rowse or Jean Le Roux, probably the man of that name who was the brother of the printer Nicolas Le Roux of Rouen.[49] In the following column comes "henry Pepwell," followed by "Will*i*am bona*m*" (who was twice a subtenant of John Rastell in Paternoster Row, outside St. Paul's Churchyard, and who worked with Pepwell and Henry Tab, and who was one of the youngest of those present, being born in 1492);[50] "ric*ar*dus ffawk*es*"; Petit; one "michaell," possibly either Michael Morin, last recorded in a colophon of 1506, or Michael Pulleyn, an importer of books from 1520 to 1535;[51] "henric*us* dab" (better known as Henry Tab); "Joh*anne*s Toye"; "Joh*anne*s Gowghe"; "Ric*ardus* pynson"; "Robert*us* Redman"; "Robert*us* copland"; "Joh*anne*s Scott"; "robertus wyer"; "Thom*as* Bartlett" (Berthelet, who took over from Richard Pynson as King's Printer on the latter's death);[52] and the multifaceted "M*aster* Rastell," that is, the lawyer, dramatist, theatrical producer, and printer John Rastell, who in fact was one of the few, together with Gough, mentioned in the Second Monition whose change in religious beliefs contributed to his downfall.[53] (By way of contrast, there is every indication from Colyns's will that he remained a staunch Catholic, bequeathing his soul to "allmyghtei god. The holly trynite, our blessed ladye saint marye, And / all the Cumpanye of heuen.")[54] Furthermore, some, though by no means all, of these individuals were possessors of considerable wealth. De Worde's taxable wealth, for instance, was £201 11s 1d, while Richard Pynson was assessed at £60 (the discrepancy not necessarily the result of any comparative profitability in the chosen areas of specialization of the two men);[55] and Pynson's successor as King's Printer, Berthelet, received an annuity of £4.[56] It is not known whether any of those listed reached the wealth of the bookseller and binder "Johannes Raynes," whose stock, at the time of his death, was valued at over £1,000.[57] Others, like Robert Redman, were of far more modest means, his evaluation being £10.[58] But that Colyns was not alone in his comparative lack of funds is indicated by the lay subsidy rolls of 1524 and 1544. In the former, Robert Wyer is enrolled as having goods worth £4, despite having a career as printer and bookseller which spanned over thirty years (although he had probably not begun to print by the time of the Second Monition);[59] in the latter, Colyns's possible collaborator, Copland, was assessed at 20s.[60]

Of the remaining eight men, most of those who can be identified were stationers. "Lodwic*us*," or Lewis, Sutton, also a bookbinder, was joint warden of the Stationers' Company in early October 1526, along with the printer Henry Pepwell;[61] "henricus harmon" in 1541 is mentioned as factor, or agent, for the Cologne stationer Arnold Byrckman, in St. Paul's Churchyard, and may be identical to the stationer from Deventer in the bishopric of Utrecht who took out denization in 1535. The man whose first name only appears fourth on the monition list may have been Arnold Harrison, another alien.[62] "Simon*us* coston" was an original member of the Stationers' Company on its incorporation in 1557 and following this monition was set to become "the principal builder and landlord of the bookshops adjoining the cathedral walls" in St. Paul's Churchyard.[63] "Joh*an*nes Groot" was a native of Normandy who took out letters of denization in 1535;[64] and "Nicholas Sutton" was a stationer who died sometime before April 30, 1530.[65] This leaves only two names unaccounted for. "Coverd," Peter Blayney suggests, was one Govaert van der Haeghen;[66] and "Edwardus Isengold," whose name appears first on the list, and who may have been a merchant, even perhaps an alien or a Hansard, trace of whom I have not been able to find.

So where does this additional information to be drawn from the monition list lead in terms of an understanding of John Colyns, mercer and bookseller of London, and what is it possible to learn from it? To put the matter one way, it embeds him in temporal and physical matrices in a way in which a study of his manuscript book alone cannot do. In addition, the fact that the location of individuals connected with the book trade is of importance both in the age of manuscript and printed book production has been made abundantly clear by the work of C. Paul Christianson and Peter Blayney.[67] The evidence I have gathered here is suggestive of a similar, if smaller, clustering of booksellers and producers around the Stocks Market, which future work may further substantiate. The evidence gives substance and materiality to Colyns as a man, as a collector of texts both literary and nonliterary, and as a seller of what the Mercers, somewhat dismissively, termed "Prynted bokes and other small tryfylles"—in the process perhaps offering a corrective to what Paul Needham has described as "the proud words of one of the great London companies."[68] Ultimately, and perhaps most important, it gives "a local habitation and a name" to the life and work of John Colyns.

Notes

I wish to express my gratitude to Professor Peter W. M. Blayney for his kindness in allowing me to see extracts, prior to publication, from his book *The Stationers' Company and the Printers of London, 1501–1557*, 2 vols. (Cambridge: Cambridge University Press, 2013), vol. 1, and for his generosity in reading an earlier draft of this paper. For any remaining errors I am alone responsible.

I should like to thank Derek Pearsall for all his support and for the opportunity given to me by speaking at the 1981 conference; and also the late Elizabeth Salter, for the interest she took and the encouragement she gave me to work on the manuscript and its owner.

1. F. S. Siebert, *Freedom of the Press in England, 1476–1776* (Urbana: University of Illinois Press, 1965), 46. The first account of this monition was given by A. W. Reed, "The Regulation of the Book Trade before the Proclamation of 1538," *Transactions of the Bibliographical Society* 15 (1918): 157–84, 170–71, reprinted in A. W. Reed, *Early Tudor Drama* (London: Methuen, 1926), 160–87, 173–74. On Tunstall, see D. G. Newcombe, "Tunstal, Cuthbert (1474–1559)," in *Oxford Dictionary of National Biography* (Oxford: Oxford University Press, 2004), online ed., May 2006.

2. All documents held by the City of London, London Metropolitan Archives, are quoted in this essay with the permission of the Senior Archivist.

3. A convenient overview of medieval and Tudor censorship is Howard W. Winger, "Regulations Relating to the Book Trade in London from 1357 to 1586," *Library Quarterly* 26 (1956): 157–95; but see, more recently, Lotte Hellinga and J. B. Trapp, eds., *The Cambridge History of the Book in Britain*, vol. 3, *1400–1557* (Cambridge: Cambridge University Press, 1999), s.v., Index, "Control of the press and book-trade." Also Blayney, *The Stationers' Company and the Printers of London*, vol. 1, chap. 4.

4. E. Gordon Duff, "Notes on Stationers from the Lay Subsidy Rolls of 1523–24," *The Library*, 2nd ser., 9 (1908): 257–66.

5. A similarly capacious definition applies to those describing themselves as stationers; see Peter W. M. Blayney, *The Stationers' Company before the Charter, 1403–1557* (Cambridge: Worshipful Company of Stationers and Newspapermakers, 2003), 15. Cf. the analysis of stationers in the monition list given below.

6. His brief will, dated July 10, 1538, of which execution of goods was granted to his wife Alice, in the person of "henrici browne" on July 4, 1541, is City of London, London Metropolitan Archives DL/C/B/004/MS 9171/011, fol. 56v. Fol. 133v of the Harley manuscript is illustrated in Carol M. Meale, "London, British Library Harley MS 2252, John Colyns' 'Boke': Structure and

Content," in *Tudor Manuscripts 1485–1603*, ed. A. S. G. Edwards, English Manuscript Studies 1100–1700 (London: British Library, 2009), 15, 66.

7. Carol M. Meale, "The Compiler at Work: John Colyns and BL MS Harley 2252," in *Manuscripts and Readers in the Fifteenth Century: The Literary Implications of Manuscript Study, Essays from the 1981 Conference at the University of York*, ed. Derek Pearsall (Cambridge: D. S. Brewer, 1983), 99.

8. L. Lyell, assisted by F. D. Watney, ed., *Worshipful Company of Mercers; Acts of Court of the Mercers' Company, 1453–1527* (Cambridge: Cambridge University Press, 1936), 509.

9. Carol M. Meale, "Wynkyn de Worde's Setting-Copy for *Ipomydon*," *Studies in Bibliography* 35 (1982): 156–71, and see 169–70 for Copland; also Mary Carpenter Erler, *Robert Copland: Poems* (Toronto: University of Toronto Press, 1993), 76–77.

10. E. Gordon Duff, *A Century of the English Book Trade* (London: Bibliographical Society, 1948), 7–8; supplemented by private communication, Derek Keene. I am most grateful to Professor Keene for discussing Colyns and his environs with me.

11. Blayney, *The Stationers' Company and the Printers of London*, vol. 1, 248; Duff, *A Century*, 7–8.

12. Pers. comm. Derek Keene.

13. C. Paul Christianson, "The Rise of London's Book-Trade," in Hellinga and Trapp, *The Cambridge History of the Book in Britain*, 128–47, 138; Duff, *A Century*, 137.

14. BL MS Harley 2252, fol. 165r; Carol M. Meale, "London, British Library Harley MS 2252, John Colyns' 'Boke,'" 115, no. 82. He bequeathed 20d to "the brotherhede of our Lady and Saint Anne." Another of the auditors was "Stephen warde wexchaundler," whose wife, Margaret (daughter of Richard Pynson: pers. comm. Peter W. M. Blayney), participated in the baptism of the fifth child of Richard Hill, grocer and merchant adventurer, who compiled Oxford, Balliol College MS 354. This does not, of course, prove or even indicate that the compilers of two of the most famous personal compilations of the sixteenth century in London knew each other, but it is of note that *if* Colyns lived in the same area in the early years of the century as he did in 1517, another of his neighbors would have been Henry Wyngar, alderman and later mayor of the City: Hill described himself in the earliest section of his book as "s*er*uant" to Wyngar (fol. 176r), and he would have lived with Wyngar as his apprentice. See Roman Dyboski, ed., *Songs, Carols, and Other Miscellaneous Poems, from the Balliol MS. 354, Richard Hill's Commonplace Book*, EETS, e.s., 101 (1908), xiv, xv; and on Hill's life, W. P. Hills, "Richard Hill of Hillend and Balliol 354," *Notes and Queries* 177 (1939): 452–56; R. A. B. Mynors, *Catalogue of the Manuscripts of Balliol College Oxford* (Oxford: Clarendon

Press, 1963), 352–54; and Heather Collier, "Richard Hill—A London Compiler," in *The Court and Cultural Diversity: Selected Papers from the Eighth Triennial Congress of the Courtly Literature Society*, ed. Evelyn Mullally and John Thompson (Cambridge: D. S. Brewer, 1997), 319–29.

15. Duff, *A Century*, 58; Mary D. Lobel, ed., *The City of London from Prehistoric Times to c. 1520*, British Atlas of Historic Towns, 3 (Oxford: Oxford University Press in conjunction with the Historic Towns Trust, 1991), map 3. Peter W. M. Blayney's study, *The Bookshops in Paul's Cross Churchyard*, Occasional Papers of the Bibliographical Society, 5 (London: Bibliographical Society, 1990), demonstrates for a similar period in the sixteenth century the importance of this different location within London for the book trade, though it should be noted that he offers a critique of its reconstruction on the map in Lobel, *The City of London*, 91–96.

16. He occupied part of John Rastell's shop at the sign of the Mermaid near Paul's Gate, 1523–26: Duff, *A Century*, 69.

17. Blayney, *The Stationers' Company and the Printers of London*, vol. 1, 248.

18. Alexandra Gillespie, "Petyt, Thomas (b. in or before 1494, d. 1565/6)," *ODNB*, online ed., January 2008.

19. On Hutton's specialization I am indebted to information from Peter W. M. Blayney.

20. For these last three men, see, most recently, Christianson, "The Rise of London's Book-Trade," 138, 141, 142; and Anne F. Sutton, "William Bretton, Publisher of Fine Books, 1506–10," *The Library*, 7th ser., 14 (2013): 3–17.

21. Anne F. Sutton, *The Mercery of London: Trade, Goods and People, 1130–1578* (Aldershot: Ashgate, 2005), 444.

22. Lyell and Watney, *Acts of Court*, 241; Gavin Bone, "Extant Manuscripts Printed from by Wynkyn de Worde with Notes on the Owner, Roger Thorney," *The Library*, 4th ser., 12 (1932): 285–36. On Colyns being made free of the company and for older men of that name (hence his appellation "Junior"), see text and n. 27 below. On the division of the company into bachelors, or yeomen, and liverymen, see Jean Imray, "'Les Bones Gentes de la Mercerye de Londres': A Study of the Membership of the Medieval Mercers' Company," in *Studies in London History Presented to P. E. Jones*, ed. A. E. J. Hollaender (London: Hodder & Stoughton, 1969), 457–67; Lyell and Watney, *Acts of Court*, x–xii. Colyns probably remained outside the Livery, if his petition to the company (which mentions his dealing in printed books) in which he asks to engage an apprentice on the lesser terms accorded to vestment makers gives an indication of his wealth and status.

23. Lyell and Watney, *Acts of Court*, 384. On these lengthy negotiations with the house of St. Thomas of Acre which finally concluded with the purchase in 1542, see Sutton, *The Mercery of London*, 360–73.

24. Lyell and Watney, *Acts of Court*, 384, 438–39.

25. See above, n. 14; see also Meale, "London, British Library, Harley MS 2252, John Colyns' 'Boke,'" 115, no. 81, for his election in November 1525 to a committee to decide on payments to be made for tolling of bells and for burials in the parish.

26. Blayney, *The Stationers' Company and the Printers of London*, 247–49: "It can hardly be imagined that these thirty-one names represent a majority of the retail booksellers in the London area, but they probably include nearly all of the wholesale distributors" (249). Blayney points out that the only printer active in the London area but not present was Peter Treveris, because he was based in the diocese of Winchester (248).

27. The Register of Freemen was compiled in 1527 by the company's clerk from sources which are now lost. Two other men named John Colyns were admitted to the company, in 1474 and 1476, but these dates would make them too old to be the compiler of BL MS Harley 2252, who would probably have been born ca. 1465–70, which would allow for a suitable apprenticeship period of ten years. He would then have been about seventy years old when he died. I am grateful to Jean Imray, former archivist to the Mercers' Company, for information drawn from the Register. On the death of one of these older men in 1506/7, see Carol M. Meale, "The Social and Literary Contexts of a Late Medieval Manuscript: A Study of BL MS Harley 2252 and Its Owner John Colyns," 2 vols. (DPhil dissertation, University of York, 1984), vol. 1, 98; vol. 2, 77, nn. 32, 33.

28. N. F. Blake, *Caxton's Own Prose* (London: Andre Deutsch, 1973), 60–61; Anne F. Sutton, "Caxton Was a Mercer: His Social Milieu and Friends," in *England in the Fifteenth Century: Proceedings of the 1992 Harlaxton Symposium*, ed. Nicholas Rogers, Harlaxton Medieval Studies, 4 (Stamford, U.K.: Paul Watkins, 1994), 141–47.

29. Pratte's will is TNA, PRO Prob.11/7, fols. 192r–v; Tenacre's (who was only in his forties when he died) is TNA, PRO Prob. 11/10, fols. 119v–121r. He does not mention Colyns in his will.

30. Sutton, "Caxton Was a Mercer," 147.

31. Pers. comm. Derek Keene.

32. City of London, London Metropolitan Archives, DL/C/B/001/MS 09168/009, fol. 222v, reads that on April 15 "comp*aru*it Bru*ne* & iura*vit* q*uod* nulla bona dict*ae* def*unctae* remanent penes ips*am*." Anne Sutton, former archivist to the Mercers' Company, has informed me in correspondence that if Alice had petitioned them the Mercers might have relieved her but that she was not admitted to the Whittington almshouse.

33. Colin Richmond, *The Paston Family in the Fifteenth Century: Endings* (Manchester: Manchester University Press, 2000), 153.

34. Colin Richmond, *John Hopton: A Fifteenth-Century Suffolk Gentleman* (Cambridge: Cambridge University Press, 1981), 196.

35. Joan Corder, transcriber and ed., *William Harvey: The Visitation of Suffolk 1561* (London: Harleian Society, 1981), 178–81; S. Wilton Rix, *The Diary and Autobiography of Edmund Bohun Esq.* (Beccles: privately printed, Read Crisp, 1853), viii.

36. Bridget Wells-Furby, ed., *The Bohun of Fressingfield Cartulary*, Suffolk Charters XIX (Woodbridge: Boydell Press for the Suffolk Records Society, 2011).

37. Richmond, *John Hopton*, 195 (she died in 1498); for her small collection of books, including a Hoccleve, see TNA PRO Prob. 11/11, fols. 151r–152r; and Carol M. Meale, "The Morgan Library Copy of *Generides*," in *Romance in Medieval England*, ed. Maldwyn Mills, Jennifer Fellows, and Carol M. Meale (Cambridge: D. S. Brewer, 1991), 103 and n. 60.

38. Richmond, *John Hopton*, 195; Richmond, *The Paston Family: Endings*, 153.

39. Norman Davis, ed., *Paston Letters and Papers of the Fifteenth Century*, 2 vols. (Oxford: Clarendon Press, 1971, 1976), vol. 1, 593, no. 364. For further letters mentioning Bohun, see 598, no. 368; and 599, no. 369.

40. Richmond, *The Paston Family: Endings*, 154 n. 86.

41. Meale, "The Social and Literary Contexts of a Late Medieval Manuscript," vol. 1, 106; Wells-Furby, *The Bohun of Fressingfield Cartulary*, 13. Katherine de la Pole, great-aunt of John de la Pole, second duke of Suffolk, was responsible for the building of the superb south porch of Fressingfield church ca. 1420, in memory of her husband and son, who had died in Henry V's French wars; and the initials of John's mother, Alice Chaucer/de la Pole, are carved into the end of one of the set of church benches of ca. 1470 in the north aisle. The arms of Edmund Bohun "de Scaccario domini Regis," dated 1516, some fifteen years after his death, were once in a window of Fressingfield church: Rix, *The Diary and Autobiography of Edmund Bohun*, viii n.

42. John and Alice were married at some time between when Colyns was made free in 1492 and the drawing up of her father's will in 1497, in which she is described as "Alicia Colyns filia mea."

43. TNA, PRO Prob.11/13, fols. 59r–60r; for his landholdings, see Wells-Furby, *The Bohun of Fressingfield Cartulary*, 14–15; his estate was said to be worth about £40 per annum.

44. TNA, PRO ECP/C1/247/45; PRO ECP/C1/259/29; PRO ECP/C1/309/56; Wells-Furby, *The Bohun Cartulary of Fressingfield*, 16–17.

45. P. H. Reaney and Marc Fitch, eds., *Feet of Fines for Essex*, vol. 4, *1423–1547* (Colchester for the Essex Archaeological Society, 1964), 112. The conveyance consisted of one messuage, one garden, fifty acres of land, six acres of meadow, thirty acres of pasture, and three acres of wood.

46. City of London, London Metropolitan Archives, Wills and Pleas, Court of Hustings CLA/023/DW/01/238 (54). In relation to Colyns's wealth it

is of note that although he was deemed insufficiently solvent to pay toward Thomas Wolsey's "loan," or tax, of 1522 (Blayney, *The Stationers' Company and the Printers of London*, 1, 219), in July 1517 he became a surety for the orphans of a grocer of London and in July 1518 a surety for those of a goldsmith (155 and n. 140). As Blayney has explained to me in private correspondence, this probably did not entail a great deal of financial risk for Colyns (or the orphans), the person listed first as surety managing "the whole sum while the others were simply sureties for payment." If this first surety defaulted, then the others were collectively liable. For Colyns's involvement, see City of London, London Metropolitan Archives, Letter Book N, fols. 47r, 78v, 134v.

47. It is also one which is in stark contrast to those of the women whose lives are documented in Caroline M. Barron and Anne F. Sutton, eds., *Medieval London Widows, 1300–1500* (London: Hambledon Press, 1994).

48. A. S. G. Edwards, "Andrewe, Laurence (*fl.* c. 1520–1539)," *ODNB*, online ed.; Duff, *A Century*, 3; Blayney, *The Stationers' Company and the Printers of London*, vol. 1, 248.

49. Christianson, "The Rise of London's Book-Trade," 145, for the record of an older man of the same name. Duff, *A Century*, 91–92, does not mention two men identically named, but the suggestion that the man named in the monition is the older of the two was mentioned in private correspondence from Peter W. M. Blayney.

50. Blayney, *The Stationers' Company and the Printers of London*, vol. 1, 249.

51. Ibid., 104.

52. K. F. Pantzer, "Berthelet, Thomas (*d.* 1555)," rev. *ODNB*, online ed., January 2008.

53. Cecil H. Clough, "Rastell, John (*c.* 1475–1536)," *ODNB*, online ed.; Alec Ryrie, "Gough, John (*d.* 1543/4)," *ODNB*, online ed., January 2008. De Worde, of course, had been summoned in December 1525, together with John Gough, to appear before Geoffrey Wharton, Tunstall's vicar general, for printing Gough's translation of a book which the authorities deemed heretical, titled *The Image of Love*, by John Ryckes, which exercise had apparently been carried out as a New Year's gift for the nuns of Syon Abbey. See, most recently, Blayney, *The Stationers' Company and the Printers of London*, vol. 1, 245–46.

54. City of London, London Metropolitan Archives, DL/C/B/004/MS 9171/011, fol. 56v; he also asked for "vij Masses at scala celi / yeu*en* whillstes I do lye In extremis and other . . . iiij as sone after my / deceasse as may be done conuenyentlye."

55. Duff, "Lay Subsidy Rolls," 261.

56. Pantzer, "Berthelet," Thomas.

57. E. G. Duff, "Reynes, John (*d.* 1545)," rev. Anita McConnell, *ODNB*, online ed., October 2008; Duff, *A Century*, 135–36. In the Return of Aliens in

1523 he was assessed at £40 3s 4d, while in those returns for 1541 and 1544 he was assessed at £100.

58. Duff, "Lay Subsidy Rolls," 261; Duff, *A Century*, 132–33.

59. N. F. Blake, "Wyer, Robert (*fl.* 1524–1556)," *ODNB*, online ed.

60. Mary C. Erler, "Copland, Robert (*fl.* 1505–1547)," *ODNB*, online ed., January 2008; Duff, *A Century*, 31–32.

61. Reed, "Regulation of the Book Trade," 171.

62. Blayney, *The Stationers' Company and the Printers of London*, vol. 1, 249.

63. Duff, *A Century*, 33; Blayney, *The Bookshops in Paul's Cross Churchyard*, 19.

64. Duff, *A Century*, 61.

65. Ibid., 154.

66. Blayney, *The Stationers' Company and the Printers of London*, vol. 1, 249.

67. See the work of C. Paul Christianson, especially *A Directory of London Stationers and Book Artisans, 1300–1500* (New York: Bibliographical Society of America, 1990); Blayney, *The Bookshops in Paul's Cross Churchyard.*

68. See Paul Needham, "The Customs Rolls," in Hellinga and Trapp, *The Cambridge History of the Book in Britain*, 163.

CHAPTER 11

Selling Lydgate Manuscripts in the Twentieth Century

A. S. G. Edwards

Few have done more to stimulate the study of fifteenth-century English manuscripts in modern times than Derek Pearsall. And no one has done more to stimulate the study of John Lydgate over this period. The conjunction of these facts prompts me to offer as a small tribute to him some consideration of a largely ignored aspect of the study of Lydgate's manuscripts.

What a manuscript has cost as it has passed from owner to owner generally has been a matter of no interest to scholars. It is easy to understand why this should be so. Such information is often difficult to obtain and rarely is included in the published record for particular copies of a work. And yet prices are an important part of the historical record since they are linked to provenance and the history of a manuscript's ownership and also provide an obvious indicator of both material and cultural value over time. In what follows I would like to examine the history of the sale in the twentieth century of manuscripts of John Lydgate's major and most widely circulating works, *The Fall of Princes*, the *Troy Book*, *The Life of Our Lady*, and *The Siege of Thebes*.[1] This period is one for which far more information exists than for earlier periods and one that has witnessed the most remarkable reorientation in critical perceptions of this poet's literary significance in the last quarter of the century. There may therefore be some value in looking at the history of the selling of Lydgate's manuscripts over the past hundred or so years.

I would stress, however, both the limitations on and the difficulties of retrieving and assessing this evidence. Retrieval is complicated by the inadequacy of the surviving records in some libraries, which have not always preserved details of purchases. Also, some libraries are not inclined to disclose prices even for items bought many years ago. And in some instances it is not possible to establish final purchase prices. Most manuscripts discussed here were bought at auction, generally through an agent acting on behalf of an end purchaser. While the auction price is usually establishable, the final markup charged by the agent to his client for his services is not. This is not a major issue: most dealers acting for a client have historically charged a fee of 10 percent, though on occasions it may be less (or—less likely—more) depending on the number of items that are purchased on commission for a client at one time or the nature of the agent's relationship with the purchaser (good clients can expect to pay less in commission). When a dealer buys an item for stock the markup is less predictable and depends on such factors as the amount of time it remains unsold and the relationship of the ultimate purchaser to the dealer. But, with such qualifications, usually sufficient information can be retrieved to permit reasonably secure generalizations regarding the implications of the commerce in Lydgate manuscripts in the twentieth century.

The most frequently sold work of Lydgate's in this period was his longest poem, *The Fall of Princes*. When Henry Bergen completed his edition of this poem in 1927,[2] he was able to describe thirty manuscripts of it, of which twenty-five were either already in public or institutional collections or in private libraries where they still remain.[3] Some of the manuscripts Bergen records had had a commercial history earlier in the twentieth century prior to finding permanent homes; these are discussed below.[4] In addition, a number of others of which Bergen was aware were to subsequently move to new homes.[5] And several others have come to light since Bergen's edition, namely, those now in the Newberry Library, Chicago; the McPherson Library, University of Victoria;[6] the University of Illinois Library, Urbana-Champaign; and English Heritage. In total, there are thirteen manuscripts in these various categories that were sold, sometimes more than once, in the twentieth century. It is with these that I am concerned here.

The earliest of the manuscripts of *The Fall of Princes* to be sold was what is now Pierpont Morgan Library MS M 124 (described in Bergen, 84–86). It was sold at Sotheby's on April 21, 1902, lot 285, and bought for stock by the book dealer Bernard Quaritch for £251. It appeared in the firm's Catalogue 217 (July 1902), no. 3, with a 50 percent markup, at £375, and was subsequently purchased at this price by J. P. Morgan in April 1903 for his library.[7] A return of nearly 50 percent within a year and no quibble about asking price would gladden the heart of any book dealer. Morgan had bought and continued to buy regularly from Quaritch as he developed his collection, and his wealth and firmness of resolve perhaps made him disinclined to argue with Quaritch's price for a good copy.

The commercial success of this manuscript can be set against the failure of the next manuscript to be sold. What is now Columbia University Plimpton 255 (described in Bergen, 103–5) was sold at the Anderson Gallery, New York, January 25, 1904, lot 157, for $107.50. There are obvious reasons for the lower price. This is only a fragment, albeit a large one, comprising fifty-four leaves, and most of those leaves that had been excised were likely those containing decoration. As Bergen notes, "It is probable that there were illuminated borders at the beginning of each [of the nine] books . . . but unfortunately the first one or two leaves of every book is missing" (105). In contrast to the Plimpton fragment, the Morgan manuscript has several full-page illuminated borders and other decoration. Completeness and decoration were always likely to be significant factors in the commercial demand for any medieval manuscript.

Lack of decoration probably had some bearing on the sluggish movement from dealer to collector of what is now Princeton University Library, MS Garrett 139 (*olim* Phillipps 8117; described Bergen, 94–97). Quaritch had bought this manuscript at Sotheby's, June 10–17, 1896, lot 845, for £70, but it did not find a buyer until 1905 in the American collector Robert Garrett.[8] Its slowness to sell may have been partly a consequence of its lack of any illumination or other decoration apart from red painted initials and some rubrication.

Concerns with condition and completeness are probably also reflected in the poor performance of *olim* Phillipps 8118 (described Bergen, 97–99). This was offered for sale for the first time in the twentieth century at Sotheby's, December 3–5, 1906, lot 374, in the sale of the manuscripts of the noted English collector, Laurence Hodson. This manuscript too was imperfect, with very little decoration and on paper. It was bought by the great scholar and collector (and dealer), Sir Sydney Cockerell, for £37.[9] He very quickly sold it to John Gribbel (1858–1936) of Philadelphia, presumably for a modest profit. It was sold after Gribbel's death, in New York at the Parke-Bernet Galleries, on April 16, 1945, lot 253, for $650 and in the same rooms on December 4, 1962, lot 181, for $6,000 when it was bought by Esther Rosenbaum; it is now University of California, Berkeley, Bancroft Library 75. It was only at its final sale that it achieved a price that could be deemed commercial.

Another Phillipps manuscript was the next to be sold, *olim* Phillipps 4255 (described Bergen, 92–94), at Sotheby's on April 24, 1911, lot 662, for £29/10 to Quaritch. It was in Quaritch Catalogue 344 (June 1916), no. 24, for £60. Whether it remained solely in the firm's possession is unclear, but Quaritch appears to have owned it in 1927 according to Bergen (94). It seems to have been acquired by the University of Chicago (MS 565) in the 1930s.

The next copy to come on the market was initially part of what was probably the most extensive single dispersal of Lydgate manuscripts in this century. The *Catalogue of Very Important Illuminated and Other Manuscripts, the Property of Lord Mostyn*, sold at Sotheby's on July 13, 1920, included five Lydgate manuscripts, one of the *Fall* (lot 73), as well as two of his *Life of Our Lady* and one each of his *Siege of Thebes* and *Lives of SS Edmund & Fremund*, the sales of which are discussed below. The *Fall* (described Bergen, 86–88) was sold on this occasion for £250 to the dealer Francis Edwards, the same price (within a pound) that Quaritch paid in 1904 for the Morgan copy. This, like the Morgan copy, was a substantially complete manuscript, on vellum, but without extensive decoration. It will emerge again.

As will be clear the importance of decoration was clearly a factor in early-twentieth-century sales of *Fall* manuscripts. But it may have been only one element in a wider disinclination to see Middle English manuscripts in general and Lydgate ones in particular as possessing any great commercial allure. When on July 24, 1924, at Sotheby's, the great American dealer A. S. W. Rosenbach paid £1,100 for lot 24, a manuscript of *The Fall of Princes*, this was the highest price ever paid for a manuscript of Lydgate's poem up to that time, more than quadrupling the price for the Mostyn copy four years earlier. There were obvious reasons for this surge. The manuscript is of clear artistic significance. It contains fifty-six miniatures of high quality. Rosenbach sold it quickly to the Huntington Library, where it is MS HM 268 (Bergen, 99–103). Only one manuscript, BL Harley 1766, has more illustrations, but they are not as good.

This high price needs some contextualization. It was not the highest price paid in the sale. Rosenbach himself paid £3,100 for a printed book, a copy of Caxton's 1482 *Chronicles*. This is not a particularly rare Caxton (over fifty copies survive in varying degrees of completeness as well as a lot of single leaves). Clearly a fairly common early printed book was seen as substantially more valuable than even a high-quality Middle English manuscript in the commercial scheme of things at the time. And for the *Fall* itself, its extensive illustration clearly outweighed any sense of relative historical significance, a fact evident elsewhere in the same sale: a manuscript of *Piers Plowman*, lot 129, brought only £700 (now Huntington Library MS HM 143), even though manuscripts of it were much rarer commercially than those of Lydgate's poem. This sale suggests that, in relative terms, Middle English manuscripts were not generally seen as works that warranted high prices. Early printed books, particularly Caxtons, even common Caxtons, were the price setters.

But the sale in 1924 of what became the Huntington manuscript represented a commercial high point for manuscripts of Lydgate's poem. What followed was a period of decline that was to continue for over fifty years. This melancholy commercial phase is exemplified by the fate of the Wollaton Hall manuscript (described Bergen, 81–84). It was sold at Christie's on June 15, 1925, lot 169, for £180 to Quaritch. It was to remain in the firm's hands for a very long time. In 1931 it was included in one of their most famous catalogs, *A Catalogue of Illuminated and Other Manuscripts*, no. 100, and priced at £1,000. As with most of the items in this catalog, it failed to sell. Two years later, in Quaritch's Catalogue 472 (1933), no. 554, it was reduced to £800;[10] ten years later, in 1943, it was still in Quaritch's possession and was offered again, in Catalogue 613, *A Catalogue of Illuminated and Literary Manuscripts*, no. 3, at a further discounted price of £700. At some time after this, possibly in 1945, it was bought by the English collector Harvey Frost (1873–1961), very probably at a further discount.[11] However, it did not stay with Frost for long. By 1952 Quaritch had it back, and it was on offer in Catalogue 699, *Manuscripts, mostly from the Collection of the Late J. P. R. Lyell*, no. 28, for £1,000, the same price it had been offered for over twenty years previously. It was still with Quaritch in 1956, when it appeared in Catalogue 77, no. 5; even the price was the same. It was quite probably around this time that it was bought by the American collector Robert H. Taylor (1909–85) and became his MS 2. After more than thirty years Quaritch was finally permanently rid of it. The manuscript is now in Princeton University Library with the rest of Taylor's collection.

If this is depressing testimony to the commercial failure of a good copy of Lydgate's poem in times of depression and war and their aftermath, it was also typical of the fate of even very good copies. The best salesmen were not exempt from economic misfortune where Lydgate's *Fall of Princes* was concerned, as even the redoubtable Rosenbach was to discover. In his 1941 catalog *English Poetry to 1700* he included three complete manuscripts of the poem. One of these, no. 475 (described as "A HITHERTO UNKNOWN LYDGATE MANUSCRIPT"), was offered at $6,000; Rosenbach sold it to Louis H. Silver, the Chicago collector, possibly after a considerable interval.[12] It is now MS 33.3 in the Newberry Library in Chicago.[13] Another copy, no. 477, priced at $2,400, the former Mostyn copy, was sold to Arthur Houghton; it will turn up again. The third, no. 476 (*olim* Phillipps 4254; described Bergen, 88–92), was by far the most expensive. Rosenbach had bought it eighteen years before, in 1923, and it had remained as stock since then. With inaccuracy born perhaps of desperation, it was described in Rosenbach's catalog as "THE FINEST KNOWN MANUSCRIPT OF LYDGATE'S 'THE FALLS OF PRINCES,' WITH SEVEN FINE LARGE ILLUMINATED MINIATURES." Rosenbach offered it for $18,500. There were no takers. Ever. It remained with him and is now in the Rosenbach Foundation in Philadelphia, MS 439/16.[14] Such failure to attract a buyer is all the more striking because this is a fine copy, virtually complete, on vellum, and—apart from two others—"the most elaborately decorated of all the manuscripts of the *Fall of Princes*" (Bergen, 89).[15] Its complete lack of commercial success parallels that of the Wollaton Hall manuscript and underscores the resistance of collectors and librarians to this poem.

After World War II, prices for *The Fall of Princes* plummeted even further. In 1947 it was possible to buy a manuscript of it for £5 at auction. One was sold for this sum at Sotheby's on July 14, as lot 181. Admittedly it was not in very good condition, on paper, undecorated, and lacking some leaves; nonetheless, it was substantially complete and previously unrecorded.[16] On March 1, 1949, lot 499, another unrecorded copy, in good condition, fetched £48 at Sotheby's to the American dealer C. A. Stonehill; it was sold the following year to the University of Illinois Library, where it is now MS 84. Such pitiful prices were not yet the nadir. Twenty-one years later, July 8, 1970, at Sotheby's, lot 98, another copy, also previously unrecorded, came up for auction. This one was in good condition and with an interesting provenance: it had been owned and annotated by members of the family of Philip Sidney. Even though it was much more extensively cataloged and had an accompanying plate, it failed to find a buyer.[17]

The first and probably the only sign of an upward trend in prices came almost ten years later, in 1979, with the last complete copy to come on the market.[18] This was from the collection of Arthur Houghton, sold at Christie's on June 14, lot 295. Houghton had bought this, the former Mostyn copy from Rosenbach in 1941, when the asking price was $2,400. At the Christie's sale it brought the not inconsiderable sum of £19,000; it is now MS 40 in the Takamiya collection in Tokyo. The sale price represents a significant advance in value over the course of a decade for a good copy that was probably still inferior in quality and significance to that which failed to sell in 1970. In strictly numerical terms this was the highest price ever paid for a Lydgate manuscript. The rise in market value is not simply a factor of inflation. It is at least in part a reflection of scholarly and bibliophilic acumen since Professor Takamiya has inhabited both of these worlds. He was hence in a position to appreciate both Lydgate's rising academic stock and the growing rarity of manuscripts of this kind.

Lydgate's other extremely long poem, his *Troy Book*, seems to have circulated less widely than *The Fall of Princes*. Only twenty manuscripts together with a few fragments or extracts survive, and only three of these manuscripts were sold in the twentieth century.[19] Two did not fare at all well in commercial terms. Harvard University, Houghton Library 752, *olim* Ashburnham App. CXXXI, was sold at Sotheby's on May 1, 1899, lot 6, to the London book dealers J. J. Leighton for £3/10 (Bergen, *Troy Book*, 43–46) and subsequently bought from them by Harvard; it is now Houghton Library MS f. 752. The price Harvard paid is not now recoverable, but the most generous markup would not have made it noteworthy.

The manuscript that was *olim* Phillipps 3113 (Bergen, *Troy Book*, 53–54) was twice sold, first by Quaritch, in Catalogue 344 (1916), no. 23, for £50 and then at Sotheby's, October 15, 1945, lot 1963, in the Sixth Portion of the Harmsworth Sale, when it was acquired by Maggs for £240. It was bought on the latter occasion by the Swiss collector Martin Bodmer and became MS 110 in the Fondation Bodmer in Cologny-Geneva. As in other instances, prices both during and immediately after world wars were significantly depressed.

The final manuscript of the *Troy Book* sold in this period is one that had been in the notable collection at Helmingham Hall, in Suffolk, since at least the sixteenth century (Bergen, *Troy Book*, 21–25). It was sold by private treaty in 1956 to the Pierpont Morgan Library and is now MS M 876 there.[20] The Morgan paid $16,000 for it, a substantial sum and probably more, in real terms at that time, than that paid for any Lydgate manuscript. Such a price must be justified both by the rarity of Lydgate's poem (this was the last manuscript in private hands) and on aesthetic grounds: the manuscript contains a number of unfinished miniatures, space for others, and other evidence of high-quality production. As Bergen notes:

> Had the work of the illuminator, so abruptly broken off, been completed, the Helmingham MS. with its six or seven large miniatures, initials and elaborate floriated borders might have been, with the possible exception of [Rylands English 1] the most sumptuous of all the *Troy Book* MSS. (*Troy Book*, 23)

Once again, it is the production values of the manuscript itself that are the primary factor in determining its material value.

The most frequently sold work of Lydgate's in manuscript after *The Fall of Princes* was his *Life of Our Lady*, another widely circulating poem, of which nearly fifty copies survive.[21] Six copies, one extract, and one fragment have been sold in the twentieth century.[22] These sales do little to strengthen any sense of Lydgate's marketability. The earliest, sold in the Henry White sale at Sotheby's, April 21–May 1, 1902, lot 1398, sold to Maggs for two guineas. Although the catalog does not identify it, this is actually a copy of Caxton's [1483] printed edition. It is now Liverpool Cathedral Library MS Radcliffe16.[23] The next to be sold did quite well. This is the copy that is now Huntington Library HM 115, a manuscript with a distinguished provenance, formerly in the collections of John Towneley, Laurence Bragge, and Robert Hoe.[24] It was in Hoe's sale at the Anderson Galleries, New York, in 1911, lot

2148, where it was sold to G. D. Smith, then Henry Huntington's main agent, for $700.

The two copies that were in the Mostyn sale in 1920, lots 75 and 76, had mixed fates. The first (*olim* Mostyn 85) did not sell at all and was only resold more than fifty years later, at Christie's on October 24, 1974, lot 1480, for £950 to Quaritch. It is now National Library of Wales 21242C. The other, lot 76, was sold to Quaritch for £200. It is now University of Illinois MS 85; it was purchased from C. A. Stonehill, the American dealers, in 1947.[25]

After World War II, prices did not pick up significantly even for fine copies. What is now Beinecke 281 was sold at Hodgson's in London on April 23, 1953, lot 200, for £555. This is a handsome manuscript, complete, with the arms of an identifiable very early owner and some possible connection to English royalty. But it was not until 1960, seven years later, that it was purchased by Yale from C. A. Stonehill as the gift of Edwin J., Frederick W., and Walter Beinecke.[26]

Over twenty years after Yale bought this copy there were signs of a change in commercial values. The marquess of Bute's copy was sold at Sotheby's on June 13, 1983, lot 9. Although this was an undecorated and rather undistinguished copy, the fact that it was hitherto unrecorded and was conjoined uniquely with the prose *Privite of the Passion* made it commercially attractive. It was bought by H. P. Kraus for £16,500 and again went to the Beinecke, as MS 660.

Lydgate's *Siege of Thebes* is at least potentially one of the most commercially attractive of his longer poems because of its status as a continuation of Chaucer's *Canterbury Tales*, to which it is conjoined in a number of manuscripts.[27] Only four separate manuscripts have been sold in the twentieth century.[28] One of these, Pierpont Morgan Library MS 4, was acquired as part of the block purchase of the library of Theodore Irwin in 1901 and hence is not considered here. Of the other three, one was sold in the Gurney sale, Sotheby's, March 30, 1936, lot 150, for £125 to Quaritch, who bought it on behalf of Cambridge University Library; it is now the library's MS Add. 6864. If this price offers a further depressing commentary on the perceived value of Lydgate manuscripts, the situation had changed a decade later when W. H. Robinson Ltd. offered another copy in its catalog *Rare Books and Manuscripts* (1946), no. 233, for £600, the highest price in the catalog. It quickly found a buyer and is now Boston Public Library MS fmed 94.

The final one to be sold illustrates most dramatically the upward trend in prices for this work. This is the former Mostyn copy, first sold in the Mostyn sale at Sotheby's, July 13, 1920, lot 77, and bought in. It was offered again at the next Mostyn sale at Christie's, October 24, 1974, lot 1481, and was bought by the collector John Wolfson of New York. He resold it to Quaritch in whose Catalogue no. 1054, *English Books, 1450–1900* (Winter 1985), no. 114, it was offered for $55,000. It was acquired by the New York dealer, H. P. Kraus, and sold to the Beinecke Library in New Haven, where it is now MS 661.[29]

For anyone who might see Middle English manuscripts as an investment, this is not an encouraging series of stories. Certainly, in commercial terms, Lydgate manuscripts have not done well in the twentieth century. The commercial record for his works is largely a dismal one. To what extent, one wonders, is this a general reflection of his perceived lack of historical importance through much of the century? One wonders what prices would be like now when the long-term scholarly consequences of the publication of Derek Pearsall's *John Lydgate* in 1970 have led to a heightened sense of Lydgate's achievements and of the value of studying the manuscripts of his verse. Is there a correlation between the rise in a sense of scholarly significance and increased commercial value? This is not a question that can be answered in our present circumstances when so few Lydgate manuscripts are now likely to come up for sale. Certainly those libraries that scooped up copies in the first half of the twentieth century at bargain prices may now justifiably congratulate themselves on their prescience.

Notes

For help of various kinds in the preparation of this essay I am much indebted to Alex Day, Richard Linenthal, and Roger Wieck.

1. This discussion does not include smaller works of Lydgate's that usually form part of more disparate manuscripts; for example, the copy of his *Dietary*, the only verse content in the manuscript, included in a collection chiefly of hunting treatises, sold at Christie's, January 27, 2006, lot 501, for £170,000 and is now in a private continental collection.

2. Henry Bergen, ed., *Lydgate's Fall of Princes, Part IV*, EETS, e.s., 124 (London: Oxford University Press, 1927), provides excellent descriptions of

many of the manuscripts discussed here. This volume is generally henceforward cited parenthetically as "Bergen" by page numbers.

3. Those still owned by the duke of Rutland, in Belvoir Castle, and by the marquess of Bath at Longleat House, Warminster.

4. Those now in the Pierpont Morgan Library MS M 124, the University of Columbia Plimpton MS 255, and Huntington Library HM 264.

5. Notably those from the collection of Sir Thomas Phillipps: Philadelphia, Rosenbach Foundation 439/16 (*olim* Phillipps 4254), University of Chicago MS 565 (*olim* Phillipps 4255), Princeton University Garrett 139 (*olim* Phillipps 8117), and University of California, Berkeley, Bancroft Library 75 (*olim* Phillipps 8118) but also including those Bergen designates as Wollaton Hall (now Princeton University Library, Taylor 2) and Mostyn (now Takamiya 40).

6. This manuscript was bought privately by the university and does not figure in the following discussion.

7. My thanks to Roger Wieck, Curator of Medieval and Renaissance Manuscripts, Pierpont Morgan Library, for this information.

8. It was offered in Quaritch's Catalogue 220, *Catalogue of a Choice Collection of Illuminated Manuscripts* (February 1903), no. 9*, for £150.

9. See further Christopher de Hamel, "Medieval and Renaissance Manuscripts from the Library of Sir Sydney Cockerell (1867–1962)," *British Library Journal* 13 (1987): 186–210, esp. 190. The price Gribbel paid cannot be established.

10. This catalog provides another, very striking gloss on relative prices. The preceding entry, no. 553, was a copy of Pynson's 1494 printed edition of *The Fall of Princes*, of which eleven other copies were then known. It was priced at more than three times the price of the manuscript, at £2,500.

11. Frost bought heavily in the mid-1940s from the 1931 catalog, so could drive a hard bargain over manuscripts that Quaritch had had in stock for over fifteen years.

12. It was in his hands by 1962, when it is so recorded in the *Supplement to the Census of Medieval and Renaissance Manuscripts in the United States and Canada* (New York: Bibliographical Society of America, 1962), 176. It is unclear when he acquired it, but Rosenbach does not seem to have known Silver before 1947; see Edwin Wolf II with John Fleming, *Rosenbach: A Biography* (London: Weidenfeld & Nicolson, 1961), 557.

13. It is described in Paul Saenger, *A Catalogue of the Pre-1500 Western Manuscript Books at the Newberry Library* (Chicago: University of Chicago Press, 1989), 60–61.

14. This manuscript had not been viewed as commercial a generation earlier; it was in Quaritch Catalogue 344 (1916), no. 24, where it was priced at £63, a price probably reflecting general wartime depression.

15. For a recent description, see James R. Tanis, ed., *Leaves of Gold: Manuscript Illumination from Philadelphia Collections* (Philadelphia: Philadelphia Museum of Art, 2001), 210–12 (with color plate).

16. It was bought by a private collector and subsequently sold privately to the McPherson Library, University of Victoria, British Columbia; for a description and brief discussion, see A. S. G. Edwards, "Lydgate's *Fall of Princes*: A 'Lost' Manuscript Found," *Manuscripta* 22 (1978): 176–78.

17. It was not offered for sale again and is now owned by English Heritage.

18. I leave out of consideration here various fragments of the poem that occasionally appeared on the market; all those of which I am aware in the postwar period are now in the Takamiya collection in Tokyo; see his MSS 30, 78, 79. A fragment of some textual significance sold earlier is now McGill University Library MS 143. This was bought in 1923 from Maggs with other material for £9/9. (I owe this information to Richard Virr, Head and Curator of Manuscripts, Rare Books and Special Collections, McGill University Library.)

19. For descriptions of Lydgate's *Troy Book* manuscripts, see Henry Bergen, ed., *Lydgate's Troy Book*, EETS, e.s., 126 (London: Oxford University Press, 1935), cited henceforward parenthetically as "Bergen, *Troy Book*."

20. See also *The Pierpont Morgan Library: A Review of Acquisitions, 1949–1968* (New York: Pierpont Morgan Library, 1969), 5. For the price the Morgan paid I am indebted to Roger Wieck.

21. For details of these manuscripts, see Julia Boffey and A. S. G. Edwards, *A New Index of Middle English Verse* (London: British Library, 2005), no. 2574.

22. Neither the extract, Huntington Library MS HM 144, nor the fragment, part of an album assembled by the seventeenth-century antiquary John Bagford, now University of Missouri Library, Fragmenta Manuscripta, fol. 178, are discussed here since they have never had any distinct commercial value.

23. I am indebted to Mary Wellesley for clarification of this point.

24. See Consuelo Dutschke et al., *A Guide to the Medieval and Renaissance Manuscripts in the Huntington Library* (San Marino, CA: Huntington Library, 1989), vol. 1, 152–53.

25. I omit from this discussion the manuscript of *The Life of Our Lady* that is now University of Chicago 566. This was bought by the great scholar and bibliophile Sir Sydney Cockerell, at auction at Puttick & Simpson, December 21, 1904, lot 179, for a price I cannot determine. He sold it in 1931 to a buyer who subsequently donated it to the University Library. See de Hamel, "Medieval and Renaissance Manuscripts from the Library of Sir Sydney Cockerell," 199, no. 34. (I slightly supplement here the information given there.)

26. See Barbara Shailor, *Catalogue of Medieval and Renaissance Manuscripts in the Beinecke Rare Book and Manuscript Library Yale University*, vol. 2:

MSS 251–500 (Binghamton, NY: Medieval & Renaissance Texts & Studies, 1987), 48–50.

27. The present discussion omits those manuscripts sold during the twentieth century in which *The Siege of Thebes* appears as part of *Canterbury Tales* manuscripts, namely, British Library Egerton 2864 and University of Texas MS 143 (formerly the Cardigan Chaucer); for these, see A. S. G. Edwards, "What's It Worth? Selling Chaucer's *Canterbury Tales* in the 20th Century," *Chaucer Review* 48 (2014): 239–50.

28. Two manuscripts of this poem cannot be found: the "Prince Frederick Duleep Singh's MS" described in Axel Erdmann and Eilert Ekwall, eds., *Lydgate's Siege of Thebes*, Part II, EETS, e.s., 125 (London: Oxford University Press, 1930), 45–47; and one sold at Sotheby's, November 6, 1899, lot 408.

29. See Daniel Huws, "Sir Thomas Mostyn and the Mostyn Manuscripts," in *Books and Collectors, 1100–1700: Essays Presented to Andrew Watson*, ed. James P. Carley and Colin G. C. Tite (London: British Library, 1997), 463, no. 34, where the current location of this manuscript is not noted.

Part IV

Newer Directions in Manuscript Studies I

Regional and Scribal Identities

Foreword to Part IV

Consider two moments in Derek Pearsall's long and rich publication history. First, the modest introduction to a book that was to become one of the most important monuments in English manuscript studies, *Book Production and Publishing in Britain, 1375–1475*, edited by Derek Pearsall and Jeremy Griffiths and published in 1989. Derek's introduction begins by suggesting, "In the present state of scholarship, any book on publishing and book-production in England in the century before the introduction of printing is bound to be limited in its ambitions, tentative in its statements, and, to some extent or in some ways, premature."[1] Setting aside the degree to which the contents of this seminal volume belie the almost apologetic introduction, we can see how much had changed about a decade later, by considering a second Pearsallian introduction, this one to *New Directions in Later Medieval Manuscript Studies*, one of several volumes arising from the York Manuscripts Conferences. Here, Derek presents the essays to follow by noting that "codices are no longer treated as inert witnesses to a culture whose character has already been determined by the modern scholar, but are active participants in a process of exploration and discovery. All aspects of the manuscript's physical existence are relevant to such an enquiry." By 2000, when this second set of remarks was published, enough scholars had been busy "filling in pieces in a large jigsaw" that, Derek suggested, we were "beginning to see what the large picture looks like."[2]

It was of course thanks to Derek that all those pieces of the jigsaw had entered discussion in the first place. Collaborative projects like *Book Production* and the York Manuscripts Conferences brought together manuscript scholars from different institutions, countries, and generations and facilitated the process by which manuscript studies was brought into the spotlight and into conversation with the literary studies from which it had often seemed to operate in isolation. Another York conference volume, *Manuscripts and Readers in Fifteenth-Century England: The Literary Implications of Manuscript Study*, had made the connection explicit,[3] but even before this collection appeared, the simple fact that one person embodied at once the sensitive literary critic and the skilled manuscript scholar had already begun to set the stage for one of the most important revolutions in the study of the literature of medieval Britain. While it would not be true to say that everyone who sits down to write about a medieval text today must take its production—whether by that we mean its material context or the reading contexts in which it circulated—into account, it is certainly true that manuscript studies have entered the mainstream consciousness of medieval literary studies. By "manuscript studies," we may mean traditional paleography, codicology, and descriptive and enumerative bibliography, or we may mean the practice of bibliography as what D. F. McKenzie has memorably called the "sociology of texts"—the New Philology, to give it its medieval studies name.[4] The point is that manuscripts matter, and Derek has done much to make that so.

It is fitting, then, that in this section of a volume dedicated to Derek, three new scholars should turn their attention to production contexts and questions that have been hitherto overlooked (in the case of the two essays dealing with Anglo-Irish literary production and circulation) or looked over from a rather different perspective (in the case of the famous *Gawain* manuscript). Hannah Zdansky, Hilary E. Fox, and Theresa O'Byrne continue to add pieces to the jigsaw puzzle, and in particular to expand its edges, as they consider places and languages that have sometimes operated on the margins of British medieval literary studies. Of course this move too has been anticipated by Derek; one thinks of his introduction, with Nicolette Zeeman, to the posthumous publication of Elizabeth Salter's *English and International*, in which he draws attention to Salter's focus on the "international and polyglot dimensions" of the "cultural contexts of literature in medieval England."[5] Derek's honoring of that legacy resides not simply in his editorial work on Salter's scholarship but also in his own acute awareness of how, for example, a trilingual poet such as John Gower needs to be understood at least in part in terms of that linguistic fluidity (and in material terms as well, of course, as Gower scholars will be forever indebted to Derek's descriptions of Gower manuscripts).[6] These essays, then, in engaging with texts in their myriad material, linguistic, cultural, and historical contexts, model a practice for which we can in large part thank Derek, his colleagues, and his many generations of students.

Two of these essays concern themselves with Anglo-Irish literary production in the fifteenth century. Hilary Fox considers the translation of the *Secreta secretorum* by James Yonge, a Dublin bureaucrat who was, for a time, a supporter of the important magnate James Butler, fourth earl of Ormond and one of Yonge's more prominent clients. Threads forming the weft here include medieval translation practice, transmission channels running from Latin to French to Hiberno-English, the processes of adaptation and accretion characteristic of a text like the *Secreta*, and the vexed history of the Ricardian and Henrician occupation of Ireland, particularly in its economic manifestations. Against this backdrop Fox shows how Yonge, a notary and clerk, through careful observation of contemporary tensions, crafts his message about fiscal malfeasance in such a way as to reflect indirectly on the exploitative and divisive system of coign and livery. By offering a somewhat manipulated version of Stephen Scrope's reformed fiscal management in his second term as deputy in Ireland and linking that (temporarily) sound economic regime to military success, Yonge attempted to influence policy and politics in the Anglo-Irish sphere. Instead, he found himself imprisoned after Butler's death, a point noted as well by Theresa O'Byrne, whose essay expands on the interconnectedness of legal and literary spheres in the Anglo-Irish areas.

Fox closes her essay by noting that both the *Secreta* and *Piers Plowman* were to be found almost simultaneously in the Ormond affinity, and O'Byrne's delineation of the career of Nicholas Bellewe adds further detail to the picture of literary production, consumption, and circulation in Ireland and between Ireland and England. Bellewe was a legal scribe in Dublin whose hand can be identified in over seventy-five documents, some of them signed, from a range of more than forty years. There is a practical element to the identification of Bellewe and his corpus, in that O'Byrne is able to suggest that his two literary manuscripts, Bodleian e. Museo 232 and Longleat 29, are likely to have been written in Dublin (where there are documents written by Bellewe from almost every year of his career) rather than, as had previously been suggested, by an Anglo-Irish expatriate working in England. This relocation of the manuscripts is important in itself, as it allows us to think about how these Irish manuscripts made their way to England. O'Byrne's identification of Bellewe's hand also gives us a new Anglo-Irish literary author, as the colophon naming the translator of Edmund Rich of Abingdon's *Speculum ecclesie* in the Bodleian manuscript can now be confirmed as authorial. By showing the circles in which Bellewe moved, in particular in his association with the FitzWilliam family, O'Byrne sketches the possibility of female lay patronage for one of Bellewe's literary manuscripts, while the other, she argues, might also be connected, via his professional practices, to the Dublin Guild of St. Anne. As we now know to be the case for London, then, a picture for Dublin emerges of a circle of scribes engaged in both legal and literary production and a circle of readers that might include other, similarly employed clerks, along with patrons from both the aristocratic and merchant classes.

One of the perplexing features of Bellewe's literary manuscripts is their mixed linguistic profile, a feature O'Byrne explains by noting that Dublin clerks were surrounded by, and attempted to copy the practices of, English documents. Hannah Zdansky takes on the decidedly peculiar hand of Cotton Nero A.x, the *Gawain* (or *Pearl*) manuscript, by arguing for a similar kind of purposeful mixing. Paleographers have of course noted before the strange *textura* used in this famous manuscript. Zdansky notes resemblances between this hand and that of some Anglo-Norman romance manuscripts and several Welsh manuscripts, including *The Red Book of Hergest*, to explore whether the hand—like the poetry itself, perhaps—is an example of conscious hybridization. Several of the manuscripts she explores are trilingual, reminding us again of the importance of linguistic fluidity throughout the medieval "English" period, and she draws our attention to the possibility of a unique production culture in the Welsh borderlands. Thus, like Fox and O'Byrne, Zdansky directs her attention at historically peripheral areas that might become central to the continually developing narrative of medieval British literary production.

All three pieces take seriously Derek's lifelong attempt to complicate what he once called the "innocent" assumptions of literary scholars about where their texts come from, who read them, and how.[7] Instead of an often featureless landscape marked only by a few tall, isolated hills labeled "Chaucer" or "Langland" or "Gower," now we see a vast panorama crowded with books and documents, clerks and scribes, magnates and merchants, patrons and patronesses, all shuttling back and forth across "Britain" in the broadest sense, and literally speaking in tongues. A fair field of folk, indeed.

Siân Echard

Notes

1. Derek Pearsall, Introduction to *Book Production and Publishing in Britain, 1375–1475*, ed. Jeremy Griffiths and Derek Pearsall (Cambridge: Cambridge University Press, 1989), 1.

2. Derek Pearsall, Introduction to *New Directions in Later Medieval Manuscript Studies: Essays from the 1998 Harvard Conference*, ed. Derek Pearsall (York: York Medieval Press, 2000), xi, xii.

3. Derek Pearsall, ed., *Manuscripts and Readers in Fifteenth-Century England: The Literary Implications of Manuscript Study. Essays from the 1981 Conference at the University of York* (Cambridge: D. S. Brewer, 1983).

4. The first term is taken from the title of the 1986 Panizzi lectures; see D. F. McKenzie, *Bibliography and the Sociology of Texts* (London: British Museum, 1986). The "New Philology" was the subject of a special issue of *Speculum* (65, no. 1) in 1990, edited by Stephen G. Nichols.

5. Derek Pearsall and Nicolette Zeeman, Foreword to Elizabeth Salter, *English and International: Studies in the Literature, Art and Patronage of Medieval England*, ed. Derek Pearsall and Nicolette Zeeman (Cambridge: Cambridge University Press, 1988), xii–xiii.

6. See Derek Pearsall, "The Manuscripts and Illustrations of Gower's Works," in *A Companion to Gower*, ed. Siân Echard (Cambridge: D. S. Brewer, 2004), 73–98.

7. In "The *Troilus* Frontispiece and Chaucer's Audience," *Yearbook of English Studies* 7 (1977): 68–74, Derek questioned the assumptions made about Chaucer and his audience on the basis of the famous frontispiece to the Corpus Christi College Cambridge MS 61 copy of *Troilus and Criseyde*. He suggested that literary critics were making an "innocent assumption" (73) in associating literary activity at court with the king himself, and made an argument instead for the importance of recognizing the broader reading circle to which—especially given the linguistic character of Richard's court—the poem might have been addressed. Other innocent assumptions of course included the idea that the frontispiece represented a record of an actual performance.

CHAPTER 12

"And fer ouer þe French flod"

A Look at Cotton Nero A.x from an International Perspective

Hannah Zdansky

Throughout his work, Derek Pearsall has not hesitated to engage the multicultural and multilingual nature of medieval Britain, as attested in his many books and articles and especially in his dedication, along with Nicolette Zeeman, to the editing and publishing of Elizabeth Salter's intellectual labors in this area. As they noted in their foreword, "The literature of medieval England was written in Anglo-Norman, French and Latin as well as in English."[1] Such a view is the kind that bids those who follow to think outside of the box (as the other essays in this part also attest), to entertain seriously the notion that people and communities were not as divided along linguistic lines as academic departments today. Pearsall has also been very influential with regard to romance.[2] Recent work in the field points to an interesting development in the sociolinguistics of the time period, one that suggests that throughout much of the fourteenth century, Anglo-Norman and Middle English were in use concurrently, not in competition with Middle English eventually winning out, as the dynamic is often described.[3] Authors and scribes did not function in monolinguistic vacuums, and neither, then, should we study them in that way. This essay explores the scribe of Cotton Nero A.x and the image of the manuscript he[4] had in mind when he set out to put pen to parchment. What did he want his copy to look like? And why? What could he have seen that would have influenced his choices, especially with regard to script? It is upon this that I shall focus.

In his introduction to the facsimile of London, British Library, MS Cotton Nero A.x, Art. 3—the only surviving copy of the four Middle English alliterative poems *Pearl*, *Cleanness*, *Patience*, and *Sir Gawain and the Green Knight*—Israel Gollancz remarks that the main text hand is unlike that of any other (fig. 12.1).[5] No two scholars seem to be able to agree on the type of script used.[6] Ian Doyle refers to it as "a species of Bastard Anglicana."[7] Anthony Petti asks if it could be "*Fere-textura rotunda facilis*."[8] Jane Roberts posits that the anonymous scribe writes a "Gothic *textualis rotunda media*," a script more prevalent in the thirteenth century, not the second half of the fourteenth century.[9] While no definitive conclusions may be reached here, my intention is to suggest possible influences and to broaden our scope of thinking about the *Gawain*- or *Pearl*-poet Manuscript, as it is often called.

Concerning our single, relatively humble copy of four of the most important poems in the Middle English canon, likely owned by a single person or family belonging to the middle class, it seems odd that a *textura* script would be employed.[10] Jane Roberts states, "A *cursiva* would be more usual late in the fourteenth century for poetry in English," as with manuscripts of rhymed poetry, such as Chaucer's, and alliterative, as with Langland's.[11] This is true, indeed, but even more so given the characteristics of the manuscript itself: the codex is not impressive and certainly not *de luxe*, though it is decorated with pen-work flourishing and a series of illustrations, likely added at a later date. What is more, Ian Doyle notes, "The main text-hand in the majority of its forms, because they are so traditional, tells one little except that its awkwardnesses and anomalies (e.g. the final *s* and the *w* which occur in Bastard Anglicana) reveal that the scribe was more at home in more cursive script."[12] So the question is: why the switch to *textura* for this particular manuscript when so many other Middle English manuscripts, of rhyming or alliterative poetry or prose, are in *cursiva* and the scribe himself is more comfortable with a cursive script? The logical conclusion seems to be that the choice of a *textura* script was deliberate, which carries with it implications when one asks why. Of course, the scribe could have been instructed to copy it this way by either his supervisor or his patron, but even still, why would the scribe's director have insisted on that particular choice? The date typically supplied for the manuscript is the second half of the fourteenth century, often thought to be in the final quarter.[13] Since Cotton Nero A.x is the only copy of the works of the *Pearl*-poet that has endured, "it is difficult to theorize as to the relation of the MS.

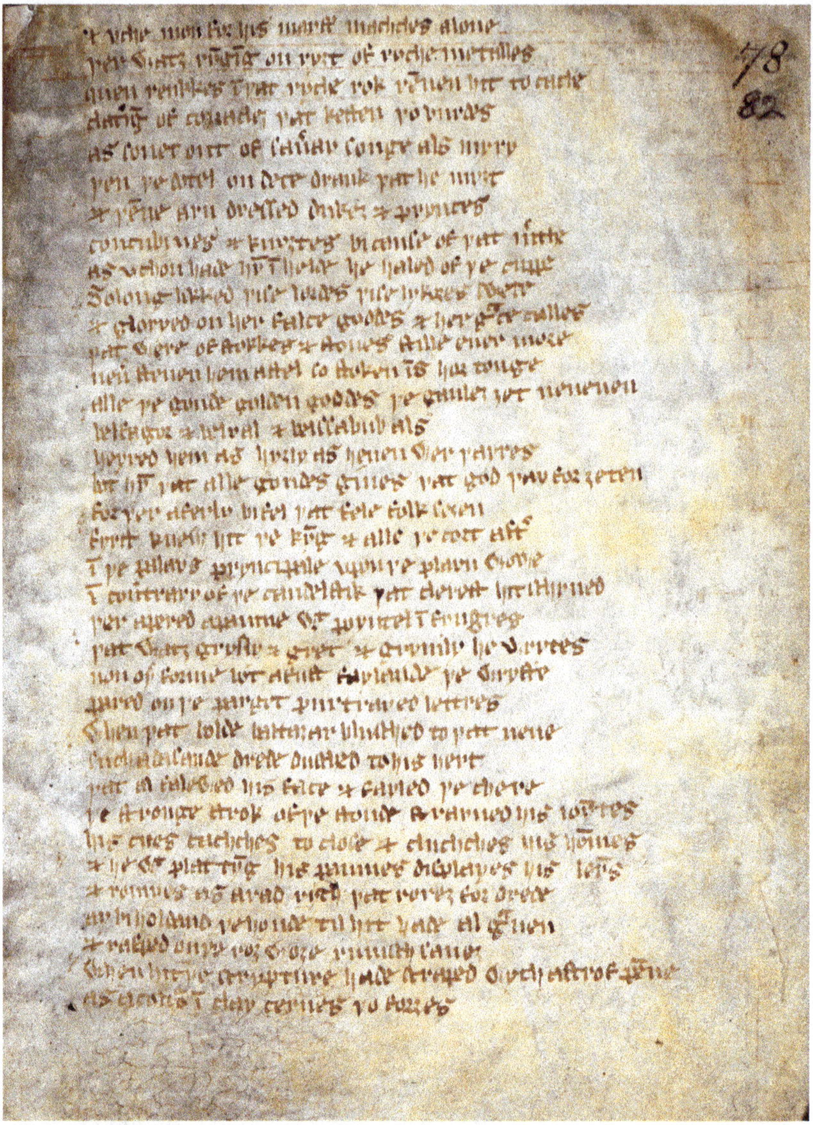

Fig. 12.1. London, British Library, MS Cotton Nero A.x, Art. 3, fol. 82r (formerly fol. 78r) (last quarter of the fourteenth century). © British Library Board.

to the original script of the poet";[14] but while Cotton Nero A.x may be several stages of copying removed from the actual drafting of the poems, the choices that the scribe made in laying out the text and in the script at which he labored may nevertheless reflect on the poems themselves.

After noting the oddity of the hand, Gollancz observes, "Apart from its 'small, sharp, irregular character,' " the letter combination *tȝ* is sometimes used to represent what would otherwise be *z* or *s*, and he says that this is "derived evidently from an Anglo-French scribal mannerism."[15] Doyle suggests that the scribe could have adopted his spelling and style of writing from Anglo-Norman models, for he tells us that "parallels may be found in Anglo-Norman manuscripts, appropriately with regard to the sources of *Gawain*."[16] He then points us to one manuscript—British Library, MS Egerton 3028—which, he says, is of a "similar duct and size, early-mid-fourteenth-century."[17] On a purely orthographic level, the scribe (or poet) could have encountered such a spelling as *tz* or *tȝ* in works predating the sound change in French from /ts/ to /s/ which resulted in a revised spelling; thus he may be—consciously or not—making his text seem older by reproducing the spellings of his exemplars (or sources). However, he could also be preserving his own pronunciation, something difficult to ascertain. With regard to script, that of Cotton Nero A.x does bear some resemblance to Egerton 3028, which is of English origin and provenance (fig. 12.2).[18] The example given is drawn from the Charlemagne romance of *Fierabras*, added to an abridgment of Wace's *Brut* that is continued up to the beginning of the Hundred Years' War. In effect, Egerton 3028 presents a history of Britain from the time of the British through the Anglo-Saxon and then Norman kings up to the time of the codex's creation, while making certain to include some Charlemagne material—even the characters of Roland and Olivier (ever important in any French history). The text of *Fierabras* is written in alexandrine lines comprising *laisses* which are unified by assonance and sometimes by monorhyme, a style typical of the chanson de geste.[19] Coming back, then, to Cotton Nero A.x, Rosalind Field posits as a possible impetus behind and influence upon the fourteenth-century revival[20] of Anglo-Saxon alliterative forms that such Francophone literature could have played a part by way of Anglo-Norman romance. A development such as this could have been significant for the *Pearl*-poet as well as our scribe.

To begin with, the localities of production of Anglo-Norman romance are "in many cases close to those later associated with alliterative poetry."[21] And while the length of a century separates the flowering of

Fig. 12.2. London, British Library, MS Egerton 3028, fol. 93r. From the text of *Fierabras*. © British Library Board.

Anglo-Norman romance from the height of the Middle English alliterative revival, both corpuses exhibit similar thematic tendencies in contrast to continental French literature. They do not "share the enthusiasm . . . for the excesses and intricacies of love and chivalry."[22] By this, Field means that "the themes and the didacticism associated with *courtoisie* and *amour courtoise* are less important in such romances than the portrayal of feudal society, its ethics and ideals."[23] And furthermore, many of the dozen or so complete romances which survive from the period of Anglo-Norman literary flourishing show a preference for treating the "history" of England, drawing on local legends and the chronicle tradition of, indeed, works like Wace's *Brut*.[24] This preference for the heroic/historic as opposed to the courtly/chivalric can be seen, to some extent, in the forms chosen for Anglo-Norman romance. While the majority of Anglo-Norman romances, despite their differences in theme, maintain the prevailing use of the octosyllabic rhyming couplet, a few works are composed in the same style as the earliest examples of French heroic literature, like the *Chanson de Roland*. This is the case with *Fierabras* and others like the *Roman de Horn*, both mid-twelfth-century compositions. A separate but related version of the *Horn* story exists in the mid-thirteenth-century *King Horn*, which is the earliest extant romance we have in Middle English, save for Laȝamon's *Brut*. Field advances the possibility that poets may have found parallels between the Old French *laisse* with its long alexandrine lines and assonance and the alliterative lines of Anglo-Saxon poetry, with both forms developing in conversation with one other and audiences cultivating an appreciation for both over time and through linguistic interaction, given the similarities of both types of versification.[25] Such parallels certainly exist, for in addition to the characteristic assonance or alliteration and the long line, both meters make use of a caesura around which is organized a series of stress patterns. The decision of writers of the alliterative revival to use such a style may lie in the fact that it invokes two earlier, grand ages of cultural history and lends the authority of two major poetic traditions to the material with which the poets worked.

Perhaps such conscious hybridization is what the *Pearl*-poet undertakes when he composes *Sir Gawain and the Green Knight*. To be sure, modern scholars point to French materials as sources for many aspects of the text.[26] That the scribe would choose to employ a script for Cotton Nero A.x similar to that found in a romance like *Fierabras*, written in French and composed in an analogous poetic style, would suggest that he too seeks to create this link by the letters he writes, lending authority to the manuscript he is crafting. There is, however, nothing particularly "French" or "Anglo-Norman" about the script of Cotton Nero A.x, but neither is there anything particularly "English." The works of most of the famous Middle English poets, as mentioned before, all seem to be in various versions of Anglicana or Secretary script. Only a few Anglo-Norman works appear in cursive hands, including Anglicana Formata, but the majority are written in variations of a Gothic minuscule book hand, as Cotton Nero A.x has been categorized.[27] Thus, I suggest that we continue to look for more Anglo-Norman examples that resemble the script of Cotton Nero A.x in certain ways. I have been able to locate a few. The first one might be that offered by British Library, MS Cotton Caligula A.ix, specifically the script used for the late-twelfth-/early-thirteenth-century *Vie des Set Dormanz* by Chardri, with the manuscript dating to the second half of the thirteenth century (fig. 12.3).[28] Another potential example might be something like the script used in Oxford, Bodleian Library, MS Auctarium F. 5. 31, for *La Novele Cirurgerie*, a rhymed medical treatise of the early to mid-thirteenth century, with the manuscript again dating to the second half of that century (fig. 12.4).[29] A third possibility may be that found in volume Va of Cambridge, Corpus Christi College, MS 405, containing Raymond du Puy's *Regula*, preceded by miracles recounting the foundation of the Hospital of St. John in Jerusalem, also known as the Anglo-Norman *Hospitallers' Riwle* and thus a vernacular version of the *Miracula et regula hospitalis Sancti Johannis Jerosolimitani*. The hand likely dates to the first decade of the fourteenth century.[30] This trilingual manuscript, consisting of six different codices, belonged to the brethren of St. John of Jerusalem at Waterford in Ireland, but the volume under question likely originated in the southwest of England (fig. 12.5).[31] Granted that much more work remains to be done and many more manuscripts need to be considered, these instances at least suggest that the scribe of Cotton Nero A.x might have looked to Anglo-Norman models in order to create—and with due reason perhaps—his distinctive style.

On the other hand, such a comparison represents only one possibility. In the same way that the first poets of the alliterative revival may have had both Anglo-Saxon verse and the Old French *laisse* in mind, the Cotton Nero A.x scribe may have tried to make his text look like older examples of English writing. Some of Kathryn Kerby-Fulton's most recent work points to older Middle English scripts, something like those found in Oxford, Jesus College, MS 29, or British Library, MS Arundel 292—both mid- to late-thirteenth-century trilingual compilations—as

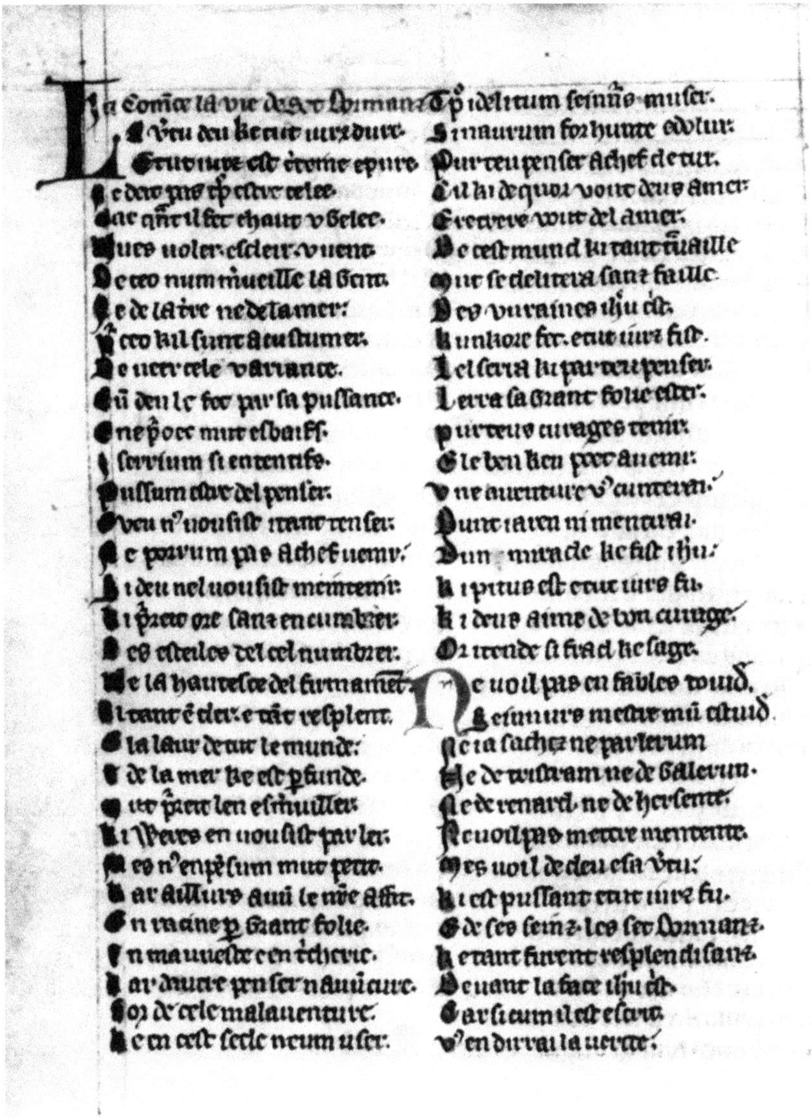

Fig. 12.3. London, British Library, MS Cotton Caligula A.ix, fol. 216v (second half of the thirteenth century). Beginning of Chardri's *La Vie des Set Dormanz*. © British Library Board.

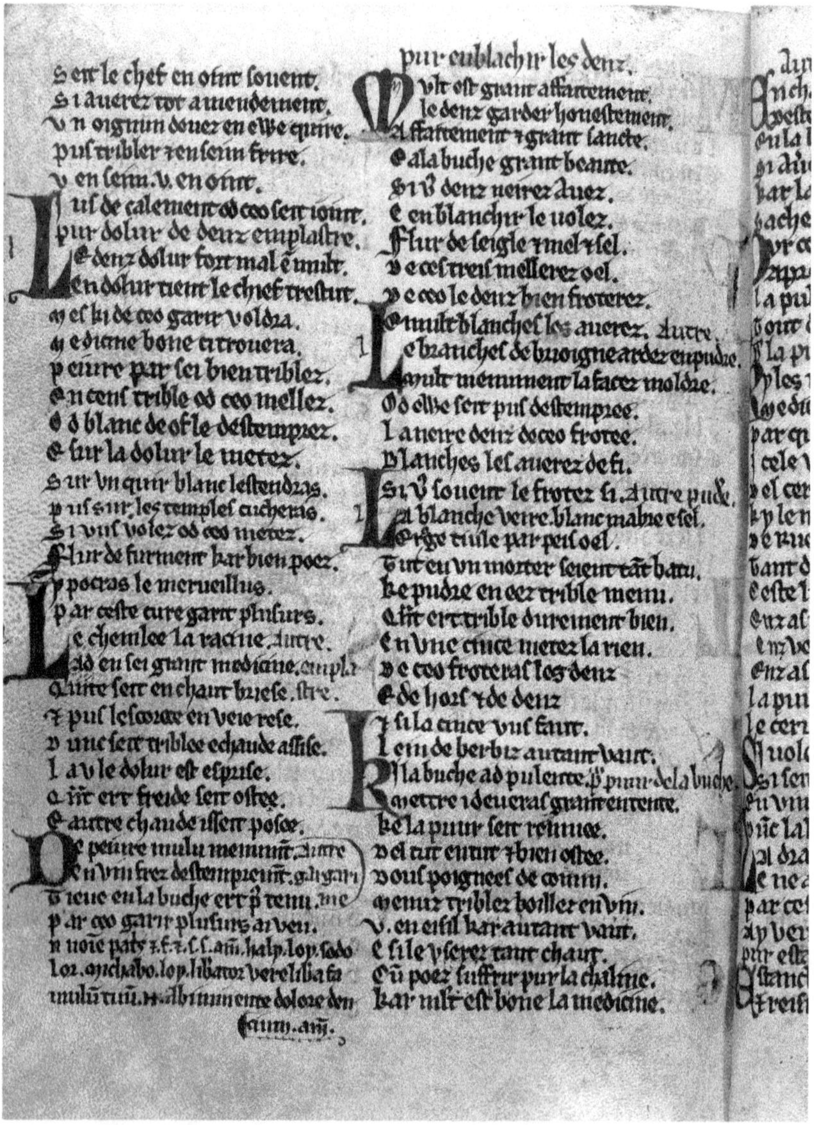

Fig. 12.4. Oxford, Bodleian Library, MS Auct. F. 5. 31, fol. 63v (second half of the thirteenth century). From *La Novele Cirurgerie.* Reproduced by kind permission of the Bodleian Libraries, University of Oxford.

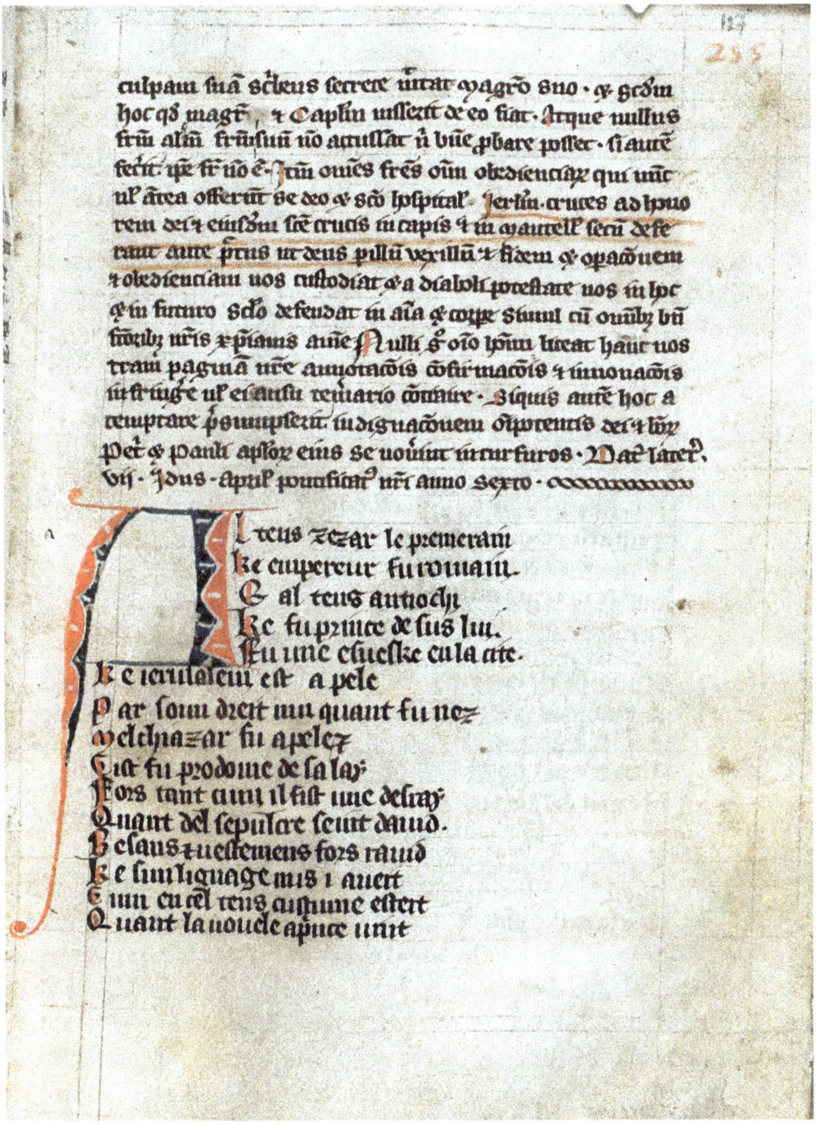

Fig. 12.5. Cambridge, Corpus Christi College, MS 405, fol. 127r (early fourteenth century). Raymond du Puy's *Regula*, preceded by *Miracles Recounting the Foundation of the Hospital of St. John in Jerusalem.* Reproduced by kind permission of the Master and Fellows of Corpus Christi College, Cambridge.

possible antecedents for what the Cotton Nero A.x scribe strives to produce.[32] Indeed, Roberts suggests that the script of *The Owl and the Nightingale* of Jesus College 29 and of the bestiary in Arundel 292 is a Gothic *littera textualis rotunda media*, very similar to what she says of Cotton Nero A.x (figs. 12.6 and 12.7).[33] Roberts also notes that with Jesus College 29, "There is an interesting overlap in contents, both English and Anglo-Norman, with Caligula A.ix.," the manuscript, dating from roughly the same time period—not likely to be before 1256, according to Roberts—preserving the most complete version of Laȝamon's *Brut* and the only other copy of *The Owl and the Nightingale*.[34] Both manuscripts likewise share copies of Chardri's *Vie des Set Dormanz*. The creation of Jesus College MS 29 can be located in East Herefordshire,[35] but the manuscript ends up in the possession of Thomas Wilkins, rector of Saint Mary Church in the Vale of Glamorgan, one of the most assiduous antiquarians in seventeenth-century Wales.[36] Quoting Laȝamon, Roberts tells us that he lived in Worcestershire and that this "is advanced as the likely place of origin" for that codex, Cotton Caligula A.ix.[37] Perhaps even if the scripts are not quite the same, the two manuscripts share both English and Anglo-Norman materials, sources, and influences, not to mention a similar place of origin. Worth noting is the fact that *The Owl and the Nightingale*, in particular, is not alliterative but written in octosyllabic rhyming couplets, a form derived from French versification. In this, we can see, once again, a possible overlap between the two vernaculars in the adoption of a common French poetic form for use with early Middle English. It may be that the Cotton Nero A.x scribe was consciously archaizing his writing, making his hand (and text) seem more old-fashioned than it was in order to echo visually a more antique period of vernacular poetry in English, as with Anglo-Norman.

Throughout the strains of these arguments, one may notice a narrative, in its variously recast forms, which continues to resurface: the legend of Brutus. If one remembers, Geoffrey of Monmouth, likely to have been Welsh or Breton, writes the Latin *Historia Regum Britanniae* (ca. 1135–38) from the point of view of the Britons, continued later in the Brythonic languages with works like the *Brut y Tywysogion* (Chronicle of the Princes) (beginning in the year 682 and ending in 1282 with the death of Llywelyn ap Gruffudd). Wace uses this "history" to support Anglo-Norman claims to the island in the *Roman de Brut* (1155). And Laȝamon asks in his *Brut* (ca. 1190–1225) that King Arthur return once again but this time to aid the English against

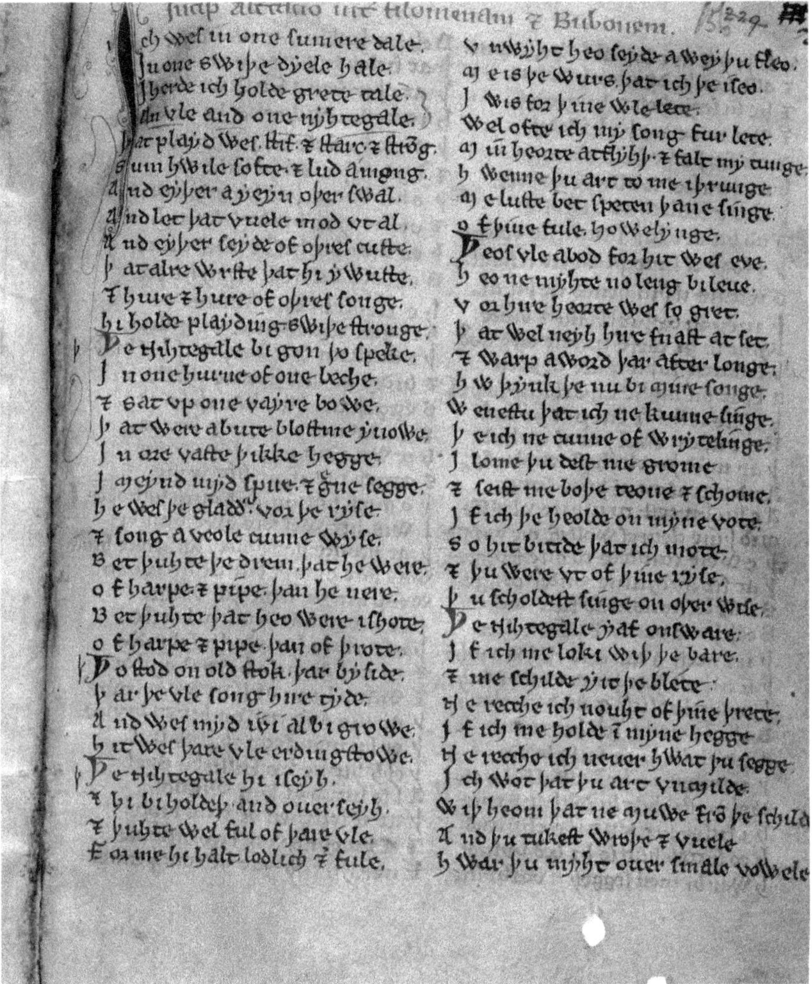

Fig. 12.6. Oxford, Jesus College, MS 29, fol. 156r (second half of the thirteenth century). Beginning of *The Owl and the Nightingale*. © Jesus College. Reproduced by kind permission of the Principal and Fellows of Jesus College, Oxford.

Anglo-Norman rule. While in each case peoples are opposed, they—nonetheless—write and view their histories based on the same myth. In fact, many of the manuscripts listed so far contain some version of a chronology of kings (British, English, and Norman) or demonstrate an interest in the history of the island. And lest we forget, the culminating work of Cotton Nero A.x begins and ends by recalling the mythological

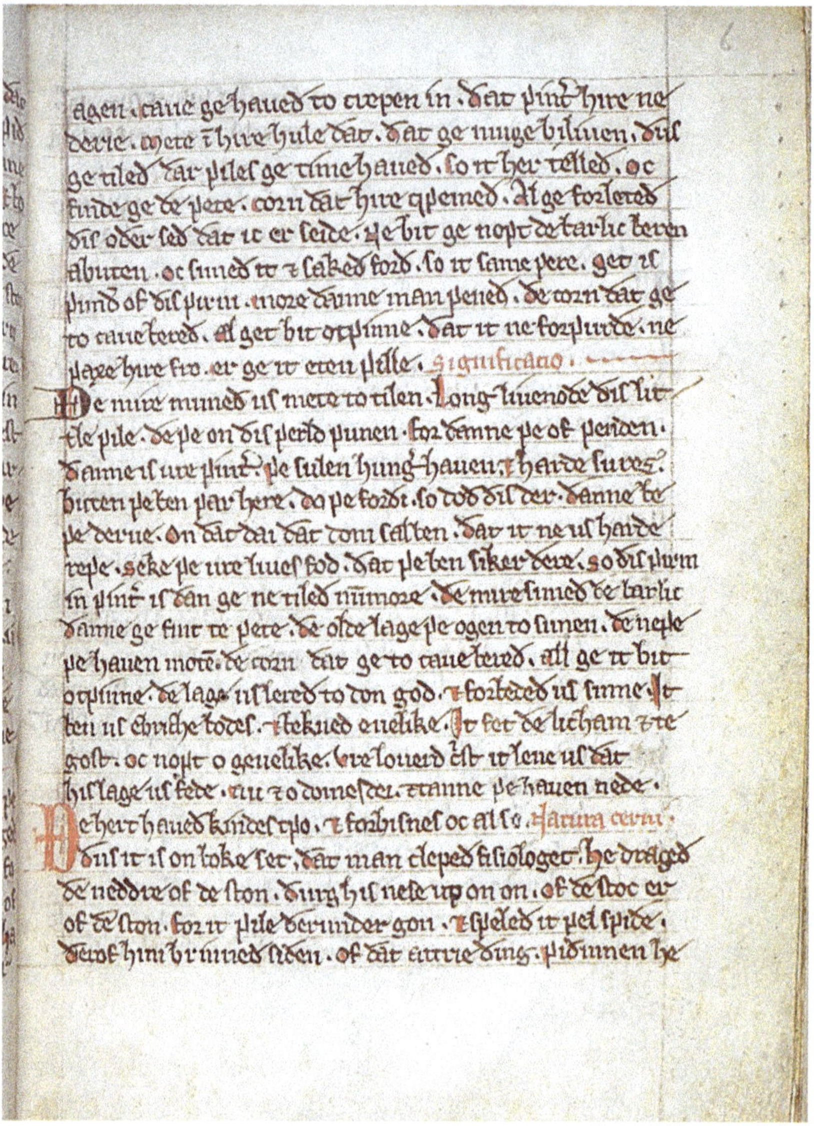

Fig. 12.7. London, British Library, MS Arundel 292, fol. 6r (last quarter of the thirteenth century). From the *Bestiary*. © British Library Board.

founding of Britain. But by the fourteenth century, these peoples share much more than a legendary history.

The final, striking similarity between many of the texts and manuscripts considered thus far is their origin and provenance within the Welsh borderlands, that region where vestiges of Anglo-Saxon culture persisted and where Anglo-Norman lords ruled almost as monarchs but with the understanding that on the other side of Offa's Dyke was another ancient people. What follows now depends, to a certain extent, on whether we continue to accept a Cheshire dialect for the *Pearl*-poet (a locale that makes sense given the poet's detailed knowledge of the region and Welsh geography), with scribal dialect placed in Staffordshire.[38] While some scholars are looking to Yorkshire, we would do well to consider also looking at manuscripts in another vernacular language. Many important Welsh manuscripts have their origin in the borderlands as well, though we must remember that what we term the Welsh Marches during the fourteenth century was actually quite extensive, including large swaths of North and Mid-Wales and nearly the entire South.[39]

The first example we might entertain comes from Oxford, Jesus College, MS 111 (*The Red Book of Hergest*), in particular the text of the *Brut y Tywysogion*, a continuation of Geoffrey of Monmouth mentioned above with reference to the *Brut* tradition (fig. 12.8). In this manuscript, the *Brut y Tywysogion* (fols. 58r–89v) is copied by "Hand I," as he is known in the scholarship. Other sections of the manuscript were copied by one Hywel Fychan ap Hywel Goch of Buellt (Builth) and another known as the scribe of *Y Llyfr Teg* (Aberystwyth, National Library of Wales, Peniarth MS 32).[40] Of these, "Hand I" and Hywel Fychan are considered professional scribes.[41] The catalog reads, "The MS. is named for its former home, Hergest, in Herefordshire." More specifically, it was likely compiled for Hopcyn ap Tomas ab Einion of Ynysforgan, whom Hywel Fychan will refer to in a colophon as his "master," before it passed into the hands of the Vaughans of Tretŵr in 1465.[42] Interesting also is that the same individual who gave Jesus College MS 29 to Oxford University—Thomas Wilkins the younger—also donated this manuscript. The date provided by Denholm-Young is ca. 1375–80.[43] However, the catalog pushes the date forward to after 1382. Perhaps we can consider this hand as representative of developments around the same time frame as the operation of the Cotton Nero A.x scribe. Denholm-Young is even compelled to remark on the "spiky" nature of the script, much like that of Cotton Nero A.x, a feature which can be more

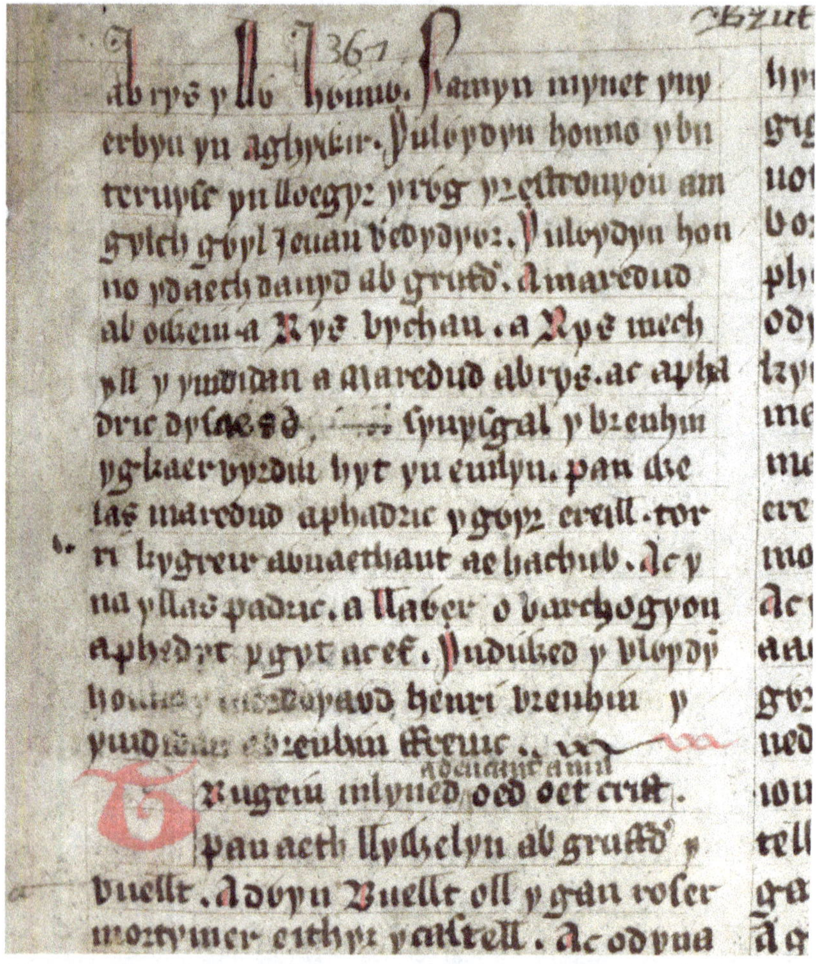

Fig. 12.8. Oxford, Jesus College, MS 111, fol. 87v (*The Red Book of Hergest*, after 1382). From the *Brut y Tywysogion* (The Chronicle of the Princes). Scribe = "Hand I." © Jesus College. Reproduced by kind permission of the Principal and Fellows of Jesus College, Oxford.

characteristic of court hands as opposed to book hands, that is, those employed in everyday life for various reasons, most notably record keeping, and that would be of a *cursiva* variety, something with which Roberts too observes that the scribe of Cotton Nero A.x is more comfortable.[44] The greatest disparity between the two scripts concerns the execution of *g* and *w*. The scribe of Cotton Nero A.x has a double-compartmented *g*, whereas the scribe who copied the *Brut y Tywyso-*

gion seems to have a single-compartmented one. However, high resolution images of the manuscript folios of the *Brut y Tywysogion* show a hair-stroke closing off the *g*'s. In some cases, this line is actually quite prominent. As for the *w*, the Cotton Nero A.x scribe utilizes a version which, as Doyle mentioned, looks more akin to a cursive script. The *w* of Jesus College MS 111 is far neater and more rigid. Nonetheless, examples can be found that bear similarity. See, for instance, near the beginning of the second line on fol. 82r (formerly fol. 78r) of Cotton Nero A.x. Both *w*'s, moreover, are formed on the same principle: two bridged *l*'s curved to the left followed by a *ȝ*. We shall leave the comparison thus for the moment and broaden our search.

The next two examples are drawn from the same manuscript but are written by a different scribe, Hywel Fychan (mentioned above), a rather prolific copyist, as there are several other manuscripts in his hand. He copied here the *Ystorya Dared* (The Story of Dares), a Middle Welsh adaptation of the *De excidio Troiae* attributed to Dares Phrygius, and a short historical text on Gildas, *Gildas Hen Broffwyd* (Gildas the Old Prophet) (figs. 12.9a and 12.9b). Compare these, though, with the same hand, slightly less formal, in another manuscript of mostly religious texts, National Library of Wales, Llanstephan MS 27 C (part of *The Red Book of Talgarth*), dating to approximately 1400 (fig. 12.10).[45] D. Simon Evans has suggested that this manuscript could stand as a religious companion to *The Red Book of Hergest*, as both were made for the same patron.[46] One can observe side by side "Hand I" and Hywel Fychan by going to fol. 89v of Oxford, Jesus College, MS 111. It is not my intention to claim that these scripts and that of Cotton Nero A.x are the same, but that similarities are evident, as manifest as they are with the Anglo-Norman or earlier Middle English examples already examined. And if the scribe of Cotton Nero A.x was seeking to make his writing appear intentionally old-fashioned, contemporaneous Welsh scripts may certainly have seemed so to him, at least until cursive scripts became more prevalent in the fifteenth century.[47]

As research is making increasingly clear, the border culture of the Marches was profoundly shaped by commerce with Wales and by contact with its culture, as the work of Robert W. Barrett Jr. and Michael J. Bennett, for example, has shown.[48] While only a small number of Middle English texts exhibit linguistic borrowing from Middle Welsh—for example, *Ancrene Wisse* and a few of the Harley lyrics—and literary borrowings are difficult to trace, given the long-term intermixing among Welsh, Anglo-Saxons, Anglo-Normans, and even Bretons in this

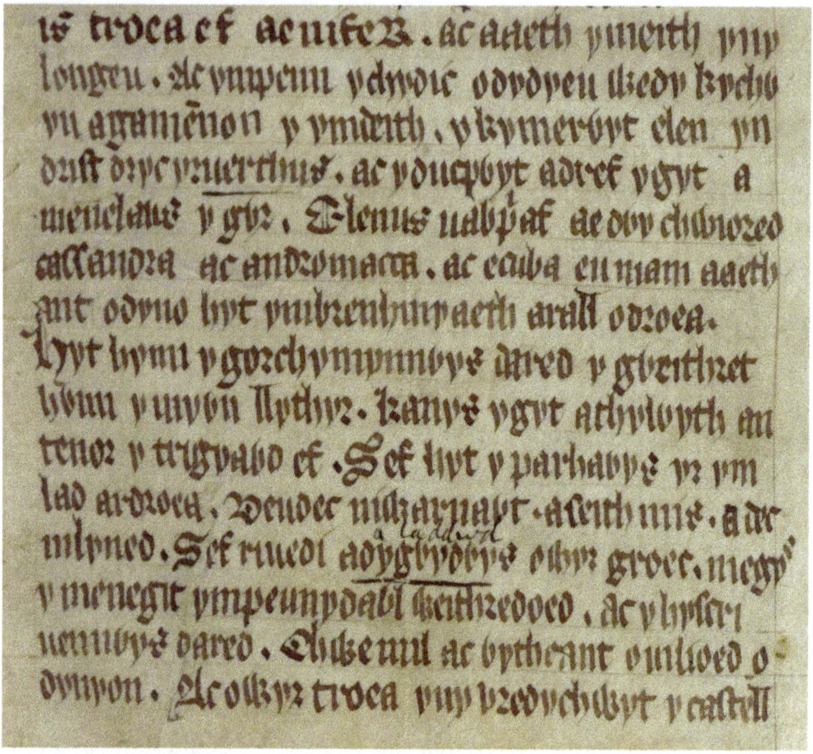

Fig. 12.9a. Oxford, Jesus College, MS 111, fol. 8r (*The Red Book of Hergest*, after 1382). From the *Ystorya Dared* (The Story of Dares). Scribe = Hywel Fychan ap Hywel Goch of Buellt (Builth). © Jesus College. Reproduced by kind permission of the Principal and Fellows of Jesus College, Oxford.

region, evidence has been brought forward to suggest metrical influences. Ordelle G. Hill, following the example of A. T. E. Matonis,[49] has examined the influence of Middle Welsh verse on Middle English poetry from the region of the Marches, namely, the Harley lyrics and also that of Cotton Nero A.x. What he presents are similarities between a complicated but very common poetic device of fourteenth-century Welsh verse known as *cynghanedd*, in which lines and stanzas are bound through alliteration following a fixed pattern that could be varied by internal and end rhyme, and the types of alliteration that appear in Middle English poetry from this period. A particular poetic form he compares to the bob and wheel pattern of *Sir Gawain and the Green Knight* is the *englyn unodl union*, a monorhymed *englyn*, one of eight possible types.[50] While Helen Fulton had earlier voiced some doubts as

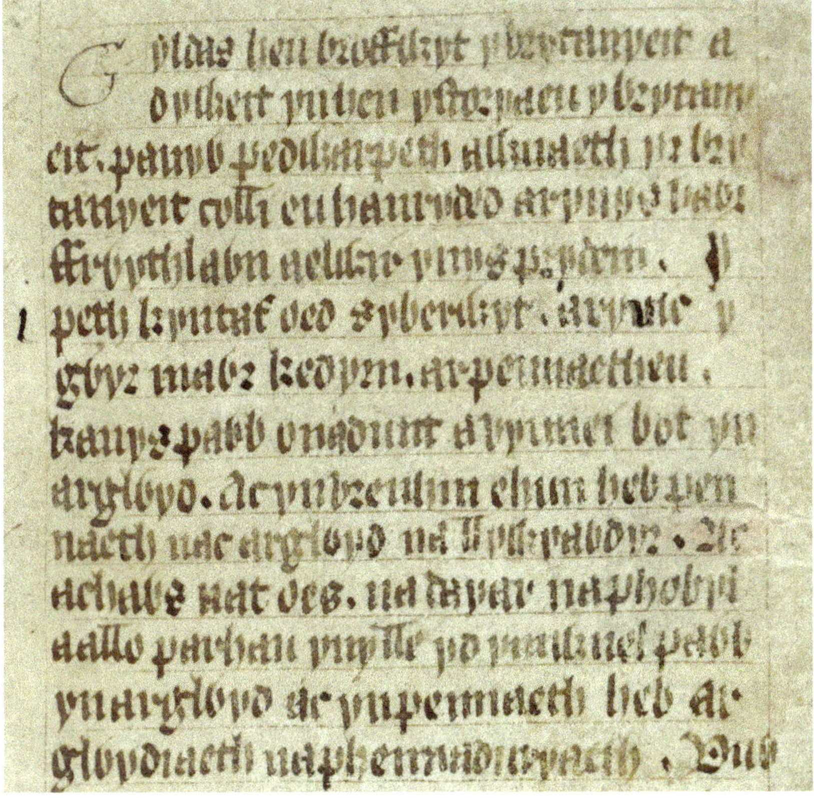

Fig. 12.9b. Oxford, Jesus College, MS 111, fol. 89v (*The Red Book of Hergest*, after 1382). Beginning of *Gildas Hen Broffwyd* (Gildas the Old Prophet). Scribe = Hywel Fychan ap Hywel Goch of Buellt (Builth). © Jesus College. Reproduced by kind permission of the Principal and Fellows of Jesus College, Oxford.

to the possibility of such influence,[51] more work remains to be done in this area. What we can say, though, is that, as with the likelihood of Anglo-Norman influence on Middle English alliterative tradition, especially in the West Midlands and Marches, so too may alliterative Middle Welsh poetry also have contributed to the changes we observe in English poetic forms. Lest we overlook the obvious, such influence may also be present in the very writing itself.

If scripts such as the ones examined here could have functioned as models for that of the Cotton Nero A.x scribe, then, as with the foundation myth preserved in so many of these codices, three different languages and cultures are united in that they share in the history of Britain

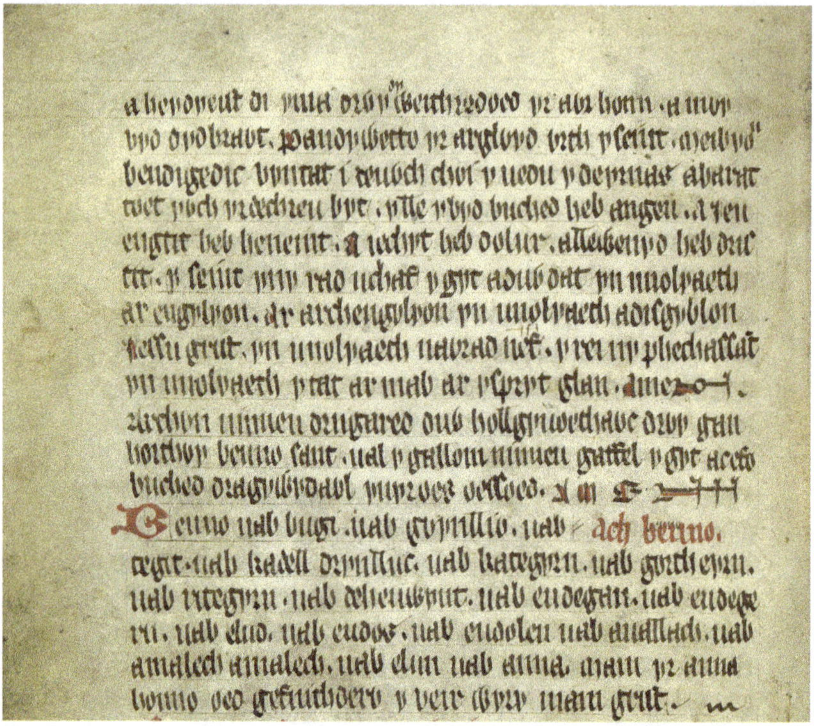

Fig. 12.10. Aberystwyth, National Library of Wales, Llanstephan MS 27 C, fol. 76v (part of *The Red Book of Talgarth*, ca. 1400). End of *Buchedd Beuno* (The Life of St. Beuno). Scribe = Hywel Fychan ap Hywel Goch of Buellt (Builth). Reproduced by kind permission of Llyfrgell Genedlaethol Cymru/The National Library of Wales.

and its literary output. And one just might be absorbing the result of these exchanges of influence in the very lettering of Cotton Nero A.x, which visually links the work of the *Pearl*-poet with more archaic forms of writing and thereby both authoritative histories (the *Brut* tradition) and long-established, respected poetic practices (the Old French *laisse* structure, the Anglo-Saxon alliterative line, the Middle Welsh *cynghanedd*). This, however, should come as no great surprise. The romance of *Sir Gawain and the Green Knight* has been shown many times to have its roots in Celtic mythology and literature. That this should be picked up in Old French/Anglo-Norman sources and reformulated thence into one of the greatest poems of Middle English alliterative poetry once again demonstrates the interrelated currents between these groups of peoples. The Cotton Nero A.x scribe adopts his script, as the *Pearl*-poet borrowed material for his verse, from the multiple cultures and traditions available to him. Working in a far-flung corner of English society, closer in physical proximity to Welsh circles of influence than to London, there seems little reason that our scribe could not have known or been exposed to a script like the ones used in Jesus College MS 111 or Llanstephan MS 27 C. If we can accept that French- and English-speaking sections of society were not as segregated as once thought and that an impressive fluidity existed among these two vernacular languages and literatures, then we should likewise not refuse to acknowledge the importance of Welsh culture, one that existed—literally—right alongside the rise of Middle English alliterative verse and that, along with the other related Brythonic languages, gave to both French and English a wealth of the Western world's most enduring characters, including Gawain himself. In his choices, the scribe of British Library, MS Cotton Nero A.x, Art. 3, despite his relative remoteness from the Continent and more cosmopolitan centers of production, created a remarkably inter-*natio*nal (*natio* in the Latin sense of the word) manuscript.

I hope, if nothing else, I have shown that far from being isolated by the "French flod"—a notably Franco-centric way of viewing the English Channel—the poems of Cotton Nero A.x and the very script employed by the scribe demonstrate the exceptionally multicultural and multilingual situation in the British Isles. We have the work of Elizabeth Salter and Derek Pearsall's continuing labor to thank for opening our eyes to this and for seeking to elucidate the complex matter. We cannot but express our deep gratitude and clamor for more.

Notes

1. Elizabeth Salter, *English and International: Studies in the Literature, Art and Patronage of Medieval England*, ed. Derek Pearsall and Nicolette Zeeman (Cambridge: Cambridge University Press, 1988), xii.

2. See, e.g., Derek Pearsall, "The Development of Middle English Romance," *Medieval Studies* 27 (1965): 91–117; and also "The English Romance in the Fifteenth Century," *Essays and Studies* 29 (1976): 56–83.

3. See the very enlightening piece by Rosalind Field, "Patterns of Availability and Demand in Middle English Translations *de romanz*," in *The Exploitations of Medieval Romance*, ed. Laura Ashe, Ivana Djordjević, and Judith Weiss

(Cambridge: D. S. Brewer, 2010), 73–89. See also Colin Baker, "Bilingualism," in *The Linguistics Encyclopedia*, ed. Kirsten Malmkjær, 2nd ed. (New York: Routledge, 2002), 64–75; C. A. Ferguson, "Diglossia," *Word* 15 (1959): 325–40; and J. A. Fishman, "Bilingualism and Biculturalism as Individual and as Societal Phenomena," *Journal of Multilingual and Multicultural Development* 1 (1980): 1–15.

4. A male gender is attributed to the scribe of Cotton Nero A.x throughout, but since we lack any hard evidence as to the identity of this individual, this is purely an assumption.

5. Israel Gollancz, Introduction to *Pearl, Cleanness, Patience, and Sir Gawain: Reproduced in Facsimile from the Unique MS. Cotton Nero A.x. in the British Museum*, EETS, o.s., 162 (London: Oxford University Press, 1931), 8.

6. The University of Calgary has headed an ambitious project of assessing the script of Cotton Nero A.x, uploading digital images of letter forms, both majuscule and minuscule, ligatures, and abbreviations. A digital facsimile is now available of the entire manuscript as well as a complete transcription and a diplomatic edition of *Cleanness*. To accompany this, they have also supplied an extensive bibliography. See http://people.ucalgary.ca/~scriptor/cotton/.

7. A. I. Doyle, "The Manuscripts," in *Middle English Alliterative Poetry and Its Literary Background: Seven Essays*, ed. David Lawton (Cambridge: D. S. Brewer, 1982), 92.

8. Anthony G. Petti, *English Literary Hands from Chaucer to Dryden* (Cambridge, MA: Harvard University Press, 1977), 49 (pl. 4).

9. Jane Roberts, *Guide to Scripts Used in English Writings up to 1500* (London: British Library, 2005), 170 (pl. 37).

10. Doyle, "The Manuscripts," 92. Maidie Hilmo suggests further, "The modest size of the *Pearl* manuscript of 90 vellum leaves, about 4¾ by 6¾ inches, makes it easily portable and so particularly suitable for private reading." See Maidie Hilmo, "Creating a Visual Narrative of the Spiritual Journey to the New Jerusalem in the *Pearl* Manuscript," in *Medieval Images, Icons, and Illustrated English Literary Texts: From Ruthwell Cross to the Ellesmere Chaucer* (Burlington, VT: Ashgate, 2004), 138. In an insightful essay, Julia Boffey calls into question the rather narrow and rigid classifications utilized by codicologists. Perhaps the term *household book* could be extended to include something more than collections of recipes and remedies and other such information. She looks at Bodleian Library, MS Arch. Selden. B. 24 and suggests that "it might be defined as a book *in use* in a specific household, or group of households, possibly compiled without recourse to commercial networks." See "Bodleian Library, MS Arch. Selden. B. 24 and Definitions of the 'Household Book,'" in *The English Medieval Book: Studies in Memory of Jeremy Griffiths*, ed. A. S. G. Edwards, Vincent Gillespie, and Ralph Hanna (London: British Library, 2000), 129. It would be interesting to consider fur-

ther the implications of such thinking with regard to the contents and creation of Cotton Nero A.x.

11. Roberts, *Guide to Scripts*, 170.

12. Doyle, "The Manuscripts," 92.

13. A. S. G. Edwards, "The Manuscript: British Library MS Cotton Nero A.x," in *A Companion to the Gawain-Poet*, ed. Derek Brewer and Jonathan Gibson (Rochester, NY: D. S. Brewer, 1997), 198–99.

14. Gollancz, Introduction, 8.

15. Such a usage can be explained given the developments of Anglo-Norman and Middle English as languages existing side by side. The *Oxford English Dictionary* (2009) explains under the entry "Z," "In French, the reduction of /ts/ to /s/ brought about a change of spelling from *z* to *s* (often alternating with *x*, e.g. *vois*, *voix*), and this helped to set free *z* to denote the voiced *s*. . . . In English, by the end of the 13th c., *z* is found with the later OF value /z/ in 'learned' words, e.g. *zizanny* tares (Cursor Mundi 1138); . . . by the end of the 14th c., the character had become general, e.g. *gaze*, *mazed*, *canonize*. In MSS of 1300 onwards, the tailed *z* and *ȝ* came to be indistinguishable in form; hence, in modern editions are found many instances of spellings such as *ȝelot* zealot, *Sarȝine* Saracen." The scribe (or poet) of Cotton Nero A.x regularly uses *ȝ* to denote a final /z/ and sometimes /s/. However, the sound combination /ts/ or /z/ can be represented more or less successfully by spelling it with *tȝ* (*tz*). This possibility, though, is only employed from time to time, especially in the word *watȝ* 'was.' See, for example, line 8 of fol. 92v in Gollancz's facsimile (now fol. 96v): "there gode gawan watȝ g*ray*þed gwenore bisyde." Most modern editions simply change all of the yoghs to zeds. While this could attest to an Anglo-Norman textual connection in many ways, it may also represent an idiosyncratic or antiquated pronunciation, something which requires further dialectical research.

16. Doyle, "The Manuscripts," 92.

17. Ibid., 143 (n. 12).

18. For more information about this manuscript, its contents, and the romance of *Fierabras* specifically—with a detailed outline summary—refer to the British Library catalog entry at www.bl.uk/catalogues/manuscripts/HITS0001.ASP?VPath=html/33768.htm&Search=Eg.+3028&Highlight=F.

19. Rita Lejeune and Jacques Stiennon, *La Légende de Roland dans l'art du Moyen Âge*, vol. 1 (Brussels: Arcade, 1966), 215–18.

20. The use of the term *revival* is one that Derek Pearsall would rightly question, as he does in his chapter, "The Origins of the Alliterative Revival," in *The Alliterative Tradition in the Fourteenth Century*, ed. Bernard S. Levy and Paul E. Szarmach (Kent, OH: Kent State University Press, 1981), 1–24. Regarding influences, he generally sides with Elizabeth Salter's earlier work in "The Alliterative Revival I," *Modern Philology* 64 (1966): 146–50, and in "The Alliterative Revival II," *Modern Philology* 64 (1967): 233–37. He posits a continuum of

poetic practice poorly attested in surviving records that was shaped by changes of historical and cultural context (5–6).

21. Rosalind Field, "The Anglo-Norman Background to Alliterative Romance," in *Middle English Alliterative Poetry and Its Literary Background: Seven Essays*, ed. David Lawton (Cambridge: D. S. Brewer, 1982), 58.

22. Ibid., 56, 58.

23. Ibid., 57.

24. Ibid., 55, 57.

25. Ibid., 58, 62. In the introduction to the second volume of the Anglo-Norman Text Society's edition (nos. 12–13) of the *Romance of Horn* (Oxford: Basil Blackwell, 1964), Mildred K. Pope and T. B. W. Reid provide a detailed explanation and diagram of *laisse* structure on pages 21–27. In "The Origins of the Alliterative Revival," Pearsall too acknowledges the similarity between the alexandrine lines of Old French/Anglo-Norman *laisses* and the alliterative long line of English poetry (5).

26. As W. R. J. Barron notes, "A number of French analogues have traditionally been cited for one of the twin plots," but sources for the other and the motif which connects them are still somewhat uncertain. See his essay "Alliterative Romance and the French Tradition," in Lawton, *Middle English Alliterative Poetry and Its Literary Background*, 73. For a more in-depth discussion on this topic, see Elisabeth Brewer, *From Cuchulainn to Gawain: Sources and Analogues of "Sir Gawain and the Green Knight"* (Totowa, NJ: D. S. Brewer, 1973). Both John Matthews, *Gawain: Knight of the Goddess: Restoring an Archetype* (Wellingborough: Aquarian, 1990), and Laura Hibbard Loomis, "Gawain and the Green Knight," in *Arthurian Literature in the Middle Ages: A Collaborative History*, ed. Roger Sherman Loomis (Oxford: Clarendon Press, 1959), 528–40, have more to add to the debate concerning influences.

27. In his book *Handwriting in England and Wales* (Cardiff: University of Wales Press, 1954), N. Denholm-Young provides an example of what he thinks represents the most common Anglo-Norman script on plate 15, found in Bodleian Library, MS Hatton 82 (*S.C.* 4092), which contains the *Perlesvaus*, with the hand dating to the middle of the thirteenth century. Plates of Anglo-Norman texts written in *cursiva* exist in the editions of the works published by the Anglo-Norman Text Society. Examples I have looked at that are written in a *cursiva* include *The Crusade and Death of Richard I* (mid-fourteenth century); *The Anglo-Norman Text of Le Lai du Cor* (ca. 1272–82); *The Anglo-Norman Pseudo-Turpin Chronicle of William de Briane* (first third of the fourteenth century); *Fouke le Fitz Waryn* (ca. 1325–40); *Corset* (late thirteenth or early fourteenth century); *Rossignos* (late fourteenth century).

28. Brian S. Merrilees, ed., Chardri, *La Vie des Set Dormanz*, ANTS 35 (London: Westfield College, 1977), 7–8.

29. Constance B. Hieatt and Robin F. Jones, eds., *La Novele Cirurgerie*, ANTS 46 (London: Birkbeck College, 1990), xii. The Bodleian Library catalog

posits a date sometime in the first half of the thirteenth century; however, in "The 'Novele cirurgerie' in MS London, British Library Harley 2558," *Zeitschrift für romanische Philologie* 103 (1987): 271–99, Tony Hunt argues for a date in the second half of the thirteenth century. Languages used in the manuscript are Anglo-Norman and Latin.

30. K.V. Sinclair, ed., *The Hospitallers' Riwle* (*Miracula et regula hospitalis Sancti Johannis Jerosolimitani*), ANTS 42 (London: Anglo-Norman Text Society, 1984), xxv. I must extend my heartfelt thanks to Prof. Maureen B. McCann Boulton for helping me to find this example and for her words of wisdom and guidance as I began my work on this project.

31. Ibid., xxiii. While many of the texts, including papal bulls and royal charters, focus on the interests of Waterford and surrounding areas, the compilation includes charters and customs documents for Drogheda, Bristol, and Haverford. Not all of the material is utilitarian, however, as the manuscript preserves a copy of the *Prophecies of Merlin*, Bede's *De temporibus liber*, a text on the interpretation of dreams, the *Disticha Catonis*, poems on the Fall, the Harrowing of Hell, and the Passion of Christ, etc. For information about this manuscript, including images, refer to the *Parker Library on the Web*: http://parkerweb.stanford.edu/parker/actions/manuscript_description_long_display.do?ms_no=405.

32. Kathryn Kerby-Fulton, Maidie Hilmo, and Linda Olson, *Opening Up Middle English Manuscripts: Literary and Visual Approaches* (Ithaca: Cornell University Press, 2012), 56–57.

33. Roberts, *Guide to Scripts*, 146, 154 (pls. 32 and 34).

34. Ibid., 148. In *English Vernacular Hands: From the Twelfth to the Fifteenth Centuries* (Oxford: Clarendon Press, 1960), 7, C. D. Wright says of the text of *The Owl and the Nightingale* in Cotton Caligula A.ix that it is written "in a hand very closely related to that of Laȝamon, perhaps a little later and with some peculiarities." Presumably what he means by "Laȝamon" is the hand of the scribe who copied the *Brut*.

35. Roberts, *Guide to Scripts*, 148.

36. Prys Morgan, "Glamorgan and the Red Book," *Morgannwg* 22 (1978): 42.

37. Roberts, *Guide to Scripts*, 152.

38. Angus McIntosh, Michael Louis Samuels, and Michael Benskin, *A Linguistic Atlas of Late Mediaeval English* (Aberdeen: Aberdeen University Press, 1986), 1:23–24, 106; 3:37–38; LP 26 Cheshire. The provenance of Cotton Nero A.x after this point is still under debate, but according to Roberts, it was part of Henry Savile of Banke's (d. 1617) library before it became part of Sir Robert Cotton's by about 1621 (172).

39. Ordelle G. Hill, *Looking Westward: Poetry, Landscape, and Politics in "Sir Gawain and the Green Knight"* (Newark: University of Delaware Press, 2009), 15. For more information about the Welsh manuscripts discussed here

as well as others, see Daniel Huws, *Medieval Welsh Manuscripts* (Cardiff: University of Wales Press and the National Library of Wales, 2000).

40. For information about this manuscript and a digitized version, see "Jesus College MS. 111," in *Early Manuscripts at Oxford University: Digital Facsimiles of Complete Manuscripts, Scanned Directly from the Originals* (Oxford Digital Library, Oxford University, 2001), http://image.ox.ac.uk/show?collection=jesus&manuscript=ms111.

41. Gifford Charles-Edwards, "The Scribes of the Red Book of Hergest," *National Library of Wales Journal* 21 (1980): 246–50.

42. Morgan, "Glamorgan and the Red Book," 44, 47, 52.

43. Denholm-Young, *Handwriting in England and Wales*, pl. 19b.

44. Charles Johnson and Hilary Jenkinson provide an excellent sketch of the development and features of court hands in *English Court Hand A.D. 1066 to 1500, Illustrated Chiefly from the Public Records* (Oxford: Clarendon Press, 1915), xx–xxi. Denholm-Young refers to their work in his assessment of court hands and, as he says, the "spiky" quality that arises among them in the latter half of the fourteenth century (35).

45. For more information about National Library of Wales, Llanstephan MS 27 C, and a digitized version, see http://digidol.llgc.org.uk/METS/DAF00024/frames?div=0&subdiv=0&locale=en&mode=thumbnail. One can also observe Hywel Fychan's hand in Oxford, Jesus College, MS 57, likewise of ca. 1400. See the digitized manuscript online at http://image.ox.ac.uk/show?collection=jesus&manuscript=ms57.

46. D. Simon Evans, Introduction to *Buchedd Dewi* (Cardiff: University of Wales Press, 1959), xxxvii.

47. Interestingly, Llanstephan MS 27 C includes a few folios written in Anglicana at the very beginning.

48. See Robert W. Barrett, *Against All England: Regional Identity and Cheshire Writing, 1195–1656* (Notre Dame: University of Notre Dame Press, 2009); and Michael J. Bennett, *Community, Class and Careerism: Cheshire and Lancashire Society in the Age of Sir Gawain and the Green Knight* (Cambridge: Cambridge University Press, 1983).

49. See A. T. E. Matonis, "An Investigation of Celtic Influences on MS Harley 2253," *Modern Philology* 70 (1972): 91–108; and "The Harley Lyrics: English and Welsh Convergences," *Modern Philology* 86 (1988): 1–21.

50. Hill, *Looking Westward*, 26–31.

51. See Helen Fulton, "The Theory of Celtic Influence on the Harley Lyrics," *Modern Philology* 82 (1985): 239–54.

CHAPTER 13

Langlandian Economics in James Yonge's *Gouernaunce*

Translation and Ethics in Fifteenth-Century Dublin

Hilary E. Fox

In 1423 the Anglo-Irish notary James Yonge was moved from Trim Castle, where he had been incarcerated since the previous year, to Dublin Castle.[1] The circumstances of his imprisonment and transfer provide an interesting conspectus of the literary and scribal landscape of colonial Ireland as much as they do the political climate in the years after Henry IV's death. One possible reason for Yonge's incarceration was his authorship of the *Gouernaunce of Prynces*. While its proclamation of Yonge's loyalty to James Butler, fourth earl of Ormond, is likely what got him into trouble, the *Gouernaunce* is intriguing for its international flavor: it is a Hiberno-English translation of an Anglo-Norman French text—itself a translation from the Latin—composed in Paris by an Irish Dominican with the aid of a Walloon and eventually returned to Ireland. The man overseeing Yonge's transfer to Dublin was his then-apprentice Nicholas Bellewe, who, after Yonge's eventual release in 1424 and pardon in 1425, joined him in the circle of legal secretaries working in Dublin. Theresa O'Byrne's essay in this volume addresses Bellewe's career in the years during and after Yonge's time in prison; the present essay addresses the work that put Yonge there.

Just as medieval manuscript production responded to scribes and readers, so too did the texts themselves respond to the needs of their authors. And just as Derek Pearsall's work has been influential in the study of the former, so too has his work on the economics of *Piers Plowman* helped to shape the melding of ethics and historicist inquiry into late medieval authorial practice. Pearsall's examination of the socioeconomic influences on the versions of *Piers Plowman*, for example, reflects the inextricable ties between the metamorphosis of that text and its critique of the economies of fourteenth-century London. In "Langland's London," Pearsall points to the development of images in the C-text that equate London and the urban with the "social and economic malpractice" epidemic in the government, the chapel, and the streets.[2] The extended narrative of Lady Meed (Passus II–IV), with its descriptions of the bribe- and reward-driven economy of the London courts and mercantile circles, represented by Meed and her attendants, is set against the sufferings of the urban underclass, for whom poverty is a way of life (IX.86–87).[3] For Langland, in Pearsall's reading of *Piers*, economy and ethics cannot be separated: the circulation of money and goods is simultaneously the reaffirmation of codes of behavior that tie citizens together. The consequences of fiscal corruption in the cities increase exponentially for those least able to defend themselves against it: when Falseness, Guile, and Liar find refuge with the friars, merchants, and frauds of all types (II.220–44), the result is corruption that "don most harm to þe mene peple" (III.81).

The purity of economy and social stability were also crucial for Yonge, whose major surviving literary foray is his Hiberno-English translation of the thirteenth-century *Segré de segrez* of the Dominican Jofroi of Waterford and Servais Copale, undertaken (according to him) at Butler's behest.[4] The bulk of his production, on the other hand, is found in a wider documentary context that embraced the circle of scribes and lawyers responsible for the textual creation and maintenance of Dublin's legal records. As a member of Dublin's "clerical proletariat," to borrow a phrase from Kathryn Kerby-Fulton, Yonge was in a position uniquely suited to observe and appreciate the vagaries of a colonial economy and the practices that enabled or hindered it. It is this economy and its corruption that I want to examine in light of Yonge's modifications to his source, as well as the criticism Yonge levels at the unreliable system of Anglo-Irish governance. By way of laying out a prospectus for the rest of the essay, I begin with a brief review of the *Secretum secretorum* tradition in the Middle Ages, before moving on to the relationship between the *Segré* and the *Gouernaunce*. Finally, I consider the motivations for Yonge's focus on fiscal malfeasance and how the advice text functions as a veiled critique of aristocratic authority. Fundamentally, Yonge's changes, in the form of interpolations and his own exempla, argue for a mind closely and critically engaged both with his source text(s) and with the system of ethics that governed (or ought to govern) the financial relationships between lord and followers.

The tradition of the *Secretum secretorum*, of which the *Segré* and the *Gouernaunce* form a part, stems from a letter to Alexander the Great attributed to Aristotle.[5] No Greek source has been found; rather, the *Secretum* derives from the tenth-century *Kitāb sirr al-asrār*.[6] It was transmitted to the West in two forms: one translation by Iohannes Hispalensis in the twelfth century and another in the first half of the thirteenth by Philippus Tripolitanus, the latter of which Jofroi took as his foundation for the *Segré*.[7] To say that the *Secretum* was hugely popular may be to understate the matter: in his 2003 study of the tradition throughout the High Middle Ages, Steven Williams counts above 130 manuscripts in Latin alone plus those of translations into vernaculars from across Europe. (The manuscript count from the later Middle Ages is considerably higher.)[8] The tradition itself was one of change and accretion and became, as its copyists and translators required it, "a sort of encyclopedic work comprising, in addition to its original moral and political component, much miscellaneous information on occult and pseudo-scientific subjects."[9] Rotating in and out were batteries of quotations from the authorities and exempla meant to demonstrate the truth of whatever ethical point the author was interested in making. The flexible nature of the *Secretum* thus meant that it was just as much a book about anything its author wanted it to be as "a book about everything." In the context of ethical works like the *Gouernaunce*, *translatio* could also mean the *translation* of advice into self-reformation and into ethical choices that reflected the lessons inculcated by the text's exempla.

This flexibility means that Yonge was by no means alone in his choice to translate "Some good boke of gouernaunce of Prynces" (122.7) for the edification of his patron, nor was he innovative either within the genre of the *Secretum* or advice literature or within the wider scope of medieval translation practices. With reference only to the *Secretum* tradition in the isles, he has parallels in his English near-contemporaries of the late fourteenth and fifteenth centuries, including John Gower (*Confessio Amantis*, completed ca. 1399 with dedications to Richard II and

Henry IV) and Thomas Hoccleve (*Regiment of Princes*, ca. 1411–12), as well as minor and anonymous English authors.[10] He was also not innovative in his decision to produce a translation that is faithful to its source in some places while departing in others. His base text, the *Segré*, as a result of its authors' "toutes sortes de suppressions et d'additions," is itself "un livre nouveau qui est sorti de leur plume."[11] It is to some of those differences that I would now like to turn. In the absence of infinite space, the present essay concentrates on *Segré* 6, "Pourquoi font a eschiuer forlargeche et escarsetez qui apent a franchise" (Bibliothèque nationale de France, MS fr. 1822, fols. 85v–86r) and its correlate, *Gouernaunce* 5, "Wher-for byth to Enchu folargesse and scarcite. And whate longyth to Fraunchis" (131.32–134.35).[12]

Both *Segré* 6 and *Gouernaunce* 5 are concerned with the meanings and political ramifications of *franchise* and its negatives, stinginess and excessive prodigality. *Franchise* is a complicated term: in French and Middle English, it means not only "generosity" or "liberality," but extends through related fields having to do with political freedom and enfranchisement, the rights of freedmen, the special privileges accorded to towns or organizations such as guilds, and the legitimate authority of the king.[13] Even though the chapters are interested in responsible economy, the political overtones in their use of *franchise* cannot be divorced from the other ideas attached to it; the king's exercise of franchise is intimately related to his power—if the king does not exercise franchise his power is either imperiled or illegitimate—and to the enfranchisement of his subjects, whose lives depend on his largesse and his honoring of his debts. On either side of franchise sit the extremes of *folargesse* and *scarcite*: the former is the excessive generosity that can bankrupt a realm; the latter withholds payment from those who deserve it.[14] *Scarcite* can also refer to lack in general, with reference to the necessaries of life or the money needed to acquire them; in the context of the *Segré* and *Gouernaunce*, poverty of goods and money may also be related to a bad ruler's failure to provide the capital that keeps the economy going or wrongfully appropriation of money and property under color of office.

This sort of *scarcite*, in which ethical failure and a failing economy are intimately related, is of special importance to Yonge, who departs at length from *Segré* 6 in order to offer an extended discussion of the evils of "unrighteous" kingship as expressed through fiscal malfeasance. Jofroi merely observes that "in a king it is a sovereign virtue, subtlety and understanding, a sure sign of knowledge and of law, with the demonstration of perfect virtue if [he] refuses to seize and deprive his subjects of their goods and possessions, because this destroys a realm; and wherefore all those who do so cannot endure long because of it" (ken roi est souerainne bontei, cointise dentendement, sourse de sauoir et de loi mostrance de parfite uirtu se il escieue aprendre et atolir a ses suges lur biens et lur auoirs: car ce destruit les roalmes tous, ceus qui ce funt, que durer ne puele ne por ce; BnF fr. 1822 fol. 86r/a, 20–27). However, Yonge adds to this observation a selection of quotations drawn from the scriptures and commentaries (132.11–18) and a diatribe against extortion under the color of law:

> Many pryncis and lordis for nede takyn goodis of the commyn pepill moche agayne har willis, And ham therwyth fro myschefe defendyth. Suche a kynge is tollerabill, as many men thynkyn, for the more myschefe to Enchu. But Sum Pryncis ther bene, that for thar owyn Synguler auauntage, as they wenyth, by coloure of har Pryncehode and coloured defense of the commyn Pepill, takyn atte har talent trew men goodis. Suche Prynces bene wors than Sathanas, lasse than thay amendis make.[15] (*Gouernaunce* 132.18–32)

Yonge is careful to distinguish between the rightful extraction of taxes or fees—or even excessive taxes that are necessary to prevent "the more myschefe"—and extractions levied "by coloure." *Color* in juridical French had already acquired the ancillary legal definition of a wrongful legal pretext, as well as an action or document having the semblance or appearance of legality but without any legal reality behind it.[16] Yonge's introduction of the term in its legal sense, playing on the idea of the claiming of princely authority ("by coloure of har Pryncehode") and the pretense of the need to defend the commons ("coloured defense of the commyn Pepill"), asserts that a ruler who operates for personal gain under cover of his office possesses only an image of legitimacy, not its reality. The fact that, in Ireland, the practices involved in acquiring money for "Synguler auauntage" involved gross harm to the commons in the form of extortion or black rent is brought home in one of Yonge's first extended historical interpolations, the career of Stephen Scrope, which follows his initial expansion on the *Segré*.

Stephen Scrope served in the government of Ireland twice, once as lieutenant to his brother William, who was made justiciar during the reign of Richard II (1394–97), and again under Thomas of Lancaster, beginning in 1401 and continuing on and off until his death at Castledermot in September 1409.[17] Yonge elides the details of Stephen's first term of service in favor of a general observation on his activities in maintaining—or not maintaining—the king's rule:

> This wyrchipphul knyght Syr Stewyn Scrope, in kynge Richarde-is tyme and Kynge Henry-is tyme the fourth Also, Hauynge the gouernaunce of Irlande, many extorcionys did, Lyuereȝ takynge, lytill good Paynge, moche he traualit, lytille espolid in the Iryssh, enemys he had al the mene tyme. (133.13–17)

Yonge reduces his account of Stephen's early career and his role in Richard's successful foray into Ireland in favor of focusing on the relationship between his fiscal malfeasance and his ineffectiveness as a governor. As I suggest, Yonge's elisions not only aid in his construction of an instructive exemplum, but serve as a method by which Yonge can offer comment on pressing contemporary issues. As such, the nature of Yonge's historiography should be understood before assessing how he deploys historical exempla in the service of his larger ethical goals. In particular, the history of Stephen Scrope—who was connected with the earl of Ormond, Yonge's patron, and with that family's advancement in the early fourteenth century—needs to be reconstructed, insofar as it can be. Yonge's changes to Stephen's biography suggest multiple concerns are at work, not only the issue of extortion as general (mal)-practice, but as a specific issue that plagued the rivals for the Butlers' governorship—particularly the Talbots—as well as the Butlers themselves and, because of that, plagued the administration of the colony.

Stephen was the third son of Richard, first Lord Scrope of Bolton. Unlike his older brother, executed for his support of Richard II,[18] and his father, who had lost influence in Richard's government due to his support of the Lords Appellant, he managed to negotiate difficult waters with some success; his competence meant the development of an advantageous relationship with Henry IV after Richard's deposition.[19] His early career benefited from his brother's intimacy with Richard, which William leveraged to keep Stephen in Ireland as his lieutenant following Richard's 1394 campaign.[20] His experiences in Ireland, despite his family's Ricardian sympathies, led Henry IV to reinstate him as deputy governor under Thomas of Lancaster in 1401.[21] Both Stephen's first and second tenures in Ireland were marked by some successes: he replaced his brother William as justiciar in 1396 due in part to his role in bringing the Irish lords to rapprochement with Richard,[22] and, by securing the submissions of several Irish nobles, he continued to demonstrate his usefulness to Henry's interests.[23]

Yonge's remark, "moche he traualit, lytille espolid in the Iryssh," may refer to the undoing of Richard's advances in Ireland, especially to the oaths of fidelity he had extracted from MacMurrough and the other Irish lords.[24] Yonge attributes this to Stephen's habit of "Lyuereȝ takynge, lytill good Paynge," a practice that was hardly limited to Stephen alone; the reality was significantly more complex, involving as it does the politics of colonial economics. For all of Yonge's complaints that Stephen failed to despoil the Irish, the Irish continued to revolt because of English failure to honor promises given in 1394, and their rebellion was aided by alliances of English lords both against the Irish and against each other, as well as a chronic lack of funding to prosecute war or establish peace.[25] What Stephen's role in Anglo-Irish bickering happened to be is unclear; he was clearly unsuccessful in keeping Leinster under wraps, as attested by MacMurrough's continued agitation and the death of Roger Mortimer, earl of March and Richard's heir, near Carlow (in Leinster) in 1397.[26] At the same time Stephen may have been trying to assert himself in Leinster, James Butler, third earl of Ormond, was engaged in a power struggle with the Geraldines, one that would last from 1394 until Richard's deposition; in September 1399, according to a letter from the king's council in Ireland to Westminster, the earl of Desmond had allied with MacMurrough against Ormond and marched from Munster with the express purpose of "destroy[ing] the Earl of Ormond."[27] Finally, the peace Richard imposed in 1394 was only as stable as the currency used to finance the garrisons that helped to keep it. This stability did not last long; as John Lydon writes, "as so often happened at this stage in Irish history, financial expediency was allowed to dictate a retreat from a policy which had been found to work."[28]

Stephen's inability to keep the "Irish enemies" in line was thus complicated at one level by England's failure to honor its promises, at another by the uncooperativeness of powerful magnates, and finally by the government's inability to fund the military, which led to the financial exploitation of which Stephen stands accused in the *Gouernaunce.* Both Stephen's Ricardian and Lancastrian appointments do not seem to differ substantially in terms of the sorts of complaints raised by the Commons or the chronicles: historically, the system of coign and livery and assignment that had plagued Ireland in the fourteenth century continued to do so into the fifteenth. Yonge's familiarity with the documents lying behind the history of English governance may also inform his treatment of Stephen's first lieutenancy. A 1399 letter of the Irish Commons to the newly crowned Henry IV sets up a refrain that would be repeated for the next two decades and beyond: in it, the Commons complained that the country "has been laid waste and destroyed through the coign of soldiers" (este degaste et destructe graundement par coyngez dez kernys).[29]

Yonge's reference to Stephen's "Lyuereȝ takynge, lytill good Paynge" may be a reference to disputes that were contemporary to the *Gouernaunce*, and to larger problems regarding the economics and rule of the colony. The exaction of coign and livery—the quartering, paying, and supplying of soldiers at the commons' expense—was illegal but, without funds from the crown, was used by Anglo-Irish lords to support their troops. In theory, liveries levied on tenants were to be paid at full market price, but because payments to magnates were often in arrears they were taken on tallies, a system of assignment in which the payee was made responsible for recovering the funds owed.[30] However, the already overtaxed system (which had been abused since before the inception of Lancastrian rule) could rarely provide payment; the lords taking liveries from their tenants either could not or would not provide reimbursement. The practice was closely implicated in the removal of John Talbot, Ormond's rival, from the lieutenancy in 1419; Ormond, among his many other attacks on Talbot, asserted that Talbot's expeditions against the Irish had required Ormond's soldiers to be fed and billeted at the expense of the people, who had gone uncompensated, and Talbot (according to Ormond) was flagrantly guilty of oppression and extortion against all classes of Anglo-Irish society.[31]

Fortunately for Stephen, he was able to find a second chance during his appointment to the deputyship of Ireland under Thomas of Lancaster—and incentive to amend his ways, thanks to the petitioning of his wife, who refused to accompany him unless he swore to commit no extortions. As a result, he met with unprecedented military success:

> Into the londe he came, good Pament to al men he makyd, Grete grace to al gentil endaunger anent the kynge for lyfe and landis he grauntid. And therfor in his baner, trewe men blessynge he bare. The vertue of thes armes was so myche that in one day, the grete

> prowte Artoure Macmurrough-is countrey, in yowre presence tendyr of age, he brente, many of his he Slow . . . good pees in leynstere that yere, and many othyr commendable dedis of armes he did elsware. Al this grace hym befelle that yere as y vndyrstond, For-thy that he al that yere noone extorcioun did. (*Gouernaunce* 133.25–39)

Stephen not only made "good Pament" to those men he owed, but he also rewarded those who served the king faithfully with favors and property.[32] The return on Stephen's investment came in the form of victory against the long-troublesome Art MacMurrough, the rebel lord Walter Bourke, and the Irish chief O'Carroll (133.28–35). Yonge's account of Stephen's Lancastrian tenure is also telescoped: the events Yonge narrates occurred not in 1401, when Henry IV appointed Stephen as Thomas's deputy, but in September 1407, six years after Stephen's first commission.[33] This compression of Stephen's career also further obscures some troubles in his Lancastrian appointment. A response to a 1405 petition at Dunboyne, from the citizens of various demesne lands, appointed Lawrence Merbury to look into the possibility of wrongful distraints of income exercised against various tenants.[34] Two years later, Stephen was summoned back to England on account of "various arduous reasons concerning the King and his estate in Ireland"; the precise nature of Henry's grievances with Stephen's administration is unknown, but the colony's unrest—and unprofitability—were likely to have been at issue.[35]

Compressing the time line of Stephen's career, in addition, highlights military successes that were crucial to the Butlers' eventual exercise of power in Ireland and the family's dominance in Irish politics. The victories over MacMurrough, Bourke, and the O'Carrolls would have had an extra significance for James IV himself: not only was he present at the battles, but that December he was appointed chief governor during Stephen's return to England.[36] By connecting fiscal rectitude with military success, Yonge collates good policy with good tactics; if he were, as Peter Crooks argues, translating the *Gouernaunce* for Butler at the beginning of his 1420 term of office, he may have wanted to remind Butler of an exemplary tale from his own youth and connect the successful Scrope-Butler expeditions both with Stephen's honoring his promise to his wife and with his fulfillment of his economic obligations. If, on the other hand (as the dedication suggests), he had carried out the translation at the end of Butler's tenure, just after Henry V's accession, he would have wanted to emphasize (for Henry) Stephen's military and economic success as living on in Butler's governorship.[37]

Yonge's "understanding" that Stephen's effective governance is due to his vow to behave with fiscal rectitude hints at other possibilities behind that success—possibilities Yonge elides in his focus on Stephen-as-example. Specifically, what Stephen accomplished in his first years as de facto lieutenant was a series of diplomatic and military successes: O'Connor Faly offered his fealty in September 1401, with O'Byrne and MacMahon joining him later that year; O'Reilly gave his allegiance in 1402, and MacMurrough was defeated at Wexford.[38] These submissions and victories were backed by Henry IV's support, which represented a significant investment in Irish security.[39] With at least some money and manpower coming in, Stephen would not have had to resort to the sorts of practices that had characterized his Ricardian term of service. However, after that one year of financial support, Henry's policy regarding Ireland very quickly became of a piece with Richard's: by 1402 the Lancastrian government was already in arrears in the payment of stipends to its governors, along with payments to the armies meant to enforce the king's authority. This meant, naturally, the reintroduction of coign and livery and the loss of the gains initially made after Henry's accession.[40] Yonge's knowledge of Ormond history alongside the history of English policy would have prevented him from making any sweeping statement about the permanence and nature of Stephen's reform. Instead, the "one yere" of Stephen's lieutenancy under Thomas of Lancaster—combining Stephen's first successes and some of his last—would have stood out as a year of promise in nearly two decades of frustration and conflict.

The twenty years that passed between Stephen's first Lancastrian deputation and the election of Ormond to the governorship saw the continuing deleterious effects of factionalism in Anglo-Irish government and the economic scandals, accusations, and counteraccusations that attend almost any political unrest.[41] For Yonge, those twenty years, with their attendant financial difficulties (and the bureaucratic chaos that certainly attended them), also threatened the legitimacy of English rule in Ireland, a legitimacy which Yonge is anxious to establish both in its own right and with respect to Butler as the viable representative of ideal English lordship. This legitimacy, which Yonge considers to be established from the earliest days of the conquest of Ireland, was imperiled by the use of extortion in the perpetual feuds waged among the Anglo-Irish lords.

After reform Stephen's successful subduing of the "rebele Waltere Bourke" refers directly to the additional difficulties English lords, in the absence of their king, brought on the populace of both loyal English and Irish subjects. A handful of proceedings from the King's Council in Ireland for 1393 suffices to give a sense of the problem. In that year, Thomas Snelle, John de Desmond, and Thomas Butler petitioned the council for relief not only from the ravages of the Irish, but the rebel English. Meanwhile, Thomas, bishop of Lismore and Waterford, sought a petition "to treat and hold parley . . . as well with English rebels as with Irish enemies whatsoever, although they may be indicted or outlawed . . . and to reform them to the peace of our Lord the King,"[42] one of the few men to do so before Richard II's arrival in 1394 to subdue the Irish *and* the rebel English.[43] A report of the Council of Ireland to the king in 1399 indicates the ongoing state of affairs: not only is the army underfunded, but the rebel English remain "sturdy robbers and not amenable to the law." In many ways, Henry IV's reassertion of royal power on the island following his accession had as much to do with halting the English rebellion as quelling the Irish one.

Stephen was only the tip of the iceberg. Alongside their own feuds the English found time to rob and despoil "the poor liege people of the land," the class to which Yonge belongs. The same 1399 council letter gives, in exhaustive detail, the failure of the government to derive revenue owed to it from rents and fees, due to the deplorable state of the Exchequer (which Yonge, as a bureaucrat, would have lamented) and the inability of officials to collect rents due to the violence endemic in counties beyond Dublin. While Yonge does not grant the enemy Irish much (or any) leeway, he may have been aware that their uprisings in the 1390s had much to do with the failure of the crown to redress wrongs done to them by the rebel English; he is careful to remark that "Fraunchis and largesse auere, makyth longe a royalme to Endure and wel y-kepid" (132.1–2). Alongside the administration's failure, as exemplified by the prereform Stephen, to honor its commitments, the ongoing abuses of the tallage system question the ability of legitimate rulership to coexist with fiscal irresponsibility.

Legitimate authority is not merely Yonge's gloss for authority of which he approves, but is tied up with his understanding of how the lordship of Ireland was rightfully held by English kings. Even as Yonge's interpolation of translations from Gerald of Wales's *Expugnatio Hibernica* serves to assert the ancient rights of English monarchs to the kingship of Ireland, Yonge places those assertions alongside demonstrations of the sorts of behaviors that threaten legitimacy. To Gerald's original five reasons, Yonge adds his own three: the decision of the 1171 Council of Armagh (also taken from the *Expugnatio*), the oaths of obedience sworn by the Irish lords to Richard II in 1395, and the hostages the lords gave to guarantee the peace.[44] The care that Yonge takes to emphasize the historical precedents for English rule should not be read as blindly uncritical support for English dominion. Rather, in the context of the *Gouernaunce*, legitimate power can only be exercised through an ethical code that ties the cultivation of private virtue to public practice—this is the hinge on which the theory of advice literature turns. However, even as Yonge reiterates the claims of English kings—and, thus, their deputies' authority to govern for kings in absentia—he also hints, by his insistence on the evils of extortion under color of authority, at the real-world consequences of dereliction of ethical obligations and how that dereliction endangers even that authority which is supported by historical precedent.

Consequently, Yonge's excursus on extortion in the *Gouernaunce* is not only a conveniently moralized pro-Lancastrian history lesson or a covert anti-Talbot treatise; rather it insists on the relationship between good economic policy and a ruler's right to rule. In the context of Ireland, which was beset by centuries of bad governance and a vicious cycle of underfunding and extortionate demands to make up the shortfall, Yonge's concern over fiscal responsibility and its ability to distinguish the "true" ruler from the usurper becomes more than a moral point for him to harp on: it becomes an issue of the survival of the state and the preservation of the class of "loyal" English whose existence was imperiled by internecine conflict.[45] It is worth noting that Yonge is translating the *Gouernaunce* while Henry V is busy asserting his claims in France and may well have completed it not long before Henry's unexpected death near Paris in August of that year. Richard's various difficulties in Ireland, and his eventual loss of his kingdom, have been detailed above; his loss of authority came at a time when the stability of English control required the assertion of it. Before he could bring the Irish and the English under control, however, Richard headed back to England to deal with Bolingbroke; the chaos left in his wake would be addressed by the Irish Commons in its letter of complaint to Henry IV and would plague the Irish government throughout Yonge's career. The English kings' pursuit of their own dynastic interests in England and on the Continent meant that Ireland was left to fend for itself, with the English and Irish prosecuting their own feuds at the expense of the commons. As a notary, Yonge would have been in a unique position to observe the havoc colonialist hostilities wrought on the populace and the government designed to look to its interests; and as a translator of an advice text, he translated his reservations with the Ricardian and Lancastrian governments' handling of English lordship on the island.

It seems a long way to travel to get back to Langland's London, but the way may be brief. One of the proverbial statements in *Piers*, "When all tresores ben tried, Treuthe is þe beste," is spoken first by Holy Church (I.81) in reference to the ruling orders' responsibility to serve Truth by defending the realm from *transgressores* and administering justice. "Ho-so passeth þat point is appostata of knyghthed," Holy Church argues. "And neuer leue for loue in hope to lacche silver" (I.98–100). Her reference to bribery and corruption anticipates the discussions of meed, reward, and the avarice that destroys the social fabric of the *comune* in the Meed Passus.[46] For Yonge, the desire of English knights *to lacche silver* led to sets of abusive practices that impaired the Irish economy; the acquisition of money under "coloured defense of the commyn Pepill" endangered the economies of the court as well as those of the commons who found their resources exhausted. The treatment of Stephen's career alongside Yonge's disquisitions on extortion offers the disease and the cure, suggesting that past systematic abuses need not (and, under Butler's rule, will not) be a pattern for the future. As such, a Yongian reading of the *Piers* aphorism might be, "when all treasures are exhausted, duty to one's subjects is the best treasure one has"—that is, the duty to honor good economic policy ought to override all other financial exigencies. When it does, the ruler is more effectively able to preserve the *treuthe* he owes to his subjects.

In "Professional Readers of Langland at Home and Abroad," Derek Pearsall's student Kathryn Kerby-Fulton points to the near-simultaneous presence of the *Secreta* and *Piers Plowman* within the Ormond affinity, with modes of reading inflected by Langlandian ethical interpretations of history and society. The production of the illustration program in the Douce 104 *Piers*, Kerby-Fulton notes, owes a great debt to the Dublin branch of the English bureaucracy; *Piers* also likely influenced the versions of the *Modus tenendi parliamentorum* held by members of

Ormond's circle and used in the parliamentary disputes in the years immediately preceding the translation of the *Gouernaunce*.[47] While Kerby-Fulton concentrates primarily on Langlandian meritocracy as informing Yonge's translation, I believe it is possible to detect strains of political and economic criticism that focus on the wrongful exchange of money and the relationship between a leader's legitimacy and the legitimate circulation of capital. Some of this criticism may have been the result of Yonge's frustration with the fact that the demands placed on the colonial government wreaked havoc with the state of the Irish Exchequer—the system of tallies and assigns was perpetually broken and in arrears, and the system of coign and livery was oppressive and pernicious—and thus interfered with his own work. But, I believe, Yonge's criticism of Ireland's financial affairs may also have come out of how those systems unfairly burdened those faithful *subiectis*—that in attempting to wrongfully acquire the treasure of their subjects, the English (whether the prereformed Stephen Scrope or the rest of the English captains) have forsaken the *treuthe* that ought to bind them to those to whom they have obligations.

NOTES

It is my pleasure to be indebted to several friends and colleagues for their assistance with the present work, in addition to that which I owe to Derek Pearsall. Kathryn Kerby-Fulton, among her many kindnesses, invited the submission of this paper to the conference and its proceedings. Hannah Zdansky assisted me with correcting the transcriptions from Jofroi's *Segré* and supplying difficult readings; any lingering errors or infelicities should be laid at my door. Last but not least, Theresa O'Byrne has been endlessly generous with her time, conversation, and expertise in the details of Yonge's biography and political and social background. Her contribution in this volume provides further insights into the bureaucratic culture of fifteenth-century Dublin and the members of the audience for Yonge's *Gouernaunce*, without which this essay would be incomplete.

1. A fuller treatment of Yonge's career can be found in Theresa O'Byrne, "Dublin's Hoccleve: James Yonge, Scribe, Author, and Bureaucrat, and the Literary World of Late Medieval Dublin" (PhD diss., University of Notre Dame, 2012). I am grateful to her for allowing me to see various aspects of the work in progress.

2. Derek Pearsall, "Langland's London," in *Written Work: Langland, Labor, and Authorship*, ed. Steven Justice and Kathryn Kerby-Fulton (Philadelphia: University of Pennsylvania Press, 1997), 187.

3. For the narrative of Lady Meed, see Pearsall, "Langland's London," 187–89. For the C-text, see William Langland, *Piers Plowman: The C-Text*, ed. Derek Pearsall (Exeter: University of Exeter Press, [1978] 1994); all references to *Piers* will be by passus and line number. A fuller discussion of urban poverty in medieval Europe as the context for Langland's thought on poverty and charity can be found in Derek Pearsall, "Poverty and Poor People in *Piers Plowman*," in *Medieval English Studies Presented to George Kane*, ed. Edward Donald Kennedy, Ronald Waldron, and Joseph S. Wittig (Woodbridge: D. S. Brewer, 1988), 167–85.

4. To distinguish between Yonge's text and Jofroi's, I will refer to Yonge's work as the *Gouernaunce* throughout; citations are given by page number and lineation according to the edition, which is Robert Steele, ed., *Three Prose Versions of the "Secreta secretorum,"* EETS, e.s., 74 (London: Kegan Paul, 1898). Jofroi's text is designated as the *Segré*.

5. Needless to say, the bibliography for the *Secretum* and medieval exemplary literature is vast. Those texts most helpful to my understanding of the tradition include W. F. Ryan and Charles B. Schmitt, eds., *Pseudo-Aristotle: The "Secret of Secrets." Sources and Influences*, Warburg Institute Surveys 9 (London: Warburg Institute, 1982); Steven J. Williams, *The "Secret of Secrets": The Scholarly Career of a Pseudo-Aristotelian Text in the Latin Middle Ages* (Ann Arbor: University of Michigan Press, 2003), a comprehensive treatment of the Latin tradition in the West until about 1330; Jacques Monfrin, "La place du *Secret des secrets* dans la littérature française médiévale," in Ryan and Schmitt, *Pseudo-Aristotle: The Secret of Secrets*, 73–113, and "L'Exemplum médiéval, du latin aux langues vulgaires, techniques de traduction et diffusion," in *Les exempla médiévaux: Nouvelles perspectives*, ed. Jacques Berlioz and Anne-Marie Polo de Beaulieu (Paris: Champion, 1998), 243–65, which explore the relationship between Latin sources and vernacular traditions; Judith Ferster, *Fictions of Advice: The Literature and Politics of Counsel in Late Medieval England* (Philadelphia: University of Pennsylvania Press, 1996), on the *Secretum* within English vernacular advice literature; Steven J. Williams, "The Vernacular Tradition of the Pseudo-Aristotelian *Secret of Secrets* in the Middle Ages: Translations, Manuscripts, Readers," in *Filosofia in volgare nel Medioevo*, ed. Nadia Bray and Loris Sturlese (Louvain-la-Neuve: Fédération Internationale des Instituts d'études médiévales, 2003), 451–82. For modern theorizing on the exemplum, see Larry Scanlon, *Narrative, Authority, and Power: The Medieval Exemplum and the Chaucerian Tradition* (Cambridge: Cambridge University Press, 1994); and J. Allan Mitchell, *Ethics and Exemplary Narrative in Chaucer and Gower* (Cambridge: D. S. Brewer, 2004), esp. 1–21.

6. Williams, *The "Secret of Secrets,"* 7–11.

7. Jacques Monfrin, "Sur les sources du *Secret des Secrets* de Jofroi de Waterford et Servais Copale," in *Mélanges de linguistique romane et de philologie médiévale offerts à M. Maurice Delbouille, professeur à l'Université de Liège*, ed. Jean Renson, 2 vols. (Gembloux: J. Duculot, 1964), vol. 2, 509–30. For other source studies, see George L. Hamilton, "The Sources of the *Secret des secrets* of Jofroi de Waterford," *Romanic Review* 1, no. 3 (1910): 259–64; and Yela Schauwecker, "Dimensionen der Wissenvermittlung im *Secré des segrez* von Jofroi de Waterford," in *Transfert des savoirs au Moyen Âge. Wissenstransfer im Mittelalter. Actes de l'Atelier franco-allemand, Heidelberg, 15–18 janvier 2008*, ed. S. Dörr and R. Wilhel (Heidelberg: C. Winter, 2008), 129–38.

8. Williams, *The "Secret of Secrets,"* 1.

9. Ryan and Schmitt, *The "Secret of Secrets": Sources and Influences*, 2.

10. The *Confessio* has been edited most recently in John Gower, *Confessio Amantis*, 3 vols., ed. Russell A. Peck and trans. Andrew Galloway (Kalamazoo, MI: TEAMS, 2000–2004); the relevant book is Book VII, on the education of the king, which folds the material derived from the *Secretum* into Genius's wider philosophical and educational program. *Confessio* Book VII probably takes the *Segré* as the format for its discourse, although of course Gower freely improvises and adapts his material. For the *Regiment*, see Thomas Hoccleve, *The Regiment of Princes*, ed. Charles R. Blyth (Kalamazoo, MI: TEAMS, 1999). A selection of late medieval and early modern English translations can be found in *Secretum Secretorum: Nine English Versions*, ed. Mahmoud Manzalaoui, 2 vols., EETS, o.s., 276 (Oxford: Oxford University Press, 1977). Anonymous prose versions in London, British Library, Bibl. Reg. MS 18 A ii, and London, Lambeth Palace Library, Lambeth MS 501, are both printed with the *Gouernaunce* in Steele's edition.

11. Monfrin, "Sur les sources du *Secret des Secrets*," 509–10.

12. For the sake of clarity in reading, abbreviations and suspensions are silently expanded in both in-paragraph quotations and block quotations. BnF fr. 1822 can be found online as part of the Bibliothèque nationale's *Gallica* project to digitize the library's facsimiles and manuscripts; see http://gallica.bnf.fr/ark:/12148/btv1b9059033v/f89.zoom for the incipit to the *Segré*.

13. Hans Kurath, ed., *Middle English Dictionary* (Ann Arbor: University of Michigan, 1952–2001), s.v. *fraunchise*; William Rothwell, Louise W. Stone, T. B. W. Reid, eds., *Anglo-Norman Dictionary* (London: Anglo-Norman Text Society, 1992), s.v. *franchise.*

14. For *folargesse*, see *MED*, s.v. *folargesse;* and *AND*, s.v. *follargesse.* For *scarcite*, see *MED*, s.v. *scārsetē;* and *AND*, s.v. *escharseté.*

15. There may be echoes of Chaucer's Parson's sermon on the correction of Avarice and Covetousness by Mercy. The Parson asserts that one "manere of remedie agayns avarice is resonable largesse" but also cautions his audience

against being generous for the sake of praise: "But for as muche as som folk been unmesurable, men oghten to eschue fool-largesse, that men clepen wast. Certes, he that is fool-large ne yeveth nat his catel, but he leseth his catel. Soothly, what thing that he yeveth for veyne glorie, as to mynstrals and to folk for to beren his renoun in the world, he hath synne therfor and noon almesse"; see Larry D. Benson, ed., *The Riverside Chaucer*, 3d ed. (Boston: Houghton Mifflin, 1987), 316. Later in the *Gouernaunce*, Yonge warns Butler against similar (fool)-largesse: "And therefore he is an onwyse man that audyence or Yeftis yeweth to Rymoris othyr any Suche losyngeris, for thay Praysith hare yeueris be thay neuer So vicious." To give to poets or minstrels also violated the Statutes of Kilkenny (1367) and merited punishment by the bishops (157.25–30).

16. *AND*, s.v. *colur*.

17. A. J. Otway-Ruthven, *A History of Medieval Ireland* (London: Ernest Benn, 1968), 341–46. Stephen's commission was formally registered at Dublin on December 19, 1401; *Rotulorum patentium et clausorum cancellariae Hiberniae calendarium, Hen. II–Hen. VII*, ed. E. Tresham (Dublin: Irish Record Commission, 1828), 162.84 (hereafter *RCH* followed by page and document number), in Peter Crooks et al., eds., *A Calendar of Irish Chancery Letters, c. 1244–1509* (Dublin: Trinity College, 2012), accessible online at http://chancery.tcd.ie/.

18. Pro-Lancastrian sources viewed William as a traitor and enabler of Richard's tyrannies, as well as an extorter in his own right. See, e.g., Thomas Walsingham, *Historia anglicana*, ed. Henry Thomas Riley, 2 vols. (London: Longman, 1863–64), vol. 2, 213; Walsingham further wrote that William had plotted against important nobles (including Henry of Lancaster), scheming to murder them and then, as treasurer, use their escheated property for his own ends; see Anthony Tuck, *Richard the II and the English Nobility* (London: Edward Arnold, 1973), 199. Adam Usk refers to William, along with his allies Sir John Bussy and Sir Henry Green, as the "regis pessimos conciliarios et eius malicie principales fautores" (most evil counselors of the king, the chief aiders and abettors of his malevolence): *The Chronicle of Adam Usk, 1377–1421*, ed. and trans. C. Given-Wilson (Oxford: Clarendon Press, 1997), 52–53. Given Yonge's own unfavorable attitude toward Richard—for example, he asserts later that Richard loses his kingdom due to his fiscal irresponsibility (*Gouernaunce* 136.21–137.14)—he may have such outrages in mind.

19. A summary of Stephen's career is detailed in Alastair Dunn, "Loyalty, Honour and the Lancastrian Revolution: Sir Stephen Scrope of Castle Combe and His Kinsmen, c. 1389–c. 1408," in *Fourteenth Century England III*, ed. W. M. Ormrod (Woodbridge: Boydell, 2004), 169–70.

20. King Richard went to Ireland personally in order to resolve the Irish rebellion; Yonge refers to Irish perfidy in Art MacMurrough's refusal, in 1399, to honor his pledge of fidelity to Richard at *Gouernaunce* 166.31–37. For

discussion of Richard's maneuverings in Ireland, see Otway-Ruthven, *History of Medieval Ireland*, 309–38; and James Lydon, *The Lordship of Ireland in the Middle Ages* (Dublin: Gill and Macmillan, 1972), 231–40.

21. Dunn, "Loyalty, Honour and the Lancastrian Revolution," 181.

22. Ibid., 171. In his capacity as a knight (*miles*) Stephen also witnessed the submission of Brian O'Brian, along with James, third earl of Ormond, and Edward Perers (who appears in the *Gouernaunce* at 129.28–40) at Dublin in 1394; see Edmund Curtis, ed. and trans., *Richard II in Ireland, 1394–5, and Submissions of the Irish Chiefs* (Oxford: Clarendon Press, 1927), 94.

23. Dunn, "Loyalty, Honour and the Lancastrian Revolution," 181–82.

24. James Lydon, "Richard II's Expeditions to Ireland," *Journal of the Royal Society of Antiquaries of Ireland* 93, no. 2 (1963): 135–49; reprinted in Peter Crooks, ed., *Government, War and Society in Medieval Ireland: Essays by Edmund Curtis, A. J. Otway-Ruthven and James Lydon* (Dublin: Four Courts Press, 2008), 229–30.

25. Otway-Ruthven, *History of Medieval Ireland*, 334–38.

26. Lydon, "Richard II's Expeditions to Ireland," 229; Otway-Ruthven, *History of Medieval Ireland*, 335–36. Following Richard's first expedition, William had been appointed justiciar for Leinster, Munster, and Louth.

27. Dorothy Johnston, "The Interim Years: Richard II and Ireland, 1395–99," in *England and Ireland in the Later Middle Ages: Essays in Honour of Jocelyn Otway-Ruthven*, ed. James Lydon (Dublin: Irish Academy Press, 1981), 183, 190–91; and Peter Crooks, "Factionalism and Noble Power in English Ireland, c. 1361–1423" (PhD diss., University of Dublin, 2007), 201–43. The Desmond-MacMurrough alliance and the general circumstances of the feud with Ormond are discussed in Crooks at 233–42, and the letter is quoted at 233.

28. Lydon, "Richard II's Expeditions to Ireland," 229; also Lydon, *The Lordship of Ireland in the Middle Ages*, 238.

29. *Proceedings and Ordinances of the Privy Council of England, 12 Henry IV to 10 Henry V*, ed. Harris Nicolas, vol. 2 (London: Public Records Office, 1834), 49.

30. Lydon, *Lordship of Ireland in the Middle Ages*, 255–56, gives the definitions for coign and livery, detailing the intricacies of the tally system and its chronic abuse at 245–54. In part, coign and livery were exploited to the extent they were because the crown persistently refused to provide adequate funds for the administration of government on the island, a problem from which even Thomas of Lancaster, the king's son, was not exempt. Ferster has suggested that the *Gouernaunce*, as part of its agenda, sought to remind Henry V of his financial obligations to his magnates, given that Ormond had been forced to fund his governorship out of his own money (*Fictions of Advice*, 64–66).

31. M. C. Griffith, "The Talbot-Ormond Struggle for Control of the Anglo-Irish Government, 1414–47," *Irish Historical Studies* 2, no. 8 (1941): 380–82; Otway-Ruthven, *History of Medieval Ireland*, 357–58. Ormond's allegations against Talbot should be taken with a grain of salt. However, the specific accusations of the extortion of food, lodgings, and supplies—factual or not—are likely present as subtext in the behaviors with which Stephen is charged. See n. 49 below.

32. A pair of 1405 grants survives in the Irish chancery records: one dated to June 24, which grants land and privileges to John Dongan, bishop of Down, "for labours sustained in Ulster" (*RCH* 179.23), and one dated June 1 to Robert Harbrik, King's esquire, for £10 per year from the coket of Waterford on account of "his good service to Richard II and the present King in the wars in Ireland" (*RCH* 202.29).

33. Crooks, "Factionalism and Royal Power," 296–99.

34. *RCH* 184.144.

35. Edmund Curtis, ed., *Calendar of Ormond Deeds, 1172–1603*, 6 vols. (Dublin: Irish Manuscripts Commission, 1932–43), vol. 2, 391.

36. Crooks, "Factionalism and Royal Power," 300.

37. E. A. E. Matthew, "The Governing of the Lancastrian Lordship of Ireland in the Time of James Butler, Fourth Earl of Ormond, c. 1420–1452" (PhD diss., Durham University, 1994).

38. Otway-Ruthven, *History of Medieval Ireland*, 341–42. The initial defeat of MacMurrough may be elided with his loss in 1407, further compressing Yonge's description of Stephen's career.

39. Lydon, *The Lordship of Ireland in the Middle Ages*, 244–45.

40. Otway-Ruthven, *History of Medieval Ireland*, 342–44; and Lydon, *The Lordship of Ireland in the Middle Ages*, 244–48, 255–56.

41. Claims of extortion and fiscal oppression were rife in the dispute between the Ormonds and Talbots. Yonge's inveighing against extortion and his discussion of livery and nonpayment may be a reference to the document drawn up by Ormond and his allies in parliament in 1421 that, among many other detailed complaints, explicitly accused Talbot of committing "several great and monstrous extortions and oppressions"; Henry F. Berry, ed. and trans., *Statutes and Ordinances, and Acts of the Parliament of Ireland: King John to Henry V* (Dublin: Alexander Thomas, 1907), 571; hereafter *ESI, John–Hen. V*). In addition, petitions of accusation against Talbot for abusing coign, wrongfully imprisoning the king's lieges, and allowing the retinues of lieutenants and governors to oppress and extort their subjects were filed with the Privy Council in London; see Griffith, "The Talbot-Ormond Struggle," 380–82, for a discussion of the Privy Council petitions. Talbot may lie behind Yonge's depiction of Dermot of Ireland as "an oppressoure and an extorcionere of vertues men, and a

crowel Tyraunt ontollerabill" (182.20–22), an echo of the *plusoures greindres et excessiues extortiones et oppressiones* of which Ormond's 1421 petition accused Talbot (*ESI, John–Hen. V*, 570).

42. James Graves, ed. and trans., *A Roll of the Proceedings of the King's Council on Ireland* (London: Longman, 1877), 114–16.

43. Lydon, *The English in Medieval Ireland*, 168.

44. Gerald of Wales, *Expugnatio Hibernica*, ed. and trans. T. W. Moody, F. X. Martin, and F. J. Bryne (Dublin: Royal Irish Academy, 1978), 148–49. For Yonge's translation and additions, see *Gouernaunce* 184.1–186.15. For the Council of Armagh, see *Expugnatio Hibernica*, 168–71.

45. Around fifteen years after the *Gouernaunce*, the anonymous author of the *Libelle of Englyshe Polycye* would complain of the underfunded English presence in Ireland. He obliquely cites an exchange with "a lorde of ful grete astate"—James Butler, fourth earl—who informs him, "That expensis of one yere don in Fraunce. . . . Myght wynne Yrelonde to a fynalle conquest / In one sole yere"; see *Political Poems and Songs Relating to English History Composed during the Period from the Accession of Edward III to That of Richard III*, ed. Thomas Wright, 2 vols. (London: Longman, 1861), vol. 2, 189–90.

46. As Theology argues to Simony, "Hit semeth sothly riȝt so on erthe / That Mede may be wedded to no man bot Treuthe" (II.135–36). The falseness of Meed's marriage thus implies the illegitimacy of any authority that props itself up with money acquired by deceit or malfeasant practices.

47. Kathryn Kerby-Fulton, "Professional Readers of Langland at Home and Abroad: New Directions in the Political and Bureaucratic Codicology of *Piers Plowman*," in *New Directions in Later Medieval Manuscript Studies: Essays from the 1998 Harvard Conference*, ed. Derek Pearsall (York: York Medieval Press, 2000), 115–16.

CHAPTER 14

Manuscript Creation in Dublin

The Scribe of Bodleian e. Museo MS 232 and Longleat MS 29

Theresa O'Byrne

In his introduction to *Manuscripts and Readers in Fifteenth-Century England*, a volume issuing from a 1981 conference at the University of York, Derek Pearsall writes:

> It seemed and seems important to recognise that palaeography, codicology and manuscript studies generally are now more than ever before to be seen as an integral part of the study of literature and literary history, and vice versa. The fact of their interdependence becomes clearer and clearer as research advances, and the nature of that interdependence needs to be similarly clarified. The days are gone when a palaeographer could be dismissed as soon as his job of dating a manuscript was done, or a manuscript dismissed as soon as it was discerned to be of little value to 'the critical edition.'[1]

Pearsall encouraged a new, integrated approach to the study of medieval literary texts and manuscripts, a method embraced by his graduate students—embraced so wholeheartedly that as one of Pearsall's many "academic grandchildren," I have taken his methodology, so new in 1981, as a given in my own research. No study of a literary work is complete without an investigation of its manuscript exemplars, and no study of a manuscript as a medieval artifact is complete without a consideration of its contents, scribes, illuminators, owners, and readers. Pearsall's approach and scholarship has inspired countless scholars to ask new questions of the sources and to conduct studies in annotation, illumination, dialect and linguistics, literary networks, and regionalism, to name just a few. One of the most significant outcomes of Pearsall's methodology is the recognition and exploration of the extreme interconnectedness of the legal and literary spheres of late medieval England. I have attempted to bring Pearsall's approach across the Irish Sea to explore the lives of fifteenth-century Anglo-Irish authors and their texts. If my own regionally based codicological research sheds new light on the late medieval Anglo-Irish literary environment, it is only because—to slightly paraphrase a quotation ascribed to Bernard of Chartres—*sum quasi nano, gigantis humeris insidens* (I am like a dwarf, sitting on the shoulders of a giant).[2]

In the previous essay in this volume, Hilary Fox investigates the genesis and afterlife of a popular didactic text, the *Secreta secretorum*, a text given a uniquely Anglo-Irish stamp by its Dublin translator, James Yonge. Yonge worked as a legal scribe in the politically fraught heart of England's first colony. The colony was a polyglot culture of shifting political and cultural allegiances. Caught between the dictums of English law and the familiar and advantageous cultural practices of their native Irish neighbors, the Anglo-Irish—descendants of twelfth- and thirteenth-century English and Anglo-Norman colonists—wove together their own culture out of the many strands offered to them. They produced and read literature in four languages: English, French, Irish, and Latin. In the fifteenth century, Dublin, the seat of colonial power, was under increasing political and cultural pressure. England repeatedly ordered its Dublin government to resist Irish acculturation and exert control over the island but failed to provide the necessary monetary and military support to do so. The Gaelic-Irish had recaptured much of the territory they lost in the thirteenth century, and English culture was increasingly limited to the tiny community of Dublin and the emerging Pale. Yonge's translation of the *Secreta secretorum*, a work he titled the *Gouernaunce of Prynces*, promotes English culture over Irish culture and supports the political aspirations of one of the powerhouses of Anglo-Irish politics, the faction of James Butler, fourth earl of Ormond. An unintended consequence of Yonge's 1422 publication of the *Gouernaunce of Prynces* was the arrest and imprisonment of the author.

Yonge was a minor government official, but in publishing the *Gouernaunce of Prynces* he made himself and his support of the Butler faction too public. Yonge's patron, James Butler, had been the king's lieutenant in Ireland, but Butler's control was wrested away by the Talbot family in late 1422, after the death of Butler's friend and patron, King Henry V.[3] Yonge, a legal clerk, was imprisoned *in ferris et in magna duricia* (in chains and in great hardship) in Trim Castle for nine months in 1423. During his imprisonment, Yonge apparently made impassioned arguments on his own behalf, but it was only a shift in the Anglo-Irish political wind that prompted an order that Yonge be transferred from Trim Castle to Dublin Castle in October 1423.[4] Yonge was pardoned in May 1425, but extant legal deeds in his hand suggest that he was free by at least November 1424 to resume his former career.[5] Fascinating as Yonge's case may be, especially in light of the forces of patronage and power that conspired to place a mere clerk in chains, and much as I think Yonge himself—ever the self-promoter—might resent it, this is not Yonge's story. This is, instead, the story of one of the bit players in Yonge's drama, an apprentice clerk named Nicholas Bellewe.

The 1423 record of Yonge's transfer is the earliest extant record naming Nicholas Bellewe. It appears in the patent rolls of the Irish Chancery, a set of documents that were among the casualties of the explosion and fire at Dublin's Four Courts in 1922. Luckily, they were calendared by Edward Tresham in 1828 and are now available in digital format on the *Calendar of Irish Chancery Letters* (CIRCLE) website.[6] According to the record of Yonge's transfer, Bellewe was assigned the task of escorting Yonge safely from Trim to Dublin. In late 1423, Bellewe would have been a young man, perhaps in his late teens or early twenties. He went on to have a long career as a legal scribe and author in the Dublin area, and his distinctive, somewhat rounded Anglicana hand appears on over seventy-five extant documents dating from 1428 to 1474. During the early fifteenth century, Dublin legal scribes were beginning to imitate their London counterparts in signing the documents they penned. While this practice was not yet common, we are fortunate to have a few extant deeds signed by Bellewe. (For an example of one of these documents, see fig. 14.1, below.) Given such a body of signed material, it is possible to use these documents to positively identify several unique characteristics of Bellewe's hand and to trace changes in Bellewe's handwriting over the course of a long and productive career. Comparison of Bellewe's legal hand to the main hand of Bodleian

e. Museo MS 232 and Longleat MS 29 reveals that these manuscripts were penned by the Dublin scribe. Moreover, several texts in the Longleat manuscript and one of the texts in the e. Museo manuscript were translated or written by Bellewe.

In her edition for the Early English Text Society of texts by Richard Rolle in Longleat MS 29, S. J. Ogilvie-Thomson recognizes a common hand in Bodleian e. Museo 232 and Longleat 29. Neil Ker also confirmed that the main hand of both manuscripts does indeed belong to the same scribe.[7] Using the dialectical markers identified by Angus McIntosh and M. L. Samuels, Ogilvie-Thomson also concludes that the dialect of the English texts in both manuscripts is that of English-controlled Ireland. In his descriptive catalog of Rolle manuscripts, Ralph Hanna agrees, describing the dialect of the Longleat and e. Museo manuscripts as Anglo-Irish and noting that the *Linguistic Atlas of Late Mediæval English* (*LALME*) suggests that the dialect is that of Dublin.[8] Because of the scribe's inconsistent use of Hiberno-English dialectical forms, however, Ogilvie-Thomson argues that the Longleat scribe "had left his native country sometime before [writing the manuscript], retaining only traces of his linguistic habits."[9] Ogilvie-Thomson may have been influenced in making this assertion by the relatively fast manner in which the Longleat manuscript made its way into the hands of Elizabeth Goldwell, daughter of the London merchant John Goldwell, soon after its creation.

It is my contention, however, that both the Longleat 29 and e. Museo 232 manuscripts were written by Nicholas Bellewe in or near Dublin rather than in England by an Anglo-Irish expatriate, as Ogilvie-Thomson asserts. Given that there are extant Dublin area legal deeds in Bellewe's hand from nearly every year of the scribe's career, which spanned from 1428 to 1475, if Bellewe did leave Ireland at all, it is unlikely that he remained away for long. Bellewe's *Mischsprache* might be attributed to one or more factors: first, he may have been influenced by the dialect of his exemplars; second (and I believe less likely), he may have been writing for a client who was not Anglo-Irish and was attempting to adjust his own dialect to his client's needs; or third, he may have been trying to imitate English dialectical conventions for personal or political reasons. Dublin bureaucrats were surrounded by examples of documents from England, and they often strove to imitate English practices in document production. There is insufficient research as of yet to determine if this clerical culture of imitation might have extended also to copying the dialectical features of English-language documents, especially those of London. Furthermore, a certain amount of caution ought to be exercised in using dialectical features alone to locate a manuscript.[10] The editors of *LALME* astutely point out that several factors can muddy the linguistic waters. Dialects can vary at borders (which English-controlled Dublin could be argued to be). The written dialect of a given manuscript can reflect the dialect of the exemplar, the dialect of the scribe, or a mixture of both. Scribes themselves can exhibit mixed dialects, and fifteenth-century manuscripts in particular display a wide range of spellings.[11] Moreover, there are so few localizable manuscripts for Ireland (and for many areas in England) that the *LALME* dot maps are extremely sparse for these areas, making an identification based upon dialect extremely difficult for manuscripts with Anglo-Irish provenance. Bellewe's manuscripts are an example of a case where manuscript dialect does not fully reflect provenance, and the appearance of the Longleat manuscript in England soon after it was written has added extra challenge to the task of locating the manuscript and its scribe. It is extremely likely that both the Longleat and e. Museo manuscripts were copied in Dublin, and after assessing Bellewe's career, I offer below possible scenarios accounting for the creation of these important manuscripts and suggesting a means by which the Longleat manuscript might have traveled to London early in its history.

Bellewe's script is one of several fifteenth-century Anglicana legal hands characterized by a large minim height relative to other Dublin area legal hands. These scripts also share certain characteristics, such as a hornless **g**, and a tendency for the descender of **h** to trail off beneath the letter obliquely or parallel to the line of writing rather than curving or hooking back up toward the baseline. The characteristics and evolution of this script subtype in Dublin are, however, a topic for a different time. Nicholas Bellewe and the other possessors of this script type worked at various times for the City of Dublin; the sole surviving city memoranda roll from the fifteenth century preserves an example of one of these hands.[12] Other examples of this large-format script are present in the legal deeds of an anonymous scribe active around the turn of the fifteenth century whom I have elsewhere termed "Hand M" and in the deeds of James Yonge and Thomas Baghill.[13]

Some of the key characteristics of Nicholas Bellewe's hand (fig. 14.1) are a flat-backed, two-chambered **a**; a two-chambered hornless **g**, usually with a flat or slightly curved vertical line forming the right side of

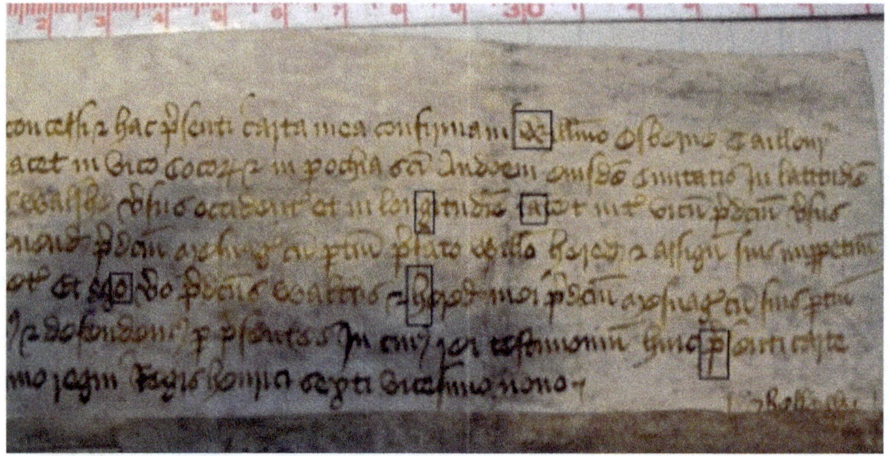

Fig. 14.1. Detail of Dublin, Royal Irish Academy, MS 12. S.22–31, no. 357, a deed dated November 20, 1450. Note **a, g, h, o, p, w,** and Bellewe's signature in lower right corner. Author's image reproduced by permission of the Royal Irish Academy © RIA.

the top chamber and a rounded or teardrop-shaped bottom chamber rather than the broken one used by many of Bellewe's contemporaries; a round **o** with a point at the top; a **p** in which the base of the bowl is made by a horizontal or slightly downward-sloping line which falls at the baseline and clearly crosses the stem; and a fistlike VB-style **w** with four distinct chambers that was often executed without lifting the pen. Bellewe also tended to cut his pen more narrowly than his contemporaries. Like James Yonge, Bellewe had two grades of script, a formal version that tended to be more upright and calligraphic (fig. 14.2) and a workaday script with more ligatures and a tendency for the letters to lean slightly to the right (fig. 14.3). The latter grade is far more common in the legal documents penned by Bellewe.

Bellewe's hand appears in three manuscripts: the Longleat and e. Museo manuscripts and the Chain Book of Dublin, a book containing laws and customs of the City of Dublin that was chained to the wall or a podium in the Tholsel—Dublin's city hall—for public access. A few differences exist between the script Bellewe used for his legal documents and that which he used in these manuscripts (fig. 14.4). Bellewe's book hand employs a slightly wider pen, thus creating more shading than is present in his legal hand. His book hand has feet on all the minims of **m**

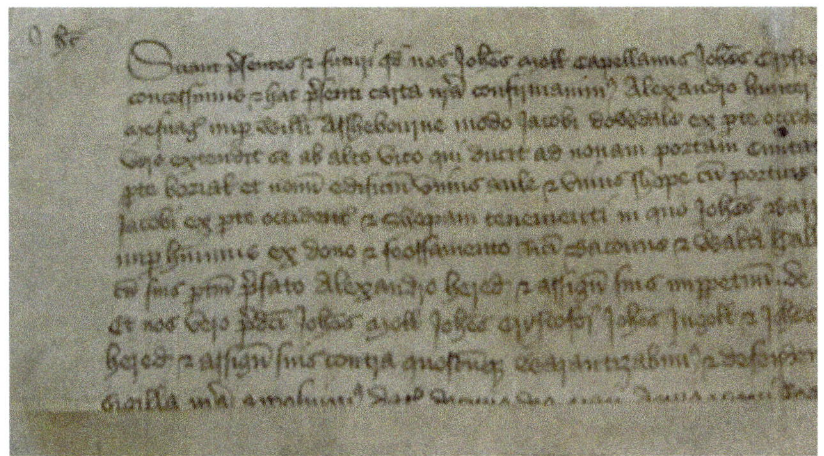

Fig. 14.2. Detail of Dublin, Royal Irish Academy, MS 12. S.22–31, no. 172, a deed dated May 10, 1434. Example of Bellewe's more formal legal hand. Author's image reproduced by permission of the Royal Irish Academy © RIA.

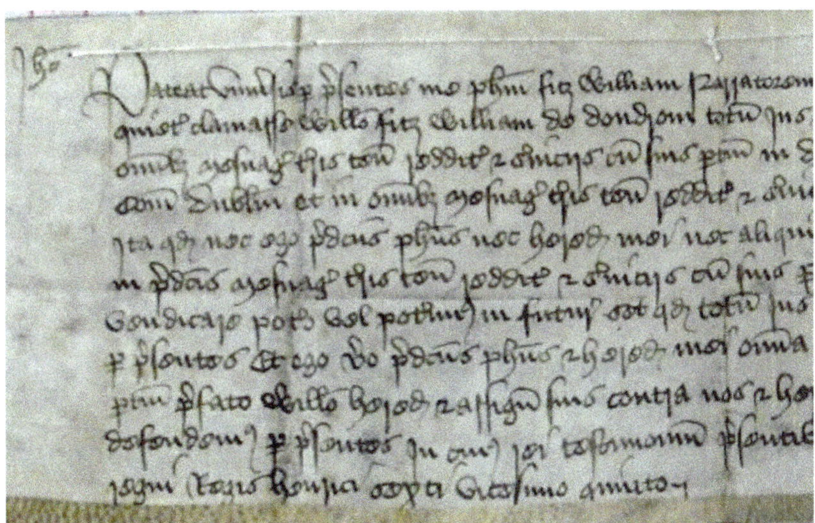

Fig. 14.3. Detail of Dublin, National Archives of Ireland (NAI): Pembroke Estate, 2011/1/164, a deed dated July 6, 1447. Example of Bellewe's less formal legal hand. Author's image reproduced by permission of the Director of the National Archives of Ireland.

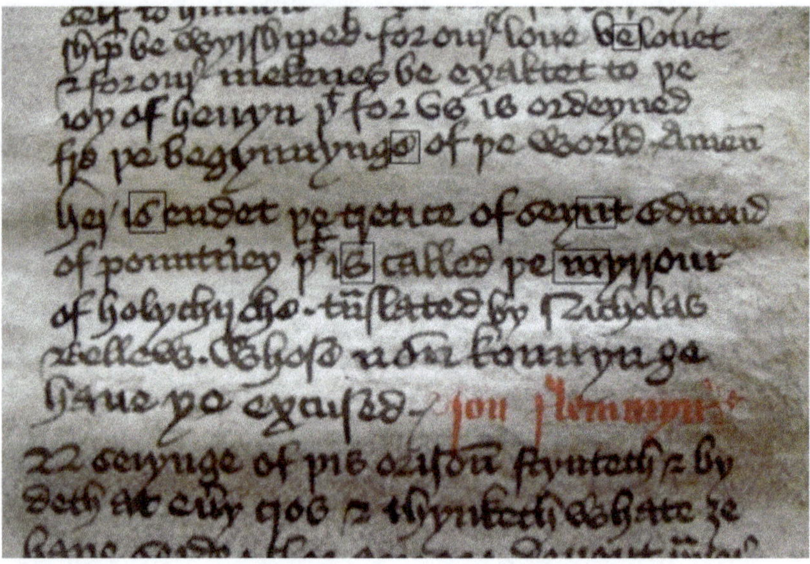

Fig. 14.4. Oxford, Bodleian, e. Museo MS 232, detail of fol. 62r, end of Bellewe's translation of *The Mirror of St. Edmund*, introduction to the prayer on the Passion. Note open **e**, rare round **e**, **m**, **n**, rare final sigma-**s**, final B-**s**, Bellewe's colophon, and the signature of John Flemyng. Author's image reproduced with permission of the Bodleian Libraries, University of Oxford.

and **n**. Bellewe also frequently employs open **e** in his book hand, whereas he uses round **e** almost exclusively in his lower-grade legal script. Words ending in *-s* usually end in a sigma-**s** on legal documents, while Bellewe often uses a B-shaped **s** in his book hand. These differences are all reflective of the more formal nature of manuscript production.

Bellewe and several other scribes belonging to the same school were associated at various points in their careers with the Seal of the Provostship of Dublin, a seal that was used in lieu of the city's official seal to authenticate documents in property transfers where the seals of the grantors were not well known. There were usually no more than two or three scribes designated as bearers of the Seal of the Provostship at any one time, and these scribes may have been assistants to the city clerk. Bellewe's stint as a bearer of the seal was a relatively short one in the 1450s.

Bellewe wrote two documents in 1428 to which the Seal of the Provostship was attached.[14] He was, however, probably not a bearer of the seal at that time. The association of his hand with the seal in 1428 is likely the result of the young scribe's relationship with James Yonge. I believe that Bellewe was a student of Yonge's, hence his designation in 1423 as Yonge's escort from Trim to Dublin. In 1428 Bellewe was at the end of his apprenticeship. On February 4 of that year, a number of documents were written for a group that would become the inaugural members of the powerful Guild of St. Anne; of these legal deeds, three survive.[15] The documents' scribes were Yonge and Bellewe. Among the extant records from Dublin, it is extremely rare to find more than one scribal hand on documents that were executed in the same place and on the same date. Dublin's professional scribes were highly mobile, carrying with them the tools of their trade. Usually when a client such as a parish church needed to have several documents written, an individual scribe would set up shop on site and write all the requested documents; these could sometimes cover several separate transactions. The only exceptions to this rule I have thus far found are cases in which a master and advanced apprentice worked together. For instance, deeds written for a property transfer in 1422 are just such a rare set. Two are penned by Thomas Baghill, and a third is written by Yonge.[16] Baghill was certainly the student of James Yonge, as the handwriting and notarial crosses of the two scribes are strikingly similar.[17] The 1428 cluster of documents penned by Yonge and Bellewe represent the latter's first extant foray into professional document production. Yonge penned a quitclaim for one property transfer, and Bellewe wrote a grant and deed of attorney for another transfer. All three documents had the Seal of the Provostship of Dublin appended to them. In 1428 Yonge and Baghill were the bearers of the seal, and it was probably Yonge who affixed it to Bellewe's documents.

After ending his apprenticeship with Yonge, Bellewe soon found steady employment as a household secretary for the FitzWilliam family, who owned the manor of Dundrum, south of the City of Dublin. Bellewe's hand appears in many of the family documents throughout the 1430s and 1440s. His hand is especially prevalent in the documents and rental rolls of William FitzWilliam, his wife, Ismaia FitzWilliam, née Perers, and their son Philip FitzWilliam. It is possible that Bellewe found work with the FitzWilliam family through Yonge's social and scribal circle. Ismaia FitzWilliam was the daughter of Edward Perers, marshal of the English army in Ireland. Yonge implies in his 1422 *Gouernaunce of Prynces* that he knows Edward Perers and has spoken with him about the struggle of James Butler's grandfather against the Irish McMurroughs.[18] Several documents relating to Edward Perers were written by Yonge's probable master, Hand M, and when Ismaia needed a notary—a specialized type of legal scribe—she called on Yonge's student, Baghill.[19] She was unable to employ Bellewe for the task because, unlike Yonge and Baghill, Bellewe never became a notary. There may also have been family connections which led to or emerged from Bellewe's employment. A 1435 document written by Nicholas Bellewe grants ten marks annually to Philip, Richard, and John Bellewe for the term of the lives of Thomas FitzWilliam, the son of William and Ismaia, and Thomas's wife, Rosie Bellewe.[20] Philip, John, and Rosie Bellewe were siblings or cousins to Nicholas. More research on the Bellewe family is necessary to establish whether the marriage of Rosie Bellewe to Thomas FitzWilliam occurred before or after Nicholas Bellewe's employment by the FitzWilliam family.

In the late 1440s, Bellewe's work for the FitzWilliam family became more sporadic, probably due to the death, ca. 1445, of Ismaia FitzWilliam. Around that time, the scribe began doing bespoke work for the Flemyng family of Kilmainham, a region about a mile west of the walls of medieval Dublin. He also had the occasional client in the City of Dublin. One of his major clients in Dublin was the Guild of St. Anne, founded in 1430, whose membership consisted mainly of well-to-do individuals and families from the mercantile class. The Guild built a fine hall onto the south side of the Church of St. Audoen, just within the western walls of Dublin;[21] part of this hall is still extant. James Yonge and Thomas Baghill both penned a large number of legal deeds for the Guild. Indeed, they appear to have been the legal scribes preferred by the Guild. Yonge's hand predominates as the Guild was forming in the late 1420s and is slowly supplanted in the 1430s by Baghill's hand. Yonge died ca. 1438, and Baghill's hand disappears from the record in late 1439. The Guild of St. Anne used four or five different legal secretaries between about 1440 and 1450, but Bellewe appears to assume the role of his predecessors, Yonge and Baghill, beginning in late 1450. From 1450 until 1471, when Bellewe's handwriting begins to show signs of old age and possibly failing eyesight, his hand dominates the papers of the Guild of St. Anne, almost to the exclusion of others. Between 1471 and 1474, the scribe seems to have entered into semiretirement, executing a few documents for old clients, the FitzWilliam and Flemyng families. These documents display an increasingly loose script with great variation in the weight of individual strokes. Nonetheless, it retains the hallmarks of Bellewe's hand at the height of his career (fig. 14.5).

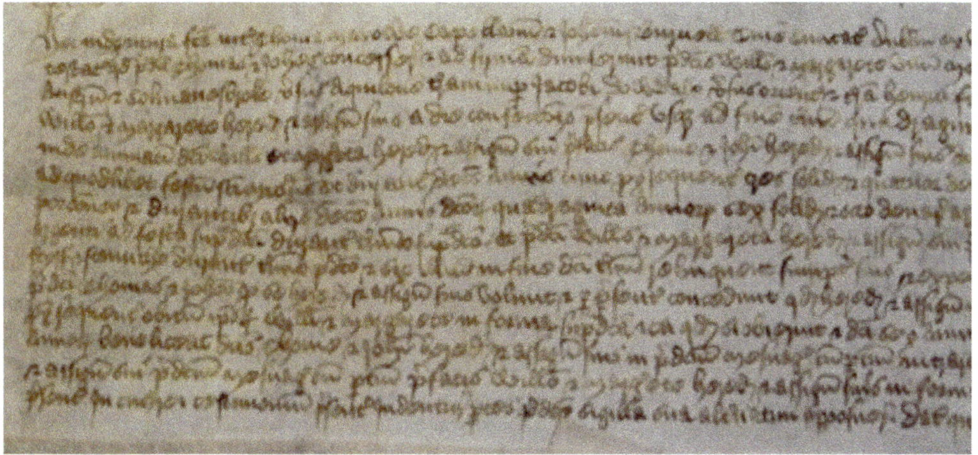

Fig. 14.5. Detail of Dublin, Royal Irish Academy, MS 12. S.22–31, no. 624, a deed dated July 4, 1471. Late example of Bellewe's hand showing the unevenness that characterizes the documents of the scribe's final years. Author's image reproduced by permission of the Royal Irish Academy © RIA.

The two literary manuscripts that Bellewe wrote—Longleat 29 and e. Museo 232—are best known as manuscripts containing works of Richard Rolle of Hampole (1290–1349). The Longleat manuscript is also known as a Chaucerian manuscript, as it contains a copy of Chaucer's "Parson's Tale" that is closely related to the text in the Ellesmere Chaucer. For this reason, Longleat 29 is included on the recently launched *Late Medieval English Scribes* website, where Bellewe's hand is described as "Hand 1" of that manuscript.[22] Both the Longleat and e. Museo manuscripts are miscellanies of works of a religious nature; they have both prose and poetry, and the Longleat manuscript contains texts in both English and Latin. Many of the works are enumerative and didactic and encourage affective piety. They are works that would appeal to a pious lay audience, and the Longleat manuscript appears to be aimed at a female audience. Along with Chaucer's "Parson's Tale" (fols. 81r–128v), Rolle's *Form of Living* (fols. 30r–v, 32r–43v), *Ego dormio* (fols. 43v–47v), *The Commandment* (fols. 47v–50v), *Desire and Delight* (fols. 50v–51r), *Ghostly Gladness* (fol. 51r), an excerpt from *Meditation on the Passion A* (fol. 58v), and lyrics, including "Love Is Life," "Jesus God's Son," and "All Sins Shall Thou Hate" (fols. 51v–55r), the Longleat manuscript contains the short text of Hilton's

Medled Life (58v–69r), English translations of Flete's *De remediis contra temptaciones* (fols. 69r–73v), and the *Fifteen Ooes of St. Bridget* (fols. 149r–152v); it also contains an account of a woman mystic's vision of purgatory, Marian prayers, and several meditations. The manuscript includes a number of unique texts, including a Latin meditation on the Eucharist mentioning several Irish saints with an accompanying English translation (fols. 19r–24v), an enumerative didactic text called the *Laddre of Heuyn* (fols. 4v–11r), a prose meditation on the Five Wounds known only in the Longleat and e. Museo manuscripts (Lt fols. 148v–149r; eM fols. 65v–66v), and an English prosimetric text addressed to a woman that offers spiritual instruction, beginning "Loue of kynde & car*e* / me byndeth lady ȝow to ler*e*" (fols. 131r–142r).[23]

Along with the meditation on the Five Wounds shared with the Longleat manuscript, the e. Museo manuscript preserves a copy of the B-version of Rolle's *Meditation on the Passion* (fols. 1r–18r). It also has a verse prayer on the Passion (fols. 62r–65v), a compilation on meekness derived from the writings of Saints Gregory and Bernard (fols. 18r–23v), and an English translation of the *Speculum ecclesie* of Saint Edmund Rich of Abingdon (ca. 1175–1240) (fols. 24r–62r).

The English translation of the *Speculum ecclesie* is particularly important in the study of fifteenth-century Anglo-Irish literature. Literary works were certainly being produced in fifteenth-century Anglo-Ireland, but with the exception of two compositions by James Yonge—the English *Gouernaunce of Prynces* and a Latin account of a Hungarian knight's visions in St. Patrick's Purgatory known as the *Memoriale*—all the works written by late medieval Anglo-Irish authors are anonymous. We can now add the name of one more author to the fifteenth-century corpus of Anglo-Irish literature: Nicholas Bellewe. The English *Mirror of St. Edmund* in the e. Museo manuscript ends with the note, "T*rans*lated by Nicholas Bellew, whose non konnynge haue ye excused" (see fig. 14.4). This short colophon has commonly been assumed to have been copied from an exemplar by a scribe unconnected with the translation. However, coupled with the evidence for Bellewe's hand provided by extant legal documents, we can now confirm that Nicholas Bellewe the Dublin legal scribe is also the scribe of the e. Museo manuscript and therefore the same Nicholas Bellewe named as translator of one of its major texts; moreover, the scribe of the e. Museo manuscript wrote the colophon himself.

By localizing the Longleat and e. Museo manuscripts to Dublin, the corpus of literary texts known to be circulating in Anglo-Ireland is now greatly expanded. In addition, the Anglo-Irish origin of the Longleat manuscript suggests similar Anglo-Irish origins for some or all of the texts it uniquely carries. These include the prose meditation on the Five Wounds that appears in both manuscripts, short florilegia, which may be merely collections of quotations of interest to Bellewe or his patrons, the prayer "Almyghty Iesu" (fol. 154r), the prose *Laddre of Heuyn*, another prose text offering spiritual consolation beginning *O thou soul myn* (fols. 11r–16v), and the prosimetric instructional tract addressed to a woman, "Loue of kynde and care."[24] In its form in the Longleat manuscript, the English and Latin meditation on the Lord's Prayer almost certainly has Anglo-Irish origins, as several Irish saints are incorporated into the litanies which accompany short prayers connected to each line of the Lord's Prayer.[25] These saints are included in both versions of the meditation, and the list includes both well-known saints such as Patrick, Brigit, and Columba and a panoply of lesser-known saints, some of them very localized: Finian, Canice, Brendan, Moling, Kevin, "Synok" (possibly Suibhne), Laserian, Mo Chua, Abbán, Éoghan, and Colman.

Bellewe's translation of Saint Edmund's *Mirror* raises a question about other possible translations or original compositions by the author-scribe. An initial survey of the unascribed texts in the Longleat manuscript indicates strongly that *The Laddre of Heuyn* is a Bellewe translation or composition. Not only does he go out of his way to introduce the text on a separate page, but phrasing and word choice also closely match those of Bellewe's translation of the *Mirror of St. Edmund*. For instance, Bellewe uses "as anent" to mean "regarding," or "with respect to," and he uses "rer(e) up" to mean "raise." When transitioning from one idea to another or restating a major point, Bellewe uses "þat is (to sey)" as a connecting phrase. The words and phrases cited here occur several times in both texts. They can also be found in Bellewe's translation of *O Thou Soul Myn*, discussed briefly below. As a compiler, author, and scribe, Bellewe had a particular affinity for enumerative texts of spiritual instruction. Into the Longleat manuscript he copied *The Fifteen Ooes of St. Bridget*, the text of the nine virtues shown to a holy man, and a confession structured around the seven deadly sins and the Ten Commandments. Marginalia in the manuscript is in his hand, and often consists merely of Latin numerals marking the beginning of each enumerated point of a text, for easy reference. Given his fondness for these texts, it is reasonable to assume that he might have written or compiled a similar work of his own such as the *Laddre of Heuyn*.

O Thou Soul Myn may have been written originally for a convent, as the text portrays Christ addressing the reader as "doghtre" and "spouse." Bellewe appears to have translated the text into the Longleat manuscript directly from a Latin exemplar. At one point, he forgets himself and copies a line of the Latin text into the manuscript, then crosses it out and proceeds to continue translating the text into English. Further research concerning Bellewe's style and translation techniques coupled with textual analysis of the Longleat texts is ongoing.

Other texts in the Longleat manuscript offer clues about the types of texts circulating in fifteenth-century Dublin and about the preoccupations of Bellewe. In the florilegium on fol. 3r, Bellewe has included a quotation that he ascribes to Anselm: "Aspice vulnera pendentis, sanguinem morientis, cicatrices resurgentis, precium tradentis, conuicium redimentis, haec quantum valent pensari in statera [. . .] vt totus nobis sit fixus in corde, qui totus [. . .] fuit fixus in cruce" (Behold the injuries of the one hanging here, the blood of the dying one, the wounds of the one rising again, the reward of the one offering deliverance, the outcry of the redeemer; how greatly these may be weighed out in the scales . . . so that he, who was wholly fastened upon the cross, may be wholly fixed upon our heart). This is a shortened, somewhat corrupt version of the same pseudo-Augustinian sermon that Yonge used in composing a short sermon in his 1412 *Memoriale*.[26] Although Yonge and Bellewe operated within the same scribal circle, it appears that they worked from very different textual sources, which suggests that this pseudo-Augustinian sermon—or at least this portion of it—was a fairly popular text in later medieval Dublin.

Other textual choices indicate that Bellewe may have once considered entering into religious life or that he had concerns about the roles of religious and laypeople. These concerns may have been shared by his patrons. Hilton's *Mixed Life* offers advice to a wealthy layman who has been considering entering a religious community; Hilton advises against it and counsels his addressee on how best to lead a good Christian life while remaining in the world. For his translation of the *Mirror of St. Edmund* in the e. Museo manuscript, Bellewe supplied the few marginal notes. Most enumerate items in the text, but the most striking note is a manicule drawn in the same brown ink of the main text which points out the complaint of a religious man that he cannot provide for the poor and sick, as he is enclosed and under the power of another. The manicule points to the line, "& þ*er*for hit wer*e* bettre to me to be a seculer man þ*at* I myȝt do þese werkes of m*er*cy." Bellewe's strong affinity for religious texts, especially those which might appeal to laypeople, coupled with this note, suggests that Bellewe was a deeply religious man who may have been trying to reconcile his faith with his life as a secular scribe.

The Longleat manuscript can be described as quite messy; it varies considerably in quire structure, *mise en page*, rubrication, and even the level of formality of Bellewe's script. These factors, coupled with the manuscript's contents, suggest that it was produced over a period of time—a few months or years—and was intended for the scribe's personal use or more likely for the personal use of someone close to him. Given the large number of the texts in the manuscript that directly address or might have appealed to a pious laywoman, including the Rolle texts, *The Fifteen Ooes of St. Bridget*, three short Marian texts, "Loue of kynde and care," and a narrative of a woman's vision of purgatory, it is plausible to assume that the Longleat MS was written for a female lay patron. One possible scenario is that Bellewe compiled the Longleat manuscript sometime between 1433 and 1445, when he was working for the FitzWilliam family, and that it was intended as a household book of pastoral care for Ismaia FitzWilliam, with whom Bellewe had a close professional relationship.

Sometime after they were written, the five individual booklets constituting the complete manuscript were brought together in a single binding. At that time, Bellewe added a booklet of prefatory material including a florilegium and a table of contents. Bellewe's table of contents is not comprehensive, often leaving out shorter texts or lumping texts together under one heading. For instance, all of the Rolle material is listed simply as "Item, a notable tretice of Ric' heremyte to Margaret, Recluse of Kyrkeby of conta*m*platif lyf." Other texts, such as a prayer and meditation on fols. 153r–154r, are not listed at all. The table of contents may have been executed with some haste, perhaps for an English purchaser. The prevailing theory concerning the Longleat manuscript's *Nachleben* places it in the hands of John Goldwell, a London merchant, prior to his death in 1466. It then passed to his daughter Elizabeth and made its way to Wiltshire via her marriage to Richard Pole (d. 1517).

Richard was the grandfather of Giles Pole, a friend of Sir John Thynne, builder of Longleat House.[27] The name Ioh*annes* Goldewell appears on fol. 168r, and John Thynne's name appears on fols. 2r and 166r.[28] To place it in London before the death of John Goldwell in 1466, our *terminus ante quem* for the manuscript is 1465; it remains only to fix the *terminus post quem*. The "notable reuelac*i*on of þ*e* peyns of p*ur*gatory shewed to a deuout Woman solitary" has an internal date of August 10, 1422. Ogilvie-Thomson also asserts that internal evidence in the exposition on the Pater Noster pushes the earliest date of composition of the manuscript to 1429, and she concludes that the manuscript was written ca. 1430–50.[29] Using the broader set of dates established here, it seems likely that Bellewe wrote the manuscript between 1429 and 1465; this fits with my theory that Bellewe composed the manuscript for Ismaia FitzWilliam. Ismaia died sometime soon after 1445, leaving two sons. There is no record of a daughter, and perhaps the family had no immediate use for such a religious manuscript aimed at a female audience; thus the manuscript might have been sold or given away at the time of her death. I believe it may have passed to the clerk who wrote it, Bellewe.

Communication between government offices in London and Dublin necessitated frequent shipments of documents back and forth. Dublin's quays were also a clearinghouse for trade goods, exporting Irish wool, timber, and hides and importing wine, pottery, and fine cloth. As a merchant, John Goldwell may have had reason to travel to Dublin for the purpose of dealing in Irish goods, and he or one of his agents could have purchased the manuscript. Several conduits for Goldwell's acquisition of the manuscript present themselves. Goldwell might have known members of the FitzWilliam family. If Bellewe retained the manuscript (or the individual booklets) after Ismaia's death, it might have come to Goldwell via Bellewe or his familial connections. Nicholas Bellewe's brothers or cousins, Philip and John, were both merchants, and it is clear that by 1444 Philip Bellewe was living in Dublin a few steps from the dockside area now known as Merchant's Quay. Philip became involved in the city administration, serving variously as treasurer and mayor of Dublin between 1451 and 1458. Nicholas Bellewe was appointed Keeper of the Crane and Weights in 1456, an office that he held until his death around 1475. As Keeper of the Crane, Bellewe probably oversaw the maintenance and use of the cargo crane located on Dublin's quayside; he probably also ensured that duties were collected, duly recorded, and paid to the City of Dublin.[30] Because he was intimately involved with shipping, Bellewe himself may have sold the manuscript to Goldwell or his agent. Goldwell's access to the Longleat manuscript may also have come from Bellewe's connections to the Guild of St. Anne ca. 1434–71. The Guild claimed many Dublin merchants among its members. If the manuscript was given to or purchased by the Guild, Goldwell or his agent might have purchased it directly from the Guild's wardens.

Bodleian e. Museo 232 represents Bellewe's later, more accomplished work. It is smaller in format and has a consistency in quire structure, *mise en page,* and rubrication lacking in the Longleat manuscript. The names Annes Helperby and Elizabeth Stoughton appear on the flyleaves of the manuscript in a sixteenth-century hand. These surnames may be derived from place-names. Helperby is located in Yorkshire, near Ripon, and Stoughton is located near Leicester. Prior to 1680, the e. Museo manuscript was in the hands of Alexander Fetherston, vicar of Wolverton and prebendary of Lichfield Cathedral. The closer proximity of Stoughton to Wolverton and Lichfield suggests that the manuscript may have spent parts of the sixteenth and seventeenth centuries in the Midlands. Unfortunately, clues concerning how the manuscript might have passed from the hands of Nicholas Bellewe to Annes and Elizabeth are not currently forthcoming. Many Dublin families had close connections with the Midlands, Yorkshire, and London, and it is quite possible that the manuscript made its way to England via a family connection.

The date of the e. Museo manuscript is also uncertain. Ogilvie-Thomson asserts that the e. Museo manuscript was written ca. 1430–50.[31] Given the evidence from Bellewe's legal career, it is possible to adjust this date range slightly and to provisionally narrow it down. Since Bellewe's handwriting was deteriorating by 1470, we can assume that the manuscript was penned prior to that year. On fol. 62r of e. Museo 232, the name "Ion Flemmyn" appears (see fig. 14.4, above). It is written in red in a hand other than Bellewe's, and Neil Ker has suggested that it may be that of the rubricator, a conclusion with which I am inclined to agree.[32] The rubrication of the manuscript is distinctive, displaying a pattern of folded leaves inside the voids created by the letters, and pen work that features wavelike and leaf-shaped forms ending in trefoils. Rubrication in a similar style appears with the late-fifteenth-century entries in Trinity College Dublin MS 525, a registry of the Priory of All Hallows, and somewhat cruder designs in the same style are present on fols. 74r–128v of the Longleat manuscript. It is possible that all three rubricators received similar training. The "Ion Flemmyn" of e. Museo 232 may be a friend and colleague of Bellewe. In 1449, Bellewe wrote the legal deeds in which John Flemyng, the son and heir of Katherine fitz Adam, deeded his inheritance from Katherine—eight and a half acres and half a mesuage in Kilmainham—to David Cornewalshe of Dublin. Flemyng may have been pursuing a clerical education at or just after that time. By 1463, he was a clerk and notary public; he was entered in the Dublin City Franchise Roll as a clerk in 1468. He also appears as a witness in Christ Church deeds of 1484 and 1485.[33] Unfortunately, no deeds known to be in Flemyng's hand are now extant.

Our knowledge of clerical life in Dublin is very incomplete, but it seems plausible that Bellewe and Flemyng worked together sometime between 1449, when Bellewe assisted Flemyng with the legal transfer of the latter's property, and 1470, when Bellewe's hand began deteriorating and Flemyng was likely carrying out notarial and clerical duties for a variety of clients. Bellewe's initial work for the Flemyng family of Kilmainham is a little early for John Flemyng's active scribal career. It seems most likely that the manuscript was written ca. 1460–70, when both Bellewe and Flemyng were active in Dublin. This pushes Ogilvie-Thomson's date for the e. Museo manuscript slightly later. The years 1450–70 also mark the period in which Bellewe was the predominant legal scribe for the Guild of St. Anne. This raises the intriguing possibility of a connection between the Guild and the e. Museo manuscript or its exemplars. It is even possible that the manuscript was originally commissioned by the parish of St. Audoen, the Guild, or a Guild member. No inventory of Guild property survives, but it is clear that it owned a considerable amount of real estate both in Dublin and in its suburbs; the Guild also looked after the interests of St. Audoen's Church, and the textual exemplars for the e. Museo manuscript may have been part of the property of St. Audoen's Church or on loan to the church or Guild from a Dublin area religious institution or from a Guild member.

Nicholas Bellewe, author, legal scribe, translator, and manuscript copyist, was a member of a circle of scribes and notaries based around the offices of the City of Dublin and the Guild of St. Anne. Both Bellewe and his probable mentor James Yonge were engaged in producing legal documents and literary texts for the Anglo-Irish community. Yonge's *Memoriale* and *Gouernaunce of Prynces* served as examples to Bellewe, who translated *O Thou Soul Myn* and Saint Edmund's *Speculum ecclesie* into Hiberno-English and who was the likely author of the *Laddre of*

Heuyne, among other religious and didactic works. The two extant manuscripts created by Bellewe—Longleat MS 29 and Bodleian e. Museo MS 232—demonstrate the connection of Bellewe and his scribal circle to other Dublin-based professionals, such as the rubricator and notary John Flemyng; they also demonstrate that this circle and the Anglo-Irish colony were connected in multiple ways to the legal and literary world of England. Both the Longleat and the e. Museo manuscript contain literary texts that originated in England but circulated in English-controlled Ireland, including works of Rolle, Hilton, and Chaucer. Both manuscripts also eventually found their way to England—in the case of Longleat 29, quite soon after the manuscript was finished. In 1427, a similar circle of legal scribes based at the Irish Exchequer produced Bodleian Douce MS 104, which contains the C-text of Langland's *Piers Plowman*.[34] Although Yonge and his circle cannot yet be connected to the group of scribes that produced the Douce manuscript, in the case of Bellewe, Yonge, Hand M, Baghill, and Flemyng, an image emerges of a circle of scribes who were, like the Exchequer scribes, engaged in both legal and literary production. While Bellewe and his circle were Dublin area locals, received their training in Dublin, and worked for Dublin area clients such as the potential patron of the Longleat manuscript, Ismaia FitzWilliam, they were far from insular; they worked in and contributed to a much broader arena of English literary culture. Much like London, Dublin's scribal and literary cultures were intertwined, with individuals such as Nicholas Bellewe contributing to both legal and literary production. Like his mentor, Yonge, Nicholas Bellewe can be counted among the growing number of scribes known to have left their marks as authors on fifteenth-century literary culture.

Notes

1. Derek Pearsall, *Manuscripts and Readers in Fifteenth-Century England: The Literary Implications of Manuscript Study. Essays from the 1981 Conference at the University of York* (Cambridge: D. S. Brewer, 1983), 1.

2. John of Salisbury, *Metalogicon*, ed. J. B. Hall, Corpus Christianorum: Continuatio Mediaevalis 98 (Turnhout: Brepols, 1991), bk. III.4, 116.

3. Margaret Griffith, "The Talbot-Ormond Struggle for Control of the Anglo-Irish Government, 1414–1447," *Irish Historical Studies* 2 (1941): 381–82; Peter Crooks, "Factions, Feuds and Noble Power in the Lordship of Ireland, ca. 1356–1496," *Irish Historical Studies* 35 (2007): 425–54.

4. Edward Tresham, ed., *Rotulorum patentium et clausorum cancellariae Hiberniae calendarium* (Dublin: Irish Record Commission, 1828), 234b, no. 37.

5. Ibid., 236b, no. 44. See also Royal Irish Academy MS 12. S.22–31, nos. 539 and 562–64; and Trinity College Dublin MS 1477, no. 107.

6. Tresham, *Rotulorum . . . cancellariae Hiberniae calendarium*; "CIRCLE: A Calendar of Irish Chancery Letters, *ca.* 1244–1509," *CIRCLE*, 2012, http://chancery.tcd.ie.

7. Richard Rolle, *Richard Rolle: Prose and Verse, Edited from MS Longleat 29 and Related Manuscripts*, ed. Sarah Ogilvie-Thompson, EETS 293 (Oxford: Early English Text Society, 1988), xxxi–xxxii.

8. Ralph Hanna, *The English Manuscripts of Richard Rolle: A Descriptive Catalogue*, Exeter Medieval Texts and Studies (Exeter: University of Exeter Press, 2010), 170–71, 211–12.

9. Rolle, *Prose and Verse*, xxxiv–xxxv.

10. For instance, see Ad Putter and Myra Stokes, "The *Linguistic Atlas* and the Dialect of the *Gawain* Poems," *Journal of English and Germanic Philology* 106, no. 4 (2007): 468–91; John J. Thompson, "Books beyond England," in *The Production of Books in England, 1350–1500*, ed. Alexandra Gillespie and Daniel Wakelin (Cambridge: Cambridge University Press, 2011), 260–61.

11. Angus McIntosh, *Guide to "A Linguistic Atlas of Late Mediaeval English"* (Aberdeen: Aberdeen University Press, 1987), 9.

12. Dublin City Archives Memoranda Roll 6. I am grateful to Mary Clark for bringing this source to my attention.

13. Theresa O'Byrne, "Dublin's Hoccleve: James Yonge, Scribe, Author, and Bureaucrat, and the Literary World of Late Medieval Dublin" (PhD diss., University of Notre Dame, 2012); Theresa O'Byrne, "Notarial Signs and Scribal Training in the Fifteenth Century: The Case of James Yonge and Thomas Baghill," *Journal of the Early Book Society* 15 (2012): 133–45.

14. Royal Irish Academy MS 12. S.22–31, nos. 631 and 639.

15. All dates have been adjusted to reflect modern reckoning, with the year beginning on January 1.

16. Royal Irish Academy MS 12. S.22–31, nos. 188–90.

17. O'Byrne, "Notarial Signs and Scribal Training."

18. James Yonge, "*Secreta Secretorum*," in *Three Prose Versions of the "Secreta Secretorum,"* ed. Robert Steele, EETS, e.s., 74 (London: Published for the EETS by K. Paul, Trench, Trübner & Co., 1898), 129.

19. National Archives of Ireland, Pembroke Estate Papers, 2011/1/141.

20. National Archives of Ireland, Pembroke Estate Papers, 2011/1/143.

21. Henry F. Berry, "History of the Religious Guild of St. Anne, in S. Audoen's Church, Dublin, 1430–1740," *Proceedings of the Royal Irish Academy; Archaeology, Linguistics, and Literature* 25 C (May 1904): 21–24.

22. Linne Mooney, Simon Horobin, and Estelle Stubbs, "Late Medieval English Scribes," *Late Medieval English Scribes*, July 31, 2012, www.medievalscribes.com.

23. For descriptions and a full listing of the contents of Longleat 29, see Hanna, *English MSS of Rolle*, 208–12; Rolle, *Prose and Verse*, xvii–xxxi.

24. Editing of these texts is ongoing, but basic editions of the *Mirror of St. Edmund*, the meditation on the Five Wounds, the *Laddre of Heuyn*, and *O Thou Soul Myn* can be found as edited texts 3–6 in O'Byrne, "Dublin's Hoccleve."

25. This text is currently being edited by Katherine Stevenson.

26. For an edition, see edited text 1, ll. 210–15, in O'Byrne, "Dublin's Hoccleve." See also Hippolyte Delehaye, ed., "Le Pèlerinage de Laurent de Paszttho au Purgatoire de S. Patrice," *Analecta Bollandiana* 27 (1908): 51. Cf. "Eleuate capita uestra et corde aspicite uulnera saluatoris nostri in ligno pendentis poenas morientis pretium redimentis cicatrices resurgentis. Quid aliud uidere poterimus nisi caput inclinatum ad uocandum et parcendum cor apertum ad diligendum brachia extensa ad amplexandum totum corpus expositum ad redimendum. Haec quanta sint cogitate uos qui doletis haec in statera uestri cordis appendite ut totus uobis figatur in corde qui pro uobis totus fixus fuit in cruce." Augustinus (pseudo) Belgicus, *Sermones ad fratres in eremo commorantes* (*Sermons to Brothers Dwelling in the Desert*), ed. J.-P. Migne, Patrologia Latina 40 (Turnhout: Brepols, 1841), Sermo 32, col. 1293, ll. 33–41.

27. Rolle, *Prose and Verse*, xx–xxi.

28. Manly and Rickert and Harley argue that the manuscript came to Thynne from his uncle William Thynne, who obtained the manuscript at the dissolution of the monasteries. However, this theory is predicated on the idea that the manuscript was created at Canterbury, possibly in a religious house, which is certainly not the case: John M. Manly and Edith Rickert, *The Text of "The Canterbury Tales": Studied on the Basis of All Known Manuscripts*, vol. 1 (Chicago: University of Chicago Press, 1940), 347–48; Marta Powell Harley, *A Revelation of Purgatory by an Unknown, Fifteenth-Century Woman Visionary*, Studies in Women and Religion 18 (Lewiston, NY: Edwin Mellen, 1985), 43–44.

29. Rolle, *Prose and Verse*, xxi.

30. John Thomas Gilbert, ed., *Calendar of Ancient Records of Dublin*, vol. 1 (Dublin: Joseph Dollard, 1889), 276–350.

31. *Prose and Verse*, xxxiii.

32. Ibid., xxxii.

33. Michael Joseph McEnery and Raymond Refaussé, eds., *Christ Church Deeds* (Dublin: Four Courts, 2001), paras. 341–42, 349.

34. Kathryn Kerby-Fulton and Denise Despres, *Iconography and the Professional Reader: The Politics of Book Production in the Douce "Piers Plowman"* (Minneapolis: University of Minnesota Press, 1999).

Part V

Newer Directions in Manuscript Studies II

Women, Children, and Literacy at Work in Late Medieval and Early Tudor England

Foreword to Part V

I was delighted to be invited to contribute to this volume recording the memorable 2011 conference with its extraordinary range of scholarship and fittingly celebrating not just the great breadth of Derek Pearsall's contributions to medieval studies but also his pivotal role in the development of so many scholarly lives and careers. The three essays in Part V, by Nicole Eddy, Karrie Fuller, and Maura Giles-Watson, have a particular resonance for me, recalling Derek's support and encouragement over thirty years ago when I, too, was what is now called an early career researcher.

Nicole Eddy's essay offers detailed, contextualized analysis of marginal annotations to produce new evidence for the readership and reception of MS Lambeth 491. This speaks to Derek's long-standing engagement with the question of the audience for medieval texts, as Eddy points out, and is entirely in the spirit of his passionate credo, his "conviction of the centrality of manuscript studies to the discipline of medieval studies," as lucidly laid out in the opening paragraph of his introduction to the volume of essays from the 1998 Harvard Manuscripts Conference.[1] As there explained, it is a credo unchanged from the beliefs that animated Derek's original series of conferences at York in the 1980s. Derek captures the sense of new directions at the first York conference on the study of fifteenth-century manuscripts and late medieval English literature in July 1981, the sense that previously held scholarly assumptions were changing, as he writes of the liberation of manuscript studies from "the tyranny exerted by the 'critical edition.'"[2] It was an exciting experience for an early career researcher, having had the pleasure of speaking to Derek's research seminar at King's Manor that January, to be invited to the conference, and to share ideas with people involved in cutting-edge manuscript scholarship. Eddy's essay interacts with these recollections in its discussion of the manuscript that was then the focus of my research, NLS MS Adv. 19.3.1, and has been the subject of ongoing conversations with other scholars interested in the kind of evidence of readership that Eddy highlights in MS Lambeth 491 as well.

Karrie Fuller is equally concerned with the significance of marginalia, as she focuses in her essay on the engagement of scribe and readers with the text of *Piers Plowman* in MS Digby 145: a case that perfectly illustrates Derek's emphasis on the continuing role of a manuscript as "an active witness to the culture of its reception, in the scope it offers for readers' marginal and other comments."[3] Fuller relates this case to that of another *Piers Plowman* manuscript, MS Douce 104, edited by Derek in a facsimile marking, as Kathryn Kerby-Fulton observes, the beginning of serious scholarly attention to that manuscript.[4] There Derek recalls George Kane's appreciation of *Piers Plowman*'s power to "elicit response, to generate active participation in the literary and social experience it evidently constituted for near-contemporary readers," and notes in this respect the "special case" of MS Digby 145, "with annotation simultaneously contemporary and late."[5] Fuller fruitfully develops such insights into the potential for participation inherent in the manuscript text, as she analyzes the unique interaction between the three annotators of this copy of *Piers Plowman*, conducting conversations between themselves as well as with Langland's text.

Maura Giles-Watson's essay takes a different tack. It begins, as scholarly papers on medieval topics often do, by positioning itself in relation to one of Derek's critical pronouncements, noting his lack of enthusiasm for medieval and early Tudor drama. Indeed, the provocative tone of Derek's judgment on early modern verse drama seems calculated to draw a response, seeking the kind of spirited exchange of views that he celebrates in his introduction to the collection of essays from the 1985 York conference: "The subject, it will be seen, is in the happy state of being much argued about and disagreed over."[6] Contesting Derek's views has been a fruitful point of departure for many a paper, and his incisive comments have helped to hone many an argument. It was Derek's challenge on the question of Lydgate's readability, for instance, at the London New Chaucer Society Congress in 2000 that spurred me to dig deeper into the subject of Lydgate's versification and syntax. Giles-Watson's essay also notes, however, Derek's characteristic and generous readiness to change his views in light of new developments: in this case, in relation to the lasting significance of feminism (see her note 5); and I was equally "stunned and delighted" at the 2008 Romance in Medieval Britain conference at St. Andrew's when Derek recanted (to some extent, at least) his previously low critical opinion of Middle English popular romance.[7]

Let us turn now to the three essays in more detail. Eddy, in "The Romance of History: Lambeth Palace MS 491 and Its Young Readers," briefly sketches the character of the manuscript and points to recent work identifying the hand of its London scribe, then turns her attention from the major contents to the apparently haphazard scribbles in the manuscript's margins,[8] most of them in the hand of one of the individuals making up what she suggests was a "network" of young writers whose names appear repeatedly among the scribbles. She uses the "echoes of the schoolroom" heard in the extensive marginalia to evoke the milieu in which the manuscript circulated from an early stage and conjures up the shadowy presence of the teaching materials behind them: collections of rhymed proverbial wisdom; model examples of epistolary forms of address and closure. Eddy is surely right to see the couplet sententiae as "evidence for a tradition of proverbial poetry, featuring borrowings and cross-connections"; there is an example of the synthetic manner in which such a "poem" might be constructed out of diverse sources in the Heege MS, where a stanza of rhyming proverbs based on Cato is grafted onto a frequently excerpted stanza on deceit and fraud from Lydgate's *Fall of Princes* and followed by a set of couplet sententiae like those in the margins of MS Lambeth 491, all presented as a coherent, proverbial whole (MS Adv. 19.3.1, fol. 61v). The same manuscript also offers a supportive parallel to the case of Lambeth 491 in its pattern of marginalia: annotations on the texts by the primary scribe, with later unrelated additions in a number of juvenile hands, drawing simple images, practicing writing, copying English sententiae and Latin vocabulary, reproducing standard letter-writing formulas.[9] From the marginal additions to Lambeth 491, Eddy reads back into the texts of this "schoolroom-adjacent" manuscript, to argue for the didactic potential of its combination of history, romance, and the art of hunting, and while space does not permit an extensive discussion of these texts, there is rich potential for development in this analysis of such a good example of Felicity Riddy's succinct characterization of the concerns expressed by manuscript collections of this kind: "good manners, right conduct and the claims of the next world[,] . . . and a concern with the past."[10] But it is the careful work of teasing out the relations between the marginal fragments and the surviving echoes of the schoolroom maxims in their contemporary culture that forms the heart of Eddy's essay. They are clearly fragments of an elementary educational experience so widespread that writers including Chaucer and the *Gawain*-poet could confidently quote a phrase shared with the marginalia in MS Lambeth 491, knowing that it would evoke the whole context that Eddy describes,[11] and so long-lived that Thomas Morley could playfully use "Christes crosse be my speede, in all vertue to proceed" and the alphabet as the text set to music in his instructions on composing part songs two centuries later.[12]

Fuller, in "Langland in the Early Modern Household: *Piers Plowman* in Oxford, Bodleian Library, MS Digby 145, and Its Scribe-Annotator Dialogues," investigates a very different case of marginal additions to a manuscript (though there is a fortuitous slight connection in the fact that the final item copied by the scribe in MS Digby 145 is a collection of proverbial sayings). These are not scribbles exploiting the resource of available blank space for practical needs but deliberate, thoughtful annotations, revealing interaction with the text of *Piers Plowman* over time by a number of interrelated reader-annotators: the original copyist, Sir Adrian Fortescue, his second wife, Anne Rede, and an unidentified third hand, which Fuller suggests may be that of a son or another family member. Fuller gives a brief account of Sir Adrian's family circumstances and political career to set the context for her interpretation of the manuscript annotations, and the life story thus sketched out has all the fascination of proximity to power, fluctuating fortunes in turbulent times, and mysterious silences that attracts historical novelists (e.g., Hilary Mantel's projected trilogy on Thomas Cromwell, patron of William Stonor, Fortescue's opponent in the lawsuit over his wife's inheritance).[13] The annotations on which Fuller focuses here are precisely those that seem to provide us with the tiny glimpses of personal relationships that can enliven the sketch of political and social upheaval: the wife writing in partnership with her husband; the younger relative occasionally intervening in the conjugal conversation, perhaps even essaying an awkward joke, and taking an increasingly independent direction in response to the text, especially with regard to the papacy. These are not lengthy annotations, and Fuller properly notes the caution with which the modern scholar must attempt any interpretation of the ideologies or affiliations they may represent, but it is hard to resist the appeal of the "shifting dynamic" she describes between the older man and the younger relative played out in their ongoing marginal conversations.

In the third essay in this part, "Playing as Literate Practice: Humanism and the Exclusion of Women Performers by the London Professional Stages," Maura Giles-Watson not only takes a new direction in the way she situates it vis-à-vis Derek's work; she moves away from close study of manuscripts to consideration of the historical and cultural circumstances of later medieval and early modern drama, focusing in particular on the reasons for the "putative absence of women players" from dramatic performances in England in the later Middle Ages and their known absence from early modern London theaters. As Giles-Watson makes clear, the scarcity of documentary evidence renders the tracing of women's participation in medieval drama very difficult: the unusual stage direction in *Wisdom* that describes six women "disguised" points only to mimed, not spoken, roles, and while educated women might have performed in private dramatic events such as mummings, the likelihood is that theirs would have been nonspeaking parts. In light of this, it is interesting to note that Derek pays Lydgate a rare compliment in relation to his seven mummings: "They are of great importance in the history of drama, and one of them is a considerable achievement in its own right"; "the *Mumming at Hertford* is one of Lydgate's unexpected triumphs."[14] The piece Derek singles out for praise, which was performed before the king "holding his noble feest of Cristmasse in the Castel of Hertford" in 1427,[15] is remarkable for its inclusion of female characters with a speaking role: "The striking innovation is the wives' reply, which is spoken in their own person."[16] Derek does not raise the question of who played the women's parts, though James Stokes, in a recent article on the participation of women in dramatic performances, notes that "records of women performing in East Anglia" (Lydgate's area) are "voluminous and varied" and include entertainments staged for visiting royalty "spanning a wide temporal range" from 1311 to

1620.[17] However, whether women's performances in the Middle Ages would have included long speeches is, as Giles-Watson points out, still a matter of "conjecture and dispute." There is no doubt, however, about the exclusion of women from the new professional stage culture of sixteenth-century London, and Giles-Watson's essay provides a succinct guide to current scholarly debate on this imperfectly explained "cultural aberration,"[18] before offering a new intervention which elegantly supplements previous arguments on economic or religious grounds by focusing on the impact of humanism via two features of sixteenth-century culture: the general cult of literacy and the particular development of academic drama. The combined requirements suggested here for players in the new London theaters—a high level of literacy, experience of grammar school or university, and professionalization—create an all too familiar barrier to female participation. The essay's final quotation, from Alberico Gentili, contrasting the contemporary mixed-gender practice of the Italian theater with the all-male playing tradition attributed to the classical past, has an unmistakable air of nostalgia as he looks back to that golden age in which "they say (*tradunt*) that men first acted women's parts," much as Charles in *As You Like It* constructs the pastoral idyll in which "they say" the Duke and his men "fleet the time carelessly, as they did in the golden world" (I.i.101–3).

Phillipa Hardman

NOTES

1. Derek Pearsall, ed., *New Directions in Later Medieval Manuscript Studies: Essays from the 1998 Harvard Conference* (York: York Medieval Press, 2000), xi.

2. Derek Pearsall, ed., *Manuscripts and Readers in Fifteenth-Century England: The Literary Implications of Manuscript Study. Essays from the 1981 Conference at the University of York* (Cambridge: D. S. Brewer, 1983), 1.

3. Pearsall, *New Directions*, xi.

4. *A Facsimile of Bodleian Library, Oxford, MS Douce 104*, with an introduction by Derek Pearsall and a catalog of the illustrations by Kathleen Scott (Cambridge: D. S. Brewer, 1992); Kathryn Kerby-Fulton and Denise L. Despres, *Iconography and the Professional Reader: The Politics of Book Production in the Douce "Piers Plowman"* (Minneapolis: University of Minnesota Press, 1999), xiii.

5. Facsimile, x; xxiv n. 20 (for sigil *Ch*, read *K*).

6. Derek Pearsall, ed., *Manuscripts and Texts: Editorial Problems in Later Middle English Literature. Essays from the 1985 Conference at the University of York* (Cambridge: D. S. Brewer, 1987), 2.

7. A revised version of Derek's conference paper appears as "The Pleasure of Popular Romance: A Prefatory Essay," in *Medieval Romance, Medieval Contexts*, ed. Rhiannon Purdie and Michael Cichon (Cambridge: D. S. Brewer, 2011), 9–18.

8. It is interesting to note how many of the early uses of Eddy's appropriate word *scribble* cited in the *OED* refer either to marginal annotations or to letter writing.

9. *The Heege Manuscript: A Facsimile*, introd. Phillipa Hardman, Leeds Texts and Monographs 16 (Leeds: Leeds Studies in English, 2000).

10. Felicity Riddy, *Sir Thomas Malory*, Medieval and Renaissance Authors 9 (Leiden: Brill, 1987), 23.

11. "The firste vertu, sone, if thou wolt leere, / Is to restreyne and kepe wel thy tonge; / Thus lerne children whan that they been yonge" (Chaucer, *Manciple's Tale*, 332–34); "He sayned hym in syþes sere / And sayde, 'Cros Kryst me spede' " (*Sir Gawain and the Green Knight*, 761–62).

12. *A plaine and easie introduction to practicall musicke* (London, 1597; repr. 1608), 36–53; cited in Andrew W. Tuer, *History of the Horn-Book* (London, 1897), 31, 81. See also Nicholas Orme, *Medieval Children* (New Haven, CT: Yale University Press, 2001), 253.

13. Hilary Mantel, *Wolf Hall* and *Bring Up the Bodies* (London: Fourth Estate, 2009, 2012); Richard Rex, "Fortescue, Sir Adrian (*c.* 1481–1539)," *Oxford Dictionary of National Biography* (Oxford: Oxford University Press, 2004); online ed., January 2008, www.oxforddnb.com/view/article/9936.

14. Derek Pearsall, *John Lydgate* (London: Routledge, 1970), 184, 187.

15. Derek Pearsall, *John Lydgate (1371–1449): A Bio-bibliography*, ELS Monograph 71 (Victoria, BC: English Literary Studies, 1997), 28.

16. Pearsall, *John Lydgate*, 188.

17. James Stokes, "Women and Performance in Medieval and Early Modern Suffolk," *Early Theatre* 15, no. 1 (2012): 28–29.

18. Quoting James Stokes, cited by Phyllis Rackin, "Afterword," in *Women Players in England, 1500–1660,* ed. Pamela Allen Brown and Peter Parolin (Burlington, VT: Ashgate, 2005), 316.

CHAPTER 15

The Romance of History

Lambeth Palace MS 491 and Its Young Readers

Nicole Eddy

One of the great themes running through Derek Pearsall's body of work—and it is a wide-ranging and comprehensive body of work indeed—is his engagement with issues of audience.[1] For whose eyes (or, as Pearsall himself would be the first to remind us, ears) was a work intended? And, perhaps more answerably, who is it that actually read a work? If manuscript studies, in directions both new and old, preoccupy Pearsall's scholarly attention, it is not (only) because of the allure of the manuscript as artifact but, frequently, because it provides another toehold on that precarious question of audience. In our examination of literary history's physical evidence, we can uncover clues to the identities of the audiences for these Middle English texts, and as Pearsall has taught us, the nature of these audiences will have determined interpretation and the *expectation* of interpretation.

As Pearsall warns, "certain aspects of the reception of the text and of our assumptions with regard to the text [are] perilous for us to ignore": "tradition impregnates reading, even when, and perhaps especially when, the reader consciously seeks to dissociate himself from it."[2] Audience does not limit interpretation but must necessarily inform it. Pearsall's work on romance has been instrumental in breaking the hold on the modern scholarly imagination exerted by the courtly recitation or the performance of the traveling minstrel (or, perhaps more properly, *disour*), perceptions of romance audience that are romantic indeed, dependent on these texts' own sometimes disingenuous self-presentation. Such models for the consumption of romance must not, of course, be rejected entirely but should instead be understood more capaciously, the limits of audience embracing a greater complexity and all "the variety of contexts within which a literary work may properly be said to live."[3] If we locate for romance audiences larger than, more complex than, or otherwise different from those we have traditionally been brought to expect, it will necessarily give rise to larger, more complex, and different ways of reading meaning.

In the case of Lambeth Palace MS 491, our expectations for its texts may be broadened if we take in all the evidence that manuscript has to offer as to its earliest audience. Over the course of the Middle English prose *Brut* chronicle,[4] which fills the first two hundred folios of the manuscript, unfolds an extensive body of notes in the hand of the scribe, as well as annotation by a later, sixteenth-century reader. The greater part of the marginal material in Lambeth 491, however, does not engage directly with the content of the text. As Gisela Guddat-Figge observes in her catalog of Middle English romances, the manuscript has been "spoilt by innumerable scribbles by former owners,"[5] inconsiderate owners whose spoiling of the codex's margins has had the fortunate consequence that we can attempt some deductions about their identities.

A composite manuscript in its present state, the first, fifteenth-century portion contains, in addition to the *Brut* chronicle, copies of the *Siege of Jerusalem*,[6] the *Three Kings of Cologne*,[7] the *Awntyrs off Arthure*,[8] and a verse treatise on hunting.[9] All the texts in this part of the manuscript were copied by a single scribe, the man also responsible for copying Huntington HM 114 and recently identified by Linne Mooney and Estelle Stubbs as Richard Osbarn, clerk of the chamber in London from 1400 to 1437 and one of a cadre of scribes associated with the London Guildhall.[10] On the basis of the manuscript's contents, among which the *Brut* clearly takes pride of place as it also consumes the largest number of folios, Guddat-Figge characterizes the manuscript as "written for a private collector interested in history, though probably not professionally."[11] All the items, including the *Awntyrs off Arthure* romance, can be interpreted as speaking directly to this historical interest. This postulated original owner is unidentified, as the manuscript is mentioned in no records before appearing in the possession of Richard Bancroft, archbishop of Canterbury, in the first decade of the seventeenth century.[12] By consulting the marginal scribbles, however, we can offer further nuance to this picture. While the driving interest of the manuscript is, certainly, history, it is more specifically a pedagogical and didactic history. The ownership marks, evidence of the manuscript's use in the late fifteenth century, do not appear to be the casual jottings of an amateur historian but are instead the scribbles of schoolboys. We find in them the echoes of the schoolroom, and of young readers who had the texts of an elementary education very much at the forefront of their minds and on the tips of their pens.

It is obvious from the beginning that young children have played at least some role in the production of marginal material in Lambeth 491. A crude drawing in the left margin of fol. 133r (at Brie, *Brut*, 1:212.1–2; see fig. 15.1) depicts a smiling figure, his stick of an arm raised in a jaunty wave. The drawing is easily recognizable as that of a very young child, perhaps around four to six years old.[13] It is by no means unusual to find such evidence of a manuscript being allowed in dangerous proximity to a very young child armed with a writing implement—dangerous, that is, to any effort to maintain the book in a pristine original condition. By far the greater amount of Guddat-Figge's "scribbles by former owners," however, are textual. As this cheerful doodle is to the art of illustration, these products of uncertain penmanship are to the acts of reading and writing.

There are a large number of simple signatures in the margins of the manuscript, among which the most frequent names, appearing often over the length of the manuscript, are those of Thomas and John Pattsall.[14] Over the large number of examples, it is extremely difficult to determine whether widely varying scripts represent the same individual experimenting with different writing styles or more than one individual, writing perhaps years apart but having the same name. It is also possible—even likely—that the variation in script reflects developments in the handwriting of one or more individuals as they matured and became more skilled: handwriting at six or eight looks very different from handwriting at twelve or fourteen. On fol. 8r, the names of John Pattsall and Thomas Pattsall are written in hands so similar they may in fact be the same (fig. 15.2)—perhaps one has signed his brother's name as well as his own? Yet on fol. 65r, "this ys Jhon Patsall ys boke" is written in a very different script (fig. 15.3). This script appears again on fol. 22v, in another signature apparently affirming identity, this time under the name of Thomas, the inhabitant of a town just outside London: "be me

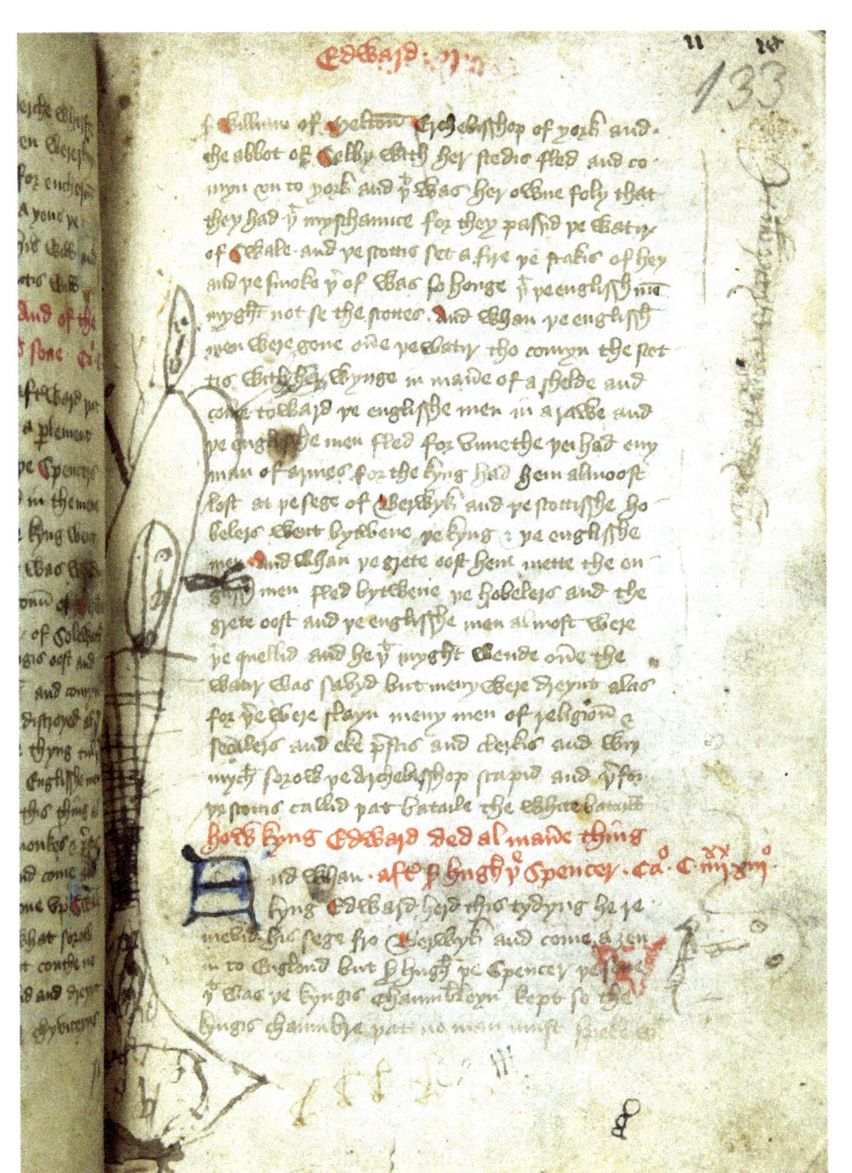

Fig. 15.1. A child's drawing of a human figure. London, Lambeth Palace MS 491, fol. 133r. Reproduced by permission of Lambeth Palace.

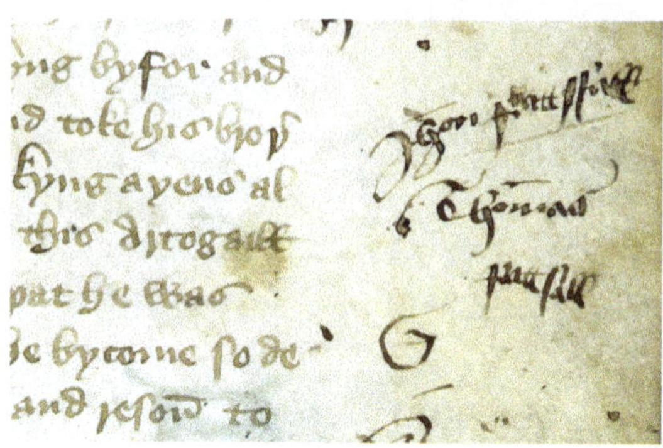

Fig. 15.2. Marginal signatures, with the names of John and Thomas Pattsall. London, Lambeth Palace MS 491, fol. 8r. Reproduced by permission of Lambeth Palace.

Tomas Patsall dellyng in the tene of barakyng" (by me, Thomas Pattsall, dwelling in the town of Barking). As is evident particularly in the last two cases, the handwriting of at least some of those signing under the Pattsall name is extremely difficult to make out, with a spelling rather inconsistent and idiosyncratic. Already there seems to be in these notes a certain uneasiness with the script in use, as though that of a child, not yet fully master of his pen.

It is clear, then, that a number of children have "gotten at" this manuscript and have left their marks on many of its pages. But what, exactly, do the scribbles say: what is it that these children are choosing to copy down in the margins of the book? The vast majority of the scribbles are fragmentary, copied or (perhaps more accurately) reproduced from some other context. They are of several types, including short, formulaic epistles (discussed in greater detail below) and, most frequently, verse proverbs, in English and, rarely, Latin, most commonly in the form of a single rhyming couplet. These couplets are often badly spelled and nearly illegible, and often in only very fragmentary form. They are all apparently in the same hand, attributable at least tentatively to Thomas, or perhaps John, Pattsall. It is perhaps best to think of these fragments as productions of a "Pattsall network" of writing, collectively associated with the names of Thomas and John, as well as with some rather less frequent names in very similar scripts, like those of John Presson (fol. 54v), John Pysant (fol. 203v), or Richard Persy (fol. 172r).[15] The most commonly appearing of these proverbs is perhaps also the most illuminating: the simple couplet "In my beginning God me speed / In grace and vertue to proceed." The couplet appears in numerous fragments throughout the

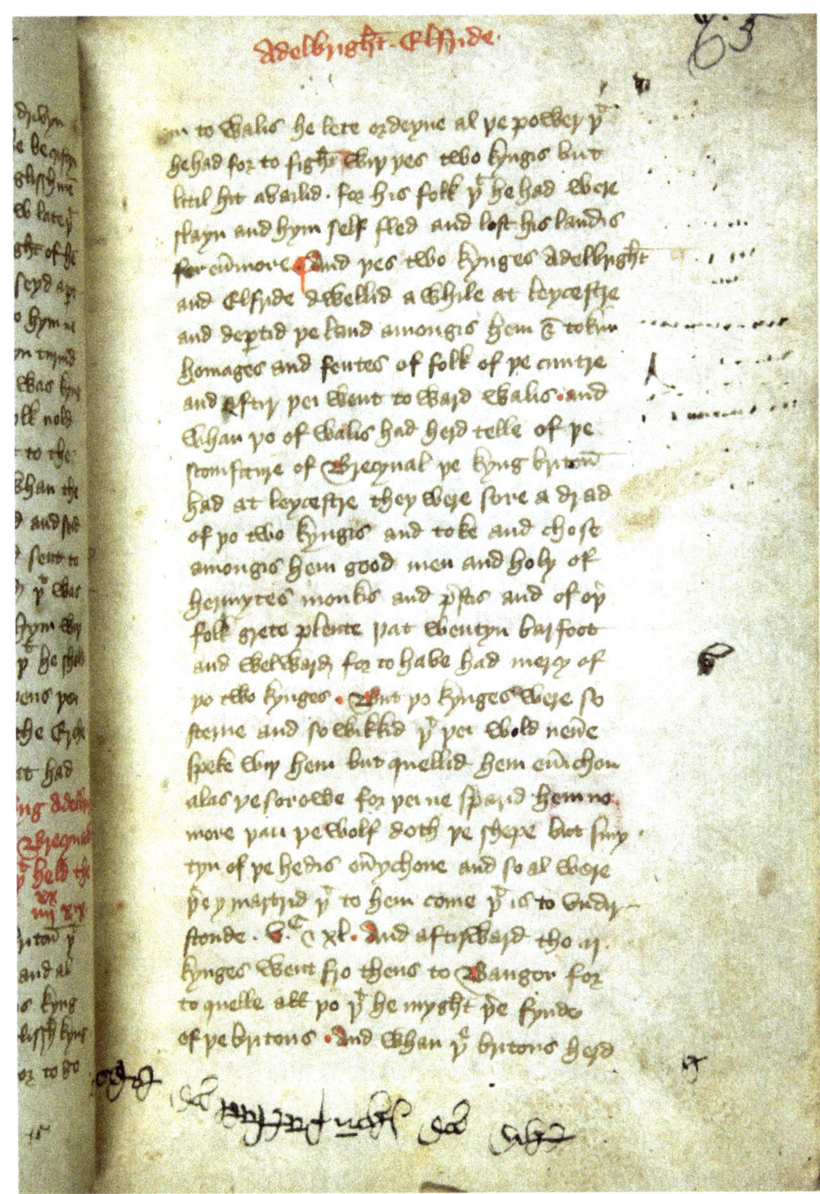

Adelbright. Elfride.

...to Wales he lete ordeyne al ye power yt
he had for to fight wt yes two kyngis but
litil hit availed. for his folk yt he had were
slayn and hym self fled and lost his landis
for euermore. And yes two kynges Adelbright
and Elfride dwellid a while at leycestre
and departid ye land amongis hem & token
homages and feutes of folk of ye cuntre
and aftir yei went to ward Walis. and
whan yo of Walis had herd telle of ye
scomfiture of Reygnal ye kyng briton
had at leycestre they were sore adrad
of yo two kyngis and toke and chose
amongis hem good men and holy of
heremytes monkis and prestes and of oyr
folk grete plente yat wenten barfoot
and wolward for to haue had mercy of
yo two kynges. But yo kynges were so
sterne and so wikkid yt yei wold neuer
speke wt hem but quellid hem euerichon
alas ye sorowe for yei ne spared hem no
more yan ye wolf doth ye shepe but slow
tyn of ye heuedes eueryschone and so al were
yey martyred yt to hem come yt is to vndyr
stonde. ij.C. xl. And aftirward tho ij
kynges went his thens to Bangor for
to quelle all yo yt he myght ther fynde
of ye britons. And whan ye britons herd

this ys Jhon Patsall ys boke

Fig. 15.3. Statement of ownership by John Pattsall, "this ys Jhon Patsall ys boke." London, Lambeth Palace MS 491, fol. 65r. Reproduced by permission of Lambeth Palace.

manuscript, with variations of wording including "God us speed" and "Jesus be my speed in grace and virtue to proceed."[16] Spelling varies widely; especially in longer words like *beginning*, the writer seems sometimes to lose control of his *N*s and *Y*s, producing a variety of nonstandard spellings. The fullest and clearest presentation of the proverb is that on fol. 193v: "be me Thomas patsal genttylman | Inmy be gynnyng god vs sped | in grace & vertu to p*r*oced be the" (fig. 15.4).

The incipit "In my beginning" appears, in a number of variations, in a few different entries of the *Digital Index of Middle English Verse*, including one entry describing its addition by readers to manuscript margins and flyleaves, naming it "A tag to be learned as a child, or at the beginning of a book."[17] Proverbs like this one were a significant part of the curriculum for elementary education in the Middle Ages, useful texts of moral instruction offered as a tool for learning to read and write. The best-documented example of this is the *Distichs* of Cato, used for elementary Latin instruction. While the "In my beginning" couplet is not a translation of one of the *Distichs*, it is similar in form to this more famous work and has a deep pedigree associating it with medieval education.

In 1615, John Boys, later the dean of Canterbury Cathedral, wrote a series of expositional sermons. Looking back on the practices of a former age he does not further specify, he asserts, "the first character our forefathers taught their children was *Christs crosse*, and the first lesson in their Primer, was, *In the name of the Father*, and the first copie in their schoole, was, *In my beginning God be my speed*."[18] Boys, assuming his audience will recognize the techniques of elementary pedagogy in reading and, more important, writing, does not elaborate further. But a manuscript schoolbook of ca. 1500 (London, British Library, Royal MS 12 B. xx, fols. 35–49) is surviving evidence of what was likely a much more widespread practice.[19] It contains passages of Latin prose followed by their English translations, the first passage of which opens: "God helpe us at owre begynny*ng*, w*ith*-owt whos helpe we can not p*r*ofet, for likewise as *the* bowes of trees if *the* be cut vp from *the* royttes sone wether and wanysshe a-waie, so we if we lacke *the* helpe and grace of god son fall and come to nowght."[20] We may gain an even more expanded view of the practice in a poem by John Trevisa that opens his translation of *On the Properties of Things* and seems to play with the forms and phrasings of the elementary primer:

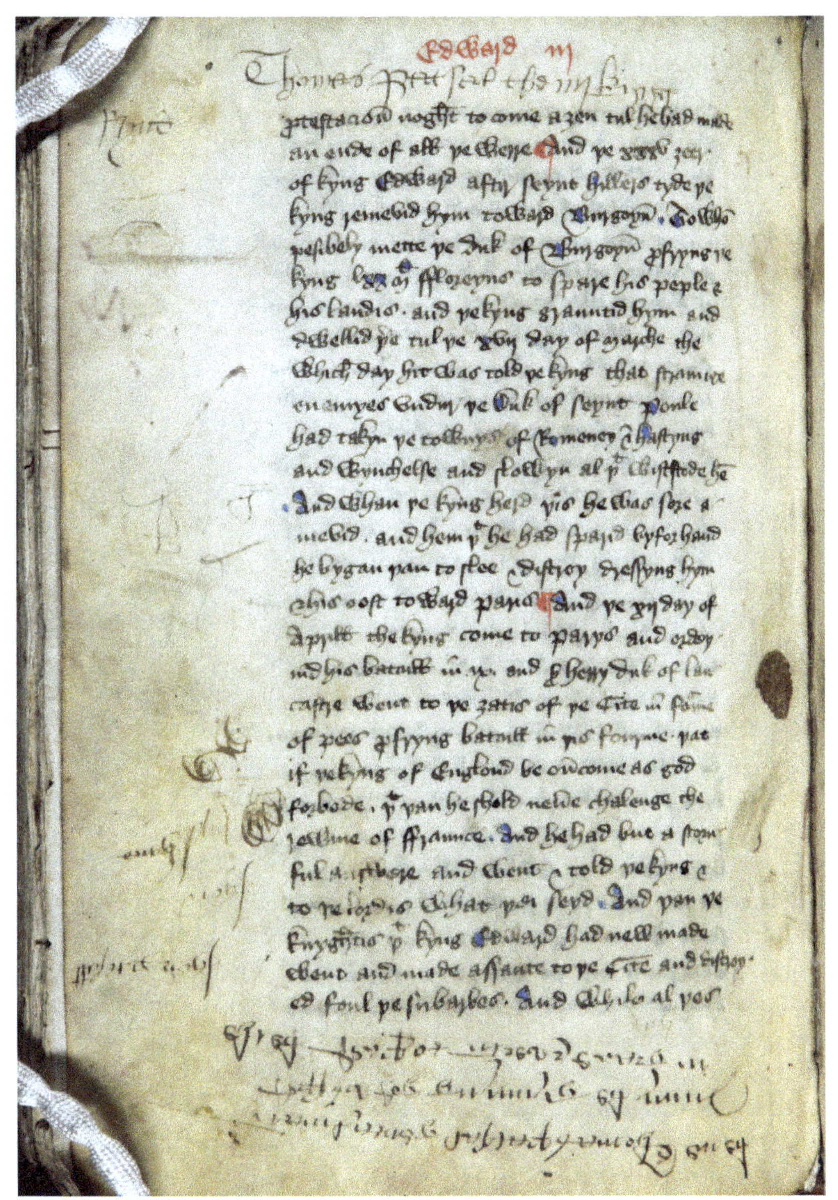

Fig. 15.4. Proverb beginning "In my beginning, God us speed . . ." signed by "Thomas patsal genttylman." London, Lambeth Palace MS 491, fol. 193v. Reproduced by permission of Lambeth Palace.

Croys was maad al of reed
In þe bigynnynge of my book
That is clepid God me spede.
In þe firste lessoun þat I took
Thanne I lerned *a* and *be*
And oþir lettres by here names.
But alwey God spede me
That is me nedeful in alle games
If I pleyde in felde oþir in medes.[21]

The red cross of his opening line clearly references the "Christs crosse" mentioned also by Boys, a prominent and nearly universal feature of early primers and horn books, dating back at least to the late fourteenth century.[22] It was, moreover, evidently intimately associated with a variation on the "In my beginning" text. "When children recited the alphabet," Nicholas Orme explains, "they began by making the sign of the cross and saying 'Christ's cross me speed.'"[23] Moreover, the formulas of beginning (and of ending) and of speed (in both its connotations, of success as well as of physical rapidity) form a leitmotif of wordplay throughout Trevisa's poem. He expects his readers to identify these phrases instantly, to find them as recognizable in their own way as the iconic red cross at the beginning of a child's alphabet.

Bearing in mind these pedagogical associations for the couplet, then, we may find a compelling reason for their reproduction in this manuscript's margins. Thomas and John Pattsall, accustomed to these verses as appropriate copy-texts, are practicing their newly learned skills with a pen, with the same texts they are routinely set to copy. This picture is more fully fleshed out by the realization that "In my beginning," while certainly one of the most frequently appearing of Lambeth 491's scribbled marginal couplets, is by no means the only one associated with education. On the contrary, all Lambeth's couplets seem to spring from a collection or collections of related poems, used for a single purpose.

While it is not now possible to identify among the extant corpus the poems that the Pattsalls must have been reading, other similar poems that do survive can give us an impression of what it must have looked like. The "In my beginning" incipit opens at least two poems that consist of a series of proverbs in rhymed couplets, presented as instruction from a father to his son. One of these, found without title in the Welles Anthology (Oxford, Bodleian Library, Rawlinson C.813), begins its eighty lines with "Att my begynning criste me spede / In grace and vertue to procede / Soo that I may through vertue and grace / Fenishe my matter to my purpasse."[24] The second poem is in London, British Library, Harley MS 2252, and opens "At ow*ur* begynny[*n*]g*e*, god be ow*ur* spede / In grace & v*er*tue to p*ro*sede! / Be petu*us* & eke m*er*ciabyll; / To nedy folke be Cherytabyll."[25] This latter poem continues, some fifty lines later, with a nugget of paternal advice: "Beware, my son, ev*er* of 'had-I-wyste.' "[26] The address to a "son" of such proverbial wisdom—saws of the same kind that, in the form of the *Distichs* of Cato, had such a prominent and long-lived place in the elementary curriculum—surely functions as a literal indication of imagined (young) readership, as well as a literary fiction.

The degree to which similar, but not identical, proverbial poems would have been available in the late Middle Ages is illustrated by comparison of the Harley 2252 "At ow*ur* begynny[n]ge" variant back again to the Welles Anthology poem, where the initial "Att my begynning criste me spede" incipit is followed in the very next stanza by the variant "Bewarre my sonne off hadde I wiste / itt ys harde to knowe whome thou may truste / A trustye Frende ys harde to Fynde / For hadde I wyste commethe euer by hynde."[27] These two stanzas are not the only ones in the Welles Anthology that share very similar wording to the Harley 2252 poem. The two poems are, if not precisely variants of a single composition, then at the very least decisive proof that verses like "in my beginning" and "a trusty friend" could travel together—along with other, similar proverbial verses—in loosely connected contexts that shifted in precise form but nevertheless had a clearly defined didactic presentation. More important, however, while the dialogue between father and son may be a conventional device within the wisdom literature genre, that device reflected its real-world application. Cato's *Distichs*, after all, carried in the Middle Ages a prologue that shares this trope ("Nunc te, fili carissime, docebo" [Now, dearest son, I will teach you]).

The maxim that "a trusty friend is hard to find" is, furthermore, not unknown to the marginal scribblers of Lambeth 491. Another couplet, or rather pair of couplets, appears in various fragmentary forms in the manuscript at irregular intervals, its first appearance being on fol. 106r (within the stretch of the manuscript containing the *Brut*) and its last on fol. 253r (alongside the *Three Kings of Cologne*), where it also finds its fullest development: "The peliccan saythtome inded a trusty | frynd ys good at need euer bare thys | in thy mend a trusty frynd ys hard to | fynd." The "peliccan" is a bird with, of course, overdetermined allegorical significance, as a type of Christ, pecking at its own breast to feed its young with the blood. But it is difficult to determine what the bird's presence here might be intended to mean. What is clear, however, is the similarity in type between the "pelican says" verses and the "at my beginning" couplet, a fact driven home by their mutual inclusion (or, at any rate, by the mutual inclusion of "at my beginning" and one—but not all four—of the lines spoken by the pelican) in the "Proverbs of Good Counsel" poem from Harley 2252: "Beware, my son, ev*er* of 'had-I-wyste' / hard ys to know who*m* on may tryst[e]; A tr[u]sty frende ys hard to fynde, / none ys more foo þen on vnkynd[e]."[28]

Lambeth 491 has other proverbial material in its margins as well. On fol. 198v, we find "he that in yowth no good can nor noonewyl lerne | yf he never thryfe / who shal hyme warne,"[29] and fol. 230v bears the observation "The begynnyg of wysdom ys god to dred | mekyns ys the gru*n*der of ieury good ded."[30] Although there is no indication in Lambeth that these couplets should be taken together, a tantalizing point of comparison can be found in a poem from the fifteenth-century London, British Library, Harley MS 3810: "For the begynnyng of wysdom is / For to drede Goddys ryȝtwysnes. / He that in ȝouthe no vertu usit, In age alle honure hym refusit."[31] Harley 3810 also contains a copy of the verse romance *Sir Orfeo*, a text whose particular appropriateness for a juvenile audience has been proposed before.[32]

Besides their didactic associations, all these couplets have one more thing in common: they are, like the manuscript's main texts, in English. This is not to say that Lambeth's readers were wholly unfamiliar with Latin, but their use of the language is rather hesitant, as of a language that is being learned, and that imperfectly. The margins' major use of Latin is in a script associated with a Pattsall signature, that of Thomas. On fol. 58v appears, written upside down in the bottom margin, "fleo damna Reru*m* sed plus | Thomas Patsal." This is more fully expanded, sans signature, on fol. 163v, also upside down: "fleo damna Reru*m* sed plus fleo damna <quis> dieru*m* | Quisquis potesset suc ledere damna Reru*m* sed nemo." The former quotation is clearly an abbreviated version of the latter, which is more fully—but not for all that necessarily better—reproduced. Indeed, in this latter, garbled version, it is possible to get a better feel for the tenuous grasp the writer (Thomas?) has on his Latin. The couplet is a traditional Latin proverb, reproduced in various manuscripts, commonplace books, and even printed works.[33] In its more standard version, the proverb runs: "Damna fleo rerum, sed plus fleo damna dierum / Quisque potest rebus succurrere, nemo diebus" (I lament the losses of things, but [even] more do I lament the losses of days. / Anyone can restore things, [but] no one [can restore] days). Even making allowances for the casual circumstances of the Pattsall reproduction of the couplet, with its canceled false start on "Quisquis" and omission of the final "diebus," nonstandard forms, in particular "potesset" (no such Latin form exists) and "suc ledere" (presumably in error for "succedere"), suggest an unfamiliarity with the language and an attempt to reproduce the couplet by rote, without fully parsing its syntax. It is possible to see in this marginalia, therefore, both an extension of the Pattsall practice of copying proverbial couplets and a foray into Latin that is not fully competent, representing instead an intermediate or even beginner's grasp of the language, at a stage when the budding Latinist might reproduce vocabulary or copy out short texts provided for instructional purposes.

The margins of Lambeth 491 are dominated by these fragments of couplets, all of which seem to display associations with the didactic: they are the tools of instruction in reading and writing. Such couplets are not, however, the only brief texts copied by the Pattsalls and their contemporaries. And these texts too seem to bolster rather than undermine the argument for young readership. One particularly charming note appears upside down in the bottom margin of fol. 54v. The handwriting, in a script similar to that elsewhere associated with Pattsall signatures (although here associated with the name John Presson), appears to be the record of Christmas presents, including one from the writer's father: "I Jhon*e* presson*e* haue Resauyd of | youer cristmas as mvch mony for final candyl & wagyng candyl morouer I haue Ressauyd | of fader Red huse." The particular attention to a parent, an immediate family member within even the circumscribed connection network of a child, gives this note a youthful feel.

Family members also play important roles in some other marginal fragments, these once again with Pattsall signatures. Like the couplets, they are often incomplete, and include many errors and repetitions. Still, the sense, if not always the precise wording, is fairly clear. The documents are letters. They are short and highly formulaic: an example on fol. 248v is illustrative of the type:

> Trusty & wyl be loyd Ant I hartily Recome | nd me vnto you & wold gadly here of | youer good here of youer god helth Ant yet | so that I maruyl gretly that so oftyn as | I haue wryttyn to you for my bokis yt can | nat haue thym be me Thomas Patsal

Thomas Pattsall writes to his aunt, hopes to find her in health, and asks after some books in her keeping. The "Trusty & wyl be loyd" (trusty and well beloved) formula is one that occurs again and again in Lambeth's letters (most signed by Thomas Pattsall). Compare, to name only one example, "Trusty & wyl be louyd mwther I hartyly Recomend me vnto you | & wold gadly here of youer good helth mwther yt ys so that I & my | bruther cantnat het . . ." (fol. 258v). The addressees of these letters are predominantly, perhaps even exclusively, family.

"Trusty and well beloved" is a formula that stretches beyond its appearance in this manuscript. Variants are found in the Paston letters ("To my most reuerent and worchepfull maister, John Paston þe eldest, esquier, be this delieueryd in hast. Right trusty and welbeloved, I grete yow hartily well"),[34] as well as the Stonor collection ("My right trusty and well enprovyd Brothyr, y recommend me unto yow").[35] Any comparison between the Lambeth letters and these other documents must, however, begin and end with this salutation. The short length of Thomas Pattsall's notes both adapts the form to the scanty available space and renders the documents almost entirely empty of specific material. The formulas, here, are by far the most important aspect.

The formality and rigid structure of the epistolary form is one which was theorized in the medieval period itself as an *ars dictaminis* that was developed from classical models and, perhaps, more honored by academic theory than by actual letter-writing practice.[36] More influential as a model than this classical system was the royal letter issued by government agencies such as the Chancery or Privy Seal, ultimately developed from the *ars dictaminis* but having taken on a formulaic character uniquely its own.[37] As Malcolm Richardson describes it, the "royal missive style," adopted "as a model for private business letters in the years before about 1475," was carried out by letters that were typically "short, highly structured, and worded mainly by stock phrases."[38] The style that Richardson describes is clearly that followed by Thomas Pattsall. "Trusty cousin," Richardson quotes with modernized spelling, "I recommend me unto you, praying you to loan me £10."[39] Such letters as this one would be used for real-life business transactions but would also appear in formularies, which gathered together large numbers of model letters to be used as style guides. While Richardson stresses again and again the brevity and concision of these letters, however, most come nowhere near the laconic slenderness of Thomas's attempts at the form. Perhaps the closest parallel to the Pattsall letters is one Richardson quotes in modern orthography, sent by one Thomas Hales to his mother, "probably in the 1430s":

> Right worshipful mother, I commend me to you, desiring to hear of your welfare, the which I pray God keep you there in all, so I pray you of your blessing, the which is better to me than any worldly good. Also, I thank you for the cheeses that you sent to my masters and to me. And I pray you to send me the casket that I had at Winchester. And no more to you at this time, but God have you in his keeping. Amen. Written at London the twenty-eighth day of September.[40]

Thomas Pattsall clearly draws his style from the same page.

Such exaggerated brevity as shown in the Lambeth 491 letters and letter fragments and such absolute reliance on the repetition of formulas—astonishing even within a genre that honors the formulaic above the particular—render them of limited utility. Even Thomas Hales's slightly more developed document is quoted by Richardson as evidence of the poverty of the medieval model in supplying the full range of desired expression. Hales's age is not addressed by Richardson, and this thank-you note may well be the product of a fully mature if taciturn pen. The Pattsall jottings, however, wear rather uncomfortably the roles of wording and rewording for a letter to be sent later, or of the composition of a letter intended to do real "work" in the world. Instead, these jottings seem better suited to two other tasks: first, the internalization of wording and arrangement for a set of fixed epistolary forms, and, second, an exercise in the simple act of writing or copying. And in light of the nature of the other material jotted down by Thomas and John Pattsall, another scenario presents itself, that these letters represent a watered-down form of the more adult productions, a form more suitable for children. A student set to copy or even compose exercises such as these might thereby learn formulas that would serve him well in later business correspondence.

The question that inevitably arises, then, is this: ought we to dismiss these clumsy jottings of letters and proverbs as evidence that children are merely "spoiling" the margins of this book indeed, that their scribbles here are evidence only of children's "mess" and not of their engagement with the manuscript's actual contents? Not, I contend, entirely. It would be pushing the argument too far, I think, to term Lambeth 491 a "schoolbook," but even if it is not itself a schooltext, it is surely schoolroom-adjacent. Significantly, nearly *all* the fifteenth- and early-sixteenth-century marks in this manuscript can be associated with the Pattsall network of scribbling; there are no marks of identifiably adult readership. Its circumstances of use, therefore, so far as there is evidence for us to make a determination, are entirely juvenile. And these young readers have been acting with the rudiments of an education in English letters very much at the front of their minds. With these associations at the front of our own minds, then, we may begin to view Lambeth 491's texts in a new light as well.

The role of the young in the reading audience of medieval romance is one that is just beginning to be fully explored. Nicholas Orme observes that "almost any genre of adult literature" was fair game to be shared with the children within the household and includes romances and chronicles prominently among the works that would have been adopted for such use.[41] Orme quotes one late-fourteenth- or early-fifteenth-century author as disapproving of the widespread use of works without an immediate program of religious instruction in the education of the young: "som men setteþ here chyldren to lerne iestes of batailles and of cronycles and nouelleryes of songes þat stereþ hem to iolyte and to harlatrye."[42]

Phillipa Hardman has examined more closely the role of so-called household miscellanies in the education of children within the home. A single household book can carry texts directed toward the entire family, comprising a wide audience of all ages, male and female—and such miscellanies frequently include romances within their pages. A number of important books noted for their inclusion of romances (the Auchinleck manuscript, the Lincoln Thornton, the Heege manuscript, etc.) fall into this category and are picked out by Hardman as particularly adapted to young readers.[43] The Lincoln Thornton even shows direct evidence of a pedagogical preoccupation on the part of its readers: on one heavily reader-marked page is "a set of Latin mnemonics," whose utility may be "in helping the reader both to memorize the elements of doctrine and to rehearse the lists of Latin words," which Hardman compares to "a school vocabulary exercise."[44]

The Heege manuscript (National Library of Scotland, MS Advocates 19.3.1) also shows, in its codicology and evidence of use, a distinctively didactic bent. Hardman has found in this manuscript strong evidence for a booklet construction, the production of a series of standalone units that could be used simultaneously by different members of a family or household.[45] Mary Shaner further proposed that the editing of the Heege manuscript's romances, an "adaptation," in Hardman's words, "to suit the prearranged plan of the booklets,"[46] was in service of an educational program, evidenced by the pairing of each romance with a didactic text, and specifically directed toward the suitable entertainment and, even more important, *education* of young boys.[47] For Shaner, the inclusion of such didactic texts makes clear the booklets' direction not, as the traditional view of a romance audience would hold, toward a broad audience encompassing a large range of readers but specifically to children and children alone: the short courtesy-manual companion pieces would have held little charm for adults, fully educated and not in need of such instruction.[48] If Hardman finds Shaner's claims of an exclusively juvenile audience for the Heege romances, over and above similar examples of the genre, to perhaps overreach, such conservatism only strengthens the basic argument. Romances could be considered appropriate for the young, even without undergoing a transformation into a specifically "children's literature," and the Heege manuscript booklets, by their physical form and inclusion of didactic texts, as well as by the moral exemplarity of their romances, were, Hardman concurs, "prepared for children to read."[49]

The case of the Heege manuscript and its booklets is particularly intriguing, because, in Hardman's view, its very production—as well as its later use—provides a model for elementary education as carried out in a noble household. Richard Heege, she hypothesizes, may have been a professional educator or tutor in such a household, and those portions of the manuscript not in his hand may well be the handiwork of his students, exercises in writing carried out with the additional purpose of creating a book of suitable texts that could be used by future pupils, both male and female.[50] And Lambeth Palace 491 resembles the Heege manuscript in many ways. The didactic materials Heege chooses are of a type singled out also by Orme as directed particularly toward children. Within this genre, Orme affords special notice to one text "oriented towards adolescent males," the "well-known fifteenth-century treatise on hunting, the so-called *Tristram* ascribed to Dame Julian Barnes," the same hunting treatise that appears immediately after the *Awntyrs off Arthure* in Lambeth 491.[51] And in an even more striking parallel between the circumstances of use between the Heege and Lambeth manuscripts, Hardman cites the copying of some rudimentary epistles, suitable to a basic instruction in the epistolary art.[52]

With these considerations in mind, then, Lambeth 491's texts begin gradually to emerge in a slightly different light from that implied by Guddat-Figge's "private collector interested in history." We may, from the outset, be emboldened to take very seriously indeed the opening lines of the "Boke of Huntyng," framing the poem as words of instruction from a mother to her son:

> My dere sone, wher so ȝe fare by frith or by fell,
> Takith good heed how Trystram wold tell
> How many man*ere* bestis of venery ther were.
> Lystenith ȝe to ȝo*ur* dame and y shal ȝow lere.[53]

The *Brut* chronicle, for its part, is now legible as a text of educational value, instilling its young readers with a knowledge of English history. And the *Three Kings of Cologne* and the *Siege of Jerusalem* may work in similar ways, enriching the study of history with connections to a larger world history outside England and, particularly in the case of the *Siege*, embellishing that history with a poetic presentation and a relish for depictions of dramatic violence.

As for the *Awntyrs off Arthure*, while the broad strokes and bashing together of knights at the tournament in the romance's second half may seem more typical romance fare, the enigmatic first half may now appear more directly to the point. Once again, we find instruction from a parent to a child—this time the moral admonitions and advice offered by the ghost of Guinevere's deceased mother to her adult daughter, spoken with the wisdom of one now in the grave, fully cognizant of the dire eternal consequences for the queen's worldly vanity and sins of the flesh. Felicity Riddy has seen in the household miscellany, and in particular the romances these miscellanies contain, a program of instruction in "Good manners, right conduct and the claims of the next world."[54] In particular, she quotes Caxton's prologue to *Blanchardyn and Eglantine*, a manifesto well thumbed by scholars plumbing the relationship between romance and the didactic:

> in my Iugement / it is as requesyte other whyle to rede in Auncyent hystoryes of noble fayttes & valiau*n*t actes of armes & warre, whiche haue ben achyeued in olde tyme of many noble prynces, lordes, & knyghtes / as wel for to see & knowe their walyau*n*tnes for to stande in the specyal grace & loue of their ladyes, And in lykewyse for gentyl yonge ladyes & damoysellys, for to lerne to be stedfaste & constau*n*t in their parte. . . . As it is to occupye theym and studye ouer moche in bokes of contemplacion[55]

"Auncyent hystoryes" and books of romance are tools of moral instruction just as important as the "bokes of contemplacion" that some, including "yong noble gentylmen & wymme*n*,"[56] as well as "yonge ladyes & damoysellys," may "studye ouer moche." The moral lessons of Guinevere's mother in the *Awntyrs*, as well as her warning of the eternal consequences of immoral behavior, should not, if the romance is read as Caxton advises for *Blanchardyn*, be taken as an empty literary exercise. Rather, it speaks directly to the moral education of the book's projected young readers.

If Lambeth 491 is part of an extended instructional program for the young, then it is the instructional value of these texts that directed their selection, both chronicle and romance alike. The *Awntyrs off Arthure*, however else it might be read in other contexts,[57] emerges here as morally instructive, calling on the lessons of the past for present education. Guinevere's mother, with the wisdom of experience, presents herself to her daughter as negative exemplar. If we know from other texts that Guinevere does not follow her mother's advice, then the readers, a new generation of students, may find in the queen a new negative exemplar. Guinevere's mother may perhaps model the appropriate spirit in which to take the episodes of the chronicle: her return from the grave gives her the opportunity to speak in words the moral lessons that the chronicle's characters may only express through their actions. Meanwhile, the pageantry and rough violence of the romance's second half, the *briȝt brondes* and *byrnies be-bled*, along with the poetic trappings of verse itself, contribute to the framing of such moral didacticism within an attractive and entertaining package.

My object here is not to pigeonhole the *Awntyrs off Arthure*, or any of Lambeth 491's other texts, as "children's literature": to do so would be to constrict rather than expand our appreciation of their audience. But the assumption of a purely adult readership—an assumption that, in the absence of extensive evidence for children's reading habits, has frequently been made for medieval romance—leaves unexplored an important dimension of the relationships among history, romance, and the morally didactic. In its early-fifteenth-century context, the *Awntyrs*, with its extended battle scene splashed liberally in a primary color of red, perhaps joins the "lower end of the romance-market," a "popular literature" so difficult to retrieve because frequently ephemeral in its orality.[58] Or we may find in its association with a prose text like the *Brut*, unwieldy for oral performance, hints too of the influence of the same Burgundian-style de-versifying ("*dérimage*") and de-oralizing that Pearsall identifies in Malory's *Morte Darthur*.[59] But the relationship between the oral and the written is all the more deeply implicated in the presence of an audience itself inhabiting a no-man's-land of more than functional but still incomplete literacy: those learning to write, still actively pursuing an education not just in literature, but in *letters*. Moreover, "popular romance" bears reexamination in the terms of an audience unsophisticated not by nature but by age, and hungry for the spoonful of sugar to sweeten a moral or historical lesson chosen for—not by—them by an interested parent or educator. If the young readers of Lambeth 491 read the manuscript for the lessons of history, they were not, for all that, required to neglect history's romance.

NOTES

1. To name but a few examples, see Derek Pearsall, "The English Romance in the Fifteenth Century," *Essays and Studies*, n.s., 29 (1976): 56–83; "The Development of Middle English Romance," in *Studies in Medieval English Romances: Some New Approaches*, ed. Derek Brewer (Cambridge: D. S. Brewer, 1988), 11–35; "The *Canterbury Tales* and London Club Culture," in *Chaucer and the City*, ed. Ardis Butterfield, Chaucer Studies 37 (Cambridge: D. S. Brewer, 2006), 95–108.

2. Derek Pearsall, "Middle English Romance and Its Audiences," in *Historical and Editorial Studies in Medieval and Early Modern English for Johan Gerritsen*, ed. Mary-Jo Arn, Hanneke Wirtjes, and Hans Jansen (Groningen: Wolters-Noordhoff, 1985), 37.

3. Ibid., 45.

4. Friedrich W. D. Brie, ed., *The Brut or The Chronicles of England: Edited from MS. Rawl. B171, Bodleian Library*, 2 vols., EETS, o.s., 131, 136 (London: Oxford University Press, 1906).

5. Gisela Guddat-Figge, *Catalogue of Manuscripts Containing Middle English Romances*, Münchener Universitäts-Schriften 4 (Munich: Wilhelm Fink Verlag, 1976), 227. Ralph Hanna identifies them more specifically as "fifteenth-century owners." Ralph Hanna, "The Scribe of Huntington HM 114," *Studies in Bibliography* 42 (1989): 123. For other catalog descriptions of this manuscript, see Lister Matheson, *The Prose* Brut*: The Development of a Middle English Chronicle*, Medieval and Renaissance Texts and Studies 180 (Tempe, AZ: Medieval and Renaissance Texts and Studies, 1998), 91–92; and M. R. James, *A Descriptive Catalogue of the Manuscripts in the Library of Lambeth Palace: The Medieval Manuscripts* (Cambridge: Cambridge University Press, 1932), 681–84.

6. Ralph Hanna and David Lawton, eds., *The Siege of Jerusalem*, EETS, o.s., 320 (Oxford: Oxford University Press, 2003). See also J. R. Hulbert, "The Text of *The Siege of Jerusalem*," *Studies in Philology* 28, no. 4 (1931): 602–12.

7. Frank Schaer, ed., *The Three Kings of Cologne: Edited from London, Lambeth Palace MS 491*, Middle English Texts 31 (Heidelberg: C. Winter, 2000).

8. Robert Gates, ed., *The Awntyrs off Arthure at the Terne Wathelyne: A Critical Edition* (Philadelphia: University of Pennsylvania Press, 1969).

9. Arne Zettersten, "The Lambeth Manuscript of the *Boke of Huntyng*," *Neuphilologische Mitteilungen* 70 (1969): 106–21. See *IMEV* 4064.

10. Linne R. Mooney and Estelle Stubbs, *Scribes and the City: London Guildhall Clerks and the Dissemination of Middle English Literature, 1375–1425* (York: York Medieval Press, 2013), esp. chap. 2.

11. Guddat-Figge, *Catalogue*, 227.

12. Mooney and Stubbs argue that the manuscript was unbound and in Osbarn's possession for an extended period, perhaps until his death, and that its intended purpose (along with that of Huntington HM 114) was as a repository of exemplars "for [Osbarn's] own use, or for use by the community of clerks at the Guildhall"; *Scribes and the City*, 37. As Mooney and Stubbs admit, however, identifying the scribe as Osbarn "raises more questions than it answers with respect to the quality of the texts he copied," as well as to why, if he intended these manuscripts as models for future copying, he was not more careful to ascertain that they were indeed the best texts available (35).

13. No studies have been done of children's drawing in the Middle Ages, but this figure is similar to ones appearing in studies of modern children across

cultures. The young artist has progressed beyond the "tadpole" stage, where the figure is represented as a large, torsoless head, but the drawing still exhibits "segmentation" rather than the "contouring" usually developed by age seven, and while its identifiable details include eyes, nose, mouth, neck, and simple lines for arms, flourishes like hair, ears, hands, and fingers and are absent; Maureen V. Cox, *Children's Drawings of the Human Figure*, Essays in Developmental Psychology (Hove, Sussex: Lawrence Erlbaum Associates, 1993), 52. See also Angela Anning and Kathy Ring, *Making Sense of Children's Drawings* (Maidenhead, Berkshire: Open University Press, 2004), 23.

14. As Julia Boffey and Carol Meale outline, Pattsalls, many of them named Thomas and John, abound in late-fifteenth- and especially early-sixteenth-century records, often in connection with properties in London and Essex; "Selecting the Text: Rawlinson C.86 and Some Other Books for London Readers," in *Regionalism in Late Medieval Manuscripts and Texts: Essays Celebrating the Publication of "A Linguistic Atlas of Late Medieval English,"* ed. Felicity Riddy, York Manuscripts Conferences Proceedings 2 (Cambridge: D. S. Brewer, 1991), 162 n. 63. It is not possible to identify any of these Thomases or Johns definitively with the Lambeth 491 scribblers, but the dates of these documents, in the 1520s and beyond, could suggest that these men are the sons and nephews of the Lambeth Pattsalls—or that the Lambeth writers were fairly young when making their late-fifteenth-century signatures.

15. Compare, however, fol. 109v, where the name "Rycharde Persey" is written in a very different, even decorative script.

16. Some examples include "At my be genynyg God be my" (fol. 38v), "God vs sped" (fol. 43r), "At oure begynnyng G[o]d vs speed / In grace and vertuis" (fol. 130r), "Ihesus be me sped in grace & | & wert uto p*ro*ced" (fol. 162v), and "Ihon*e* | Ihesus be my sped [in] G[race] (fol. 167r).

17. Linne R. Mooney et. al., The *DIMEV*: An Open-Access, Digital Edition of the *Index of Middle English Verse*, no. 709, www.dimev.net/record.php?recID=709; *IMEV* 430.5.

18. John Boys, *An Exposition of the Dominical Epistles and Gospels, Vsed in our English Liturgie, Throughout the Whole Yeere* (London: Edward Griffin for William Aspley, 1615), 203 (italics in original).

19. Nicholas Orme, *Education and Society in Medieval and Renaissance England* (London: Hambledon Press, 1989), 123–51.

20. Ibid., 134. Compare also British Library, Harley MS 4733, which bears the inscription of John Pynnyngton, master of the King's School in Worcester in 1487: "Master John Penyngton schole master of Worcestur ys possessed of thys booke" (fol. 2v; for John Pynnyngton, see Alec MacDonald, *A History of the King's School Worcester* [London: Ernest Benn, 1936], 16). Sandwiched between Cato's *Distichs* (in both Latin and Benedict Burgh's English translation) and the historical romance *The Destruction of Jerusalem* is the verse "Proverbs of

Old Philosophers" with the incipit "The wyse man in his boke hat thys seying | that the begynnyng of good lyvyng | Over all thyng ys god to drede | And hym to wurship with all oure spede" (fol. 30r; see *IMEV* 3501).

21. John Trevisa, *On the Properties of Things: John Trevisa's Translation of "Bartholomaeus Anglicus De Proprietatibus Rerum": A Critical Text*, ed. M. C. Seymour, vol. 1 (Oxford: Clarendon Press, 1975), 40.4–12. My profound thanks to Eleanor Pettus for her sharp eye in spotting this adaptation of the "In my beginning" incipit.

22. See Nicholas Orme, "Children and Literature in Medieval England," *Medium Aevum* 68, no. 2 (1999): 226.

23. Ibid.

24. Sharon L. Jansen and Kathleen H. Jordan, eds., *The Welles Anthology: MS. Rawlinson C. 813: A Critical Edition*, Medieval and Renaissance Texts and Studies 75 (Binghamton, NY: Medieval and Renaissance Texts and Studies, 1991), 106.1–107.4; *IMEV* 430.

25. Frederick J. Furnivall, ed., *Queene Elizabethes Achademy*, EETS, e.s., 8 (London: Trübner, 1869), 68–70; *IMEV* 432.

26. Furnivall, *Queene Elizabethes Achademy*, 69.56.

27. Jansen and Jordan, *Welles Anthology*, 107.5–8.

28. Furnivall, *Queene Elizabethes Achademy*, 69.56–70.59.

29. A variant of *IMEV* 1151, where the standard form is given as "He that in youth no virtue used / In age all honor him refused." Even in the list of manuscript witnesses cited there, however, eccentric versions appear. One variant of the verse, in London, British Library, Royal MS 17 D. xviii, fol. 99v, was written in a sixteenth-century hand in the lower margin of one of the final pages of a copy of Hoccleve's *Regiment of Princes*. The circumstances behind its addition are not entirely clear, but roughly contemporary inscriptions on the next page (fol. 100v) include "hartely commende me vnto" and "Ryght worshyfull" (apparently epistolary fragments), as well as a Latin translation of the first two lines of Homer's *Odyssey*.

30. See Proverbs 9:10 and Psalms 110:10.

31. Thomas Wright and James O. Halliwell, *Reliquiae Antiquae: Scraps from Ancient Manuscripts, Illustrating Chiefly Early English Literature and the English Language* (London: John Russell Smith, 1845), 92.1–4.

32. Bennett A. Brockman, "The Juvenile Audiences of Sir Orfeo," *Children's Literature Association Quarterly* 10, no. 1 (1985): 18–20.

33. See Hans Walther, *Carmina Medii Aevi Posterioris Latina II: Proverbia Sententiaeque Latinitas Medii Aevi: Lateinische Sprichwörter und Sentenzen des Mittelalters in Alphabetischer Anordnung* (Göttingen: Vandenhoeck and Ruprecht, 1963), 4893; and J. Wegeler, *Philosophia Patrum Versibus Praesertim Leoninis, Rhythmis Germanicis Adiectis, Iuventuti Studiosae Hilariter Tradita* (Koblenz: R. F. Hergt, 1869), 211.

34. "Perhaps to Thomas Howes: Draft 1462, 02, 09?," in *Paston Letters and Papers of the Fifteenth Century: Part I*, ed. Norman Davis (Oxford: Clarendon Press, 1971), 104.

35. "William Harleston to Thomas Stonor [1474 or earlier]," in *The Stonor Letters and Papers, 1290–1483*, ed. Charles Lethbridge Kingford (London: Offices of the Royal Historical Society, 1919), 140 (no. 135).

36. From the eleventh century on, the most popular doctrine on letters prescribed an ideal epistle of five major phases: "the *salutatio*, or formal greeting," "the *captatio benevolentiae*, or introduction proper in which goodwill was sought," the "*narratio* . . . explaining background," the "*petitio*," or petition, laying out the request that is presumed to be the business of the letter, and the "*conclusio*," or conclusion. James J. Murphy, "Introduction: The Medieval Background," in *Three Medieval Rhetorical Acts*, ed. James J. Murphy (Berkeley: University of California Press, 1971), xvi.

37. See Malcolm Richardson, "The Fading Influence of the Medieval *Ars Dictaminis* in England after 1400," *Rhetorica* 19, no. 2 (2001): 225–47.

38. Ibid., 230.

39. Ibid., 231. Richardson has found this letter, dating to the 1440s, in London, Public Record Office, Ancient Correspondence, *SC* 1/44, no. 29.

40. Malcolm Richardson, "The *Ars Dictaminis*, the Formulary, and Medieval Epistolary Practice," in *Letter-Writing Manuals and Instruction from Antiquity to the Present: Historical and Bibliographic Studies*, ed. Carol Poster and Linda C. Mitchell (Columbia: University of South Carolina Press, 2007), 62. Richardson has found this letter, "probably" dating to the 1430s, in London, Public Record Office, Ancient Correspondence, *SC* 1/44, no. 33.

41. Orme, "Children and Literature," 226.

42. Ibid., 227. Orme quotes London, British Library, Harley MS 2398, fol. 94v.

43. See especially Phillipa Hardman's "Popular Romances and Young Readers," in *A Companion to Medieval Popular Romance*, ed. Raluca L. Radulescu and Cory J. Rushton, Studies in Medieval Romance 10 (Cambridge: D. S. Brewer, 2009), 150–64; "'This Litel Child, His Litel Book': Narratives for Children in Late-Fifteenth-Century England," *Journal of the Early Book Society* 7 (2004): 51–66; and introduction to *The Heege Manuscript: A Facsimile of National Library of Scotland MS Advocates 19.3.1*, Leeds Texts and Monographs, n.s., 16 (Leeds: Leeds Studies in English, 2000).

44. Phillipa Hardman, "Domestic Learning and Teaching: Investigating Evidence for the Role of 'Household Miscellanies' in Late-Medieval England," in *Women and Writing c. 1340–c.1650: The Domestication of Print Culture*, ed. Anne Lawrence-Mathers and Phillipa Hardman (York: York Medieval Press, 2010), 23.

45. Philippa Hardman, "A Mediaeval 'Library *In Parvo*,'" *Medium Aevum* 47 (1978): 262–73; and Hardman, introduction to *The Heege Manuscript*.

46. Hardman, "'Library *In Parvo*,'" 267.

47. Mary E. Shaner, "Instruction and Delight: Medieval Romances as Children's Literature," *Poetics Today* 13, no. 1 (1992): 5–15.

48. Ibid., 9.

49. Hardman, "'This Litel Child,'" 59.

50. Hardman, introduction to *The Heege Manuscript*.

51. Orme, "Children and Literature," 227.

52. "'Right reue*re*nt and Worshipfull master I recum*m*end me unto you as mekely as I can desiryng more hartely / Most enterly and Wellbelouyd Fader and Moder I recu*m*mend / Ryghtt Reverantt And Wyrshipfull' (fol. 202v)"; Hardman, introduction to *The Heege Manuscript*, 42.

53. Zettersten, "The Lambeth Manuscript of the *Boke of Huntyng*," 114.

54. Felicity Riddy, *Sir Thomas Malory*, Medieval and Renaissance Authors 9 (Leiden: Brill, 1987), 23.

55. Leon Kellner, ed., *Caxton's Blanchardyn and Eglantine*, EETS, o.s., 58 (London: Trübner, 1890), 1.13–22.

56. Ibid., 1.11–12.

57. Rosamund Allen, for example, identifies the *Awntyrs* as originating within a circle of patronage around the Neville family and argues for a reading of the ghost of Guinevere's mother not as a maternal instructress but as a warning of the dangers of insufficient provision for the soul, perhaps with specific reference to the adultery of Joan Neville's parents, Catherine Swynford and John of Gaunt. Rosamund Allen, "Place-Names in *The Awntyrs Off Arthure*: Corruption, Conjecture, Coincidence," in *Arthurian Studies in Honour of P. J. C. Field*, ed. Bonnie Wheeler, Arthurian Studies 57 (Cambridge: D. S. Brewer, 2004), 193–95.

58. Pearsall, "Middle English Romance and Its Audiences," 42.

59. Pearsall, "The English Romance in the Fifteenth Century," 76.

CHAPTER 16

Langland in the Early Modern Household

Piers Plowman in Oxford, Bodleian Library MS Digby 145, and Its Scribe-Annotator Dialogues

Karrie Fuller

Derek Pearsall's inspiriting promotion of manuscript studies permeates his oeuvre and scholarly activity, from his organization of manuscript-themed conferences at York and at Harvard to numerous, similarly themed lectures presented on both sides of the Atlantic. Among the many sentiments expressed by Pearsall in support of this burgeoning discipline, I can only hope to pick up on two: first, that manuscript marginalia by scribes and early readers "constitutes an attempt to govern interpretative activity;"[1] and second, that "there are no texts that were not embedded in the machinery of their production."[2] In the case of the second statement, it is the circumstances of production and the relationship of the manuscript producers with the text produced that is the focus of this essay. Using a single manuscript example and current methodologies for examining textual reception, I hope to contribute one more piece to the "large jigsaw" of manuscript studies that began to take a more concrete shape at Pearsall's first "New Directions in Later Medieval Manuscript Studies" conference over a decade ago.[3]

The manuscript in question, Oxford, Bodleian Library MS Digby 145, contains a highly personalized version of William Langland's *Piers Plowman*, an amalgamation of the A and C texts copied by its owner, Sir Adrian Fortescue, in 1532.[4] Why Adrian, a professed Catholic, courtier to Henry VIII, and distant relative of Anne Boleyn, produced his own household copy remains a conundrum due to the complexity of his conflicting religious and political affiliations. By the time he copied *Piers*, he had already served for several years as a courtier, as a justice of the peace in Oxfordshire, and as a knight in the king's wars against France.[5] This manuscript's production also coincides with his remarriage to Anne Rede after the death of his first wife, Anne Stonor. Over the course of multiple readings during a tumultuous period of his life, he, with the help of his new wife, filled the margins of his manuscript with copious annotations.[6] In the years coinciding with these readings, Adrian lost his homestead at Stonor Park in a prolonged lawsuit instigated by his first wife's relatives and was arrested because of his familial ties to the earl of Kildare, a rebel against the king. As both Richard Rex and Thorlac Turville-Petre point out, his complicated Catholic background and political associations, especially at the time of Henry's excommunication, created a situation in which his divided allegiances might have led to the unspecified act of treason that caused Henry to imprison and execute him in 1539.[7] Although the extent to which Adrian's major life experiences informed his reading of *Piers* cannot be determined with certainty, his complex and fluctuating allegiances suggest a great deal about his social and theological interest in Langland.

Adrian's unique version of *Piers* shows a fair amount of scribal editorialization and, therefore, involvement with the text as he copies it out. In the earlier sections of the poem, he overlays parts of his C-text exemplar onto his A text and supplements it throughout with extensive marginalia and what James Weldon describes as " 'structural' decoration," which includes any scribal practices contributing to the manuscript's *ordinatio*.[8] In this way, Adrian creates an individualized text available to a small circle of readers in his household. However, he limits his editorial choices in certain ways: as George Russell notes, Adrian makes no "attempt to renovate the lexis and syntax" for the early modern reader, nor does he make "any detectable attempt to intervene or censor" the more controversial parts of the poem.[9] To this latter point I would add, based on his annotations, that he sometimes chooses potentially contentious passages to highlight, such as the Tearing of the Pardon scene.[10] Throughout the first half of the poem, Adrian marks passages where religious and political counsel either succeed or blatantly fail, or where much-needed counsel remains conspicuously absent.[11] Those moments when he identifies spiritual and administrative cracks in Langland's carefully orchestrated representations of society, such as Hunger's morally questionable attempts to reorganize Piers's disintegrating community, reveal Adrian's awareness of the fragility of religious and social order.[12] He repeatedly acknowledges the impending threat of sin, moral degeneracy, and poor counsel, perhaps seeing a series of arguments in *Piers* that reinforce and justify his moral positions in a turbulent political climate overseen by a capricious monarch.[13] These annotations early in the text set the tone for how his interests, especially his theological ones, develop over the course of the poem until its apocalyptic ending with the dissolution of Holy Church's community.

As *Piers* progresses, the scribe's interests continue to range from the highly political or social to the deeply religious, and patterns revealing the diversity of his concerns begin to manifest as early as the Prologue and evolve throughout the narrative. Friars, theological concepts such as "charite," old age, and marriage all make repeat appearances, and Digby 145's other annotators, Anne and the slightly later, unidentified "Hand B," share some of the responsibility for the manuscript's emphasis on these and related topics.[14] Anne, as mentioned above, worked alongside her husband and contributed at least five annotations in the form of a distinctive manicule, two of which she signs in Latin.[15] Hand B, less consistent but more argumentative than Adrian, shows up at irregular intervals throughout *Piers*. Despite his anonymity, readers of Digby 145 can ascertain a great deal from his interpretive and emotional annotations about his attitudes toward Langland, especially in relation to the pope and the Antichrist. Although Adrian's annotations establish a foundation for how the other two annotators approach the text, what makes Digby 145 unique among *Piers* manuscripts is the interactions and relationships between the annotators, who compose their responses not only to Langland, but to each other as they converse among themselves to an unprecedented extent.[16]

Anne's conversation with Adrian occurs on somewhat uncertain terms because she marks different passages than her husband, but their joint efforts at highlighting, for example, friars and marriage-related issues are more than a chance occurrence. Hand B's more pronounced responses answer directly to Adrian's work as he regularly finishes or expands Adrian's annotations, repeats them in the opposite margin as in agreement, or, by the end of the poem, reacts against them. He becomes inflamed at the end of *Piers* as he divulges some theological and potentially Protestant, or proto-Protestant, sentiments that diverge from Adrian's neutral and more levelheaded readings in later passūs. Eventually, when Elde flies over the dreamer's head and causes him impotence, he too enters the marginal conversation about marriage, rejecting the wife's discontent over her husband's condition and Adrian's unbiased acknowledgment of it.[17] The wider trajectory of the relationship between Adrian and Hand B has, until now, been left unexamined because Marie-Claire Uhart's edition of Digby 145's annotations identifies Hand B only in the last few passūs of the poem, leaving his earlier marginalia labeled as Adrian's.[18] As a result, I argue that Hand B's dialogue with Adrian develops over the course of the poem, shifting from a mostly peaceful exchange to total disagreement. As this exchange progresses, Hand B expresses a level of outrage at the pope characteristic of a reform-minded sixteenth-century reader reacting against the church's hierarchical infrastructure and deep-seated corruption. He applies Langland's reformist agenda in a nonreformation text to fit his own early modern initiatives and crosses a line that Adrian's annotations never approach even when he marks anticlerical material. When the institution of marriage comes under discussion at the end of this exchange, Hand B, aware or not, participates in what feels like a personal husband-wife conversation, challenging their commentary with his own humorous but somewhat uncomfortable contribution.

Although initially peaceful, Hand B's interactions with Adrian's terse responses evolve as he becomes agitated about the pope. The progression of their relationship emerges most clearly in three major topics that appear in the final third of the poem: *caritas*, the Antichrist, and old age.[19] By the time *caritas* becomes a dominant theme in *Piers*, Hand B works in accordance with Adrian's running apparatus. In Passus XVI, for example, when *Liberum Arbitrium*, or Free Will, defines the concept of charity at Will's request, the words *charite*, written in the vernacular by Adrian, and *caritas*, written in its Latin form by Hand B, show up nine times over the space of two folios alongside a variety of manicules, brackets, and other related short notes. While both annotators maintain their interest in charity at regular intervals throughout the manuscript, this dialogue between Will and *Liberum Arbitrium* receives the longest and most sustained treatment, even more than the description of the tree of charity. This section defines charity when *Liberum Arbitrium* tells Will,

"Charite is a childishe thyng, as Holy Churche witnesseth—
Nisi efficiamini sicut parvuli—
As proud of a peny as of a pounde of golde,
And as glad of a goune of a gray russet
As of a cote of cammaca or of clene scarlet.
He is glad with alle glade, as gurles þat lawhen alle,
And sory when he seth men sory—as thow seest childerne
Lawhe þer men lawheth and loure þer oþere louren."
(C.16.296–302; fol. 84r)[20]

The passage continues to describe the childlike qualities that characterize this concept: trusting, honest, and humble in the face of adversity. Their conversation then proceeds with an account of the routine acts of piety, care of the poor, and preaching required of charitable behavior. A list of people with whom charity does and does not keep company concludes this discussion, echoing a similar list for the character False at the conclusion of the Mede episode. What makes this particular definition of charity stand out to these readers, as we will see, is the way it reconfigures the traditional biblical description of charity in 1 Corinthians 13 by combining it with a seemingly unrelated New Testament passage found in Matthew 18.

Much of the marginalia corresponding to these lines are limited to one to three words and come across as what Uhart labels "subject guides" to the events and themes playing out in the narrative.[21] These types of short notations also exemplify the kind that lead David Benson and Joshua Eyler to call attention to "the difficulty in interpreting manuscript evidence that is almost always scanty and terse: if, for example, a passage has a nota bene in the margin, how can we know what it was that the writer found so notable?"[22] Their warning about the limits imposed on scholars trying to use this evidence to understand early readerships of *Piers* should always inform our critical reconstructions of these reading communities. At the same time, however, even Uhart acknowledges in her analysis of Digby 145's marginalia that the annotators chose specific themes, characters, and events to highlight, and, according to a few of her own examples, these one-word responses can function interpretively and comment on Langland in a decisive if often vague manner.[23] It should be noted that Benson works more heavily on B-text copies of *Piers*, which tend to provide terser and fewer annotations than the more fulsome and provocative examples found in many

C-text manuscripts.[24] Following a pattern more in line with annotated C texts, Digby 145's annotations, in effect, "govern interpretive activity," according to Pearsall's more general formulation.[25] In addition to indicating what they care about as readers, Adrian's and Hand B's marking of Passus XVI's definition of charity draws the reader's eye through a text providing a unique definition that, in itself, offers up further clues about these readers' interests.

The scribes' agreement about charity becomes apparent not only in the sheer number of times they write this word in the margins but also in their combined efforts to point out where Langland offers his most precise definition. The annotators sandwich the line cited above in which *Liberum Arbitrium* introduces charity as a "childish thyng" between the word *charite* in the left-hand margin by Adrian and the phrase *caritas parvulus est* by Hand B on the right-hand side of the page.[26] Adrian's one-word notation echoes the first word of this line and the last word of the previous line, functioning as a marginal guide to the subject of this dialogue and emphasizing the concept's importance. Hand B's phrase brings the reader's focus to the Latin tag that inspires Langland's interpretation of charity, that is, his citation of Matthew 18:3, "*Nisi efficiamini sicut parvuli, etc.*"[27] Matthew 18 does not mention *caritas*, but its message to assume the humility of a child and to remove all barriers to salvation for anyone who goes astray supplies Langland with the material to supplement the biblical definition of *caritas* in 1 Corinthians 13, a passage Will cites twice right before *Liberum Arbitrium* speaks.[28] This annotation borrows the adjective *parvulus* from the Latin tag and translates Langland's Middle English *charite* into *caritas*, imitating in Latin what Langland does in the vernacular when he connects charity with the salvific childish qualities of the Matthew 18 verse he quotes in the next line. Thus Hand B's comment brings Langland's discussion of the Pauline version of charity and the supplemental passage from Matthew together in a single phrase, *caritas parvulus est*, connecting the various dimensions of charity at play in the poem while reinforcing Adrian's vernacular, one-word annotation by setting its Latin equivalent beside it for the reader to consider.

Hand B, then, expresses a clear interest in the conflation of two New Testament passages that recast the traditional biblical definition of charity in new terms. Adrian's less interpretive response calls attention to charity on a more topical level that nevertheless brings this unique definition into focus as a response to an issue raised by Will, who cannot find the charity of 1 Corinthians among "clerk noþer lewed" or religious in London (C.16.290; fol. 83v). The particularity of the definition stems from Will's inability to observe examples of charity in action. *Liberum Arbitrium* never quite resolves this problem, but his reconfiguration of 1 Corinthians with the quality of childishness promoted in Matthew 18 infuses Will's already established definition with character traits or behaviors associated with children, namely, innocence, humility, guilelessness, and empathy. The condition of childishness that *Liberum Arbitrium* associates with charity depends on neighborliness and a willingness to trust in the care of God.[29] It points to a Father-child relationship in which the child submits wholly to the will of the Father and lives the life of Dowel, a familial image appropriate to this book's household context.[30] In fact, the connection between behavior and works as outward signs of charity might account for the readers' greater interest in this definition than the Passus XVIII description of the tree of charity, which offers a more symbolic and less practical account of the concept.

As the poem progresses from this discussion of charity toward its turbulent apocalyptic conclusion, the number of annotations rapidly multiplies as Adrian and Hand B become at once more vocal and more distinct. Their initial remarks on the Antichrist remain in sync, at least on the surface, when, in Passus XXI, Grace prophesies the Antichrist's arrival and the two scribes once again sandwich the text with their response, making its impact on the reader stronger. Adrian writes the single word "antecriste," while Hand B writes "Nota the Antechrist" next to "For Auntecrist and hise al the world shal greue, / And acombre þe, Concscience, bote yf Crist the helpe" (C.21.220–21; fol. 117v). Hand B also sees fit to expand some of Adrian's notes in this section, adding, for example, the phrase "Then pryde be" to Adrian's note, "the pope and the cardenalles," a few lines down.[31] The two readers notice the Antichrist and the effect he has on the clergy, including the pope, but Adrian's notes never take this connection any further.[32] Hand B, in contrast, becomes incensed as he continues reading Langland's commentary on the pope and conflates the pontiff and the Antichrist outright. When Langland criticizes the pope in a passage alluding to the papal schism, Hand B exclaims, "O Very Antichrist," in larger than average letters.[33] A vicar, the speaker at this point in the narrative, complains of murder among Christian brethren:

And God [the Pope amende], þat pileth Holi Churche,
And claymeth bifore þe Kynge to be kepare ouer Cristene,
And counteth nat thow Cristene be culde and yrobbed,
And fynde folke to fihte and Cristene bloed to spille
Aȝen þe Olde Lawe and þe Newe Lawe, as Luk bereth witnesse.
(C.21.445–49; fol. 121v)

Hand B's interpretive annotation here suggests more than a simple disgust at papal behavior. Casting the pope as the greatest of apocalyptic evils, Hand B identifies him not just as a key player in the apocalypse, but as the face and heart of the apocalypse itself, blurring lines Adrian never approaches. To what extent Hand B acknowledges the schismatic context of Langland's remark remains unclear, but his strong reaction conveys an unmistakable sense of the pope's negative disposition in the reader's mind. His reaction relates quite naturally to the chaotic sixteenth-century religious climate in which reformist and Protestant movements pick up steam, rejecting the same kinds of extreme corruption in papal circles that Langland reiterates in his last few passūs. The instability of the papal seat during the schism would, moreover, resonate with both Adrian and Hand B in a period when the seat of religious authority in England oscillated between Rome and the English monarch until Henry's final break with Catholicism and supersession over the English Church. This situation created serious problems for those who wished to remain loyal to Rome, such as Thomas More and, possibly, Adrian himself, but not necessarily for Hand B, who may have been writing his responses after the dissolution and with no obligation to adhere to papal law.

Hand B's emotional, reformist commentary reappears in Passus XXII as he repeats the pope-Antichrist conflation that separates him from Adrian. He identifies the Antichrist, after his official arrival in the narrative, as "puppa [*sic*]" next to the line, "And a false fende Auntecrist ouer all folk regnede" (C.22.64; fol. 124r). Here the poem describes the Antichrist's burgeoning number of followers, including friars and religious. This passage, depicting the Antichrist in his leadership capacity, lends itself almost naturally to Hand B's interpretation since the Antichrist's power extends across Christendom and includes the submission of kings to his will. He represents a leader with the long reach of the pope's worldly jurisdiction. Thus, no matter what distinctions Langland, or Adrian, makes between the pope and the Antichrist, Hand B has solidified them into one entity in his mind, one figure wreaking havoc and catastrophe the world over. These antipapal sentiments, especially this latter one, transform the notion Langland develops in Passus XXI of Piers the Plowman as the inheritor of Rome into its antithesis. It replaces Piers, the Christlike figure whose association with the papal seat allows him to establish the church, with the Antichrist, whose papal authority, in the mind of Hand B, destroys the church from the same seat of power that helped to create it. Thus the distinction between the Antichrist and the corrupt pope, which Langland maintains for the most part even at his most condemnatory moments and which Adrian never challenges, blurs with the addition of one reader's distressed reaction to the pope, who he interprets as the harbinger of the apocalypse and instigator of an eschatological crisis.[34]

Contrary to Uhart's reading, however, Hand B's antipapal annotations betray no clear sign of misinterpretation on his part. While he does indeed resist the distinctions made by Langland and Adrian, his emotional reactions do not necessarily prohibit "constructive engagement with the poem's fundamental issues" or demonstrate a "limited understanding" of the poem.[35] In fact, Hand B's interest in Piers's barn earlier in the passage suggests that he recognizes Piers's role in the establishment of Holy Church, and he even notes "the barne vnytye" where the poem describes its construction and its synonymous name "Holi Chirche an Englisch" (C.21.330; fol. 119v).[36] That he takes this association between Piers and the foundation of the church to its opposite extreme by conflating the pope with the source of Holy Church's destruction only makes his position more emphatic. He plays here on Langland's ability to encode two opposite meanings in one character or theme the way, for example, Mede comes to simultaneously embody beneficial and detrimental forms of reward and bribery. Langland frequently imbues his characters with variable, shifting, or developing identities, and, in the final two passūs, he also presents a major shift between the founding of Holy Church and its destruction. Thus when Langland identifies the prideful pope as a servant of the Antichrist, Hand B has only to take this turn of events one step further to push a slightly more extreme agenda in what might very well constitute a "constructive engagement" with the poem in the mind of this reader.

Despite his emphatic protestation against the pope, Hand B's religious affiliations cannot be firmly pinned down the way that Adrian's can. His response reflects either a wish for Catholic reform or an alliance with the Protestant movement. Uhart first observes the evidence of Hand B's potential Protestant leanings given his interest in the pope and its relevance to the Reformation occurring in England during the production and early life of this manuscript. She also notes the difficulties of determining when a commentator expresses reform-minded versus Reformation ideas. Her discussion references Hand B's responses to the pope as well as the censoring of Thomas Becket's name elsewhere in Digby 145 to make this argument.[37] Uhart also correctly identifies the difference in tone between Hand B and Adrian in these last two passūs, stating that Hand B "points out chiefly negative aspects of the text in an exclamatory style."[38] However, because she does not know that Hand B shows up throughout the manuscript, she overlooks the earlier interactions between the annotators where they coexist peacefully and sometimes reinforce each other's interpretations, as in the passage on charity. The two scribes permanently part ways in their treatment of the Antichrist after an extended running commentary throughout most of the poem, and this disagreement occurs at a moment in which the stakes are high due to the threat imposed by the apocalyptic attack on Holy Church, which mirrors the deterioration of religious unity in England at the time these scribes recorded their responses.

The case for a Protestant or proto-Protestant reader proves even more complicated given the manuscript's early provenance: this household manuscript stayed in the family after Adrian's death, and many of Adrian's descendants held on to their Catholic backgrounds. This provenance increases the likelihood that Hand B is a relative or close associate of Adrian's; nevertheless, the annotations suggest a reform-minded reader with strong opinions, and no conclusive evidence exists to stymie arguments about Hand B's potentially Protestant leanings. Unlike other well-known sixteenth-century annotators of *Piers* such as Robert Crowley or Stephan Batman, none of the annotators in Digby 145 use any obvious examples of Reformation language. Just as Rex concludes that Adrian "was untouched by the 'reformist' jargon of the Protestant Reformation," Hand B, though more controversial in his responses, also exhibits none of the explicit markers of Protestantism employed by Crowley or Batman around the same time as, or shortly after, Hand B's scribal activity.[39] Because the language of the annotations so often echoes that of the text itself, it could be that Langland influences Hand B's diction more than any outside influences, but this explanation only serves to muddy the water further since it makes any external ideologies Hand B might sustain more difficult to discern. Moreover, as Larry Scanlon points out, even Crowley edited and commented on *Piers* in a way that called attention to "the convergence of Langland's Catholicism with a Protestant virtue," indicating that the Protestant agenda could ally itself with some Catholic polemics even while distancing itself from others.[40] Hand B, then, could be working from any number of reformist perspectives, ranging anywhere from that of a reform-minded Catholic to that of a radical Protestant.

When it comes to the Antichrist, Adrian, who, according to the external documents discussed by Rex, maintained his conventional Catholic piety during his life, recognizes the perils of the corruption that the Antichrist sows among the clergy, but he stops short of making any accusations of his own against anyone in the church's infrastructure. He respects the boundaries set in place by church authorities, the same boundaries Hand B crosses with a vehemence toward the pope that surpasses Langland's criticisms of the church. This difference between them is all the more striking in light of their harmonious relationship beforehand, since it reveals a shifting dynamic that complicates Digby 145's presentation of Langland's work. Interestingly enough, the Antichrist's presence in the poem has the same effect on these readers as it does on Langland's portrayal of Christendom in that it creates disunity and ruptures the peace between them, breaking apart a link established over the course of the poem by their combined efforts to guide future readers through the text. It does so, furthermore, over the sensitive issue of papal authority at a crucial moment in English history when Catholicism and Protestantism vied for power in the hostile political setting of Henry VIII's reign. These readers, like their contemporary Catholic and Protestant counterparts, agree on basic interpretations of the Gospels such as the notions of *caritas* Langland presents, but on questions of temporal governance they no longer share as much common ground, a difference made no less interesting if the Protestant attitudes Hand B's annotations so seductively evince turn out to belong to a reform-minded Catholic.

Rather than resolve the disruption between Adrian and Hand B, the final events in the narrative intensify their divergent responses to Langland. Their liveliest exchange takes place as Conscience sends Elde to combat the sinful behaviors the character Lyf indulges in as the Antichrist wreaks havoc over Holy Church. During the encounter between Elde and Lyf, Elde afflicts the dreamer, who suffers from the physical ailments of old age:

And Elde aftur hym [Lyf], and ouer myn heued ȝede,
And made me balled bifore and baer on þe crowne;
So harde he ȝede ouer myn heued hit wol be sene euere.
"Syre euele ytauȝt Elde," quod Y, "vnhende go with the!
Sennes whanne was þe way ouer menne heuedes?
Haddest thow be hende," quod Y, "thow wost haue asked leue!"
"Ȝe—leue, lordeyne?" quod he, leide on me with age,
And hitte me vnder þe ere—vnnethe may Ich here.
He boffeded me about þe mouthe and beet out my wangteeth,
And gyued me in gowtes—Y may nat go at large.
And of þe wo þat Y was ynne my wyf hadde reuthe,
And wesched wel witterly þat Y were in heuene.
For þe lyme þat she loued me fore, and leef was to fele—
A nyhtes, nameliche, when we naked were—
Y ne myhte in none manere maken hit at here wille,
So Elde and heo hit hadde forbete. (C.22.183–98; fols. 126r–v)

Next to the beginning of this passage, Adrian remarks with a tinge of humor and irony uncharacteristic of his normal annotations, "Nota age and his giftes."[41] Once the dreamer proceeds to complain about his wife's disappointment in his impotence, emphasizing a private household matter, Adrian inserts "Nota þe wyfe." Hand B, however, responds to this second remark with two comments of his own, possibly extending the joke, but with a more interpretive tone.[42] First, he writes underneath Adrian's note in the bottom margin of the page, "ye but nota for what cause"; then he continues on the top of the next folio in the upper margin with "the wief is woo but why."[43] Although a humorous scribal interaction, Hand B's interpretation simultaneously rejects Adrian's nonargumentative reaction to a funny scene and the wife's disappointment in her husband. His response to the cause of the wife's discontent, her husband's bodily dysfunction, implies that he takes issue with it and calls her distress into question. Even if Hand B intends his remarks to carry a jocular tone, he treats the deterioration of the marriage as problematic, perhaps due to the wife's emphasis on the husband's physical body, his worldly existence, rather than his immaterial soul. Whatever humor Hand B sees, or fails to see, in this passage, he insists on reading it interpretively, whereas Adrian contentedly brings it to the reader's attention without commentary. Hand B might read this marital discordance as unsettling appropriate Christian paradigms because Elde, the defender of Conscience and Unity, causes the disruption of their sacred union.

What makes Hand B's commentary on Will's marriage somewhat uncomfortable is the way it interrupts what feels like a husband-wife conversation. Adrian's comment here in relation to a wife suffering from her husband's impotence could be read as a response to one of Anne's earlier annotations next to a passage about a befuddled husband, Wit. In this passage, Dame Study, angry at her husband's foolish lessons about Dowel, Dobet, and Dobest, teaches Will that learning belongs to the clergy rather than the laity, who tend to misconstrue their biblical interpretations. Anne playfully places her characteristic manicule and her Latin signature alongside Wit's silent reaction to Dame Study's speech:

> And whanne þat Wyt was war how his wif tolde,
> He becom so confus he couþe nouȝt mele,
> And also doumb as a dore drouȝ hym aside. (A.11.93–95; fol. 52r)

Even before Anne's annotation, Adrian annotates Wit's explication of marriage, including his justification of lawful marriage as pleasing to God and his comment about the unsavory union of a young woman and an old man.[44] It is impossible to know for certain whether Adrian marks these arguments in reference to his own marriage with his young wife, but if so, Anne supersedes them with Dame Study's muting of Wit's voice. Since this husband-wife team of annotators shared this household manuscript, such an exchange comes across as more than mere coincidence. This series of annotations indicates that these two readers, probably reading the poem together, read it with a sense of humor. That Anne's joking message to her spouse in this passūs elicits Adrian's later noting of the sexually frustrated wife fits perfectly within this framework. However, Hand B's participation in the Elde scene, whether intentionally or not, turns the conversation into a less private one and adds a subtle hermeneutic or critical bent to the commentary. If Adrian directs his response to his wife, or at least keeps Anne in mind when highlighting this marital turmoil, then Hand B's reaction interferes with the private context of this spousal dialogue. His remarks make better sense outside the context of Digby 145's spousal annotators and within the realm of Adrian's and Hand B's tenuous exchanges, but Hand B's presence alongside Adrian's in this instance connects his reader response to this original spousal conversation. In doing so, it also connects Hand B's commentary with the implied association made between Langland's fictional wife and Adrian's real wife.

Blatant disagreements such as the one between Adrian and Hand B rarely occur in the margins of *Piers* manuscripts, and few if any annotators have the kind of evolving and dynamic dialogue that these two have by the end of *Piers*. The commentary found in the final sections of the poem and even those spousal responses produced by Adrian and Anne exemplify the level of emotional engagement, interpretation, and argumentation that can appear in the margins of Langland's work. Adrian and Hand B's responses provide crucial evidence for an ongoing tradition of reform-minded reactions to Langland, beginning with the marginalia found in earlier copies of *Piers* such as those discussed in detail by Kerby-Fulton in Oxford, Bodleian Library, MS Douce 104, and continuing down through the sixteenth century to Digby 145.[45] The unique household circumstances of this manuscript's production and early provenance, however, become particularly striking in light of the strong possibility of Hand B's familial ties to Adrian. Hand B could easily be one of Adrian's own children, perhaps his son Thomas whose name appears in an inscription, or a member of his extended family, meaning that their marginalia represent not only a religious but a family dispute as well.[46] In the case of Digby 145, the marginalia in the final passūs of *Piers* conveys the Antichrist's power to stir up disagreement, destroy unity, and silence the voice of charity within and without the dreamer's world, speaking to the sensibilities of two, or possibly three, family members who experience the real sting of religious instability and turmoil in Reformation England even within the private space of their own home.

Notes

1. Derek Pearsall, "The Uses of Manuscripts: Late Medieval English," *Harvard Library Bulletin* 4.4 (1993–94): 35.

2. Derek Pearsall, "The Text of *Piers Plowman*: Past, Present, and Future," *Poetica* 71 (2009): 87.

3. Derek Pearsall, Introduction to *New Directions in Later Medieval Manuscript Studies: Essays from the 1998 Harvard Conference*, ed. Derek Pearsall (Woodbridge: York Medieval Press, 2000), xii.

4. *Piers* functions as the centerpiece of Digby 145; the only other texts copied in it are Sir John Fortescue's *The Governance of England*, a much shorter piece written by Adrian's great-uncle, and a collection of proverbs. For a description of the manuscript, see George Kane, ed., *Piers Plowman: The A Version* (London: Athlone Press, 1988), 9–10. Another short description of the manuscript can be found in R. W. Hunt and A. G. Watson, *Bodleian Library Quarto Catalogues: Digby Manuscripts*, vol. 9 (Oxford: Bodleian Library, 1999), 143.

5. The best and most recent account of Adrian's biography can be found in Richard Rex, "Blessed Adrian Fortescue: A Martyr without a Cause?," *Analecta Bollandiana* 115 (1997): 307–53.

6. Evidence in the form of ink color and slight variations in handwriting suggests that this manuscript was perused and annotated during multiple sittings. For the identification of Anne's hand, see Kathryn Kerby-Fulton, "The Women Readers in Langland's Earliest Audience: Some Codicological Evidence," in *Learning and Literacy in Medieval England and Abroad*, ed. Sarah Rees-Jones (Turnhout: Brepols, 2002), 121–34. Note also that because this essay discusses both Adrian and Anne Fortescue I have chosen to call them by their first names to avoid confusion.

7. Rex, "Blessed Adrian," 339–41, 349–51. Thorlac Turville-Petre's similar argument can be found in "Sir Adrian Fortescue and His Copy of *Piers Plowman*," *Yearbook of Langland Studies* 14 (2000): 29–48.

8. Turville-Petre speculates that Adrian's use of two exemplars determines his approach to copying the poem: "Fortescue seems to have had two manuscripts of *Piers Plowman* in front of him, one an A text and the other a C text. The A text was the source of his copy until the end of A.11 (fol. 56v); the C text becomes the source from C.11.296. Though he was basing himself on the A text, he was from the opening lines continually looking across to his C text, introducing the odd line, a paragraph, or a passage of 100 lines or more that was not in A." For this excerpt and the rest of Turville-Petre's explanation, see "Sir Adrian," 34–35. The manuscript maintains only a small reading circle throughout its early provenance. It seems to have stayed within the family until Bodley bought it. The manuscript's readership only widens at this later point in its history. For analysis of the *ordinatio*, especially of the rubrication, of Digby 145, another method of determining a reader's interpretations, see James Weldon's "Decorative Reading: Some Implications of *Ordinatio* in *Piers Plowman*," *Florilegium* 14 (1995–96): 142.

9. George Russell, "'As They Read It': Some Notes on Early Responses to the C-Version of *Piers Plowman*," *Leeds Studies in English* 20 (1989): 180.

10. A.8.3–4; fol. 40r. The scribe simply writes "a pardone" in the left-hand margin and then continues to annotate the entire episode, including the content of the pardon, where he writes "pers pardone" at A.8.96; fol. 41v. For ease of comparison between the A- and C-text sections of Digby 145, all *Piers*

citations come from A. V. C. Schmidt's edition in *Piers Plowman: A Parallel-Text Edition of the A, B, C, and Z Versions*, 2nd ed., 2 vols. (Kalamazoo, MI: Medieval Institute Publications, 2011).

11. Of particular interest to Adrian is the rat parliament in the prologue, which he inserts into his A text from his C exemplar and then annotates throughout. Likewise, he takes special interest in the plowing of the half acre, responding to Piers's character and actions repeatedly as well as the Knight and Hunger, whom Piers hires to help him lead his community more effectively. Significantly, Adrian expresses little to no interest in the masses, for example, the thousand men who throng together and come under Piers's care. Instead, he focuses on the administrative side of governance by highlighting only the leaders.

12. Hunger's poor behavior receives Adrian's attention in relation to his extravagant dining at lines A.7.262–63 where Adrian writes "Hynger wil dyne" (fol. 39r) and again when he writes "plenty & glotony" (fol. 39r) next to A.7.283–85.

13. It is important to understand that Adrian's exact religious positions remain unclear and that his "unwavering" Catholic faith has an element of myth or legend to it. Both Rex and Turville-Petre discuss the complications involved in Adrian's religious affiliations during Henry's reign, and the manuscript evidence of his reform-minded attitudes as well as his obedience to the king, or at least his show of obedience by erasing the words *pope* and *Beckett* in his Book of Hours, points to the necessary limitations of his religious practices. However, as his execution suggests, his obedience to Henry was neither blind nor wholehearted.

14. The name "Hand B" comes from Turville-Petre, "Sir Adrian," 39. There is not space here to discuss every recurrent topic that appears in Digby 145. Thus a selection of prominent themes that occupy the readers' attention and are shared by all three readers take precedence.

15. For a fuller account of Anne Fortescue's contributions to Digby 145 and for an edition of the five annotations known for certain to belong to her, see Kerby-Fulton, "Women Readers."

16. While other examples of annotators responding to each other exist, this level of interaction is unprecedented in the *Piers* manuscripts known to me. Another example of annotator interaction can be found in the editions of two C-text manuscripts by Carl Grindley, "Reading *Piers Plowman* C-Text Annotations: Notes towards the Classification of Printed and Written Marginalia in Texts from the British Isles, 1300–1642," in *The Medieval Professional Reader at Work: Evidence from Manuscripts of Chaucer, Langland, Kempe, and Gower*, ed. Kathryn Kerby-Fulton and Maidie Hilmo (Victoria, BC: University of Victoria Press, 2001): 73–141.

17. C.22.193–98; fols. 126r and 126v.

18. Marie-Claire Uhart, "The Early Reception of *Piers Plowman*" (PhD diss., University of Leicester, 1986). Turville-Petre first points out this shortcoming of Uhart's edition, but as it is outside the scope of his article he provides only minimal discussion of the annotations. Turville-Petre, "Sir Adrian," 39.

19. Examples of their harmonious coexistence appear as early as the Prologue, but they are outside the parameters of this essay. For example, Hand B expands Adrian's annotations at C. P.162 when Adrian notes "lernd men" and Hand B adds "of law" (fol. 4v). It happens again at C. P.167–68 when Adrian writes "counsellours" and Hand B adds "of the lawe" (fol. 4v).

20. At lines 298–99 Adrian's copy reads with some variation: "and as glad of a gown of blak as of a gray rosett / and of a cote of cotton as of a clene scarlet."

21. Uhart, "Early Reception," 113.

22. C. David Benson and Joshua R. Eyler, "The Manuscripts of *Piers Plowman*," *Literature Compass* 2, no. 1 (2005): 5.

23. Uhart, "Early Reception," 124–30.

24. See especially the introduction to David Benson and Lynne Blanchfield, *The Manuscripts of Piers Plowman: The B-Version* (Woodbridge: D. S. Brewer, 1997), 9–27. For examples of C-text annotations, in addition to Grindley's edition cited above, see Kathryn Kerby-Fulton and Denise Despres, *Iconography and the Professional Reader: The Politics of Book Production in the Douce "Piers Plowman"* (Minneapolis: University of Minnesota Press, 1999). See also Tanya Schaap, "From Professional to Private Readership: A Discussion and Transcription of the Fifteenth- and Sixteenth-Century Marginalia in *Piers Plowman* C-Text, Oxford, Bodleian Library, MS Digby 102," in *The Medieval Reader: Reception and Cultural History in the Late Medieval Manuscript*, ed. Kathryn Kerby-Fulton and Maidie Hilmo (New York: AMS Press, 2001): 81–116.

25. Pearsall, "The Uses of Manuscripts," 35.

26. Fol. 84r, which corresponds to C.16.296 quoted above.

27. In its fuller context, Matthew 18:3–5 reads, "Truly I tell you, unless you become like children, you will never enter the kingdom of heaven. Whoever becomes humble like this child is the greatest in the kingdom of heaven. Whoever welcomes one such child in my name welcomes me." *The New Oxford Annotated Bible*, 3rd ed. (Oxford: Oxford University Press, 2001). The passage refers to C.16.296a.

28. C.16.289–95.

29. In expounding neighborliness as an important quality, Langland even cites Matthew 7:12 at line C.16.307a, "Quodcunque vultis vt faciant vobis homines, facite eis."

30. On fol. 123v, Anne annotates another kind of Father-Son relationship where the poem, discussing Need, suggests that God, the Father, became mankind, the Son. This annotation occurs at C.22.40–41 next to "And God al his grete ioye goestliche he lefte, / And cam and toek mankynde and bicam nedy."

31. C.21.223–24; fol. 117v. In this example, Adrian calls attention to some potentially controversial material and provides some suggestion that he is not averse to reformist ideas despite his Catholic background. This kind of evidence might reflect an ideology that informs his complex relationship with Henry.

32. C.21.224; fol. 117v. This passage distinguishes between the Antichrist and the pope because it prophesies that Pride will become pope upon the reign of the Antichrist. This factor might account for Hand B not conflating the two here, unless he interprets Pride as synonymous with the Antichrist, but there is no evidence to confirm this reading. Moreover, there is not much to disagree about in this section since the prophecy that the Antichrist will come is so commonplace.

33. C.21.448; fol. 121v. Although Wyclif's followers were still present in sixteenth-century England, there is no evidence that Hand B expresses Wycliffite sympathies in his interpretations of the pope.

34. For further discussion of Langland's Apocalypse, see Kathryn Kerby-Fulton, *Reformist Apocalypticism and "Piers Plowman"* (Cambridge: Cambridge University Press, 1990).

35. Uhart, "Early Reception," 149, 151.

36. Hand B also expands Adrian's annotation "pers barne" by placing "tymber for" in front of it a few lines earlier, at C.21.322–24; fol. 119v.

37. Uhart, "Early Reception," 150–51.

38. Ibid., 151. Turville-Petre notices the different emotional register of Hand B's marginalia as well, in "Sir Adrian," 42.

39. Rex, "Blessed Adrian," 317. For discussions of Crowley and Batman, see Larry Scanlon, "Langland, Apocalypse and the Early Modern Editor," in *Reading the Medieval in Early England*, ed. Gordon McMullan and David Matthews (Cambridge: Cambridge University Press, 2007), 51–73; and Simon Horobin, "Stephan Batman and His Manuscripts of *Piers Plowman*," *Review of English Studies* 62, no. 255 (2010): 358–72.

40. Scanlon, "Langland," 60.

41. Fol. 126r, at line C.22.183–84.

42. Fol. 126r, at line C.22.193.

43. Fols. 126r and 126v.

44. Adrian writes "wedlok" next to A.10.131–32; fol. 48v. He also places, "Nota marage" next to A.10.186–87; fol. 49v. Note that Adrian's interest in marriage begins early in the narrative as he follows the Mede episode closely. The Passus X examples, however, relate more easily to the context of his own marriage.

45. Kerby-Fulton and Despres, *Iconography*.

46. This inscription appears on the manuscript's second flyleaf.

CHAPTER 17

Playing as Literate Practice

Humanism and the Exclusion of Women Performers by the London Professional Stages

Maura Giles-Watson

Derek Pearsall is not a big fan of medieval drama. Except for a few mentions scattered in the footnotes, he excludes drama from his magisterial anthology, *Chaucer to Spenser*. In *Old and Middle English Poetry*, Derek devotes just seven pages to dramatic verse, and he concludes that section by chiding the Chaucer-loving Tudor playwright John Heywood for clumsy versification. For the earlier Tudor playwrights as a group, Derek has this critique: "The learning, wit, and sophistication of these plays should not be underestimated[,] . . . but the kind of intelligence one would appreciate from the point of view of poetry, namely, to use prose, is not there."[1] In this essay, I do not try to reform Derek, and I abstain from discussing drama and dramatic verse per se and instead speculate on an aspect of early English dramatic culture neglected until recent years: the reasons for the putative absence of women players[2] from the public stages in late medieval England and their certain absence from the newly professionalized London stages in the Renaissance.[3]

In 1959, the same year Derek Pearsall began his university teaching career, Glynne Wickham published the first volume of *Early English Stages*, a work that revolutionized the study of medieval and Renaissance dramatic culture. Yet Wickham places his discussion of women performers at the very end of his analysis of amateur and professional acting, and he begins his brief comments with this concessionary remark: "A last small point worth mentioning is the position of women in relation to the mediaeval stage."[4] The position of women may have been considered a small point in 1959, but, as Derek has pointed out, feminism has forever altered the way we view women in early English literature and culture.[5]

The culture of performance underwent major changes in late medieval and early Renaissance England. The professionalization of both playing and musicianship over the sixteenth century effected significant changes in the working lives of all performers,[6] and London's female performers were perhaps most profoundly affected, as their previous opportunities dried up and they were excluded from performing on the city's new professional stages. In England, as on the Continent, women performed publicly throughout the Middle Ages, although the extent to which women acted in stage plays remains the subject of conjecture and dispute. But we do know that female minstrelsy was not uncommon and that women sang, played instruments, danced, mimed, recited, jested, and participated in public spectacles and festivities.[7] As a result, audiences would have accepted both the reality and the notion of women as performers and entertainers. Nevertheless, with the opening of the public theaters—the moment when a wide range of opportunities suddenly emerged for performers—women were excluded from taking what would seem to be their rightful place. In this environment, as Natasha Korda observes and documents, women instead performed supporting tasks ancillary to the primary public theatrical activities of men, namely, the staging of plays and the playing of spoken interpretive dramatic parts.[8]

James Stokes has "suggested that the all-male companies that performed in London from the 1570s to the late 1630s constituted a 'cultural aberration,'"[9] and Phyllis Rackin notes that "the reason the English professional companies excluded women from the stage has never been satisfactorily explained."[10] I do not claim to resolve the matter here, but I would like to suggest that we consider explanations beyond those that have been offered to date. The received reasons have tended to be either religious or economic. The economic explanations include the assertion that the acting companies kept expenses low by supporting boy apprentices rather than paying women players, but the long-term obligation and expense of feeding, clothing, and housing boys—sometimes up to the age of twenty-five—renders this assertion doubtful.[11] The religious reasons include the fact that sixteenth-century antitheatricalists trumpeted the indecency of women's public performances, but religious polemicists argued even more vehemently that cross-dressed boys pretending to be female presented a greater risk to public morals.[12]

In late-sixteenth-century London, religion and economics were surely factors in limiting the opportunities for women performers, but they were not the only factors. Rather, this exclusion of women was an integral part of the process of professionalization and specialization of performance practices. Performers' desire for the recognition and rewards that attended their new professional status meant that they could not associate themselves and their new playing ventures with performers such as minstrels—both male and female—who carried with them the menial connotations of prior and provincial performance conditions and practices.[13] As Southworth observes, "It is not just that the status of the minstrel was low; for many of his contemporaries he was altogether beyond the pale of social acceptance."[14] Yet a minstrel could rise in social status, and becoming literate was one way to open up opportunities for advancement.[15]

Earlier in the sixteenth century, the Tudor humanist movement and its educational reforms contributed to social aspirationalism and to the realization of desires for upward mobility, particularly among the merchant class. And while the influence of humanism and humanists on drama and dramatic representation has been ably and thoroughly studied,[16] there remain gaps in our understanding of humanism's impact on England's wider performance culture and the emergence of the professional theater. One might expect Renaissance humanist protofeminism to have opened doors for women performers, but instead certain aspects of humanism appear to have been detrimental to their working lives. Indeed, I would argue that the marginalization of women performers by the late-sixteenth-century professional playing companies was, at least in part, the result of two cultural forces with roots in Renaissance humanism, namely, the cult of literacy and the academic drama.

The Cult of Literacy and the Illiterate Performer

Arguably, the primary activities of Renaissance humanism in England were reading and the cultivation of reading.[17] Humanist pedagogy relies upon reading and perceives education to be fundamental to every person's ability to conduct a moral and meaningful life. In the humanists' view, educated women were as capable of moral reasoning as were educated men.[18] But while English humanists advocated liberal education for the moral development of girls, they did not see their way clear to implementing a program of humanist education for females equivalent to that provided to males in the new schools. The New Learning benefited males of the merchant class and above whose families could afford school fees or tutors, but when humanist education was made available to women, it was chiefly to aristocratic women. Meanwhile, humanist education afforded middle-class males the opportunity to advance socially and equipped them with comprehensive literacy.[19] In the process, boys were exposed to and drilled in both classical and contemporary dramatic models in the classroom; few girls enjoyed such opportunities.[20] Humanist education's cult of literacy was thus predominantly male and middle to high status and in this way played an overlooked but significant role in effecting the exclusion of low-status and illiterate women performers from professional playing.

Although the question of whether women played spoken, interpretive dramatic roles in interludes and biblical plays remains contested,[21] the *Records of Early English Drama* project has demonstrated clearly that women performed in a tremendous range of ways and settings—from convents and aristocratic households to churches and the streets—during the later Middle Ages. Evidence from the plays is scarce, but what there is points to the presence of women in nonspeaking roles. In *Wisdom*, for example, a stage direction calls for the entrance of six costumed women who personify the vices of the brothel:

> Here entreth six women in sut thre disguised as gallontys and thre as matrons wyth wondyrfull vysurs congruent. (752*sd*)[22]

The women then proceed to dance to the accompaniment of a minstrel with a hornpipe. Greg Walker notes that this stage direction is "valuable as one of the few surviving references to female actors in the medieval period."[23] However, in this dramatic context these "actors" are not actually players; they do not perform spoken interpretive or expository parts. Instead, the women interpret their roles by means of a mime or dance that is likely to have included lascivious gestural improvisations and thus may not have been considered suitable for cross-dressed boys.

In the earlier Tudor period, aristocratic women were not likely to have performed in public, but they probably performed nonspeaking parts in private disguisings, pageants, and mummings during Henry VIII's reign and even earlier. During a 1501 disguising at Richmond, for instance, in addition to a singing "chylde of the chappell," the performers included "ii mermaydes, one of them a man mermayde, th'other a woman."[24] However, the extent to which aristocratic women may have performed speaking parts in household plays before the court masques of the Stuart period is unknown; such roles would frequently have required the memorization of scripted parts. During the late Middle Ages and the early Renaissance, aristocratic women enjoyed higher rates of literacy than did poor and working-class women, so they certainly could have studied and memorized written parts, although it is by no means certain that they did.[25]

Although there were no legal bars to women performing on the stage during the sixteenth century, there were limitations placed on the literacy of women—and of working-class men. Apparently with no irony intended, the 1543 Act for the Advancement of True Religion specifies the categories of people forbidden to read the English Bible: "no women or artificers, 'prentices, journeymen, servingmen of the degrees of yeoman or under, husbandmen, nor labourers."[26] In reality, the women this act prohibited from Bible reading would have occupied the same social strata as the men who are listed by occupation. Despite what it says, the act was not intended to prevent all women from reading the vernacular Bible. Rather, its intention was to ensure that literacy did not trickle down far enough into the social substrata to empower poor and working-class people, regardless of gender, to question or try to change their living and working conditions.[27]

Women who performed in public for their livings were poor or working class, and some of these women probably possessed limited functional literacy, but few would have been literate in any comprehensive sense of the term.[28] Although there is disagreement on the rates of female literacy at different levels of society and at various times,[29] it is clear that during the Middle Ages "many of the jongleurs . . . were probably scarcely literate,"[30] and in all likelihood most of the female performers were illiterate or nearly so. Up through the sixteenth century, women's culture was primarily oral and women's performance primarily improvisational, so literacy was not a prerequisite for female performance.[31] Illiterate performers possessed and utilized highly developed mnemonic and improvisational skills but lacked the level of literacy necessary for participation in the London professional theater's script-dependent culture. As John Astington points out, "even the youngest actors had to be literate in order to learn the scripts they had to read,"[32] and the youngest actors in the professional companies were boys playing women's parts. Because female performance culture had always been largely unscripted and had relied upon aural, rather than literate, memorization skills, the emergence of the professional stages put illiterate women performers at a serious disadvantage. To be sure, in the English Middle Ages and Renaissance there was a "relatively hidden tradition of female performance."[33] This tradition has been hidden not only because the relatively lower status of women resulted in a shortage of documentary evidence but also because women's performance was more often improvisational and ephemeral, and men's performance, while often unscripted, was also frequently scripted.[34] In the Middle Ages and the Renaissance, improvisation was crucial to every category of women's performance—representational, presentational, musical, physical, minstrel, mountebank, singing, dancing, jesting. Among the new professional companies, improvisation was associated with both illiteracy and a lack of professionalism.

Clifford Davidson notes that the range of performative activities in the Middle Ages included scripted "plays which make available considerable space for improvisation,"[35] but the Renaissance reacted against this practice. On the professional stages, improvisational performance, and the improvisers themselves, contained a potential for disruption that threatened to undermine both the performance itself and the authority of the dramatic script. In this way, improvisation—which had always been the primary performative mode for illiterate and marginally literate women who made their livings as performers[36]—fell out of favor with the professional companies whose work was both script driven and script dependent. Like illiteracy, improvisational performance was both class-bound and gender-bound. Hamlet's instructions to the players make explicit the playwright's desire to protect his play text from degradation at the hands of improvisers:

> let not your Clowne speake
> More then is set downe, there be of them I can tell you
> That will laugh themselues, to set on some
> Quantitie of barren spectators to laugh with them,

Albeit there is some necessary point in the Play
Then to be obserued: O 'tis vile, and shewes
A pittifull ambition in the foole that vseth it. (III.2)[37]

The transgressive connotations of "*ambition*"—the desire to rise above one's position—imply the lower status of improvisers and suggest that professional players were anxious to maintain their superior rank over the improvising performers whom they sought to restrict. What is more, "garrulous and frequently 'illiterate' women are often viewed as threatening androcentric values and institutions; the satirical caricature of these women as 'gossips' is an attempt to silence them."[38] Improvisers, including women, were silenced, marginalized, and controlled by the privileged status afforded to the script and its literate performance.[39]

Over the sixteenth century a radical change also occurred in the preparation and memorization methods of script-dependent performers. Illiterate players would no longer be coached orally/aurally as they memorized their roles. Instead, all players required some degree of literacy in order to read and memorize their own parts.[40] Like Peter Quince's rude mechanicals in *A Midsummer Night's Dream* (V.1), players would be provided with manuscript rolls that had been prepared by a scribe; these rolls contained only their own cues and parts. The actors would then take these rolls away and memorize their parts on their own. In some cases, actors who possessed comprehensive vernacular literacy might copy their cues and lines from a master script or, more rarely, write them down during an out-loud reading of the play.[41] In this way, as playing became increasingly professionalized, it also became a literate practice from which illiterate performers would be entirely excluded. Women were among these illiterate performers; boys, however, were not.

Although Tudor humanist educators did tend to regard the education of women as a positive development for the family and for society, from what little is known about female schooling it is certain that girls and young women were not provided with the same schooling as boys. Humanistic education from the petty school on was intended for boys, including those of the merchant and landed classes whose families sought the opportunity to prepare their sons for professions. In the implementation of the humanist vision, education is, among other social goods, a means of advancement. Rhetorical training played a significant role in this program, and drama played a significant role in rhetorical training, particularly in delivery, memorization, personation (*ethopoeia*), and impersonation (*prosopopoeia*).[42] In particular, Erasmus, More, and other humanists had advocated the inclusion of Terence in the New Learning, and indeed Terence's plays were frequently taught. But the classics were not the only plays that boys read in school, and not every schoolmaster selected edifying material for his pupils. In Ben Jonson's *The Staple of Newes*, Censure complains bitterly about schoolmasters who teach contemporary, rather than classical, drama to their charges:

> They make all their schollers Play-boyes! Is't not a fine sight, to see all our children made Enterluders? Do we pay our money for this? Wee send them to learne their Grammar, and their Terence, and they learne their play-books?"[43]

In the humanist schoolroom, rhetorical exercises required that such "play-boyes" dramatically personate and impersonate females with some frequency. In a 1565 case, an eleven-year-old pupil, William Badger, wrote and performed a Latin poetic lament in the voice of an emotionally upset nymph, Sylvia. From within this performative persona, William-Sylvia refers to the present audience of classmate-nymphs as "infelix turba puelli."[44] At first glance, Badger seems to be employing ungrammatically an unusual form of *puer* (boy), *puellus* (little boy), to denote "an unhappy crowd of little boys." In this pedagogical exercise, however, Badger might instead be making a different and more intriguing mistake in conflating *puer* with *puella* (girl) to arrive at an equally ungrammatical "unhappy crowd of boy-girls." But, regardless of the performative gender of the audience, the rhetorico-dramatic transgendering of William into Sylvia represents routine practice in humanist schooling. And, as Eugene Kintgen points out, "schooling, or rather the habitus of schooling, forms the basis for the structuring of all subsequent experience."[45]

Academic Drama and the Normative All-Male Stage

By 1565 somewhat older "boy-girls" had already been performing plays in the universities for over a century, and student-acted drama continued to flourish at both Oxford and Cambridge until 1642. As Alan Nelson points out, "Cambridge and Oxford reflected a tradition of academic drama shared with England's grammar schools."[46] In the universities, all-male dramatic performance of ancient and contemporary Latin plays, and of vernacular English plays, set in motion an elite performance culture that mirrored the popular tradition evinced by the all- or almost-all-male performance of the popular biblical plays. By the emergence of the London professional stages in the late sixteenth century, all-male performance was not a cultural aberration at all but rather a performative norm firmly grounded in both popular and academic drama, and so readily translated to the new performance conditions.

Under the rubric of rhetorical training, the humanist educational movement had introduced boys to playing and had extended theatrical training to young men who were being prepared for respectable professions in the church and at the law. This situation created what Jacques Rancière has termed an "aesthetic community," which he distinguishes from "a community of aesthetes." An aesthetic community is rather "a community of sense, or a *sensus communis*," bound together by "a certain combination of sense data: forms, words, spaces, rhythms and so on."[47] Out of this community, the so-called university wits brought their experience of academic theatricality with them to the professional stages. What is more, many of the men who had inhabited the all-male aesthetic community of the academic drama as students went on to complete their degrees and pursue professions off the stage. These men took with them into the wider culture an imprinted understanding of scripted dramatic performance as an academic ritual with both didactic and festive implications. This ritual simultaneously contained and authorized male transvestism, thereby institutionalizing homosocial theatrical culture among educated men both on and off the professional stages. Transferred to the professional stages, this all-male culture readily effected the exclusion of women from the new performance opportunities.

Shakespeare, who had probably never been to university himself, represented academic drama onstage. After Hamlet instructs the players in their craft, he makes metatheatrical small talk with Polonius:

> HAMLET. my lord, you play'd once i'th' universitie, you say?
> POLONIUS. That I did my lord, and was accounted a good Actor.
> HAMLET. What did you enact?

POLONIUS. I did enact Iulius Caesar. I was kild i'th' Capitall. Brutus kild mee.
HAMLET. It was a brute part of him to kill so capitall a calfe there. (III.2)[48]

Shakespeare's relations with academic drama have been illuminated by Alan H. Nelson, who further distinguishes between the "dynamic" staging of plays at the Rose and the Globe and the "academic" staging of plays at Cambridge, Oxford, and the Inns of Court.[49] He notes that *The Comedy of Errors* was written for performance at Gray's Inn and that both *Love's Labor's Lost* and *The Taming of the Shrew* contain academic tropes and call for static staging; taken together, these elements suggest performance for an academic audience in an academic venue.[50] But men and boys played all the parts regardless of the site of performance, and Shakespeare's academically themed plays further demonstrate that even a playwright with no direct experience of university dramatics operated under the influence of that tradition both in the writing and in the staging of plays.[51] Indeed, a number of academic plays were, like the *Liber apologeticus de omni statu humanae naturae* by Oxford Chancellor Thomas Chaundler (ca. 1465), rather dull humanist concoctions written as stilted Latin dialogues and debates for the moral and rhetorical edification of students. But not all university plays were tedious and pedantic. In fact, many may be termed "academic" only because they were written and performed in university settings or express scholarly preoccupations.[52]

A final point worth considering is the question of the extent to which the Renaissance humanist cult of classicism and its adherents were aware of, and sought to emulate, Greek and Roman theatrical practices as they revived, read, and performed ancient dramatic texts.[53] Appreciation for the talents of the Roman actor Roscius had resurfaced during the Ciceronian revival, but more general and genuine knowledge of classical acting appears to have been limited. In the epistolary debate over theatrical transvestism between John Rainolds and Alberico Gentili, the latter points to classical practices in his defense of cross-dressing in academic drama:

For . . . there can be tragedies and comedies without female characters, such as the *Philoctetes* of Sophocles, Euripides' satyr play *Cyclops*, the *Equites* of Aristophanes, and also Plautus' *Captivi*

> and *Trinummi*. Actors who play for hire have used female mimes and players for a long time now, although it was not always so; rather they say (*tradunt*) that men first acted women's parts.[54]

Gentili's assertion certainly suggests that the sixteenth century was aware of classical practice and viewed theatrical cross-dressing in light of both the tradition and the humanists' classicizing notion of *verum vetus*. As Binns observes, the contemporary employment of women players to which Gentili refers reflects Italian performance practices of the time, not English.[55] Indeed, it appears that the emulation of stage traditions with classical origins is yet another humanist factor in the English theater's marginalization of women performers.

Notes

I would like to thank Phillipa Hardman, Rhonda Garelick, Pamela Starr, Abraham Stoll, Yasmine Hachimi, and the anonymous readers for their insightful critiques of and contributions to this essay. I would also like to express my gratitude to Kathryn Kerby-Fulton and Sarah Baechle for all their work in organizing the New Directions in Manuscript Studies and Reading Practices Conference in Honour of Derek Pearsall's 80th Birthday and for making it such a stimulating and convivial event.

1. Derek Pearsall, *Old and Middle English Poetry*, Routledge History of English Poetry, 1 (London: Routledge & Kegan Paul, 1977), 258.

2. Throughout this essay I am careful to distinguish between *performers* (a capacious category that includes players, reciters, musicians, mimes, minstrels, dancers, etc.) and the more specific *players* (actors who perform spoken parts, whether interpretive or expository, in scripted plays).

3. Among important works on women and performance are *Early Theatre* 15, no. 1 (2012), an entire issue of fine essays that includes James Stokes, "Women and Performance in Medieval and Early Modern Suffolk" (27–43); Natasha Korda, *Labors Lost: Women's Work and the Early Modern English Stage* (Philadelphia: University of Pennsylvania Press, 2011), a monumental work on women who did not perform on stage but instead performed work that supported the professional London stages; the important essay collection, *Women Players in England, 1500–1660*, ed. Pamela Allen Brown and Peter Parolin (Burlington, VT: Ashgate, 2005), especially James Stokes, "Women and Performance: Evidences of Universal Cultural Suffrage in Medieval and Early Modern Lincolnshire" (25–44); Ann Thompson, "Women/'women' and the

Stage," in *Women and Literature in Britain, 1500–1700*, ed. Helen Wilcox (Cambridge: Cambridge University Press, 1996), 100–116; Claire MacManus, "Women and English Renaissance Drama: Making and Unmaking 'The All-Male Stage,'" *Literature Compass* 4, no. 3 (2007): 784–96, and her *Women on the Renaissance Stage* (Manchester: Manchester University Press, 2002). Earlier groundbreaking treatments of the subject include James Stokes, "Women and Mimesis in Medieval and Renaissance Somerset (and Beyond)," *Comparative Drama* 27, no. 2 (1993): 176–93; and Clifford Davidson, "Women and the Medieval Stage," *Women's Studies* 11 (1984): 99–113.

4. Glynne Wickham, *Early English Stages, 1300–1660*, vol. 1 (London: Routledge & Kegan Paul, 1959), 271.

5. A year after his retirement from Harvard, Derek returned to give a very humorous paper in which he reminisced about his forty-year academic career. At the end of his talk, a member of the overflow Warren Hall audience asked Derek which school of theory he thought would have a lasting impact on scholarly practices. After pondering the question for about two seconds, Derek responded, "Feminism." Having had feminist arguments with Derek in classes a decade earlier, I was both stunned and delighted by his response.

6. For a concise discussion of this transformative phenomenon, see William Ingram, *The Business of Playing: The Beginnings of the Adult Professional Theater in Elizabethan London* (Ithaca: Cornell University Press, 1992), esp. chaps. 3 and 5; and Timothy McGee, "The Fall of the Noble Minstrel: The Sixteenth-Century Minstrel in a Musical Context," in *Medieval and Renaissance Drama in England*, vol. 7, ed. Leeds Barroll (London and Toronto: Associated University Presses, 1995), 98–120.

7. The *REED* project has provided vital documentation of the compensation of female performers, but such records suggest that an invisible culture of women's performance existed alongside the documented culture. See also John Southworth, *The English Medieval Minstrel* (Wolfboro, NH: Boydell Press, 1989), esp. chap. 1 and pp. 35, 62–63.

8. See Korda, *Labors Lost.*

9. Quoted by Phyllis Rackin, "Afterword," in Brown and Parolin, *Women Players in England,* 316.

10. Rackin, "Afterword," 316.

11. On the apprenticeship system for boy actors, see John Astington, *Actors and Acting in Shakespeare's Time* (Cambridge: Cambridge University Press, 2010), 76–107. Michael Shapiro, "The Introduction of Actresses in England: Delay or Defensiveness?," in *Women and Dramatic Production, 1550–1700*, ed. Alison Findlay, Stephanie Hodgson-Wright, with Gweno Williams (Harlow: Pearson, 2000), 183–84. Shapiro notes too that "perhaps the strongest reason for the continued exclusion of women from the stage was a desire on

the part of male actors to preserve the profession of acting as a site for male employment" (185).

12. For a succinct discussion of the religious controversies, see J. W. Binns, "Women or Transvestites on the Elizabethan Stage? An Oxford Controversy," *Sixteenth Century Journal* 5, no. 2 (1974): 95–120; for gender and cross-dressing on early English stages, see esp. Lisa Jardine, " 'As boys and women are for the most part cattle of the same colour': Female Roles and Elizabethan Eroticism," in *Still Harping on Daughters: Women and Drama in the Age of Shakespeare* (New York: Columbia University Press, 1983), 9–36; Jean Howard, "Power and Eros: Crossdressing in Dramatic Representation and Theatrical Practice," in *The Stage and Social Struggle in Early Modern England* (New York: Routledge, 1994), 93–128; Stephen Orgel, *Impersonations: The Performance of Gender in Shakespeare's England* (Cambridge: Cambridge University Press, 1996); Viviana Comensoli and Anne Russell, eds., *Enacting Gender on the Renaissance Stage* (Urbana: University of Illinois Press, 1999); and Findlay, Hodgson-Wright, and Williams, *Women and Dramatic Production*. On cross-dressing in medieval performance, see Meg Twycross, " 'Transvestism' in the Mystery Plays," *Medieval English Theatre* 5 (1983): 123–80; Richard Rastall, "Female Roles in All Male Casts," *Medieval English Theatre* 7 (1985): 25–50; and Claire Sponsler, "Counterfeit in Their Array: Cross-Dressing in Robin Hood Performances," in *Drama and Resistance: Bodies, Goods, and Theatricality in Late Medieval England* (Minneapolis: University of Minnesota Press, 1997), 24–49; Robert Weimann and Douglas Bruster, *Shakespeare and the Power of Performance: Stage and Page in the Elizabethan Theatre* (Cambridge: Cambridge University Press, 2008), 117–37; Tracey Sedinger, " 'If sight and shape be true': The Epistemology of Crossdressing on the London Stage," *Shakespeare Quarterly* 49, no. 2 (1997): 63–79; and Peter Stallybrass, "Transvestism and the 'Body Beneath': Speculating on the Boy Actor," in *Erotic Politics: Desire on the Renaissance Stage*, ed. Susan Zimmerman (New York: Routledge, 1992), 64–83.

13. I date the beginnings of the London professional theater to John Rastell's public stage at Finsbury during the 1520s; see Maura Giles-Watson, "John Rastell's London Stage: Reconstructing Repertory and Collaborative Practice," *Early Theatre* 16, no. 2 (2013): 171–84.

14. Southworth, *The English Medieval Minstrel*, 4.

15. Ibid., 5.

16. See Kent Cartwright, *Theatre and Humanism: English Drama in the Sixteenth Century* (Cambridge: Cambridge University Press, 1999), esp. chap. 5, "Humanism and the Dramatizing of Women."

17. Daniel Wakelin, *Humanism, Reading, and English Literature, 1430–1530* (Oxford: Oxford University Press, 2007), makes this point effectively as he attends to "vernacular humanism" during the long fifteenth century (3 and passim).

18. See, for instance, Thomas Elyot, *Defense of Good Women* (London: Thomas Berthelet, 1540), STC2/7657.5 (EEBO).

19. Alan Stewart, *Close Readers: Humanism and Sodomy in Early Modern England* (Princeton, NJ: Princeton University Press, 1997), esp. 104; Anthony Grafton and Lisa Jardine, *From Humanism to Humanities: Education and Liberal Arts in Fifteenth- and Sixteenth-Century Europe* (Cambridge, MA: Harvard University Press, 1986), xiv, 141–42; Lynne Enterline, *Shakespeare's Schoolroom: Rhetoric, Discipline, Emotion* (Philadelphia: University of Pennsylvania Press, 2012).

20. Margaret More Roper stands as the exception that proves the rule. It is noteworthy that Erasmus credited Thomas More with converting him to the cause of female education: "Scarcely any mortal man was not under the conviction that, for the female sex, education had nothing to offer in the way of either virtue or reputation. Nor was I myself in the old days completely free of this opinion: but More has quite put it out of my head" (*Collected Works of Erasmus: Epistles* [Toronto: University of Toronto Press, 1992], 1233:112–15).

21. For instance, Meg Twycross points out that available evidence supports the claim that "women's roles" in the popular medieval biblical plays, "as in the Elizabethan theatre, were played by male actors" ("Theatricality of Medieval English Plays," in *Cambridge Companion to Medieval English Drama*, 2nd ed., ed. Richard Beadle and Alan Fletcher [Cambridge: Cambridge University Press, 2008], 32), but others note specific incidents of female stage performance that may or may not be indicative of wider cultural practice (Stokes, "Women and Mimesis," 176–77, 181). Indeed, the scarcity of documentation of women's stage performances may be consistent with the scarcity of documentation of other aspects of women's lives in the later Middle Ages.

22. *Wisdom*, in *The Macro Plays*, ed. Mark Eccles, EETS 262 (London: Oxford University Press, 1969).

23. Greg Walker, ed., *Medieval Drama* (Oxford: Blackwell, 2000), 235.

24. Glynne Wickham, *Early English Stages*, vol. 1, pt. 1, *1300–1576* (New York: Columbia University Press, 1959), 213.

25. I am intentionally omitting discussion of the question of convent performance by women religious, the nature and extent of whose literacy is a complex and unsettled question. Nuns enjoyed higher rates of literacy than women in the general population, and their convent performances would have been all female. On the literacy of nuns, see Katherine Zieman, "Reading, Singing, and Understanding: Constructions of the Literacy of Women Religious in Late Medieval England," in *Learning and Literacy in Medieval England and Abroad*, ed. Sarah Rees Jones (Turnhout: Brepols, 2003), 97–120.

26. 34 and 35 Henry VIII. For a discussion of this act's wider social implications, see David Cressy, *Literacy and the Social Order: Reading in Tudor and Stuart England* (Cambridge: Cambridge University Press, 1980), 44.

27. By the close of the sixteenth century, women were encouraged to read the Bible. Juan Luis Vives's *Instruction of a Christian Woman*, the eighth edition of which was printed in 1592, allowed that "on holy days continually and some time on working days let her read or hear such as shall lift up the mind to God." See Alison Findlay, *A Feminist Perspective on Renaissance Drama* (Oxford: Blackwell, 1999), 11.

28. I am employing here chiefly the notion of comprehensive *vernacular* literacy rather than a wider definition of "comprehensive literacy" that might include Latin and the reading of learned texts; see, for instance, the discussion of Julian of Norwich's literacy in Julia Boffey, "Women Authors and Women's Literacy in Fourteenth- and Fifteenth-Century England," in *Women and Literature in Britain, 1150–1500*, ed. Carol Meale (Cambridge: Cambridge University Press, 1991), 162.

29. See Cressy, *Literature and the Social Order*, 176–77 and chap. 6; Keith Thomas, "Literacy in Early Modern England," in *The Written Word: Literacy in Transition*, ed. Gerd Bauman (Oxford: Clarendon Press, 1986), 101–3; James Daybell, "Interpreting Letters and Reading Script: Evidence for Female Education and Literacy in Tudor England," *History of Education* 34, no. 6 (2005): 695–715; Patricia Parker, " 'On the Tongue': Cross Gendering, Effeminacy, and the Art of Words," *Style* 23, no. 3 (1989): 445–65; Sara Mendelson and Patricia Crawford, *Women in Early Modern England, 1550–1720* (Oxford: Oxford University Press, 1998), esp. 212–18; and Susan Schibanoff, "Taking the Gold out of Egypt: The Art of Reading as a Woman," in *Gender and Reading: Essays on Readers, Texts, and Contexts*, ed. Elizabeth Flynn and Patrocino Schweickart (Baltimore, MD: Johns Hopkins University Press, 1986), 83–106, esp. 88–89.

30. Andrew Taylor, "The Myth of the Minstrel Manuscript," *Speculum* 66 (1991): 51.

31. Kathleen McGill, "Women and Performance: The Development of Improvisation by the Sixteenth-Century Commedia dell'Arte," *Theatre Journal* 43, no. 1 (1991): 59.

32. Astington, *Actors and Acting*, 2.

33. Thompson, "Women/'women,' " 103.

34. Women's improvisational practices on the Continent offer intriguing comparisons. See Kathleen McGill, "Women and Performance," and also her "Improvisatory Competence and the Cueing of Performance: The Case of the Commedia dell'Arte," *Text and Performance Quarterly* 10 (1990): 111–22.

35. Clifford Davidson, "Improvisation in Medieval Drama," in *Improvisation in the Arts of the Middle Ages and Renaissance*, ed. Timothy J. McGee (Kalamazoo, MI: Medieval Institute Publications, 2003), 194.

36. See McGill, "Women and Performance," esp. 59–63.

37. William Shakespeare, *Hamlet*, Q1 (1603), fol. 2r; STC2/22275 (EEBO).

38. Schibanoff, "Taking the Gold out of Egypt," 106 n. 38.

39. Tiffany Stern notes the controlled use of extemporaneous performance, especially that of clowns, on early modern stages during and after scripted performances: *Documents of Performance in Early Modern England* (Cambridge: Cambridge University Press, 2009), 245–56. These performances, however, represent examples of a hybrid form termed "planned improvisation" by David Klausner, in "The Improvising Vice in Renaissance England," in McGee, *Improvisation in the Arts of the Middle Ages and Renaissance*, 273–85.

40. Simon Palfrey and Tiffany Stern, *Shakespeare in Parts* (Oxford: Oxford University Press, 2007), 60–70.

41. Stern, *Documents of Performance*, 174–90, 232–44.

42. On drama in Tudor educational practice, see especially Ursula Potter, "Performing Arts in the Tudor Classroom," in *Tudor Drama before Shakespeare, 1485–1590*, ed. Lloyd Kermode, Jason Scott-Warren, and Martine van Elk (Houndmills: Palgrave Macmillan, 2004), 143–66; and Enterline, *Shakespeare's Schoolroom*, 14.

43. Ben Jonson, *The Staple of Newes* (Third Intermean), in *The Workes of Ben Jonson* (London: John Beale et al., 1640/1), 49–50. STC2/14754 (EEBO).

44. Enterline, *Shakespeare's Schoolroom*, 85.

45. Eugene Kintgen, *Reading in Tudor England* (Pittsburgh: University of Pittsburgh Press, 1996), 9.

46. Alan H. Nelson, "Emulating Royalty: Cambridge, Oxford, and the Inns of Court," *Shakespeare Studies* 37 (2009): 67.

47. Jacques Rancière, *The Emancipated Spectator*, trans. Gregory Elliott (London: Verso, 2009), 57.

48. William Shakespeare, *Hamlet*, Q2 1604/5, H. STC2/22276 (EEBO).

49. Alan H. Nelson, "The Universities," in *A New History of Early English Drama* (New York: Columbia University Press, 1997), 66.

50. Nelson, "The Universities," 66.

51. Nelson observes that Shakespeare may have "learned of the academic performance tradition at the grammar school in Stratford" ("The Universities," 67 n. 6). It is also likely that Shakespeare learned additional skills and techniques from university-trained playwrights with whom he collaborated and whose plays he saw onstage.

52. Astington, *Actors and Acting*, 59–75; and Sarah Knight, "Fantastical Distempers: The Psychopathology of Early Modern Scholars," in *Early Modern Academic Drama*, ed. Jonathan Walker and Paul Streufert (Aldershot: Ashgate, 2008), 129–52.

53. Edith Hall, "The Ancient Actor's Presence since the Renaissance," in *Greek and Roman Actors: Aspects of an Ancient Profession*, ed. Pat Easterling and Edith Hall (Cambridge: Cambridge University Press, 2002), 419–34; Charles Garton, *Personal Aspects of the Roman Theatre* (Toronto: University

of Toronto Press, 1972), 203–29; Eva Keuls, "The Two Kinds of Women: Splitting the Female Psyche," in *The Reign of the Phallus* (Berkeley: University of California Press, 1985), 204–28. While there certainly were female performers in antiquity, they tended to be, or to be depicted as, slaves and prostitutes.

54. "Dicere enim potuissem sine faeminarum personis esse tragaedias posse et comoedias ut Sophoclis Philoctetes, Euripidis Cyclops tragicosatyra Aristophanes Equites, Plauti Captivi etiam et Trinummi. Mercenarii histriones inducunt mimas et scenicas iamdudum, neque enim ita semper fuit, sed primum agisse partes mulierum viros, tradunt." Corpus Christi College MS 352, 216, quoted by Binns, "Women or Transvestites?," 111 (I have modified Binns's translation). The lengthy Rainolds-Gentili correspondence on this topic took place in the early 1590s.

55. Binns, "Women or Transvestites?," 112. See also McGill, "Women and Performance" and "Improvisatory Competence." Women performed improvisational roles—unscripted parts based on scenarios—in the commedia dell'arte, and Gentili would have had firsthand knowledge of this performance practice.

Part VI

Chaucerian and Post-Chaucerian Reading Practices

Foreword to Part VI

For those of us fortunate enough to have been Derek Pearsall's students, the study of Chaucerian and post-Chaucerian reading practices is inexorably interwoven with Pearsallian reading practices, some of which have been outlined in Part I of this volume. Of course the depth of his perceptions and the breadth of his knowledge have made him perhaps the best-known and most widely read medievalist of recent decades, but another aspect of his scholarship deserves equal attention: his remarkable sense of caution. Almost as frequently as he makes a brilliant assertion, he warns readers of medieval texts not to go too far or become too speculative in their readings of literature and research about its writers. Nowhere is this cautionary attitude more thoughtfully presented than in the introduction to Derek's *Life of Chaucer: A Critical Biography*, in which he cites previous biographers' enthusiastic predilection for making Chaucer look like themselves so that he comes across as "a decent sort of fellow." Derek suggests a far more balanced and nuanced position for himself in a paragraph that bears rereading by every professor at the beginning of every course devoted to Chaucer.

> Perhaps one could adopt a differently prejudiced view of Chaucer, and represent his life, and its importance in his writings, as that of a time-serving opportunist and placeman, who pictured his own

> pliability in all that he saw. He might be seen as one who had outlived the idealisms of chivalry and faith but found nothing to fill the vacuum that they left; who exposed the meretriciousness of institutionalized religion, but retreated into its most inflexible dogma when his humanity was exhausted; who recognized no central social value in law and other forms of contract, but saw only what was hollow and saleable; who made many generous gestures toward women, but returned generally to a conventional misogyny; who viewed life in a spirit of pessimism interspersed with irrepressible hilarity.[1]

To extend the metaphor in one of the *moralitates* of the Nun's Priest's Tale, the Canterbury tale often thought to be the most Chaucerian (an idea reinforced by Elizabeth Scala here), Derek provides plenty of "fruyt" in his work while letting the "chaf" be still, but he is thoughtful enough to point out where it lies and why it must be avoided—and this habit of his has provided a very useful example for his students. Good Pearsallians that they are, each of the four scholars in this section has done the same in their readings of Chaucerian and post-Chaucerian texts.

For the writer and glossator in the works discussed by Sarah Baechle and Elizabeth Scala (who while at Harvard named her dog Derek after her dissertation adviser), to read is to remember and to relate intertextually. Scala shows us Chaucer reading himself in the Nun's Priest's Tale, reminding us of Derek Pearsall's 1983 *Variorum Edition* of the tale,[2] so magisterial that she almost criticizes him for being too thorough in filling in the allusional and citational blanks in the tale, removing us from the experience of the medieval reader who might have recognized only a few of them. Dealing with medieval texts and their glosses in Latin, Baechle is also appropriately cautious about whether the knowledge that readers brought to a vernacular text would allow more than a handful of them to understand the meaning of the allusions and quotations, much less their full context in the work from which they were taken; she aptly notes the "ambiguous potentiality" of these glosses. But at the risk of stating the obvious, readers have always brought different degrees of expertise and interest to texts, resulting in different levels of understanding of the texts' allusions and scholastic apparatus. As any professor knows who has taught from *The Riverside Chaucer*, the explanatory notes identifying allusions and quotations set readers, like so many Custances, adrift in a sea of too much information in what ultimately may become a test of their faith in the editor. Such is the privileged position of post-Chaucerian readers. On the other hand, surely there are readers of Chaucer who remain high and dry, reading only for the "story" (though now probably very few do so in Middle English). Anyone reading this book in honor of Derek is likely to belong to the former category, so we can appreciate the diplomacy of Derek's editorial voice while noting (as Chris Cannon does in his foreword here) that diplomacy does not preclude negative critical judgments.

Scala's essay necessarily makes use of Correale and Hamel's *Sources and Analogues of the Canterbury Tales*, the important revision of Bryan and Dempster's volume published some sixty years earlier, in which Derek also had a hand as an editorial board member: as the editors put it, he was "an early and zealous promoter of this project, even assuming leadership of it for a brief period and playing a crucial role in moving it forward."[3] This is yet another reminder of how frequently his work has been indispensable in organizing and contributing to significant scholarly projects that are in turn foundational for further research.

For the adapter of Hoccleve's *La Male Regle* in Huntington Library MS HM 111, to read is to revise. Peter Brown argues persuasively that the Balade in this manuscript is basically a chrestomathy of Hoccleve's longer work that would have had particular meaning for a monastic record keeper and his audience. The essay clearly shows that when winnowed correctly, this text that appeared to earlier scholars to be chaff would have been a fruitfully "complete and coherent poem with its own priorities" as an ethically informed postscript to what seems basically an account book. The work that the Balade does in the codex exemplifies with uncanny precision some of the ideas of John Dagenais, whose scholarship on ethics in manuscript culture remains useful: "The production of medieval text takes place . . . in that same ethical world to which it also points. These 'ethical' modalities are certainly as significant in constituting 'medieval literature' as are the processes of authorial creation or textual play that have been its major focuses until now."[4]

Brown's suggestion that the Balade may have been related to the fifth jubilee of Saint Thomas of Canterbury in 1420 is particularly interesting inasmuch as the poem serves as an ethical addendum to a codex largely concerned with business matters of a monastic community making money from pilgrims. The Balade nicely highlights the Chaucerian ethical division, effectively outlined by Alcuin Blamires,[5] between secular ethics based on the classical tradition of rational philosophy, apparent in the poem's frequent allusions to the virtuous power of reason, and the Christian moral impulse, which appears only in its last eight lines. As the compiler of the poem read Hoccleve, was he in a sense rendering unto Caesar what was Caesar's before the final turn to the Christian God?

For Stephen Partridge, to read is to rethink, finding greater codicological complexity than has been previously noted in a manuscript in the Houghton Library at Harvard. We might read a Pearsallian sense of caution at work here inasmuch as Partridge, another former student of Derek's, makes a strong case about different scribal hands but poses significant questions about methodology, both his own and others', in manuscript studies. His assertions, counterbalanced by ongoing questions, are a reminder of Derek's role in helping to define manuscript studies as the field took a new, revitalized form after the publication of such books as *Book Production and Publishing in Britain, 1375–1475* and *New Directions in Later Medieval Manuscript Studies*.

Just before the Nun's Priest tells his audience to reject the "chaf" in favor of the "fruyt," he reminds them, "For Seint Paul seith that al that writen is, / To oure doctrine it is ywrite, ywis" (VII.3441–42). While the meaning of this scriptural citation in the Nun's Priest's Tale remains ambiguous, it is clearly applicable to Derek's half century of chaffless work on Chaucer, which not only bears carefully nurtured fruit of its own but continues to go forth and multiply in the work of those who follow him.

Edward Wheatley

Notes

1. Derek Pearsall, *The Life of Chaucer: A Critical Biography* (Oxford: Blackwell, 1992), 8.

2. Derek Pearsall, ed., *A Variorum Edition of the Works of Geoffrey Chaucer, Part II: The Canterbury Tales, Part Nine: The Nun's Priest's Tale* (Norman, OK: Pilgrim Books, 1983).

3. Robert M. Correale and Mary Hamel, eds., *Sources and Analogues of the Canterbury Tales*, vol. 1 (Cambridge: D. S. Brewer, 2002), viii.

4. John Dagenais, *The Ethics of Reading in Manuscript Culture: Glossing the "Libro de Buen Amor"* (Princeton: Princeton University Press, 1994), 18.

5. Alcuin Blamires, *Chaucer, Ethics, and Gender* (Oxford: Oxford University Press, 2006).

CHAPTER 18

Quoting Chaucer

Textual Authority, the Nun's Priest, and the Making of the *Canterbury Tales*

Elizabeth Scala

A variorum edition is hardly the place one expects to find new readings. By definition, a variorum edition collects, organizes, and largely rehearses a text's critical reception, attending to what has already been written. This essay examines Derek Pearsall's *Variorum Edition* of the Nun's Priest's Tale to go one better in the very same direction the edition itself does.[1] By collecting, organizing, and largely rehearsing claims that Pearsall has drawn to our attention, I focus on these points to offer something new. Within the *Variorum* lies evidence for reading the tale as Chaucer's subtle act of self-quotation. Pearsall's *Variorum* shows us that the Nun's Priest's Tale makes its witty claims by an excessive display of quotation and allusion to various texts, many used repeatedly by Chaucer elsewhere, as well as to the larger work in which the tale is contained.

The tale's capacity for echoing other pilgrims' stories has long been recognized by critics arguing for the thematic relations between tales. But the total force of the Nun's Priest's citational practice has not yet been fully calibrated. Through an elaborate system of quotation and allusion, the Nun's Priest echoes a number of Canterbury tales in the same way he references other sources. By quoting Chaucer, the Nun's Priest's self-conscious literary performance transforms scattered tales told upon a journey to Canterbury, which have been referring to each other all along, into the canonical work now known as the *Canterbury Tales*.

Much has been written of late about Chaucer's fifteenth- and sixteenth-century inheritors, the poets responsible for the creation of a Chaucerian tradition and their imitation of Chaucer's works. The past decade has witnessed an increase in studies of Hoccleve and Lydgate, two figures most responsible for canonizing Chaucer's works through their imitations and allusions. Attention to the Nun's Priest's acts of quotation does not detract from their acts of laureation but instead reveals another of their sources. If "his later fifteenth-century scribes, readers, and poetic imitators" subject Chaucer to acts of laureation, as Seth Lerer has shown, by "draw[ing] on . . . figures from Chaucerian fiction to articulate their understanding of authorial and interpretive control," the Nun's Priest's subtle quotations form yet another Chaucerian model.[2]

For a supposedly simple fable, the Nun's Priest's Tale is impressively complex. Its comedy of literate chickens weaves a fabric of authorial references, textual allusions, and well-worn quotations in the form of a deceptively simple story. A famous example appears in the narrator's complaint about the misfortunes of his protagonist Chauntecleer by way of an elaborate set of apostrophes to destiny, to Venus, and to "Gaufred" (VII.3347). This last is an allusion to Geoffrey of Vinsauf's *Poetria Nova* and his lament on the death of Richard I, an event which occurred on the same day of the week as the rooster's capture—"And on a Friday fil al this meschaunce" (VII.3341). Pearsall's *Variorum Edition* marks clearly the textual authorities cited in the Nun's Priest's Tale. It may even mark them *too* clearly, since it offers names and titles where the tale commonly addresses "oon auctor" or paraphrases with no attribution at all. Indeed, as a retelling of Marie de France's fable of the cock and fox, influenced by various versions of the *Renart* story, the Nun's Priest's comedy reads as a dense texture of authoritative quotation, allusion, and adaptation, which its many scholarly readers delight in identifying.[3]

Cautioning us about the seductions of allusive identification, A. C. Spearing questions Chaucer's audience's ability to identify or even recognize such gestures. These are the talents of modern scholars, trained in multiple languages and with copies of these books at hand. Chaucer's audience, even one of similarly educated London bureaucrats and civil servants, could not possibly have known his sources so intimately, especially rare Italian ones. Spearing differentiates the use of source from allusion by the importance of recognition, which allusion depends upon. Failure to recognize an allusion may result in "diminished understanding," whereas a writer may never intend an audience to know his dependence on and use of a source.[4] Spearing's caution here is needed, as it reveals differing assumptions about dependency, originality, and intent for premodern texts. I want to take his reservations a step further, querying the parameters of vernacular quotation. Given the anonymity of such texts and the lack of standard formatting for them, is the quotation—in the modern sense of exact lexical rendering—of vernacular texts even possible? Where punctuation guarantees the exactitude of one's reference and marks it authoritatively in print, no such marks guarantee medieval texts, particularly those with secular interests. But Chaucer everywhere engages in such acts of quotation, to the point that modern editors add the quotation marks even when they have little information about who or what is being quoted. In the Nun's Priest's Tale itself, the happy song the chickens sing, "Myn lyf is faren in londe," provides just such an example. Susan Cavanaugh explains the line in the *Riverside*'s explanatory notes as "a popular song" and prints its entirety from Robbins's edition of *Secular Lyrics of the Fifteenth Century*, giving the impression that the lyric is widely attested. Pearsall offers a corrective. The only witness for the lyric is Trinity College Cambridge, MS R.3.19, which postdates the Nun's Priest's Tale by a century. We have no evidence that the lyric in the Trinity MS is the "popular" love song to which the Nun's Priest alludes. In fact, Pearsall raises "the possibility that the little song [in the sixteenth-century manuscript] is prompted by the Nun's Priest's Tale" itself (155).

Despite the fact that we can't identify the text of the lyric or verify the nature and extent of its popularity, we know we are in the presence of some form of quotation—even if Chaucer is the originator of the line, working with "collocational sets."[5] Along with the more general kind of references to his own work, which include the Man of Law's frustration with a poet named "Chaucer" who has told too many stories in English (II.47) and the reference to the wisdom of the Wife of Bath from within the fiction of the Merchant's Tale (V.1685), Chaucer does, of course, make conventional references to authorities, calling out specific sources as he quotes, paraphrases, and often translates: "Salomon seith" (VII.1002); "For it is writen that" (VII.1846); "For the commune proverbe seith thus" (VII.1030); "The Apostle Paul unto the

Romayns writeth" (VII.989). All of these examples are taken from the Tale of Melibee, a veritable patchwork of quotation, paraphrase, and allusion to the best-known proverbs of schoolroom learning. It is a tale that gives its editors some difficulty in punctuating since its wisdom is often given by Prudence in the form of quotation and paraphrase. Thus, Chaucer quotes prudently not merely at one level, and not at all certainly or literally, since he is often translating as he cites from the texts (and his citations are often wrong).[6] All of this goes to say that quotation's form in the Middle Ages and before the advent of print (and its increasing advances in uniformity) has to be considered in looser terms. And it is precisely such terms I wish to invoke for Chaucer's self-quotation in the Nun's Priest's Tale.

A telltale trait of his hapless dream-vision narrators and the personally inexperienced servant of love's servants transmitting *Troilus and Criseyde*, such bookishness itself appears quintessentially Chaucerian. As so much of its long critical tradition suggests, the *Canterbury Tales* is woven out of the books Chaucer has read and is littered with textual references—some in the voices of the pilgrim narrators, others in the mouths of their fictional inventions. But the density and productiveness of quotation in the Nun's Priest's Tale remains striking, particularly because, as many of its readers have noticed, such "auctoritee" contrasts with its supposedly simplistic genre and its animal characters. The list of authorities the birds cite is impressive: not only Geoffrey of Vinsauf, but Augustine, Boethius, Saint Kenelm, the Books of Daniel and Ecclesiastes, *Lancelot du Lak*, *Eneydos*, and the *Distichs* of Cato are mentioned by name.[7] In addition, the Nun's Priest alludes to Cicero, Robert Holkot, Vincent of Beauvais, Macrobius, Bartholmaeus Anglicus (possibly via John Trevisa), Valerius Maximus, Giraldus Cambrensis, Albertus Magnus, Guido delle Colonne's *Historia Destructionis Troiae*, and Nigel Wireker's *Speculum Stultorum,* beside herbals, various scriptural quotations, proverbial materials, and schoolroom exercises.

Despite, or rather in contrast to, these many authoritative texts and the "sentence" with which they imbue the tale, there is little agreement about interpreting the Nun's Priest's overblown story. In fact, the many morals adduced by the narrator, as well as those within his characters' stories, make impossible a clear-cut interpretation and, for some, have threatened its generic status.[8] Spearing believes that "Chaucer shows little interest in hidden meanings or allegorical interpretation," both generally and in the Nun's Priest's Tale in particular.[9] Yet the use of fables as sermon exempla has led a number of scholars to press various exegetical readings, hotly contesting the correct "sentence" that one should take as the fruit is separated from its chaff. These contests have recently prompted John Finlayson to respond to the "clerkly fashion" of such readers, whom he finds "impervious" to the best aspects of the tale: its literary self-awareness and its sense of humor.[10] Finlayson would read these exegetes as products of the Nun's Priest's comedy, unaware of the tale's hilarious excess. In their efforts to make earnest out of game, they unwittingly dramatize the central comic "act" of Chauntecleer's story—a rooster's parody of the fall that turns tragedy into game. In turning Chaucer's game back into tragedy and morality, such readers miss (and hence themselves become) the very machinery of Chaucer's joke.[11] In opposition to these clerkly exegetes, the tale is thus better understood in literary terms as one for which "elusiveness is indeed its character."[12] But the nature of such literariness has itself been elusive, and various strategies have been deployed to find a more material answer to this condition.

The precise relations between elusiveness and allusiveness, I want to argue, are crucial to the Nun's Priest's distinctiveness. Precisely because of our appreciation of the tale's virtuoso comedy on textual authority and the authoritative pronouncements such texts make, we have yet to recognize that the Nun's Priest alludes to and quotes one work more pervasively, if more subtly, than all the others by repeating its most basic moves and gestures. While a number of the Canterbury tales refer back to a previous story—the Clerk's to the Wife's, the Reeve's to the Miller's—the loose yet widespread quotation of Chaucer's story collection in the Nun's Priest's Tale brings the *Canterbury Tales* into being as an authoritative literary work. Comparable to allusions to already existing objects of "textual" status elsewhere cited by various narrators or their fictions, the Nun's Priest's Tale makes an authoritative, textual—what we would call a *literary*—object out of the compilation of individual Canterbury tales themselves.

The particular echoes and allusions to other Canterbury tales in the collection have, of course, been noted before. As I discuss in more detail below, Pertelote echoes the Wife of Bath; the narrator's declamations on Fortune sound much like the Monk and the Man of Law; his aphoristic "Mordre wol out" repeats words recounted as recently as the Prioress's Tale. But less has been made of the effect of these sly and comic references as a whole. Neither have they been coordinated with the strategies of textual reference elsewhere pervading the Priest's performance. An important part of the Nun's Priest's comedy is wrought around the rhetorical and dramatic deployment of its textual allusions and its recourse to textual authority. The tale finds its own vernacular authority in the deauthorizations of its textual others as well as their usefulness to its project. That is, the Nun's Priest's Tale both cites its authorities in ways that ultimately empty them of any authority over his tale and, in doing so, authorizes its own comedy. Among its allusions are a number of explicit quotations and citations of *auctores*, in both the narration of the Nun's Priest and the discourse of his fictional characters, which, we have to keep telling ourselves, happen to be chickens and a fox. Chaucer weaves his comedy by exploding the simple didactic form of the fable via a mock-epic presentation; he thereby extends and proliferates the moral content—of a tale *about* the dangers of flattering presentation and epic pretension—it can contain. Through an examination of the authorities, which the tale simultaneously exalts and deflates, I will show an analogous process of local citation as a quiet exaltation of the *Canterbury Tales* itself.

The Nun's Priest's Tale foregrounds an authoritative self-fashioning uncannily similar to that taken in the Retractions appended to the Parson's Tale in the Canterbury book. Found in most of the manuscripts that preserve this story, the Retractions addendum to the Parson's penitential effort "to make an ende" (X.47) looks to "revoke" a number of works, what Chaucer calls "my giltes; / and namely of my translacions and enditynges of worldly vanitees," apologizing for "the defaute of myn unkonnynge" (X.1082–84). Yet this retrospective account also puts Chaucer's signature squarely on his writings, naming those that have come down to us as the poet's works, as well as some, like the "book of the Leoun," that do not survive (X.1086). Thus even as the Retractions presume a movement away from his own fictions, "thilke that sownen into synne," they also more firmly inscribe Chaucer's authorship over them. Like the quotations in the Nun's Priest's Tale, the Retractions solidify the "tales of Caunterbury" and their *textual* status.[13]

If the Retractions name the "tales of Caunterbury" similarly to the manuscript colophons and headings found in the majority of complete manuscripts (and thus offer a formal title to the still accreting collection), the Nun's Priest's Tale more playfully shows a similar kind of negative affirmation and self-authorization in Chaucer's fiction.

This connection makes more serious business out of the Nun's Priest's playful rhetoric. The conjunction of intent in the Nun's Priest's Tale and the Retractions also destabilizes any lingering images of a Chaucerian deathbed repentance in them, likely promulgated by Thomas Gascoigne's reading of the Retractions. Moreover, similar to the authorial book list that establishes Chaucer's canon in the Retractions (X.1085–87), we see in the Nun's Priest's Tale an embedded signature of the poet in the name of his avian protagonist. Finding the same kind of signature in these two places—one clearly ludic, the other decidedly more serious—thus unhinges those starkly penitential ideas that have firmly, if somewhat silently, haunted our readings of the end of the larger poem.

While the Nun's Priest's Tale has long been considered one of Chaucer's most self-conscious and self-reflexive efforts, critical comfort in the firm ground of modern forms of citation and source has ironically hindered our recognition of Chaucer's playful self-quotation. The authorities cited by the chickens in the tale as well as by the Nun's Priest himself have drawn less focused attention than Chaucer's external sources for the story, most likely because the sources are more allusively uncertain and thus in need of excavation. By contrast, the tale's citations appear fixed, attached to a name or the term *auctor* proximate to them. A number of *Renart* tales and exempla stand behind Chaucer's poem, which rehearses clearly no single major source. This situation has tempted some to speculate that Chaucer composed the tale from memory, out of a recollection of various versions he had previously read and with which he was familiar, perhaps from his earliest school days. These include Marie de France's "Del cok e del grupil," the *Roman de Renart*, possibly the *Roman de Contrefait*, and a number of school commentaries.[14] Indeed, some have suggested that we read the tale's misattributions as Chaucer's poor recollections.[15] In any other place such mistakes are made, they typically devolve upon the character or narrator responsible for the allusion. But the "characteristic" and self-consciously literary comedy of the Nun's Priest's Tale raises the stakes of this claim. Why should we attribute one of Chaucer's best, if not the best, Canterbury tale to mere *sprezzatura* or, worse, to a bad memory? Where Chaucer works painstakingly from various sources he adapts, modifies, and copies elsewhere in his more serious works, why should we be so quick to find him abandoning that practice in his potentially most Chaucerian of tales?

A shift in Chaucer's textual practice hardly seems likely; indeed, such a notion instead seems produced by the kinds of texts, especially school texts, lying at its source.[16] That is, our assumptions about these schoolroom exercises appear to influence negatively how we read the possible discontinuities of the Nun's Priest's Tale: as wild experiment or adolescent recollection. But we ought to exercise caution regarding this kind of speculation because such a reading effectively removes other books from a tale that keeps gesturing toward various books as well as *the* book of which it is a part. If scholarship has failed to find, despite its best efforts, a solid source text lying behind and guaranteeing the Nun's Priest's Tale, that failure might be seen as a textual effect of the tale's own representation of authority. The Nun's Priest's Tale repeats a transfer of authority from one text to another as it blinds us to the proximate origin from which Chaucer's quotations emerge.

As with the rest of the tale's citations, Pearsall's *Variorum Edition*, with its lengthy footnotes and explanatory apparatus, helps us read these allusions. More extensively than is at first apparent, we can appreciate this system of citation for reading at least three levels of textuality in the Nun's Priest's Tale. At the first level, we find a general kind of textual use that can be seen in all of Chaucer's stories and medieval textual culture, since each derives from some source. By such means we can adduce Chaucer's wide and capacious memory. The second level puts texts to comic use in the Nun's Priest's fiction of particularly well-read and articulate chickens. Beyond the kinds of references various characters make throughout the *Tales*, these barn fowl parodically signify through their textual discourse—their overt citations and allusions—because of the absolute incommensurability with their animal condition, despite whatever historicizing gestures the Nun's Priest offers: "For thilke tyme, as I have understonde, / Beestes and briddes koude speke and synge" (VII.2880–81). The third level, partially reflected at the second, returns to genre and to the ironic play upon the fable and its simplicity. That is, a good part of the humor of this story comes from the kind of expectations (for a simple tale with a clear moral) raised by its genre and exceeded by its sophistication and proliferation of morals. Fables, no less than the animals in them, are presented in this bookish way. In referring to the books he has used to such brilliant effect elsewhere, Chaucer puts the Nun's Priest's Tale into conversation with most of the other stories in the Canterbury collection, as readers have recognized. But by citing those other stories he has written, often in the position of a moral to which the fable is typically directed, the Nun's Priest makes yet another book out of the tales told by the pilgrims: the *Canterbury Tales*.

While something like a summary chart might seem to offer a synoptic catalog of the Nun's Priest's Tale's Chaucerian quotations and allusions, it would offer less new information than would a broader turn to the nature of this intertextuality, the tale's manner of using citation in its fiction. One of its most infamous quotations, for instance, comes as a conclusion to Chauntecleer's intellectual conquest of his wife regarding the importance of dreams. Pertelote dismisses Chauntecleer's dream as indigestion, an overabundance of red cholera, to be remedied by purgation with laxatives. She cites Cato in her rebuke, "Ne do no fors of dremes" (VII.2941). Even more cutting, she scolds Chauntecleer for his lack of masculinity—"have ye no mannes herte, and han a berd?" (VII.2920)—since no wife "can love a coward" afraid of a dream (VII.2911). Clearly more depends on Chauntecleer's refutation of his wife's learning than mere intellectual superiority. After relating at length two exempla showing how much "dremes been to drede" (VII.3063) that serve as a full display of his learning, Chauntecleer vaunts in conclusion:

> *In principio*
> *Mulier est hominis confusio*—
> Madame, the sentence of this Latyn is,
> 'Womman is mannes joye and al his blis.' (VII.3163–66)

This biblical quotation, and its explicit translation of the Latin maxim, exemplifies a textual behavior one encounters throughout the *Canterbury Tales*, a bookishness that is here both admired and mocked. Chauntecleer's invocation of this wisdom "in the beginning" and its (mis)translation are wonderfully inappropriate and devastatingly accurate. The Latin "*mulier est hominis confusio*"—rendered simply as "woman is man's ruin" by the *Riverside* glossator—offers a conclusion to Chauntecleer's lecture on the importance of dreams by invoking, in the authoritative language of the church, Eve's confusion, error, and originary guilt. In committing the first human error, Eve exhibits the intellectual weakness of women that Chauntecleer demonstrates in his erudite rebuttal to his wife's practical advice. The Latin quotation Chauntecleer uses puts Pertelote back in her place and into an intellectual position decidedly beneath her husband. But Chauntecleer also imagines Pertelote beneath him in much more physical terms as he speaks, becoming increasingly enamored by her attractive eyes. Verbal and intellectual mastery easily slides back into the sexual mastery that Pertelote questioned and by which Chauntecleer is here undone. More important, however, Chauntecleer's triumph over Pertelote would itself be undone were she to understand the full meaning of the Latin quotation and the force of Chauntecleer's rebuttal.

Indeed, the rooster's entire discourse on dreams seems more a recovery of his diminished masculinity than a correction to his wife's limited understanding. (It is even better that it does both simultaneously.) Because his admission of fear in the face of the dream threatens to spoil his "manly" image in the eyes of his wife, Chauntecleer's lesson and its concluding Latin quotation do far more than at first appears. For if this compliment offers a humiliation she cannot perceive without such learning, it also works more extensively and appropriately than Chauntecleer intends. The rooster's translation of the biblical quotation by which he regains power and desirability is an intentional mistranslation of the line "*mulier est hominis confusio*." Instead of "woman is man's ruin" (lit., "confusion"), he offers "womman is mannes joye and al his blis" (VII.3166) precisely in order to confuse his wife to his own benefit. But it is Chauntecleer who ultimately becomes confused. As if caught up in the act of repossessing his masculinity and desirability before her, he digresses upon the "bliss" he has experienced and hopes to have again. He reveals:

> For whan I feele a-nyght your softe syde—
> Al be it that I may nat on yow ryde,
> For that oure perche is maad so narwe, allas—
> I am so ful of joye and of solas,
> That I defeye both swevene and dreeme. (VII.3167–71)

Chauntecleer's argument for the importance of dreams devolves into an excited performance of defiance before his wife. Perhaps it is even semiheroic; conquering her intellectual resistance, he then conquers his fear and "defeye[s] both swevene and dreeme." But it is more likely that Chauntecleer is caught (and thus conquered) in a fit of passion, as he immediately "flay doun fro the beem" and "fethered" Pertelote twenty times "er it was pryme" (VII.3172, 3177–78).

While Chauntecleer's desire has clearly whipped him into a froth of defiance, the temptation to say that Pertelote convinces Chauntecleer to ignore his dream or that he simply listens to his wife remains great. In fact, one might say that the Nun's Priest himself cultivates such a response when he later offers this summary of the situation to his readers: "My tale is of a cok, as ye may heere, / That tok his conseil of his wyf, with sorwe" (VII.3252–53). Taking his wife carnally sits in place of taking his wife's counsel. For the Nun's Priest, it would seem, they are the same. Thus, while the narrator's statement is not precisely accurate, it reveals tellingly the means by which woman's "sin" is performed in the story again and again, indeed every time it is read. Chauntecleer explains causality much more effectively when he attributes his confusion to seeing her ("for whan I se the beautee of youre face / Ye been so scarlet reed aboute youre yen, / It maketh al my drede for to dyen" [VII.3260–62]) as well as to his own defiance. This performance makes Chauntecleer's manipulative mistranslation literally appropriate to the situation, though perhaps not in the way he intends. If woman is man's ruin it is *because*, of course, she is his confusion, his joy, and all his bliss. Thus Chauntecleer's mollifying mistranslation more accurately designates the work that his lesson performs. The cock's superior textual knowledge ultimately bites him back because texts—particularly those that translate from one language to another and that thus make visible the movement of the signifier—mean far more than they can say.

The entirety of the argument between Chauntecleer and Pertelote creates a web of quoted texts and cited authority that pits the proverbial and practical wisdom of wife against the textual *auctoritas* of husband. Such a description recalls, of course, the general tenor of the Wife of Bath's Prologue, to which the tale not only alludes but quotes as well. Pertelote's quotations from the *Distichs* of Cato are matched by a series of texts and their stories that end with the biblical invocation and sermonizing display described above. Chauntecleer gives us the benefit of his reading in Macrobius, the Old Testament Books of Daniel and Joseph, as well as "oon of the grettest auctors men han rede" (VII.2985)—an unnamed author whose stories of prophetic dreams trump "Cato's" wisdom. While this "grettest auctor" is sometimes presumed to be Cicero, Chaucer is also producing an "authority" because it more generally suits his textual practices, similar to the "Lollius" who licenses so much unauthorized invention behind *Troilus and Criseyde*.

Yet more than the general tenor of the Wife's Prologue has been invoked by Pertelote's citational acts. She quotes the Wife of Bath in much more direct ways. The Wife, whose Prologue and Tale are both differently structured around the question and proliferation of women's desire, has been quoted and reformulated into Pertelote's "ignorant" and emotional outburst:

> For certes, what so any womman seith,
> We alle desiren, if it myghte bee,
> To han housbondes hardy, wise, and free,
> And secree—and no nygard, ne no fool
> Ne hym that is agast of every tool,
> Ne noon avauntour, by that God above! (VII.2912–17)

Such a scolding cannot help but recall the Wife, whose carping and complaining—even through the ventriloquized voices of her difficult husbands—individuate her among the other pilgrims. However, these lines bear closest resemblance to those found at the opening of the Shipman's Tale, which begins in the voice of a secular female speaker that must once have been the Wife at an earlier stage of the *Tales*' development. The fictional merchant's wife in the Shipman's Tale recalls the revised Wife of Bath herself in a number of ways. Here, however, she provides the source of Pertelote's outburst:

> And wel ye woot that wommen naturelly
> Desiren thynges sixe as wel as I:
> They wolde that hir housbondes sholde be
> Hardy and wise, and riche, and thereto free,
> And buxom unto his wyf and fressh abedde. (VII.173–77)

This fictional wife, who can make her exchanges come out even and avoid the humiliation of husbands and suitors that other Canterbury fabliau wives cannot, operates much as we would expect from the self-proclaimed "expert" Wife of Bath (III.174). She would certainly be one who could turn the trickery of the fabliaux to her own advantage, all the while maintaining her husband's honor (or at least its illusion).

The Shipman's infamous pun on "taille," meaning tally, tail, and tale, suggests the Wife of Bath's particular areas of expertise: economics, sex, and the fabrication of stories. But the Wife's Prologue also provides a more literal "source" for the language of the Nun's Priest's and Shipman's fictional wives in the acrimonious conclusion to her otherwise happy story:

And thus they lyve unto hir lyves ende
In parfit joye; and Jhesu Crist us sende
Housbondes meeke, yonge, and fresh abedde,
And grace t'overbyde hem that we wedde. (III.1257–60)

At her conclusion, as in the rest of her Prologue, the Wife has little trouble telling "ye wives" what women want from men. But such material is not restricted to her Prologue. Spoken in the more elegant register of courtly romance and Breton *lai*, the Wife of Bath's Tale offers similar wisdom about feminine desire when its miscreant knight journeys in search of the answer to Guenevere's riddle as to "what thyng is it that wommen moost desiren" (III.905). Unable to find two creatures that agree on the matter, the knight hears an array of responses that set up the later claims of the merchant's wife and Pertelote:

Somme seyde wommen loven best richessse,
Some seyde honour, somme seyde jolynesse,
Somme riche array, somme seyden lust abedde,
And oftetyme to be wydwe and wedde.
Somme seyde that oure hertes been moost esed
Whan that we been yflatered and yplesed. . . .

And somme seyen that we loven best
For to be free and do right as us lest
And that no man repreve us of oure vice,
But seye that we be wise and no thynge nyce. . . .

And somme seyn that greet delit han we
For to been holden stable, and eek secree. (III.925–30;
935–38; 945–46)

The Wife of Bath's Tale articulates possibilities for feminine desire in drawn-out terms that dilate on female vice as much as the virtue about which women would rather hear. This part of the Wife's tale also situates what will be more economically figured in the "later" Shipman's and Nun's Priest's quotations as the desired attributes of husbands, represented here as wives' perception of their own qualities. Thus where Pertelote and the merchant's wife require husbands "hardy and wys, and rich, and therto free," the Wife of Bath claims "richesse" (III.925), "to be free" (III.936), and to be called "wys" (III.938). Similarly, where Pertelote demands a man "secree—and no nygard, ne no fool" (VII.2915), the Wife of Bath says women wish to be considered "stable, and eek secree" (III.946). In appropriating what this tidy Arthurian romance says about women and their desires, the Wife of Bath, the merchant's wife, and Pertelote each turn their ideas about themselves into qualifications for their husbands.

Pertelote's outburst may provide the most obvious citation from the rest of the *Canterbury Tales*, but other lines echo throughout the Nun's Priest's story in a fashion that makes their accidental appearance unlikely, an indication that Chaucer intends his faceless prelate to repeat the other pilgrims he has heard. A preponderance of such quotation comes from other tales in fragment seven, like the Shipman's Tale discussed above, which has been analyzed as a "literature group." Alan Gaylord's fashioning of such a group operates on the generic display of these linked tales, the assortment of genres that fragment seven offers, replicating the variety of "the story-collection in miniature."[17] But it is not merely genre, but the requotations of the texts in this "literature group" that produces the literary effect of the Nun's Priest's Tale. For instance, the Nun's Priest quotes his own superior, the Prioress, when he extols, "Mordre wol out," in the midst of one of Chauntecleer's stories about the portentiousness of dreams. Chauntecleer lectures from within his first exemplary story on dreams, just before the body of the murdered victim is discovered:

> O blisful God, that art so just and trewe,
> Lo, how that thou biwreyest mordre alwey!
> Mordre wol out; that se we day by day.
> Mordre is so wlatsom and abhomynable
> To God, that is so just and resonable,
> That he ne wol nat suffre it heled be,
> Though it abyde a yeer, or two, or thre.
> Mordre wol out, this my conclusioun. (VII.3050–57)

Situated as such a "conclusioun," this aphoristic quotation of the Prioress offers itself as a portion of the surfeit of "moralite" contained in the tale.[18] That is, not only does the Nun's Priest's story urge us to "taketh the moralite, goode men" (VII.3440) from the tale as a whole, but its inwardly framed tales, such as this one recounted by Chauntecleer to his wife, also provide "conclusiouns" as well.

Recalling the moral certainty of the Prioress, a figure about whom little is morally certain, this phrase appears first in her blood libel story:

> O cursed folk of Herodes al newe,
> What may youre yvel entente yow availle?
> Mordre wol out, certeyn, it wol nat faille,
> . . . .
> The blood out crieth on youre cursed dede. (VII.574–78)

If the certainty of such wrongdoing becoming known emerges from God's divine will, what the Prioress calls "th'honour of God" (VII.577), the difference between the Prioress's use of this proverbial sentiment and Chauntecleer's is merely that of its conclusory status. Where both speakers manipulate the emotional effects of their stories with the use of this aphorism, only Chauntecleer's threatens to become the entire meaning of his tale, while, paradoxically, his is also the only tale for which such a "moral" threatens to be forgotten.

Introducing the turn of events by which deceiver will ultimately be deceived in the Nun's Priest's Tale, another proverb appears as an allusion to the repeated theme of the recently interrupted Monk's Tale: "Lo how Fortune turneth sodeynly" (VII.4593). An indirect quotation of the Monk's story, this line epitomizes a number of exclamations about Fortune and the movement of her wheel. These serve as the explanatory device for each of the figures in the Monk's series of *De Casibus* tragedies (e.g., "Lo, who may truste on Fortune any throwe?" [VII.2136]) that the Knight happily interrupts before the Nun's Priest begins speaking. Such exclamations work similarly within the tragedies the Monk relates and inside the Nun's Priest's Tale. Each line voices the emphatic emotion of the narrator in the face of the tale's recounted events, and such emotion figures the tale's affective meaning. These variations on the theme of fortune sound a refrain in the Monk's Tale, upon which its many readers have commented. Indeed, Eric Jager hears "a comic echo of the Monk's tragical 'bewaill[ing]' (1991) of Fortune's victims" when the Nun's Priest apostrophizes, "O Chauntecleer, acursed be that morwe, / That thou into that yerd flaugh fro the bemes!" (VII.3230–31).[19] Positing an even more direct imitation, Spearing writes, "designed as a parody of exemplary tragedy," the Nun's Priest's Tale offers an inversion of the Monk's exempla and authorities.[20] In their sequence in fragment seven, "the two tales are not random" or randomly placed next to each other.[21]

Such quotations thus make clearer the Nun's Priest's larger "quotation" of the emotional affect of other Chaucerian narratives within his own. Whether they are appropriate to the events of the Nun's Priest's fable continues to be debated, but their effects are nonetheless striking. Working through these citations, the Nun's Priest's Tale operates as a framing fiction, despite its location deep within the structure of the *Tales* and late in the storytelling game, containing the energy and emotion of these preceding tales in an abbreviated and aphoristic form. Little wonder, then, that it has been called the "most Chaucerian" of tales or that fragment seven, that segment of the poem which concludes with the Nun's Priest's Tale, has been called the *Canterbury Tales* in miniature. The loose but widespread quotation of the rest of the *Tales* within the Nun's Priest's Tale silently underwrites these claims.

Yet also obfuscating Chaucer's own "textual" power, the diffuse and often inappropriate quotation of other tales in the Nun's Priest's has problematized such recognition. If the Nun's Priest's genre and humble opening set up expectations for a traditional fable with a simple moral, each Chaucerian quotation operates as a moral that makes taking the story's "fruit" all the more difficult. This placement of quotations and allusions is important in a tale supposedly identified by its moral content, a tale whose moral content is offered for the easy taking: "taketh the fruyt and lat the chaf be stille" (VII.3443). At various points, the Nun's Priest's Tale plays on the simplicity of its genre and of its absent and mystified sources. It's merely a tale about a cock that took the advice of his wife to his sorrow, or so its narrator says (VII.3253). It's an admonition against flattery (VII.3436–37). It's a slap at anyone getting tricked more than once (VII.3426–28). It's a warning against speaking when one should hold one's peace (VII.3433–35). It even seems to be a bit of a correction to the fabliau logic governing at least six of the Canterbury tales in the way it inveighs against the fool who falls prey to his own trickery. It warns against pride and then over again against an unselfconscious pridefulness skillfully aware of the pride in others—or what the Reeve terms the "balke" that the Miller cannot see in his own eye as he presumes to show the mote in someone else's (I.3920). At its most simple, then, the Nun's Priest's Tale is also the most complicated example of the Canterbury fictions and in this way comes to represent the poem as a whole.

It is thus even more significant that the quotations of the *Canterbury Tales* within the Nun's Priest's Tale occur in some of the most inconspicuous of places, registering an understatement of Chaucer's most forcefully self-justifying claims. In the midst of the tale, just as the "treacherous" fox is about to be introduced into the story in characteristically hyperbolic fashion, the Nun's Priest waxes philosophical by pausing over the deterministic nature of events and their significance with familiar sentiments offered as early as the Knight's Tale (I.1251–74). Indeed, the humorous invocation of Thomas Bradwardine in an effort to reconcile predestination and free will itself alludes to the central philosophic meditations of the Knight's romance. The Nun's Priest laments in advance of "tragic" events:

> For evere the latter ende of joye is wo.
> God woot that worldly joye is soone ago;
> And if a rethor koude faire endite,
> He in a cronycle saufly myghte it write
> As for a soveryen notabilitee. (VII.3205–9)

In concluding "for evere the latter ende of joye is wo," the Nun's Priest echoes the conclusion to the Man of Law's Tale, in which Constance is returned to her father and husband only to have the entire cast of characters dead a mere fifteen lines later. King Alla and Constance return to England "Wher as they lyve in joye and in quiete," only to have "Deeth, that taketh of height and logh his rente," show up a year later (II.1131, 1143). This allusive reference back to the Man of Law stands as a curious frame for the shift from joy to woe, from the "feathering" of Pertelote "twenty tyme" and the strutting he does surrounded by his hens to the predations of the "col-fox, ful of sly iniquitee" (VII.3215) who tricks Chauntecleer into "wink[ing] whan he sholde see" (VII.3431). It is particularly the citations from and allusions to the other Canterbury tales that inflect the Nun's Priest's Tale with its fits of high emotion and overwrought sentiment. These quotations bring the tale not to the profound heights of their original iterations but to profoundly comic effects in their delightful redeployments and appropriations.

Even the tale's opening functions in this hyper-economy of Canterbury quotation. Finlayson points to "the framing realism of the tale . . . from that fairy-tale 'whilom', once upon a time, is gently ironic from the beginning, a matter of competing perspectives and literary evocations."[22] But that "whilom" also quotes the *Canterbury Tales* in the very act of quotation itself. For, of course, that same conventional "whilom" opens the first two tales (among later others), an initial duo that operates almost wholly in terms of parodic citation of each other. The Knight's opening, "Whilom, as olde stories tellen us, / Ther was a duc that highte Theseus," provides the Miller with the form of introducing the analogous protagonist of his story: "Whilom ther was dwellynge at Oxenford / A riche gnof, that helde gestes to borde" (I.859–60; I.3187–88). This opening is only the first intimation of parodic citation in the Miller's Tale, whose redeployment of a number of lines from the Knight's Tale engineers its social and narrative critique.

Perhaps one reason that the Nun's Priest's Tale is often seen as the *Canterbury Tales* in miniature lies in the fact that so many of the tale's citations and allusions refer to those materials most important to the collection as a whole. *Aesop* itself, from which the Nun's Priest's Tale and its *Renart* source derive, appears in a number of places, as Edward Wheatley has demonstrated. More recently, Finlayson has called the tale a "gossipy re-imagining of the fable."[23] Like the *Distichs* and other proverbial materials, *Aesop* appears as one of the collection's—if not the culture's—most "basic" texts, by which we can measure Chaucer's appreciable literarity.[24] With this textual language, Chaucer establishes a cultural and citational archive for the Canterbury pilgrims. But in the Nun's Priest's Tale he also makes an archive *out* of them as well. For example, Pertelote's discourse on the insignificance of dreams cites "Cato" and its common wisdom, much like the opinion that informed the Miller's condemnation of John, the "sely" carpenter. Recourse to Cato's knowledge remains as appropriate to a wifely hen as to a Miller's carpenter, and the object of both speakers' use of Cato is unruly, impractical husbands. But as Jill Mann intimates in the quotation above, it is the "literarity," what we might call the literary effect, of this behavior that redounds on Chaucer's text—especially when he makes so much out of lines from his own Canterbury book.

The reuse of so many verbal bits and pieces of other Canterbury tales makes certain demands of the Nun's Priest's Tale. As has been widely appreciated, such virtuoso narration turns our attention not to the character of the narrator speaking but back to the tale itself and what such tales can do. In this context, such a practice merely makes that turn back to the story a (re)turn to the stories of the Canterbury collection. But it also does important work for Chaucer's literary and authoritative status and the conception of the Canterbury book. Chaucer's reputation was, of course, secured by Caxton's printing press and the Renaissance editions of the poet who created the "father Chaucer" engendering English letters. His prominence appears also in the production of fifteenth-century copies of his works, particularly the *Canterbury Tales*, consumed by a newly literate, book-buying merchant class from commercial London scriptoria.[25] These material conditions explain the place of Chaucer and his continually reworked position at the head of a native English tradition throughout the late medieval and early modern period. But Chaucer's use of his own works as citational authorities throughout the *Canterbury Tales*, in a story that plays so intently with the concept and consequences of textual authority, can be seen as an early instance of the citation of the poet his later inheritors will perform in their acts of laureation. Chaucer's place at the head of English letters is inaugurated, one might say, by Chaucer's own fiction, his act of self-quotation, highlighted to exceptional degree in the Nun's Priest's Tale. By turning to the other tales in the collection, the Nun's Priest makes "Chaucer" into a text, like the many others worth alluding to in his story, and produces the very idea of the "Chaucerian" we still depend upon.

Notes

1. Derek Pearsall, ed., *A Variorum Edition of the Works of Geoffrey Chaucer, Part II: The Canterbury Tales, Part Nine: The Nun's Priest's Tale* (Norman, OK: Pilgrim Books, 1983).

2. Seth Lerer, *Chaucer and His Readers: Imagining the Author in Late Medieval England* (Princeton, NJ: Princeton University Press, 1996), 3.

3. See the essays by Robert Pratt, "Some Latin Sources of the Nonnes Preest on Dreams," *Speculum* 52 (1977): 538–70; and "Chaucer's Title: 'The Tales of Caunterbury,'" *Philological Quarterly* 54 (1975): 19–25.

4. A. C. Spearing, "Chaucer's *Troilus and Criseyde*: The Illusion of Allusion," *Exemplaria* 2, no. 1 (1990): 264.

5. N. F. Blake, *The English Language in Medieval Literature* (Totowa, NJ: Rowman and Littlefield, 1977), 19–20; cited in Pearsall, *Variorum*, 155.

6. See Christopher Cannon, "Proverbs and the Wisdom of Literature: *The Proverbs of Alfred* and Chaucer's *Tale of Melibee*," *Textual Practice* 24 (2010): 423.

7. While Chaucer references the *Distichs* of Cato, he is likely referring to a compilation of proverbial materials widely circulated and used in the schools that went under the name of "Cato." See Jill Mann, "'He Knew Nat Catoun': Medieval School-Texts and Middle English Literature," in *The Text in the Community: Essays on Medieval Manuscripts, Writers, and Readers*, ed. Jill Mann and Maura Nolan (Notre Dame: University of Notre Dame Press, 2006), 41–74.

8. Edward Wheatley, *Mastering Aesop: Medieval Education, Chaucer, and His Followers* (Gainesville: University Press of Florida, 2000), 100.

9. A. C. Spearing, "The *Canterbury Tales* IV: Exemplum and Fable," in *The Cambridge Chaucer Companion*, 2nd ed., ed. Piero Boitani and Jill Mann (Cambridge: Cambridge University Press, 2003), 195.

10. John Finlayson, "Reading Chaucer's *Nun's Priest's Tale*: Mixed Genres and Multi-Layered Worlds of Illusion," *English Studies* 86 (2005): 494, 495; see also Derek Pearsall, *The Canterbury Tales* (New York: Routledge, 1985), 236.

11. Finlayson, "Reading Chaucer's *Nun's Priest's Tale*," 493.

12. Pearsall, *The Canterbury Tales*, 3.

13. On the form of the title and change from "Tales of Canterbury" to the *Canterbury Tales*, see Pratt, "Chaucer's Title," 22.

14. For discussions of Chaucer's schoolroom learning and its effects, see Peter Travis, "*The Nun's Priest's Tale* as Grammar-School Primer," *Studies in the Age of Chaucer, Proceedings* 1 (1984): 81–91.

15. Pearsall, *Variorum*, 16–17.

16. See Wheatley, *Mastering Aesop*, 102; and Travis, "Grammar-School Primer," 84–85.

17. Helen Cooper, *The Structure of the "Canterbury Tales"* (London: Duckworth, 1983), 5. On the "literature group," see Alan Gaylord, "*Sentence* and *Solaas* in Fragment VII of the *Canterbury Tales*: Harry Bailly as Horseback Editor," *PMLA* 82 (1967): 226–35.

18. But even further, its surfeit may also extend to another Canterbury tale in its articulation of God's reasonableness. It echoes, in reverse, Dorigen's rhetorical question about the unreasonableness of God's creation of the black rocks in the Franklin's Tale (V.868–93).

19. Eric Jager, "Croesus and Chauntecleer: The Royal Road of Dreams," *Modern Language Quarterly* 49 (1988): 15.

20. Spearing, "Exemplum and Fable," 206–7.

21. Ibid., 206.

22. Finlayson, "Reading Chaucer's *Nun's Priest's Tale*," 495.

23. Ibid., 500.

24. Jill Mann, "'He Knew Nat Catoun,'" 55.

25. See Derek Pearsall and A. S. G. Edwards, "The Manuscripts of Major English Poetic Texts," in *Book Production and Publishing in Britain, 1375–1475*, ed. Derek Pearsall and Jeremy Griffiths (Cambridge: Cambridge University Press, 1989), 257–78.

CHAPTER 19

Chaucer, the Continent, and the Characteristics of Commentary

Sarah Baechle

It is hardly exaggeration to claim that Derek Pearsall's impact on the study of medieval literature is immensely far-reaching, evangelizing close reading, the merits of attending to the letter and form of the text, and likewise promoting capability with the material object, the unique instantiation of a text in its manifold manuscript forms. Among these potentially disparate critical practices runs a leitmotif that epitomizes one of the profound influences Derek has exerted: at the intersection of the study of a text and the study of its medium lies the question of its audience. The significance of a text's formal features rests upon its readers, as much as the individualized details of its material expression—its textual permutation, illustrations, and marginalia.

In the *Canterbury Tales*, this is a question of crucial importance; with eighty-three extant manuscripts, the physical track of the poem's audience leads modern readers inexorably toward befuddlement. Over thirty of the *Tales* manuscripts, moreover, include some portion of a corpus of glosses witnessed in some of the earliest manuscripts of the poem and which continued to be copied into many of its later instantiations. Despite growing interest in vernacular English manuscripts—due, no doubt, to the scholarship of Derek and those students whom he mentored—they have received little critical attention, discounted as authorial memoranda for future revisions by modern critics who assert, based on their expectations of what the apparatus should look like, that it does not comment on the poetic text itself. Yet they discount the traces of the poem's medieval audience, and of larger reading communities of vernacular literature, whose reactions to their manuscripts suggest otherwise. The *Canterbury Tales* glosses do not direct readers to a particular, orthodox interpretation of the text, but they act, nonetheless, as commentary, and their reception in later manuscripts demonstrates medieval readers' awareness of this potential. To regard these glosses as editorial memoranda oversimplifies their function, flattening their complex hermeneutic relationship with the main text of the *Tales*. Moreover, the fifteenth-century instantiations of these glosses demonstrate a sophisticated readership that not only regarded the glosses as essential paratexts of the *Tales* but also recognized and attempted to domesticate their hermeneutic ambiguity. I will briefly address the glosses' legacy of insignificance in twentieth-century scholarship and point to a few analogues in literary manuscripts on the Continent which likewise display the qualities that relegate the Chaucerian marginalia to the status of editorial detritus, before unpacking the editorial methods employed to tame the glosses in the fifteenth century.

The evidence on which an identification of the glosses as editorial memoranda is predicated coalesces largely around concern with their lack of uniformity, both in placement and in source material.[1] The glosses are present to varying degrees in different *Tales*, with the most plentiful marginalia seen in the "Wife of Bath's Prologue." These glosses are not uniformly distributed throughout the "Prologue;" rather, they are concentrated in the first half and taper off during Alysoun's discussion of her five husbands. Daniel Silvia, arguing that the glosses indicate planned revisions, posits that this reflects the stages of the "Prologue's" composition—the latter part having been composed first—and any marginalia evident in the second half would have been incorporated into the "Prologue" or rejected.[2] He suggests, furthermore, that the lack of source glossing from Book I, chapter 47, of *Against Jovinian*—the part of the Hieronymic text with the greatest influence on the "Prologue"—is due to a similar process: Chaucer would have used this part of the letter first and discarded the marginalia after use.[3] The Latin apparatus that traveled with the *Tales*, he states emphatically, was not intended to comment on or explain the poetry; it was merely a set of Chaucer's notes to himself, which reflected a lack of completion in the "Prologue" and other texts that would not have been out of keeping for the poet.[4]

Yet why must this lack of uniformity demand the rejection of any more complex function? The manuscript tradition of the *Roman de la Rose* betrays the traces of scribes and readers who over the centuries after its composition likewise recorded their responses to the poem across its pages.[5] Their marginalia offer particularly relevant points of comparison with those in the *Tales* and display parallels to the criteria used to deem the *Tales* glosses authorial memoranda which belie the glosses' hermeneutic potentiality.[6] These manuscripts display a tradition of glossing that is more varied than that in the *Canterbury Tales*, in large part because they are copied not necessarily by the scribes, but by later readers. The first of these, BNF fr. 1560, contains few glosses—nine, to be exact—but even these few have some common ground with the *Tales* marginalia. They consist of quotations from Latin *auctoritas*—Tibullus, Macrobius, Ovid, and Aristotle (in Latin translation), among others—and are concentrated largely within the first fifteen folios.[7] The second manuscript, Arsenal 3337, is heavily glossed, by at least two different hands. The first set of glosses, added by the scribe, consists mostly of French and Latin proverbs, along with a few quotations from Ovid; the second, a set of nearly sixty glosses taken almost exclusively from the *Ars Amatoria*, is primarily clustered around the teachings of the God of Love in Guillaume's section of the poem and in Jean's discourse of Amis, with a very few in the sections of the poem containing Reason's discourse and the speeches of La Vielle.[8]

This concentration of glosses is particularly interesting as the *Ars Amatoria* is one of the most influential sources of La Vielle's dialogue, making the relative paucity of glossing in this section quite surprising—we might compare it to a third manuscript, Turin, Bibl. Univ. L. III. 22, which features a number of readers' comments, many of them quotations from Ovid, in the discourse of La Vielle—and perhaps providing a parallel to the unevenness of the distribution of *Tales* glosses, as well as the lack of glosses from particularly influential sources.[9] A fourth manuscript, BNF fr. 24390, contains a similar apparatus, with the further additions of a number of citations of relevant Latin material from Gratian's *Decretum* and Bartholomew of Brescia's commentary, all of which, like those in Arsenal 3337, are found mainly in the middle of the manuscript, from folio 51 to folio 90, tapering off with La Vielle.[10] These brief descriptions do not suffice to claim any one *Rose* manuscript as a model for Chaucer's glosses, but they point toward a tradition of glossing in vernacular verse manuscripts, which demonstrates a similar lack of uniformity that, while it may appear capricious to modern readers, does not require us to term them authorial revision memoranda, by dint of their significantly later origin. They remind us, moreover, of the danger in assuming modern expectations of what annotation in medieval literature *ought* to look like: what we perceive to be lack of uniformity or a lack of attention to the more "significant" parts of a text, quotation from its most important sources, does not necessarily reflect the interests or values of the medieval reader.

If these *Tales* glosses might be regarded as performing some hermeneutic function, how, precisely, do they operate? In *Opening Up Middle English Manuscripts*, Kathryn Kerby-Fulton posits a relationship between Latin and vernacular that provides the possibility of reading multiple interpretations into the text, commensurate with the depth a reader wishes, or is able, to read into the source quotation.[11] That is to say, selective quotation of a source text means that the text may be read literally, as it is presented on the page, or that readers with knowledge of the source text might, if they so choose, bring that exterior knowledge to bear on their reading of Chaucer.

For the sake of illustration, we might consider one example from the abundant Latin glossing in the "Wife of Bath's Prologue": at III.26–29, the Wife of Bath observes, in defense of her multiple remarriages, that God has commanded her to "wexe and multiplye" (III.28). In Ellesmere, this is accompanied by the gloss, "Crescite et multiplicamini" (Increase and multiply).[12] The quotation is not cited, but it is taken from Saint Jerome who is himself quoting Genesis 1:28 in his *Against Jovinian*. Medieval readers might, Kerby-Fulton argues, fill in the rest of the scriptural context—the exhortation to fill the earth—and find humor in the ironic textual interplay.[13] They might, however, also think of the biblical verse's use in Chaucer's direct source—Jerome—which interprets the text in a much darker fashion. The context is both physically and spiritually threatening, as Kerby-Fulton explains: readers encountering the Wife of Bath in the context of *Against Jovinian* might remember "that plants needed first 'to grow,' so that there would be that afterwards to be *cut off*—a vicious metaphor in a sexual context, suggesting marriage as emasculation . . . [and] that marriage only 'fills earth' not heaven."[14] However, to reach this interpretation of the "Prologue," readers would need not only to be literate in Latin but also to be familiar enough with the relevant source texts to recall the context whence the source gloss derives, and make the choice to interpret the text in this context.

Perhaps the most compelling evidence that, regardless of their author's intentions, the *Canterbury Tales* marginalia could be understood as commentary arrives in the form of editorial revisions to the apparatus. Fifteenth-century scribes were no less free to adapt the manuscript presentation of the poem than they were the text itself, and frequently did so, incorporating new material, removing glosses they did not care for, and adding their own comments in the margins of their manuscripts. From the larger editorial campaigns that particular later professional readers enacted in their copies of the *Canterbury Tales* emerges a characteristic reaction to the glosses as intrinsically part of a cohesive Chaucerian text, and one whose polysemous potential demanded control, in some cases, significant restraint from the exuberant ambiguity of the original apparatus.

As the Chaucerian text with the most significant Latin source glossing, the "Wife of Bath's Prologue" provides, once more, the most significant case study in later medieval attempts to lock down interpretation and restrict the unbridled intertextual production of meaning in the *Tales*' source glosses.[15] The greatest and most provocative changes are those found in two fifteenth-century manuscripts: British Library MSS Additional 5140 and Egerton 2864 (hereafter referred to as Ad1 and En3, respectively); accordingly, the remainder of this analysis focuses on these two manuscripts.[16]

The apparatus in Ad1 and En3, two manuscripts ostensibly copied from the same exemplar, occur in differing degrees of editorial intervention.[17] At their simplest, they repeat the brief Latin quotation in El but add a citation of the text's original source in scripture. Thus, at III.81, the Wife of Bath gleefully informs readers that Saint Paul could do no more than advise Christians to preserve their virginity: "But natheless, thogh that he wroot and sayde / He wolde that every wight were swich as he / Al nys but conseil to virginitee" (III.80–82). In El, and the three other manuscripts that most closely adhere to this earliest set of glosses, the marginal text reads, "Volo autem omnes homines esse sicut meipsum" (I prefer, moreover, that all men were just like myself), a quotation that Steven Partridge suggests likely comes to the author by way of Jerome's *Against Jovinian*.[18] In Ad1 and En3, however, the gloss reads, "Volo autem omnes homines esse sicut meipsum Apostolus ad Corinthios."[19] The change is simple, but its implications are far-reaching: where the original format of the gloss creates ambiguity through its refusal to disclose a specific intertext, the accompanying citation in Ad1 and En3 attempts to forestall interpretive uncertainty by directing readers away from *Against Jovinian* and instructing them to find their context in scripture.

The Latin apparatus of Ad1 and En3 is characterized by this apparent preference for narrowing the field of reference in the *Tales* glosses, but it is quite rare that they do so through citation alone. Rather, the editorial changes compass an impulse not only to direct readers away from the influence of *Against Jovinian* and toward scripture but also to fill in the larger contextual picture, particularly where the connotations of the biblical verse differ from those of Jerome's text. The glosses' editor tends to accomplish this through the addition of scriptural citation and expansion of the source quotation. In the above example of the Ellesmere gloss at III.28, with which Kerby-Fulton outlines the markedly different ways in which each source text could color Chaucer's verse, the scriptural endorsement of human sexuality devolves into a metaphoric precursor of death—physical and spiritual—and perhaps emasculation. The gloss in Ad1 and En3 echoes the text of its predecessor—with citation—but includes far lengthier quotation. El's "Crescite et multiplicamini" (increase and multiply) thus becomes[20]

> Crescite et multiplicamini Genesis ij.° viij.° et ix.° bis Quambret [properly Quamobrem] relinquet homo patrem et matrem suam et adherebit vxori sue Genesis ibid Relinquet homo patrem et matrem suam et adherebit vxori sue Apostolus ad Philippenses Siquidem et duc [properly duae] vxores Dauid captiue fuerat Achinoen Israelites et Abigail vxor Nabal Carmeli Regum primo Capitulo xxx.°
>
> ——
>
> [Increase and multiply Genesis ii° viii° and ix° twice, Therefore man shall leave his mother and father and cleave to his wife Genesis, the same place, Man shall leave his father and mother and cleave to his wife, the Apostle to the Philippians, Since two wives of David were taken captive, Achinoen the Israelite and Abigail wife of Nabal of Carmel, Kings [book] one, chapter xxx°.][21]

Where the Ellesmere gloss attends selectively to the text, highlighting only the advice to "wexe and multiplye" (III.28), arguably through the lens of *Against Jovinian*, Ad1 and En3's editorial reader attends to the larger significance of the passage, acknowledging as well Alysoun's reminder that biblical authority dictates that her husband "Sholde lete fader and mooder and take to me" (III.31), incorporating both references into a marginal approbation of marriage in which the command to increase and multiply is clearly figured as a physical mandate, the product of matrimony—the earthly bond between a man and woman, not man and the church, as Jerome envisions it—and not conversion.[22]

The gloss concludes, curiously, with a passage that is not incorporated into the Middle English verse itself: the citation of 1 Kings 30, in which David retrieves his captive wives from the Amalecites after the destruction of Siceleg. Since demonstrably not a source gloss, as the two Genesis quotations are, the excerpt from Kings must have been included for some perceived thematic relevance; at its most basic, the biblical passage provides an object lesson in the lengths to which a husband might be obliged to go in order to cleave to his wife. In this sense at least, David's pursuit of the Amalecites provides a source of *auctoritas*, in the form of an Old Testament patriarch, testifying to the importance of the marital bond. Yet if the editor of these glosses is a careful reader, as seems likely given the extensive quotation of additional appropriate scriptural material in Ad1 and En3's glosses, the story of David and the Amalecites picks up, and subtly comments on, one further part of the passage. As the Wife argues that God commanded her husbands to leave their families and take to her, she observes, "But of no nombre mencion made he / Of bigamye, or of octogamye" (III.32–33). Jerome's exegesis of the command to go forth and multiply concludes, in *Against Jovinian*, with a clear denunciation of second marriage, which, he claims, is not permitted even to birds and beasts.[23] Among the spoils, however, that David wrests away from the Amalecites are two of his wives—Achinoen and Abigail—who offer clear evidence that in the world of the Old Testament patriarchs, the injunction to be fruitful was hardly restricted to a single spouse.

Ad1 and En3 handle the subject of marriage itself, whether monogamous or plural, in a far more permissive light than its authoritative predecessor in the El glosses. Their approbation is crystallized in the treatment of a cluster of marginalia appending Alysoun's reminder that the apostle Paul advises Christians, "Bet is to be wedded than to brynne" (III.52). The vast majority of the manuscripts that contain some version of the Latin apparatus contain the gloss "melius est nubere quam vri" (It is better to marry than to burn).[24] The quotation ultimately derives from Paul's first epistle to the Corinthians, where it is used specifically to justify the remarriage of widows: "Dico autem non nuptis et viduis: bonum est illis si sic maneant, sicut et ego. Quod si non se continent, nubant. Melius est enim nubere, quam uri" (I say to the unmarried, and to widows: it is good for them if they continue thus, even as I. But if they do not hold themselves back, let them marry. For indeed, it is better to marry than to burn).[25] It is a particularly apt point of *auctoritas* for the Wife's justification of her own marriage practices, for though she speaks of bigamy, nothing of her account of her marriages suggests that she has been married to more than one man at a time. Well aware of her inability to hold back, she has followed the advice laid out in 1 Corinthians to a tee, and a reader encountering the gloss alongside Alysoun's lively screed might recognize the legitimacy of her arguments, or find humor in the way they play against the misogynist traditions she fights. In Jerome's polemical take, however, the claim that it is better to marry than to burn represents not approbation of marriage, but only the lenient suggestion of a slightly less evil alternative to fornication and subsequent perdition. Paul does not, he argues, say that marriage is *good*—merely that it is better than temptation and damnation, just as it is better to limp on one foot than to crawl with two broken legs—a violent comparison that leaves little doubt that in Jerome's mind marriage is to be equated with physical pain and the weakness of disfigurement.[26] In El, and every other manuscript apart from Ad1 and En3 that witnesses this gloss, it is presented without citation, leaving interpretation, the choice of context in which to read the English verse, to the reader.

In El, the quotation of 1 Corinthians is packaged within a frame of other glosses that significantly qualify Paul's leniency. I reproduce the text of the Wife's argument here:

He seith that to be wedded is no synne;
Bet is to be wedded than to brynne.
What rekketh me, thogh folk seye vileynye
Of shrewed Lameth and his bigamye?
I woot wel Abraham was an hooly man,
And Jacob eek, as ferforth as I kan;
And ech of hem hadde wyves mo than two (III.51–57)

At III.51, immediately preceding the Pauline gloss, El's margins read, "Si acceperis vxorem non peccasti et si nupserit virgo non peccauit sed hij domino se vouerunt Ita idem et cetera" (If you take a wife you have not sinned and if a virgin marry, she has not sinned, however, thus also, those who consecrated themselves to the Lord, et cetera).[27] The gloss attributes no sin to marriage, but in its Hieronymic context, it establishes a clear preference for virginity and a blatant condemnation of remarriage whose vitriol is not echoed in Jerome's Pauline source, where the Apostle merely acknowledges, "Si autem acceperis uxorem: non peccasti. Et si nupserit virgo, non peccavit. Tribulationem tamen carnis habebunt huiusmodi. Ego autem vobis parco" (If you take a wife, you have not sinned. And if a virgin marry, she has not sinned. They will have tribulation of the flesh, even so. However, I would spare you that).[28] Though Paul admits a preference for sparing his audience the tribulation of the flesh that accompanies marriage, he stops far short of Jerome, for whom tribulation of the flesh negates the joys of the flesh that are the sole attraction of marriage. Here, Jerome argues that those virgins who dedicate themselves to God and subsequently marry "habebit damnationem" (she will have damnation), in the same stroke deeming consecrated virgins who marry incestuous and widows who remarry adulterous: "Si autem hoc de viduis dictum objecerit, quanto magis de virginibus praevalebit, cum etiam his non liceat, quibus aliquando licuit! Virgines enim, quae post consecrationem nupserint, non tam adulterae sunt, quam incestae" (If, however, he objects that this saying is about widows, how much greater does it have force regarding virgins, since it is forbidden even to those [widows] to whom once it had been allowed. For virgins who marry after consecration are incestuous rather than adulterous).[29] In such a context, Paul's express admission that widows who cannot remain chaste may remarry is elided in the face of the assertion that to do so would be to commit adultery; the leniency extends only, in Jerome's polemics, to first marriage. Indeed, Jerome goes on to tackle a similarly permissive statement in 1 Timothy: "Volo ergo iuveniores nubere, filios procreare, matres familias esse, nullam occasionem dare adversario maledicti gratia" (I wish, therefore, that the young widows marry, bring forth children, be the heads of households, to give no occasion to the adversary to curse them).[30] The Apostle says, Jerome argues, that it is better that a woman remarry because "tolerabilius est uni homini prostitutam esse, quam multis" (it is more tolerable to be a prostitute to one man than to many).[31] If first marriage, for Jerome, is tolerable but not good, subsequent marriages, no matter the number, are always figured not as a morally acceptable alternative to fornication, not the beginning of a fruitful family life, but merely a restriction of the extent to which its inherent sin is spread, for the remarried woman is still a prostitute, even if she reserves her services for one man.

The gloss which concludes this sequence, in El, associates still worse crimes with the marital practices the Wife attempts to defend. At III.54–57, above, she clearly responds to the association of serial remarriage with bigamy, citing precedent in the Old Testament patriarchs. In El, this is accompanied by a third gloss: "Lameth qui primus intrauit bigamiam sanguinarius et homicida est et cetera / Abraham trigamus Iacob quatrigamus" (Lamech, who first entered into bigamy was bloodstained and a murderer / Abraham [was] a trigamist, Jacob, a quadrigamist).[32] There may be Old Testament *auctorites* for multiple marriage, the gloss reminds readers, but they are hardly worth emulating, their actions tainted by association with the first bigamist's bloodthirsty, murderous past. Jerome extends this violence inward: Lamech's brutality is not only to be found in his homicidal nature, but is self-inflicting as well, for in committing bigamy, he divided the single flesh of marriage between two spouses: "*Et erunt*, inquit, *duo in carne una*: non tres, neque quatuor, alioquin jam non duo, si plures. Primus Lamech sanguinarius et homicida, unam carnem in duas divisit uxores" ("And they will be," he says, "two in one flesh": not three, nor four; otherwise, they are no longer two, if they are many. Lamech, a bloodthirsty man and a murderer, first divided one flesh between two wives).[33] In order to become one flesh with a second, or third, or fourth spouse, the would-be bigamist must divide his own flesh in an act of spiritual—though literally phrased—self-violence that renders the process as uninviting as the implication that it is an act of prostitution.

Even then, these are the lesser allegations Jerome raises against multiple marriage. In Genesis, Lamech compares himself—unfavorably—with Cain, confessing to his wives that he has killed a man with his own hands and will be punished accordingly: "Dixitque Lamech uxoribus suis Adae et Sellae: Audite vocem meam uxores Lamech, auscultate sermonem meum: quoniam occidi virum in vulnus meum, et adolescentulum in livorem meum. Septuplum ultio dabitur de Cain: de Lamech vero septuagies septies" (And Lamech said to his wives, Adah and Zilah:

"Hear my voice, wives of Lamech, heed my sermon: for in my distress I have killed a man, and an adolescent, in my spite. Seven times retribution was given concerning Cain, seventy-seven times, truly, concerning Lamech").[34] In Genesis, the cause of Lamech's punishment is clear: he expects fair retribution for the murder of another. *Against Jovinian* attributes the cause, rather, to Lamech's bigamy: "fratricidium et digamiam, eadem cataclysmi poena delevit. De altero septies, de altero septuagies septies vindicatum est. Quantum distant in numero, tantum et in crimine" (Fratricide and digamy[35] together were destroyed by the punishment of the deluge. Concerning the one seven times vengeance, the other seventy times seven. As far apart as they are in number, so are they in sin).[36] The harsher punishment is to be visited upon Lamech for his graver sin, and fratricide expressly preferred to bigamy. The marginal treatment of this passage offers readers the choice of two vastly different contexts against which they might read the "Prologue." At its core, the gloss still offers readers Genesis's matter-of-fact acceptance of polygamous practice and the lenient Pauline context with which to align their interpretation, but it presents them, equally, with the misogynist, polemic Hieronymic equation of remarriage with adultery, prostitution, and murder.

In Ad1 and En3, the ambiguous field of reference is restricted to its scriptural sources. The gloss from 1 Corinthians is, here, part of a single long gloss which elaborates significantly on Alysoun's citation of both the Apostle's approbation of marriage and the Old Testament patriarchs' multiple spouses:

> Propter fornicationem autem vnusquisque suam vxorem habeat et vnaquaque suum virum habeat Apostolus ad Corintheos Melius est enim nubere quam vri Apostolus ad Corintheos Matusael genuit lameth qui accepit duas vxores Genesis iiij.° Abraham vero aliam vxorem duxit Genesis xxv.° Et Labam Vespelyam [properly vespere Lyam] filiam suam introduxit ad eum .i. Iacob Genesi xxx.° et postea ibidem et ebdomoda transacta Rachel duxit in vxorem .i. Iacob.

—

> [However, on account of fornication, let each man have his wife, and let each woman have her husband, the Apostle to Corinthians; Indeed, it is better to marry than to burn, the Apostle to Corinthians; Methuselah begat Lameth, who took two wives, Genesis iiii°;

> Indeed Abraham took another wife, Genesis xxv°. And in the evening, Laban brought his daughter Leah in to him, that is, Jacob, Genesis xxx°, and in the same place, after the week was completed, he, that is, Jacob, took Rachel as a wife.][37]

Where the El gloss prefaces the verse permitting widows to remarry with oblique praise of consecrated virginity and denigration of remarriage, Ad1 and En3 preface it instead with parallel permissiveness granted to first marriages. Just as widows who cannot remain chaste are better off if they remarry, so are virgins encouraged to marry rather than commit fornication. The passages of 1 Corinthians quoted in these two manuscripts do admit a preference for virginity—Paul begins by stating, "bonum est homini mulierem non tangere" (it is good for a man not to touch a woman)[38]—yet marriage and, more important for Alysoun's case, the remarriage of widows are presented as viable alternatives to virginity for those who are afflicted with carnal desire, rather than sinful acts.

The remainder of the gloss consists of a series of quotations from Genesis, identifying the sources of the Wife's allusions to bigamous Old Testament patriarchs. These, explicitly attributed to their original, scriptural sources, circumnavigate the condemnations suggested by the El gloss's association with *Against Jovinian*, offering readers instead a different, straightforward narrative in which marriage, multiple or otherwise, is figured as generative, the vehicle of the growth of the human race. The passages quoted and cited from Genesis are drawn from the *libri generationum* of the Old Testament patriarchs, describing the lines of descent of humanity, first from Adam, then from Noah, from Abraham and Ishmael and Isaac, and finally, from Jacob. Lamech, the gloss informs readers, was begotten by Methusaleh and then took two wives; the passage continues, in Genesis 4 and again in Genesis 5, to enumerate the descendants that he fathers with each wife; his marriages are defined by their procreativity.[39] In the first instance, Lamech is descended from Cain, and his wives are numbered and named; it is from this passage that the text of the gloss is drawn. In Genesis 5, Lamech descends, rather, from Seth, and nothing is shared of his wives. In each case, however, the unions are clearly fertile, one in a chain of men who are born, marry, and produce heirs who repeat the process.

Abraham, too, engages in additional marriages, cited in the margins of Ad1 and En3 from Genesis 25:1. The choice of citation here is curious; it passes over his union with Hagar, the handmaid of his first wife, Sarah, in silence, choosing instead to quote from the passage in which, after Sarah's death, a widowed Abraham remarries, presenting the patriarch as less a bigamist than a serial monogamist, much like Alysoun herself. His new wife, Keturah, bears him several additional children, and the text of the chapter enumerates his descendants, through Keturah, through Hagar's son Ishmael, and finally through his favored son, Isaac.[40] Abraham's polygamy is refigured like Lamech's before him as a powerful generative force, and he, as the father of nations. Readers of Ad1 and En3 might still see the ironic humor in this defense of bigamy in the hands of the Wife of Bath, whose marriages have been anything but fruitful, but the potential to read further, to the criticisms leveled by Jerome, is foreshortened by the editorial changes to the marginalia.

Alysoun's final choice of *auctorite*, Jacob, likewise presents a curious decision, as Jacob's bigamy stems from the deceit of his father-in-law, who promises him one bride and delivers another. The text of the gloss in Ad1 and En3 highlights the deception as much as it does Jacob's multiple marriages, with the quotations in the gloss bookending a narrative in which Jacob—anointed the father of a nation by God—seeks only monogamous union with Rachel. Between the two acts of marriage, recorded in the margins of Ad1 and En3, the text of Genesis unfolds a narrative in which Jacob's bigamy is definitively entered at his father-in-law's wishes, following the bait-and-switch of his first marriage.[41] The editorial hand responsible for these changes to the marginalia chooses then to privilege not the censure which the Wife claims is directed toward the Old Testament bigamists but the individual circumstances that flesh out their choices, humanizing them through the exploration of their motives, valorizing the fecundity of their marriages, and at times exercising subtle differentiation between bigamy and the remarriage of widows like Alysoun herself. Their approach, though not overtly praising the Wife's choices, does demonstrate a predilection for underscoring where the weighty authority of scripture agrees with her arguments and, more important, for narrowing readers' field of reference and restraining the avenues through which ambiguous, conflicting interpretations proliferate.

At times, this predilection gives way to more overtly restrictive editorial manipulation. At their most extreme, the editorial changes to the glosses take the form of almost wholesale rejection of certain marginalia and the substitution of scriptural quotation in the margins of the "Prologue." The manuscripts' treatment of the Pauline concept of the marriage debt—whose virtues Alysoun extols at length—offers illustrative demonstration of the extent to which later readers shaped the hermeneutic practices of the early Chaucerian manuscripts and a suitable place to conclude. El shares a kernel of glossed text in common with Ad1 and En3: as Alysoun observes that "An housbonde I wol have—I wol nat lette— / Which shal be bothe my dettour and my thral, / And have his tribulacion withal / Upon his flesh, whil that I am his wyf," almost all of the glossed manuscripts note some minor variation on "Tribulacionem tamen carnis habebunt huiusmodi" (Nevertheless, they will have tribulation of the flesh).[42] The remainder of the glossed text, however, varies significantly in source and tone. El prefaces this brief passage, from 1 Corinthians, with a gloss drawn from *Against Jovinian*. In El, the whole marginal text for this passage reads:

> Qui vxorem habet et debitor dicitur et esse in prepucio et seruus vxoris et quod malorum seruorum est alligatus / Item si acceperis vxorem non peccasti tribulacionem tamen carnis habebunt huiusmodi et cetera / Item vir corporis sui non habet potestatem set vxor / Item viri diligite vxores vestras.
>
> ———
>
> [He who has a wife is said to be a debtor, and to be uncircumcised, and the servant of his wife and, like bad servants, a bound slave / Likewise if you take a wife you have not sinned, but they will have tribulation of the flesh, et cetera / Also a man has no power over his own body, but his wife (does) / Also, husbands, love your wives.][43]

In El, this ambiguous context plays upon a deeply misogynist polemical twist to 1 Corinthians in *Against Jovinian*, in which the marriage bond is interpreted literally: the meaning of the words themselves, Jerome argues, must be taken into account, and if he who is married is a servant, a debtor, a bound slave, and uncircumcised, conversely, "Qui autem sine uxore est, primum nullius debitor est, deinde circumcisus, tertio liber, ad extremam solutus" (But he who is without a wife, first is no one's debtor, then is circumcised, thirdly is free, lastly, is unbound).[44] The discussion of the Pauline concept of the marriage debt is decidedly one-sided; a husband, Jerome points out, is said to be his wife's debtor, but he says nothing of the possibility of mutuality. Rather, the woman is figured as slave owner of an unclean—uncircumcised, removed from the Old Testament covenant with God—husband.[45] Unspoken in the letter of Jerome's text is a deeply pervasive misogynist view of femininity that corresponds closely to Alysoun's description of her first marriages: women are domineering, liberally exerting their wills on powerless, emasculated spouses.

Jerome's twist on Pauline marriage debt accords with that set out in the "Wife of Bath's Prologue," but the misogyny of his text is dampened, if not wholly absent, from his source in scripture. Paul describes marriage as a mutual debt, in which just as a husband owes his wife a debt, so too does she owe her husband: "Uxori vir debitum reddat: similiter autem et uxor viro. Mulier sui corporis potestatem non habet, sed vir. Similiter autem et vir sui corporis potestatem non habet, sed mulier. Nolite fraudare invicem, nisi forte ex consensu ad tempus, ut vacetis orationi: et iterum revertimini in id ipsum" (Let the husband render the debt to his wife: likewise, let the wife render the debt to her husband. A woman does not have power over her own body, but her husband does. Likewise, however, the husband has no power over his body, but his wife does. Do not defraud one another, unless perhaps out of consensus, so that you may be free to pray: and return again to one another).[46] In its original Pauline expression, marriage is an equal partnership: the wife, rather than a domineering harridan, may have power over her husband, but he too has power over her body. The emasculating spousal subjugation of *Against Jovinian* is neatly balanced by this mutual power, such that if the husband is in fact his wife's slave, so too is she his. El's readers might well evaluate the "Wife of Bath's Prologue" in relation to Jerome's antifeminist screed—the language of the gloss, here, echoes his text—but Paul's epistle remains at the gloss's core, so that the reader who encounters the "Prologue" in this context might also recognize the scriptural source and reevaluate the poem accordingly, correcting the Wife's one-sided understanding of marriage debt, perhaps understanding the ironic misinterpretation of scripture at play in the misogynist stereotypes to which she gives form—including those voiced in *Against Jovinian*.

In Ad1 and En3, this process of recognition and evaluation is foreshortened by the editorial changes to the gloss, which restrict its interpretive possibilities by restoring, over several lines of verse, the marginal text to its fuller Pauline context. Alysoun's first discussion of the marital debt is folded into a defense of the procreative capabilities of the sexual organs. If genitalia were intended only for purgation, why, she asks, would anyone have written "That man shal yelde to his wyf hire dette?" (III.130). Ad1 and En3 echo her one-sided understanding of marital debt here, remarking, "Vxori vir debitum reddat Apostolus ad Corinthios" (Let the husband render the debt to his wife, the Apostle to the Corinthians).[47] The gloss here, while it does preempt a Hieronymic contextualization, can only point readers toward the source that corrects Alysoun's apparent misunderstanding of the marriage debt. Yet the Wife is not finished discussing the subject, and she returns to the subject, proclaiming that she will persevere in her sexuality, to use her "instrument" whenever her husband "list come forth and paye his dette. / A housbond I wol have—I wol nat lette— / Which shal be bothe my dettour and my thral, / . . . / I have the power durynge al my lyf / Upon his propre body, and noght he" (III.153–58). Alysoun's language clearly echoes Jerome's—her husband shall be her debtor and her slave—but the author of Ad1 and En3's changes responds with a firmly Pauline gloss:

> Vxori vir debitum reddat similiter autem et vxor viro Apostolus ad Corinthios / Tribulacionem tamen carnis habebunt Apostolus ad Corinthios / Similiter autem et vir potestatem non habet sed mulier Apostolus ad Corinthios Viri diligite vxores vestras et nolite amari esse ad illas Apostolus ad Colocenses.
>
> ——
>
> [Let the husband render the debt to his wife, likewise however, let the wife to her husband, the Apostle to the Corinthians / Nevertheless they shall have tribulation of the flesh, the Apostle to the Corinthians / Likewise, however, also a husband has now power, but his wife does, the Apostle to the Corinthians, Husbands, love your wives, and do not be bitter to them, the Apostle to the Colossians.][48]

The text does not stray completely from El's gloss, or Jerome's interpretation of scripture; where *Against Jovinian* and Chaucer's tale concur with scriptural precedent, Ad1 and En3 reproduce the glosses in El, albeit with scriptural citation. They firmly acknowledge the root of Alysoun's claim that her husbands shall have tribulation of the flesh, and command husbands to love their wives. Yet the marginalia's insistence on the Pauline intertext forces something of a theological confrontation between the competing marital power dynamics, calling attention to, and correcting, the Wife's misunderstanding of Paul's epistle and shepherding readers from the misogynist polemics of Jerome's text toward an orthodox, scriptural interpretation affirming uxorial debt parallel to that which Alysoun gleefully asserts her husbands owed her.

Yet there is a distinction to maintain. While the changes to the marginalia in Ad1 and En3 steer readers away from the antifeminist hermeneutic of *Against Jovinian*, it would be rash to assert a protofeminist approach to the text at the root of these emendations. Rather, they spring from an emphasis on scriptural orthodoxy. Where Alysoun echoes misogynistic depictions of women taken from the Book of Proverbs, the author of Ad1 and En3's editorial changes adds source marginalia affirming those passages, asserting women's gifts with weeping and lying, and alleging the essentiality of their noisome qualities.[49] Inasmuch as the editorial changes to the marginal apparatus of the "Wife of Bath's Prologue" appear to assert a particular hermeneutic approach to the poem, they demonstrate a concerted and repeated investment in narrowing the field of reference enabled by the glosses and directing readers to the specific intertext of Holy Scripture. This approach must be seen not as a response to the poem itself but as a cognizant reaction against the ambiguous recontextualization of the apparatus witnessed in the earliest glossed *Canterbury Tales* manuscripts and established in the Ellesmere manuscript. It suggests, then, concrete evidence that, whatever the glosses' original purpose, they were received by medieval readers as an integral part of the text, one which they anticipated might be able, or expected, to offer some form of commentary on the poem itself; where the glosses failed to adequately indicate a particular, comprehensible textual meaning, the inherent malleability of medieval textual culture allowed the glosses to be shaped to a particular editor's chosen venture, leaving behind the track of a medieval reader's reaction to the physical object of the poem and its attendant paratexts.

Notes

1. Daniel Silvia is the main proponent of this argument, though it is first briefly suggested by Aage Brudendorf in *The Chaucer Tradition*. Aage Brudendorf, *The Chaucer Tradition* (Copenhagen: S. L. Møller, 1925), 82; Daniel S. Silvia, "Glosses to the *Canterbury Tales* from St. Jerome's *Epistola Adversus Jovinianum*," *Studies in Philology* 62 (1965): 28–39.

2. Silvia, "Glosses to the *Canterbury Tales*," 31–33, 37–39.

3. Ibid., 29–31.

4. Ibid., 38.

5. The choice of the *Roman de la Rose* manuscripts is not as capricious as it might appear. Chaucer's English contemporaries exhibit few similar glossed manuscripts. For more detailed discussion of Gower's Latin apparatus and its difference from Chaucer's, see Derek Pearsall, "Gower's Latin in the *Confessio Amantis*," in *Latin and Vernacular: Studies in Late-Medieval Texts and Manuscripts*, ed. Alastair Minnis, York Manuscripts Conferences, Proceedings Series 1 (Cambridge: D. S. Brewer, 1989), 14. The glossed texts of Chaucer's Italian sources, such as the Anonymous Latin commentary on Dante or Boccaccio's vernacular prose glosses on the *Tesseida*, are hermeneutically dissimilar from the *Tales* glosses, explaining literary allusions and unfolding textual meaning. See, in particular, Vincenzo Cioffari, ed., *Anonymous Latin Commentary on Dante's "Commedia": Reconstructed Text*, Testi, Studi, Strumenti 1 (Spoleto: Centro Italiano du Studi sull'Alto Medioevo, 1989); and Giovanni Boccaccio, *Chiose al Teseida*, in *Opere Minori in Volgare*, vol. 2, ed. Mario Marti (Milan: Rizzoli, 1970), 659–765. French literature offers more analogous examples of vernacular poetry with Latin marginalia in the *Rose* manuscripts and in at least one poem of Eustache Deschamps preserved in Bibliothèque Nationale MS fr. 20029. See also, for a discussion of (at times positive) French literary representations of this ambiguity, Deborah McGrady, *Controlling Readers: Guillaume de Machaut and His Late Medieval Audience* (Toronto: University of Toronto Press, 2006): 170–89.

6. The sticky wicket in looking to the Continent for parallel marginalia remains the question of tracing direct lines of influence. Chaucer alludes, in the *Book of the Duchess*, to a glossed version of the poem: And sooth to seyn, my chambre was / Ful wel depeynted . . . / and alle the walles with colours fyne / Were peynted, bothe text and glose, / Of al the Romaunce of the Rose" (*BD* 321–34). All quotations from Chaucer are from Larry D. Benson, ed., *The Riverside Chaucer*, 3rd ed. (Boston: Houghton Mifflin, 1987). While it is difficult to know if Chaucer had access to a glossed *Rose* manuscript, Derek's landmark *Life of Geoffrey Chaucer* reminds us that the poet spent a great deal of time abroad in France and paints a detailed picture of the influence of French literature in the English court. Derek Pearsall, *The Life of Geoffrey Chaucer* (Oxford: Blackwell, 1992), 51–55, 63–73, and 105–9.

7. Sylvia Huot offers a concise summary of certain glossing traditions in the *Rose*, to which this analysis is gratefully indebted. See Sylvia Huot, *The "Romance of the Rose" and Its Medieval Readers: Interpretation, Reception, Manuscript Transmission*, Cambridge Studies in Medieval Literature 16 (Cambridge: Cambridge University Press, 2007). See also gallica.bnf.fr for digitizations of the *Rose* manuscripts in the Bibliothèque nationale, as well as romandelarose.org for digitizations of select manuscripts in other repositories. I have not the space

here to further address the hermeneutic similarities between these manuscripts and the *Tales* glosses—here, Huot's analysis offers a compelling summary of the way these manuscripts shape the text for its readership, particularly her discussion of BnF fr. 1560—or a number of less discussed *Rose* manuscripts that are likewise glossed.

8. Huot, *The "Romance of the Rose" and Its Medieval Readers*, 55.

9. Ibid., 35–36.

10. Ibid., 63–75.

11. Kathryn Kerby-Fulton, Maidie Hilmo, and Linda Olson, *Opening Up Middle English Manuscripts: Literary and Visual Approaches* (Ithaca, NY: Cornell University Press, 2012), 217.

12. San Marino, Huntington Library MS El 26 C 9, fol. 63r (hereafter El). See also Kerby-Fulton, Hilmo, and Olson, *Opening Up Middle English Manuscripts*, 217. For the only complete edition of the glosses, see Stephen Partridge's unpublished thesis, "Glosses in the Manuscripts of Chaucer's *Canterbury Tales*: An Edition and Commentary" (PhD diss., Harvard University, 1992), III-2. All citations of scripture are taken from *Biblia Sacra: Iuxta Vulgatam Versionem*, 3rd ed., ed. Bonifatio Fischer, OSB, Iohanne Gribomont, OSB, H. F. D. Sparks, and W. Thiele (Stuttgart: Deutsche Bibelgesellschaft, 1983). All translations are my own, unless otherwise noted.

13. Kerby-Fulton, Hilmo, and Olson, *Opening Up Middle English Manuscripts*, 217.

14. Ibid. Emphasis in original.

15. Though not as prolific as in the "Wife of Bath's Prologue," the remainder of the *Tales*—particularly the Man of Law's Tale and the Franklin's Tale—also display this instinct toward editorial revision of the glosses, as later readers copied some marginalia and not others or added their own annotations.

16. A number of other glossed manuscripts of the "Wife of Bath's Prologue" demonstrate similar editorial impulses, though rarely to the same degree as Ad1 and En3; they tend to concentrate on providing citation along with the quotation, only occasionally altering the text of the quotation itself.

17. The stemma of extant *Canterbury Tales* glosses is of course rather complicated, and a direct route of transmission from Ellesmere itself difficult but not entirely impossible to trace. Manly and Rickert group Ad1 and En3 as an independent pairing, based on word difference, but based on tale order assign the two manuscripts to the same group as Ellesmere. Charles Owen seems unsure what to do with Ad1 and En3, assigning Hk as their exemplar, floating somewhere on the stemma several exemplars removed from the earliest manuscripts. However, Peter Robinson's work on computer-assisted stemmatic analysis, made possible through the *Canterbury Tales Project*, offers more promising avenues of descent in various studies of the stemmae of the "Wife of Bath's Prologue." In Robinson's grouping, Ad1 and En3 fall within Group O—which

also includes British Library MS Additional 35286 (Ad3), another manuscript witnessing the Ellesmere glosses—a disparate grouping of manuscripts that nevertheless, along with El and Cambridge University Library MS Dd.4.24 (Dd), are particularly close witnesses to Chaucer's original copy. Of course, despite the convolutions of the *Tales* stemma, the presence of glosses at the same passages of the "Wife of Bath's Prologue," often quoting similar Latin source passages built around the same kernels of scriptural text, are deeply suggestive of the influence of El and its glosses on Ad1 and En3, even if the marginalia have traveled through other exemplars along the way, making it possible to speak of editorial changes to the El apparatus, preserved in the extant witnesses Ad1 and En3. See John M. Manly and Edith Rickert, *The Text of the "Canterbury Tales": Studies on the Basis of All Known Manuscripts*, 8 vols. (Chicago: University of Chicago Press, 1940); Charles A. Owen, *The Manuscripts of the "Canterbury Tales,"* Chaucer Studies 17 (Cambridge: D. S. Brewer, 1991); Christopher J. Howe, Adrian C. Barbrook, Matthew Spencer, Peter Robinson, Barbara Bordalejo, and Linne R. Mooney, "Manuscript Evolution," *Endeavor* 23 (2001): 121–26; and Peter Robinson, "A Stemmatic Analysis of the Fifteenth-Century Witnesses to 'The Wife of Bath's Prologue,'" in *The Canterbury Tales Project: Occasional Papers*, vol. 2, ed. Norman Blake and Peter Robinson (London: Office for Humanities Communication, 1997), 69–132.

18. El, fol. 64r; Partridge, "Glosses in the Manuscripts," III-1. Partridge follows Silvia in attributing the glosses to Jerome; see Silvia, "Glosses to the *Canterbury Tales*," 29.

19. Ad1, fol. 89r; En3, fol. 82v. The three manuscripts that almost always correspond with El are Ad3, Bodleian MS Rawlinson poet. 141 (Ra1), and Cambridge, Trinity College MS R.3.15 (Tc2), the first of which is grouped, in Robinson's analysis in the O group with Ad1 and En3, and may help pinpoint, as closely as we can, the point at which the Latin apparatus underwent the changes manifested in Ad1 and En3. Robinson, "A Stemmatic Analysis of the Fifteenth-Century Witnesses," 69–132.

20. El, fol. 63r.

21. Ad1, fol. 88r; En3, fol. 81v.

22. In addition, the gloss "Relinquet homo patrem et matrem et adherebit vxori sue et cetera" can be found in a further nine manuscripts: Oxford, Corpus Christi College MS 198 (Cp); British Library, MS Harley 1758 (Ha2); Lichfield Cathedral MS 2 (Lc); Bodleian MS Laud 600 (Ld1); Northumberland MS 455 (Nl); Petworth House MS 7 (Pw); British Library MS Sloane 1685 (Sl1); Oxford, New College MS 314 (Ne); and Paris, Bibliothèque nationale fonds anglais 39 (Ps). Two of these—Ps and Ne—preface this gloss with "Crescite et multiplicamini et cetera." For Jerome's equation of marital love with love of the church, see *Against Jovinian* I.22 (16). All citations of *Against Jovinian* taken from Jerome, *Libri duo adversus Jovinianum*, ed. J.-P. Migne,

Patrologia Latina Cursus Completus 23 (Paris, 1845; repr. Turnhout: Brepols, 1997), 221–338. Citations refer to the 1997 edition.

23. "ne in bestiis quidem et in immundis avibus digamia comprobata sit" (Not even in beasts or in unclean birds may bigamy be justified). *Against Jovinian* I.22 (16).

24. Variations on this gloss exist in the following MSS: Ad1, En3, Ad3, El, Ra1, Tc2, Cp, Ha2, La, Lc, Ld1, Nl, Ps, Pw, Sl1.

25. 1 Corinthians 7:8–9.

26. "*Melius est nubere, quam uri.* Ideo melius est nubere, quia pejus est uri. Tolle ardorem libidinis, et non dicet, *melius est nubere.* Melius enim semper ad comparationem deterioris respicit, non ad simplicitatem incomparabilis per se boni. Velut si diceret: Melius est unum oculum habere, quam nullum: melius est uno inniti pede, et alteram partem corporis baculo sustentare, quam fractis cruribus repere" (*It is better to marry than to burn.* For this reason is it better to marry, because it is worse to burn. Take away the flame of lust, and he will not say, *it is better to marry*. Indeed, better always regards something worse, not simply incomparable good in itself. Just as if he may have said: It is better to have one eye than none: it is better to stand on one foot, and to support the other part of the body with a staff, than to crawl on broken legs). *Against Jovinian* I.9.

27. El, fol. 63v.

28. 1 Corinthians 7:28.

29. *Against Jovinian* I.13.

30. 1 Timothy 5:14.

31. *Against Jovinian* I.14.

32. El, fol. 63v. The gloss is likely taken from *Against Jovinian* I.20 (14).

33. *Against Jovinian* I.14.

34. Genesis 4:23–24.

35. *Digamia* covered all manner of multiple-marriage sins in Latin, including remarriage after divorce or the death of a spouse; the term *bigamy* (*bigamia*) was a medieval introduction into the language, marking a distinction perhaps available to Chaucer and his readers but not to Jerome. I use "digamy" here to retain the term's original double meaning.

36. *Against Jovinian* I.14.

37. Ad1, fol. 89r; En3, fol. 82r.

38. 1 Corinthians 7:1.

39. Genesis 4:18–22 and 5:25–31.

40. Genesis 25:2–4 and 25:12–25.

41. Genesis 29:23–28.

42. El, fol. 64v; Ad1, fol. 90v; En3, fol. 83v; WBP III.154–57.

43. El, fol. 64v; WBP.155–58.

44. *Against Jovinian* I.12.

45. For discussion of circumcision in the Old Testament, see Genesis 17:11–14; Exodus 4:24–26 and 12:48; Joshua 5:2; Isaiah 52:1; Ezekiel 28:10 and 32:17–32, where it is frequently used as a term of reproach, as Jerome appears to do.

46. 1 Corinthians 7:3–5.

47. Ad1, fol. 90r; En3, fol. 83r.

48. Ad1, fol. 90v; En3, fol. 83v.

49. For example, III.278 includes quotations from Proverbs 19:13 and 27:15–16; III.363, from Proverbs 30:21–23; and III.371, from Proverbs 30:15–16.

CHAPTER 20

Hoccleve in Canterbury

Peter Brown

La Male Regle by Thomas Hoccleve is the third item in San Marino, Huntington Library MS HM 111, one of three volumes containing holographs of Hoccleve's English poems. J. A. Burrow and A. I. Doyle have suggested that HM 111 represents an early phase of Hoccleve's project to establish an oeuvre in the four years before his death in 1426.[1] The *Male Regle* occupies ten folios (16v–26r) and comprises fifty-six eight-line stanzas, three to a page, rhyming *ababbcbc*—the same scheme that Chaucer used in the Monk's Tale. The Huntington *Male Regle* is the only complete text of the poem extant.

In content the work is vintage Hoccleve. It begins with a sustained address to health, which has now forsaken the poet. The autobiographical flavor is spiced with descriptions of his ailments, often rendered in a witty fashion. What wisdom Hoccleve, or his persona, has learned is at the expense of bitter experience. The mature man looks back regretfully on the folly and excess of his youth—what he calls twenty winters of "Excesse at borde" (112)[2]—and longs to return from a kind of exile to the land of well-being. Haunting the narrative is the shadowy presence of others, referred to loosely as "freendes" (89), two of whom are named ("Prentys and Arondel," 321) and are identifiable as clerks of the king's chapel.[3] Hoccleve is acutely aware of their perception of him. Not that he was one of the worst offenders when it came to excess. His love of wine brought him into the company of women at his favorite tavern, "Paul's Head" (143), near St. Paul's Cathedral,[4] but "Of loves aart yit touched I no deel [part]" (153). He would content himself with a kiss because he was naturally inhibited, blushing for shame at the mere mention of sex. Nor was he inclined to get into brawls. A soft-spoken manner and cowardly disposition saw to that.

The self-portrait is comic, engaging, insouciant, and discerning by turns—tricks Hoccleve learned from Chaucer. And just as his master recalled the numbing experience of after-work bookish activities (reading until "fully daswed" in the *House of Fame* [658]),[5] so the inebriated Hoccleve totters from the tavern "Hoom to the Priuee Seel" (188). Thus he lived, enjoyed respect, and was called "maister" (201) such that "Methoughte I was ymaad a man for evere" (203). But all that now seems like so much flattery. He has fallen on hard times, and his friends have deserted him. For his sickness is "As wel of purs as body" (338). So he has begun a process of introspection, addressing his alter ego, reviewing his debts and his sources of income, and concluding ruefully that he cannot sustain his former lifestyle: "Bewaar Hoccleve . . . / And to a mene [moderate] reule thow the dresse" (351–52). In trying to persuade himself to adopt a better form of living, he chatters to himself, worried that people will think him mad: "Ey, what is me, that to myself thus longe / Clappid have I? I trowe that I rave" (393–94). The poem then elides into a plea to the treasurer, "my lord the Fourneval" (417), for payment of his annuities, a detail that dates the composition of the poem to 1405 or 1406.[6] For this, Hoccleve steels himself to become more resolute, importunate, and assertive than is his natural inclination, for money will restore both him and his purse to health.

Intimations of melancholy and madness, a disabling self-consciousness, the fragmentation and negotiation of identity, alienation, anxiety about others, self-deprecation, echoes of Chaucer, specificity of place and people, a disarming performance of self, a marked sense of liminality, references to his experience as a clerk of the Privy Seal, a poem that crosses the boundaries of genre (is it a complaint, a petition, a penitential lyric, or merely a jeu d'esprit?)—all of these are hallmarks of Hoccleve's work.[7] They carry the further endorsement of his own highly distinctive Secretary hand. What could be more definitive and authoritative? But there is another witness to the *Male Regle*, and it has tended to suffer by comparison with the authenticity of the version in HM 111. In rather more cramped conditions, at thirty-six lines to the page, it occupies two endleaves of Canterbury Cathedral Archives, Register O (fols. 406v–407r), a cartulary otherwise containing records of rentals and other payments concerning the property, estates, and management of Christ Church Priory, 1275–1330.[8] Described variously as "fragmentary"[9] and as "a selected and disordered version,"[10] the poem consists of nine stanzas of the *Male Regle* (roughly a sixth of HM 111's fifty-six stanzas), of which the seventh and eighth occur in reverse order. Variants from the Canterbury manuscript do not appear in the editions of the *Male Regle*, and a critical edition of the Canterbury poem has only recently appeared in print.[11]

Its neglect is a pity, because the Canterbury *Male Regle*, taken on its own terms rather than as a pale reflection of Hoccleve's "original," is a complete and coherent poem with its own priorities. In fact, "the Canterbury *Male Regle*" is a misnomer because the poem carries its own title, "Balade," as an indication that it is a freestanding composition with a particular purpose and one that, taking its cue from Hoccleve, who wrote many ballades, has improvised its own genre. In reverting to a ballade form it harks back, whether deliberately or not, to the organizing principle, as well as the rhyme scheme, of Chaucer's Monk's Tale, which is essentially a series of ballades on the common theme of tragedy. The Canterbury Balade is an example of what Julia Boffey terms an "extracted" lyric—one taken, often without acknowledgment, from a longer work. As such it represents a recognized practice that targeted poems by Chaucer, Hawes, and Lydgate, as well as ones by Hoccleve.[12] What might the purpose of the new Balade be? It begins with line 33 of Hoccleve's poem, "But I have herd men seye longe ago," dropping the "But," beginning with the personal pronoun, and inserting an "of," probably to maintain the syllable count. It proceeds to the proverb used by Hoccleve—"Prosperitee is blynd and se ne may"—setting the tone for what follows. So while the Balade still reads as a record of individual testimony of experiences over "xx^{ti} yeres passyd contynuelly," those experiences are now more generalized. The autobiographical and topographic specifics of Hoccleve's poem are ditched, notably at line 351, where the original reads "Bewaar, Hoccleve" but the Balade has "Be war ther for." There is no speaking to the divergent self in the Balade, which is, rather, an admonitory address to others to avoid the pitfalls that the speaker has suffered: a misspent youth, rebellion against reason, the advice of solicitous friends, excess of food and expenditure. Instead, the reader or audience is encouraged to pursue moderation, self-control, and a healthy lifestyle. (The presence of a persuasive argument is also characteristic of the genre.) As Marian Trudgill and Burrow have pointed out, it is a "moral balade of the sort popular in England at the time."[13]

I want to resist the temptation to see the Canterbury poem as a facile redaction of a rather more interesting original. While it might seem like easy money to mine Hoccleve's poem for moral nuggets, there is plenty of evidence of close engagement with his text, and of an effort to create a new poem. I have mentioned one or two word changes already. In addition, the Balade is carefully punctuated with virgules, its rhymes neatly indicated with brackets, its verses marked by paraphs. Doyle dated the hand to the 1420s or 1430s, so it is roughly contemporary with Hoccleve's own fair copy of the *Male Regle*.[14] In the Balade, at the very least, we have intriguing evidence for the circulation and early reception of his poem. What appealed to its medieval reader in Canterbury is rather different from what appeals to a modern reader, but, as appeals go, it is no less authentic.[15] In all likelihood the extractor was a Canterbury monk, for there are other items on the endleaves of Register O, in the form of Latin proverbs, in his hand. If so, he would be one of a group of monks active ca. 1420 among whom literary activity in Latin and English enjoyed something of a vogue.

It is notoriously difficult to provide contexts for lyrics, but in the case of the Balade they are available. The fifth jubilee of Saint Thomas, in 1420, provoked a flurry of literary activity in Latin and English among the monks at Christ Church. They produced a Latin poem for local display and on the door of St. Paul's Cathedral, London, advertising the benefits of a pilgrimage to Canterbury; notices for posting on the pilgrim route; and a Latin treatise on pilgrimage and against Lollardy, probably by Richard of Godmersham.[16] Another self-styled "filius ecclesie Thome" wrote the prologue to the tale of *Beryn*. It describes the arrival in Canterbury of Chaucer's pilgrims, where they lodge at a pilgrim inn, the Checker of the Hope, before proceeding the following morning to the shrine of Saint Thomas, where they pay their respects and make donations.[17] It is a poem by an astute reader of the *Canterbury Tales* but also by someone—possibly one of the shrine keepers—who knows about the economics of pilgrimage.[18] Pilgrimage was an important source of income for the Benedictines at Christ Church, and their promotional labor was rewarded: their takings at the shrine and associated sites for the jubilee year were a record.[19] Pilgrims paid for their accommodation, too. The Checker of the Hope, part of which still stands, was built by Prior Chillenden between 1392 and 1395, specifically for the pilgrim trade.

This mixture of literary and economic perspectives brings us back to Hoccleve and Register O, which, with Register P (once part of the same volume), maps economic activities within Christ Church and on its estates—a feature of the original compilation that is still prominent, despite the disordered state of the folios.[20] Hoccleve, in the *Male Regle*, links bodily dysfunction with economic malaise (the absence of his annuity), but goes on—especially through a lengthy section on flattery—to foreground what Perkins calls "a vocabulary of regulation that connects the body of the poet with public governance."[21] In a similar way the Balade is both a plea for personal moderation to counteract excess and a comment on the corporate activity of the monastic community, where the production and consumption of food and money also required control and regulation. An item that precedes the Balade—to give the manuscript's fuller flavor, as it were—records payments to monastic lay servants, including women who prepare the guts for sausage skins (Register O, fol. 402v). Registers O and P also include a number of other, more substantial documents on the production and consumption of food and drink. They include Walter of Henley's treatise on husbandry, in French (Register P, fols. 139–145), composed ca. 1286. The *Husbandry* was copied a number of times in the Canterbury scriptorium, and it begins with some exhortatory remarks on the virtues of living within one's means.[22] The copy in Register P itself includes two short sequences of verse in Middle English (fols. 139 and 139v).[23] Another text relates to the work of the cellarer (Register P, fols. 76–78). It specifies the drink allocation at the principal feasts and records his receipts for expenditure on provisions, the weekly bread allowance for the refectory, his budget for fish, vegetables, meat, and other food—in other words, ways of regulating "excess at board" and of guarding against the blinding effects of prosperity, or what the anonymous compiler of the entry for the Royal Commission on Historical Manuscripts calls "carefully constructed calculations of how the income [from rents] was to be, and was, expended: how much the wheat for the diet of the monks and their guests cost in the year; how much barley was due from the tenants; how much beer this would make and who were entitled to draw rations of the several qualities of this beer."[24] From records at the Westminster convent, it is clear that the regulation of diet was central to the governance of a Benedictine house, and what individual monks enjoyed "at board" a topic of keen discussion.[25]

What I am suggesting is that the Balade should be read not as merely an inferior version of Hoccleve's *Male Regle*, but as an extracted lyric with its own independent life, one that is informed by its manuscript and cultural contexts.[26] That it was seen as integral to Registers O and P is clear from the medieval table of contents for the two registers, where it is listed as "A Balade Anglice" (Register P, fol. 8v) together with its original folio number, 419, itself still visible on the right-hand corner of the second leaf of the Balade. I am further suggesting that the Balade was the work of a monk who was a relatively sophisticated reader of the *Male Regle* and a person of some literary accomplishment—possibly Walter de Norwich, cellarer and monk warden of the East Anglian estates ca. 1304–29, an area of the country to which a number of the contents refer.[27] He was probably a member of a group of monks—his natural immediate audience—who were receptive to contemporary vernacular literature, including that produced by both Hoccleve and Chaucer.

The Canterbury Balade

I am aware of five occasions on which the Balade has been transcribed in whole or in part. The anonymous compiler of the entry for Register O in the *Ninth Report* published by the Royal Commission on Historical Manuscripts recorded the sixth and ninth stanzas and part of the eighth (lines 41–48 and 61–72).[28] Over a century later, Trudgill and Burrow provided best readings of the words at the beginnings of lines 1–36 on fol. 207v where cockling of the parchment as a result of fire damage has affected legibility. They also published complete transcriptions of stanzas 7 and 8 (lines 49–64).[29] More recently, Peter Rowe, an MA student at the University of Kent's Canterbury Centre for Medieval and Tudor (now Early Modern) Studies, copied out the entire Balade for a coursework project. It remains unpublished, but the author has generously made it available for the purposes of this essay.[30] A transcription without variants appears in the recent article by Rory G. Critten, and David Watt has produced one with collations from HM111.[31]

The text that appears here has been newly transcribed direct from the manuscript. It records only those words and letters that are visible to the naked eye either on the parchment or in a magnified digital image kindly provided by Canterbury Cathedral Archives. Lacunae and illegible words or letters are indicated by ellipses in square brackets. Two punctuation marks are reproduced: the virgule and *punctus*. Missing paraphs and the bracketing of rhymes have not been supplied. There are no conjectural readings, although a number of the missing components might be supplied by referring to the text of the *Male Regle*. For instance, the second word in line 2 of the Balade is doubtless *prosperite*, and the phrase in line 36 recorded as "[...]itil and [...]il" is likely to be "litil and litil," following "lyte and lyte" in the full version of the poem. However, the extent of the differences in detail between the Balade and the *Male Regle*, discussed more extensively below, urges caution in using the latter as a means of reconstructing the former.

The accompanying apparatus provides all the available materials for recovering the complete text of the Balade. The variants are of two kinds: collations with the Huntington *Male Regle*, using the facsimile introduced by Burrow and Doyle (H); and, indented below, readings of the Balade that differ from my own: those of the anonymous author of the Historical Manuscript Commission entry for Register O (A), Trudgill and Burrow (T), Rowe (R), and Critten (C). Watt's variants appeared too late for inclusion. Matching stanzas from the *Male Regle* are indicated in the right-hand margin as [*MR5*], and so on.

Balade [fol. 406v]

¶ Y haue he*r*d / of men ful [...]re a go [*MR5*]
That p*ro*sp[...] blynd / ande se ne may
And verifye / y may wel hit is so
[...] y my self / haue put hit in*n* a say
[...] y was wel / cowde y co*n*sydere hit • nay
what [...] longyd aftyr nouelrye
[...] / ȝerny*n* day be day
and [...]e smert / accusyth me my folye
[...] war ȝowth / knew noȝt what he wroghte [*MR6*]
[...] wot y wel / whan fro the twyin*n*ed he
[...]t of his ignoraunce / him self he soghte

[...] knewe not / that he dwellyng was wyth the
[...] y[...]t / were to gret nycete
[...]ys lord or frend / wytyngly for to offende
[...] that the wyghte / of his adu*er*syte
[...] fool opp*re*sse / and make of hym an ende
[...]d [...]yt for the more part / ȝowth ys rebel [*MR*9]
vn to resoun / and hatyth his doct*ri*ne
And re[...]yng that / hit may noȝt stonde wel
Wyth ȝouthe as fer / as wyt can ymagyne
o • ȝowthe alas / why wolt thow noȝt enclyne
and þ*er*to rewlyd resoun / bowyn the
syn resoun / ys the verry streghte lyne
That ledyth folk / yn to felycite
Ful selde ys seyn / that youthe takyth hede [*MR*10]
Of p*er*ils / that ben emynent to falle
[...] haue‸^{he} take a po*ur*pos / he wol nede
[...]h[...]elle hit / and no conseyl to hym calle
hys owyn wit / he demyth best of alle
and forth ther wyth / he rennyth Brydilles
[...] he / that noȝght betwyxt hony and galle
[...]n iuge / ne the werre fro the pees
[...]y ffrendes / seyde to me ful ofte [*MR*12]
[...]y mysrewle / wolde me cause a ffyt
[...]nd reddyn m[...]n esywyse and softe
[...]itil / and [...]il / to withdrawe hit
But that noȝt / myghte synke in to my wit [fol. 407r]
so was the lust / rotyd in to my*n* herte
and y am so rype / vn to my pyt
that scarsly / y may noȝt hit a sterte
¶ Resoun me bad and redde / as for the best [*MR*14]
To ete and drynke / in tyme and temprely
But wylful ȝouth / nat obeye lest
vn to hys red / he sette noȝt ther by
he of hem bothe / hath take outrageously
ant out of tyme / not two or thre
But xx^{ti} ȝeres / passyd contynuelly
Excesse at borde / hys knyf hath leyd wyth me
¶ Who so that passyng mesure desyryth [*MR*45]

as that wytnessyn / olde clerkys wyse
hym self encombryth / ofte sythe and myryth
And therfore / let the mene the suffyse
yf such conceytys / in thyn herte ryse
as thy profyt / mowe hyndre or thy renoun
yf ~~h~~ they were execut / in any wyse
Wyth manly resoun / thryst thow hem a dowun
¶ And al so despenseʒ large / en haunce a mannes loos [*MR*44]
Whyl they endure / and whan ther is more
Hys name is ded / me*n* kepe her mowthis cloos
as noʒt a peny / hadde be spent a fore
my thank ys queynt / my purs his stuf hath lore
and myn karkeys / replet of heuynesse
Be war ther fore / y rede the‸the more
and to a mene rewle / now dresse the
¶ O • god / o • helthe / vn to thyn ordynaunce [*MR*51]
Thow weleful lord / lowly su*b*mytt y me
y am contryt / and of ful repentaunce
that euyr y swam / in swych nycete
As was dysplesaunt / to thy deyte
Now scew on me / thy m*er*cy and thy grace
hyt syttyth a god / to be of g*ra*ce free
For yeue me lord • / and y no more wole *tre*space

1 Y] But I | he*r*d] herd | men] of men | ful [...]re a go] seye longe ago H
a go] ago C
2 p*ro*sp [...]] Prosperitee is | ande se] and see H
That p*ro*sp[...]] that ys T
3 verifye y may] verifie I can | hit] it H
verifye] verefye R
4 [...] y] For I | haue put hit in*n* a say] put haue it in assay H
my self] myself C | in*n*] in RC
5 [...] y] Whan I | wel cowde y co*n*sydere hit] weel kowde I considere it H
co*n*sydere*e*] consider C
6 what] But what | [...] longyd aftyr nouelrye] me longed aftir nouelrie H
7 [...] ʒerny*n*] As yeeres yonge yernen | be] by H
8 and [...]e] And now my | accusyth] accusith | folye] folie H
accusyth] acwsyth R
9 [...] war ʒowth knew noʒt] Myn vnwar yowthe kneew nat | he] it H

10 [...] wot y] This woot I | the twyin*n*ed he] thee twynned shee H
[...]] ys R | wot] oot T | twyin*n*ed] twymyd TC | twym*m*ed R

11 [...]t] But | his ignoraunce him] hir ignorance hir | he] shee H
[...]t] [...]hy[...] R

12 [...] knewe not that he] And kneew nat þ*at* shee | wyth the] w*ith* thee H

13 [...] y[...]t were to gret nycete] For to a wight wer it greet nycetee H
[...] y[...]t] For to [...]ygt R

14 [...]ys] His | frend wytyngly] freend wityngly | to offende] toffende H

15 [...] that] Lest þ*at* | wyghte] weighte | adu*er*syte] aduersitee H

16 [...]] The | hym] him H
fool] ffool C

17 [...]d [...]yt] As | part ȝowth ys] paart youthe is H
[...]yt] ȝyt TC

18 vn to resoun] Vn to reson | hatyth his doct*ri*ne] hatith hir doctrine H
vn] Vn C

19 re[...]yng that hit] Regnynge which it | noȝt stonde] nat stande H
And re[...]yng] and reyneng T | re[...]yng] regnyng R

20 Wyth ȝouthe] With yowthe | wyt] wit H

21 ȝowthe alas] yowthe allas | wolt] wilt | noȝt] nat H
o] O C | alas] a las C

22 and þ*er*to rewlyd] And vn to reuled | bowyn the] bowe thee H
þ*er*to] to C

23 syn] Syn | ys] is | verry streghte] verray streighte H

24 That ledyth] þ*at* ledith | yn] vn | felycite] felicitee H

25 selde ys seyn that youthe takyth hede] seelde is seen þ*at* yowthe takith heede H

26 that ben emynent] þ*at* been likly for | falle] fall H

27 [...]] For | po*ur*pos he wol nede] purpos þ*at* moot neede H

28 [...]h[...]elle hit] Been execut | conseyl to hym calle] conseil wole he call H
[...]h[...]elle] Welle R

29 hys owyn] His owne | demyth] deemeth | alle] all H

30 and forth] And foorth | wyth] with | rennyth Brydilles] renneth brydillees H

31 [...]] As | that noȝght betwyxt] þ*at* nat betwixt | galle] gall H
betwyxt] be twyxt C

32 [...]n] Can H
I] were R

33 [...]y ffrendes seyde] My freendes seiden vn H

34 [...]y mysrewle wolde me cause] My mis reule me cause wolde | ffyt] fit H

35 [...]nd reddyn m[...]n esywyse and] And redden me in esy wyse a*nd* H
reddyn m[...]n] raeddyn met in R | reddyn] in C

36 [...]itil] A lyte | [...]il] lyte | withdrawe hit] withdrawen it H

37 that noȝt myghte] þ*at* nat mighte H
noȝt] niȝt R | in] up R

38 so] So | rotyd] y rootid | my*n*] myn H
so] So C

39 and y] And now I | pyt] pit H
and] And C

40 that scarsly y] Þ*at* scarsely I | noȝt hit a sterte] it nat asterte H
that] That C

41 Resoun] Reson | as for the best] a*nd* beste H

42 and temprely] a*nd* attemprely H

43 wylful ȝouth] wilful youthe | obeye lest] obeie leste H
ȝouth] routh A

44 vn] Vn | red he] þ*at* reed ne | noȝt] nat H
vn] Vn C | vn to hys] Unto his A | noȝt ther by] nat therby A

45 hath take] I take haue H
he] He C | hath] hathe A

46 ant] And | not two] nat two yeer | thre] three H
ant] And AC | not] nat A | thre] three A

47 ȝeres passyd contynuelly] wyntir past continually H
ȝeres] yeres A | contynuelly] contynually A

48 hys knyf hath leyd wyth me] hath leyd his knyf with me H
borde] bord A | knyf] knyff A

49 passyng] passynge | desyryth] desyrith H
desyryth] desyrth R

50 as that wytnessyn] As þ*at* witnessen | clerkys] clerkes H
as] As C

51 hym] him | encombryth ofte] encombrith often | and myryth] a*nd* myrith H
hym] Hym C

52 therfore] for thy | the suffyse] thee souffyse H
mene] men R

53 yf such conceytys] If swich a conceit H
yf] Yf C

54 as] As | mowe] may H
as] As C
55 yf ~~h~~ they were] If it wer H
yf] Yf C
56 Wyth] With | thryst] thriste | hem a dowun] it doun H
57 And al so despenseȝ] Despenses | en haunce] enhaunce H
despenseȝ] despensez C | mannes] manne*s* T | loos] loss R
58 Whyl] Whil | and] a*nd* | ther is more] they be forbore H
59 Hys] His | ded me*n* kepe her mowthis] deed men keepe hir mowthes H
is] ys C
60 as noȝt] As nat | hadde] had | a fore] tofore H
as] As C
61 my] My | ys queynt] is qweynt H
my] My C
62 and myn karkeys replet of] And my Carkeis repleet with H
and] And C | heuynesse] hevynesse A
63 war ther fore y] waar Hoccleue I | the ‸the more] thee therefore H
64 and] And | rewle now dresse the] reule thow thee dresse H
and] And C
65 ordynaunce] ordenance H
helthe vn to] Helth unto A
66 lowly su*b*mytt y] meekly submitte I H
lowly su*b*mytt] loly summyt A | su*b*mytt y] summytty T | suurytty R | su*m*mytty C | me] mee A
67 y] I | and] a*nd* | repentaunce] repentance H
y] I A | Y C | of ful] full of A
68 that euyr y swam] Þ*at* eue*re* I swymmed | swych nycete] swich nycetee H
that] That C | euyr] evyr A | swych] swiche A
69 dysplesaunt] displesaunt | deyte] deitee H
dysplesaunt] dysplesaunte A | dysplesaulnt R | thy] they A
70 scew] kythe | and] a*nd* H
scew] sceu A
71 hyt syttyth] It sit | to be] been | g*ra*ce] his grace H
hyt] It A | Hyt C | free] fre A
72 For yeue me lord and y no more wole] Foryeue, a*nd* neue*re* wole I eft H
For yeue] Foryeve A | y] I A | wole] will A

Some of the more general changes to the *Male Regle* stanzas, introduced by the author of the Balade, are discussed above. Immediately noticeable from a more detailed comparison is the extent of the differences. No line from the Balade is an exact match of the equivalent line in the Huntington manuscript. Of course, it is highly unlikely that the Balade author had access to a holograph of the *Male Regle.* It is more reasonable to presume that he was working from another copy then in circulation but now lost. That would account for some of the differences. So too would the familiar scribal habits of altering spellings, changing word orders, and misreading. But there are some particular disparities between the Balade and the *Male Regle* that point to more conscious and deliberate small-scale interventions on the part of the copyist.

At lines 10, 11, and 12, the gender of "ȝowth" (line 9) is altered from female to male, entailing four changes to personal or possessive pronouns. Similarly, at line 18, "reson"—following French usage, a feminine noun in Hoccleve's poem—reverts to a masculine one for the Canterbury author. Again, Hoccleve's "conceit" becomes a plural, "conceytys," at line 53, necessitating two further changes: "it" to "hem" in line 56 and "it" to "they" in the preceding line. In the latter case it is almost possible to see the scribe in action. In copying the "it," he began by writing an "h," presumably the first letter of "hit" which he tends to substitute for "it" (e.g., at line 4). Then he deleted the letter *h* in order to write the plural form, "they." Technically, it might be argued that the pluralizing of "conceit," in the sense of "preoccupying idea," is correct, for two such ideas are referred to in line 54. They are the temptations of personal reputation ("profyt") and of individual reputation ("renoun")—subversive conceits that are to be kept under control by "manly resoun" (56). So what this particular order of revision may indicate is a redactor alert to the niceties of grammar. His liking for consistency, and desire to improve his original, is indicative of someone with the mentality of a modern copy editor, used to engaging with texts at close quarters. So if Hoccleve's reson is "manly" (56) it had better be referred to earlier as "his" (18). The scribe's gender-changing tendencies in the case of "ȝowth" are more difficult to fathom.

His more substantive changes are no less instructive. There are six visible occasions when he deviates from the lexicon provided by Hoccleve to substitute vocabulary of his own. The most prominent of these interventions, previously noted, is when he anonymizes the Balade by removing the word *Hoccleue*. At line 63 he changes the *Male Regle*'s "waar Hoccleue" in favor of the anodyne "war ther fore." One alteration necessitated another. Hoccleve continues with "I rede thee therfore," but the scribe has already used one "ther fore" so he emends the closing words to "I rede the the more," thus redeeming some of the line's emphasis and application. The second "the" is an insertion, perhaps to reclaim the syllable count. Other substitutions are of straightforward homonyms indicating little more than personal preference on the part of the redactor. Hoccleve's "xx^{ti} wyntir" as a measure of the time he has been guilty of excess becomes the less baleful and threatening "xx^{ti} ȝeres" at line 47. In line 70, where Hoccleve has *kythe* meaning "make known" as he prays to Health to show mercy and grace, the Canterbury author has the more common *scew*.[32]

Revisions of this kind are not all plain sailing. Just five lines before the anonymized line, and in the same stanza, the Balade author introduces another revision, at line 58. In the *Male Regle* Hoccleve is here describing the beneficial effect of extravagant expense on a man's reputation and the contrasting outcome when the expenditure dries up: "Despenses large enhaunce a mannes loos [reputation] / Whil they endure and whan they be forbore / His name is deed." The Balade author decided to replace "forbore" (dispensed with) but in the process dispenses with sense: "despenseȝ large en haunce a mannes loos / Whyl they endure and whan ther is more / Hys name is ded" (57–59). Clearly, he has omitted the word "*no*" before "more" that would have captured Hoccleve's meaning (and maintained the decasyllabic line). It is a minor error, though quite fatal in its effect, committed perhaps because attention is focused on the significance of individual words rather than on syntax or on maintaining the rhyme. The most resonant example of this kind of attention to individual words is at line 26, where Hoccleve's line about youth's being oblivious "Of perils þat been likly for to fall" becomes the sonorous "Of p*er*ils that ben emynent to falle." *Emynent* here means "exposed (to a certain contingency), liable," but can also convey the sense of "imminent."[33] It is an exceptionally rare word, one for the cognoscenti, a Latinate coinage of the early fifteenth century and an aureate embellishment not unworthy of that other Benedictine poet writing in a vernacular idiom, John Lydgate, who was also the author of ballades and a widespread dietary that stressed moderation.[34]

Effective though the Balade author's revisions of Hoccleve's English words can be, he is less confident or focused when dealing with vernacular rhyme and meter. All of the Balade's rhyme words are legible, and they follow Hoccleve's to a fault except in the accident-prone penultimate stanza. There, having secured the rhyme at line 63 with the substitution of "the more" for "therfore," the author proceeds to abandon it in the following line. For no apparent reason, he revises the order of Hoccleve's words, "And to a mene reule now the dresse," to read "and to a mene rewle now dresse the." The end word should rhyme with "heuynesse" at line 62 but hardly does so (although the author of the Royal Commission entry begs to differ).[35] The Balade's neglect of line length is yet more lax, even though Hoccleve keeps religiously to a ten-syllable count. For instance, the omission of Hoccleve's "now" before *y* at line 39 is not made good. Again, the absence of an intermediate *e* in "scarsly" in the following line, or of final *e* in "ȝouth" at line 43, or "swam" at line 68—all of which deplete the standard length of the line—might suggest that this is a reviser not overaccustomed to the sound of English poetry. Alternatively, it may indicate someone who simply had a poor ear for rhythm. Lines such as 71 (one extra beat) or 72 (two extra) or 57 (that troublesome stanza again!), which notches up thirteen syllables with the addition of a gratuitous "And al so," are otherwise difficult to explain.

On the other hand, the folios bear clear indications that the Balade was created in order to be sounded out, either in the head of an individual reader or aloud, perhaps in the presence of others. The paraphs, bracketing of rhymes, and punctuation would have helped such a performance. One wonders what sort of reception a reading of the poem might have elicited. Its primary audience is likely to have been the one posited earlier: a select group of Canterbury monks with literary leanings that included an inclination toward vernacular literature. They would have appreciated the volte-face at the close of their brother's compilation, when the Balade ends, conventionally, with a prayer. Yet the prayer is of an unusual kind since it targets not the Christian God who was the object of their daily devotions but another deity, named "helthe." Such manipulations and endorsements of Hoccleve's poem argue for a coterie monastic audience that was urbane and sophisticated, one that would have had no difficulty finding an application for the Balade both in its manuscript context and in their wider experience and calling. The Balade's emphasis on moderation, and especially on a rule to counter misrule, as in the line "and to a mene rewle now dresse the" (64), would surely have gone down well with individuals dedicated to the rule of Saint Benedict, with its stress on temperate behavior and the measured consumption of personal and collective resources.[36] It might also have had a topical application: in 1421 Henry V initiated an attempt to reform what he perceived as the laxity of the Benedictine rule.[37]

Notes

1. Thomas Hoccleve, *A Facsimile of the Autograph Verse Manuscripts: Henry E. Huntington Library, San Marino (California), MS HM 111 and HM 744; University Library, Durham (England), MS Cosin V. III. 9*, introd. J. A. Burrow and A. I. Doyle, EETS, s.s., 19 (2002), xi.

2. References are to Thomas Hoccleve, *"My Compleinte" and Other Poems*, ed. Roger Ellis (Exeter: University of Exeter Press, 2001).

3. Jenni Nuttall, *The Creation of Lancastrian Kingship: Literature, Language and Politics in Late Medieval England* (Cambridge: Cambridge University Press, 2007), 68–69.

4. Thomas Hoccleve, *Selections from Hoccleve*, ed. M. C. Seymour (Oxford: Clarendon Press, 1981), 107.

5. Geoffrey Chaucer, *The Riverside Chaucer*, 3rd ed., ed. Larry D. Benson (Boston: Houghton Mifflin, 1987).

6. Thomas Nevill, fourth Baron Furnivall, d. 1407, and one of two war treasurers appointed by Henry IV after a meeting of Parliament in November 1404. See Lee Patterson, "'What is me?': Self and Society in the Poetry of Thomas Hoccleve," *Studies in the Age of Chaucer* 23 (2001): 455; and J. A. Burrow, *Thomas Hoccleve*, Authors of the Middle Ages, 4: English Writers of the Late Middle Ages (Aldershot: Variorum, 1994), 14–15.

7. On the *Male Regle,* see especially Ethan Knapp, *The Bureaucratic Muse: Thomas Hoccleve and the Literature of Late Medieval England* (University Park: Pennsylvania State University Press, 2001), 36–43, the chapter being a revised version of his "Bureaucratic Identity and Construction of the Self in Hoccleve's *Formulary* and *La male regle*," *Speculum* 74 (1999): 357–76; Nicholas Perkins, "Thomas Hoccleve, *La Male Regle*," in *A Companion to Medieval Literature and Culture, c. 1350–c. 1500*, ed. Peter Brown (Oxford: Blackwell, 2007), 585–603; and Sarah Tolmie, "The Professional: Thomas Hoccleve," *Studies in the Age of Chaucer* 29 (2007): 341–73. For commentary on Hoccleve's

persona, see, e.g., John Burrow, "Autobiographical Poetry in the Middle Ages: The Case of Thomas Hoccleve," *Proceedings of the British Academy* 68 (1982): 389–412; his "Hoccleve's *Series*: Experience and Books," in *Fifteenth-Century Studies: Recent Essays*, ed. R. F. Yeager (Hamden, CT: Archon Books, 1984), 259–73; James Simpson, "Madness and Texts: Hoccleve's *Series*," in *Chaucer and Fifteenth-Century Poetry*, ed. Julia Boffey and Janet Cowen, King's College London Medieval Studies 5 (London: Centre for Late Antique and Medieval Studies, King's College, 1991), 15–29; Derek Pearsall, "Hoccleve's *Regement of Princes*: The Poetics of Self-Representation," *Speculum* 69 (1994): 408–10; Knapp, *Bureaucratic Muse*, chap. 6; and Patterson, " 'What is me?' "

8. Reference number CCA-DCc-Register/O at www.canterbury-cathedral.org/conservation/archives/, accessed July 21, 2014.

9. Burrow, *Thomas Hoccleve*, 14.

10. Julia Boffey and A. S. G. Edwards, *A New Index of Middle English Verse* (London: British Library, 2005), item 2538. Register O is omitted from their list of manuscripts in Canterbury Cathedral Library [*sic*], 295.

11. Thomas Hoccleve, *Hoccleve's Works: The Minor Poems*, ed. Frederick J. Furnivall and I. Gollancz, rev. Jerome Mitchell and A. I. Doyle, EETS, e.s., 61 and 73 (1970), does not mention the Balade. Some account of it is taken in Hoccleve, "*My Compleinte*," ed. Ellis, 77 and note to lines 42–44; and in Hoccleve, *Facsimile*, introd. Burrow and Doyle, p. xii, item 3. See now David Watt, "Thomas Hoccleve's *La Male Regle* in the Canterbury Cathedral Archives," *Opuscula* 2 (2012): 1–11. The Balade is beginning to attract critical attention, if only as a variant of the *Male Regle*. See Perkins, "Thomas Hoccleve," 600–601; and Rory G. Critten, " 'Her heed they caste awry': The Transmission and Reception of Thomas Hoccleve's Personal Poetry," *Review of English Studies* 64 (2013): 389–93.

12. Julia Boffey, *Manuscripts of English Courtly Love Lyrics in the Later Middle Ages*, Manuscript Studies 1 (Woodbridge: D. S. Brewer, 1985), 69–71; and A. S. G. Edwards, "Manuscripts and Readers," in Brown, *Companion to Medieval English Literature and Culture*, 102–3.

13. Marian Trudgill and J. A. Burrow, "A Hocclevean Balade," *Notes and Queries* 243 (1998): 179. On the popularity and development of the ballade genre in the period prior to Hoccleve's, see James I. Wimsatt, *Chaucer and His French Contemporaries: Natural Music in the Fourteenth Century* (Toronto: University of Toronto Press, 1991), 29–30, 58–69, 116–26.

14. Trudgill and Burrow, "Hocclevean Balade," 178–79.

15. For a development of this theme in relation to the Balade and other poems by Hoccleve, see Critten, " 'Her heed.' "

16. Raymonde Foreville, *Le Jubilé de saint Thomas Becket du XIIIè au XVè siècle (1220–1470): Étude et documents* (Paris: S.E.V.P.E.N., 1958), 47–59, 109–13, 129–37.

17. John M. Bowers, ed., *The Canterbury Tales: Fifteenth-Century Continuations and Additions* (Kalamazoo: Medieval Institute Publications for TEAMS, 1982), 60–79.

18. Peter Brown, "Journey's End: The Prologue to *The Tale of Beryn*," in Boffey and Cowen, *Chaucer and Fifteenth-Century Poetry*, 143–74.

19. C. E. Woodruff, "The Financial Aspect of the Cult of St Thomas of Canterbury," *Archaeologia Cantiana* 44 (1932): 22.

20. The Priory and Chapter registers were rebound in 1711–53 under the direction of the auditor, Samuel Norris, after the Audit House fire of 1670.

21. Perkins, "Hoccleve, *Male Regle*," 597; also Patterson, " 'What is me?,' " 454–56; and Nuttall, *Creation*, 58–71.

22. Dorothea Oschinsky, *Walter of Henley and Other Treatises on Estate Management and Accounting* (Oxford: Clarendon Press, 1971), 46–47, 58–61, 308–11.

23. Boffey and Edwards, *New Index*, items 2698 and 4113.

24. *Ninth Report of the Royal Commission on Historical Manuscripts*, Part [Vol.] 1: *Report and Appendix* (London: HMSO, 1883), 107.

25. Barbara Harvey, *Living and Dying in England: The Monastic Experience* (Oxford: Clarendon Press, 1993), chap. 2, esp. 45–46.

26. This is the tendency of the argument put forward by Trudgill and Burrow, "Hocclevean Balade," to which the present essay is indebted.

27. Reference number CCA-DCc-Register/P at www.canterbury-cathedral.org/conservation/archives/, accessed July 21, 2014.

28. *Ninth Report*, 108.

29. Trudgill and Burrow, "Hocclevean Balade," 178–80.

30. Peter Rowe, "A Canterbury Monk Rewrites Hoccleve's *Malregle* in the Early Fifteenth Century" (n.d.). Sixteen photocopied pages containing a monochrome reproduction of the Balade in Register O, a synopsis of the *Male Regle*, transcription of the Balade, and a transcription of the equivalent stanzas from the *Male Regle*.

31. Critten, " 'Her heed,' " 23–24; Watt, "Hoccleve's *Male Regle*," 8–11.

32. *MED* scheuen (7a) http://quod.lib.umich.edu.m/med/, accessed September 5, 2012.

33. *MED* (3) http://quod.lib.umich.edu/m/med/, accessed September 5, 2012. *OED* (6), www.oed.com.chain.kent.ac.uk, accessed September 5, 2012. See Trudgill and Burrow, "Hocclevean Balade," 180 and n. 6.

34. Claire Sponsler, "Eating Lessons: Lydgate's 'Dietary' and Consumer Conduct," in *Medieval Conduct*, ed. Kathleen Ashley and Robert L. A. Clark, Medieval Cultures 29 (Minneapolis: University of Minnesota Press, 2001), 1–22. Lydgate's continuation of the *Canterbury Tales* includes lines on the regulation of monastic diet that humorously invert cautions against excess. See the prologue to the *Siege of Thebes*, ed. Bowers, in *Canterbury Tales: Fifteenth-Century*

Continuations, ll. 86–118. On Lydgate's aureate diction, see Derek Pearsall, *John Lydgate* (London: Routledge & Kegan Paul, 1970), 262–63; Lois A. Ebin, *Illuminator, Makar, Vates: Visions of Poetry in the Fifteenth Century* (Lincoln: University of Nebraska Press, 1988), 25–27; and Seth Lerer, *Chaucer and His Readers: Imagining the Author in Late-Medieval England* (Princeton: Princeton University Press, 1993), chap. 1.

35. *Ninth Report*, 108.

36. *The Rule of St Benedict*, ed. and trans. Justin McCann (London: Sheed and Ward, 1972), 94–98 (chaps. 39 and 40) on food and the dangers of excess; and 80–83 (chap. 31) on the work of the cellarer.

37. John Bowers, "Controversy and Criticism: Lydgate's *Thebes* and the Prologue to *Beryn*," *Chaucer Yearbook* 5 (1998): 94–95.

CHAPTER 21

The Legacy of John Shirley

Revisiting Houghton MS Eng 530

Stephen Partridge

Early in 2011, I was fortunate to spend nearly three months at Harvard, my first extended stay since I finished my PhD twenty years ago. In addition to enjoying the inexhaustible resources of the libraries, I attended the English department's long-running medieval colloquium and other academic and social events for medievalists. These happily reminded me of Derek Pearsall's large role during my own era in creating an environment for graduate students in Middle English that was both convivial and demanding, and of how unusually lucky we were to have trained as researchers and teachers under his mentorship.

The specific project that brought me to Harvard's Houghton Library was an embryonic one on the "Shirleian" manuscripts—that is, those manuscripts not in John Shirley's own hand but which include texts derived from copies Shirley had made. Houghton MS Eng 530 is one such manuscript. Here I would like to record some observations about this anthology and its several published descriptions, and pose a few questions about how far along we are in understanding the milieu into which Shirley's texts passed, and about the challenges this manuscript and others like it may pose to current practices in Middle English paleography.[1]

The first published description of Eng 530 was one undertaken by Harvard's F. N. Robinson in 1896.[2] Robinson observes, and a note in the manuscript confirms, that the University Library bought Eng 530 at the sale of manuscripts owned by William Medlicott of Longmeadow, Massachusetts, on September 2, 1878.[3] Rodney Dennis seems to have been unaware of this purchase when he wrote his 1983 essay on the history of collecting early manuscripts at Harvard. There Dennis states that although donors had given manuscripts to Harvard through much of the nineteenth century, the first time manuscripts were bought for the library was in 1896.[4] I wonder therefore if the purchase of Eng 530 some eighteen years earlier means that it was the first of the early manuscripts, or among the first, bought by the Harvard library. These are the contents of Eng 530:

1. *The Complaint of God* by William Lychefelde, fols. 1–4r (*NIMEV* 2714) (begins imperfectly).[5]
2. John Lydgate's *Guy of Warwick*, fols. 4v–12v (*NIMEV* 875).
3. *The Three Kings of Cologne*, fols. 13r–33r.
4. *The Governance of Princes*; titled in the manuscript and in the modern edition *The III Consideracions Right Necesserye to the Good Governaunce of a Prince*, fols. 34r–48r.
5. Lydgate's *Serpent of Division*, fols. 49r–57v.
6. The prose *Brut*, fols. 59r–211v.

Robinson reproduces a letter written by Henry Bradshaw in 1866, in which Bradshaw offered some observations on this manuscript to the then-owner, Mr. Lilly, who had put it up for sale.[6] This was apparently the point at which Medlicott bought it, despite Bradshaw's expressed desire that "it ought to be in the British Museum or in the Record Office." Bradshaw asserted that the manuscript was in the hand of John Shirley, but Robinson observes that items 4 and 5 are in a different hand from the others.[7]

These two texts are indeed in a hand which does not, so far as I have determined, appear elsewhere in Eng 530. This hand writes a Secretary script, which is the most polished in the manuscript. In blank space below the end of item 5, on fol. 57v, appears the word *darshyll*. I agree with the judgment of Ryan Perry and Jason O'Rourke, in their description of Eng 530 for the *Imagining History* project, that this word is in the scribe's hand, though it is in a less formal script than that he uses for his texts.[8] Darshill is a village in the southwest Midlands, and given where the scribe writes the word, it is a distinct possibility that he is signing his work here. Robinson also noticed the lack of "Shirleian" rubrics in the two items written by this scribe and the provision of large initials, whereas in other texts large spaces have been left for initials that were never supplied. On these bases, Robinson supposed Eng 530 to be a case of two distinct manuscripts having been brought together.[9] Because blank leaves are found at the ends of both items 4 and 5, as well as at the end of item 3, which precedes them, the former do appear to be written in one or perhaps two separate booklets, probably consisting of three quires.[10] (Unfortunately Eng 530 has been so heavily trimmed that it is impossible to determine its quire structure with confidence.) I will suggest below, however, some reasons for supposing that while items 4 and 5 probably were a distinct unit (or units) of production, they may well have been brought together with the remaining items before they were all completed.

Items 2 and 6 contain elaborate rubrics of the kind which appear in Shirley's own manuscripts and in those that derive from him. The specific rubric about Lydgate's authorship which precedes his *Guy of Warwick* also appears in British Library MS Harley 7333.[11] In her catalog of Middle English manuscripts at Harvard, Linda Voigts gave credit to Ian Doyle for correcting the earlier attribution of Eng 530 to John Shirley and thereby shifting the manuscript to the "Shirleian" category.[12] Voigts refined the picture of scribal stints in Eng 530 by observing that a scribe not present elsewhere in the manuscript wrote the final few surviving folios of the *Brut*.[13] These folios are devoted to a continuation which Lister Matheson has asserted Caxton wrote for his 1480 printing of the *Brut*.[14] For the preceding parts of the manuscript, it is difficult to assign a specific date, but those who have described it generally agree that Eng 530 appears to have been written around the middle of the fifteenth century or slightly later. Thus this final scribe seems to have provided the continuation of the *Brut* on blank leaves he found at the end of the manuscript two or three decades after the preceding portions had been copied.

Voigts's description reflects uncertainty about who was responsible for writing the remaining leaves of Eng 530, aside from those I have suggested we attribute to "Darshyll" and those containing the *Brut* continuation which she noticed were in a later Secretary hand. She refers to a "primary hand" which "is one of several cursive Anglicana hands."[15] This uncertainty about how many scribes worked to produce this manuscript has continued in other references to Eng 530. In her book on

Shirley and his influence, Margaret Connolly suggests that "many" scribes were involved in the production of Eng 530.[16] In her survey of the Shirleian manuscripts, Linne Mooney emphasizes the disjunctive, booklet quality of Eng 530's production and attributes it to "several scribes apparently working independently."[17] Perry and O'Rourke's description for the *Imagining History* project distinguishes seven scribes: A for item 1; B for items 2 and 3; C for items 4 and 5, the second hand distinguished by Robinson, which I have suggested might be "Darshyll"; three hands, D–F, in the bulk of the *Brut*; and G, the scribe distinguished by Voigts as writing in Secretary script the Caxton continuation of the *Brut*.[18] When outlining these stints, Perry and O'Rourke attribute three distinct segments of the *Brut* to scribes D–F; respectively, these are fols. 59r–85r, 85r–109r, and 109r–204r. But Perry and O'Rourke also offer "the opinion that it is difficult to ascertain a changeover between scribes E and F, and that hands E and F may in fact be one scribe who does not practice a consistent script." Moreover, in a later part of their description, they notice an apparent overlap, or switching off, between scribes D and E, and they also note that scribe F "either goes through a change in style . . . or else there is another scribe at work." In other words, the boundaries between these three scribes seem less clear than that initial list might suggest. In fact, the script in the *Brut* varies enough, and in short enough stints, to lead Perry and O'Rourke to remark that "it could be argued that a number of (junior? Amateur?) scribes are taking the opportunity to attempt different styles of script and rubrication. Poss. scribal school?"[19]

We need to arrive at more definite conclusions about how Eng 530 was produced before its evidence can inform any study of how Shirley's manuscripts passed to other scribes and early printers. The *Brut* occupies a considerable majority of its folios, so we must determine how many scribes were involved in writing that text. Moreover, we need to consider whether Perry and O'Rourke are justified in distinguishing the scribes of *The Complaint of God*, on the one side, and Lydgate's *Guy* and *The Three Kings of Cologne*, on the other, from one another and from all other scribes in Eng 530.

We can begin to reexamine these issues by observing the characteristics of the writing, including its variability, in the two texts that Perry and O'Rourke attribute to scribe B, Lydgate's *Guy* and *The Three Kings of Cologne*. In the former, the scribe generally writes around 32 lines per page (see fig. 21.1, which illustrates some though not all of the following features). The scribe uses a cursive form of *e*; mixes long-stemmed and short-stemmed forms of *r*, and as the text progresses, also employs a third, Secretary form of *r*; extends the final strokes of *h* and *y* well below the line; and similarly extends the final stroke of *d* downward when the letter occurs at the end of a word. He also extends *f* below the line; its vertical stroke is slightly tilted to the right, and its somewhat daggerlike shape can make this letter stand out from the adjacent ones. The scribe mixes single-compartment and double-compartment forms of *a*. The upper compartment of the latter form is quite open to the left, and its "back" stroke to the right is regularly separated from the lower compartment. This form of *a* can begin well above the line and appear somewhat oversized relative to adjacent letters. As the scribe's copying progresses in *Guy*, long *s* becomes more frequent than short *s*. He occasionally begins words within the line with a large or "capital" letter. His favorite form of large *I* descends below the line and often appears to be set or centered about a half-line below the rest of his writing. He frequently abbreviates "and" and employs other abbreviations as well, including strokes added to short- and long-stemmed *r*; a semi-circle enclosing a dot for *n*; w^t for "with"; abbreviations for *per* and *pro* at the beginnings of words; and a final loop for *-es* or *-is* as a sign of the plural. He sometimes attaches otiose strokes to final *m* and *n*; these curve back above these letters and then return in a straight horizontal to the right. With noticeable frequency, he separates initial syllable *a* from the remainder of a word; on folios 9 and 10, for example, can be found "a noon," "a woke," "a geynst," "a syde," "a qwytt," "a byde," "a veyle." The scribe mixes *i* and vocalic *y*, and uses the yogh infrequently or not at all.

In *The Three Kings of Cologne* we find all of these letter forms and many similar patterns or habits. Although this text is prose, in contrast to the verse of *Guy*, the first few folios of *The Three Kings*, in particular, resemble those of *Guy* in their general appearance. As the writing progresses, however, it becomes more cursive. I have reproduced here a folio where that cursiveness becomes most extreme in order to demonstrate how different an initial impression the writing of *The Three Kings* can sometimes make from that of *Guy* (fig. 21.2). While that difference is due partly to a general reduction in the number and variety of pen strokes, a few features seem to contribute especially to the change. The scribe here relies heavily on the long-stemmed *r*, which increases the amount of writing below the line. On the other hand, the scribe

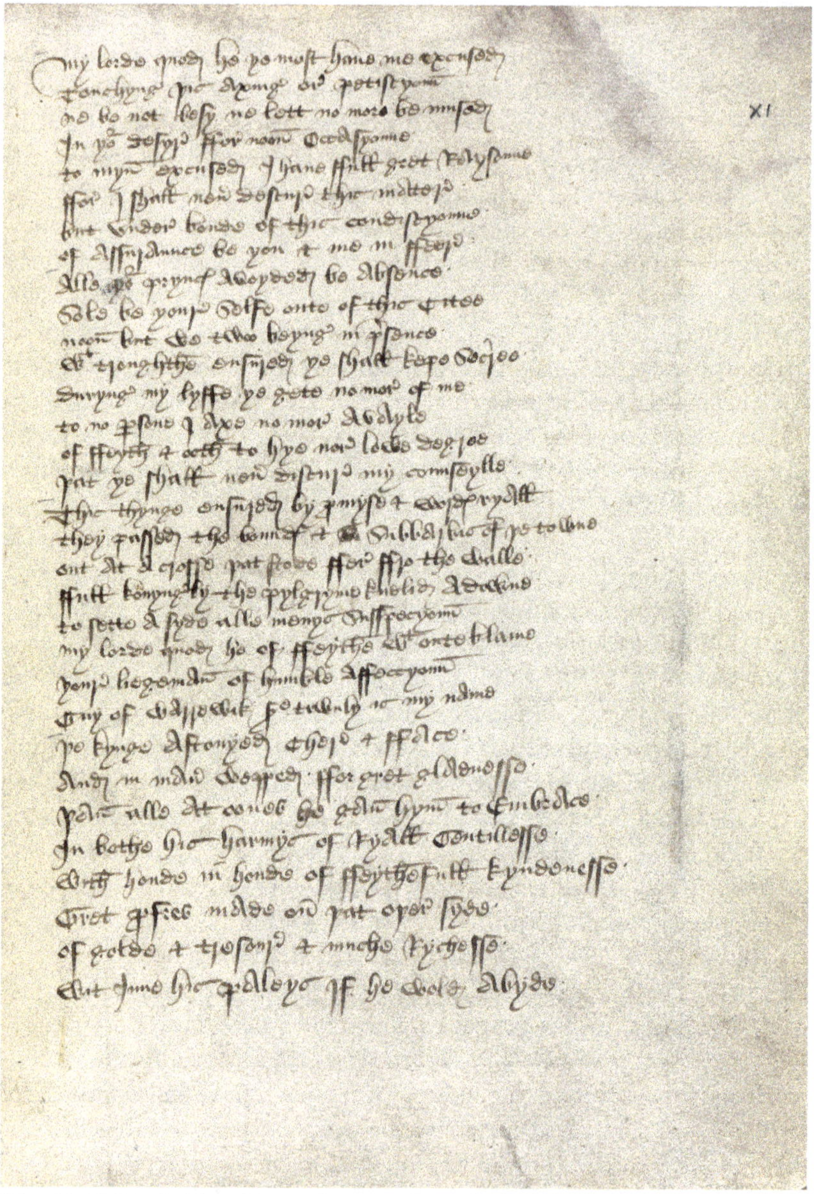

Fig. 21.1. Cambridge, Massachusetts, Houghton Library MS Eng 530, fol. 11r. Reproduced by permission of Houghton Library.

tends to write descenders as simple downstrokes; the vertical stroke of *f*, in particular, is thinner than it is in *Guy*, though in the first few folios of *The Three Kings* it is instead more daggerlike than in *Guy*. While on subsequent folios, such as 18v and following and especially on fol. 29r and after, the writing becomes somewhat more formal and similar to *Guy* again, the strokes sometimes appear thinner and finer than in *Guy*. Another factor that contributes to the cursive quality on fol. 17r, and elsewhere in *The Three Kings*, is the greater frequency of abbreviation. Like the scribe's reliance on the long-stemmed *r*, this pattern increases the amount of writing away from the line and thus makes the lines appear less neat. This change in the scribe's practice may be due to the influence of his exemplars; or it may be a response to pressure on space created by a longer prose text (though see comments below on the *Brut*); or it may reflect a tendency for the scribe to return to habits he finds most comfortable as he progresses through the writing of a given text. The presence of the yogh for *gh* and for consonantal *y* in *The Three Kings* similarly may be due either to the influence of exemplars or to a reversion to the scribe's own preferences. Toward the end of *The Three Kings* (fols. 28 and following), the scribe appears to have had difficulty controlling the amount of ink being dispensed from his quill, another factor that contributes to the occasional messiness of this text.

The *Brut* differs in general appearance from either *Guy* or *The Three Kings*, especially at its beginning. Folios of the *Brut* contain more lines, usually between forty and forty-five but sometimes up to fifty or even slightly more.[20] Not only is the writing smaller, but particularly in the opening folios it is more compact and efficient than in *Guy* or *The Three Kings* (fig. 21.3). A few changes in specific letter forms and habits seem especially responsible for this change. For example, the two-compartment *a*, which is predominant at the beginning of the *Brut*, is much more closed up and more consistent in size with other letters than it was earlier. In addition, the writing now includes a neat Secretary form of *e*. In figure 21.3 this is visible in the heading, though it occurs in the text of the *Prologue* on preceding folios. That a cursive form of *e* has come to predominate in the text after only a couple of folios, as illustrated in figure 21.3, is perhaps the strongest early hint that scribe D is actually scribe B of the preceeding texts, reverting to his preferred forms. Another element that contributes to the impression of control at the beginning of the *Brut* is the presence of a more compact

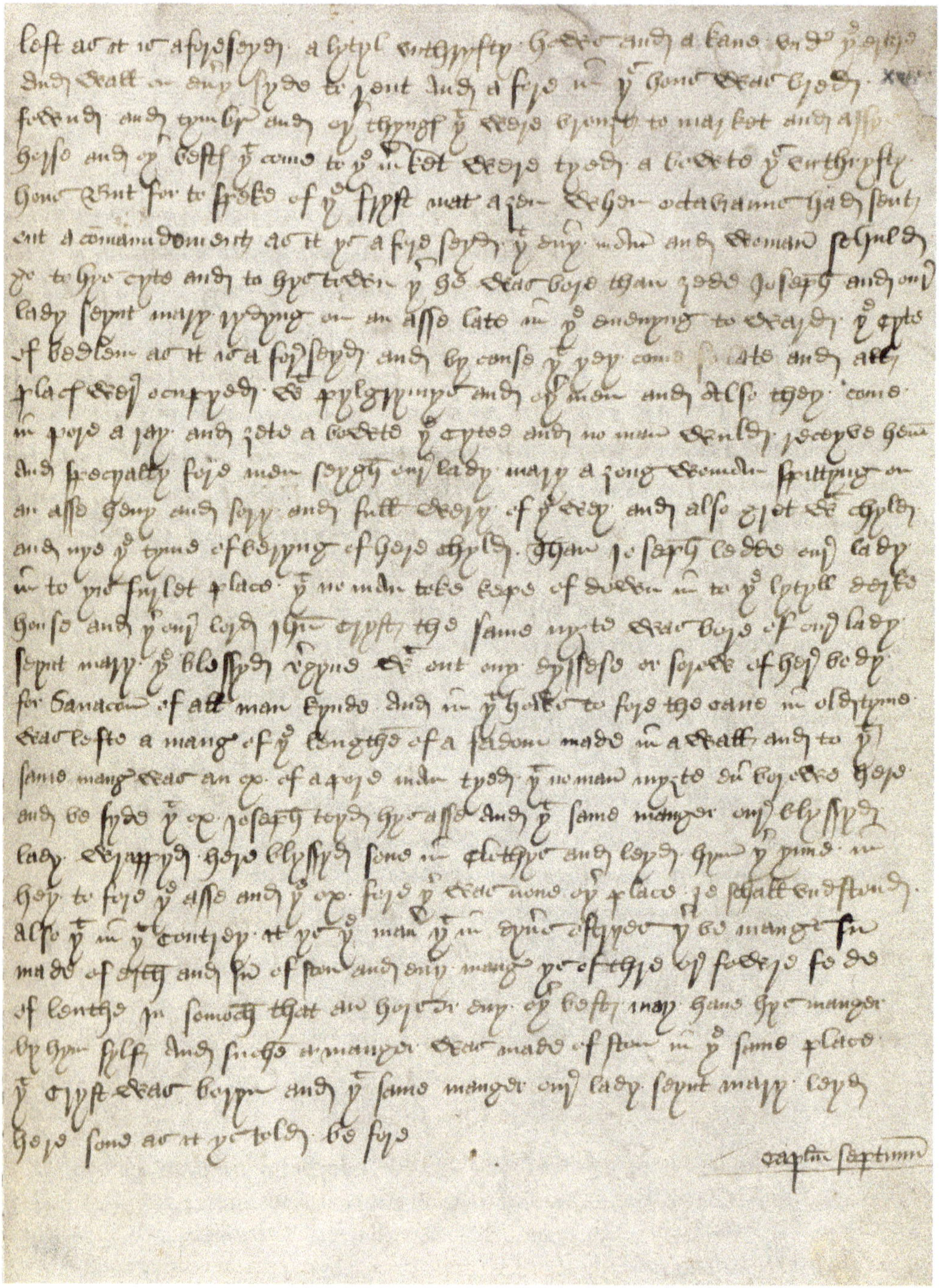

Fig. 21.2. Cambridge, Massachusetts, Houghton Library MS Eng 530, fol. 17r. Reproduced by permission of Houghton Library.

w than appears in *Guy* or *The Three Kings*, but on subsequent folios the scribe returns to the more splayed form visible in the earlier texts. As he begins the *Brut*, the scribe relies on short and Secretary forms of *r*, though a few long-stemmed forms appear on fol. 60 and become steadily more frequent on subsequent folios. The scribe omits any downward stroke on final *d* at first, but this habit also reasserts itself as the *Brut* progresses. While *f* and long *s* are at first more strictly vertical than they were earlier, they begin to slant to the right in a familiar way. In the opening folios of the *Brut*, the large *I* is set more on the line than it was before, but by fol. 66v there can be found several instances in their familiar position, set or centered below the line. Some other changes in the writing continue, to a degree, further into the *Brut*. For example, there are more broken and horned strokes in letters such as *g*, *b*, *m*, and *n*; while these are not obtrusive on individual letters, they have a cumulative effect on the script's appearance. Moreover, abbreviations are less frequent than in *The Three Kings*; for example, the scribe rarely abbreviates "and," though this abbreviation and others are more noticeable in later sections of the *Brut*. While this scarcity costs the scribe some efficiency in transcribing his text, it contributes to the impression of compactness and adherence to the line, which enhances legibility in spite of the rather compressed writing. As in *The Three Kings*, it is difficult to be sure whether the patterns of abbreviation (and lack thereof) result from the influence of exemplars or the scribe's preferences.

Like some of the other trends I have described, the treatment of *a* also suggests that the scribe of *Guy* and *The Three Kings* has attempted to modify and discipline his script as he begins the *Brut* but gradually has returned to his habitual forms. By fol. 71r, where, for example, the tilting of *f* and long *s* has become noticeable, the two-compartment form of *a* more often has the elevated and extended initial stroke visible in the earlier texts of Eng 530, and its upper compartment is more open than it was in the first folios of the *Brut*. At this point or a little later, single-compartment *a* begins to appear, in chapter headings and in the text, and on some folios of the *Brut* is more frequent than the two-compartment form. Perhaps as the scribe returned to his larger and more open two-compartment *a*, he shifted to frequent use of single-compartment *a* as a way of maintaining economy in his use of writing space. The scribe's habit of detaching an initial syllabic *a* from the

Here endiþe þe prologe of þis cronycle of þe yle of Albyone and Filosophe howe þis noble man Brut was borne and goten and in what wyse he slowghe boþe his fader and moder and in what maner he conquered Albyone and after his name cleped it Bretayne // which nowe is called England after þe name of Engest of Saxoyne þat putte oute Brut and his peonyes

In þe noble cite of grete Troye was a noble knyghte and a myghty man of grete power which men cleped þee Eneas and whanne þe cite of Troye was lost and destroyed thorough hem of Grece þis Eneas with alle his meyne fledde þens and came into lombardye of which contrey þat tyme was gouernoure and lorde þat tyme a kyng þat men called Latyn a noþer kyng þer was in þoo contrey cleped Turnelyn which maynteined grete werre ageyns latyn thorowe which he resceyued grete harme and miche disease and whanne þis kyng latyne herde þat Eneas was comen he resceyued hym with honoure and with hoolde hym bycause he hade herde wel telle he was a ful honourable and a manly knyghte of his handes þis Eneas holpe kyng latyne in his werre and schortly for to telle so wele and worþely he did þat with inne shortnesse of tyme he slowghe Turnelyne and descomfyted alle his people for which cause kyng latyne gaf al þat lande þat was Turnelynes unto Eneas in mariage with his doughter lamane þe fayrest creature þat was euer knowen in þoo dayes þe whiche Eneas and lamane lyueden and lyuweden with þeyre procreacion in ioye and grete felycite alle her lyues whane Eneas was ded Ascanyus his sone which came with hym frome Troye succeded and possessed þat regioun al his lyfes tyme after his fader which Ascanius with inne short proces of tyme wedded hym and hade issu Silvan þe which at resonable age acqueynted hym with þe Cosyns lamanes doughter a fayre creature which loued hym so paramours þat he gate hur with childe and whane Ascanius his fader wist he sent for þe grettest maysters of astronomye or nygromancye to wit of hem of þe childe þat she shulde bere to þe whome þey answerd and sayde þat she scholde bere a sone which shulde slee boþe fader and moder his

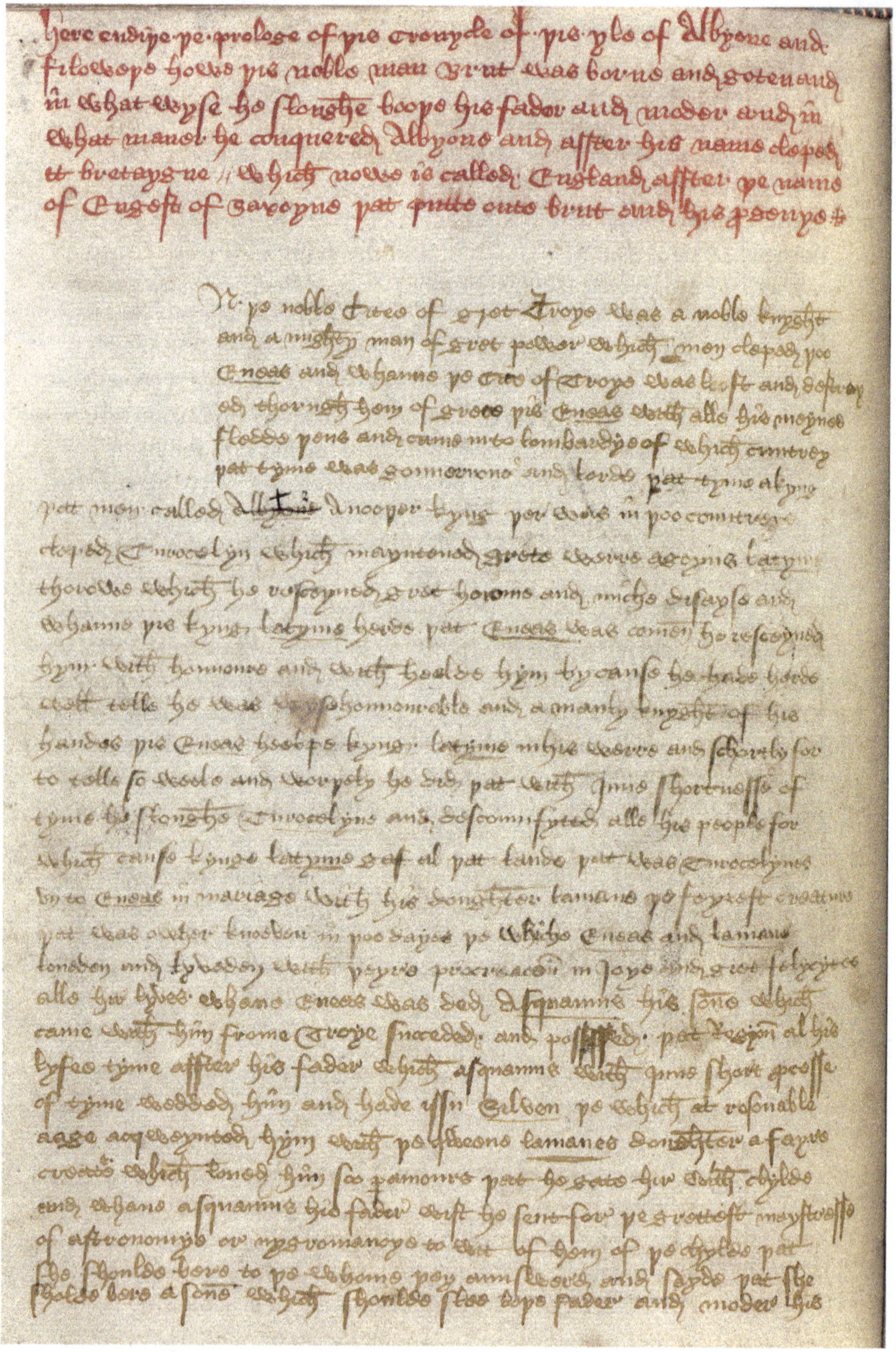

Fig. 21.3. Cambridge, Massachusetts, Houghton Library MS Eng 530, fol. 60v. Reproduced by permission of Houghton Library.

remainder of a word also resurfaces, such as on fol. 81, where "a boute," "a venge," and "a gayne" appear.

The effect of these changes, together with a general, gradual relaxation into a more rounded, cursive script, is to return the writing to a form that might be described as a more compact and calligraphic version of the script used in Lydgate's *Guy* (fig. 21.4). The folio reproduced, 77v, draws attention to some issues in the treatment of the chapter headings that affect an attempt to determine the number of scribes. In the first fifteen folios of the *Brut*, the chapter headings are more often in red, and in a script influenced by Secretary and comparable to that used at the opening of the text. On folio 74, however, two chapter headings are in a shade of black that is darker than that of the folio's text, though comparable to a shade that can be found in the text and headings elsewhere in the *Brut*. These headings are also in a larger script than has appeared in chapter headings so far in the *Brut* but which resembles that used for the heading and colophon to *Guy*—and these are certainly by scribe B, who wrote the text of *Guy*. Moreover, corrections in the same script and ink appear on fol. 74v and some subsequent folios. This pattern indicates that the scribe wrote some chapter headings and corrections on a separate, later pass through Eng 530. Furthermore, continuing shifts between scripts and inks in the chapter headings suggest that the scribe returned multiple times to the first fifty folios or so of the *Brut* and, when he did, did not write all the chapter headings in sequence. For example, some headings in red, such as on fol. 86r, are in the large, rounded script, though on the verso of fol. 86 the same script is written in black.

Such variation in the treatment of headings is especially frequent on folios 85–89 and is accompanied by comparable changes in the writing of the text. This concentrated variation explains the judgment by Kelly and O'Rourke that "scribes D and E share the copying of a few fols. after 85r, with D ceasing to contribute on fol. 89r," but the more widespread variation in the writing of the *Brut* argues that no shift of hand occurs here. Rather, it appears that this is still scribe B, writing in unusually short stints. It is impossible to be certain why his writing should vary so much at this point. The variation may be due to external circumstances, such as an unusual lapse of time between stints, or to his departing from strictly sequential copying of the text. Or it may reflect a series of experiments as he tries to find a script with which he can comfortably and efficiently copy this especially long text. If the

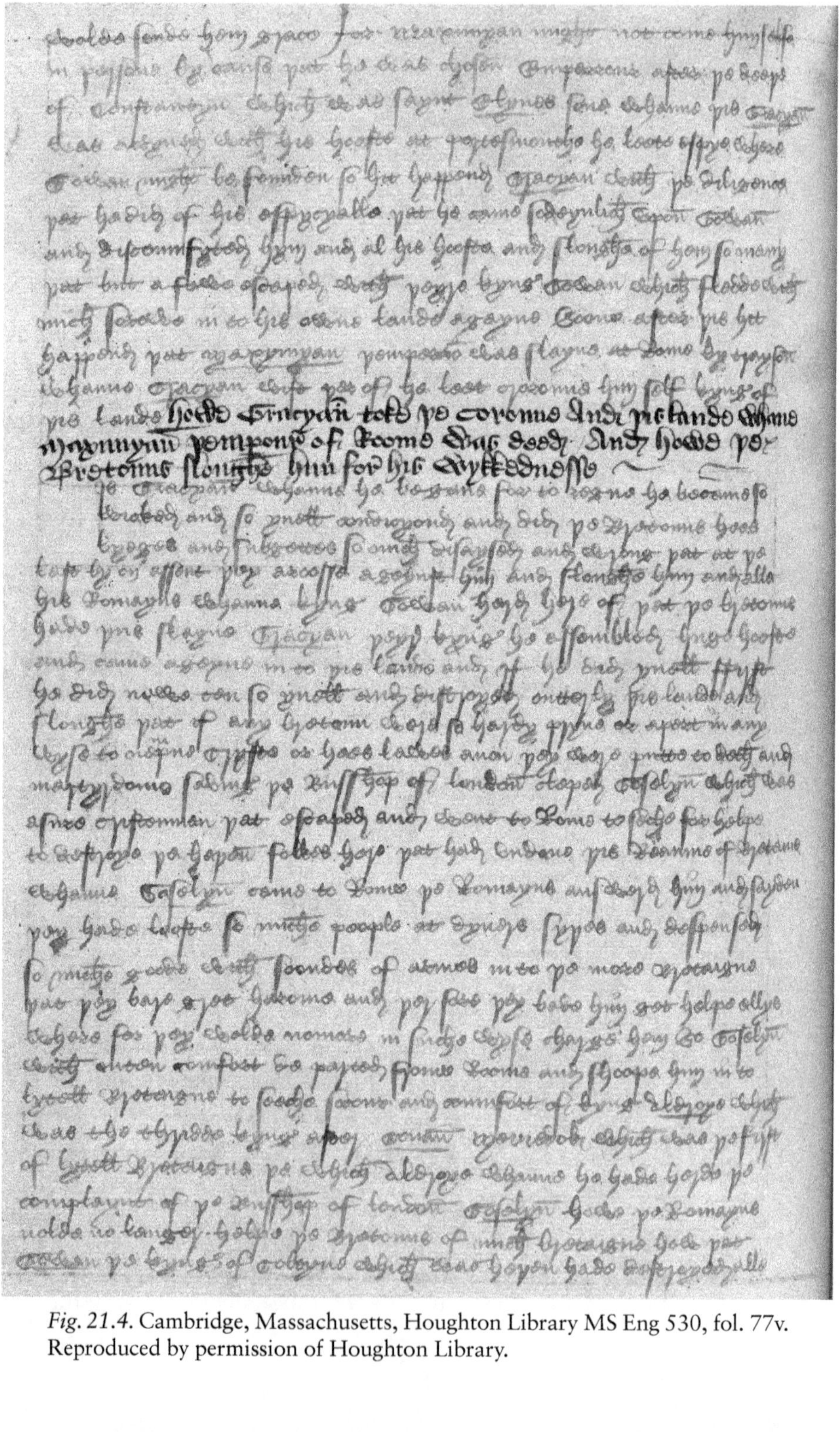

Fig. 21.4. Cambridge, Massachusetts, Houghton Library MS Eng 530, fol. 77v. Reproduced by permission of Houghton Library.

latter is the case, the evolution of his script seems to continue for another twenty folios, to fol. 109r, after which point the scribe's writing is quite consistent to the end of his copying of the *Brut*. The chapter headings on fol. 109r seem to represent the latest point in the *Brut* where the scribe has used the more calligraphic, Secretary-influenced script of some earlier chapter headings and text. Thereafter, although the ink of both text and headings can vary from a rather light shade of brown to black, the ink of the chapter headings tends to be much closer to that of the immediately surrounding text than was the case earlier in the *Brut*. In addition, the script of the headings more closely resembles that of the text, in size and style. These changes suggest that sometime after fol. 109r, the scribe began writing chapter headings more or less as he copied the text rather than in separate passes. This shift in his practice may have resulted partly from the fact that in this latter part of the *Brut* chapters generally become longer and thus headings for them less numerous; their copying thus may have demanded less of the scribe's attention.

Those headings on fol. 109r include a *g* with a bar across the top. This form is visible in some chapter headings from the beginning of the *Brut*, but one further significant development in the scribe's writing from fol. 109r forward is his increasing use of this form of *g* in the text. This form always alternates, however, with forms of *g* that are familiar from earlier parts of Eng 530 (fig. 21.5). Thus the treatment of *g* exemplifies the more general tendency in the *Brut*: while new letter forms and habits of writing appear, these all remain mixed with elements familiar from Lydgate's *Guy* and *The Three Kings* and from preceding parts of the *Brut*. The initial impression derived from Eng 530, that a large number of scribes were involved in its production, results partly from factors that do not actually constitute proof of changes in hand. These include, for example, shifts between verse and prose; large differences in the number of lines per folio; different shades of ink among various stints of writing; and differences in script among headings, and between headings and text, as well as the occasional use of red in headings. There are, moreover, changes in the writing of scribe B which seem to result from two different tendencies. First, he disciplines his writing in an attempt to produce a more calligraphic style of writing, perhaps under the influence of Secretary, at the beginnings of some stints and especially as he begins the *Brut*, but then reverts to the cursive Anglicana forms with which he seems to have been more familiar and which perhaps allowed him to write more quickly.[21] The second general

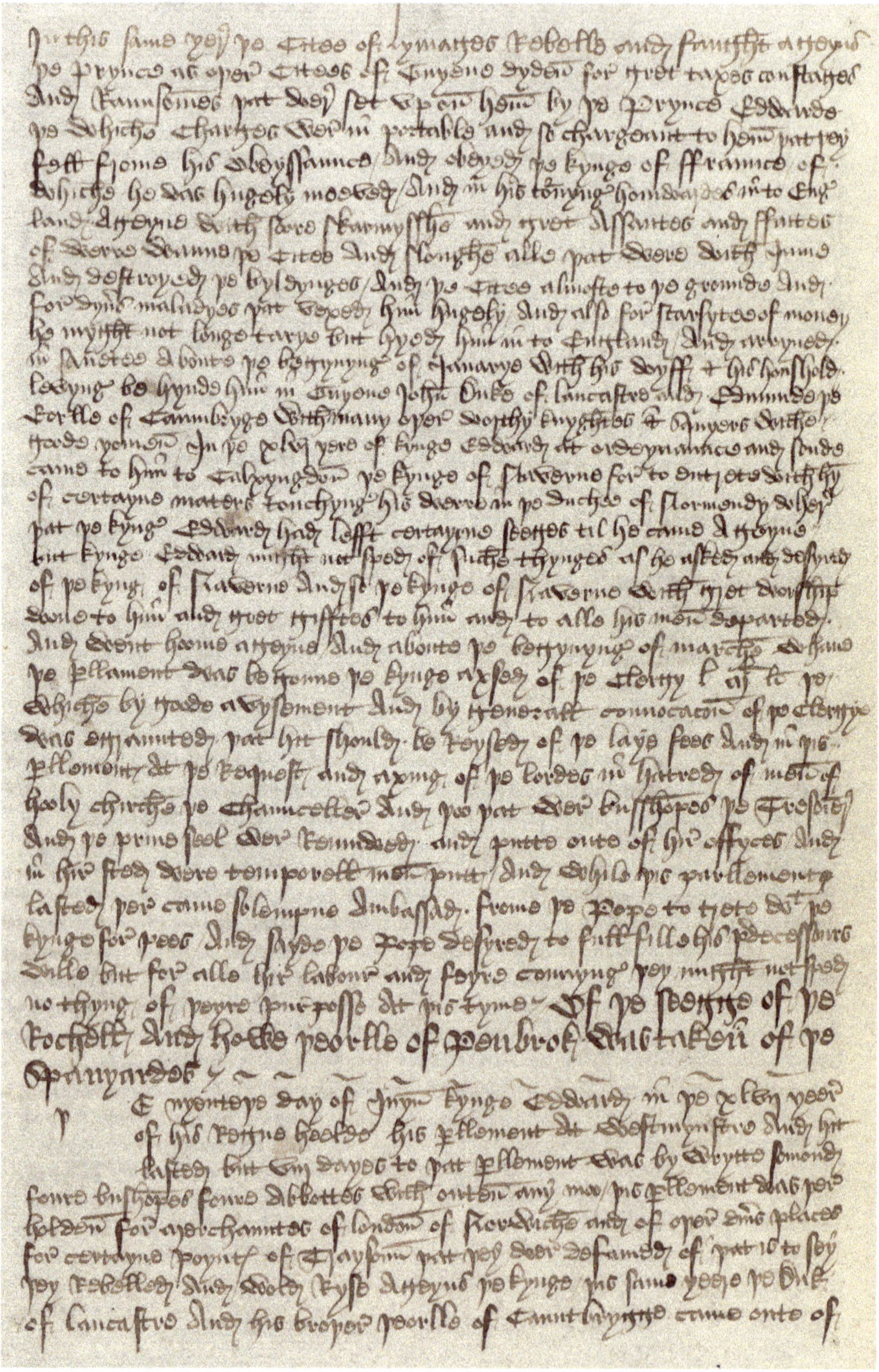

Fig. 21.5. Cambridge, Massachusetts, Houghton Library MS Eng 530, fol. 177r. Reproduced by permission of Houghton Library.

pattern seems to be the growing influence of aspects of the Secretary script with which scribe B was in fact comfortable—those he internalized, so to speak, such as the barred *g*, and made part of his standard repertoire.

Once the variability of this scribe's writing is recognized, it is difficult to distinguish him from Perry and O'Rourke's scribe A, copyist of the first text surviving in Eng 530, the *Complaint of God* (fig. 21.6). The folios of this text present a somewhat different appearance from those of others in Eng 530, partly because the short lines of verse are written in two columns. Yet an examination of individual letter forms reveals much that is familiar, such as the scribe's preference for long *s*, cursive *e*, and long-stemmed *r*; the curls at the ends of descending strokes in *h* and *y*; the descender added to word-final *d*. The large *I*, frequent in this text, is centered or set below the level of other letters. The two-compartment *a* is open and expansive. The headings for the sections of the *Complaint* are written in a larger script similar to that used for headings elsewhere. At least two characters appear with unusual frequency in the *Complaint*—the yogh and vocalic *y*—and these contribute to the distinctive appearance of these folios, but these differences from the other texts of Eng 530 may well result from the influence of the scribe's exemplars. The identification of the *Complaint*'s scribe with scribe B is important because the scribe appears to sign his work in the space below the conclusion of the *Complaint* on fol. 4. Unfortunately, despite repeated attempts, I have not been able to transcribe the scribe's name with confidence. My best guess at individual letters would produce *thys Iudonfeu mad*, but this does not seem very plausible. I hope others may be more successful.

What is the relationship of this scribe's texts to items 4 and 5, written by "Darshyll," which precede the *Brut*? I have not identified any point of overlap in the writing of these two scribes; that is, I do not find the main scribe's hand on the pages of Darshyll's booklet(s), or vice versa. Thus there is, so far, nothing to prove that these scribes worked together. The use of red in Eng 530, however, suggests that the main scribe may have been responsible for bringing Darshyll's booklets together with his own texts while his writing was still in progress. Those large initials, which Robinson observed are unique to Darshyll's items, are in red, as are chapter headings, explicits, page headings, and paragraph marks. In item 5, Lydgate's *Serpent of Division*, red was used to highlight the initial letters of many words. Red does not appear in the

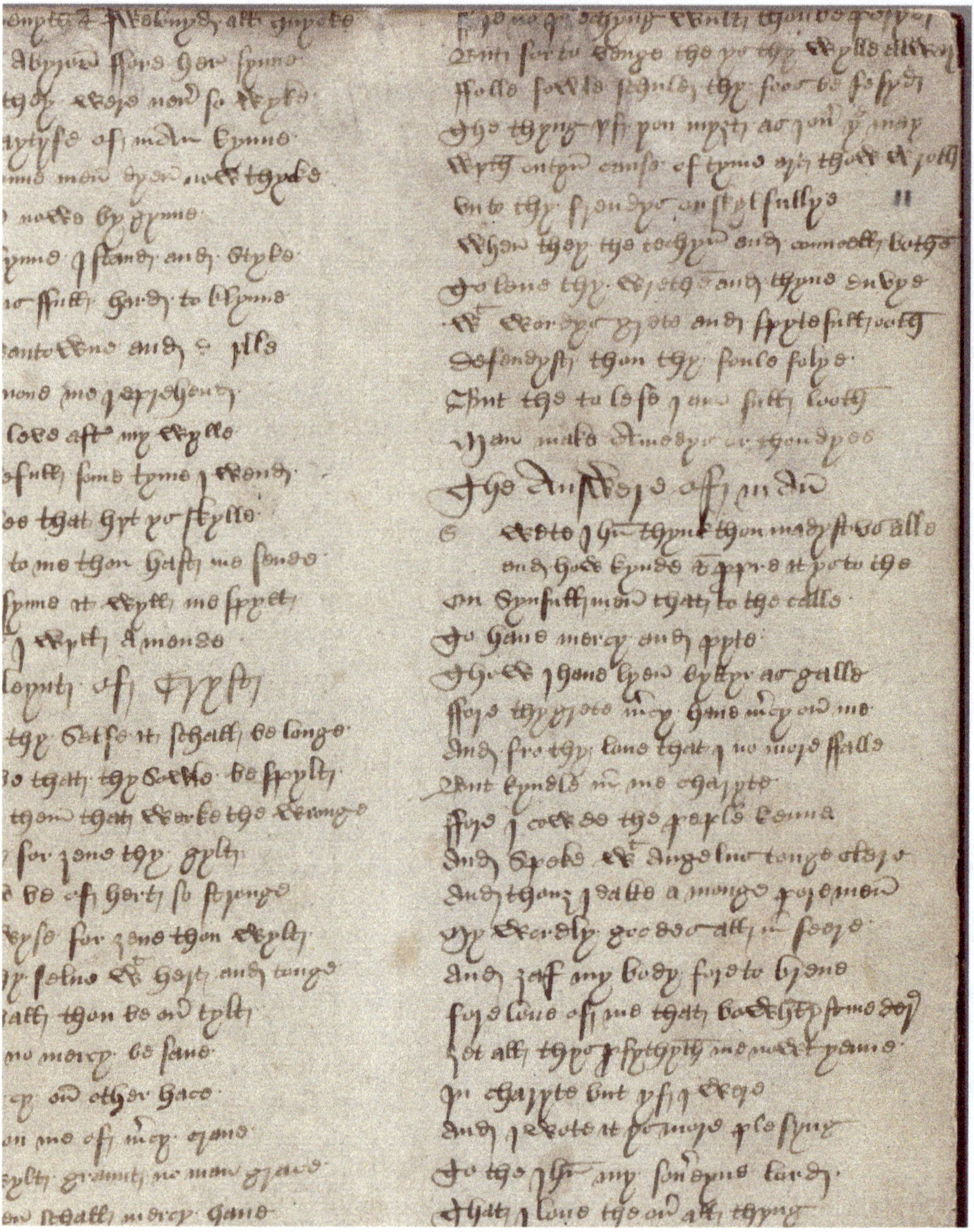

Fig. 21.6. Cambridge, Massachusetts, Houghton Library MS Eng 530, fol. 2r. Reproduced by permission of Houghton Library.

main scribe's first three items, but when he writes the *Brut*, he uses red for the Shirleian "blurb" preceding its prologue, for the incipit to its text, and for many (though not all) chapter headings through the first forty folios or so of the chronicle. This change might suggest that the main scribe had come across (or commissioned?) Darshyll's items 4 and 5 and added them to his own items 1–3, before going on to copy the *Brut*, and began using red in the *Brut* in a short-lived effort to make the folios of the *Brut* somewhat resemble those of Darshyll's items.

Though they can tell us nothing definite about the process by which the manuscript reached its present form, we might notice a few points of connection between the texts copied by Darshyll and others in Eng 530. One of these is Lydgate's authorship of items 2 and 5 and the attribution, in a Shirleian heading, of the *Brut* chapters concerning Richard II's reign to Lydgate. In addition, after the first two items in verse, the bulk of Eng 530 is in prose. We can perceive, in varying proportions in the different texts of Eng 530, a group of themes related to English and British history and to good governance, of self and subjects. This might be characterized as a "legitimating" manuscript, designed to promote and attest to a gentle patron's "natural" status as well as his piety and probity. One suspects that this was a kind of manuscript household clerks were often called on to produce for their masters. Determining that most of Eng 530 was the work of a single scribe, possibly over an extended period, seems to point toward a model of a clerk or another person in household service copying and assembling texts as time and opportunity allowed. Though the manuscript is not in Shirley's hand, this is a somewhat Shirleian model of scribal labor. Whether or not a single Shirley anthology lies behind the combination of items 2 and 6 in Eng 530, Shirley's texts seem, in one sense, not to have traveled far before arriving in that manuscript.[22]

All this, however, remains only hypothesis for now, as there remains much to be discovered about Eng 530. For instance, I have not yet been able to analyze the language of this manuscript. Such an analysis may help us determine how accurate is my guess that the word *darshyll* is a scribal signature rather than an indication of where the manuscript was copied or owned. Names written in the manuscript might also provide evidence for its early provenance, a topic that has received virtually no attention to date. The appearance of their scripts suggests that Darshyll was a professional scribe but that the main scribe very possibly was not.[23] The former's writing is distinctive enough that it should be fairly recognizable if it is found elsewhere. The main scribe's writing, by contrast, seems quite typical of the mid-fifteenth century. This, together with that writing's variability, may make it difficult to recognize that scribe readily if and when we encounter his writing in another manuscript.

Simply ascertaining how many scribes worked on Eng 530, however, may help refine our ideas about the environments into which Shirley's manuscripts passed. If it was written by as many as seven or eight scribes, as suggested by *Imagining History,* we might be inclined to think that it was produced in a well-developed commercial copying environment or perhaps in a religious house—a place where there would have been large numbers of scribes of comparable competence. If Eng 530 is instead primarily a single-scribe production, with a couple of texts in booklets copied by a second scribe, this might better support the model I have proposed of a household clerk gathering and copying texts for his employer over an extended period. Intriguingly, another instance I know of such marked scholarly disagreement over how many scribes worked on a manuscript relates to another Shirleian manuscript, London, BL MS Harley 7333. Manly and Rickert attribute this manuscript to "six to nine or more hands."[24] In a 1999 essay that critiques Manly and Rickert's account in several respects, Timothy Shonk attributes Harley 7333 to three scribes.[25] Yet Mooney in her article on the Shirleian anthologies distinguishes eight hands, though in its details her analysis differs significantly from Manly and Rickert's.[26] This fundamental issue needs to be resolved through more extended analysis of Harley 7333 before our understanding of who received Shirley's manuscripts can be advanced.[27]

Scholarly uncertainty over how many hands are present in Eng 530 also raises questions about paleographic method. I find interesting the general tendency, from Bradshaw and Robinson through *Imagining History*, to record more and more hands in Eng 530, which might suggest that the drawing of one distinction between scribes in a given manuscript creates a bias toward distinguishing additional ones—a bias to be conscious of in describing Middle English manuscripts, perhaps especially those of the mid-fifteenth century. There might also be in this history of descriptions a familiar lesson about the value of consulting manuscripts in situ rather than relying on microfilm or even excellent images like those of Eng 530 that the Houghton Library has made available online.[28] The ability rapidly to compare many different folios was crucial in enabling me to determine how many hands were present in Eng 530. Furthermore, we might consider how the project of identifying hands from one Middle English manuscript to another may or may not be informed by cases like these, where writing that can appear very different among various folios of one manuscript seems on further examination most likely to be that of the same scribe. We are often predisposed to identify work within a given manuscript as by the same scribe, but we require a high standard of proof in arguments that the same hand appears in more than one manuscript. Is our method consistent?

Finally, Robinson's study of Eng 530 remains useful, despite its antiquity. Those who have subsequently offered descriptions of Eng 530 have in certain ways refined his account of this interesting manuscript but have also created elements of confusion that might have been avoided by giving greater weight to Robinson's observations.[29] The study of Middle English manuscripts has of course been vastly expanded and transformed since Robinson's day—and Derek Pearsall has directly and through his influence played a major part in those changes. Those changes continue and may well accelerate with the advance of technology. For example, libraries making images of entire manuscripts available online, as the Houghton Library has done with Eng 530 and other manuscripts, should make more practically possible the wiki-style descriptions that the *Imagining History* project so admirably pioneered. As we move forward, we must remember what those who have gone before have given us and consider how best to make use of their gifts.

Notes

I wish to express my deep gratitude to the Houghton Library for the award of a Katharine F. Pantzer Jr. Fellowship in Descriptive Bibliography, which enabled me to carry out the research described in this essay.

1. Digital images of the entire manuscript are now available online; see http://pds.lib.harvard.edu/pds/view/7835965.

2. F. N. Robinson, "On Two Manuscripts of Lydgate's Guy of Warwick," *Harvard Studies & Notes in Philology & Literature* 5 (1896): 177–220.

3. Ibid., 180.

4. Rodney G. Dennis, "Collecting Early Manuscripts at Harvard," *Harvard Library Bulletin* 31 (1983): 287: "The Library first became actively involved at a Phillipps sale in London in June 1896." The entry for Eng 530 in the

Harvard Library's online catalog, HOLLIS Classic, does record the information about the manuscript's early ownership and purchase.

5. *NIMEV* refers to Julia Boffey and A. S. G. Edwards, *A New Index of Middle English Verse* (London: British Library, 2005).

6. Robinson, "On Two Manuscripts," 179–80 n. 1.

7. Ibid., 180–81. Robinson, however, did not challenge the attribution of the remainder of the manuscript to Shirley. Robinson's study reproduces fol. 39v, part of *The Gouvernance of Princes*, to illustrate this second scribal hand (183).

8. The description of Eng 530 is at www.qub.ac.uk/imagining-history/resources/short/results.php?record=84 (accessed November 27, 2012). In the section on "Graffiti?" the word is transcribed as "a n[d n?] shyll." Previous descriptions had not noticed the word.

9. Robinson, "On Two Manuscripts," 181.

10. Fols. 33v, 48v, and 58 (recto and verso) were left blank by the scribes.

11. Robinson, "On Two Manuscripts," transcribes the Shirleian rubric to Lydgate's *Guy* on 197 and the Shirleian rubrics to the *Brut* on 185.

12. Linda Ehrsam Voigts, "A Handlist of Middle English in Harvard Manuscripts," *Harvard Library Bulletin* 33, no. 1 (1985): 17. I do not find a specific statement about the scribe(s) of Eng 530 in either A. I. Doyle, "English Books in and out of Court from Edward III to Henry VII," in *English Court Culture in the Later Middle Ages* (London: Duckworth, 1983), 163–81, or A. I. Doyle, "More Light on John Shirley," *Medium Aevum* 30 (1961): 93–101.

13. Voigts, "A Handlist of Middle English," 18: "ff. 204–211v [P4B], a current secretary."

14. Lister M. Matheson, *The Prose "Brut": The Development of a Middle English Chronicle* (Tempe, AZ: Medieval and Renaissance Texts and Studies), 164–65, 258. The continuation breaks off in Eng 530, due to a loss of leaves from the end of the manuscript.

15. Voigts, "A Handlist of Middle English," 17–18.

16. Margaret Connolly, *John Shirley: Book Production and the Noble Household in Fifteenth-Century England* (Aldershot: Ashgate, 1998), 172.

17. Linne Mooney, "John Shirley's Heirs," *Yearbook of English Studies* 33 (2003): 194.

18. See "Number of Scribes," in Perry and O'Rourke, *Imagining History*; see note 8 for website.

19. These remarks are in the section "Style of Hand," in Perry and O'Rourke, *Imagining History;* see note 8 for website. They acknowledge that their description is based on a microfilm ("Credits and acknowledgments") and that "the hands responsible for copying the *Brut* need further examination" ("Number of Scribes"). Their description records many details not provided in Robinson, "On Two Manuscripts," or Voigts, "A Handlist of Middle English."

20. The writing area is framed but unruled on the folios of Eng 530.

21. Cf. M.B. Parkes, *English Cursive Book Hands, 1250–1500* (Oxford: Clarendon Press, 1969), pl. 21, "Variations in the Handwriting of a Single Scribe within the Same MS." The example is London, Society of Antiquaries, MS 223, a copy of the *Brut* from the second half of the fifteenth century. The scribe begins writing "a calligraphic well-spaced Secretary book hand," but by fol. 30v his script has become "a typical example of late-fifteenth-century Anglicana."

22. Mooney, "John Shirley's Heirs," 195, speculates that some other texts in Eng 530 may also have derived from Shirley exemplars.

23. See Doyle, "English Books," 177–78, who refers to Shirley's texts passing into the hands of "very amateurish-looking copyists"; and Mooney, "John Shirley's Heirs," 195, who characterizes the writing and decoration of items 4 and 5 as "distinctly more professional in appearance than the rest of the volume"; and comments on the *Imagining History* website.

24. J.M. Manly and Edith Rickert, *The Text of The Canterbury Tales,* 8 vols. (Chicago: University of Chicago Press, 1940), vol. 1, 209.

25. Timothy A. Shonk, "BL MS Harley 7333: The 'Publication' of Chaucer in the Rural Areas," *Essays in Medieval Studies* 15 (1999): 81–91. For his outline of the booklets and scribal stints, see 84–85.

26. Mooney, "John Shirley's Heirs," 190–94, 198.

27. When I examined Harley 7333 in 1993, I could distinguish only three scribes.

28. See http://pds.lib.harvard.edu/pds/view/7835965 for a complete digital facsimile of Eng 530.

29. For example, Robinson, "On Two Manuscripts," 197 and 185, offers more accurate and complete transcriptions of the Shirleian rubrics to Lydgate's *Guy* and the *Brut* than does Voigts, "A Handlist of Middle English," 18 and 20–21; Mooney reproduces Voigts's transcriptions in "John Shirley's Heirs," 195 and 194 n. 31.

Part VII

What a Poet Is "Entitled to Be Remembered By"

Editorial Philosophies and the Langlandian Legacy of Derek Pearsall

Foreword to Part VII

The very different essays that follow offer a number of insights into current concerns in Langland studies. Jill Mann brings pragmatism and detail to long-standing critical anxiety about George Kane and E. Talbot Donaldson's strict conception of the poet (an anxiety articulated early on in Lee Patterson's celebrated defense of their editorial systematics).[1] Melinda Nielsen and Kathryn Kerby-Fulton exemplify the way that scholarship placing Langland in his historical context currently seems to be moving on from earlier (highly productive) questions about Langland's relation to the Peasants Revolt, labor legislation, and Wyclifitism to other versions of a "*Piers Plowman* tradition."[2] Whether focused on the poem's textual transmission or its legacy in later writings, however, the three essays show that Langland's reception is always simultaneously clarifying and complicating, both ordinatory (concerned with manuscript *ordinatio*) and reviserly, at once "scribal" and "writerly." And in all these respects, of course, these modes of reception look remarkably like Langland's own writing practices. Mann's fluid and pragmatic view of Langland has much in common with the vision of London textual and scribal culture that Kerby-Fulton has for a while now been developing in dialogue with scholars such as Denise Despres, Linne Mooney, and Ralph Hanna.

The interventionist scribes and writers described in these essays are all engaged in the perpetuation of a self-consciously complex exegetical and glossatory poetic, one that is characterized by dialogism, dialectic, and even contradiction. But they are also concerned with "making sense"—with methods of textual organization and manuscript rubrication designed to focus meaning and render texts usable and accessible. This is perhaps not quite the same as the fifteenth-century courtly and Chaucerian literary tradition, with its easy cultivation of narrative variation and imaginative ambiguity: this is a religious, political, and legal milieu in which poetry is often ostentatiously difficult and yet preoccupied with being understood.

Mann does not question Kane and Donaldson's extraordinary advances in editorial theory and the new benchmark for editorial systematicity represented by the Athlone edition of *Piers Plowman*; but in her discussion of the work of the C-reviser she is surely correct to remind us of the very problematic determinations that result from Kane's commitment to his edition of the A text. She is surely right that an editorial project cannot be judged only on its theoretical premises but must also be assessed on the pragmatics of its local decision making in light of those premises. This she documents in her responses to nine instances of supposed B-manuscript "corruption," not to mention Kane and Donaldson's claim that the C-reviser is systematically trying to improve them. Her examples illustrate the well-known partiality of some of their local judgments about Langland's "difficult" or "pregnant" poetry and what the author could or could not have intended, a partiality that results directly from their distinctively formalist and purposive version of Langland's "authorial originality." Other examples spring to mind: Kane and Donaldson's assertion that the use of the word *megre* for Envy is impossible because he is in fact swollen (B 5.129), when the whole point about Envy is that he is both *lene* (unable to eat) and *bollen* with bile; or their insistence that the wonderfully vivid and alliterating "gnawen with the gorge" is impossible because it "is actually non-sense" (B 10.58); or the idea that Mede cannot be using the insulting words *wernard* and *gabbe* at B 3.180 because she "is speaking more in sorrow than in anger," when of course this is just what she wants us to believe.[3]

As it has long been recognized, the corollary of Kane and Donaldson's view of the poet is their have-it-all-ways characterization of the scribe—both overemphatic and flat, both crassly clear and obscure. And while there is clearly no risk of returning to earlier twentieth-century notions of Langland as an unsophisticated writer and thinker, Mann is surely right to ask if Langland does not sometimes make what it suits Kane and Donaldson to describe as "scribal" choices, writing in ways that are emphatic, clear, obvious, or simply banal. What Mann is prepared to countenance is, to me, a much more recognizable Langland, the most sophisticated of thinkers but also an impulsive and experimental writer, constantly rereading and reworking his text (and sometimes just fiddling with it): a writer for whom the tension between two different urges, one to complicate and nuance and the other to clarify and embolden, is a fundamentally productive one. This is also a view of the poet that connects much more meaningfully with the critical, risk-taking, and iconoclastic ethos that governs his poem. If Langland was concerned that we should use, not reify, things, terms, or concepts, it would be slightly surprising if he turned out to be a fetishist of his own poetry. But of course this view of Langland would not really have been news to Kane and Donaldson; it was they, after all, who said of him, "There is . . . no evidence that his revision was systematic. . . . All indications are that he revised and rewrote rather than restored his text. . . . [H]is revision was neither systematic nor thorough."[4] It was Kane and Donaldson who first introduced the specter of a C-reviser who, if he was not actually disorganized, then was at least not a textual pedant—no longer in possession of a clean copy of his own text.

The textual culture in which Kerby-Fulton has located the John Wells copy of the Z text (Oxford, Bodleian Library, MS Bodley 851) is similarly unsettled (or "scrambled," as Nielsen says in her essay), with Wells himself moving and possibly carrying his carefully frontispieced manuscript of religious, historical, and satirical texts between Ramsey Abbey in East Anglia and the Benedictine house in Oxford. In this context, the Z text's omission of the Tearing of the Pardon, the addition of the Tearing by Scribe Q1, and Scribe Q2's continuation of the C text do not just pose editorial questions about the relation of the Z text to the A text (which includes the Tearing) and the C text (which does not); they also epitomize a culture in which manuscripts and their revision, or even cancellation, represent a site of special concern. Could this in turn suggest that a writerly or scribal valuation of the manuscript may have played a part in Langland's revisions of this scene? Was manuscript tearing just too inflammatory?

Whatever the answer to this question, such equivocations over the Tearing also reveal in Langland and his disseminators the same urge toward the simplification, or even removal, of troublesome elements but also toward the production of new textual excrescences. In her exploration of the acrostic as a method of "freezing" long and complex texts, Nielsen has drawn our attention to a similar interplay of textual control and elaboration, this time by rubrication. Nielsen describes the acrostic as a response to endemic reviserliness, an attempt to fix texts in flux, such as Thomas Usk's *Testament of Love* or Ranulph Higden's *Polychronicon*; such acrostics are thus an example of authorial (and not scribal) determination to circumscribe complex textuality. They surely represent an impulse similar to that which introduced the *Visio*, and *Vita de dowel*, *dobet*, and *dobest* rubrics into Langland's poem—rubrics whose disputed authorship once again reveals the difficulty of separating Langland from his disseminators.[5]

Kerby-Fulton comments on "Langland's ability . . . to inspire readers to become writers," his capacity to create readers in his own image. However, the other specter that her work has long raised is that of a Langland who sees himself in the mirror of the community of contemporary religious, political, and legal controversialists, writers, and scribes. Although none of the famous *Piers Plowman* "autobiographical" passages describes him in this way, the various authorial signatures that have been identified in the poem, most notably by Anne Middleton (not acrostics but certainly marked by an interest in word games), surely bear the mark of these scribal workers as much as they do that of the manual workers targeted by the 1388 Statute of Labourers. This scribal community must, after all, have constituted Langland's first readers and interlocutors, as he went about the business of getting his work disseminated. Like his, their work was to carve a path between a poetic text that testified to its poet's obsessive revising and the need for a clean, rubricated, and readable text. Like Langland, too, they made their presence manifest in the manuscripts they produced, although they only rarely named or referred to themselves.

Derek Pearsall has always been very much in tune with the dynamic, "in-process" version of Langland and his textual community that we see in these essays. Elizabeth Salter once said to me that the world of medieval studies was full of avuncular male medievalists whom students tended to mistake for Chaucer. Perhaps this is less true than it once was. However, it seems to me that Derek's capacious and flexible modes of scholarship might in fact be rather Langlandian. What distinguishes Derek's writing and editing is an indefatigable drive to engage and to get traction with the opposition, as well as, when it seems right, to take some of that opposition on board. This is very different from the tenacity with which Kane and Donaldson clung to Kane's A text. It is something that is absolutely in evidence in Derek's own revised edition of the C text, marked not least by his generosity to Kane and Donaldson, as he gives credit for—and adopts—their "particularly striking and successful emendations."[6] It is an edition that reveals Derek's tenacity and his readiness to revise his opinion (as, for example, on the personification Rechlessness), as well, of course, as the exploitation of these skills in the service of that ultimately desirable clean, rubricated, and readable text. In all these respects, Derek is, although by no means *recheles*, a true Langlandian.

Nicolette Zeeman

Notes

1. Lee Patterson, "The Logic of Textual Criticism and the Way of Genius: The Kane-Donaldson *Piers Plowman* in Historical Perspective," in his *Negotiating the Past* (Madison: University of Wisconsin Press, 1987), 77–113.

2. See, e.g., Kathryn Kerby-Fulton, *Books under Suspicion: Censorship and Tolerance of Revelatory Writing in Late Medieval England* (Notre Dame: University of Notre Dame Press, 2006); Ralph Hanna, *London Literature, 1300–1380* (Cambridge: Cambridge University Press, 2005). See also Rita Copeland, "*Pathos* and Pastoralism: Aristotle's *Rhetoric* in Medieval England," *Speculum* 89 (2014): 96–127.

3. George Kane and E. Talbot Donaldson, eds., *Piers Plowman: The B Version. Will's Visions of Piers Plowman, Do-Well, Do-Better and Do-Best*, rev. ed. (London: Athlone Press, 1988), 102, 103, 106.

4. Ibid., 125–26.

5. Robert Adams, "Langland's *Ordinatio*: The *Visio* and the *Vita* Once More," *Yearbook of Langland Studies* 5 (1991): 51–84.

6. William Langland, *Piers Plowman: A New Annotated Edition of the C-Text*, ed. Derek Pearsall (Exeter: University of Exeter Press, 2008), 18.

CHAPTER 22

Was the C-Reviser's Manuscript Really So Corrupt?

Jill Mann

One of the most startling features of Kane and Donaldson's edition of the B text of *Piers Plowman* was their contention that the manuscript of B that was used by the C-reviser contained a highly corrupt text.[1] The first evidence for this claim comprises one hundred or so instances where B and C agree with each other but differ from A. (It is important to note here that by "A," Kane meant his own edition of the A version, not the totality of readings in the surviving A manuscripts.) One might assume that differences between A and BC were due to revision, but Kane and Donaldson rejected this assumption because of the "positively scribal character" of the BC readings (101). This "positively scribal character" is confirmed, they claim, by the occurrence of "more than half" of these BC readings as scribal variants in "the post-archetypal tradition of A, that is, in surviving A manuscripts" (101–2).

The presence of these readings in A manuscripts might of course indicate that these readings could be authorial without being revisions; that is, such ABC agreement creates a presumption of originality for such readings and so might prompt a reassessment of the A edition (which Kane had, of course, produced without consulting BC readings, a procedure that he later acknowledged to have been mistaken).[2] But with astonishing firmness, Kane maintained confidence in his ability to distinguish original A readings from scribal variants. This confidence was so great that he never even addressed the problem posed by these BC readings in A manuscripts, namely, how did they get there?[3] By contamination? By convergent variation? If so, why could they not have appeared in the C archetype (Cx) by the same route? Convergent variation resulting in such BC agreement is indeed a possibility mentioned by Kane and Donaldson, who say it "could not be theoretically excluded" but declare themselves willing to admit it only "when there is no reasonable alternative" (103). The "reasonable alternative" that they prefer is that "our identifications of originality in A and unoriginality in BC are correct; the BC readings were produced by scribal variation in the prearchetypal B tradition, that is before the exclusive common ancestor of the surviving B manuscripts was copied; and they are present in the C archetype because Langland, when he revised B to C, used a scribal B manuscript where they occurred and let them stand, for whatever reason" (103).[4]

As has been shown by David Fowler, Charlotte Brewer, and Robert Adams,[5] Kane's procedure in editing B was heavily influenced by his need to defend his A text. If BC agree against A, they must be wrong, *unless* there are compelling reasons to suppose revision. This, despite the fact that in 1988 Kane produced a second edition of A in which he revised numerous earlier decisions and several times cited BC support for the change. Kane's need to defend A, as we shall see, underpins the theory of the "corrupt B manuscript." It is significant that that theory is outlined, not in the Russell-Kane edition of C, but in Kane and Donaldson's edition of B; that is, it is not aimed at establishing a basis for editing C but is rather a rearguard action in defense of A against the BC agreements of which Kane had become aware. However, in his article in Kane's festschrift, George Russell accepted the theory of the C-reviser's "corrupt" B manuscript, which in theory ought to mean editing the C text to make it conform with A, just as had been done for B.[6] But when the C text finally appeared, a sort of compromise had been reached: it was admitted that "errors" in B had been allowed to stand in the C revision (whether by Langland or by a "literary executor"), and thereby had a kind of authorial sanction, so they were not expunged in Russell-Kane's C.[7]

The strength of George Kane's work is that he was not afraid to present the detailed evidence on which his judgments were based and the reasoning he applied. My own reexamination of this detailed evidence leads me to conclude that although the differences between

(Kane's) A and BC can certainly be explained by typical scribal habits, it is just as possible to argue, using Kane's own classification of scribal practices, that it is A rather than BC that is "scribal" in character. In other words, Kane either made the wrong choice between variants when editing A or did not even realize he *had* a choice since he excluded consideration of BC variants. I propose to illustrate this by presenting as much of the detailed evidence as can be fitted into this brief essay.

The first group of examples are some cases where Kane and Donaldson claim that BC are not only "manifestly inferior in sense" to A but also show "incomprehension" of A readings, and so their version cannot be attributed to Langland (102–3). Of Kane and Donaldson's eight examples, I select three. I give the A, B, and C texts as printed in the Athlone editions, with the readings at issue in bold, and the manuscript variants relating to them.

1. A 3.145–51 Be Iesu, wiþ hire Iuelx ȝoure Iustice she shendiþ,
And leiþ aȝen *þe lawe* & lettiþ þe treuþe
Þat feiþ may not haue his forþ, hire floreynes go so þikke.
She let **lawe** as hire list & louedaies makiþ;
Þe mase for a mene man þeiȝ he mote euere.
Lawe is so lordlich & loþ to make ende,
Wiþoute presentis or panis he plesiþ [wel] fewe.

148 lawe] þe lawe VEKWN; þe lawis H.

B 3.155–62 By Iesus! wiþ hire Ieweles youre Iustices she shendeþ
And liþ ayein *þe lawe* and letteþ *hym* þe gate
That feiþ may noȝt haue his forþ, hire floryns go so þikke.
She ledeþ **lawe** as hire list and louedaies makeþ,
And doþ men lese þoruȝ hire loue þat lawe myȝte wynne;
The maȝe for a mene man þouȝ he mote euere!
Lawe is so lordlich and looþ to maken ende;
Wiþouten presentȝ or pens [he] pleseþ wel fewe.

158 lawe] þe lawe *all B mss.*

C 3.193–200 By iesu! with here ieweles the Iustices she shendeth;
He lyth aȝeyn *þe lawe* and le[tte]th *hym* þe gate
That fayth may nat haue his forth, here floreynes goth so thykke,
And le[deth] **þe lawe** as here luste and louedayes maketh,

Thorw which loueday is loste þat leute myhte wynne;
The mase for a mene man thow he mote euere!
Lawe is so lordliche and loth to make ende;
Withoute presentes oþer pans he pleseth [wel] fewe.

196 þe lawe] *no C variants.*

The B manuscripts all agree in reading "þe lawe" in line 158, a reading that is also found in some A manuscripts. But Kane had preferred "lawe" in his edition of A, and Kane and Donaldson substitute this reading in B, on the grounds that the definite article "destroys the personification" (102) which has been established by the personal pronoun "him" in B 3.156 (the personal pronoun is lacking in A's corresponding line, 146). *But in that very line* in B, "him" follows "þe lawe," not "lawe" (indicated by my italics). If the definite article is not felt to destroy the personification there, why should it do so in line 158? The main reason for claiming that the definite article is an error seems to be that Kane had rejected it in his edition of A (reasonably enough, as on its own it might well look like scribal overexplicitness). This passage seems to me a classic example of Langland's use of what might be called intermittent personification: the vacillation between "þe lawe" (abstract noun) and "Lawe" (a fully fledged personification, who is "so lordlich . . . ") continues throughout.

2. A 5.129–30 My wyf was a **wynstere** & wollene cloþ made,
And spak to þe spynstere to spynnen it softe.

129 was a wynstere] at westmynstre H; at westmunstre V.
wynstere] wynnestre RDL; vynnestre N; wyndster E; weuester (? wenester) Ch; wevester K; webbestere M; webstere AWH³; webster J; webbere H²; breustere U.

B 5.213–14 My wif was a [**wynnestere**] and wollen cloþ made,
[And] spak to [þe] Spynnester[e] to spynnen it [softe].

213 wynnestere] webbster GCr; webber C²; webbe WHmYOCBLMRF (= *all B mss; H is out*).

C 6.221–22 My wyf was a **webbe** and wollone cloth made
[And] spak to þe spynnester[e] to spynnen [hit] oute.

221 webbe] *altered to* webbster *in another ink* P².

To Kane, A's "wynstere," as against "webbestere," no doubt looked like a marvelous instance of a *lectio difficilior*. As he says, the scatter of scribal substitutions for this word in the A manuscripts shows that it gave the scribes difficulty. But it is *so* much a *difficilior* that its very existence is doubtful in the extreme. The *MED* gives only this example from *Piers Plowman* A and glosses it as a "female winder of wool." Kane's *Glossary* gives its meaning as "successful businesswoman," deriving it from the verb "wynnen."[8] Kane and Donaldson reject the majority B reading "webbe" as "totally inappropriate," since they claim that this could apply only to a male weaver (102). The *OED*'s citation of an example of "webbe" as applied to a woman in one manuscript of *Cursor Mundi* is vigorously rejected as "an example of the consequences of using corrupt texts for lexicographical purposes" (102 n. 4)—a remark that might be better applied to "wynstere." The *MED* not only repeats the example from *Cursor Mundi* but offers in addition an instance of a woman named in a thirteenth-century manorial record as "Alicie la Webbe." In any case it is not clear why the B and C manuscripts themselves would not provide support for the application of "webbe" to a woman. If B and C were resorting to a "desperate substitution for an evidently very difficult term," as Kane and Donaldson claim (102), why would they not have simply substituted "webbstere," if that was the exclusive term for a female weaver? (Presumably that is what Kane and Donaldson think happened with the variant readings in the A tradition.) It seems to me more likely that the nonce-word "wynstere" arose by anticipation of copy under the influence of "spynstere" in the following line—a kind of scribal error that Kane elsewhere shows to be common.[9]

3. A 7.88–89 My wyf shal haue of þat I wan wiþ treuþe, & namore,
And dele among my **frendis** & my dere children.

89 frendis] freondis L; children H.

B 6.96–97 My wif shal haue of þat I wan wiþ truþe and na moore,
And dele among my [**frendes**] and my deere children.

97 frendes] douȝtres WHmCrGYOC²CBLMRF (= *all B mss; H is out*).

C 8.105–6 My wyf shal haue of þat y wan with treuthe and no more
And delen amongus my **douhteres** and my dere childre[n].

106 douhteres] *no C variants.*

Alliteration would seem to support "douȝtres,"[10] even if it seems odd that Piers's testament should specify his female children first (though alliteration, as we know, does produce unusual lexical choices from time to time). Kane and Donaldson, however, attribute this alliteration on *d* to an improving scribe who failed to perceive the original alliteration on *m*: a**m**ong **m**y **m**y (102). This is implausible in the extreme. And it seems exaggerated to claim that "douȝtres" "makes nonsense of the line" (102 n. 6), especially as paired with "children." I also fail to see how "douȝtres" could demonstrate a failure on B's part to understand A's "frendis." (The opposite would be more plausible.)

These examples may be taken as representative of B's supposed "incomprehension" of A, which might be better described as simple divergence from Kane's A text. A much larger set of examples supposedly illustrates the following set of interconnected circumstances:

(i) A furnishes a "presumably original" reading, while the B archetype's reading appears "scribal."
(ii) B cannot derive from C but must derive from A.
(iii) C is evidently a revision and agrees with (or otherwise reflects) the corrupt B form rather than "the putative original common to A and B" (Kane and Donaldson 104) (which is allegedly preserved in A).

That is, although there is no evidence of "incomprehension" in these cases, C reflects what is held to be a scribal corruption in B and is unable to restore the "correct" reading (assumed to be that of Kane's A text) out of his own resources.

The examples adduced by Kane and Donaldson under this heading seem to me to be open to two objections: first, B is not more evidently "scribal" than A, and second, C's revision is not evidently responding to corruption in B. Again I shall have space to discuss only a sample, but it is representative of the whole. Since Kane and Donaldson's B text is emended to match A in these instances, for clarity I here cite, in addition to the Athlone texts and relevant variants, the reading of the B archetype (Bx) as given by Kane and Donaldson, so that judgment as to its corruption or otherwise is easier. I also cite extra lines where context is useful in establishing authenticity or corruption.

4. A 2.5–6 "Loke on þi left half, & lo where he standis,
Boþe fals & fauel & **hise** feris manye."

6 hise . . . manye] many of here ferys vnfeythful to knowyn M. hise] al his V; here A; alle her H.

B 2.5–6	"Loke [o]n þi left half, and lo where he stondeþ, Boþe Fals and Fauel and **hi[s]e** feeres manye."

6 hise . . . manye] many of her ferys H; hise] hire WHmCr-GYOC²CLMF (= *all B mss; R is out*).

Bx	Boþe Fals and Fauel and **hire** feeres manye.
C 2.5–7	"Loke [o]n thy left half, and loo where he standeth, [Boþe] fals and fauel and fikel tonge lyare And mony mo of **here** maners, of men and of wymmen."

7 here] *no C variants.*

The difference here is between "hise," relating only to "fauel," and "hire," relating to "fals and fauel" both. The A manuscripts are overwhelmingly in favor of "hise," and in the absence of serious competition it is not surprising that Kane adopted it in his A text. Called upon to defend this reading against B's "hire," Kane and Donaldson say the B reading is "easier" because "to identify the referent of *hise* calls for attention and reflection" (105); in addition, they say, *hire* could have been "subconsciously induced by the shape of the following word," *feris*. C retains B's plural *hire*, but the recasting of this line as two lines is said to indicate the C-reviser's "dissatisfaction with the form it took in his B manuscript." So C's "here maners" is said to be evidence that he was looking at (but dissatisfied with) B's "hire feris" (105).

If A's "hise" is a harder reading, it is only—in my view—because it makes much less good sense (why are the companions of "fauel" in particular and not of "fals"?). Was "hise" provoked by the singular "he" in the preceding line? At any rate, B's "hire" is not self-evidently "corrupt"; furthermore, it is difficult to see how the C-reviser could have remembered the A version of the line well enough to register his "dissatisfaction" by rewriting the line as two but not well enough to get rid of the unsatisfactory "hire" by correcting it to "hise." In short, it looks to me as if B's "hire" is original, confirmed by C, and A's "hise" is a scribal misreading.

5. A 3.86–87	Among þise lettride lordis þis latyn amountiþ Þat fuyr shal falle & **forbrenne at þe laste**

87 forbrenne] brenne VHLEAW; brennyn JM. at þe] atte VJNM; at Ch. at] al at H²; right at U.

B 3.97–98 Among þise lettrede l[or]des þis latyn [amounteþ]
That fir shal falle & [**forbrenne at þe laste**]

98 forbrenne . . . laste] brenne al to bloo askes *all B mss.*

Bx That fir shal falle & **brenne al to bloo askes**

C 3.125–26 Amonge thise lettred lordes this latyn is to mene
That fuyr shal falle and **forbrenne al to blew aysches**

126 forbrenne] forbrent D; tobrenne S; brenne P²AG; brennen R; eke brenne F. al] on VA; *om.* G. blew] blak VAG; plake N; brown QS; *om.* P²D.

Alliteration on *f* requires "forbrenne" rather than "brenne," so B's "brenne" may plausibly be taken as a scribal corruption. But the variant readings in the A and C manuscripts show how easily the variation between different forms of the verb can be made by scribes who were insensitive to alliterative requirements. And there is no reason, in my opinion, to extend B's corruption to embrace "al to bloo askes," which Kane and Donaldson claim as "more emphatic and explicit" but at the same time a "less meaningful reading" than A's "at þe laste" (106). Here we are in one of Kane's favorite cleft sticks: scribal variants can be so identified *either* because they are weaker and more conventionally phrased than the alternatives *or* because they are more "emphatic," expressing the scribe's enthusiastic participation in the text he is copying.[11] To me, it is "at þe laste" that seems more likely to be a conventional scribal substitution "in the direction of flat statement" (Kane, *A Version*, 134), but at the very least I would say that "al to bloo askes," confirmed by C, is not self-evidently corrupt.

6. A 4.18–19 "Sette my sadil vpon suffre til I se my tyme,
And let warroke hym wel wiþ [**wy**]**tful gerþis**."

19 wytful] DJLKWN; wittful A; full wyght E; riȝtful TRUChH²; swiþe fele H; swiþe feole V; to goode M.

B 4.20–21 "Set my Sadel vpon suffre-til-I-se-my-tyme
And lat warroke hym wel wiþ **wit**[**ful**] **gerþes**."

21 witful gerþes] gyrtys þat is with witty wordis F; witful] witty wordes WHmCr-GYOC²CBLMR; wyse wordis H (= *all B mss*).

Bx . . . wiþ **witty wordes gerþes**

C 4.17–21 And kalde Catoun his knaue, Corteys of speche,
And also th[omm]e trewe-tonge-telle-me-no-tales-
Ne-lesynges-to-lauhe-of-for-y-louede-hit-neuere.
"Sette my sadel vpon soffre-tyl-y-se-my-tyme
And lat warrokye [hym] w[e]l with **auys[e]-þe-byfore.**"

21 auyse] YJPERMQSFKN; a vise UDVAG; auyseth X. þe] *om.* DPERMVAQ.

Kane and Donaldson claim that Bx's "witty wordes" is "a scribal substitution of an easier reading," in place of A's "manifestly difficult" expression (107)—its difficulty being attested in the rash of scribal variants in the A manuscripts. B's "witty wordes" is also said to have the added attraction (for the scribe who produced it) of increasing the alliteration. One could equally well explain A's omission of "wordes" as attributable to homoarchy ("witty wordes"). The *MED* glosses "witful" as "wise, cunning, ingenious." "Wise girths" does not quite make sense. What is needed by the allegory here is a noun, not an adjective: the girths *are* "witty wordes." The C-reviser, according to Kane and Donaldson, "rejects *witty wordes*," but "he reproduces the sense of the expression which he could not tolerate: *auyseth-þe-byfore* (IV 21) are in fact *witty wordes*" (107). I have to admit that I do not understand the logic of this last proposition at all. And why would the C-reviser be "unable to tolerate" the expression "witty wordes"? (What is obviously unacceptable about it?) If he *did* find it unacceptable, why would he be keen to preserve its sense? Why not just delete "wordes," if A's version is correct? An alternative way of looking at the C version is to suggest that it is "enthusiastically" increasing the number of hyphenated personifications at this point, as it also does in the added lines 18–19, so that "soffre-tyl-y-se-my-tyme" is both preceded and followed by similar constructions.

Finally, it should be noted that the A version of the second half of line 4.19 is suspect because it does not fit the standard requirements of the b-verse—namely, that it should contain one long dip. Everything suggests, therefore, that the B version of this line is original, A is a corruption, and C a revision (whether authorial or scribal).

7. A 7.107–8 Þanne seten somme & sungen at þe ale,
And holpen [to] ere **þe** half akir wiþ "hey trolly lolly."

108 þe . . . akir] *om.* VHJN. þe] þat RH[3].

B 6.115–16 [Th]anne seten somme and songen atte Nale
And holpen ere **þ[e]** half acre wiþ "how trolly lolly."

116 ere . . . acre] hym so to heryȝe F; þe] þis W; his HmCrGYOC²CBLMR (= *all B mss; H is out*).

Bx . . . holpen ere **his** half acre

C 8.122–23 Thenne seet somme and songen at the ale
And holpe erye **this** half aker with "hey trollilolly."

123 this] *no C variants.*

Kane and Donaldson say that unless the B-reviser "specifically intended to attribute ownership of the land to Piers," the archetypal B reading *his* "must be explained as scribal substitution, either of a (mistakenly) more explicit term, or of one induced by the alliteration" (108). But why should not B's "his" be original, with A's "þe" and C's "þis" as scribal variants of a very familiar kind? Piers is named in line 112 as overseeing the plowing, so it seems quite natural to speak of "his" half-acre in line 116. C's "þis acre" is said by Kane and Donaldson to show that the C-reviser had B's "his" in front of him and was responding to the shape of the word. But it could equally well be an independent scribal variation (as B's ms W testifies; see Kane and Donaldson, 108 n. 17), or else a carryover from "þis half aker" in line 113 (where, interestingly, eleven C manuscripts read "hus" instead of "this"). This strikes me as a clear example of Kane's premise that the reading of his A edition *must* be original, and any variations from it have to be either authorial revisions or scribal corruptions.

8\. A 7.280 **Hungir [eet] þis** in haste & askide aftir more.

280 *line om.* W. Hungir] UVHJLANH³; And hungir TRDChKM. eet] VHJL; ete RUDKN; hente TChAmH³. þis in] in þat L. þis] al þis UJN; hit H; *om.* M.

B 6.296 **[Hunger eet þis]** in haste and axed after moore.

296 Hunger . . . þis] Al hunger eet WHmCrGYOC²LMR; & all þo hungir eet F; An hunger ete C; Ac hungur ete B (=*all B mss; H is out*).

Bx **Al hunger eet** in haste

C 8.318 **Hunger eet al** in haste and askede aftur more.

318 Hunger eet al] *no C variants.*

Bx's "Al hunger eet" is said by Kane and Donaldson to be a "more emphatic variation" and thus "a scribal substitution" (109). They note that "al" also appears in some A manuscripts, which they think supports the notion that it is scribal. But in that case, why not assume that C's "al" is likewise an independent scribal variation rather than a reflection of the C-reviser's B manuscript? Then again, one could equally well explain the A version of this line as a typical scribal restoration of normal word order and claim that B's inversion of object and subject ("Al hunger eet") is proof of its originality (as Kane often does elsewhere). Kane and Donaldson claim that in A and C, "the rhythmic stress . . . falls more significantly on the personification," but this seems to me tenuous in the extreme. In short, the B version has a rather better chance of being authorial than the other two, and C's restoration of normal prose word order is most likely scribal.

9. A 9.16–20 "*Contra*," quaþ I as a clerk & comside to dispute:
"*Sepcies in die cadit iustus.*
Seue siþes, seiþ þe bok, [synneþ] þe riȝtful;
Ac whoso synneþ, **I seiȝe, sertis, me þinkiþ**
[Þ]at dowel & do euele mowe not dwelle togidere.
Ergo he nis not alwey at hom among ȝow Freris;"

18 Ac] Bot Ch; and RUDVJAKW; *om.* M. I] as I A; he RU. seiȝe] saie Ch; say DJAM; seiþ U; seide V; sayde RW; said K. sertis] I wot he doth ille Certys J; me] as me VKWM. þinkiþ] þinkyt M; thinkes R.

B 8.20–24 "*Contra*!" quod I as a clerc & comsed to disputen:
"*Sepcies in die cadit Iustus.*
Seuene siþes, seiþ þe book, synneþ þe rightfulle;
A[c] whoso synneþ, **I sei[e, certes], me þynkeþ**
[That] dowel and do yuele mowe noȝt dwelle togideres.
Ergo he nys noȝt alwey [at hoom] amonges yow freres;"

22 Ac] And *all B mss (H is out)*. I seie] I say Cr; I seide WGYLMR; as seyde Hm; he seyde OC²C; seide he B; in doynge he F (= *all B mss; H is out*). certes] doþ evele F; dooþ yuele as WHmCrGYOC²CBLMR (= *all B mss; H is out*). þynkeþ] thynke C.

Bx **And** whoso synneþ **I seide dooþ yuele as me þynkeþ**
And dowel and do yuele mowe noȝt dwelle togideres

C 10.20–28 "*Contra*!" quod y as a Clerk & comsed to despute
And saide, "sothly *sepcies in die ca[d]it iust[u]s*,
Fallyng fro ioye, iesu woet þe sothe!
Seuene sithe, sayth þe boek, synegeth day by day
The rihtfulluste ren[k] þat regneth [o]n erthe.
And hoso synegeth," **y sayde, "certes he doth nat wel;**
For hoso synegeth sicurly doth euele
And dowel and do euele may not dwelle togyderes.
Ergo he [n]is nat alwey at hom amonges ȝow freres;"

25 *line om.* A; *as one line with* 26 ZF. y . . . wel] *om.* Z. y] he P²UG. sayde] say F. certes . . . wel] is voided fro Dowel N²; *om.* F. he] *om.* PERMVQKGN.
26 *line om.* P²N². For . . . synegeth] *om.* ZF; For] And AN. so] *om.* D; synegeth] that syneth R. doth euele] mot nede do vuele N. doth] he doþ DR.

Kane and Donaldson think that the Bx version is proved scribal by its "more explicit statement, markedly easier grammar, and less pregnant meaning" (109). I cannot see what "pregnant meaning" the A version contains; rather, the first half of line 18 seems to be abruptly abandoned in midstream, and "I seiȝe, sertis, me þinkiþ" to be no more than fussy padding. B's version, in contrast, is exactly suited to Langland's humorous adoption of a slightly ponderous logic-chopping style here: "*Contra*, quod I as a clerk. . . . *Ergo* . . . " The argument takes the form of a three-part syllogism: "The book says that the just man sins seven times a day, and whoever sins does evil, and dowell and do evil might not live together, *ergo*, dowell does not live with you." C expands line 22 into two lines (26–27) but follows B's line of thought exactly. Kane and Donaldson think that C takes over three "errors" from B: "And" for A's "Ac"; preterite "sayde" for A's "seiȝe," and "doth euele" for A's "sertis" (109). In all three instances, B seems to me to be right. Kane has a declared preference for "Ac" as authorial as against scribal "And," but in this case the argument requires a copulative rather than an adversative conjunction. The preterite "sayde" is entirely in line with the preceding preterites "quod" and "comsed," if one is assuming that it represents reported rather than direct speech. And as already noted, "doþ yuele" is essential to the line of argument here. Once again C is simply engaging in minor revision and expansion (and "improving" the alliteration) rather than taking over B's supposed corruption.[12]

If I had time (and my readers had patience), I could work through the rest of Kane and Donaldson's examples in the same way. But I hope that this selection will suffice to show the weakness of Kane and Donaldson's case for the "corruption" of the C-reviser's B manuscript. All too often, what is driving the argument is Kane's anxiety to defend the readings of his A edition as original; if C supports B readings, therefore, the BC agreements must be explained away as due to the C-reviser's inability to identify the true original. Forgive me if I note in passing that both the A variants that agree with BC and the A variants that I have identified as scribal are more easily explained by the assumption that A derives from B rather than the reverse,[13] but this assumption is not a necessary foundation for skepticism about Kane and Donaldson's case for the C-reviser's "corrupt" B manuscript.

I said earlier that Kane's great strength was his willingness to document his case with the examples on which it is based, so that readers may follow his train of thought. But of course not every reader has the time or the stamina to work through the long lists of examples in the Athlone editions—it takes months of full-time work, as I can testify—and the absence of Russell and Kane's C edition in 1975 made the task of comparison more difficult. Perhaps for that reason the theory of the "corrupt" B manuscript was widely accepted, strange as it seemed.[14] There are now some signs that it is being treated with skepticism;[15] I hope that the examples I have discussed may help to increase that skepticism.

Notes

This essay is offered in affectionate homage to Derek Pearsall, in gratitude for his own work on the C text of *Piers Plowman* and for a friendship which began when he was my PhD examiner forty years ago.

1. I cite *Piers Plowman* from the Athlone edition, as follows: *Piers Plowman: The A Version*, ed. George Kane (London: Athlone Press, 1960, rev. 1988); *Piers Plowman: The B Version*, ed. George Kane and E. Talbot Donaldson (London: Athlone Press, 1975, rev. 1988), hereafter cited as Kane and Donaldson, with page numbers in the body of the text; *Piers Plowman: The C Version*, ed. George Russell and George Kane (London: Athlone Press, 1997). Reference will also be made to the edition by A. V. C. Schmidt, *Piers Plowman:*

A Parallel-Text Edition of the A, B, C and Z Versions, vol. 1 (London: Longman, 1995); vol. 2 (Kalamazoo, MI: Medieval Institute Publications, 2008). Since this essay focuses on the Athlone editions, I use their manuscript sigla rather than the partially altered set introduced in *The Piers Plowman Electronic Archive* (ed. Hoyt Duggan et al.).

2. Kane and Donaldson, 75 n. 15.

3. The problem is raised and discussed by Robert Adams, "Editing *Piers Plowman B*: The Imperative of an Intermittently Critical Edition," *Studies in Bibliography* 45 (1992): 54–56.

4. Lawrence Warner has recently argued something like the opposite case; namely, that the B archetype (Bx) was contaminated by C; see his *The Lost History of "Piers Plowman": The Earliest Transmission of Langland's Work* (Philadelphia: University of Pennsylvania Press, 2011). While highlighting some intriguing agreements between different branches of the manuscript tradition, his argument is highly complicated, often implausible, and leaves numerous things unexplained; it also puts undue weight on the presence of a C rubric in two key manuscripts of B. See the balanced review by Simon Horobin in *Yearbook of Langland Studies* 25 (2011): 205–7.

5. David C. Fowler, "A New Edition of the B Text of *Piers Plowman*" [review of Kane-Donaldson], *Yearbook of English Studies* 7 (1977): 23–42; Charlotte Brewer, "The Textual Principles of Kane's A Text," *Yearbook of Langland Studies* 3 (1989): 67–90; Charlotte Brewer, "George Kane's Processes of Revision," in *Crux and Controversy in Middle English Textual Criticism*, ed. A. J. Minnis and Charlotte Brewer (Cambridge: D. S. Brewer, 1992), 71–96; Adams, "Editing *Piers Plowman B*."

6. G. H. Russell, "The Imperative of Revision in the C Version of *Piers Plowman*," in *Medieval English Studies Presented to George Kane*, ed. Edward Donald Kennedy, Ronald Waldron, and Joseph S. Wittig (Woodbridge: D. S. Brewer, 1988), 234.

7. See *C Version*, ed. Russell and Kane, 62–63, 82, 90–94. Cf. Kane's revised edition of A, 463, where he discusses (what he sees as) scribal errors in A which survived Langland's revisions to B and/or C and thus have "a kind of sanction."

8. George Kane, *Will's Visions of Piers Plowman, Do-Well, Do-Better, and Do-Best: A Glossary of the A, B, and C Versions as Presented in the Athlone Editions* (London: Continuum, 2005), s.v. "wynnestre, wynstere."

9. *A Version*, ed. Kane, 121–22.

10. As pointed out by Hoyt Duggan, "Notes towards a Theory of Langland's Meter," *Yearbook of Langland Studies* 1 (1987): 66.

11. See *A Version*, ed. Kane, 134 (scribal change "in the direction of flat statement") and 138 (scribal enthusiasm leading to an increase in "the emphasis of statements"); and cf. Adams, "Editing *Piers Plowman B*," 43.

12. The *aaa/xx* alliterative pattern is accepted as authorial by Kane and Donaldson (137–39) and Schmidt, *Parallel-Text Edition*, 2:256 (Type IIa), but the A and C versions might represent scribal dissatisfaction with the lack of an alliterating word in the b-verse.

13. For an argument that this is the case, see Jill Mann, "The Power of the Alphabet: A Reassessment of the Relation between the A and the B Versions of *Piers Plowman*," *Yearbook of Langland Studies* 8 (1994): 21–50.

14. See, e.g., Derek Pearsall, "Editing the C Text: The Athlone Press Edition of 1997," *Yearbook of Langland Studies* 24 (2010): 24–26.

15. Schmidt (*Parallel-Text Edition*, 2:50–54, 62–64, 124, 158, 163 n. 4) discounts the evidence presented in Kane and Donaldson, 98–127 (the section from which the examples in this essay are taken), though he finds other signs that the C text "unquestionably reflects errors present in the text of B he [Langland] worked from, which must therefore have been a scribal product" (2:287). Schmidt's edited text of B agrees with the Bx readings in all the examples I cite, except that at B 3.98 he sensibly emends "brenne" to "forbrenne."

CHAPTER 23

Emending Oneself

Compilatio and *Revisio* in Langland, Usk, and Higden

Melinda Nielsen

In 1978 Derek Pearsall's pioneering edition of Langland's C-text challenged new critical conceptions of the finished, self-referential text to celebrate its "continuous life in the mind of its creator over a period" and its revision, "piecemeal, outward from certain cores of dissatisfaction, rather than systematically."[1] While the similarities between William Langland and Thomas Usk's clerical backgrounds and their "Tree of Charity" imagery has long fostered scrutiny of the *Testament of Love*'s relationship to *Piers Plowman*, the specific debate about direct borrowings has obscured their shared modus operandi of composition and authorship. This essay seeks to adapt Pearsall's scrupulous attention to the material circumstances, constraints, and opportunities of manuscript culture to the *Testament of Love*. In particular, I explore possible implications of Usk's acrostic, "Margarete of virtw have marci on thin Usk," for our understanding of the dynamic process of composition, publication, and authorial intent in London documentary culture. Internal evidence from the only surviving version, the 1532 print edition by William Thynne, and comparable Middle English and Anglo-Latin manuscripts suggests that the form of "prose acrostic" used by Usk is a strategy to stamp and freeze revision of a preexisting text. Likely, the *Testament of Love* as we know it was produced within and reflects upon multiple sets of circumstances, and not exclusively the Northampton affair.

LANGLANDIAN COMPOSITION

Pearsall's edition of Langland's C-text made the poet's final revision available to scholars and students for the first time since Skeat's 1885 edition. The corruptions of William Skeat's base manuscript would have been motive enough for a new edition of the medieval dream vision, but Pearsall's introduction suggests several reasons to counterbalance the B-text's dominance, including the mild statement that the "C-text, put quite simply, makes better sense."[2] Pearsall observes that, like it or not, "the author's latest revision presumably represents his latest thinking, and therefore, *a priori*, what he is entitled to ask to be remembered by, unless it is marred by evident senility. Discrimination of relative merit is in such a case a highly subjective matter . . . but the prima facie authority of an authorial revision is not similarly arguable."[3] Devotees of either version may debate the superiority of their favorite passages, but Pearsall's limpid introduction navigates shoals of authorial intent and reception that have shipwrecked many a scholar while suggesting principles that have properly guided Langlandian studies since. Indeed, Pearsall's approach has situated the poet alongside such figures as William Shakespeare and William Blake in terms of authorial complexity, particularly when parsing implications of revision, property, and ownership.

While making a case for the C-text's value, Pearsall manages to step out of the B versus C binary to manifest the poem as a dynamic work, the reoccurring fruit of Langland's thought "over a period of some twenty-five years."[4] Pearsall's observation that "the poem is, to all intents and purposes, Langland's whole known existence and his whole life's work" is valid existentially, as well as historically.[5] The restoration of the C-text to scholarly dialogue has illuminated "the great good fortune we have in possessing all three versions of Langland's poem, and a unique and compelling record, therefore, of the growth of a poet's mind over the whole of his mature life."[6] Although ruminative composition is not unique to Langland, treating medieval writing as continuous work rather than a completed work—perhaps not dissimilar to the liturgical *opus dei*—has often not translated easily into the inherited rubrics of literary criticism, particularly in a period of criticism dominated by Chaucerian critical practices.

Yet the dynamic, multilayered approach that Pearsall brings to Langland's great London poem productively illuminates many other literary processes of manuscript culture, not the least the *Testament of Love*, the external textual witness that Pearsall and many others use to date the expansive life of *Piers Plowman*. The *Testament of Love* has long been the poor relative of Chaucerian literature, tolerated about the Ricardian house for its serviceable moments of historical information. Since Henry Bradley's discovery that the *Testament of Love* was the work of the clerk Thomas Usk, hanged, drawn, and quartered in 1387, rather than Geoffrey Chaucer to whom it had been attributed for nearly four centuries, the *Testament*'s literary career has been largely divided between debates on its usefulness for the dating of *Piers Plowman*'s C-text and as a first and failed appearance of a Chaucerian imitation, due to extended borrowings chiefly of *Troilus and Criseyde*. Allusions to other *auctores* have been noted—and large chunks of arguments and passages are taken over wholesale from Boethius and Anselm—but the uneven merit of the work has discouraged much consideration of the text itself, even as Usk's role in the heart of documentary and factional London has become more evident.

Usk's contributions to London's literature may not appear most forcibly, however, when viewed as a frozen monument to the greatness of others, whether Chaucer or Langland, Boethius or Anselm. Even less does the *Testament of Love* appear to advantage as a monument to Usk himself in his account of the events leading up to his change of allegiance from John of Northampton's party to that of Nicholas Brembre in the London power struggles of 1384. But while *Piers Plowman* has been recognized as a work spanning the decades and with layers of meaning in even the most seemingly straightforward statements, the *Testament of Love* has been continually referred to the London events surrounding that one date, 1384. Such tunnel vision may seem solicited by Usk himself; after all, it is Usk who translates and dresses up his *Appeal* against his former leader Northampton in order to recycle it in Book I of the *Testament*. It is Usk who encodes another type of "appeal" in his chapter-initial acrostic, "Margarete of virtw have marci on thin Usk," which grants some unified structure to Usk's often sprawling prose. However, fourteenth-century acrostic strategies suggest that the *Testament of Love* would benefit from approaches similar to Pearsall's treatment of *Piers Plowman*, as a fluid, ongoing, and revisionary testament of one man's lifework—work considered personally, textually, socially, and professionally—in which missteps and triumphs alike participate.

USK AND LANGLAND

Thomas Usk's relation to Langland has long been a contentious topic, often mired in controversies over perceived verbal borrowings, the Tree of Charity passages in particular. And while the list of Usk's "borrowed" passages compiled by Skeat and Sister Mary Aquinas Devlin does not prove direct knowledge beyond possibility of doubt, their strong verbal similarities have proved enough to obscure other resonances between the two London clerks. For example, while it is certainly possible that Usk consciously echoes Langland, the likelihood that they were reading similar books is perhaps more fascinating. As Joanna Summers has noted, Usk merits consideration not only according to the Chaucerian status that he deliberately advertised but in respect to other contemporary writers as well. Summers lists parallels between the *Testament of Love* and John Gower's *Vox clamantis*: "Both texts present a narrator who foolishly leaves home to become lost in a forest; witnesses the rampages of domestic animals, like swine, who have turned wild; is rescued by a ship, but then is subject to a treacherous storm; and is finally driven to an island."[7] Such structural parallels are intriguing, not least because of their potential illustration once again of Usk's familiarity with Latin, "contemporary" as well as antique, and the proximity of London literatures across languages. At the same time, Usk's Book I, chapter 3, may resemble Langland's first-person urgency and visionary imagery as much as the fill-in-the-blank political allegory of *Vox clamantis*. Such resemblances need not establish deliberate borrowing between lines like *TL* I.3.135–36 and *PP* B 18.4/C 21.212 (although it is not unlikely that Usk was familiar with *Vox clamantis* and especially with *Piers Plowman*, in light of the latter's pervasive London distribution and popularity and Usk's obvious interest in vernacular experimentation). What they do suggest, however, is a similitude of modus operandi, particularly in terms of first-person authorship, anonymity, ownership, and English composition amid the scramble of London documentary culture. For now, speculation about direct personal knowledge between the two writers seems premature, despite the marked similarities between their skill sets and backgrounds. Fresh information continues to trickle out every year about Usk's connections and reinforces his location in the midst of London documentary culture, from low-ranking cleric or lawyer to scribe of the Goldsmiths; from amateur scholastic to patient of medical author John Ardenne, in addition to his better-known roles as John Northampton's textual handyman and then king's bureaucrat.[8]

Although lacking the complex manuscript tradition of *Piers Plowman*, the *Testament of Love* presents certain evidences of an ongoing multistage compositional process closer to that of Langland's *ruminatio* than a "sit down and hammer it out in jail" model. I would suggest at least two stages of composition, perhaps more, and that Usk had in some sense been preparing himself to be an *auctor* before the turmoil of the mid-1380s apparently gave him a reason to turn to extrapolitical writing to try to retrieve his reputation.[9] Both internal textual evidence and Anne Middleton's reconstructed manuscript description suggest that Usk may have worked "piecemeal" on the *Testament of Love*—that the first two books probably date from the 1384–85 period, the final book later as an "extensive but incomplete rewriting" with "exposed seams where new material has been patched [on] with little care for detailed congruence," as Pearsall describes Langland's C-text, and the prologue either prior or anterior to both and probably originally intended to preface a different sort of composition altogether.[10]

Discordance between the various sections has long been observed—to Usk's discredit. However, two other levels of textual issues have overshadowed its significance: first, the large-scale obvious corruptions of the *Testament*'s textual tradition that are inextricable in its sole surviving edition by William Thynne; and second, the syntactical incoherencies which are, at least in large part, due to Usk's lack of authorial discipline. Yet three modes of disjunction—on a verbal level, on a thematic level, and the *ordinatio* of Thynne's reconstructed physical manuscript—line up surprisingly well in the midscale structural fissures discussed above. Their confluence suggests that Usk may have been composing portions of the *Testament* during several different periods or sets of circumstances and that such a mode of composition may bear partial responsibility for the episodes of textual inconsistency.

Ruptures in the *Testament of Love*

The text's ruptures warrant closer examination, as do the explanations for them previously put forward. There are three potential ruptures: the Prologue; Book I–Book II.11/12; and Book II.12–end. The most significant of these is the break toward the end of Book II; it is the dynamics of this rupture operating across several modes of discourse that is my first focus and which prompted Stephen Medcalf to posit that the *Testament of Love* was composed in multiple sets of circumstances.[11] Medcalf calls the first and longer portion the "Boethian Testament," due to its dependence on the *Consolation of Philosophy* for its setting and arguments, and the second portion the "Anselmian Testament," as Usk relies on Saint Anselm's treatise *De concordia praescientiae et praedestinationis et gratiae Dei cum libero arbitrio* to resolve the free will questions posed by the "Boethian Testament." Such nomenclature is a useful shorthand to distinguish the thematic and literary movements of the *Testament of Love* regardless of one's historical dating of the respective portions, and it is followed here in the summary of the discrepancies between the two portions.

The most obvious discrepancies arise between the portions' respective source matter. As Medcalf's terminology indicates, the first portion of the *Testament of Love* makes explicit its dependence on Boethius's *Consolation of Philosophy*: one need not elaborate upon Usk's usage of the prison motif, an initial lament, the celestial *magister*, and parsing of the *summum bonum*, reimagined rather thoughtfully as "the knot" in the *Testament*. Like her exemplar Lady Philosophy, Love examines the frail value of riches, fame, and high office in turn to show in what true happiness does *not* consist (Usk removes Philosophy's belittling of precious stones, probably out of deference for the "Margarete-pearl"). Although readers should be wary of taking Usk's self-referential details at their literal face value, the narrator draws upon and even recites word for word parts of Usk's legal *Appeal*, apparently to create a parallel, even identity between the first-person narrator and himself, the author and scribe of both texts.[12]

As such, it is significant to note that the first two books contain several references to the narrator's imprisonment.[13] Such allusions are typical of the genre (one thinks of the *Confessio Amantis*, written in the decade after Usk's death), but unlike Gower's use of the prison motif, the *Testament*'s self-referential quality has circumstantial credibility as well in light of the frequency with which Usk found himself in jail. Many lines have the ring of historicity, such as Love's account of how "whan thou were arested and fyrste tyme enprisoned thou were loth to chaunge thy way, for in thy hert thou wendest to have ben there thou shuldest" (II.4.95–97). Usk adds an unwonted note of realism to the tradition, however, when one recalls that in the Latin tradition Boethius himself does not talk about being in prison but exile;[14] the *vita* tradition alternates between *in carcerem* and *in exilio*; and even Chaucer translates it "solitarie place of myne exil."[15] Yet for Usk, even the most fanciful references disappear by midway through Book II, with the final allusion of being contemporarily in prison, according to Leyerle, occurring at II.10.50—that is, just before the "Anselmian Testament." Even if one takes Usk's prison references at face value, their cessation does not necessarily mean a break of composition: Usk could as easily have been released from prison and continued his writing as he could have broken off and finished at a later date. Yet just as the prison references are missing from the "Anselmian Testament," the "Boethian Testament" displays no knowledge of *De concordia*, leading to a scholarly consensus that he was unaware of Anselm's text until late in the project, but after discovering it, preferred its treatment of the issues of free will and predestination to that of the *Consolation of Philosophy*. Not only has the leading *circumstantia* changed, but there appears to have been a shift in Usk's access to materials.

Other factors may indicate a change of time, as well as a change of circumstance. In the "Anselmian Testament," there is a shift of rhetorical pattern beyond that attributable to the change of source alone—and after all, the last three books of the *Consolation of Philosophy* are nearly as dry and densely argued as Anselm's text. Even considered in respect to form, however, the first two books are different from the third. Books I and II each have a highly ornate self-professed "verse" prologue, despite being written in prose like the entire *Testament*.[16] Book I commences with the Boethian-Ovidian, "Alas! Fortune! Alas! I, that somtyme in delycyous houres was wont to enjoy blysful stoundes, am nowe dryve be unhappy hevynesse to bewayle my sondrye yvels in tene" (I.1.1–3). Book I concludes with Love's injunction, "thanne lette us syngen," followed by Book II's Ecclesiastes-style prelude.[17] The chapter culminates as "this comfortable lady ganne synge a wonder mater of enditynge in Latyn. . . . Certes, they were wonder swete of sowne, and they were touched al in lamentacion-wyse and by no werbles of myrthe. Lo, thus ganne she synge in Latyn, as I may constrewe it in our Englysshe tonge" (I.10.13; II.2.1–6). On the contrary, Book III plunges the reader deep into the scholastic argument with no lyric transition: "Of nombre, sayne these clerkes that it is naturel somme of discrete thynges, as in tellynge one, two, thre, and so forth. But amonge al nombres thre is determyned for moste certayne."[18] Here there is no "verse" prologue, despite Usk's previous elaborate markings and textual emphasis on these passages, which seem to have been an important way for him to strut his stuff as an author, as his over-the-top modesty *topos* seems to serve primarily to draw attention to the ornate "kunstprose" that follows it. As the narrator observes humbly in Book II, "But trewly, the noble colours in rethorik-wyse knytte were so craftely that my connyng wol not stretche to remembre; but the sentence, I trowe, somdele have I in mynde." Such moments only partly fulfill the dictums of the Prologue, in which the various colors of rhetorical language are sketched out but here fulfilled in play between genre, complicating the linguistic differences. In short, then, in the *Testament of Love*, the rhetorical forms and patterns shift between II.2 and III.1; the prison references disappear after II.10 or 11; the Boethian material ends at II.11; and the Anselmian material commences at Book III, chapter 2. Such indications point to a shift of circumstance, probably corresponding to a break in the times of composition, somewhere between II.11 and III.2 at the broadest and more probably between II.12 and II.14.

Making and Misreading the *Testament of Love*

Along with the indications of rupture present in the *Testament of Love*'s textual structure, Middleton's hypothetical manuscript reconstruction encounters a similar break, and in the same locale. As no manuscript of the *Testament of Love* is known to survive, Middleton works backward from William Thynne's corrupt print text, which now constitutes the only textual witness to the book. As Middleton shows, however, the corruptions themselves testify eloquently to the manuscript's layout, appearance, and *ordinatio*. The printer's misreadings of the manuscript provide valuable clues to its appearance and arrangement, particularly Thynne's large-scale misplacements of several chapters of Book III, which scrambled the authorial acrostic "Margarete of virtw have marci on thin Usk." With this acrostic absent and with little interest in the text other than the eulogy to Chaucer, Usk's authorship was unrecognized for centuries until Henry Bradley noted the similarities between the political scrivener Thomas Usk and the *Testament*'s narrator and rearranged the displacements of Book III to uncover the acrostic.[19] By working backward from Thynne's misreadings, both large and small, Middleton divides Thynne's text into manuscript lines and quires to discover what arrangement best accounts for the errors. Among her many fascinating deductions, Middleton finds that either the amplitude of the manuscript's hand seems to have become slightly denser or the hand itself changed around the final chapters of Book II or the beginning of Book III. Through most of the first two books—the "Boethian Testament"—the acrostic initial of each chapter always begins on the upper left side of the text box, in the page-initial position and, she suggests, on the flesh side of the leaf, whereas from II.12 on through the third and final book—or "Anselmian Testament"—five or six initials appear on the hair side. Middleton suggests that in addition to the shifts of chapter-initial position, other "transitions in decorative code" may have occurred in the marking of the acrostic's initials. For example, a change of decoration from inks to coals to chalks as Usk mentions in his prologue to Book I might have caused the typesetter to miss the cues for a new chapter break.

Such a reconstruction is particularly valuable in light of Paul Strohm's previous suggestion that Thynne's base manuscript may have been a holograph like Usk's surviving *Appeal.* Although Middleton does not quite commit herself, she agrees that "the semiotics of the scribal and spatial *ordinatio* of the book and those of its composition as a verbal artifact were in some fashion, and at some stage of its making, linked in its production as a book."[20] If Middleton's reconstruction of Thynne's manuscript is to be accepted—and other accounts of his misreadings are tortuous at best—the base manuscript itself has a shift of *ordinatio* within a hundred lines of II.12; and this shift in the physical nature of the manuscript is likely to be as authorial as the shifts in the text itself. Yet the acrostic, the very tool which has enabled the flourishing of Bradley's, Bressie's, and Middleton's sleuth work, appears to argue against a multipart composition as it stitches together the various parts into a single coded message—*have mercy!*—a message that seems most applicable to the events of 1384–85. Yet because of the convergence of these significant ruptures—source, style, *ordinatio*, and internal autobiographical references—at the brief span of chapters II.11–12, it is worth considering what evidence the acrostic may furnish pro or contra approaching the *Testament of Love* as one integral work.

Acrostics in Action

Despite the obvious shortcomings of the text as presented in Thynne's early print edition, it makes a claim upon the reader as being itself complete, from the ambitious English project outlined explicitly in the Prologue to the concluding couplet: "God graunt us al therin to be frended. And thus the *Testament of Love* is ended" (III.9.100–101). More significantly, when Skeat reconstructed and Ramona Bressie revised the sequence of the authorial acrostic, "Margarete of virtw have marci on thin Usk," a unity seemed implicit in the whole text. Spanning the initial letters of the *Testament*'s thirty-three chapters, the acrostic seemingly knits the body of the text into one cohesive message: a plea for pity from some feminine figure to the supplicating author. Since its discovery, numerous attempts have been made to identify "Margarete," who, indeed, has a life within the text as well, through the central image of the Margarete-pearl.[21] Perhaps the only message that can be with confidence extracted from the acrostic is that the author hopes to get something from his book—what exactly, we cannot say (Freedom? Fame? Prayers? A job?), nor from whom. In the end, it is not "Margarete" but Usk's ulterior motive that has been seen as stitching together the various disparate parts of the text.

However, the extent to which the *Testament of Love*'s acrostic functions as a unifying agent is dubious at best, in part because of the wide-ranging nature of the literary device itself. The acrostic is a venerable form of visual and textual play whose semiotics and history of usage deserve greater attention. Technically, of course, any literary device in which the initial letters of a segment of text (word, line, stanza, paragraph, chapter) spell out a message counts as an "acrostic," but this catchall term obscures the full range of semiotic possibilities. A glance at the device's many iterations shows that it is necessary to discriminate among types of acrostics according to how they mark space and the degree to which they may act as surety of a text's integrity, or only relatively superficial decoration of the text's—or of the author's, or scribe's, or even in a case like Usk's, the author-scribe's—ingenuity.

And, indeed, when attention is paid to acrostics' functions as well as their form, the differences are significant enough to justify distinguishing three different types based on the interdependence of their textual and spatial arrangement. The first kind could be called a "tight" acrostic such as would be found in poetry, spelling out a woman's or a saint's name in a lyric praising her merits. This sort of acrostic genuinely possesses the unity of message attributed to the device by literary handbooks. Here, the acrostic itself must be planned first and the total body of the text composed in accordance with the coded message. That is, the acrostic is prior to the text, even if a general message may be prior to both. One can imagine an author sitting down and penciling in the proper letters vertically on his "foul papers" to achieve the acrostic, then filling in the blank lines with pertinent material. In the abstract there is no set limit on how long such an acrostic could be, but its difficulty tends to keep it within a short space. The difficulty can be multiplied by making a double acrostic, in which the first and final letters of the lines spell out messages, or even interior acrostics with further complications. While such elaborations are plentiful in literary history, the single or initial letter acrostic is most common in Middle English. Such lyrics may have an occasional, even ephemeral character. Indeed, of the eleven acrostics listed in the *Index to Middle English Verse*, most occur in the same text, that is, the Capesthorne manuscript, or commonplace book, of Humphrey Newton (Bodleian Library, Oxford MS Lat. misc. c. 66), and none have more than two surviving attestations. Indeed, there are few Middle English acrostics of any variety: Cutler identifies only seventeen, a number which Leyerle expands to twenty-two.[22] The surviving Middle English "tight" acrostics have little distinguishing *ordinatio* to aid in spelling out the coded names. (There may well have been greater decoration to draw attention to the embedded compliment if they were presented to their human subject.) Similarly, the initial letters are not distinguished in the print edition of an acrostic "Alison" mistakenly attributed to Chaucer, printed by William Thynne in the same series as the *Testament of Love*.

A second variety is the abecedarian acrostic, notable in the Psalms, and, in Middle English, Geoffrey Chaucer's "An ABC" (fig. 23.1).[23] Here again the initials of the acrostic are predetermined once the choice of the acrostic type has been made by the author. Given that choice, the acrostic form will be prior to the words of the text, even if the letters of the acrostic and the text should be first penned at the same instant. Such form has more flexibility as to space and difficulty. It may be "tight" and compressed in space, as in Psalm 111 (112), or come in clusters like Psalm 118 (119), or spread across lengthy verses as with Chaucer's poem. In Chaucer's surviving manuscripts at least, the *ordinatio* promotes the reader's perception of the acrostic, as it does in print, although the more

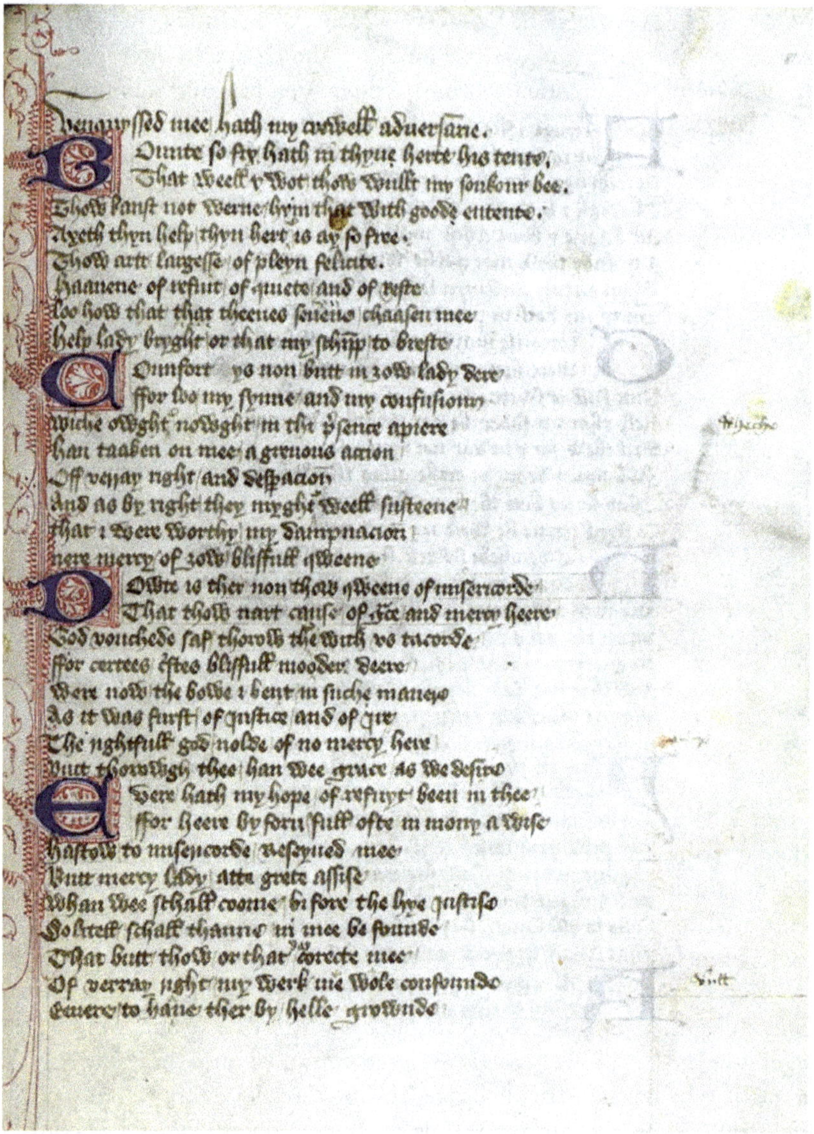

Fig. 23.1. Geoffrey Chaucer, "An ABC." Glasgow, Glasgow University Library MS Hunter 239 (U.3.12), fol. 81r. By permission of the University of Glasgow, Department of Special Collections.

elaborate decoration may reflect as much on the poet's fifteenth-century prestige as it does on modes of reading acrostics.

Indeed, it is worth noting the range of potential chronologies for a reader's experience of acrostics, in terms of whether they read the text first or the acrostic first or the subject of the text and acrostic simultaneously. In the tight acrostic, the chronology depends primarily on the *ordinatio*: when the *ordinatio* draws attention to and delineates the letters of the acrostic, the acrostic will likely be read before the text itself. Without suggestive decoration fully visible in a short, contained passage, the acrostic will be read *after* the text has been read, reread, and ruminated upon; only then does the hidden additional level of meaning emerge for the discerning reader. On the other hand, the abecedarian acrostic overleaps a linear approach to reading. If the initial letters are emphasized, as in MS Hunter 239 (U.3.12) fol. 81r (see fig. 23.1) and in Thynne's use of woodblock capital initials, then the reader may perceive or intuit the whole of the acrostic prior to his or her reading of the text, or even before seeing the very letters of the text that contain the acrostic initials. When decorated fittingly, the "A to Zed" scheme may manifest itself within a few lines or stanzas.

Prose Acrostics

The third form of acrostic is far looser and is the sort employed by Thomas Usk in which the acrostic sprawls out over a prolonged series of large textual segments, whether poetry or prose. Such large-scale acrostics, broken down over significant portions of text, are both far easier to devise and much harder to spot even with rubrication or woodcuts, unless one routinely extracts and aligns first letters in the hope of finding such coded messages. Whether because the simplicity of their creation removes the charm of devising them or because they are more difficult to detect, there are few such acrostics known in medieval England. Such as there are, the manuscript evidence suggests that these "loose" acrostics were used to "freeze" a previously disseminated text into a standardized and set form, as in the cases of *The Three Kings of Cologne*, the *Mappula Angliae*, and perhaps the most intriguing example, Higden's *Polychronicon*. Of the other acrostics listed in *Middle English Verse* and Leyerle's edition, none save these three—the two Middle English acrostics, *Three Kings of Cologne*, *Mappula Angliae*, and the Latin

Polychronicon—operate in the same proportion of text to letter as does the *Testament of Love.* Unlike the tight acrostics (if sufficiently decorated) and the abecedarian acrostic, which can be discerned at a glance, such prose chapter acrostics demand a separate act of decoding quite independent from one's reading of the text and words out of which the acrostic is composed.

An anonymous translation of John of Hildesheim's Latin text, *Historia trium regum* (ca. 1364–75), the Middle English text probably dates from around 1400, "before not after."[24] Like its near-contemporary, the *Testament of Love*, the Middle English text *The Three Kings of Cologne* is a prose work divided into chapters with a chapter initial acrostic. Unlike the *Testament*, however, there is a vigorous manuscript tradition through which to trace the acrostic, which appears in one half of the stemma but not the other. *Three Kings* editor Carl Horstmann describes the two sides of the manuscript tradition:

> MS. Royal (1st group), carefully written and executed, with Latin marginal notes, is of older date (beginning of the 15th century); its readings are generally the best, its language and dialect very nearly original. But its arrangement in some parts (pp. 69–78; 145, 24–152), contrary to the Latin source, and without apparent reason, is such as can hardly be deemed original. The initials of most chapters differ from those in the other MSS., and on closer examination it appears that they have been altered on purpose, and that forced turns and circumscriptions are employed for the sake of obtaining certain initials. There must be some reason for that: indeed, if the initials of the 32 first chapters are put together, we get MARGARETA MONINGTOWN, MAWDE STRANLEA. . . . But in the case of MS. Royal I cannot be brought to believe those 2 female names, Margaret Moningtown and Mawde Stranlea, to be those of the first authors, as their names are obviously forced upon an earlier text; they must be either the compilers of this single version, or the dedicatees. . . . For these reasons I cannot believe MS. Royal to contain the primitive text; it is rather to be regarded as a separate version, made after a first text.[25]

That is, the acrostic of the Middle English *Three Kings of Cologne*—containing presumably the names of either its compilers or its patrons—was used to "freeze" preexisting versions into a standardized text, with care having been taken to make such a text competitive—if not superior—to alternate forms.

Higden's *Polychronicon* is the formative example for this revisionary, standardizing function for the prose acrostic. The *Polychronicon*'s sixty chapters sprawl out an acrostic of the author's name: *Presentem cronicam compilavit Frater Ranulphus Cestrenis Monachus* ("Brother Ranulph, monk of Chester, compiled the present chronicle"). However, the acrostic appears only in the final versions of Higden's *Polychronicon*, what are known as the A, B, and E versions, and not in the shorter—and demonstrably earlier—C and D texts. V. H. Galbraith has shown that this later tradition is indeed an authorial expansion on the more primitive text and determined that Huntington MS HM 132 is a holograph manuscript of Higden's amplification and revision. In this "heavily carreted, emended, scarped, and rewritten manuscript," the rubricated acrostic initials survive to show the final stage of the *Polychronicon*'s development around 1340, after its early anonymous success and dissemination (fig. 23.2).[26] Galbraith notes:

> His task was to enlarge and revise a C and D version, though doubtless one already much changed from those of 1327 into a final, finished book that, by means of the acrostic, should perpetuate his name. That the acrostic appeared for the first time in this very manuscript seems proved by the evidence of certain of the erasures and the substituted leaf that is now fol. 23. We may guess that many months, perhaps even years, were spent in its completion; and it is certain that changes were made, possibly more than once, after the manuscript had been rubricated.[27]

Galbraith's description of Huntington MS HM 132 may be fruitfully compared to Middleton's reconstruction of William Thynne's base manuscript, from the single column layout, quire rearrangement, the greater density of the hand as the manuscript progresses, adjustment of whole chapter blocks, and the erasures of chapter initials (also situated on the top left of the text box). If Thynne faced similar manuscript acrobatics from Usk's hand, he may easily be pardoned for mistaking a few chapter initials and orderings.

Higden's authorial strategies and forms of "signature" were enormously significant for both Latin and vernacular writings, as Andrew Galloway has shown, influencing historical compilers such as Thomas

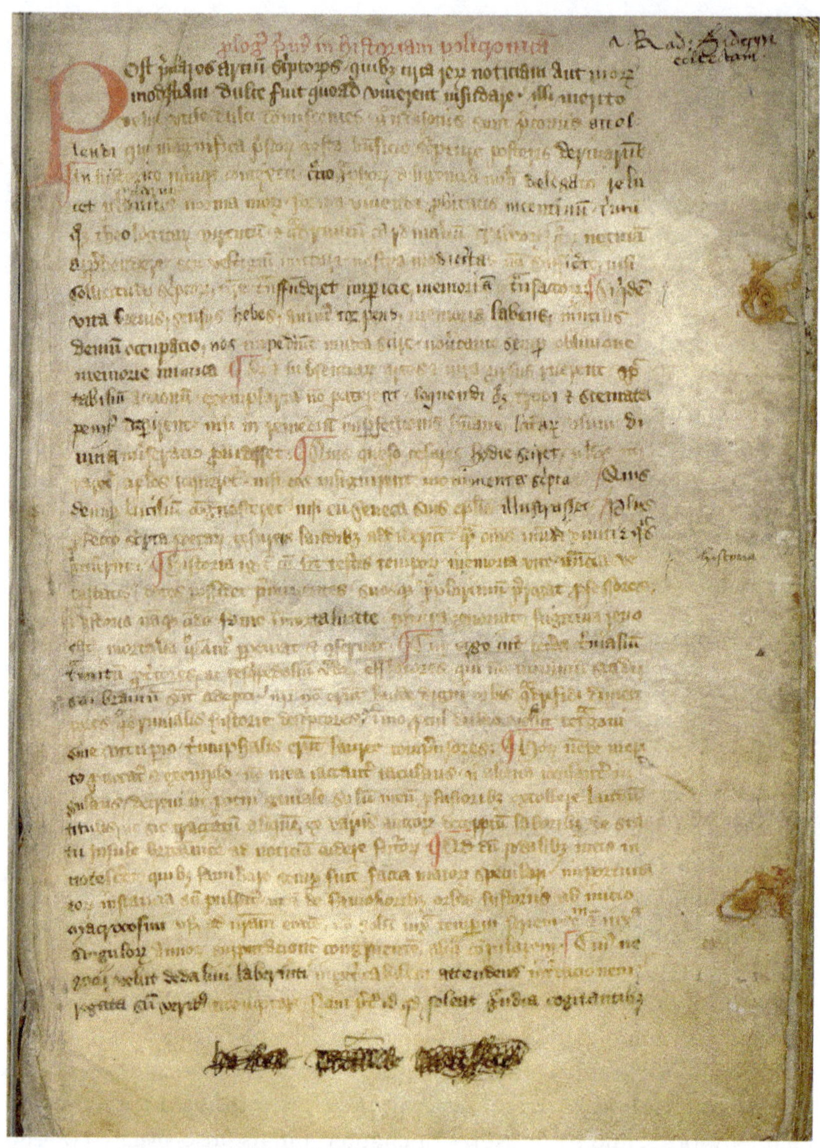

Fig. 23.2. Autograph of Ranulph Higden's *Polychronicon.* San Marino, Huntington Library, MS HM 132, fol. 1. Reproduced by permission of The Huntington Library, San Marino, California.

Gray, John of Tynemouth, Henry Knighton, and Ralph Ergom.[28] Indeed, the *Mappula Angliae* and its authorial acrostic, implanted by Bokenham to identify himself as the author of the adaptation, is itself derived from Book I of Ranulph Higden's *Polychronicon*.[29] Similarities between Higden's peculiar usage and that of Usk led Skeat to suggest that Usk borrowed the idea for the acrostic from the monk's chronicle.[30] There are a number of connections between the two textual traditions: Usk appears to draw upon Higden's Latin original at I.6.42 and III.2.20–23 and Trevisa's Middle English translation of the *Polychronicon* at I. Prol.73–98 and II.2.104–6. In addition, the Latin continuator of the *Polychronicon*, John of Malverne, or the Monk of Worchester, himself described Usk's death with vivid detail, suggesting that he was personally present at the execution.

More important, the *Polychronicon*'s textual history illustrates how, unlike tighter acrostics in which the device's formal constraints dictate the text in varying degrees of difficulty, the easier "loose" or prose acrostic allows for a text to reach an advanced and independent level of sophistication, upon which it may later be arbitrarily imposed with little change to the text's signification. Such topsy-turveydom is only possible when the acrostic is spread out over a great deal of text and the first words have plenty of leeway. As Galbraith observes, "In order to combine the professional humility and anonymity of the monk with the very human instinct for fame, the author had to 'fudge' the beginning of nearly every chapter of Book I."[31] Although Higden's changes are, on the whole, fairly unobtrusive, Horstmann finds the changed words that form the initials of the *Three Kings of Cologne* awkward.[32] Such infelicities are likely due to the acrostic being forced on a preexisting text. Like Higden, Usk pads the opening sentences of the *Testament of Love* with placeholders like "greatly" or "alas," which could be moved about indiscriminately to achieve the desired letters. The surviving fourteenth- and early-fifteenth-century prose acrostics suggest that the device was useful to writers—whether author, compiler, or self-reviser—who wished to "set" a preexisting text, usually historical in genre, into a certain authoritative version for a discerning readership. Engraved into a self-consciously literary text, Usk's prose acrostic makes a claim for the validity of his text's representations. Combined with the evidence for the ruptures and the fault lines within the text, it suggests that the acrostic is a means of stitching together and signing multiple "self-chronicles."

And that brings us back to *Piers Plowman*, the "literary" example par excellence of composition as an ongoing work, with ever-deepening levels of authorial contextualization, representation, and signature in each revision. Middleton's observation of Langland's internal signatures, from the anagramic " 'I have lyved in lond,' quod I, 'and my name is Longe Will,' " to the C 5 "apologia," suggests that "in late medieval literary texts, internal signature regulates . . . proprieties that are in the first instance grammatical and ontological rather than economic: it proclaims and governs the representative claims of the work, rather than the circulation or exchange value of the maker's hand."[33] To carve a space for Usk outside of economic value or political value might seem a desperate task. Yet immediate gain—whether tangible, indirect, or aiming for a more elusive goodwill—fails to explain the project as a whole despite the patently self-promotional tendencies of large parts of the *Testament of Love*. The Prologue reads like literary ambition, plain and simple, disguised as modesty *topos*; the bulk of the text combines confession with apologia and a curriculum vitae of superior literacy; yet the scholastic density of the "Anselmian Testament" seems unlikely to persuade any patron that Usk would make an effective undersheriff. If a sentence like "But nowe, thou reder, who is thylke that thou wyl not scorne laughe to here a dwarfe, or els halfe a man, say he wyl rende out the swerde of Hercules handes; and also he shulde set Hercules Gades a myle yet ferther; and, over that, he had the power of strengthe to pul up the spere that Alisander the noble might never wagge" has any meaning at all, it is as an indication of Usk's pleasure in composition, in *making*, even if occasionally manifested with self-defeating zeal. If Usk is a poor relation of Chaucer and Langland, tolerated at the board of fourteenth- and twenty-first-century dinner parties to circulate the wine and tell Ricardian anecdotes, he still triumphs as the medieval Micawber to their Copperfield. Like that incorrigible beggar, Usk might have been hard pressed, if offered the alternative, to choose between a lucrative "advance money by bearer" note and an uncertain but gorgeous begging letter that gave greater scope to his "bibliographic ego."[34] Although expressed according to a different sensibility than that of Langland, Usk's *Testament of Love* appears to be the result of an "ongoing process of composition," in which the events of 1384–95 are of great but not all-encompassing significance. The prose acrostic bridges the disparate parts that a purely print tradition has elided and functions according to its usage in medieval chronicles to compile and "freeze" Usk's writing as one integrated, if not quite polished, work.

Notes

1. Derek Pearsall, ed., *Piers Plowman: The C-Text* (Exeter: Exeter University Press, 1978), 9, 10.
2. Ibid., 11.
3. Ibid., 10.
4. Ibid., 9.
5. Ibid.
6. Ibid., 11.
7. Joanna Summers, "Gower's *Vox Clamantis* and Usk's *Testament of Love*," *Medium Aevum* 68 (1999): 57
8. Melinda Nielsen, "Scholastic Persuasion in Thomas Usk's *Testament of Love*," *Viator* 42, no. 2 (2011): 183–203; Marion Turner, "Thomas Usk and John Arderne," *Chaucer Review* 47, no. 1 (2012): 95–105. Unfortunately, Linne Mooney and Estelle Stubbs's *Scribes and the City: London Guildhall Clerks and the Dissemination of Middle English Literature, 1372–1425* (Suffolk: Boydell and Brewer, 2013), appeared after this essay was in press and thus could not be incorporated.
9. The first two books present an apolitical fiction which the text is not able to sustain uniformly, and which scarcely qualify as extrapolitical, even in comparison to his judicial *Appeal* and work as a factional scribe. Cf. A. Marotti, "Love Is Not Love: Elizabethan Sonnet Sequences and the Social Order," *English Literary History* 49, no. 2 (1982): 396–428. The bulk of the third book, on the other hand, is not directly political in any meaningful sense.
10. Pearsall, *Piers Plowman*, 10. Ronald Waldron, who summarizes Usk's career in his 2004 *Oxford Dictionary of National Biography* entry, construes the passage "and that, passyng al thynge, to ben mayster of Fraunce by myght, there-as the noble gracyous Edwarde the thyrde, for al his great prowesse in victories, ne myght al yet conquere?" as an indication that the prologue may have been composed before Richard II ascended to the throne, and remained unrevised thereafter. Pers. comm., October 22, 2011. Skeat, on the other hand, construes the passage thus: "and who says that, surpassing all wonders, he will be master of France by might, whereas even King Edward III could not conquer all of it" (452). For a summary of dating issues surrounding the *Testament of Love*, see Gary W. Shawver and John F. Leyerle, eds., *The Testament of Love* (Toronto: University of Toronto Press, 2002), 24. All quotations from the

Testament of Love are hereafter taken from this edition unless otherwise noted. The Prologue leads us to expect a rather different sort of text than we actually receive: "And bycause this boke shal be of love, and the pryme causes of sterynge in that doynge, with passyons and dyseases for wantynge of desire, I wyl that this boke be cleped THE TESTAMENT OF LOVE. . . . Certes, I wote wel, ther shal be made more scorne and jape of me, that I, so unworthely clothed altogyder in a cloudy cloude of unconnynge, wyl putten me in prees to speke of love, or else of the causes in that matter" (Book I, Prologue, 69–72, 80–82). While it is possible that this material was crafted to introduce the *Testament* as we know it with its interlocutor "Love," the combination of the "first stirrings of love, with its passions and diseases," and the emphasized hierarchy of Latin-French-English would lead one rather to expect a treatise more in keeping with one similar, perhaps, to the *Roman de la Rose*.

11. "The World and Heart of Thomas Usk," in *Essays in Ricardian Literature in Honour of John Burrow*, ed. A. J. Minnis, Charlotte C. Morse, and Thorlac Turville-Petre (Oxford: Clarendon Press, 1997), 232. Rebecca McNamara's recent work on Usk's linguistic register appears to corroborate Medcalf and this essay as well. See " 'Diversity in Setting of Words Makes Diversity in Understanding': Bureaucratic and Political Language in Thomas Usk's *Testament of Love*," *New Medieval Literatures* 14 (2012): 170.

12. Cf Ramona Bressie, "A Study of Thomas Usk's *Testament of Love* as an Autobiography" (PhD diss., University of Chicago, 1928).

13. Shawver and Leyerle assemble the references to Usk's imprisonments: I.1.14, 33–34; I.2.23–25; I.3.102; I.3.127; I.6.67–72; II.4.95–96; II.4.103–4; II.10.5, II.11.4. The references range from the flagrantly picturesque example of Sir Daunger holding him "in stockes" (I.3.127) to the explicitly autobiographical (II.4.103–4) and everything in between (*The Testament of Love*, 24).

14. See S. J. Tester, *Philosophiae Consolationis* in *Boethius: The Theological Tractates and the Consolation of Philosophy*, ed. H. F. Stewart, E. K. Rand, and S. J. Tester (Cambridge, MA: Harvard University Press, 1973), Bk.I.pr.iii.6; Bk I.pr.v.4.

15. For the *vita* tradition, see R. Peiper, *Anicii Manlii Severini Boetii Philosophiae consolationis libri quinque. Accedunt eiusdem atque incertorum opuscula sacra* (Leipzig, 1871), xxxi. *Boece* I.pr3.10–11, in *The Riverside Chaucer*, ed. Larry D. Benson (Oxford: Oxford University Press, 1987).

16. The one exception appears to be the *Testament*'s concluding couplet: "God graunt us al therin to be frended. And thus the *Testament of Love* is ended" (III.100–101).

17. "Very welth may not be founden in al this worlde, and that is wel sene. Lo, howe in my mooste comforte, as I wende. and moost supposed to have hadde ful answere of my contrary thoughtes, sodaynly it was vanysshed" (*TL* II.1.1–3).

18. *TL* III.1.1–3. Ramona Bressie notes the oddity of this *ad media res* introduction and accounts for it by supposing some of the text has been lost. See Ramona Bressie, "The Date of Thomas Usk's *Testament of Love*," *Modern Philology* 26 (1928): 28 n. 1. For Anne Middleton's alternate account of these displacements, see "Thomas Usk's 'Perdurable Letters': *The Testament of Love* from Script to Print," *Studies in Bibliography* 51 (1998): 63 ff.

19. Henry Bradley, *Athenaeum* 3615 (February 6, 1897), 184.

20. Middleton, "Perdurable Letters," 99.

21. Margaret Berkeley, Anne of Bohemia, Richard II himself—all have been variously suggested as plausible historical options, along with the spiritualized possibilities of Saint Margaret; or that Margaret exists purely as a romantic, ideal, or allegorical figure. In the final book, Usk as author glosses the meaning of the pearl: "Margarite, a woman, betokeneth grace, lernyng, or wisdom of God, or els holy church" (III.9.91–92).

22. J. L. Cutler, "A Middle English Acrostic," *Modern Language Notes* 70 (1955): 88; Shawver and Leyerle, *Testament of Love*, 8. Both concentrate on poetic acrostics and omit the three prose acrostics in the *Three Kings of Cologne*, *Mappula Angliae*, and *Secreta secretorum*. I am very grateful to Tony Edwards for drawing my attention to these prose acrostics. Their inclusion brings the total of known Middle English acrostics up to twenty-five (or thirty-one when including the abecedarian acrostics), with surely more remaining to be identified.

23. *The Index of Middle English Verse* lists six abecedarian acrostics, including Chaucer's. See Carleton Brown and Rossell Hope Robbins, *The Index of Middle English Verse* (New York: Columbia University Press, 1943), 740.

24. C. Horstmann, ed., *The Three Kings of Cologne*, EETS 85 (1886; rpt. 1988), vi.

25. Introduction to Horstmann, *The Three Kings of Cologne*, vi. Horstmann notes that the following chapter initials consist of AA and then subsequently are the same as in the other manuscripts.

26. Andrew Galloway, "Latin England," in *Imagining a Medieval English Nation* (Minneapolis: University of Minnesota Press, 2004), 49.

27. V. H. Galbraith, "An Autograph MS of Ranulph Higden's *Polychronicon*, *Huntington Library Quarterly* 23, no. 1 (November 1959): 14–15.

28. Andrew Galloway, "Writing History in England," in *The Cambridge History of Medieval English Literature*, ed. David Wallace (Cambridge: Cambridge University Press, 2002), 276; Galbraith, "An Autograph MS," 21.

29. See C. Horstmann's edition of the *Mappula Angliae* in *Englische Studien* 10 (1886).

30. "Thomas Usk and Ralph Higden," *Notes and Queries* 109 (March 26, 1904): 245. Galbraith, Galloway, and Shawver and Leyerle concur.

31. Galbraith, "An Autograph MS," 5.

32. Horstmann, *Three Kings of Cologne*, vi.

33. Anne Middleton, "'Langland's Kynde Name': Authorial Signature and Social Identity in Late Fourteenth-Century England," in *Literary Practice and Social Change in Britain: 1380–1530*, ed. Lee Patterson (Berkeley: University of California Press, 1990), 27.

34. See Kathryn Kerby-Fulton, "Langland and the Bibliographic Ego," in *Written Work: Langland, Labor, and Authorship* (Philadelphia: University of Pennsylvania Press, 1997), 67–143.

CHAPTER 24

Confronting the Scribe-Poet Binary

The Z Text, Writing Office Redaction, and the Oxford Reading Circles

Kathryn Kerby-Fulton

> Said Donaldson and Kane, "When we edit
> We don't give the scribes any credit
> In a flash we divine
> The poet's each line
> And if we say he said it, he said it."
>
> —A limerick about Kane and Donaldson's edition of *Piers Plowman* composed by Marie Boroff

It would be hard to imagine an editorial philosophy more diametrically opposed to Derek Pearsall's than George Kane and E. Talbot Donaldson's.[1] Not that as editors they do not share a great deal: devotion to Langland, first and foremost, as a great poet worth recovering; an uncanny ability to resolve a crux by working backward, almost mathematically, through a tangle of scribal error; a sixth sense for the poet's instincts that only years of closeness to a text and its variants can give. What the rest of us can know pales by comparison to any sensitive editor's intimacy with the text. But the differences in these two editorial philosophies are also large and real, and they may arise even from the deepest social values each man holds (or held). I have never known Derek Pearsall, for instance, to disrespect a scribe's work simply because the man was a scribe—someone who worked for someone else. When, as a young doctoral student, I first knew Derek, I was deeply impressed that he had Marxist posters on the wall of his office. Clearly his view of scribal labor, of the dignity and integrity of the worker's contribution, was going to be more sympathetic than the norm. The field owes Derek (and probably Marx) an enormous debt: a new approach to editing, to textual transmission, and to scribal craftsmanship, finally resulting in a whole new field. Middle English manuscript studies took root here, glimpsed first in Derek's 1981 conference, as John Thompson notes in this volume. In the mid-twentieth-century scholarly world in which Derek's ideas were forged, this took serious independence of mind. Editors and critics—themselves the product of print culture, with its immovable type and equally immovable ideas of what a poet's "finished" text must have looked like—were determined to restore Langland's ur-text to an idealized pristine, immovable glory. But anyone who works with manuscripts, as Derek has always done, knows that our poets weren't bound by immovable type. We now know, thanks to recent research, that most medieval writers continued to revise and experiment—even immediately after they "published"—and that rough notes were leaked and that looseleaf insertions (the common way of adding new passages) could have intriguing afterlives.[2] But most of that work had not yet been done when Derek was shaping his own independent sense of how to balance the "mouvance" of medieval poetry and the modern ideal we all share of the sanctity of the poet's text.

The recent publication of volume 2 of A. V. C. Schmidt's *Parallel-Text Edition of Piers Plowman* will revive the debate over whether Oxford, MS Bodley 851's copy of the poem (named for its sigil Z) is a heavily editorialized A text or an early authorial version of Langland's poem.[3] Talented scholars can be found on either side of this debate, although even the supporters of Z's canonicity, such as Schmidt himself, acknowledge that it has not achieved widespread acceptance. Citing George Kane's famous dismissal of Z as "useless for editing, if not actually misleading,"[4] Schmidt notes, "this verdict has already been shown to be mistaken . . . even if Bodley 851 is taken as no more than a wayward **A** copy similar to F of the **B** Version and N^2 of **C**."[5] This is a brilliant observation, and though also a partial admission, an exciting one: what he is saying is that recent work on maverick manuscripts like F and N^2 potentially offers parallels to the crux of Z and new ways of looking at the question of authorial text versus scribal redaction.

Any such process, however, as I hope to show here, must now be nuanced in light of recent work on professional scribes. No longer viewable simply as the ham-fisted minor functionaries Kane usually assumed them to be—an assumption that gave him and his fellow Athlone editors free rein in interventionist editing—scribes have now been shown in plenty of studies to display intelligent scribal behavior, some of it virtually inextricable from sophisticated Langlandian imitation—or Langland himself. The Ilchester Prologue is a great case in point: Scribe D's copy of this text uniquely carries an alliterating version of an otherwise metrically deficient C Prologue passage, alliteration so skillful that it had been attributed to Langland. But, as Derek Pearsall showed years ago, it was the work of Scribe D himself.[6] This man—the long-suffering scribe of eight works of Gower and two of Chaucer—has just been identified by Linne Mooney and Estelle Stubbs as John Marchaunt, a civic scribe working in various important official positions for the City of London between 1380 and 1417.[7] This proposed identification would give us even further reason to know him as an educated, sensible man, and also someone situated within easy reach of London's Langlandian reading circles even during the author's lifetime. A second instance is the "But Ending" found in three A texts: even Kane himself admitted that the skills of John But were sufficient to baffle definitive editorial judgment about where Langland stopped and But took over.[8] Of course, John But shows soon enough that he is no Langland, but no one knows exactly *how* soon.[9] These instances can be multiplied: the important point is that three groups we used to think of as distinct—scribes, poetic imitators, and authors—can no longer always be seen quite so separately.

This essay examines what some of the Z text's moments of "free composition" might tell us about who—or rather what *kind* of writer or poetic imitator—composed it.[10] And it offers some further evidence of the Z redactor's writing office connections, pointing toward a likely London origin for its composition and more certainly an Oxford provenance for its home in MS Bodley 851. It also offers historical evidence about why John Wells, Bodley 851's owner, might have *personally* wanted a copy of *Piers Plowman* to add to his complex personal collection of Latin satires. Too much about 851 has gone unnoticed amidst overheated authorship disputes of the past. It is time for a fresh look.

THE NATURE OF Z AND ITS WRITING OFFICE INFLECTIONS

In the 1999 *Cambridge History of Medieval English Literature* chapter on *Piers Plowman*, I offered an overview of the distinctive and often disruptive character of Z's interpolations, beginning with this brief description of the difficulties one needs to get over to accept Z as authentic:

> The most straightforward explanation of the evidence (and the one preferred here) is to see it as a conjoint **A-C** manuscript, the **A** portion of which is doctored with **B** and **C** readings and heavily elaborated by an enthusiastic 'editor'—hereafter, to give him his due, the Z 'maker'. In 1983, Rigg and Brewer challenged this view, publishing the unique text of Z's Prol.-VIII, and arguing that 'Z's peculiarities can all be explained more satisfactorily as early and rejected readings than as corruption of the A-text'.[11] But to make this view tenable one has to accept that Langland wrote many lines for Z which he then cancelled in **A**, but reinscribed in **B** or **C**. One also has to be willing to accept that when composing Z Langland (**1**) wrote a good deal of radically inferior verse, often illogically disruptive to the sense of a passage; (**2**) that he held some opinions markedly different from, indeed contrary to, those in **A**, **B**, and **C** (for instance, the avid and unLanglandian *defense* of physicians at Z.VII.260–278); and, finally, (**3**) that he adopted some styles of writing not found in any other text of *Piers Plowman* (such as the outburst of nature mysticism at Z.VI.68–75).[12] None of this is impossible, but the combined weight of it, compounded by doubts cast on the paleographical and textual evidence by Kane, Doyle and Hanna, makes it unlikely.[13] However, Z is an invaluable witness to the early transmission of the poem, and a striking, but by no means isolated instance of Langland's ability *to inspire readers of his text to become writers*. (Emphasis added.)[14]

Schmidt's recent, careful review of the case for authenticity offers this explanation for the awkward question of Z's lines from B or C: "suspected echoes of BC may have been introduced by scribe X or the copyist of his exemplar" (II.77). Of course this is not impossible, albeit cumbersome, but it still does not explain the mysterious Z poetic passages that differ from Langland in style or content. Take, for instance, a couple of lines from the nature mysticism passage mentioned above, which meditate on the power of God:

> **W*yth* the lest word that a wil, the wynd ys aredy**
> **To blowe or to be stille or to brethy softe**
> **Ant all the water of thys world wolde in his gloue.**
> **He hath fuyr *wythouten* flint ys foes to brenne.**
> (Z. VI.69–72, retaining Rigg and Brewer's boldface for text designated unique to Z)

If this is not Langland's writing (and it doesn't exactly sound like him), whose is it? Langland shows little inclination to this type of nature mysticism, but bits of his poem might have inspired it: for example, Z's metaphor of Truth's glove may have been inspired by the Latin line from an Annunciation hymn at C. XIX.114a ("mundum pugillo continens" [holding the world in his fist]), to which, I would note, other early interpreters, such as the Douce 104 illustrator, also responded.[15] Or, as Kane noted, Langland's mention of the day star in A. VII.80 might have triggered this reminiscence of the Judaic God's governance of the elements in Job 37, Psalm 146/147, or Isaiah 40.[16] The Z poet had already played with the alliteration of word and wind (see Z. V.34–40), but here the extrapolation from Langland's A text makes more sense (extrapolations don't always in Z) and these are some of Z's best lines.

To explain such instances, Schmidt notes that Z's "peculiar passages are *beyond the capacity of a literate scribe*" (II.77; my emphasis). The working assumption here is that there is no gray area between the categories "literate scribe" and "poet." But this does not really take account of Langland's ability, as I noted above, *to inspire readers to become writers*—nor his many known professional readers and interpreters especially among intelligent writing-office scribes.[17] Men such as Thomas Usk and Thomas Hoccleve—to take but two identifiable ones—were also "literate scribes" but nonetheless capable of invention.[18] In fact, by good fortune, Melinda Nielsen's neighboring contribution to this volume discusses how Langland inspired Usk. Both Schmidt and Hoyt Duggan defend the authenticity of Z on the basis that only Langland and, as Duggan notes, the author of *Pierce the Plowman's Crede* were known to wield a particular type of alliterative line.[19] But, surely we must ask, if one imitator of Langland could learn the technique, why couldn't another? Or, to take Duggan's evidence to one possible, though extreme, logical conclusion, what then prevents the *Crede* author from being the Z poet instead of Langland?[20]

My point here is not to revisit older attribution disputes but rather to stress that a great deal of Middle English poetry was inspired by *imitative adulation* and written with an audience *already* familiar with the poet being imitated in mind.[21] Examples survive in both Langlandiana and Chauceriana, and some (e.g., Scribe D's and John But's) were even written *within* the text being imitated. Only understanding the sophistication of London book producers during Langland's lifetime, and his earliest readership there and abroad, can help us historicize the production of Bodley 851.[22] In the case of Z much still remains to be done, and, given the extreme constraint on space here, this discussion is only a beginning.[23] But the balance of this essay examines anew the contested early provenance issues of 851 and explores the textual affiliations of Z's mysteriously truncated ending. Finally, I hope to illuminate the acute *scribal* self-awareness of Z's unique passages, which are sometimes clever though not always *Langlandian* in character.

JOHN WELLS AND THE POLEMICAL CONTEXT OF BODLEY 851: THE SHIFTING GEOGRAPHIES OF Z'S REDACTION

Previous scholarship has laid an excellent foundation for uncovering 851's provenance, even if controversy has often obscured our view of it. Among contra arguments beyond Kane's, Hanna's analysis of Bodley 851 is brilliant and groundbreaking. Even so, unsolved cruxes remain. Hanna argued persuasively for Ramsey Abbey (East Anglian) origins of Z's text (found in Part III, fols. 124–39) on the basis of its textual affiliation with a group of A texts, though Rigg had argued for Oxford origins of many of the Latin satirical contents (especially in Part I, fols. 7–77). These Latin text affiliations, Rigg writes, "can best be explained by 851's participation in an Oxford 'pool' of poetic anthologies"—including sophisticated texts of high satirical quality.[24] More recently, Hanna has joined Rigg in this view of Part I especially.[25] But when did Z (in Part III), with its Ramsey-area affiliations, join the Latin satires of Parts I and II, with their Oxford ones? Hanna's earlier study of the booklet structure of Bodley 851 in fact showed that there could be as many as seven different manuscripts within its present binding, and how soon all these elements were bound together has long been a matter of dispute.[26]

As Malcolm Parkes wrote to me in 1998: "851 is one of the most difficult manuscripts I have had to do with, since the physical as well as the provenance evidence is open to different interpretations."[27] But Parkes, like Rigg, leaned toward Oxford provenance of the book, in view of ownership evidence among successive later Oxford students. He concluded, "An Oxford association for the manuscript, passed on from one owner to another, would account for how it ultimately came into the possession of young Cuthbert Ridley (. . . BA 1596, MA 1599), who gave it to the new Library established by Thomas Bodley in 1601."[28]

At the center of this dispute is 851's enigmatic ex libris inscription ("Iste liber constat Fratri Johanni de **Wellis**, monacho Rameseye*nsi*"), entered into an elaborate, custom-made grisaille "bookplate" on 6v of a four-leaf quire (now fols. 5–6), and visibly *added* at least to the older core of the manuscript (Parts I and II).[29] It names John Wells, a famous Oxford Benedictine and monk of Ramsey Abbey (fig. 24.1). Whether Part III, the Z text, was already appended when the bookplate was made is unclear. What is clear is that the hand that wrote the words of the inscription *into* the artist's scrolls of the ex libris drawing dots his *y*, indicating, I would note, that he is used to copying Middle English—not at all a common scribal specialty during Wells's lifetime. The only Middle English in Bodley 851 is in Part III: Hand X copied the Z text, later augmented by Hands Q1 and Q2 to finish *Piers Plowman*. Since the bookplate is in more formal script, it is impossible to compare it with these hands. But as Hanna has shown, X also supplied extensive corrections from multiple exemplars to the Latin Walter Map text (Part I) to which the bookplate is appended.[30] To this I can add tentative evidence that X was active as a corrector in another Latin satire, Nigel Whiteacre's *Speculum stultorum*, in Part II.[31] This suggests that the Z text's *Piers* scribe was active throughout the manuscript and that his investment in copying Z was no random afterthought, however indeterminate its time of arrival remains.

Now, much ink has been spilled on the question of whether Wells owned Part III (Z) during his lifetime. Fortunately, we are now in a position to add some new observations. First, Hanna had ruled out John Wells's ownership of Z before his death in 1388 on the basis of its C-text content because C is "a version of the poem inferentially not available until after 1388."[32] But, I would suggest, the Z maker might well have

Fig. 24.1. Oxford, Bodleian Library, MS Bodley 851, fol. 6v, John Wells's ex libris "bookplate." By permission of the Bodleian Libraries, University of Oxford.

had access to the C tradition or the *relevant* parts of it in its nascent or developing form ("work in progress") any time after 1381, and especially (though not only) if he were a Londoner. Even Anne Middleton, author of the hypothesis that the C text was not finished until 1388, believes it to have been substantially done before then.[33] Second, as noted, Hanna also magisterially showed why Z *as we find it in 851* is likely derived from an A-text group circulating in the East Anglian area (Z is closely related to EAMH^3, three of which come from either East Anglia or Norfolk) and suggested that its provenance remained in the east, at Ramsey Abbey.[34] Similarly, Simon Horobin notes the East Anglian dialect of a later *Piers* addition to 851 but puzzles over its affinities with London area *Piers* texts.[35] But, I would suggest, there is a way to explain all these puzzles of provenance and dialect. Manuscripts *travel*, especially along monastic grapevines and most especially to and from Oxford.[36] Monks from Ramsey were going back and forth all the time to Oxford's Benedictine college of Gloucester, where in fact the owner of Bodley 851, John Wells, was prior of students for thirteen years. Moreover, I would note, the Royal Commission on Historical Monuments evidence—known since 1939 but not to Z scholars—showed Ramsey having its own house or "rooms" (*camarae*) in Gloucester College, which means that a group of Ramsey monks lived together there, supervised by Wells.[37] These monks carried with them not only books, but dialects. And evidence that Benedictines often brought books from their abbeys to Oxford abounds: Malcolm Parkes established in his study of Oxford book provisions that ex libris inscriptions were normally added to books that monks were taking from their home abbeys for use at Oxford.[38] This would explain in part why Wells (whether or not the Z *Piers* had yet been added) recorded both his ownership and his home abbey so explicitly. Befitting his stature as a great man of the order, he did so in this striking, professionally made bookplate that also bespeaks access to some major artistic center. It is hard to imagine, I think, going to this kind of trouble and expense to create a personalized bookplate if one's book wasn't traveling or regularly on loan outside of one's home convent or Oxford room.

The stunning and playful nature of this bookplate I have discussed elsewhere,[39] but a few key observations can be made here. First, the lion image, if we consult contemporary bestiaries, is of a specific type: its curly mane indicated meekness in medieval natural histories, and its tail, protruding forward between its legs (in this case almost obscenely), indicated a nonaggressive stance (hunted and hunting lions hold their tails behind them, supposedly to cover their tracks).[40] Fittingly for an image attached to the opening of Walter Map's irreverent *De nugis curialium*, and a collection of goliardic texts, the tail is drawn provocatively as if to mimic urination or ejaculation into the "well" beneath, an elaborate pun on Wells's name.[41] In the mid-fourteenth century, England had three leading centers for book artistry, London, Oxford, and various sites in East Anglia. Intriguingly, Bodley 851 or parts of it could be associated with all three, given that Ramsey Abbey itself is in East Anglia. The quality of the drawing is astonishing: the brilliant shaded scrollwork of the name "wellis" thematically linking Saint Christopher's oar and the lion are highly sophisticated for England at this date. Lucy Sandler informs me that she knows of no East Anglian or Oxford artist who could have produced comparable chain-and-scrollwork sophistication before 1388 and suggests therefore that London is the likeliest point of origin.[42] The Wells bookplate itself has never been examined before in aid of 851's provenance, partly since it was added to the manuscript at an indeterminate point in relation to the addition of Z. But we know it was added *before* Wells's death in 1388 given the present tense verb of ownership ("constat"), and likely done by a London artist.

If we look at his polemical activities, John Wells was just the kind of man who would have metropolitan connections. Ordained in 1365, Wells began his studies at Gloucester College in 1374, was *prior studentium* at Gloucester until 1381, and was known at least by 1380 as a prominent opponent of Wyclif.[43] But his greatest role was still to come: that of international Benedictine envoy to Italy, tasked with the rather dangerous job of pleading in person for the release of England's high-profile cardinal, Adam Easton, from torture in Pope Urban VI's prison during the Great Schism. Wells died in Perugia in 1388, not having succeeded in his mission

A record of Wells's life that has not so far been connected with the question of his ownership of Z involves a pro-Wycliffite Latin broadside against his role as first speaker at the London Blackfriars Council of 1382, convened as a response to Wyclif's teachings. Wells is parodied as a windbag and a feeble disputer in this Latin broadside on the council, "Heu, quanta desolacio"—a poem sporadically echoing *Piers Plowman*.[44] One stanza even contains two lines apparently referring to Piers: "Quomodo mutati sunt rogo dicat Pers" (How they [the friars] have changed, I ask that Pers say).[45] "Heu" can be very securely dated to 1382 and therefore predates *Pierce the Plowman's Crede*, so this (complicated) allusion seems to be to Langland's poem. It survives in multiple copies, in one instance as a broadside of the 1380s written on a single, foldout leaf and saved in another personalized Oxford compilation made, like 851, by many scribes (in this case by Peter Partriche and fellow Oxford academics ca. 1400).[46] So the poem was clearly circulating in Oxford in the aftermath of the London council.

This connection between *Piers Plowman* and Wells raises a new question: was Wells himself interested in having a copy of *Piers* in the wake of these events? Or perhaps Wells's students or fellow monk-compilers were? One striking thing about 851 is the presence of an epitaph poem in memory of Wells on the flyleaf, written in a fifteenth-century hand, so it is clear that the book was used by friends or followers after his death.[47] But *Piers* is the only vernacular text—and given the volume's taste for satire and topical interclerical polemic, Z seems likely to have been gathered into the collection for a particular purpose. Perhaps this was sometime after the 1382 Blackfriars Council and before Wells's death in 1388? It is impossible that Wells didn't know the Latin broadside about the council personally targeting him and circulating in Oxford. And any number of other polemical and religious interests might have made *Piers* compelling reading for Wells. Benedictines were remarkably open-minded about monastic satire, as 851's goliardic contents show repeatedly. But high-profile polemicists such as Wells were also quite studious of their opponents, as some of the Latin contents of 851 also testify.

So Rigg is right after all about Wells's Oxford ownership of 851, and Hanna is also right in suggesting that the examplar of Z in 851 had East Anglian connections. But such connections could easily have come to Oxford through the Gloucester College grapevine via Ramsey. Of course we can't know *when* Hand X was making his corrections to Parts I and II and copying Z, but we know he was in Oxford for his Part I Latin corrections (as Hanna showed) and, I would add, that his Z text could easily have had East Anglian affiliations without him having to *copy* it at Ramsey. It makes more sense that he and his fellow scribes were Ramsey students or faculty at Oxford, making use of Ramsey books on loan, as did many monks borrowing from their home abbeys. When Z was added we cannot say for sure, but the mid-1380s were when the Latin broadside was circulating and when Wells might most want a copy of *Piers* to study, which he may have commissioned himself.

If so, what he got was Z. But, oddly enough, the Z *redactor*, I would suggest, came from neither Oxford nor Ramsey, and more likely from writing office circles in London. In fact, *The Linguistic Atlas of Late Medieval English* places the dialect of Z in Worcester, but, as Simon Horobin notes of so many Worcestershire *Piers* texts "suggestive of London interferences," I would suggest that Z's may have hailed originally from metropolitan circles, too.[48]

While there is not space here to fully explore this possibility, the internal evidence of Z's writing office culture, to which we now turn, becomes more suggestive in light of London connections. Of course, we cannot know for sure by what channels the original Z redaction might have reached Wells or his circle. But we do know that very close to the St. Paul's/Paternoster Row/ Guildhall area of London, home to several scribes of Middle English literature, was also Blackfriars, a mere stone's throw from St. Paul's. There, as William Courtenay notes, the university scholars gathered in *studia*, situated roughly between the writing offices of the Inns of Court just to the west (another important source of Middle English scribes) and the scribal haunts of the St. Paul's area just to the northeast.[49] The Convent of Blackfriars was its own book production area, and a liberty of the city as Linne Mooney has explained, and a key site not only for scholarly but also for royal scribes. Here foreign scribes were able to make a living in London, initially brought to England by English intellectuals. It was here at Blackfriars, of course, in 1382, that the scholarly world convened to debate Wyclif's teachings—chief among them, John Wells himself. Although we cannot know for sure, the hints of continental sophistication in the Wells bookplate, stylistically early for English book production, might be explained by Wells's academic connections at Blackfriars. Should he have wanted a copy of Langland's controversial new poem, he would have found himself ideally situated to procure one. And this is all happening during Langland's own lifetime (so far as we know), and that of his coterie and earliest audience, among whom many were associated with the London writing offices.

Z's Scrivener Embellishments to the Pardon's Clauses on Lawyers, Merchants, and Beggars

As I have suggested elsewhere, the Z text is awash in added lines emphasizing writing office life,[50] among which the Pardon episode makes for a good, necessarily short case study. In the A, B, and C versions of Piers's Pardon from Truth, Langland brings *new* social groups (merchants, lawyers, and beggars) into the salvational covenant of the Pardon but only under certain conditions. The Z version pointedly highlights this effort, and heightens the physical legal documentary nature of the Pardon: for example, in his version of the passage about not allowing beggars into the "bull," he explicitly and physically shifts them "to the dorso, outside, by themselves":

> Beggaueres ne byddares ne but nat in the bulle
> **But yt be in the bak half wyt*h*outen, by hemsilue**" (Z. VIII.68–69)

This is a very clever, concrete scrivener's-eye embellishment of Langland's allegory. More specifically, the Z redactor is fond of inserting references to notaries (more fond than Langland in fact).[51] Take this instance, interpolated into the Lady Mede section of Z, which elaborates on notarial signs:

> Sire Simonye ys ofsent to sele the chartres
> **Ant alle the notaryes by name, that they noen fayle,**
> **To sette on here sygnes as Symonye wyl bydde.** (Z. II.39–41)

One can't help speculate whether the Z redactor was himself connected with the legal community (critique can come from *within* any group as well as from without), perhaps a London man whose career paralleled those of the Dublin notaries and embellishing translators studied by both Theresa O'Byrne and Hilary Fox in this volume. He may also have been a member of the clerical proletariat, one of many underemployed clergy eking out a living in scribal work of all kinds, with their own good reasons for hating simoniacs. Of course we cannot know, but the Pardon scene with all its documentary legalisms *fascinates* the Z redactor. In A, B, and C, the passage describing the Pardon from Truth, of course, deals first with the salvation of the standard three estates (nobility, clergy, peasantry) traditionally accepted by the church in a still vaguely feudal salvational theology. But the three "newer" groups Langland was so keen to find a place for in Truth's document, the merchants, lawyers, and beggars, are also social groups, I would note, highly relevant to writing office life and documentary work. Langland in particular goes to great lengths to squeeze in the merchants:

Marchauntes in þe margine hadde many ȝeres,
Ac no *pena et a culpa* no Treuthe wolde hem graunte
For they holde nat here haliday as holi chirch hem hoteth . . .
Ac vnder his secrete seal Treuthe sente hem a lettre.
(*Piers* C. IX.22–24 and 27)

The clause about the merchants is placed in the margin of the "bull," emphasizing their marginality in the church's schema, but the image of the "secrete seal" is anything but marginal. As Pearsall explains it, the personal seal, or "privy seal," of a pope or king was used on documents not intended for public proclamation (Hoccleve spent his life copying such documents).[52] Langland especially likes this image: he uses it again at C. IX.138 in relation to his newly added "lunatic lollars" or "godes munstrals": "For vnder godes secret seal here synnes ben keuered." This second usage, in fact, urges the kind of social outreach to beggars and the mentally disabled that merchants' guild records do in fact attest.[53] The first instance, in Truth's letter under the secret seal accompanying the Pardon, likewise urges a catalog of this kind of charitable work upon merchants, with the promise that in return Saint Michael himself will defend them at the time of death. This brings a powerful, surprisingly emotional response from the merchants—the *only* group, I would note, allowed the distinction of being able to respond to Truth's offer in the poem itself. Apparently Langland was trying to say something of special significance about and to the mercantile class:

Tho were marchauntes mury; many wopen for ioye
And preyed for Peres the plouhman þat purchased hem þis bulles.
(C. IX.41–42)

But in the A text, and of course in Z, these lines run very differently:

Þanne were marchauntis m*er*ye: many wepe for ioye,
And ȝaf wille for his writing wollene cloþis;
For he co[pie]de þus h*er*e clause þei [couden] hym gret mede.
(A. VIII.42–44)

Here Will is also an agent of the joy, having written the merchant's "clause." In Z, it is even more pointed:

And yeuen Wylle for **thys** wrytyng wollen clothus
For he coped thus here clause, couth hym gret mede.
(Z.VIII.43–44)

Note that "copiede" (as Kane points out, quite a new verb) is "coped" in Z (shared, like many other readings, with the N tradition), which—if it didn't originate simply as a slip—may be a delightful pun on the idea of clothing the words on parchment in ecclesiastical garb, the "bull" itself. As Kane says, and the variants of AC composite manuscripts like Z indicate, the text is unstable here.[54] But since Will's poem itself is the vehicle of the pardon, one can't help but see in A's version a moment of writerly vocation, indeed, even mission. In BC, the merchants weep for joy and pray for Piers, who "purchased them these bulles" (C.IX.42).[55] In Z and N (which often shares Z readings), it is *Will* who does, and the act of copying the "clause" is both allegorized and sanctified quite cleverly.

Why should merchants have such a special role? One pertinent factor may be that scribes, scriveners, and notaries did much of their daily work *for* merchants and lawyers. Examples abound of "crossover" scribes who wrote for this clientele and also copied literature: from the earlier charters of the Harley 2253 scribe to the multiple instances studied by Mooney and her associates (especially in the London Guildhall) to the work of Theresa O'Byrne and Nicole Eddy in the present volume.[56] Much internal evidence in *Piers Plowman* suggests Langland's own firsthand experience of writing office culture, which might help explain how poignantly he imagines mercantile client gratitude and relief from salvation anxieties in his Pardon scene. The language of the Z redactor is even slightly stronger (he is clearer about Will's agency) and certainly more vividly "scrivenerly" in his metaphors. The church regarded the rising merchant class as a gray area in canon law; someone like Langland must have found this intolerable, or at least unsatisfactory. Though the Z redactor is more conservative than Langland on many ecclesiastical issues,[57] he endorses him here, and his redaction evokes the smell of the inkpot and a brotherhood of scribes even more. Merchants generally were also an important early *audience* for English literature, as the texts annotated by John Shirley, for instance, show, and as Mooney and Stubbs have shown in great detail in relation to civic scribes such as Adam Pynkhurst and others.[58] Amusingly, real-life client gratitude may be something that Adam Pynkhurst himself found hard to come by, if we can judge by Chaucer's little poem "Adam Scriveyn," though in Chaucer this could mean anything from a spoof to affectionate raillery to genuine pique.

As we will see, this working relationship between scribes, scriveners, or notaries and these "new" social groups Langland brought into the Pardon may explain in some part why the Z redactor seems to have deliberately dropped the *Tearing* of the Pardon, another indicator that the Pardon itself was very important to him. Z originally ended with the Pardon unchallenged, with the merchants joyful, and the beggars legally stowed on the dorse of the document. We now have a few ideas about why the Z redactor might have ended it that way, but we can learn more by considering the textual tradition known to him and to the scribes who copied Z (Scribe X) and later its *Piers* continuation (Scribes Q1 and Q2) into Bodley 851.

THE PARDON UNTORN, THE MARGINAL EMPOWERED: Z'S ENDING AND Q1'S ADDITION

One peculiarity of Z is that, central though the Pardon is, it does not contain the *Tearing* of the Pardon: it ends with a line (A.VIII.88) that is *reminiscent* of the end of the A text, though normal A texts carry on much farther beyond the point where Z stops. Whoever created the last lines of Z was capping it off prematurely but similarly to A—likely, we might initially guess, trying to pass it off as a finished text to an audience or client who already vaguely knew the poem. But it is also possible that the Z redactor preferred *Piers Plowman without* the Tearing of the Pardon—just as, we might note, its own author preferred it in the C version. Though modern infatuation with the Tearing scene makes us apt to overlook this, the Tearing is, in many ways, a real spoiler to Piers's socially progressive project. As we saw, Piers was trying to bring new social groups (merchants, lawyers, and beggars) into the privileges of the Pardon from Truth, and the Z version highlights this effort. The Tearing of the Pardon, however, if included, would derail this visionary plan. That a scribe-redactor might reject the Tearing, preferring to end the poem on a note of triumph with all the new and upwardly mobile social groups carefully ranked—even the marginal ones—in a godly society is entirely plausible. That a scribe-redactor as engaged as Z's might have also preferred not to have Piers's Pardon questioned by the priest is also probable. But that a different scribe might later come along and want the Tearing scene added again is not only possible; it is exactly what happened in Bodley 851.

Here are the details: in fol. 139, Z ends with comments on the patient poor and these lines:

[For] loue of here **lownesse** oure lord hem hath graunted
Here penaunce ant here purgatorye vp on thys erth*e*.
(Z. VIII.91–92)

Compare the end of A (XI.310–13), whose

Pore peple, as plouȝmen, and pasto*urs* . . .
Percen wiþ a *paternoster* þe paleis of heuene
Wiþoute pen*au*nce at here p*ar*tyng, into [þe] heiȝe blisse.
(A. XI.310–13)

Why Z ends where it does has not been much studied. It ends not long after Will copies the clauses allowing merchants into the Pardon (Z. VIII.42–45), which the Z redactor (likely a writing office man) apparently thought—unlike modern readers—rather an emotional highlight of the poem, as we saw above. The second *Piers* scribe in Bodley 851 came along and added the Q1 section written in an East Anglian dialect (fig. 24.2),[59] starting immediately after Z's ending with the Pardon scene from A (VIII.89 ff), exactly where Z left it off on fol. 139, beginning, "Pers q*uo*d a prest tho .~ þi p*ar*do*u*n most I rede."

Q1's stint itself then ends soon after with the end of A. VIII (at line 189), with very slight rewriting, and with an otherwise unattested rhyming couplet such as one might expect to find in a Chaucerian context, and such as scribes did often invent for "finishing" Chaucer's tales or spurious versions of them:

And þ*at* it so mote be to God p*re*ye we all*e*,
To vs and all*e* cristin God leue it so beffall*e*. Ame*n*.
(Z. VIII.190–91)

This couplet suggests that Q1 or his source knew something of Middle English Chaucerian tradition, and that he, too (or his exemplar), was fibbing about the real end of A.[60]

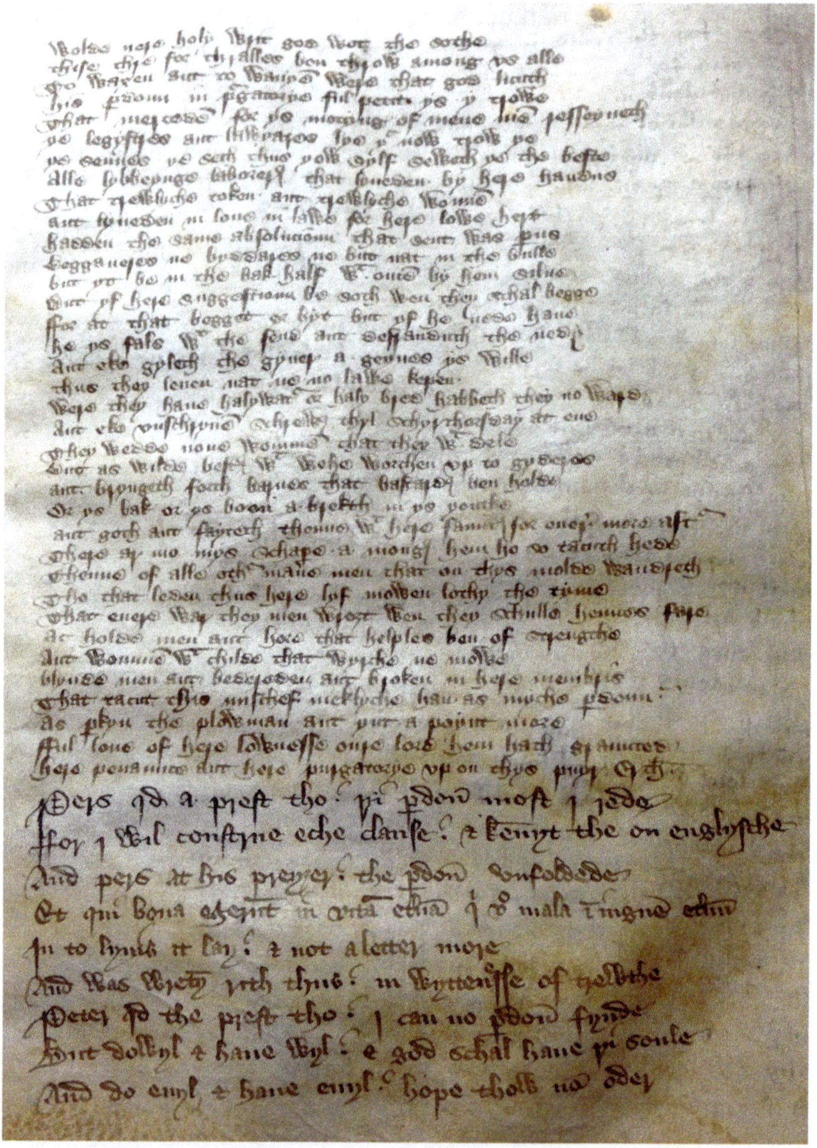

Fig. 24.2. Oxford, Bodleian Library, MS Bodley 851, fol. 139r, showing where Scribe Q1 takes over from the copyist of the Z text (Scribe X). By permission of the Bodleian Libraries, University of Oxford.

What this means is that Q1 either found or extracted a copy of the Tearing of the Pardon and its aftermath (in which Will ponders the validity of dreams and pardons) and added it to the Z text at the bottom of fol. 139–40v.[61] Why, however, did Q1, in turn, choose to end *there*? This isn't the normal end of the A text either—so neither the Z copyist (Scribe X) nor the Q1 copyist wrote out a canonical A ending. The most likely explanation, I believe, given the place Q1 ends, is that this scribe had access to the same kind of textual tradition as Kane's N (now conjoined with Russell-Kane's N^2).[62] In editing the A text, Kane did not collate Bodley 851, making this hard to notice before, but N finishes exactly where Q1 does. Apparently not fooled by the false ending of A that Z's redactor provided, Q1's idea of a complete A text nonetheless mirrors not the standard Passus XI ending of most manuscripts but rather *that of N*, the only extant A text to end at the final lines of VIII.

Figure 24.3 shows the page on which Kane's N becomes Russell and Kane's N^2—that is, where the A text ends at VIII.184 and C. X begins. Looking at this page in N, I would suggest, is likely the closest we can come now to reconstructing what Q1's scribe had in front of him. N's scribe reduces three lines of A (182–84) to this:

> Þ*at* god gif vs g*ra*ce here / or we go hennes /
> To do so þat Dowel / rehearse it att Dome.

Whether Q1's scribe would have also seen the elaborate Latin rubric that immediately follows in N, as figure 24.3 shows, we do not know since he did not copy it, but the rubric is of considerable interest to us: it shows that the N scribe knew the text was defective, and it also hints at a writing office habit of mind. It reads:

> Passus nonus de visione et vltim*us* & hi*c* desinit
> Et decet*ero* tangit auctor de i*nqui*sicionibus de Dowel—
> Do bettre & Dobest sicut patebit speculantib*us*. Inq*ui*sicio p*ri*ma

What this rubric tells us is that the scribe considered "nonus (IX)" the "vltimus" passus but states that the text leaves off incomplete ("hic desinit"). His description of the rest ("decetero," i.e., C) which follows is also startling: the author touches upon, he says, "inquisicionibus de Dowel, Do bettre & Dobest."[63] Most striking is the word "inquisicionibus," repeated again at "Inquisicio prima." The lexical domain of

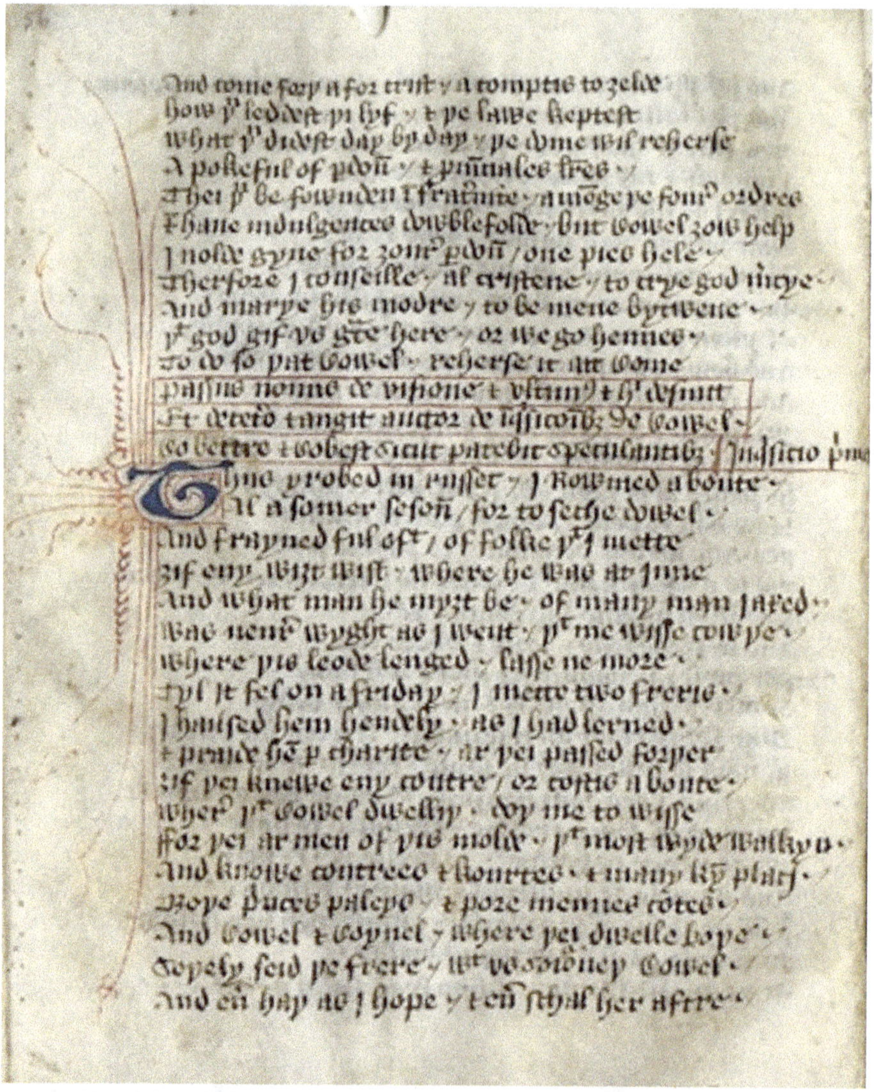

Fig. 24.3. Aberystwyth, National Library of Wales, MS 733B, p. 56. The end of the A text (N) and Latin rubric marking the splice to the C text (N^2). By permission of the Llyfrgell Genedlaethol Cymru/National Library of Wales.

this word is nearly entirely legal, where it can refer to examinations or audits of nearly anything from mundane financial accounts to religious heresy. In scholastic circles a very different kind of word, probably *questio*, would be used to describe academic questioning—and that is more what we would expect in the context of an ostensibly devotional/theological work such as *Piers*. Scholastic-style disputation occurs all over the poem, in fact, within a few lines of this rubric in C. X. Alternatively, "dialogus"—more appropriate to the genre of *Piers*—does occur in some other *Piers* manuscript rubrics, but N's term *inquisicio* is also used in two important and early B texts: M and L.[64] Hanna, in fact, notes the term's use in the heading to Passus VIII in M, which in turn "lies behind a heading at the same point in the B-conflated A+C copy of" [N] . . . , 'incipit inquisicio prima de dowell.' " These "two generic markers, 'dialogue' and 'inquisicio' show the production teams either responding to or passing on Langland's indication of the unfixed and non-visionary properties of the text."[65] In other words, Hanna believes the "inquisicio" rubric may be authorial. This would be exciting, but even if it's not authorial, I would note at the very least, its author had writing office experience somewhere where *inquisiciones* and other examinations of records of all sorts were routine.

Of course, we cannot know what motivated the Q1 scribe to add the Tearing scene back into the text, but a Ramsey monk or Ramsey Oxford student-novice would certainly value Piers's conversion there to the contemplative life. We do know that Q1's dialect is consistent with the Ramsey Abbey area, but we now also know that he could easily be working in the Ramsey *camerae* at Oxford. Q1 copied only this strange, shorter version of the A ending: it was not Q1, as Rigg and Brewer first thought, who copied the long C text portion that follows but rather another scribe, Q2.[66] So the Z and the Q1 portions are mysteriously unique, and in different dialects. But, like the Z interpolations, our extant copy of N, Q1's likeliest *type* of textual source, seems to have stemmed originally from bureaucratic culture.

To conclude: Z originally ended with the Pardon unchallenged, with the merchants joyful, and with the beggars stowed on the dorse. While there might be *Piers* redactors anywhere who, like the later Langland himself, *preferred* the Pardon untorn, it seems especially possible that the Z redactor, who took so much trouble to intrude scribal and writing office culture into his text, might have worked in the London area.[67] And while the scribe who *copied* Z looks likely to have been a member of Ramsey Abbey's Oxford contingent in Gloucester College, perhaps having procured the poem on account of their *prior studentium*'s polemical concerns, the original redaction need not have been composed in either Oxford or Ramsey but rather in London. Z teaches us that scribal redactors can rise to poetic and intellectual heights we can *at moments* mistake for a great poet. And in the generation beyond George Kane's, a gifted redactor like this can even be celebrated, and scribes can assume a more dignified place in our cultural histories at last. But then, Derek Pearsall was ahead of us all on this point.

NOTES

The chapter epigraph is cited from Jill Mann, "The Poetics of Editing: In Memory of George Kane," King's College London Centre for Late Antique and Medieval Studies, *Occasional Papers* 3 (2011): 9–10.

I am grateful to Professor Mann for her advice and also to Ralph Hanna for his acumen and generosity in reading the whole essay in draft. I am also grateful to Lucy Freeman Sandler for her expert advice on the Bodley 851 bookplate and to Karrie Fuller for her enthusiasm and for sharing her own work on Z. Two anonymous press readers have also helped make this a better paper, as have Sarah Baechle, Amanda Bohne, and our press copy editor, Sheila Berg. My biggest debt of gratitude, by now nearly infinite, is to Derek Pearsall himself, whose love of William Langland, William Blake, and "the Poetry of Hope" first enticed me to University of York in 1979 to do my D. Phil and guides me still.

1. But see also Nicolette Zeeman's foreword to Part VII of this volume on Derek Pearsall's admiration of Kane and Donaldson as gifted editors.

2. See note 6 below for sample Langland studies; and on revisionary publication methods more generally, Daniel Hobbins, *Authorship and Publication before Print* (Philadelphia: University of Pennsylvania Press, 2009).

3. A. V. C. Schmidt, *Parallel-Text Edition of Piers Plowman*, 2 vols. (Kalamazoo: Western Michigan University Press, 2008; vol. 1 originally published by Longmans in 1995, repr. 2008).

4. Ibid., vol. 2, 75, citing George Kane, ed., *Piers Plowman: The A Version*, 2nd ed. (London: Athlone Press, 1988), "Retrospect," 459.

5. On N^2, see the bold thesis proposed by Lawrence Warner in "The Ending, and End, of *Piers Plowman* B: The C Version Origins of the Final Two Passus," *Medium Aevum* 76 (2007): 225–50; but see also the persuasive refutation in Ralph Hanna, "George Kane and the Invention of Textual Thought: Ret-

rospect and Prospect," *Yearbook of Langland Studies* 24 (2010): 1–20, esp. 13–14. For the F copy of **B**, see Robert Adams et al., *The Piers Plowman Electronic Archive*, vol. 1, *Corpus Christi College, Oxford MS 201 (F)* (Ann Arbor: University of Michigan Press, 2000).

6. See Derek Pearsall, "The 'Ilchester' Manuscript of *Piers Plowman*," *Neuphilologische Mitteilungen* 82 (1981): 181–93; and, most recently, Kathryn Kerby-Fulton, Maidie Hilmo, and Linda Olson, *Opening Up Middle English Manuscripts* (Ithaca: Cornell University Press, 2012), 69–75.

7. Linne Mooney and Estelle Stubbs, *Scribes and the City: London Guildhall Clerks and the Dissemination of Middle English Literature, 1375–1425* (York: York Medieval Press, 2013).

8. George Kane, "The 'Z Version' of *Piers Plowman*," *Speculum* 60 (1985): 910–30.

9. Kathryn Kerby-Fulton, *Books under Suspicion* (Notre Dame: University of Notre Dame Press, 2006), 388–91, summarizing previous textual scholarship on the John But ending.

10. See also the detailed analysis of Karrie Fuller, "The Craft of the Z-Maker: Reading the Z Text's Unique Lines in Context," *Yearbook of Langland Studies* 28 (2014): 15–43.

11. A. G. Rigg and Charlotte Brewer, *Piers Plowman: The Z Version* (Toronto: Pontifical Institute of Mediaeval Studies, 1983), 2.

12. Z.VII.245 is a good instance of Z's enthusiastic types of elaboration: here he elaborates Hunger's advice to Piers (that he and his workers have eaten too much) to include the fact that they have also drunk too much!

13. Conveniently summarized in Ralph Hanna, "Bodley 851 and *Piers Plowman*," in *Pursuing History: Middle English Manuscripts and Their Texts* (Stanford: Stanford University Press, 1996), 195–203.

14. Kathryn Kerby-Fulton, "*Piers Plowman*," in *Cambridge History of Medieval English Literature*, ed. David Wallace (Cambridge: Cambridge University Press, 1999), 513–38, esp. 518–19. On Z, see also my "Professional Readers of Langland at Home and Abroad," in *New Directions in Later Manuscript Studies: Essays from the 1998 Harvard Conference*, ed. Derek Pearsall (Cambridge: D. S. Brewer, 2000), 101–37.

15. See Pearsall's note to XIX.114a. For Oxford, Bodleian Library, MS Douce 104, see fol. 88; and on the image, Kathryn Kerby-Fulton and Denise Despres, *Iconography and the Professional Reader: The Politics of Book Production in the Douce "Piers Plowman"* (Minneapolis: University of Minnesota Press, 1999), 189.

16. Kane, "The 'Z Version,'" 922.

17. On "professional readers" as scribes and other book production specialists appointed to prepare and sometimes filter texts for the reading public,

see Kerby-Fulton and Despres, *Iconography,* 6–7. On *Piers* manuscripts and bureaucratic scribes, including the Z text, see Kerby-Fulton, "Professional Readers of Langland."

18. On Usk and Hoccleve as readers of Langland, see Kathryn Kerby-Fulton and Steven Justice, "Langlandian Reading Circles, and the Civil Service in London and Dublin, 1380–1427," *New Medieval Literatures* 1 (1997): 59–83.

19. See Hoyt Duggan, "The Authenticity of the Z-Text of *Piers Plowman*: Further Notes on Metrical Evidence," *Medium Aevum* 56 (1987): 25.

20. See Kane, "The 'Z Version.' "

21. Kerby-Fulton, Hilmo, and Olson, *Opening Up Middle English Manuscripts*, 83 ff., for some Chaucerian examples, and 69–75 for Langlandian ones.

22. See Hanna, *Pursuing History*, 195.

23. For more detail on 851's Oxford context, see my "Oxford," in *Europe: A New Literary History, 1348–1417*, ed. David Wallace (Oxford: Oxford University Press, forthcoming); and for more on Z's clerical proletarian nature, see my "The Clerical Proletariat: The Underemployed Scribe and Vocational Crisis," forthcoming in *Journal of the Early Book Society.* See also Fuller, "The Craft of the Z-Maker."

24. Charlotte Brewer and A. G. Rigg, eds., *Piers Plowman: A Working Facsimile of the Z-Text in Bodleian Library, Oxford, MS Bodley 851* (Cambridge: D. S. Brewer, 1994), 29; and 26 for the parts. For Hanna, see note 30 below.

25. Ralph Hanna and Traugott Lawler, eds., *Jankyn's Book of Wikked Wyves* (Athens: University of Georgia Press), vol. 1, esp. 171 n. 70.

26. Hanna, *Pursuing History*, 196–98.

27. Malcolm Parkes, private correspondence, November 5, 1998. I am grateful to the late Professor Parkes for his extensive communication.

28. Ibid. For these names, see Brewer and Rigg, *Facsimile*, 32.

29. The part numbers refer to Brewer and Rigg's chart, *Facsimile*, 26; see also Hanna's helpful appendix, *Pursuing History*, 201–2.

30. Hanna and Lawler, *Jankyn's Book of Wikked Wyves*, 2 and n. I am grateful to Professor Hanna for his advice on this.

31. E.g., fol. 100v, col. 1, correcting "*con*tem*p*ta" to "*con*tenta" (!), and active elsewhere.

32. Hanna, *Pursuing History*, 198.

33. See Anne Middleton, "Acts of Vagrancy: The 'C' Version Autobiography and the Statute of 1388," in *Written Work: Langland, Labor, and Authorship*, ed. Steven Justice and K. Kerby-Fulton (Philadelphia: University of Pennsylvania Press, 1997), 208–318.

34. Hanna, *Pursuing History*, 200.

35. Simon Horobin, "The Scribe of Bodleian Library Digby 102 and the Circulation of the C-Text of *Piers Plowman*," *Yearbook of Langland Studies* (2002): 108–9.

36. For instance, the Oxford Benedictine, Uthred de Boldon, asked for books to be sent to him from his Durham priory; for this and other instances, see, most recently, Mark Faulkner and W. H. E. Sweet, "The Autograph Hand of John Lydgate," *Speculum* 83 (2012): 767 and n. 9.

37. See *Royal Commission on Historical Monuments: An Inventory of the Historical Monuments in the City of Oxford* (London: Her Majesty's Stationery Office, 1939), 123–24 and pl. 197; and, more recently, A. B. Cobban, "Colleges and Halls, 1380–1500," in *The History of the University of Oxford*, ed. Jeremy Catto and Ralph Evans (Oxford: Clarendon Press, 1992), pl. XIX, for a picture of Ramsey's chambers (*camerae*), once part of Gloucester College.

38. M. B. Parkes, "The Provision of Books," in Catto and Evans, *History of the University of Oxford*, vol. 2, 450.

39. See Kerby-Fulton, "Oxford."

40. See, e.g., the six images of lions reproduced from MS Bodley 764 in Richard Barber, *Bestiary* (Woodbridge: Boydell, 1994), 21–22, and accompanying thirteenth-century commentary, 23, which is explicit on the significances of the curly mane and the position of the tail.

41. Visual punning, as Denise Despres suggested to me, is a feature of the de Bohun artists, highly sophisticated and often clerically trained. Lucy Sandler kindly informs me, however, that the Bohun manuscripts offer few real parallels to the 851 bookplate, "except for the Italianate rocks." Generally speaking, given that illuminated manuscripts produced in England during the 1370s and 1380s are quite scarce, she notes that "finding *comparanda* remains a problem." Private correspondence, November 6, 2013. See Lucy Freeman Sandler, "A Note on the Illuminators of the Bohun Manuscripts," *Speculum* 60 (1985): 364 ff.

42. Lucy Sandler writes in addition, "Since 'constat' really sounds as if the owner was living, before 1388 would be strikingly early for this kind of thing, although the figure form is certainly fourteenth century." Private correspondence, April 2, 2013.

43. See Brewer and Rigg, *Piers Plowman: A Working Facsimile of the Z-Text,* 29; and *Dictionary of National Biography* entry for John Wells by Christina von Nolcken, online at www.oxforddnb.com/view/article/29014.

44. See Kerby-Fulton, *Books under Suspicion*, 174–87.

45. Ibid., 183. *Crede*, in the version now extant, must postdate 1393.

46. This is Digby 98, on which see the discussion in Kerby-Fulton, *Books under Suspicion*, 174–87 and fig. 14.

47. The key line, "Doctor erat gratus, prudens, pius, hic tumulatus," suggests an epitaph (for the text, see Rigg and Brewer, *Z Version*, 5). The presence of this epitaph in the manuscript in a fifteenth-century hand suggests that he was not forgotten among the monks who used the book.

48. See Angus McIntosh, M. L. Samuels, et al., *Linguistic Atlas of Late Medieval English*, 4 vols. (Aberdeen: Aberdeen University Press, 1986), vol. 1,

146, for analysis of the three hands of Bodley 851's *Piers* Z–C texts by Scribes X, Q1, and Q2, respectively: LP 7700 (Worcs. Hand A, beginning to fol. 139); 1.146 ("Language of Suffolk or SE Norfolk": Hand B, fols. 139–40); 1.146 (Worcs. Hand C, fols. 141–208), online at www.hrionline.ac.uk/mwm/browse?type=ms&id=102&titleid=7. See also Simon Horobin and Linne Mooney, "A *Piers Plowman* Manuscript by the Hengwrt and Ellesmere Scribe," *Studies in the Age of Chaucer* 26 (2004): 65–112.

49. William Courtenay, *Schools and Scholars in Fourteenth-Century England* (Princeton: Princeton University Press, 1987), 96–98; and the map in Paul Christianson, *London Stationers and Book Artisans, 1300–1500* (New York: Bibliographical Society, 1990), 58; see also Linne R. Mooney, "Locating Scribal Activity in Late-Medieval London," in *Design and Distribution of Late Medieval Manuscripts in England*, ed. Margaret Connolly and Linne R. Mooney (Woodbridge, UK: York Medieval, 2008), 183–204, esp. 198–99 on Blackfriars, 191 on the St. Paul's area, and 193 on the Inns of Court.

50. Kerby-Fulton, "*Piers Plowman*" and "Professional Readers."

51. In addition to these instances, see also Z. II.99 ff. and II.119 ff.

52. Derek Pearsall, *Piers Plowman: A New Annotated Edition of the C-Text* (Exeter: Exeter University Press, 2008), note to l. C. IX.27.

53. See also III.182.

54. Kane, *A Version*, 450.

55. C is more daring politically (see IX.16 ff.) and spiritually, where the pope has been edged out by Truth.

56. See Kerby-Fulton, Hilmo, and Olson, *Opening Up Middle English Manuscripts*, 11, on Harley 2253; Horobin and Mooney, "A *Piers Plowman* Manuscript."

57. For a list of passages in Z, see Kerby-Fulton, "*Piers Plowman*"; see also Fuller, "The Craft of the Z-Maker." On the church's view of mercantile professions, see Pearsall's note to IX.27.

58. See Kathryn Veeman, "'Sende þis booke ageyne hoome to Shirley': John Shirley and the Circulation of Manuscripts in Fifteenth-Century England" (PhD diss., University of Notre Dame, 2010).

59. See note 48 above for the *Linguistic Atlas* dialect analysis of the three scribal segments.

60. See Kerby-Fulton, Hilmo, and Olson, *Opening Up Middle English Manuscripts*, 83 ff.

61. See Rigg and Brewer, *Z Version*, 28.

62. I would like to thank Lawrence Warner for sharing information on N. See the online description listing missing lines and defective elements in N (National Library of Wales, MS 733 B): http://faculty.washington.edu/miceal/PiersA/Introduction_Knott_Fowler.html.

63. The word *speculantibus*, meaning "to the watchers"(?), is a puzzle, but it is a sense used in apocalyptic works. Alternatively, "to those who look in a mirror"? (Anticipating the Mirror of Middle Earth?) There are many possibilities here, ranging from apocalyptic to the contemplative to the Langlandian.

64. Schmidt, *Parallel-Text Edition*, vol. 2, 378. Schmidt notes the use in M and L, though he does not comment on its use here.

65. Ralph Hanna, *London Literature, 1300–1380* (Cambridge: Cambridge University Press, 2005), 246–47. I would like to thank Ralph Hanna for his extensive advice. See also Hanna's "George Kane and the Invention of Textual Thought," 8–12.

66. Kane, "'Z Version.'"

67. See Kerby-Fulton, "The Clerical Proletariat: The Underemployed Scribe and Vocational Crisis."

Contributors

Sarah Baechle, Postdoctoral Fellow, English Department, University of Notre Dame

Julia Boffey, Professor, Queen Mary University of London

Peter Brown, Professor, University of Kent, Canterbury

Katie Ann-Marie Bugyis, Mellon/ACLS Dissertation Completion Fellow, University of Notre Dame, and Visiting Scholar, University of Washington

Christopher Cannon, Professor, New York University, New York

A. I. Doyle, Emeritus Professor of Paleography, University of Durham

Martha W. Driver, Distinguished Professor of English and Women's and Gender Studies, Pace University, New York

Siân Echard, Professor, University of British Columbia, Vancouver

Nicole Eddy, Postdoctoral Fellow, Medieval Institute, University of Notre Dame, and Consultant, Les Enluminures, Ltd., Chicago

A. S. G. Edwards, Professor, University of Kent, Canterbury

Hilary E. Fox, Assistant Professor, Wayne State University, Detroit

Karrie Fuller, Gerald Bruns Distinguished Dissertation Fellow, University of Notre Dame

Maura Giles-Watson, Assistant Professor, University of San Diego

Phillipa Hardman, Reader in Medieval English Literature, University of Reading

Kathryn Kerby-Fulton, Notre Dame Professor of English, University of Notre Dame

Jill Mann, Emeritus Notre Dame Professor of English, University of Notre Dame, and Life Fellow of Girton College, Cambridge

William Marx, Reader in Medieval Literature, University of Wales, Trinity St. David, Lampeter

Sarah McNamer, Associate Professor, Georgetown University, Washington, DC

Carol M. Meale, Senior Research Fellow, University of Bristol

Linne Mooney, Professor of Middle English Paleography, University of York

Melinda Nielsen, Assistant Professor, Baylor University, Waco, TX

Theresa O'Byrne, Postdoctoral Fellow, Rutgers University, New Brunswick, NJ

Stephen Partridge, Assistant Professor, University of British Columbia, Vancouver

Oliver Pickering, Honorary Fellow, University of Leeds

Susan Powell, Professor, University of Salford, Manchester

Elizabeth Scala, Associate Professor, University of Texas at Austin

A. C. Spearing, William R. Kenan Jr. Professor, University of Virginia, Charlottesville

John J. Thompson, Director, Institute for Collaborative Research in the Humanities, and Professor, Queen's University Belfast

Edward Wheatley, Professor, Loyola University Chicago

Jocelyn Wogan-Browne, Thomas F. X. and Theresa Mullarkey Chair in Literature, Fordham University, Bronx, NY

Hannah Zdansky, PhD candidate, University of Notre Dame

Nicolette Zeeman, Fellow of King's College Cambridge

Index of Manuscripts and Incunabula

Page numbers in *italics* refer to figures and are followed by their respective figure number in parentheses when available. Sigla in **bold** have been included for manuscripts referred to by sigla.

General Index